New York

timeout.com/newyork

Time Out Guides Ltd
Universal House
251 Tottenham Court Road
London W1T 7AB
United Kingdom
Tel: +44 (0)20 7813 3000
Fax: +44 (0)20 7813 6001
Email: guides@timeout.com
www.timeout.com

Published by Time Out Guides Ltd, a wholly owned subsidiary of Time Out Group Ltd.
Time Out and the Time Out logo are trademarks of Time Out Group Ltd.

© **Time Out Group Ltd 2009**
Previous editions 1990, 1992, 1994, 1996, 1997, 1998, 1999, 2000, 2001, 2002, 2003, 2004, 2005, 2006, 2007, 2008.

10 9 8 7 6 5 4 3 2 1

This edition first published in Great Britain in 2009 by Ebury Publishing.
A Random House Group Company
20 Vauxhall Bridge Road, London SW1V 2SA

Random House Australia Pty Ltd 20 Alfred Street, Milsons Point, Sydney, New South Wales 2061, Australia

Random House New Zealand Ltd 18 Poland Road, Glenfield, Auckland 10, New Zealand

Random House South Africa (Pty) Ltd Isle of Houghton, Corner Boundary Road & Carse O'Gowrie, Houghton 2198, South Africa

Random House UK Limited Reg. No. 954009

For further distribution details, see www.timeout.com.

ISBN: 978-1-84670-072-9

A CIP catalogue record for this book is available from the British Library.

Printed and bound by Firmengruppe APPL, aprinta druck, Wemding, Germany.

The Random House Group Limited supports The Forest Stewardship Council (FSC), the leading international forest certification organisation. All our titles that are printed on Greenpeace approved FSC certified paper carry the FSC logo. Our paper procurement policy can be found at http://www.rbooks.co.uk/environment.

Time Out carbon-offsets its flights with Trees for Cities (www.treesforcities.org).

Contents

Introduction

New York may have a larger-than-life image, but it's surprisingly slight in size. The island of Manhattan is only 13.4 miles long and 2.3 miles across at its widest point, and a recent land mass recalculation revealed that the five boroughs measure up to just 304.8 square miles. Even the Empire State Building, once again Gotham's tallest skyscraper after the destruction of the World Trade Center, is modest by 21st-century standards.

Yet despite its relatively small size, this fast-paced, high-voltage metropolis feels huge. Manhattanites may complain of the homogenising effect of chain stores and condos, but the island is still a densely packed deli sandwich of diverse, characterful neighbourhoods. Dozens of must-visit museums vie for attention, and even the most plugged-in locals struggle to keep up with the constantly shifting dining and arts scenes. Relax: much of the pleasure of visiting the city lies in simply being here. Take time to wander the film-set-perfect, townhouse-lined streets of the West Village, linger over a boozy brunch or get a ringside view of Central Park's promenaders from a well-positioned bench.

While ultra-modern in many ways, the metropolis is also surprisingly retro. Although locals bemoan the loss of old New York (while clamouring for the next big thing), you'll still find plenty of tin-ceilinged dives, old-school diners and bizarre anachronisms – take, for instance, the city's 10,000 wooden water towers, which stand atop many buildings.

If it's iconic vistas you're after, you won't be disappointed. Even the most jaded urbanite can't help but be dazzled by the post-sleaze Times Square – sanitised, yes, but bigger, brasher and flashier than ever. Yellow (eco-friendly hybrid) taxis still stream picturesquely up Park Avenue towards Grand Central Terminal. And Lower Manhattan's harbour views, framing a certain world-famous statue, are exhilarating.

New York's official dimensions may have shrunk, but its horizons are expanding for visitors. After regeneration, Harlem and Queens are far more welcoming places, while Brooklyn continues to evolve as a haven for hip restaurants, shops, alternative arts and nightlife. The ever-widening choices are agonising, but the best way to savour the Big Apple is through repeat visits: one bite at a time. *Lisa Ritchie, Editor*

this is your
new york™

In the heart of historic Rockefeller Center®,
Top of the Rock Observation Deck is New York's
most beautiful view from a thrilling 70 stories up.

TOP OF THE ROCK™
OBSERVATION DECK
at Rockefeller Center®

TOP OF THE ROCK OBSERVATION DECK
50th Street between 5th and 6th Avenues
Open daily from 8am to midnight
For tickets call 212-698-2000
Visit topoftherocknyc.com

New York in Brief

NEW YORK IN CONTEXT
To open the book, this series of essays tells the city's fascinating back story, covering everything from the immigrant influx that helped create its modern identity and the evolution of its iconic skyscrapers. We also look at controversial mayor Michael Bloomberg's legacy, before going on to profile other key figures that have made their mark on the metropolis.
▶ *For more, see pp17-54.*

SIGHTS
As well as in-depth insights into the city's best-known attractions – the Statue of Liberty and the Metropolitan Museum of Art, to name a couple – the sightseeing section illuminates the shifting character of local neighbourhoods. Here's where you'll find pointers about the latest art districts and fashionable areas, underrated small museums and less-celebrated architectural highlights.
▶ *For more, see pp55-149.*

CONSUME
One of the most exciting eating and drinking playgrounds is also among the most changeable, but that doesn't mean you should neglect old favourites. We've combined the best of the recent openings with trusty classics and wallet-friendly pit stops, all reviewed by critics from *Time Out New York* magazine. Insider guides to shops, bars and hotels round out this part of the book.
▶ *For more, see pp151-258.*

ARTS & ENTERTAINMENT
Beyond the razzle-dazzle of Broadway, this culture capital is also home to top-notch repertory theatre and fearless fringe companies. The underground club scene may have taken a dive, but the city holds a prominent place in rock and jazz history. Also in this section, you'll find details of everything from literary salons to gay nightclubs, children's museums to sports stadiums.
▶ *For more, see pp259-360.*

ESCAPES & EXCURSIONS
If you need respite from the non-stop activity that defines New York City, or if you simply want to explore further afield, you're in luck. Whether you crave culture in a country setting, bracing wilderness walks, a beach day, or the retro glamour and gaming tables of Atlantic City, there are many worthwhile destinations within easy reach of the city.
▶ *For more, see pp361-369.*

New York in 48 Hrs

Day 1 Downtown Delights

8AM Start your New York odyssey Downtown, where Manhattan began and where millions of immigrants embarked on a new life. Get an organic caffeine jolt at **Jack's Stir Brew Coffee** (*see p178*), then stroll down to Pier 17 for great views of the harbour and the Brooklyn Bridge. Head further south if you want to hop on the free Staten Island Ferry (*see p59*) for classic Manhattan panoramas.

11AM To get a sense of how many New Yorkers' ancestors lived, take the subway north to Delancey Street for a tour of one of the reconstructed immigrants' apartments at the **Lower East Side Tenement Museum** (*see p77*). For a more literal taste of the old neighbourhood, order a pastrami on rye at cavernous old deli **Katz's** (*see p185*), or take a detour into Chinatown for superior dim sum at the **Golden Bridge** (*see p183*).

3PM The Lower East Side has changed considerably since its 19th-century squalour. Not only is it bursting at the seams with idiosyncratic shops – boutique-cum-bar the **Dressing Room** (*see p238*), neo-dandy favourites **Bblessing** (*see p236*) and **THECAST** (*see p240*) – but it's also now a booming art district. Once you've checked out the **New Museum of Contemporary Art** (*see p80*), gallery-hop the art spaces in the vicinity, especially on Chrystie, Orchard and Rivington Streets (for highlights, *see p270*). When you've worked up an early-evening thirst, sleuth out one of Downtown's new wave of speakeasy-style bars: the **Back Room** (*see p215*) or, in the East Village, **Death & Co** (*see p217*).

8PM At this juncture, you can either stay on the island or exit to Brooklyn. You'll take Manhattan? Get a bite at one of white-hot chef David Chang's three modern Korean **Momofuku** eateries (*see p189*) and then head west for musical pot pourri at eclectic **(Le) Poisson Rouge** (*see p322*). Alternatively, cross the East River for what many consider to be New York's best steakhouse, Williamsburg's **Peter Luger** (*see p211*), before bar-crawling across to overlooked indie-music gem **Pete's Candy Store** (*see p323*).

NAVIGATING THE CITY
Thanks to the famous grid system of conveniently interconnecting streets, much of Manhattan is relatively easy to navigate. However, the older, more complex layout in Lower Manhattan and the less orderly arrangements in the outer boroughs are more of a challenge. When heading to a particular address, find out its cross-street: it may be more useful than the street number. We've included cross-streets in all our listings.

The subway is the simplest way to get around town, while the bus system is reliable. Be sure to pound the sidewalk: New York is best experienced from street level. And then there's the water: boats run all day around Manhattan. For more on transport and guided tours, *see p372*.

SEEING THE SIGHTS
Your first problem when sightseeing in New York will be deciding which sights to see: the choice is immense. Don't try

Day 2 Living in an Uptown World

9AM A short break in the Big Apple involves some tough choices: the Upper East Side alone is home to a dozen world-class institutions. Fortify yourself with doorstop slices of French toast at old-school diner **Lexington Candy Shop** (*see p203*), near the Museum Mile, before making your decision.

If you opt for the **Metropolitan Museum of Art** (*see p110*), you can either take a brisk two-hour essentials tour or forget the rest of the itinerary entirely – it's a vast place. In the warm-weather months, don't miss the view over Central Park from the Iris & B Gerald Cantor Roof Garden. But if the Met seems too overwhelming, opt instead for the more manageable **Frick Collection** (*see p109*), a hand-picked cache of masterpieces in an exquisite early-20th-century mansion.

NOON From the museum, slip a few blocks north to admire the just-restored façade at the **Guggenheim** (*see p111*). Then stroll south through the park; if you pause for a drink at the **Boathouse Restaurant**'s bar (*see p203*), you can gaze at the strange sight of gondolas on the lake. Exit at the south-east corner of the park and window-shop your way down Fifth Avenue to **MoMA** (*see p100*) – but before you start taking in more art, lunch at the more affordable of its two exemplary eateries: the **Bar Room at the Modern** (*see p201*).

5PM Once you've had your fill of Artic char tartare and modern masterworks, it's time to get high. Rockefeller Center's **Top of the Rock** (*see p101*) is a less-mobbed alternative to the Empire State Building – and affords a good view of the latter iconic structure.

8PM Evening, though, brings more dilemmas. Should you head back uptown for soul food (**Amy Ruth's**; *see p206*) and jazz (**Lenox Lounge** or **Minton's Playhouse**; *see pp327-328*) in Harlem? Or stick to Midtown for a dozen Long Island oysters at the **Grand Central Oyster Bar & Restaurant** (*see p202*), followed by a Broadway or Off-Broadway show (*see p345*) and a nightcap at any number of Midtown bars? It's simply a matter of taste.

and do too much. Your second problem will be finding the money. As most of the city's museums are privately funded, admission prices can be steep. However, a number of them either waive admission fees or make them voluntary once a week. Check the listings for details.

PACKAGE DEALS

If you're planning to visit a number of attractions, it's worth considering a pair of cards that offer free entry to a number of attractions. The New York **CityPass** (www.citypass.com) gives pre-paid, queue-jumping access to six big-ticket attractions, among them the Empire State and the Met; it lasts nine days, and costs $74 (or $54 for children). Meanwhile, the **New York Pass** (www.newyorkpass.com) grants admission to a large number of venues. The card is time-tied: it costs $69 for a one-day pass, $89 for two days, $114 for three days and $144 for seven days.

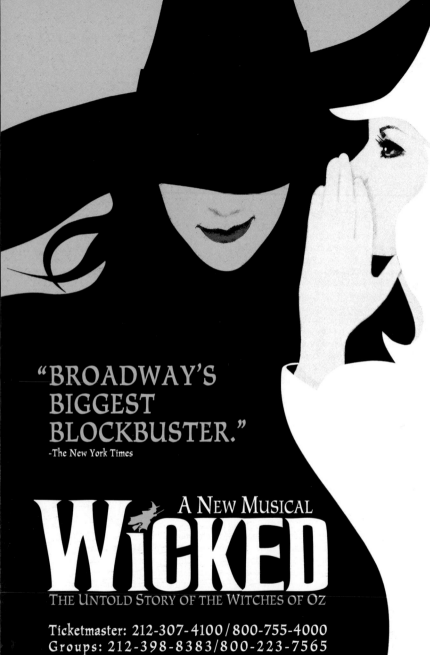

"BROADWAY'S
BIGGEST
BLOCKBUSTER."
-The New York Times

A NEW MUSICAL
WICKED
THE UNTOLD STORY OF THE WITCHES OF OZ

Ticketmaster: 212-307-4100 / 800-755-4000
Groups: 212-398-8383 / 800-223-7565
Ticketmaster.com /wicked • Premium Tickets Available: 212-220-0500
⇒N⇐ GERSHWIN THEATRE, 222 W. 51st St. • WickedtheMusical.com
Grammy® Award-Winning Cast Recording on DECCA BROADWAY

New York in Profile

DOWNTOWN

The oldest part of Manhattan is also the most happening. The tip of the island is the seat of local government and the epicentre of capitalism, but to the north-east, trendy bars, boutiques and galleries have moved into the tenement buildings of erstwhile immigrant neighbourhood the **Lower East Side**. Former bohemian stomping ground **Greenwich Village** still resounds with cultural associations; to the west, leafy, winding streets give way to the **Meatpacking District**'s warehouses, now colonised by designer stores and clubs, while the once-radical **East Village** brims with bars and restaurants. Former art enclave **Soho** is now a prime shopping and dining destination, along with well-heeled neighbour **Tribeca**. Meanwhile, **Little Italy** is being squeezed out by ever-expanding **Chinatown** and, to the north, **Nolita**.

▶ *For more, see pp62-85*.

MIDTOWN

Now New York's main gallery district, **Chelsea** is also the city's most prominent gay enclave. Along with **Union Square**, which hosts the city's best-known farmers' market, the nearby **Flatiron District** has become a fine-dining destination. Among the skyscrapers of Midtown's prime commercial stretch are some of NYC's most iconic attractions, such as the Empire State Building. Here, **Fifth Avenue** is

home to some of the city's poshest retail, while **Broadway** is the world's most famous theatreland. Love it or loathe it, garish **Times Square** is a must-gawp spectacle.

▶ *For more, see pp86-103*.

UPTOWN

Bucolic **Central Park**, with its picturesque lakes, expansive lawns and famous zoo, is the green divider between the patrician **Upper East Side** and the more liberal but equally well-heeled **Upper West Side**. Between them, these wealthy locales contain the lion's share of the city's cultural institutions: the majority of museums are on the UES – the mammoth Metropolitan Museum of Art,

plus others on Fifth Avenue's **Museum Mile**, housed in the stately former mansions of the 20th-century elite – but the UWS has the Metropolitan Opera, the New York Philharmonic and the New York City Ballet at Lincoln Center. Famed designer strip **Madison Avenue** offers more materialistic thrills. Further uptown, regenerated **Harlem** now offers vibrant nightlife, great soul food and plenty of history.

▶ *For more, see pp104-123.*

BROOKLYN

Giving Manhattan a run for its money as a fashionable hangout, the second borough now contains some of the city's best nightlife, dining and shopping. **Williamsburg** is the uncontested hipster hub, brimming with indie music spots, experimental galleries, retro eateries and interesting shops, but it's also worth exploring **Boerum Hill**, **Cobble Hill** and **Red Hook**. Former industrial district **Dumbo** affords great views of Manhattan, while **Brooklyn Heights** and **Park Slope**, where leafy streets are lined with classic brownstones, are the habitats of the intelligentsia. **Prospect Park** is the borough's answer to Central Park, and the amazing Green-Wood cemetery is the final resting place of the great, the good and the notorious.

▶ *For more, see pp124-134.*

QUEENS

The melting pot personified, this diverse borough serves up a slew of ethnic dining opportunities. **Long Island City** is also a burgeoning art district, with the MoMA-affiliated P.S.1 Contemporary Art Center and one of the most eye-popping displays of graffiti you've ever seen. Queens is also home to the rambling Flushing Meadows-Corona Park.

▶ *For more, see pp135-140.*

THE BRONX

One of the country's poorest districts, the Bronx is slowly improving through government initiatives, and provides studio space for the latest wave of priced-out artists. The inner-cityscape has some standout features: the art deco architecture of the Grand Concourse, the sprawling Bronx Zoo, the lush greenery of the New York Botanical Garden and the new Yankee Stadium.

▶ *For more, see pp141-146.*

STATEN ISLAND

Best known for the free ferry that serves it, which offers stunning harbour views, Staten Island has a small-town vibe and a handful of historic sites (the city's oldest concert venue, centuries-old fortifications). With an abundance of parkland, it also offers a tranquil urban escape.

▶ *For more, see pp147-149.*

Time Out New York

Editorial
Editor Lisa Ritchie
Consultant Editor Elizabeth Barr for
Time Out New York
Copy Editors Lesley McCave, Sarah Thorowgood
Listings Editors Covey Crolius, Julia Dodson,
Josh Frank, Amy Wang
Proofreader Cathy Limb
Indexer Anna Norman

Managing Director Peter Fiennes
Editorial Director Ruth Jarvis
Series Editor Will Fulford-Jones
Business Manager Dan Allen
Editorial Manager Holly Pick
Assistant Management Accountant Ija Krasnikova

Design
Art Director Scott Moore
Art Editor Pinelope Kourmouzoglou
Senior Designer Henry Elphick
Graphic Designers Kei Ishimaru, Nicola Wilson
Advertising Designer Jodi Sher

Picture Desk
Picture Editor Jael Marschner
Deputy Picture Editor Lynn Chambers
Picture Researcher Gemma Walters
Picture Desk Assistant Marzena Zoladz
Picture Librarian Christina Theisen

Advertising
Commercial Director Mark Phillips
International Advertising Manager Kasimir Berger
International Sales Executive Charlie Sokol
Advertising Sales (New York)
Julia Keefe-Chamberlain (Time Out New York),
Siobhan Shea Rossi

Marketing
Marketing Manager Yvonne Poon
**Sales & Marketing Director, North America &
Latin America** Lisa Levinson
Senior Publishing Brand Manager Luthfa Begum
Marketing Designer Anthony Huggins

Production
Group Production Director Mark Lamond
Production Manager Brendan McKeown
Production Controller Damian Bennett
Production Coordinator Julie Pallot

Time Out Group
Chairman Tony Elliott
Group General Manager/Director Nichola Coulthard
Time Out Communications Ltd MD David Pepper
Time Out International Ltd MD Cathy Runciman
Group IT Director Simon Chappell
Head of Marketing Catherine Demajo

Contributors
Introduction Lisa Ritchie. **History** Kathleen Squires (*An Englishman in New York, The Tainted Gov* Richard Koss). **New York Today** Howard Halle. **Architecture** Eric P Nash (*Profile* Richard Koss). **Movers and Shapers** Richard Koss. **Tour New York** Erin Clements. **Downtown** Dan Avery (*Profile* Richard Koss; *Walk* Allison Williams; *Kitchen Sink Drama* Erin Clements). **Midtown** Dan Avery (*High Point* Keith Mulvihill; *Profile* Lisa Ritchie; *Walk* Ashlea Halpern). **Uptown** Richard Koss, Lisa Ritchie (*Profile* Richard Koss; *Full Circle* Dan Avery). **Brooklyn** Angela Gaimari (*Walk* Mike Olson). **Queens, The Bronx** Richard Koss. **Staten Island** Kathleen Squires. **Hotels** Dan Avery (*Break for the Borough* Keith Mulvihill). **Restaurants & Cafés, Bars** Adapted from the *Time Out New York Eating & Drinking Guide* (*Profile, Deals on Meals* Gabriella Gershenson; *Secret Gardens* Joshua M Bernstein; *Dram Yankees!* Bret Stetka). **Shops & Services** Lisa Ritchie (*Profile* Erin Wylie; *Vinyl Solution* Nicole Tourtelot). **Calendar** Erin Clements. **Art Galleries** TJ Carlin (*Off the Streets* Camille Dodero). **Books & Poetry** Michael Miller. **Cabaret & Comedy** Adam Feldman, Jane Borden. **Children** Julia Israel (*Profile* Leanne French). **Clubs** Bruce Tantum. **Film & TV** Joshua Rothkopf. **Gay & Lesbian** Keith Mulvihill. **Music** Jay Ruttenberg, Steve Smith. **Sports & Fitness** Drew Toal. **Theatre & Dance** Adam Feldman, Elizabeth Zimmer (*The Next Stage* Helen Shaw). **Escapes & Excursions** Adapted from *Time Out New York* magazine. **Directory** Amy Wang.

Maps john@jsgraphics.co.uk, except: pages 413-416, used by kind permission of the Metropolitan Transportation Authority.

The Editor would like to thank Richard Koss, Lesley McCave, Keith Mulvihill, Cinzia Reale-Castello and all contributors to previous editions of the *Time Out New York Guide*, whose work forms the basis for parts of this book.

About the Guide

GETTING AROUND

The back of the book contains street maps of New York City, together with a full street index and a selection of local transport maps. The maps start on page 397; on them are marked the locations of hotels (❶), restaurants and cafés (❶), and bars (❶). The majority of businesses listed in this guide are located in the areas we've mapped; the grid-square references in the listings refer to these maps.

THE ESSENTIALS

For practical information, including visas, disabled access, emergency numbers, lost property, useful websites and local transport, please see the Directory. It begins on page 371.

THE LISTINGS

Addresses, phone numbers, websites, transport information, hours and prices are all included in our listings, as are selected other facilities. All were checked and correct at press time. However, business owners can alter their arrangements at any time, and fluctuating economic conditions can cause prices to change rapidly.

The very best venues in the city, the must-sees and must-dos in every category, have been marked with a red star (★). In the Sights chapters, we've also marked venues with free admission with a FREE symbol.

PHONE NUMBERS

New York has a number of different area codes. Manhattan is covered by 212 and 646, while Brooklyn, Queens, the Bronx and Staten Island are served by 718 and 347. Even if you're dialling from within the area you're calling, you'll need to use the area code, always preceded by 1.

From outside the US, dial your country's international access code (00 from the UK) or a plus symbol, followed by the number as listed in this guide; here, the initial '1' serves as the US country code. So, to reach the Metropolitan Museum of Art, dial +1-212 535 7710. For more on phones, see p374.

FEEDBACK

We welcome feedback on this guide, both on the venues we've included and on any other locations that you'd like to see featured in future editions. Please email us at guides@timeout.com.

Time Out Guides

Founded in 1968, Time Out has grown from humble beginnings into the leading resource for anyone wanting to know what's happening in the world's greatest cities. Alongside our influential weeklies in London, New York and Chicago, we publish more than 20 magazines in cities as varied as Beijing and Beirut; a range of travel books, with the City Guides now joined by the newer Shortlist series; and an information-packed website. The company remains proudly independent, still owned by Tony Elliott four decades after he launched *Time Out London*.

Written by local experts and illustrated with original photography, our books also retain their independence. No business has been featured because it has advertised, and all restaurants and bars are visited and reviewed anonymously.

ABOUT THE EDITOR

Manhattan-born **Lisa Ritchie** lived in London for two decades before returning to her native city. As well as editing numerous Time Out titles, she has written for publications including London's *Evening Standard*.

A full list of the book's contributors can be found opposite. However, we've also included details of our writers in selected chapters throughout the guide.

Brooklyn *Tourism*

WWW.VISITBROOKLYN.ORG   718.802.3846

THE BROOKLYN TOURISM & VISITORS CENTER

HISTORIC BROOKLYN BOROUGH HALL, GROUND FLOOR

209 JORALEMON ST. (BTW COURT/ADAMS), BROOKLYN, NY 11201

SUBWAY - BOROUGH HALL STOP:
OPEN MONDAY-FRIDAY 10AM-6PM (SATURDAY SEASONAL)

In Context

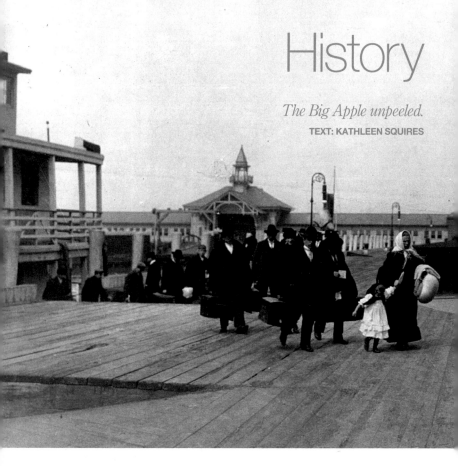

History

The Big Apple unpeeled.

TEXT: KATHLEEN SQUIRES

Kathleen Squires has contributed to publications including the New York Post and the New York Daily News.

Welcome mat to wave after wave of immigrants, New York City has evolved with the energy and aspirations of those who've called it home. Numerous intertwining cultural legacies have come to define one of the world's most ethnically diverse cities – from the wealthy and powerful Anglos who helped build the city's riches, to the fabled tired, poor huddled masses who arrived here from far-off lands and faced a rather tougher struggle to weave themselves into the fabric of their new home town. It's perhaps an exaggeration to suggest that New Yorkers' brash, outspoken reputation was formed from the expatriate's bold resolve to succeed in his adopted land. But even so, from its very beginnings, this forward-looking town has been shaped by a cast of hard-nosed, ambitious characters – and continues to be so today.

NATIVE NEW YORKERS

The area's first residents were the indigenous Lenape tribe. They lived among the forests, meadows and farms of the land they called Lenapehoking, pretty much undisturbed by outsiders for thousands of years – until 1524, when their idyll was interrupted by European visitors. The first to cast his eyes upon this land was Giovanni da Verrazano, an Italian explorer commissioned by the French to find a shortcut to the Orient. Instead, he found Staten Island. Recognising that he was on the wrong track, Verrazano hauled anchor nearly as quickly as he had dropped it, never actually setting foot on dry land.

Eighty-five years later, Englishman Henry Hudson was far more favourably disposed to the place (see p21 **An Englishman in New York**), and his tales of the lush, river-crossed countryside captured the Dutch imagination. In 1624, the Dutch West India Company sent 110 settlers to establish a trading post here, planting themselves at the southern tip of the island called Mannahata and christening the colony New Amsterdam. In many bloody battles against the local Lenape, they did their best to drive the natives away from the little company town. But the tribe were immovable.

In 1626, a man named Peter Minuit, New Amsterdam's first governor, thought he had solved the Lenape problem by pulling off the city's very first real-estate rip-off. He made them an offer they couldn't refuse: he 'bought' the island of Manhattan – all 14,000 acres of it – from the Lenape for 60 guilders' worth of goods. Legend famously values the purchase price at $24, but modern historians set the amount closer to $500. (These days, that wouldn't cover a fraction of a month's rent for a closet-size studio apartment.) It was a slick trick, and set a precedent for countless future ungracious business transactions.

The Dutch quickly made the port of New Amsterdam a centre for fur trading. The population didn't grow as fast as the business, however, and the Dutch West India Company had a hard time finding recruits to move to this unknown island an ocean away. The company instead gathered servants, orphans and slaves, and other more unsavoury outcasts such as thieves, drunkards and prostitutes. The population grew to 400 within ten years, but drunkenness, crime and squalor prevailed. If the colony was to thrive, it needed a strong leader. Enter Dutch West India Company director Peter Stuyvesant.

PEG-LEG PETE

A one-legged, puritanical bully with a quick temper, Stuyvesant – or Peg-leg Pete, as he was known – may have been less than popular but he was the colony's first effective governor. He made peace with the Lenape, formed the first policing force (consisting of nine men), cracked down on debauchery by shutting taverns and outlawing drinking on Sunday, and established the first school, post office, hospital, prison and poorhouse. Within a decade, the population had quadrupled, and the settlement had become an important trading port.

Lined with canals and windmills, and dotted with gabled farmhouses, New Amsterdam finally began to resemble its namesake. Newcomers arrived to work in the fur and slave trades, or to farm. Soon, a dozen and a half languages could be heard in the streets – a fact that made Stuyvesant nervous. In 1654, he attempted to quash immigration by turning away Sephardic Jews who were fleeing the Spanish Inquisition. But, surprisingly for the time, the corporate honchos at the Dutch West India Company reprimanded him for his intolerance and overturned his decision, leading to the establishment of the earliest Jewish community in the New World. It was the first time that the inflexible Stuyvesant was made to bend his ways. The second time put an end to the 40-year Dutch rule for good.

BRITISH INVASION

In late August 1664, English warships sailed into the harbour, set on taking over the now prosperous colony. To avoid bloodshed and destruction, Stuyvesant quickly surrendered. Soon after, New Amsterdam was renamed New York (after the Duke of York, brother of King Charles II) and Stuyvesant quietly retired to his farm. Unlike Stuyvesant, the English battled with the Lenape; by 1695, those members of the tribe who weren't killed off were

IN CONTEXT

sent packing upstate, and New York's European population shot up to 3,000. Over the next 35 years, Dutch-style farmhouses and windmills gave way to stately townhouses and monuments to English royals. By 1740, the slave trade had made New York the third-busiest port in the British Empire. The city, now home to more than 11,000 residents, continued to prosper for a quarter-century. But resentment was beginning to build in the colony, fuelled by the ever-heavier burden of British taxation.

One very angry young man was Alexander Hamilton, the illegitimate son of a Scottish nobleman who arrived in New York from the West Indies in 1772. A fierce intellectual, Hamilton enrolled in King's College (now Columbia University) and became politically active – writing anti-British pamphlets, organising an artillery company and serving as a lieutenant colonel in General George Washington's army. In these and many other ways, he played a central role in a movement that would change the city – and the country – forever.

Fearing revolution, New York's citizenry fled the city in droves in 1775, causing the population to plummet from 25,000 to just 5,000. The following year, 100 British warships sailed into the harbour of this virtual ghost town, carrying with them an intimidating army of 32,000 men – nearly four times the size of Washington's militia. Despite the British presence, Washington organised a reading of the Declaration of Independence, and patriots tore the statue of King George III from its pedestal. Revolution was inevitable.

The battle for New York officially began on 26 August 1776, and Washington's army sustained heavy losses; nearly a quarter of his men were slaughtered in a two-day period. As Washington retreated, a fire – thought to have been lit by patriots – destroyed 493 buildings, including Trinity Church, the tallest structure on the island. The British found a scorched city, and a populace living in tents.

The city continued to suffer for seven long years. Eventually, of course, Washington's luck turned. As the British forces left, he and his troops marched triumphantly down Broadway to reclaim the city as a part of the newly established United States of America. A week and a half later, on 4 December 1783, the general bade farewell to his dispersing troops at Fraunces Tavern, which still stands to this day on Pearl Street.

For his part, Hamilton got busy in the rebuilding effort, laying the groundwork for New York City institutions that remain vital to this day. He started by establishing the Bank of New York, the city's first bank, in 1784. When Washington was inaugurated as the nation's first president in 1789, at Federal Hall on Wall Street, he brought Hamilton on board as the first secretary of the treasury. Thanks to Hamilton's business savvy, trade in stocks and bonds flourished, leading to the establishment in 1792 of what would eventually be known as the New York Stock Exchange. In 1801, Hamilton founded the *Evening Post* newspaper, still in circulation today as the *New York Post*. And by 1804, he had helped make New York a world-leading financial centre. That same year, however, Hamilton was killed by political rival Aaron Burr in a duel in Weehawken, New Jersey.

THE CITY TAKES SHAPE...

New York continued to grow and prosper for the next three decades. Maritime commerce soared, and Robert Fulton's innovative steamboat made its maiden voyage on the Hudson River in 1807. Eleven years later, a group of merchants introduced regularly scheduled shipping (a novel concept at the time) between New York and Liverpool on the Black Ball Line. A boom in the maritime trades lured hundreds of European labourers, and the city – still entirely crammed below Houston Street – grew more and more congested. Where Dutch farms and English estates once stood, taller, far more efficient structures took hold. Manhattan real estate became the most expensive in the world.

The first man to conquer the city's congestion problem was Mayor DeWitt Clinton, a brilliant politician and a protégé of Hamilton. Clinton's dream was to organise the entire island of Manhattan in such a way that it could cope with the eventual population creep northwards. In 1807, he created a commission to map out the foreseeable sprawl. It presented its work four years later, and the destiny of this new city was made manifest: it would be a regular grid of crossing thoroughfares, 12 avenues wide and 155 streets long.

An Englishman in New York

Henry Hudson arrived in the Big Apple 400 years ago, but he didn't stay.

New York's first real tourist, Henry Hudson sailed into New York Harbor on the *Half Moon* on 3 September 1609. Like most explorers of the time, the Englishman was in search of an elusive shortcut to Asia, a quest he'd undertaken on two earlier voyages only to give up after floundering in the ice floes around Greenland and the Arctic Circle.

This time, Hudson sailed west from Amsterdam in the service of the Dutch East India Company. After brief stops in Maine's Penobscot Bay and Delaware Bay, Hudson arrived at the mouth of the river that now bears his name, claiming the land for his Dutch employers. After trading with the local Lenape, he ventured up the river, thinking it offered a north-west passage to Asia, but halted just south of present-day Albany when the river's shallowness convinced him it didn't lead to the Pacific. Hudson turned back; the *Half Moon* set sail for Europe on 4 October.

Hudson got a dreadful reception when he landed on his home soil, where he was imprisoned as a traitor for having claimed the land for the Dutch. However, he was released the following year; flying the British flag, he set off again in search of a new route to the East. This time, it was his crew that gave him trouble: frozen and mutinous, they cast Hudson adrift on a raft. The stretch of water was later renamed Hudson Bay in his honour.

In 2009, the 400th anniversary of Hudson's arrival, the city celebrates both the explorer and the Dutch colony that arose from his territorial claim. Events include a transatlantic race between fleets of American and Dutch vessels from Amsterdam to Newport, Rhode Island, then to New York in September; a celebration of New Amsterdam Week centred on Battery Park (2-6 September); a recreation of Hudson's journey up the river by a replica of the *Half Moon* accompanied by 35 traditional flat-bottomed boats from Holland, arriving in Albany on 19 September; and 'New Amsterdam, The Island at the Center of the World', an exhibit at the South Street Seaport Museum (*see p70*). For more, visit www.henryhudson400.com.

IN CONTEXT

'Between 1892 and 1954, the Statue of Liberty ushered more than 12 million immigrants into New York Harbor.'

Then Clinton literally overstepped his boundaries. In 1811, he presented a plan to build a 363-mile canal linking the Hudson River with Lake Erie. Many of his contemporaries thought it was simply an impossible task: at the time, the longest canal in the world ran a mere 27 miles. But he pressed on and, with a silver tongue to rival a certain modern-day Clinton, raised a truly staggering $6 million for the project.

Work on the Erie Canal began in 1817 and was completed in 1825 – three years ahead of schedule. It shortened the journey between New York City and Buffalo from three weeks to one, and cut the shipping cost per ton from about $100 to $4. Goods, people and money poured into New York, fostering a merchant elite that moved northwards to escape the urban crush. Estates multiplied above Houston Street – all grander and more imposing than their modest colonial forerunners. Once slavery was abolished in New York in 1827, free blacks became an essential part of the workforce. In 1831, the first public transport system began operating, pulling passengers in horse-drawn omnibuses to the city's far reaches.

... AND SO DO THE SLUMS

As the population grew (swelling to 170,000 by 1830), so did the city's problems. Tensions bubbled between immigrant newcomers and those who could trace their American lineage back a generation or two. Crime rose and lurid tales filled the 'penny press', the city's proto-tabloids. While wealthy New Yorkers were moving as far 'uptown' as Greenwich Village, the infamous Five Points neighbourhood – the city's first slum – festered in the area now occupied by City Hall, the courthouses and Chinatown. Built on a fetid drained pond, Five Points became the ramshackle home of poor immigrants and blacks. Brutal gangs with colourful names such as the Forty Thieves, Plug Uglies and Dead Rabbits often met in bloody clashes in the streets, but what finally sent a mass of 100,000 people scurrying from Downtown was an outbreak of cholera in 1832. In just six weeks, 3,513 New Yorkers died.

In 1837, a financial panic left hundreds of Wall Street businesses crumbling. Commerce stagnated at the docks, the real-estate market collapsed, and all but three city banks closed down. Some 50,000 New Yorkers lost their jobs, while 200,000 teetered on the edge of poverty. The panic also sparked an era of civil unrest and violence. In 1849, a xenophobic mob of 8,000 protesting the performance of an English actor at the Astor Place Opera House was met by a militia that opened fire, killing 22 people. But the Draft Riots of 1863, known as 'the bloodiest riots in American history', were much worse. After a law was passed exempting men from the draft for a $300 fee, the (mostly Irish) poor rose up, forming a 15,000-strong force that rampaged through the city. Fuelled by anger about the Civil War (for which they blamed blacks), the rioting gangs set fire to the Colored Orphan Asylum and vandalised black homes. Blacks were beaten in the streets, and some were lynched. A federal force of 6,000 men was sent to subdue the violence. After four days and at least 105 deaths, peace was finally restored.

ON THE MOVE

Amid the chaos of the mid 19th century, the pace of progress continued unabated. Compared to the major Southern cities, New York emerged nearly unscathed from the Civil War. The population ballooned to two million, and new technologies revolutionised daily life. The elevated railway helped extend the population into what are now the Upper East and Upper West Sides, while other trains connected the city with upstate New York, New England and the Midwest. By 1871, train traffic had grown so much that rail tycoon

IN CONTEXT

Cornelius Vanderbilt built the original Grand Central Depot, which could accommodate no fewer than 15,000 passengers at a time. (It was replaced in 1913 by the current Grand Central Terminal.)

One ambitious project was inspired by the harsh winter of 1867. The East River froze over, halting water traffic between Brooklyn and Manhattan for weeks. Brooklyn, by then, had become the nation's third most populous city, and its politicians, businessmen and community leaders realised that the boroughs had to be linked. The New York Bridge Company's goal was to build the world's longest bridge, spanning the East River between downtown Manhattan and south-western Brooklyn. Over 16 years (four times longer than projected), 14,000 miles of steel cable were stretched across the 1,595-foot span, while the towers rose a staggering 276 feet above the river. Worker deaths and corruption dogged the project, but the Brooklyn Bridge opened in triumph on 24 May 1883.

William M 'Boss' Tweed.

THE GREED OF 'BOSS' TWEED

As New York recovered from the turmoil of the mid 1800s, William M 'Boss' Tweed began pulling the strings. Using his ample charm, the six-foot-tall, 300-pound bookkeeper, chair-maker and volunteer fire-fighter became one of the city's most powerful politicians. He had been an alderman and district leader; he had served in the US House of Representatives and as a state senator; and he was a chairman of the Democratic General Committee and leader of Tammany Hall, a political organisation formed by local craftsmen to keep the wealthy classes' political clout in check. But even though Tweed opened orphanages, poorhouses and hospitals, his good deeds were overshadowed by his and his cohorts' gross embezzlement of city funds. By 1870, members of the 'Tweed Ring' had created a new city charter, granting themselves control of the City Treasury. Using fake leases and wildly inflated bills for city supplies and services, Tweed and his cronies may ultimately have pocketed as much as $200 million.

Tweed was eventually sued by the city for $6 million, and charged with forgery and larceny. He escaped from debtor's prison in 1875, but was captured in Spain a year later and died in 1878. But Tweed's insatiable greed hurt many. As he was emptying the city's coffers, poverty spread. Then the stock market took a nosedive, factories closed and railroads went bankrupt. By 1874, New York estimated its homeless population at 90,000. That winter, *Harper's Weekly* reported, 900 New Yorkers starved to death.

IMMIGRANT DREAMS

In September 1882, a new era dawned brightly when Thomas Alva Edison lit up half a square mile of lower Manhattan with 3,000 electric lamps. One of the newly illuminated offices belonged to financier JP Morgan, who played an essential part in bringing New York's, and America's, economy back to life. By bailing out a number of failing railroads, then merging and restructuring them, Morgan jump-started commerce in New York once again. Goods, jobs and businesses returned to the city, and very soon aggressive businessmen with names like Rockefeller, Carnegie and Frick wanted a piece of the action. They made New York the HQ of Standard Oil and US Steel, corporations that went on to shape America's economic future and New York's reputation as the centre of capitalism.

A shining symbol for those less fortunate immigrants also made New York its home around that time. To commemorate America's freedom 100 years after the Declaration of Independence, the French gave the Statue of Liberty to the United States. Between 1892 and 1954, the statue ushered more than 12 million immigrants into New York Harbor, and Ellis Island served to process many of them. The island had opened as an immigration centre in 1892 with expectations of accommodating 500,000 people annually, but it processed twice that number in its first year. In the 34-building complex, crowds of would-be Americans were herded through examinations, inspections and interrogations. Four million got through, turning New York into what British playwright Israel Zangwill called 'the great melting pot where all the races of Europe are melting and reforming'.

Many of these new immigrants crowded into dark, squalid tenements on the Lower East Side, while millionaires such as the Vanderbilts constructed huge French-style mansions along Fifth Avenue. Jacob A Riis, a Danish immigrant and police reporter for the *New York Tribune*, made it his business to expose this dichotomy, scouring filthy alleys and overcrowded tenements to research and photograph his 1890 book, *How the Other Half Lives*. Largely as a result of Riis's work, the state passed the Tenement House Act of 1901, which called for drastic housing reforms.

SOARING ASPIRATIONS

By the close of the 19th century, 40 fragmented governments had been formed in and around Manhattan, creating political confusion. So, on 1 January 1898, the boroughs of Manhattan, Brooklyn, Queens, Staten Island and the Bronx consolidated to form New York City, the largest city in America. More and more companies started to move their headquarters to this new metropolis, increasing the demand for office space. With little

IN CONTEXT

'Factory workers faced impossible quotas, had their pay docked for minor mistakes and were often locked in during working hours.'

land left to develop in lower Manhattan, New York embraced the steel revolution and grew steadily skywards. Thus began an all-out race to build the tallest building in the world.

By 1902, New York boasted 66 skyscrapers, including the 20-storey Fuller Building (now known as the Flatiron Building) at Fifth Avenue and 23rd Street, and the 25-storey New York Times Tower in Longacre (now Times) Square. Within four years, these two buildings would be completely dwarfed by the 47-storey Singer Building on lower Broadway, which enjoyed the status of tallest building in the world – but only for 18 months. The 700-foot Metropolitan Life Tower on Madison Square claimed the title from the Singer Building in 1909, but the 793.5-foot-tall Woolworth Building on Broadway and Park Place topped it in 1913 – and, amazingly, held the distinction for nearly two decades.

If that weren't enough to demonstrate New Yorkers' unending ambition, the city burrowed below the streets at the same time, starting work on its underground transit system in 1900. The $35-million project took nearly four and a half years to complete. Less than a decade after opening, it was the most heavily travelled subway system in the world, carrying almost a billion passengers on its trains every year.

CHANGING TIMES

By 1909, 30,000 factories were operating in the city, churning out everything from heavy machinery to artificial flowers. Mistrusted, abused and underpaid, factory workers faced impossible quotas, had their pay docked for minor mistakes and were often locked in during working hours. In the end, it took a tragedy to bring about real changes.

On 25 March 1911, a fire broke out at the Triangle Shirtwaist Company. Although it was a Saturday, some 500 workers – most of them teenage girls – were toiling in the Greenwich Village factory. Flames spread rapidly through the fabric-filled building, but as the girls rushed to escape, they found many of the exits locked. Roughly 350 made it out on to the adjoining rooftops before the inferno closed off all exits, but 146 young women perished; many jumped to their deaths from windows on the eighth, ninth and tenth floors. The two factory owners were tried for manslaughter but acquitted, yet the disaster did at least spur labour and union organisations, which pushed for and won sweeping reforms.

Another sort of rights movement was taking hold during this time. Between 1910 and 1913, New York City was the site of the largest women's suffrage rallies in the United States. Harriet Stanton Blatch (the daughter of famed suffragette Elizabeth Cady Stanton, and founder of the Equality League of Self-Supporting Women) and Carrie Chapman Catt (the organiser of the New York City Women's Suffrage party) arranged attention-getting demonstrations intended to pressure the state into authorising a referendum on a woman's right to vote. The measure's defeat in 1915 only steeled the suffragettes' resolve. Finally, with the support of Tammany Hall, the law was passed in 1919, challenging the male stranglehold on voting throughout the country. With New York leading the nation, the 19th Amendment was ratified in 1920.

In 1919, as New York welcomed troops home from World War I with a parade, the city also celebrated its emergence on the global stage. It had supplanted London as the investment capital of the world, and had become the centre of publishing, thanks to two men: Pulitzer and Hearst. The *New York Times* had become the country's most respected newspaper; Broadway was the focal point of American theatre; and Greenwich Village had become a world-class bohemia, where flamboyant artists, writers and political revolutionaries gathered in galleries and coffeehouses.

Cab Calloway at the **Cotton Club**. *See p29.*

The more personal side of the women's movement also found a home in New York City. A nurse and midwife who grew up in a family of 11 children, Margaret Sanger was a fierce advocate of birth control and family planning. She opened the first ever birth-control clinic in Brooklyn on 16 October 1916. Finding this unseemly, the police closed the clinic soon after and imprisoned Sanger for 30 days. She pressed on and, in 1921, formed the American Birth Control League – the forerunner of the organisation Planned Parenthood – which researched birth control methods and provided gynaecological services.

ALL THAT JAZZ

Forward-thinking women such as Sanger set the tone for an era when women, now a voting political force, were moving beyond the moral conventions of the 19th century. The country ushered in the Jazz Age in 1919 by ratifying the 18th Amendment, which outlawed the distribution and sale of alcoholic beverages. Prohibition turned the city into the epicentre of bootlegging, speakeasies and organised crime. By the early 1920s, New York boasted 32,000 illegal watering holes – twice the number of legal bars before Prohibition.

In 1925, New Yorkers elected the magnetic James J Walker as mayor. A charming ex-songwriter (as well as a speakeasy patron and skirt-chaser), Walker was the perfect match for his city's flashy style, hunger for publicity and a consequences-be-damned attitude. Fame flowed in the city's veins: home-run hero Babe Ruth drew a million fans each season to the New York Yankees' games, and sharp-tongued Walter Winchell filled his newspaper

Seedy **Times Square** in 1975. *See p30.*

'President Ford refused to bail out the city, a decision summed up by the immortal Daily News *headline: "Ford to city: drop dead".'*

columns with celebrity titbits and scandals. Alexander Woollcott, Dorothy Parker, Robert Benchley and other writers met up daily to trade witticisms around a table at the Algonquin Hotel; the result, in February 1925, was *The New Yorker*.

The Harlem Renaissance blossomed at the same time. Writers Langston Hughes, Zora Neale Hurston and James Weldon Johnson transformed the African-American experience into lyrical literary works, and white society flocked to the Cotton Club to see genre-defining musicians such as Bessie Smith, Cab Calloway, Louis Armstrong and Duke Ellington. (Blacks were not welcome unless they were performing.) Downtown, Broadway houses were packed out with fans of George and Ira Gershwin, Irving Berlin, Cole Porter, Lorenz Hart, Richard Rodgers and Oscar Hammerstein II. Towards the end of the '20s, New York-born Al Jolson wowed audiences in *The Jazz Singer*, the first talking picture.

AFTER THE FALL

The dizzying excitement ended on Tuesday, 29 October 1929, when the stock market crashed. Corruption eroded Mayor Walker's hold on the city: despite a tenure that saw the opening of the Holland Tunnel, the completion of the George Washington Bridge and the construction of the Chrysler and Empire State Buildings, Walker's lustre faded in the growing shadow of graft accusations. He resigned in 1932, as New York, caught in the depths of the Great Depression, had a staggering one million unemployed inhabitants.

In 1934, an unstoppable force named Fiorello La Guardia took office as mayor, rolling up his sleeves to crack down on mobsters, gambling, smut and government corruption. The son of an Italian father and a Jewish mother, La Guardia was a tough-talking politician who was known for nearly coming to blows with other city officials; he described himself as 'inconsiderate, arbitrary, authoritative, difficult, complicated, intolerant and somewhat theatrical'. La Guardia's act played well: he ushered New York into an era of unparalleled prosperity over the course of his three terms. The 'Little Flower', as La Guardia was known, streamlined city government, paid down the debt and updated the transportation, hospital, reservoir and sewer systems. New highways made the city more accessible, and North Beach (now La Guardia) Airport became the city's first commercial landing field.

Helping La Guardia to modernise the city was Robert Moses, a hard-nosed visionary who would do much to shape – and in some cases, destroy – New York's landscape. Moses spent 44 years stepping on toes to build expressways, parks, beaches, public housing, bridges and tunnels, creating such landmarks as Shea Stadium, Lincoln Center, the United Nations complex and the Verrazano-Narrows Bridge.

BIRTH OF BOHEMIA

Despite La Guardia's belt-tightening and Moses' renovations, New York began to fall apart financially. When World War II ended, 800,000 industrial jobs disappeared from the city. Factories in need of more space moved to the suburbs, along with nearly five million residents. But more crowding occurred as rural African-Americans and Puerto Ricans flocked to the metropolis in the 1950s and '60s, only to meet with ruthless discrimination and a dearth of jobs. Robert Moses' Slum Clearance Committee reduced many neighbourhoods to rubble, forcing out residents in order to build huge, isolating housing projects that became magnets for crime. In 1963, the city also lost Pennsylvania Station, when the Pennsylvania Railroad Company demolished the site over the protests of picketers in order to make way for a modern station and Madison Square Garden. It was a wake-up call for New York: architectural changes were hurtling out of control.

But Moses and his wrecking ball couldn't knock over one steadfast West Village woman. Architectural writer and urban-planning critic Jane Jacobs organised local residents when the city unveiled its plan to clear a 14-block tract of her neighbourhood to make space for yet more public housing. Her obstinacy was applauded by many, including an influential councilman named Ed Koch (who would become mayor in 1978). The group fought the plan and won, causing Mayor Robert F Wagner to back down. As a result of Jacobs's efforts in the wake of Pennsylvania Station's demolition, the Landmarks Preservation Commission – the first such group in the US – was established in 1965.

At the dawning of the Age of Aquarius, the city harboured its share of innovative creators. Allen Ginsberg, Jack Kerouac and others gathered in Village coffeehouses to create a new voice for poetry. A folk music scene brewed in tiny clubs around Bleecker Street, showcasing musicians such as Bob Dylan. A former advertising illustrator named Andy Warhol turned images of mass consumerism into deadpan, ironic art statements. And in 1969, the city's long-hidden gay communities came out into the streets, as patrons at the Stonewall Inn on Christopher Street demonstrated against a police raid. The protests, known as the Stonewall riots, gave birth to the modern gay rights movement.

MEAN STREETS

By the early 1970s, deficits had forced heavy cutbacks in city services. The streets were dirty, and subway cars and buildings were scrawled with graffiti; crime skyrocketed as the city's debt deepened to $6 billion. Despite the huge downturn, construction commenced on the World Trade Center; when completed, in 1973, its twin 110-storey towers were the world's tallest buildings. Even as the Trade Center rose, the city became so desperately overdrawn that Mayor Abraham Beame appealed to the federal government for financial assistance in 1975. Yet President Gerald Ford refused to bail out the city, a decision summed up by the immortal Daily News headline: 'Ford to city: drop dead'.

Around the same time, Times Square degenerated into a morass of sex shops and porn palaces, drug use rose and subway use hit an all-time low. In 1977, serial killer Son of Sam terrorised the city, and a blackout one hot August night that same year led to widespread looting and arson. The angst of the time fuelled the punk culture that rose in downtown clubs such as CBGB. At the same time, celebrities, designers and models converged on Midtown to disco their nights away at Studio 54.

The Wall Street boom of the '80s and fiscal petitioning by Mayor Ed Koch brought money flooding back into New York. Gentrification glamorised neighbourhoods such as Soho, Tribeca and the East Village. But deeper ills persisted. In 1988, a protest against the city's efforts to impose a strict curfew and displace the homeless away from Tompkins Square Park erupted into a violent clash with the police. Crack use became endemic in the ghettos, homelessness rose and AIDS emerged into a new scourge.

By 1989, citizens were restless for change. They turned to David N Dinkins, electing him the city's first African-American mayor. A distinguished, softly-spoken man, Dinkins held office for only a single term, marked by a record murder rate, flaring racial tensions in Washington Heights, Crown Heights and Flatbush, and the explosion of a bomb in the World Trade Center that killed six, injured 1,000 and foreshadowed the attacks of 2001.

Deeming the polite Dinkins ineffective, New Yorkers voted in former federal prosecutor Rudolph Giuliani. Like his predecessors Peter Stuyvesant and Fiorello La Guardia, Giuliani was an abrasive leader who used bully tactics to get things done, as his 'quality of life' campaign cracked down on everything from drug dealing and pornography to unsolicited windshield washing. As cases of severe police brutality grabbed the headlines, crime plummeted, tourism soared and New York became cleaner and safer than it had been in decades. Times Square was transformed into a family-friendly tourist destination, and the dot-com explosion brought young wannabe millionaires to the Flatiron District's Silicon Alley. Giuliani's second term as mayor would close, however, on a devastating tragedy.

IN CONTEXT

The Tainted Gov

How New York's Mr Clean turned out to be a very dirty boy.

On 10 March 2008, the news broke that an upscale international prostitution ring had been busted. That the online agency catered to politicians and aristocrats came as no surprise, but few would have expected one name to be implicated: Eliot Spitzer, whose spotless reputation and lengthy crusades against dirty dealing and sleaze had helped sweep him to the city's governorship. In a spectacularly tawdry fall from grace, Mr Clean turned out to be 'Client 9', who reputedly shelled out more than $15,000 to the Emperors Club VIP over more than six months.

Between 1998 and 2006, Spitzer built a formidable résumé as New York State Attorney General, taking on a variety of powerful concerns. He charged or investigated investment banks, mutual funds, the New York Stock Exchange and the insurance industry over various infractions, and earned the nickname of the 'Sheriff of Wall Street' for his prosecution of white-collar crime. He also brought a suit in 2003 against a Queens company that he alleged promoted Asian sex tours.

Spitzer's governorship, which began in 2007, was less stellar. A proposal to grant driver's licenses to illegal immigrants met with such opposition, even among fellow Democrats, that he was forced to withdraw it. And the revelation that he'd authorised state police to monitor the travels of Joseph Bruno, the Republican majority leader, forced him to issue a public apology.

But perhaps Spitzer was merely warming up for his ultimate expression of contrition. An investigation into his affairs was initiated after his bank reported suspicious transfers of more than $10,000 in July 2007 to what would turn out to be the front for Emperors Club VIP. The federal probe received permission to wiretap his calls and discovered his assignation (under the

'Client 9' alias) with a prostitute named 'Kristen' for a night at the Mayflower Hotel in Washington, DC, on 13 February 2008, allegedly leaving her $4,300 in cash. Within a month, four members of the ring had been charged, and the *New York Times*, which had learned of the investigation, confronted the governor.

Acknowledging his involvement publicly, Spitzer quickly became fodder for late-night television hosts, while his enemies gloated with great 'Spitzenfreude' at the private debauchery of so publicly moral a man. A week later, with his wife at his side, a grim-faced Spitzer resigned as governor; while he is expected to escape prosecution, his political career is undoubtedly over.

And 'Kristen'? Since puttin' on the Spitz, she has emerged as Ashley Alexandra Dupré, a budding singer who released two singles online in the aftermath of the scandal. There are even rumours of a career in reality television – stay tuned.

'Amid the trauma of 9/11, the attack triggered a citywide sense of unity. New Yorkers muscled together.'

IN CONTEXT

9/11 AND BEYOND

On 11 September 2001, terrorists flew two hijacked passenger jets into the Twin Towers of the World Trade Center, collapsing the entire complex and killing nearly 2,800 people. Amid the trauma, the attack triggered a citywide sense of unity, and New Yorkers muscled together and did what they could to help their fellow citizens, from feeding emergency crews around the clock to cheering on rescue workers en route to Ground Zero.

Two months later, billionaire Michael Bloomberg was elected mayor and took on the daunting task of repairing not only the city's skyline but also its battered economy and shattered psyche. He proved adept at steering New York back on the road to health as the stock market revived, downtown businesses re-emerged and plans for rebuilding the Trade Center were drawn. True to form, however, New Yorkers debated the future of the site for more than a year until architect Daniel Libeskind was awarded the redevelopment job in 2003, since when progress has been slow. David Childs' Freedom Tower rose by 15 feet in spring 2008, but just weeks later, Chris Ward, executive director of the Port Authority of New York (which owns the site), reported that 'schedule and cost estimates of the rebuilding effort that have been communicated to the public are not realistic.' It's believed that neither the 1,776-foot tower nor the proposed World Trade Center museum and memorial will be completed by their 2011 target date.

Yet despite Bloomberg's many efforts to make New York a more considerate and civil place – imposing a citywide smoking ban in bars and restaurants and a strict noise ordinance that would silence even the jingling of ice-cream vans – New Yorkers continue to uphold their hard-edged image. The 2004 Republican National Convention brought out hundreds of thousands of peace marchers who had no trouble expressing how they felt about the war in Iraq. Local belly-aching helped kill a plan to build a 75,000-seat stadium on Manhattan's West Side, squashing Bloomberg and Co's dream to bring the 2012 Olympic Games to the Big Apple. In 2007, Bloomberg jumped on the eco bandwagon and announced plans to 'green up' NYC, aiming to reduce carbon emissions by 30 per cent; fight traffic jams by making motorists pay driving fees in parts of Manhattan; and ensure that every New Yorker is no more than a ten-minute walk from a park. Whether these plans will come to fruition remains to be seen.

The most sensational news in 2008 was the stuff of made-for-TV movies: the news that Governor Eliot Spitzer, who had built his reputation as a sleaze-fighting 'white knight', had been a big-spending client of a major prostitution ring (*see p31* **The Tainted Gov**). Upon Spitzer's resignation, the affable lieutenant governor David Paterson became New York's first African-American – and blind – governor. Just days after he was sworn in, another (much smaller) scandal erupted when it was revealed he'd had an extra-marital affair. But the chatter quickly died down after he and his wife explained that they had both strayed during a rough patch in their marriage.

As Bloomberg's second term nears its end (in December 2009), he has become increasingly frustrated that some of his pet proposals – such as that London-style congestion charge, which has met with overwhelming opposition from state politicians – haven't been realised. In the midst of 2008's deepening financial crisis, he proposed a controversial bill to extend the tenure of elected officials from two four-year terms to three. Although it was narrowly passed by the New York City Council in October 2008, many politicos (and citizens) opposed the law change and at time of writing two suits had been filed against it. Come 2010, another chapter in New York's history may yet be written.

Key Events

New York in brief.

1524 Giovanni da Verrazano sails into New York Harbor.
1624 First Dutch settlers establish New Amsterdam at foot of Manhattan Island.
1626 Peter Minuit purchases Manhattan for goods worth 60 guilders.
1639 The Broncks settle north of Manhattan.
1646 Village of Breuckelen founded.
1664 Dutch rule ends; New Amsterdam renamed New York.
1754 King's College (now Columbia University) founded.
1776 Battle for New York begins; fire ravages city.
1783 George Washington's troops march triumphantly down Broadway.
1784 Alexander Hamilton founds the Bank of New York.
1785 City becomes nation's capital.
1789 President Washington inaugurated at Federal Hall on Wall Street.
1792 New York Stock Exchange opens.
1804 New York becomes country's most populous city, with 80,000 inhabitants.
1811 Mayor DeWitt Clinton's grid plan for Manhattan introduced.
1827 Slavery officially abolished.
1851 The *New York Daily Times* (now the *New York Times*) published.
1858 Work on Central Park begins.
1872 Metropolitan Museum of Art opens.
1883 Brooklyn Bridge opens.
1886 Statue of Liberty unveiled.
1891 Carnegie Hall opens.
1892 Ellis Island opens.
1898 City consolidates the five boroughs.
1902 The Fuller (Flatiron) Building becomes the world's first skyscraper.
1903 The New York Highlanders (later the Yankees) play their first game.
1904 New York's first subway line opens; Longacre Square becomes Times Square.
1908 First ball dropped to celebrate the new year in Times Square.
1923 Yankee Stadium opens.
1924 First Macy's Christmas Parade held – now the Thanksgiving Day Parade.

1929 Stock market crashes; Museum of Modern Art opens.
1931 George Washington Bridge completed; Empire State Building completed; Whitney Museum opens.
1934 Fiorello La Guardia takes office; Tavern on the Green opens.
1939 New York hosts a World's Fair.
1950 United Nations complex finished.
1953 Robert Moses spearheads building of the Cross Bronx Expressway; 40,000 homes demolished in the process.
1957 New York Giants baseball team moves to San Francisco; Brooklyn Dodgers move to Los Angeles.
1962 New York Mets debut at the Polo Grounds; Philharmonic Hall (later Avery Fisher Hall), first building in Lincoln Center, opens.
1964 Verrazano-Narrows Bridge completed; World's Fair held in Flushing Meadows-Corona Park in Queens.
1970 First New York City Marathon held.
1973 World Trade Center completed.
1975 On verge of bankruptcy, city is snubbed by federal government; *Saturday Night Live* debuts.
1977 Serial killer David 'Son of Sam' Berkowitz arrested; Studio 54 opens; 4,000 arrested during citywide blackout.
1989 David N Dinkins elected city's first black mayor.
1993 Bomb explodes in World Trade Center, killing six and injuring 1,000.
1997 Murder rate lowest in 30 years.
2001 Hijackers fly two jets into World Trade Center, killing nearly 2,800 and demolishing both towers.
2004 Statue of Liberty reopens for first time since 9/11; Republican National Convention draws huge protests.
2007 Mayor Bloomberg unveils long-term vision for more eco-friendly city.
2008 David Paterson becomes New York State's first African-American governor.
2009 Yankees and Mets prepare to move into new state-of-the-art stadiums.

IN CONTEXT

New York Today

There may be trouble ahead...

TEXT: HOWARD HALLE

Is Gotham still a place of limitless horizons? Or is the city entering an era of shrunken expectations? That, in a nutshell, may be the best way to sum up modern-day New York.

To visitors from abroad, the city remains the undisputed Capital of the World. The numbers don't lie: a record 46 million tourists came to the city in 2007, up from a record 44 million in 2006. To be sure, the weak dollar was a factor: New York has become a favourite weekend destination for British and European shoppers, arriving with empty suitcases and pockets full of pounds or Euros. Still, it's more than easy pickings that lures outsiders to New York: they're just as drawn by the city itself, by a glamorous/dangerous image reinforced by countless movies and TV series.

Americans have seen the same films and shows, and have swarmed into the metropolis despite the rising cost of air travel and gasoline. But the attitude of the rest of the country to its largest conurbation has always swung wildly between love and hate, jealousy and awe. While New York has long been seen as a place apart, the idea that the city's fate is detached from the nation's has been overstated. But although Gotham's economy purred along relatively unscathed while other Americans struggled with job losses and mounting mortgage failures in 2007, New Yorkers are confronting the same conjoined uncertainties of a faltering economy and a change of administration.

Howard Halle is Time Out New York *magazine's Editor-at-Large.*

MONEY, MONEY, MONEY

The pain has been felt most acutely in the city's crucial financial sector, which has seen major layoffs as well as the federal bail-outs of Citibank and brokerage firm Bear Stearns. Worries are also linked to the impending change of administration, although eyes may be fixed less on the White House than on City Hall: 2009 represents the conclusion of Mayor Michael Bloomberg's second term in office. Historically, this would have been his last, but in the face of 2008's financial spiral, he pushed for the law governing the term limits of elected officials to be changed so he could run for a third.

Dreamer, technocrat, billionaire: Bloomberg has become a pivotal figure in NYC history. Although, early on, he was seen as simply building on the crime-busting legacy of former mayor Rudolph Giuliani, it's now clear that Bloomberg has taken New York to a whole new level of wealth, power and international stature, beyond anything that Giuliani's polarising regime could have ever achieved. From his sponsorship of such public artworks as Christo and Jeanne-Claude's *The Gates* (displayed in Central Park in 2005) and Olafur Eliasson's *Waterfalls* (New York Harbor, 2008) to his support for major redevelopment plans (the West Side's Hudson Yards and Brooklyn's Atlantic Yards) and his green initiatives, Bloomberg has always thought big. Not all of his schemes succeeded, but the sheer scale of his ambitions were enough, it seems, to kick the city into overdrive – sometimes to deleterious effect. Indeed, if there's one thread running through the embroidery that is New York today, it's the impact of Bloomberg's vision upon the city, for good and bad.

LOOK OUT BELOW

The most conspicuous sign of New York's explosive growth under Bloomberg has been the construction projects that seem to dot nearly every block of the city. That's an exaggeration, of course, but large swathes of Gotham have been radically transformed. And the fallout from this boom has, at times, been quite literal.

On 15 March 2008, the upper reaches of a construction crane – including the operator's cab and the perpendicular swing arm – broke away from its supporting base at a site on the East Side along 51st Street. Eyewitnesses reported that the crane hurtled southwards through the air before tumbling towards 50th Street, where it made a direct hit on a four-storey townhouse and flattened it on impact. Seven people died and over a dozen were injured. Then, just two months later, another crane collapsed 40 blocks north at the site of a new condo development; this time, two people died. Speculation as to the cause of the accidents centred on whether or not there might have been poorly maintained equipment that somehow made it past city inspectors. There was talk that the worldwide demand for cranes, especially in Dubai, forced developers to cut corners while officials looked the other way. In June, the city's chief crane inspector was arrested for allegedly doing just that; he pleaded not guilty at the arraignment and at press time was awaiting trial. Links were made, by residents and in the media, about the human cost of the construction glut.

BACK TO THE BAD OLD DAYS?

There have been flipsides to this frenetic activity. Although, in 2007, New York appeared immune from the housing crisis that saddled the rest of the country, things began to change with the new year. There were 918 foreclosures in the five boroughs during the first quarter of 2008 compared to 554 the previous year – a 66 per cent increase. Most were in the outer boroughs; Manhattan reported 14 foreclosures, a relatively small number when you consider the loss of Wall Street jobs.

The slowing economy has forced plans for larger redevelopment to be stalled or put on hold. The vast Hudson Yards city-within-the-city project recently avoided being killed outright when a new developer stepped in with a $1 billion infusion, but it's still far from secure; and the Frank Gehry-designed Atlantic Yards has been increasingly hamstrung by tightening credit and community opposition. Meanwhile, the perpetually limping rebuild of Ground Zero, crippled by delays and cost overruns, hit another roadblock when Governor Paterson declared that the proposed 2011 deadline for completion had been unrealistic.

'The great wheel of gentrification churns unabated, but many New Yorkers wonder if their city has lost its soul.'

But the most alarming news for average New Yorkers has perhaps been the Transit Authority's announcement that, because of budgetary shortfalls, the number of subway stations slated for refurbishment would be slashed from 55 to 25. The notion of a financial shortfall was a surprise to New Yorkers paying increasing fares; but as the subway goes, so goes the city. The fact that the MTA was returning to its old habits of indefinitely pulling off repairs raised fears that things might revert to the Stygian conditions of 30 years ago.

CHAIN REACTION

Still, the great wheel of gentrification churns unabated, and as good as that might be for the overall quality of life, many New Yorkers find themselves wondering if their city has lost its soul – that ineffable product of countless individuals pursuing individual, idiosyncratic goals, whether in business or the arts. It's a relevant question. Along with all the new condos and corporate buildings, a veritable tsunami of chain stores has crashed on to our shores over the past several years. The worry is that New York is becoming one giant strip mall, overrun by banks and pharmacies. The huge number of Starbucks in the city is something of a local joke, but despite its ubiquity, it's not the most pervasive retailer. That honour, according to a recent survey by non-partisan think tank Center for an Urban Future, goes to the more downscale Dunkin' Donuts, which has 341 outlets throughout the city.

Things have got so out of hand that the City Council has been debating measures to slow the tide by giving local mom-and-pop stores a leg up against national competitors. Among the ideas: a tax break for small businesses, and the widening of protective zones – similar to those already in place in Harlem – that limit banks from opening branches on street-level floors.

WHITHER BOHEMIA?

But it's not just small businesses that are being threatened by relentless redevelopment: the very cultural fabric of the city is in danger of being eroded. The clearest indication of this trend is in the transformation of neighbourhoods once associated with artists and outsiders. Soho seems to have evolved into a luxe version of a strip mall; and while the West Village retains its quaint characteristics, the costs of enjoying them have gone up exponentially. Similarly, the former Meatpacking District, once a stark waterfront zone that served as the unlikely meeting ground for trannies and truck drivers, is now stuffed with upscale boutiques, hotels and boîtes. The early rough-edged pioneers have been priced out – in summer 2008, Florent, the all-night bistro that served French-style bar grub to club kids and butchers alike, closed after 23 years.

Artist nabes offering alternative scenes – such as they are – do exist in Brooklyn, especially along the border between Williamsburg and Bushwick. However, bohemia in New York has been historically associated with Manhattan. In this respect, it's the current state of affairs in the East Village and the Lower East Side, areas long known for immigrants and cutting-edge types, that best sums the contradictions of the modern city.

In summer 1988, Tompkins Square Park erupted in riots over attempts by the police to impose a midnight closing that meant the dismantling of a sprawling tent city of homeless people that had sprung up in the park the previous winter. Among the defenders of the homeless manning the barricades were local artists and anarchists. But 20 years later, most of the participants in the saga – the homeless, the anarchists, the artists – have long

Construction work continues.

since gone, and the railway tenement flats they once squatted are now being rented for thousands of dollars a month. Meanwhile, new development, in the form of luxury high-rises on the Lower East Side and swanky hotels on the Bowery, has again attracted the attention of officials hoping to stem the tide. The National Trust for Historic Preservation recently named the Lower East Side as one of the 11 most endangered places in America, and has called for the area to be designated an official historic district by the Landmarks Preservation Commission. Whether landmarking and attendant restrictions on development take place remain to be seen.

Yet alternative cultural scenes flourish as well as flounder in these locales. They're home to notable venues of New York's Off-Off Broadway theatre scene, which are under duress from rising rents. And over little more than a year, there's been a veritable eruption of more than 50 new galleries devoted to young artists in and around the New Museum of Contemporary Art, which opened in late 2007 on the Bowery.

And so the countercultural spirit of the Lower East Side and New York lives on – hard to kill, but also hard to maintain in the current climate. This paradoxical situation, perhaps, is no different from the paradox that is Michael Bloomberg himself. Whether he's re-elected for 2010 remains to be seen, but will the mayor's final legacy be that he left New York City better off or somehow diminished? At his request, the Department of City Planning recently undertook a recalculation of the city's land mass. Their finding? That the city isn't as large as it used to be. The five boroughs are 17.2 square miles smaller than previously estimated – down from 322 square miles to 304.8. Whether this becomes the ultimate metaphor for the age of Bloomberg is for history to decide.

Architecture

The building boom has stalled, but New York City continues to rise.

TEXT: ERIC P NASH

The New York Times

Manhattan, of course, is synonymous with skyscrapers. Following advances in iron and steel technology in the middle of the 19th century, and the pressing need for space in an already overcrowded island, New York's architects realised that the only way really was up. The race to reach the heavens in the early 20th century was supplanted by the minimalist post-war International Style, which saw a rash of towering glass boxes spread across Midtown. Even these days, despite less than favourable economic conditions, high-rise style is still very much in favour.

However, those with an architectural interest and an observant eye will be rewarded by the fascinating mix of architectural styles and surprising details closer to the ground in virtually every corner of the metropolis, from gargoyles crouching on the façade of an early 20th-century apartment building to extravagant cast-iron decoration adorning a humble warehouse. And it's worth remembering that under New York's gleaming exoskeleton of steel and glass lies the heart of a 17th-century Dutch city.

Eric P Nash is the author of Manhattan Skyscrapers *and other books on New York architecture.*

CUSTOM MADE

It all began at the Battery and New York Harbor, one of the greatest naturally formed deep-water ports in the world. The old Alexander Hamilton Custom House, now the National Museum of the American Indian (*see p65*), was built by Cass Gilbert in 1907 and is a symbol of the harbour's significance in Manhattan's growth. Before 1913, the city's chief source of revenue was customs duties. Gilbert's domed marble edifice is suitably monumental – its carved figures of the Four Continents are by Daniel Chester French, the sculptor of the Lincoln Memorial in Washington, DC.

The Dutch influence is still traceable in the downtown web of narrow, winding lanes, reminiscent of the streets in medieval European cities. Because the Cartesian grid that rules the city was laid out by the Commissioners' Plan in 1811, only a few samples of Dutch architecture remain, mostly off the beaten path. One is the 1785 **Dyckman Farmhouse Museum** (4881 Broadway, at 204th Street, www.dyckmanfarmhouse.org, closed Mon & Tue) in Inwood, Manhattan's northernmost neighbourhood. Its decorative brickwork and gambrel roof reflect the architectural fashion of the late 18th century. The single oldest house still standing today in the five boroughs, meanwhile, is the **Pieter Claesen Wyckoff House Museum** (5816 Clarendon Road, at Ralph Avenue, Flatbush, Brooklyn, www.wyckoffassociation.org, closed Mon & Sun in winter). First erected around 1652, it's a typical Dutch farmhouse with deep eaves and roughly shingled walls.

In Manhattan, the only building left from pre-Revolutionary times is the stately columned and quoined **St Paul's Chapel** (*see p69*), completed in 1766 (a spire was added in 1796). George Washington, a parishioner here, was officially received in the chapel after his 1789 presidential inauguration. The Enlightenment ideals upon which the nation was founded influenced the church's highly democratic, non-hierarchical layout. **Trinity Church** (*see p68*) of 1846, one of the first and finest Gothic Revival churches in the country, was designed by Richard Upjohn. It's difficult to imagine now that Trinity's crocketed, finialed 281-foot-tall spire held sway for decades as the tallest structure in Manhattan.

Holdouts remain from each epoch of the city's architectural history. An outstanding example of Greek Revival from the first half of the 19th century is the 1842 **Federal Hall National Memorial** (*see p68*), the mighty marble colonnade built to mark the site where George Washington took his oath of office. A larger-than-life statue of Washington by the sculptor John Quincy Adams Ward stands in front. The city's most celebrated blocks of Greek Revival townhouses, built in the 1830s, are known simply as the **Row** (1-13 Washington Square North, between Fifth Avenue & Washington Square West); they're exemplars of the more genteel metropolis of Henry James and Edith Wharton.

Greek Revival gave way to Renaissance-inspired Beaux Arts architecture, which itself reflected the imperial ambitions of a wealthy young nation during the Gilded Age of the late 19th century. Like Emperor Augustus, who boasted that he had found Rome a city of brick and left it a city of marble, the firm of McKim, Mead & White built noble civic monuments and *palazzi* for the rich. The best-known buildings of the classicist Charles Follen McKim include the main campus of **Columbia University** (*see p117*), begun in the 1890s, and the austere 1906 **Morgan Library** (*see p91*). His partner, socialite and bon vivant Stanford White (scandalously murdered by his mistress's husband in 1906), designed more festive spaces, such as the **Metropolitan Club** (1 E 60th Street, at Fifth Avenue) and the luxe Villard Houses of 1882, now part of the 100-year-old **New York Palace Hotel** (*see p170*).

Another Beaux Arts treasure from the city's grand metropolitan era is Carrère & Hastings' sumptuous white marble **New York Public Library** of 1911 (*see p100*), built on the site of a former Revolutionary War battleground. The 1913 travertine-lined **Grand Central Terminal** (*see p103*) remains the most elegant foyer, thanks to preservationists (including Jacqueline Kennedy Onassis) who saved it from the wrecking ball.

AIMING HIGH

Cast-iron architecture peaked in the latter half of the 19th century, coinciding roughly with the Civil War. Iron and steel components freed architects from the bulk, weight and cost of

IN CONTEXT

Tall Storeys

How NYC's architects reached for the sky.

For nearly half a century after its 1846 completion, the 284-foot steeple of Richard Upjohn's great Gothic Revival **Trinity Church** (*see p68*) reigned in lonely serenity at the foot of Wall Street as the tallest structure in Manhattan. This was the pre-skyscraper era, and building upwards was neither popular nor straightforward. The church was finally topped in 1890 by the since-demolished, 348-foot **New York World Building**. But it wasn't until the turn of the century that New York's architects started to reach for the skies. And so began a mad rush to the top, with building after building capturing the title of the world's tallest.

When it was completed in 1899, the 30-storey, 391-foot **Park Row Building** (15 Park Row, between Ann & Beekman Streets) became the tallest building in the world. However, its record was shattered by the 612-foot **Singer Building** in 1908 (which, 60 years later, became the tallest building ever to be demolished in 1968);

the 52-storey, 700-foot **Metropolitan Life Tower** (1 Madison Avenue, at 24th Street) of 1909, modelled after the Campanile in Venice's Piazza San Marco; and the 793.5-foot **Woolworth Building** (*see p71*), Cass Gilbert's Gothic 1913 masterpiece that was as famous as the Empire State in its heyday.

The Woolworth reigned in solitary splendour until skyscraper construction reached a crescendo in the late 1920s, with a famed three-way race. The now largely forgotten **Bank of Manhattan Building** at 40 Wall Street was briefly the record-holder, at 71 storeys and 927 feet in 1930. Soon after, William Van Alen, the architect of the **Chrysler Building** (*see p103*), unveiled his secret weapon: a 'vertex', a spire of chrome nickel steel put together inside the dome and raised from within that brought the building's height to 1,046 feet. But then, 13 months later, Van Alen's homage to the Automobile Age was itself outstripped by Shreve, Lamb & Harmon's 1,250-foot **Empire State Building** (*see p100*). With its broad base, narrow shaft and distinctive needled crown, it remains the quintessential skyscraper, and one of the most famous buildings in the world.

Incredibly, there were no challengers for the title of New York's – and the world's – tallest building for more than 40 years, until the 110-storey, 1,362- and 1,368-foot twin towers of Minoru Yamasaki's **World Trade Center** were completed in 1973. They were trumped by Chicago's Sears Tower a year later but reigned as the city's tallest building until 11 September 2001, when the New York crown reverted to the Empire State Building. The **Freedom Tower** (pictured) designed by David Childs of Skidmore, Owings & Merrill to replace the Twin Towers, has been bogged down by problems, but it's eventually expected to surpass the WTC with a completed height of 1,776 feet. Don't look down…

IN CONTEXT

stone construction, and allowed them to build taller structures. Cast-iron columns – cheap to mass-produce – could support a tremendous amount of weight. The façades of many Soho buildings, with their intricate details of Italianate columns, were manufactured on assembly lines and could be ordered in pieces from catalogues. This led to an aesthetic of uniform building façades, which had a direct impact on subsequent steel skyscraper and continues to inform New York's skyline today. To enjoy one of the most telling vistas of skyscraper history, gaze north from the 1859 **Cooper Union** building in the East Village (*see p82*), the oldest existing steel-beam-framed building in America.

The most visible effect of the move towards cast-iron construction was the way it opened up solid-stone façades to expanses of glass. In fact, window-shopping came into vogue in the 1860s. Mrs Lincoln bought the White House china at the **Haughwout Store** (488-492 Broadway, at Broome Street). The 1857 building's Palladian-style façade recalls Renaissance Venice, but its regular, open fenestration was also a portent of the future. (Look carefully: the cast-iron elevator sign is a relic of the world's first working safety passenger elevator, designed by Elisha Graves Otis in 1852.)

Once engineers perfected steel, which is stronger and lighter than iron, and created the interlocking steel-cage construction that distributed the weight of a building over its entire frame, the sky was the limit. New York has one structure by the great Chicago-based innovator Louis Sullivan: the 1898 **Bayard-Condict Building** (65-69 Bleecker Street, between Broadway & Lafayette Street). Though only 13 storeys tall, Sullivan's building, covered with richly decorative terracotta, was one of the earliest to have a purely vertical design rather than one that imitated the horizontal styles of the past. Sullivan wrote that a skyscraper 'must be tall, every inch of it tall… From bottom to top, it is a unit without a single dissenting line'. The 21-storey **Flatiron Building** (*see p89*), designed by fellow Chicagoan Daniel H Burnham and completed in 1902, is another standout of the era. Its height and modern design combined with traditional masonry decoration, breathtaking even today, was made possible only by its steel-cage construction.

IN CONTEXT

Haughwout Store.

Early icons: the **Flatiron Building**
(*left*) and the **Woolworth Building**.
See pp40-41.

The new century saw a frenzy of skyward manufacture, resulting in buildings of record-breaking height. When it was built in 1899, the 30-storey, 391-foot **Park Row Building** (15 Park Row, between Ann & Beekman Streets) was the tallest building in the world; by 1931, though, Shreve, Lamb & Harmon's 1,250-foot **Empire State Building** (*see p100*) had more than tripled its record. For more on the battle for the city's tallest building, *see p40* **Tall storeys**.

Although they were retroactively labelled art deco (such buildings were then simply called 'modern'), the Empire State's setbacks were actually a response to the zoning code of 1916, which required a building's upper storeys to be tapered in order not to block out sunlight and air circulation to the streets. The code engendered some of the city's most fanciful architectural designs, such as the ziggurat-crowned 1926 **Paramount Building** (1501 Broadway, between 43rd & 44th Streets) and the romantically slender spire of the former **Cities Service Building** (70 Pine Street, at Pearl Street), illuminated from within like an enormous rare gem.

OUTSIDE THE BOX

The post-World War II period saw the rise of the International Style, pioneered by such giants as Le Corbusier and Ludwig Mies van der Rohe. The International Style relied on a new set of aesthetics: minimal decoration, clear expression of construction, an honest use of materials and a near-Platonic harmony of proportions. The style's most visible symbol was the all-glass façade, similar to that found on the sleek slab of the **United Nations Headquarters** (*see p103*).

Designed by Gordon Bunshaft of Skidmore, Owings & Merrill, **Lever House** (390 Park Avenue, between 53rd & 54th Streets) became the city's first all-steel-and-glass

'The International Style had obviously reached its end when Philip Johnson began disparaging the aesthetic as "glass-boxitis".'

structure when it was built in 1952. It's almost impossible to imagine the radical vision this glass construction represented on the all-masonry corridor of Park Avenue, because nearly every building since has followed suit. Mies van der Rohe's celebrated bronze-skinned **Seagram Building** (375 Park Avenue, between 52nd & 53rd Streets), which reigns in imperious isolation in its own plaza, is the epitome of the architect's cryptic dicta that 'Less is more' and 'God is in the details'. The detailing on the building is exquisite – the custom-made bolts securing the miniature bronze piers that run the length of the façade must be polished by hand every year to keep them from oxidising and turning green. With this heady combination of grandeur and attention to detail, it's the Rolls-Royce of skyscrapers.

High modernism began to show cracks in its façade during the mid 1960s. By then, New York had built too many such structures in Midtown and below. The public had never fully warmed to the undecorated style, and the International Style's sheer arrogance in trying to supplant the traditional city structure didn't endear the movement to anyone. The **MetLife Building** (200 Park Avenue, at 45th Street), originally the Pan Am Building of 1963, was the prime culprit, not so much because of its design (by Walter Gropius of the Bauhaus) but because of its presumptuous location, straddling Park Avenue and looming over Grand Central. There was even a plan to raze Grand Central and construct a twin Pan Am in its place. The International Style had obviously reached its end when Philip Johnson, instrumental in defining the movement with his book *The International Style* (co-written with Henry-Russell Hitchcock), began disparaging the aesthetic as 'glass-boxitis'.

Plainly, new blood was needed. A glimmer on the horizon was provided by Boston architect Hugh Stubbins' silvery, triangle-topped **Citicorp Center** (Lexington Avenue, between 53rd & 54th Streets), which utilised contemporary engineering (the building cantilevers almost magically on high stilts above street level) while harking back to the decorative tops of yesteryear. Sly old Johnson turned the tables on everyone with the heretical Chippendale crown on his **Sony Building**, originally the AT&T Building (350 Madison Avenue, between 55th & 56th Streets), a bold throwback to decoration for its own sake.

Postmodernism provided a theoretical basis for a new wave of buildings that mixed past and present, often taking cues from the environs. Some notable examples include Helmut Jahn's **425 Lexington Avenue** (between 43rd & 44th Streets) of 1988; David Childs' retro diamond-tipped **Worldwide Plaza** (825 Eighth Avenue, between 49th & 50th Streets) of 1989; and the honky-tonk agglomeration of Skidmore, Owings & Merrill's **Bertelsmann Building** (1540 Broadway, between 45th & 46th Streets) of 1990. But even postmodernism became old hat after a while: too many architects relied on fussy fenestration and passive commentary on other styles, and too few began to create vital new building façades.

The electronic spectacle of **Times Square** (*see p95*) provided, and continues to provide, one possible direction for architects. Upon seeing the myriad electric lights of Times Square in 1922, British wit GK Chesterton remarked: 'What a glorious garden of wonder this would be, to anyone who was lucky enough to be unable to read.' This particular crossroads of the world continues to be at the cybernetic cutting edge, with the 120-foot-tall, quarter-acre-in-area NASDAQ sign; the real-time stock tickers and jumbo TV screens; and the news ticker on the original **New York Times Tower** (1 Times Square, between Broadway & Seventh Avenue). The public's appetite for new images seems so

IN CONTEXT

Profile Solomon R Guggenheim Museum

Frank Lloyd Wright's iconic structure gets a birthday clean-up.

While its winding, cantilevered curves have become as integral to New York's architectural landscape as the spire of the Chrysler Building or the arches of the Brooklyn Bridge, the Solomon R Guggenheim Museum ruffled feathers when it was completed in 1959. Many felt its appearance clashed with the rest of staid Fifth Avenue, while Willem de Kooning and Robert Motherwell complained that their art was not best appreciated from the museum's ramps. Some critics suggested the building was less a museum than a monument to its architect, Frank Lloyd Wright, who died six months before its completion.

To a degree, these criticisms still hold water, but they were of little concern to Wright; when someone complained that the walls wouldn't be high enough to display certain paintings, he retorted that the canvases should be cut in half. Indeed, this conflict between architect and art still courses through the museum. Wright intended that visitors take the elevator to the top and view exhibits by strolling down the winding interior ramp; however, the order of many displays goes from the bottom up. Moreover, the skylight that imbued the space with natural light was damaging to certain works – the glass was replaced with thermal panes in the 1980s.

That the Guggenheim represents the sole major building by America's greatest 20th-century architect in its most iconic architectural city (there's also a house designed by Wright in the Lighthouse Hill section of Staten Island that isn't open to the public) is hardly surprising. Wright was not really an urban architect: most of his designs were for private homes in rural or suburban sites, and he was initially reluctant to take on the Guggenheim project. But as the building celebrates its half-century, with its formerly crack-plagued façade having at last been restored to its former glory, his Gotham swansong is probably his most famous creation.

HOW TO GET THERE For full details of the Guggenheim, including details of 2009 exhibitions, *see p111.*

IN CONTEXT

insatiable that a building's fixed profile no longer suffices here – only an ever-shifting electronic skin will do. The iconoclastic critic Robert Venturi calls this trend 'iconography and electronics upon a generic architecture'.

RADICAL RETHINKS

Early 21st-century architecture is moving beyond applied symbolism to radical new forms, facilitated by computer-based design methods. A stellar example is Kohn Pedersen Fox's stainless steel and glass 'vertical campus', the **Baruch College Academic Complex** (55 Lexington Avenue, between 24th & 25th Streets). The resulting phantasmic designs that curve and dart in sculptural space are so beyond the timid window-dressing of postmodernism that they deserve a new label.

Frank Gehry's ten-storey, white-glass mirage of a building on the Lower West Side, completed in 2007, is emblematic of the radical reworking of the New York cityscape. Gehry's first ever glass building and his first office building in New York, the headquarters for Barry Diller's **InterActiveCorp** (555 W 18th Street, at West Side Highway) is composed of tilting glass volumes that resemble a fully rigged tall ship. Change is quite literally in the air in this area. Once an ugly duckling neighbourhood of warehouses and industrial buildings, it is being transformed by the much-anticipated **High Line** project, a former elevated railroad viaduct that is being reconceived as a cutting-edge urban park (*see p89* **High point**). Down south, the **Urban Glass House** (330 Spring Street, at Washington Street), one of the late Philip Johnson's last designs, sprang up in 2006 amid Tribeca's hulking industrial edifices. The mini-skyscraper is a multiplication of his iconic Glass House in New Canaan, Connecticut. Nearby, Mexican architect Enrique Norten's crisply planed 14-storey glass tower rises from an antebellum warehouse at **One York Street**.

Midtown West has recently become an unlikely hotbed of new construction, with its architectural attractions boosted in 2006 by Norman Foster's elegant, 46-storey, 597-foot crystalline addition to the art deco base of the **Hearst Magazine Building** (300 W 57th Street, at Eighth Avenue). The structure is a breathtaking combination of old and new, with the massive triangular struts of the tower penetrating the façade of the base and opening up great airy spaces within. Further north, and among the more controversial facelifts of recent years, is Brad Cloepfil's renovation of Edward Durell Stone's 1964 modernism-meets-Venetian-palazzo **2 Columbus Circle**, originally the home of A & P heir Huntington Hartford's Gallery of Modern Art. In the same way that the gallery's collection of mostly figurative painting was seen as reactionary in the face of the abstract art movement, Stone's quotation of an historicist style was laughed into apostasy. However, Stone's work is being re-evaluated as a precursor to postmodernism, and many 20th-century architecture enthusiasts lamented the loss of the original façade after a lengthy, unsuccessful battle by the Landmarks Preservation Commission. The building is the new home of the Museum of Arts & Design (*see p115* **Full Circle**).

The activity hasn't been confined to Manhattan. In Brooklyn, Richard Meier has added a glass box condo '**On Prospect Park**' (1 Grand Army Plaza), upsetting some of the long-standing residents in the process: most preferred the unbroken vista of classic apartment buildings. At $1,200 per square foot for some units, Meier's building set a new real-estate record for Brooklyn; still, it's not as inspired as his more elegantly thought-out apartment buildings at 173 and 176 Perry Street, which overlook the Hudson. The Bronx got a boost with Arquitectonica's sleek aluminium and glass addition to the **Bronx Museum of the Arts** (*see p143*), which opens up to narrow strips of windows like accordion pleats.

FUTURE SHOCKS

Some of New York's more ambitious architectural projects have been significantly scaled back in the face of new economic realities. A major draw for new visitors of the city, **Ground Zero** has seen frustratingly little progress in the years since the tragedy of 9/11. The 16-acre site's overseers, the Port Authority of New York and New Jersey, reported that construction of the 26 interrelated projects was years behind schedule and billions

'Some of New York's more ambitious projects have been significantly scaled back in the face of new economic realities.'

IN CONTEXT

of dollars over its $16 billion budget, and the planned memorials will not be ready by the tenth anniversary of the Twin Towers' fall. So far, the site, originally conceived by Daniel Libeskind, has been unable to attract private tenants, and will be mostly occupied by state and government agencies. Santiago Calatrava's spectacular plan for a shimmering, subterranean PATH train station no longer features retractable roof wings, but the ribbed ceiling will still let in the sun with a skylight. At least the final design of David Childs' centrepiece 1,776-foot-tall Freedom Tower, expected to become the tallest building in the city at a cost of $3 billion, is making some visible progress – the steel pillars rising from the ground are the foundation for the tower's concrete base, to be clad in prismatic glass.

Scaling back seems to be a key phrase as the city enters the second decade of the 21st century, and grandiose schemes are now settling earthward. The transformation of Brooklyn's **Atlantic Yards** into a mega-development started boldly as an architectural site for Frank Gehry and Enrique Norten, but is now subject to budget cutbacks that may lower the proposed high-rises and reduce the density of the $4 billion project (which would be the largest private investment in Brooklyn's history). And the proposed $1.5 billion renovation of **Lincoln Center** has foregone new construction and left a team of top-notch architects to work with what's already there. Diller Scofidio + Renfro, one of the most creative teams on the scene, is turning the travertine marble façade of Alice Tully Hall into a show window, integrating inside and out with glass walls; elsewhere, Billie Tsien and Tod Williams are transforming an atrium across from Lincoln Center, between Broadway and Columbus and 62nd and 63rd Streets, into a sky-lit 'theatrical garden' lined with ferns, moss and flowering vines for buying tickets and sipping refreshments.

Even as the age of superblock Modernism seems to be coming to a close, a new era of green, ecology-conscious architecture is emerging. Cook + Fox's near-completed **Bank of America Tower** at 1 Bryant Park bills itself as the greenest skyscraper in the city, with torqued, glass facets reaching 54 storeys. The structure boasts a thermal storage system, daylight dimmers, green roofs and double-wall construction to reduce heat build-up, and the company is even looking into an anaerobic digester that will turn leftover food into electricity. Renzo Piano's sparkling new tower for *The New York Times* at **620 Eighth Avenue** (between W 40th & W 41st Streets) also offers such green amenities as automatic shades that respond to the heat of the sun, and recycled air. The glass-walled design is a literal representation of the newspaper's desire for transparency in reporting; the lobby moss garden with birch trees is also an interesting metaphor for an old-fashioned, paper-based industry in the computer age.

Unfortunately, the pace of construction lags considerably behind fashion trends and volatile economic markets; some buildings, such as the boxy **11 Times Square**, look old as soon as they are finished. Seeing no end in sight to growth and profits, developers tend to overbuild commercial space until there's a bust – plans for Ground Zero alone call for new office space that equates to five times the amount in downtown Atlanta – and there are plenty of acres in the city ripe for redevelopment. One developer has agreed to pay $1 billion for the MTA's 26-acre train yards on Manhattan's Far West Side, along Eleventh Avenue between 30th and 33rd Streets, which could offer the opportunity to extend the urbane design of the High Line. But this may not be the proper environment for grand new schemes after the expansion of the Javits Center fell through, along with David Childs' initial scheme for a new Penn Station (now likely to be an attempt to open up the old space instead).

Santiago Calatrava (left) and his designs for **80 South Street**

Nevertheless, some exciting projects are in the pipeline. Pritzker Prize-winner Jean Nouvel's 75-storey sloped, crystalline tower, with an exoskeleton of irregularly crossing beams, is rising next door to the Museum of Modern Art. Equal in height to the Chrysler Building, it should be a glamorous presence on the city skyline, dwarfing Cesar Pelli's existing Museum Tower. And in a reversal of the city's historical pattern of development, most of the money is migrating downtown. The Blue Building, Bernard Tschumi's multifaceted, blue-glass-walled condominium, is a startling breakaway from the low-rise brick buildings that make up the Lower East Side. Also noteworthy is the Japanese firm SANAA's **New Museum of Contemporary Art** (*see p80*); its asymmetrically staggered boxy volumes covered in aluminum mesh shake up the traditional street front of the Bowery. Meanwhile, the curled and warped façade of Frank Gehry's 76-storey **Beekman Tower** across from City Hall will revitalise downtown when it's completed in 2010.

Other projects exist tantalisingly on the drafting board, such as Calatrava's proposal for an 835-foot-tall concrete core with 12 four-storey townhouses daringly cantilevered from its sides. The only thing standing in the way of the visionary project, slated for 80 South Street, is finding 12 billionaires to invest in it. And Renzo Piano has blueprints for a tiered glass downtown satellite of the Whitney Museum at the southern end of the High Line that has double the floor space of the existing museum. To keep up with what's going up in New York, visit the **AIA Center for Architecture** (*see p84*), the **Skyscraper Museum** (*see p68*) and the **Storefront for Art & Architecture** (97 Kenmare Street, between Mulberry Street & Cleveland Place, 1-212 431 5795, www.storefrontnews.org, closed Mon, Sun), a non-profit organisation that hosts a programme of exhibitions, talks, screenings and more.

They could have made it anywhere, but they made it here.

TEXT: RICHARD KOSS

Movers and Shapers

New York City is being remoulded and reshaped all the time: by longtime locals and new arrivals, born-and-bred Americans and just-arrived immigrants, men and women and children of every age. All of the world's best and most interesting cities are in a state of constant flux, and the city that never sleeps is no exception.

New York is a famously tough town, and New Yorkers are a famously and suitably tough bunch. But in this dog-eat-dog city, it's hardly surprising that some exceptional cream should have risen to the surface. Visionary developers and landscape gardeners, political activists and campaign crusaders, well-heeled philanthropists and self-obsessed artists, scenesters and sportsmen, journalists and movie-makers – all have made their mark in New York. And in doing so, all have transcended the city in which they made their name.

Over the following pages, we profile 20 big shots who all helped, one way or another, to define the Big Apple as we know it in 2009. Together, they make up a cultural and political force that has far outstretched the boundaries of the Five Boroughs.

Native New Yorker **Richard Koss** *is a travel writer and the editor of the annual* Time Out New York Eating & Drinking Guide.

Visionaries

THE PLANNER AND THE PRESERVATIONIST

Nobody did more to shape modern New York than **ROBERT MOSES** (1888-1981), the controversial urban planner who held numerous appointed municipal offices between 1924 and 1968. Seeking to bring the city into the automobile age, he built 13 bridges (including the Triborough and the Verrazano Narrows) and such urban highways as the Cross-Bronx Expressway. Fans applaud his creation of Jones Beach on **Long Island**, his role in bringing the United Nations to New York, his overseeing of the 1964/5 New York World's Fair and his construction of over 600 children's playgrounds. Foes note that the vast majority of these playgrounds were in white neighborhoods and that many of his much-vaunted expressways uprooted existing communities and left decaying ghettos in their wake. Countered Moses, 'Those who can, build. Those who can't, criticise.'

The master builder's most constructive critic was community activist and urban theorist **JANE JACOBS** (1916-2006), who saw the death of small neighbourhoods lurking in Moses's expansive vision of the big city. She successfully led the opposition to his proposed Lower Manhattan Expressway, a crosstown highway that would have connected the Holland Tunnel with the Williamsburg Bridge (and paved over Soho in the process) and defeated his attempts to extend Fifth Avenue through **Washington Square Park** (see p84). This last move would have disfigured Greenwich Village, the neighbourhood Jacobs cited in her seminal work *The Death and Life of Great American Cities* (1961) as the perfect example of a vital community that had evolved without urban planning.

THE PHILANTHROPIST

Born with a head start in life as sole heir to the enormous Standard Oil fortune, **JOHN D ROCKEFELLER, JR** (1874-1960) was a committed philanthropist. Among the city's recipients of his largesse were the **Museum of Modern Art** (see p100), co-founded by his wife Abby and built on property he donated; the **Cloisters** museum (see p122), to which he contributed art from his collection; and **Lincoln Center** (see p331), which he helped build. However, his biggest landmark in the city is the **Rockefeller Center** complex (see p101), an art deco extravaganza that he financed during the Depression.

THE MUCK RAKER

Danish-born **JACOB RIIS** (1849-1914) was a pioneering photojournalist who documented the appalling conditions of New York tenement life during the late 19th century. Riis was one of the first photographers to use flash powder, a new photographic technology that allowed him to take shots at night and further illuminate the horrific squalour, overcrowding and disease of life on the **Lower East Side** (see p75). Raking through this social muck in his books *How the Other Half Lives* (1891) and *The Battle with the Slum* (1902), Riis argued forcefully for better housing, lighting and sanitation. His call was eventually heeded with the Tenement House Act, which greatly improved living conditions for the poor.

THE CELEBRITY ARTIST

A self-described 'deeply superficial person', **ANDY WARHOL** (1928-1987) was the godfather of Pop Art, the movement that manipulated mass-produced images from popular culture. For Warhol, this meant silk-screened Campbell's soup cans or colourised Marilyn Monroe portraits, as well as deadpan commentaries on modern consumerism and the worship of celebrity. Indeed, his Factory workspace became the salon of 1960s and '70s New York, luring through its portals such luminaries as Salvador Dalí, Truman Capote, Edie Sedgwick and the Velvet Underground. Warhol's influence was international, but felt most keenly on the New York scene by such artists as Keith Haring and Jean-Michel Basquiat; a fine selection of his work can be seen at **MoMA** (see p100). A plaque outside 57 E 66th Street, between Madison and Park Avenues on the Upper East Side, identifies it as the artist's address from 1974 to 1987.

THE PRINCE OF DARKNESS

The man behind the velvet rope, not as a bouncer but as the cruel barrier's originator, was real estate developer **IAN SCHRAGER** (1946-), who first came to prominence as the co-owner of clubs such as the Palladium and Studio 54. The latter was the nexus of late '70s and early '80s hedonistic nightlife, as coked-to-the-gills celebrities packed the place out every evening. Following a stint in jail for tax evasion, Schrager reinvented himself as a pioneer of the boutique hotel concept, first with the Morgans Hotel in 1984, and then in his collaboration with artist and film director Julian Schnabel, who decorated the relaunched **Gramercy Park Hotel** (see p162) to great acclaim.

THE MASTER GARDENER

Without the talents of **FREDERICK LAW OLMSTED** (1822-1903), New York would probably now be 100 per cent concrete jungle. Olmsted believed that the city's inhabitants should have access to parklands with landscaped hills, stately trees and curved walkways that offered respite from the city's bustle. With associate Calvert Vault, he won an 1857 competition to design 'Greensward', then a sprawling marshland on the northern fringe of Manhattan; in 1876, it opened as **Central Park** (see p104). Olmsted went on to design numerous other green spaces in the city; among them were Manhattan's **Riverside** and **Morningside** parks as well as Brooklyn's **Prospect Park** (see p129). It's scary to think of New York without them.

Campaigners & Crusaders

THE CLEANER AND THE MAN OF GOD

While it's hard to view **RUDOLPH GIULIANI** (1944-) without thinking of 9/11 (and one suspects that he doesn't want you to), his mayoralty from 1994 to 2001 had an immense impact on the fabric of the city. After a high-profile career as a prosecutor, Giuliani swept to power on a law-and-order ticket. His subsequent 'war on crime' entailed aggressive policing that came down hard on minor misdemeanours (woe betide the 'squeegee men' who – at one time – sponged windshields at traffic lights) and targeted high-crime neighbourhoods. Declining crime figures suggested that he was indeed cleaning up the city, but several incidents of police brutality and the spot-checking of ethnic minority drivers outraged many. Yet the attacks on the World Trade Center obscured his polarising legacy, and Giuliani, thanks to a frequent presence at **Ground Zero** (see p66), came to be considered by many as a more unifying force.

Baptist minister and African-American political activist, the **REVEREND AL SHARPTON** (1954-) was one of Giuliani's most outspoken critics. Though he rose to prominence by vociferously championing a teenager whose 1987 gang-rape claims turned out to be concocted, the reverend has since managed to modify his more extreme advocacy (enough to sustain a presidential campaign in 2004) without abandoning civil rights causes and protests against police brutality. When Amadou Diallo, an unarmed African immigrant, was fatally shot by cops in 1999, Sharpton led the demonstrations. And while much of the world lauded Giuliani for uniting the city after 9/11, Sharpton famously remarked: 'We would have come together if Bozo [the Clown] was the mayor.'

THE FEMINIST

New York's original riot grrrl, **BELLA ABZUG** (1920-1998) was a crusader against the establishment, a collective that, she declared, 'is made up of little men, very frightened'. She first began stirring their fears as a labour attorney, before winning election to the US House of Representatives in 1970. Wearing her distinctive wide-brimmed hat, she introduced a bill calling for an end to the Vietnam War, as well as measures endorsing gay rights in the Equality Act of 1974. Campaigns for the Senate in 1976 and mayor a year later were unsuccessful, but she remained politically active, helping to found Women's Environment & Development Organization, a leading advocate at the **United Nations** (see p103), in 1990.

GAY-RIGHTS GODFATHER

LARRY KRAMER (1935-) captured gay New York's zeitgeist: first with the novel *Faggots* (1978), a tale of the fast-lane lifestyles of homosexuals post-Stonewall, then with the 1985 play *The Normal Heart*, which addressed the impact of the HIV-AIDS crisis on the gay community. Kramer's writing went hand in glove with his activism. In 1982, he co-founded **Gay Men's Health Crisis** (see p308), a community-based organisation that spread awareness of AIDS and offered assistance to its victims; however, he soon left the group because he deemed it not political enough. To that end, he founded ACT UP (AIDS Coalition to Unleash Power) in 1987, a more militant organisation worthy both of its name and its founder's advocacy.

Cultural Forces

THE PEOPLE'S IMPRESARIO

Born Yosl Papirofsky, director **JOSEPH PAPP** (1921-1991) was a theatrical innovator with a lifelong commitment to bring Shakespeare to the public. To that end, he founded the New York Shakespeare Festival – commonly known as 'Shakespeare in the Park' – in

IN CONTEXT

1954. This summer series of Shakespeare plays at the **Delacorte Theater** (*see p353*) in Central Park has featured performances from the likes of Meryl Streep and Kevin Kline and attracted untold thousands, who line up patiently for free tickets. Papp also launched the **Public Theater** (*see p353*), which has presented the works of many up-and-coming American playwrights, and funded productions by numerous smaller theatres on the off-Broadway scene.

A DUKE AND A KING

One of the major figures of the Harlem Renaissance, pianist and bandleader **EDWARD KENNEDY 'DUKE' ELLINGTON** (1899-1974) kept all-white audiences at the old Cotton Club swinging through the late 1920s. In time, Ellington's music transcended such segregation, helping set in motion the very idea of New York City as a place where nonconformity is nurtured and auspicious things are born. As the man himself said: 'It don't mean a thing if it ain't got that swing.' You can pay homage to his grave in **Woodlawn Cemetery** (*see p146*) in the Bronx.

If the mambo is Cuba's gift to the world, it's no small feat that **TITO PUENTE** (1923-2000), a Puerto Rican New Yorker, earned the title of the Mambo King. Puente's bands ruled the Latin music mecca at the Palladium Ballroom in the 1950s, making mambo, son and Afro-Cuban jazz popular among its increasingly mainstream audience. His reputation was assured once Santana covered his classic 'Oye Como Va' in 1970. Today, Tito Puente Way runs along 110th Street from Fifth to First Avenues in **Spanish Harlem** (*see p121*).

THE BIRTH OF KOOL

Long before hip hop shot straight outta New York to become the world's party jam, Clive Campbell, aka **KOOL HERC** (1955-), was the originator of its block-rockin' beats. A Jamaican immigrant who moved to the States at the age of 12, Campbell became a DJ and initiated the practice of using two turntables simultaneously to isolate, repeat and prolong the percussive 'breakbeat' that became the basis of hip hop music. Kool Herc's sound-system parties in the **South Bronx** (*see p141*) during the early 1970s offered relief from the neglected neighbourhood's troubles and earned a following that spread across the city.

BOHEMIAN RHAPSODIST

Icon and iconoclast, poet **ALLEN GINSBERG** (1926-1997) was a seminal figure of the Beat Generation, and a writer who managed to stay relevant long after most of his contemporaries had passed into oblivion. While at **Columbia University** (*see p117*), he met fellow undergraduate Jack Kerouac and Harvard graduate, author and heroin addict William Burroughs; he soon began writing in the stream-of-consciousness 'spontaneous bop prosody' style that gave voice to his 1956 epic *Howl*, a sprawling indictment of American materialist society and a homage to bohemianism. Ginsberg was a bit of a nomad, with many of his wanderings assisted by acid. However, he retained an apartment in the East Village for more than 40 years, and gave occasional readings at the **Nuyorican Poets Café** (*see p280*).

THE ARCHETYPAL LOCAL

What's the deal with **JERRY SEINFELD** (1954-)? Whatever it is, the observational stand-up comedian managed to touch a nerve with his eponymous TV sitcom, a show which ran from 1989 to 1998. Ostensibly about nothing, it focused on Jerry and his friends George, Elaine and Kramer, who live self-absorbed and superficial lives on the Upper West Side – the exterior of **Tom's Restaurant** (*see p118*) was used for the diner where they often gather – yet it achieved immense popularity way beyond their narrow milieu and continues to rerun in perpetuity. It seems Seinlanguage translates easily. Yada yada yada.

THE HEAVY HITTER

Larger than life, **BABE RUTH** (1895-1948) was America's first sports megastar, an athlete whose prodigious home runs helped turn baseball into America's main pastime. Ruth started off with the Boston Red Sox, but was sold to the rival New York Yankees in 1919, where his career really took off. He set numerous home-run records (his career total of 714 was unsurpassed until 1974) and won four World Series with the Yankees. When the team moved into **Yankee Stadium** (*see p337*) in 1923, it became known as 'the House that Ruth Built'; with its razing, the city has lost some of its hallowed lore. Fans can rest assured, however, that the old stadium's Monument Park will be transferred to the new site.

CELLULOID VISIONARIES

If the name **WOODY ALLEN** (1935-) evokes the cliché of the neurotic, self-absorbed New York Jewish intellectual, it's because that popular image owes much to his cinematic alter-egos. After working as a gag-writer for hire in the '50s, finding fame as a stand-up comic in the early '60s and even enjoying success on Broadway with a pair of plays, the Brooklyn native turned to cinema. After a succession of knockabout movies (*Take the Money and Run*, *Bananas*, *Sleeper*), Allen cemented his place in the cinematic pantheon with *Annie Hall* (1977) and *Manhattan* (1979), two autobiographical romantic comedies that eulogised the city with a compelling wistfulness. Despite the decline of his later films, his early work still has the power to spellbind audiences – much as Woody and Diane Keaton were transfixed in *Manhattan*, gazing at the sunrise over the **59th Street Bridge** (*see p140*) from Riverview Terrace.

Though their careers coincide, the New York of **MARTIN SCORSESE** (1942-) is a grittier and far more violent metropolis than Allen's. In *Mean Streets* (1973), he revisited his native **Little Italy** (*see p74*) to explore themes of Catholic guilt and Mafia loyalty, while *Taxi Driver* (1976) is a dark and alienated ride through a Gotham dystopia. Scorsese based many subsequent films on the lives of historical figures, finding most success with New Yorkers such as self-destructive prizefighter Jake La Motta, who punches his way through *Raging Bull* (1980), and mobster Henry Hill, whose rise, fall and testimony against the mob is the subject of *Goodfellas* (1990).

Sights

Tour New York

Cycle, cruise, fly or simply jog: there are plenty of ways to see the big city.

Navigating New York may at first appear to be a daunting task: it's big, it's busy and it doesn't have any interest in waiting for you while you rustle around in the bottom of your bag for your pocket map. Fortunately, there are countless options for exploring the city's attractions, whether your pleasure is cycling, sailing, bonding with fellow sightseers on a crowded tour bus, or simply hoofing it – with or without a chaperone. For additional inspiration, refer to the Own This City section of *Time Out New York* magazine, which offers weekly listings for urban outings.

SIGHTS

BY BICYCLE

For more on cycling, *see p341 and p374.*

★ Bike the Big Apple
1-877 865 0078/www.bikethebigapple.com.
Tours phone or check website for schedule.
Tickets (incl bicycle & helmet rental) $70-$80.
Credit DC, MC, V.
You don't have to be Lance Armstrong to join these gently paced 5-7hr rides. Licensed guides lead cyclists through both historic and newly hip neighbourhoods: popular tours include Harlem (the Park and Soul tour), Chinatown (High Finance to Hidden Chinatown), Williamsburg and Battery Park City.

Bite of the Apple Tours
1-212 541 8759/www.centralparkbiketour.com.
Tours *Apr-Oct* 10am, 1pm, 4pm daily. **Tickets** (incl bicycle rental) $49; $40 reductions. **Credit** AmEx, DC, Disc, MC, V.
Bite of the Apple focuses its attentions on Central Park. The main two-hour tour visits the John Lennon memorial at Strawberry Fields, Belvedere Castle and the Shakespeare Garden. Dedicated film buffs will especially enjoy the Central Park Movie Scenes Bike Tour, which passes locations from *When Harry Met Sally…* and *Wall Street.* You can also book your own tailor-made private tour.

BY BOAT

Adirondack
Chelsea Piers, Pier 59, 18th Street, at the Hudson River, Chelsea (1-646 336 5270/www.sail-nyc.com). Subway C, E to 23rd Street. **Tours**

May-Oct 1pm, 2pm, 3.30pm, 4.30pm, 6pm, 7pm, 8.30pm, 9.30pm daily. **Tickets** $40 day sails; $50 eve & Sun brunch sails. **Credit** AmEx, DC, MC, V. **Map** p403 C27.
Sailing since 1994, the *Adirondack* is a beautiful replica of a classic 19th-century, wooden-hulled 80ft schooner. Trips on board are the essence of laid-back luxury: sip your complimentary glass of wine or beer in teak and mahogany surroundings as the ship sails gracefully from Chelsea Piers to Battery Park, past Ellis Island, to the Statue of Liberty and around to Governors Island and the Brooklyn Bridge. The almost identical *Imagine* schooner joined *Adirondack* for similar tours in 2007.

★ Circle Line Cruises
Pier 83, 42nd Street, at the Hudson River, Midtown (1-212 563 3200/www.circleline.com). Subway A, C, E to 42nd Street-Port Authority. **Tours** phone or check website for schedule.
Tickets $31/3hrs; $18-$26 reductions. **Credit** AmEx, DC, Disc, MC, V. **Map** p404 B24.
Circle Line's famed three-hour guided circumnavigation of Manhattan Island really is a fantastic way to get your bearings and to see many of the city's sights and as you pass under its iconic bridges. The special themed tours include a New Year's Eve cruise, a Fourth of July celebration, an evening 'Harbour Lights' sailing and an autumn foliage ride to Bear Mountain in the Hudson Valley. If you don't have time for the full round trip, there's also a two-hour Semi-Circle tour which takes you around Downtown to the Brooklyn Bridge and back. From April to October, there's also a fun, adrenalin-inducing and splashy 30-minute speedboat ride on *The Beast.*

Running Commentary

Your cultural and physical kicks rolled into one.

Whether you're a seasoned marathoner or just a jogging junkie, getting your daily endorphin fix can be a must – even while on vacation. You may be reluctant to waste valuable sightseeing time within the confines of a hotel gym or aimlessly hitting the streets. Fortunately, you don't have to do so…

Michael Gazaleh, founder of **City Running Tours** (*see p61*), offers a dozen different routes for fleet-footed visitors to explore New York at a ten-minute-mile pace. Groups are kept small – just two or three people, on average – and so Gazaleh and the 18 guides he employs are able to customise each tour to fit the participants' athletic abilities and cultural interests. Worry not: if you want to slow down for a photograph or a closer look at a landmark, Gazaleh is happy to wait.

Gazaleh, a licensed chiropractor and lifelong exercise enthusiast, says his most popular excursion is the downtown run, a 6.6-mile trip down the Hudson River, through Battery Park and the Financial District, across the Brooklyn and Manhattan Bridges and into Chinatown and Little Italy. His personal favourites

are the eight-mile Harlem run, which takes in sites in northern Manhattan and the Bronx such as Columbia University and Yankee Stadium, and the ten-mile Brooklyn run, which traverses Green-Wood Cemetery, Prospect Park and the Brooklyn Heights Promenade. There's also a jaunt through Central Park's verdant expanse, a trip through the historic neighbourhoods of the ethnically rich Lower East Side (where Gazaleh resides) and a particularly ambitious journey that navigates the entire length of Broadway. The $60-and-up cost includes a T-shirt, a souvenir photo, product samples and discount coupons for local athletic shops.

One obvious advantage to Gazaleh's service is the vast amount of territory he covers in a mere 60-90 minutes. 'We can go as far as a bus tour, and we take people on a lot of streets that buses can't,' he notes. He also points out that guides are able to connect with participants on a personal level. 'We're runners, so we have that common interest. And we know that if they go too long without a run, they just don't feel like themselves, so we're able to give them that sense of accomplishment.'

SIGHTS

6 FAMOUS ATTRACTIONS
ONE AMAZING PRICE
AVOID MOST TICKET LINES

Empire State Building Observatory

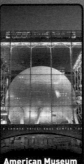

American Museum of Natural History

Guggenheim Museum

Museum of Modern Art

The Metropolitan Museum of Art

Your choice of: Circle Line Sightseeing Cruises or Statue of Liberty & Ellis Island Reserved Ticket

VALID 9 DAYS

ON SALE AT THESE ATTRACTIONS
Buy it at the first one you visit!
For more information visit
www.citypass.com or
call 877-THEPASS (877-843-7277).
Pricing and programs are subject to change.

Only $**79.00**
A $143.00 Value!
(Youth 12-17 $59.00)

Atlanta   Boston   Chicago   Hollywood   Houston   Philadelphia   San Francisco   Seattle   So. California   Toronto

Other locations Circle Line Downtown, South Street Seaport, Pier 16, by Burling Slip & Fulton Street, Downtown (1-212 630 8888).

NY Waterway
Pier 78, 38th Street, at the Hudson River, Midtown (1-800 533 3779/www.nywaterway. com). Subway A, C, E to 42nd Street-Port Authority. Tours phone or check website for schedule. Tickets $26/90mins; $15-$21 reductions. Credit AmEx, DC, Disc, MC, V. Map p404 B24.
NY Waterway's scenic 90-minute harbour tour takes you on a complete circuit around Manhattan's landmarks. Choose from the City Lights evening excursion, or a daytime cruise that focuses on the skyline of lower Manhattan. A variety of more specialist tours are also available, including the American Institute of Architects Cruise and a New York Historical Society Cruise (check their website for further information).
Other locations World Financial Center Pier, Pier 11, Wall Street, Downtown (1-800 533 3779).

Pioneer
South Street Seaport Museum, 12 Fulton Street, between Water & South Streets, Financial District (1-212 748 8786/www.southstreets eaportmuseum.org). Subway A, C to Broadway-Nassau Street; J, M, Z, 2, 3, 4, 5 to Fulton Street. Tours phone or check website for schedule. Tickets $25; $15-$20 reductions. Credit AmEx, DC, MC, V. Map p402 F32.
Built in 1885, the 102ft *Pioneer* is the only iron-hulled merchant sailing ship still in existence. Rebuilt with steel plating in the 1960s and with a restored rig, now her sails billow as you cruise the East River and New York Harbor. A range of highly educational on-board adult and children's programmes is also offered.

Shearwater Sailing
North Cove, Hudson River, between Liberty & Vesey Streets, Financial District (1-212 619 0885/1-800 544 1224/www.shearwatersailing. com). Subway R, W to City Hall; A, C, 2, 3, 4, 5 to Fulton Street/Broadway-Nassau Street. Tours mid Apr-Oct 5 times daily; phone or check website for schedule. Tickets $45-$50; $25 reductions. Credit AmEx, DC, Disc, MC, V. Map p402 D32.
Set sail on the *Shearwater*, an 82ft luxury yacht built in 1929. The champagne brunch ($79) or full-moon ($50) sail options are lovely ways to take in the skyline.

★ FREE Staten Island Ferry
Battery Park, South Street, at Whitehall Street, Financial District (1-718 727 2508/www.si ferry.com). Subway 1 to South Ferry; 4, 5 to Bowling Green. Tickets free. Map p402 E34.

During this commuter barge's 25-minute crossing, you get superb panoramas of lower Manhattan and the Statue of Liberty. Boats leave South Ferry at Battery Park and run 24 hours a day. Call or see the website for schedules and more information.
► *See p147 for details of Staten Island itself.*

BY BUS
Gray Line
777 Eighth Avenue, between 47th & 48th Streets, Theater District (1-212 445 0848/1-800 669 0051 ext 3/www.graylinenewyork.com). Subway A, C, E to 42nd Street-Port Authority. Tours phone or check website for schedule. Tickets $25-$125. Credit AmEx, DC, Disc, MC, V. Map p404 D23.
This is your grandma's classic red double-decker tour (the line runs other buses), but with something to interest everyone. Gray Line offers more than 20 bus tours, from a basic two-hour ride (with 40-plus hop-on, hop-off stops) to the guided Manhattan Comprehensive, which lasts 8.5hrs and includes lunch, admission to Top of the Rock, and a boat ride to Ellis Island and the Statue of Liberty.

On-Location Tours
1-212 683 2027/www.screentours.com. Tours phone or check website for schedule & meeting locations. Tickets $36-$42. Credit AmEx, DC, MC, V.
Whether you'd prefer to sip cosmos à la Carrie Bradshaw or visit the Bada Bing, On-Location's well-organised bus trips allow HBO enthusiasts to simulate the experiences of their favourite characters from *Sex and the City* and *The Sopranos*. Or hop aboard the New York TV and Movie Sites tour, a more varied outing that features more than 40 sites from big- and small-screen productions, such as *The Devil Wears Prada, Spider-Man* and *Friends*.

BY HELICOPTER, CARRIAGE OR RICKSHAW
Liberty Helicopter Tours
Downtown Manhattan Heliport, Pier 6, East River, between Broad Street & Old Slip, Financial District (1-212 967 6464/1-800 542 9933/www.libertyhelicopters.com). Subway R, W to Whitehall Street; 1 to South Ferry. Tours 9am-6pm daily. Tickets $130-$210. Credit AmEx, DC, MC, V. Map p402 E34.
There'll be no daredevil swooping and diving around the city (Liberty's helicopters provide a fairly smooth flight), but the views are thrilling in themselves. Even a five-minute ride (durations vary) is long enough to get a thrilling look at the Empire State Building.
Other locations VIP Heliport, Twelfth Avenue, at 30th Street, Midtown (1-800 542 9933).

SIGHTS

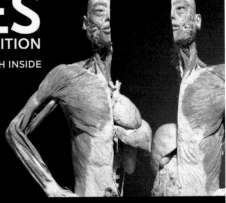

Manhattan Carriage Company

200 Central Park South, at Seventh Avenue, Midtown (1-212 664 1149/www.ajnfine art.com/mcc.html). Subway N, Q, R, W to 57th Street. **Tours** 10am-2am Mon-Fri; 7pm-2am Sat, Sun. **Tickets** from $40/20min ride (extended rides by reservation only). Hours & prices vary during hols. **Credit** AmEx, DC, MC, V (reserved tours only). **Map** p405 D22.

The beauty of Central Park seems even more romantic from the seat of a horse-drawn carriage. Choose your coach from those lined up on the streets along the southern end of the park, or book in advance.

Manhattan Rickshaw Company

1-212 604 4729/www.manhattanrickshaw.com. **Tours** noon-midnight Tue-Sun; by appointment. **Tickets** $10-$50. **No credit cards.**

Manhattan Rickshaw Company's pedicabs operate in Greenwich Village, Soho, Times Square and the Theater District. If you see one that's available, hail the driver, but determine your fare before you jump in (prices vary according to duration and number of passengers). For a pre-arranged pick-up, make reservations at least 24 hours in advance.

ON FOOT

Adventure on a Shoestring

1-212 265 2663. **Tours** daily; phone for schedule & reservations. **Tickets** $10. **No credit cards.**

The motto of this organisation, now in its 46th year, is 'Exploring the world within our reach… within our means', and founder Howard Goldberg is dedicated to revealing the 'real' New York. Walks take you from one charming neighbourhood to another, and topics can include Millionaire's Row and Haunted Greenwich Village. Special celebrity theme tours, including tributes to Jackie O, Katharine Hepburn and Marilyn Monroe, are also available.

FREE Big Apple Greeter

1-212 439 1090/www.bigapplegreeter.org. **Tours** by arrangement. **Tickets** free.

Set up in 1992, this non-profit, city-funded scheme offers visitors an alternative to the organised tour format. Sign up to the scheme through the website at least 3-4 weeks ahead and you'll be paired with a volunteer 'greeter', who'll give you a personal 2-4hr tour of one of the city's neighbourhoods (your choice or theirs). All tours are free.

Big Onion Walking Tours

1-212 439 1090/www.bigonion.com. **Tours** daily, times vary; phone or check website for schedule. **Tickets** $15; $10-$12 reductions. **No credit cards.**

New York was known as the Big Onion before it became the Big Apple. The tour guides will explain why, and they should know – all guides hold advanced degrees in history (or a related field). Check the website for meeting locations. Private tours are also available.

★ City Running Tours

1-877 415 0058/www.cityrunningtours.com. **Tours** phone or check website for schedule & meeting locations. **Tickets** from $60. **Credit** AmEx, DC, Disc, MC, V.

Get your runner's high while taking in pristine views of Central Park, the Brooklyn Bridge and other popular destinations in this energetic excursion led by veteran sneaker jockeys. *See also p57* **Running commentary**.

Harlem Heritage Tours

1-212 280 7888/www.harlemheritage.com. **Tours** phone or check website for schedule & meeting locations. **Tickets** $20-$100 (reservations required). **Credit** DC, Disc, MC, V.

Now operating more than ten bus and walking tours, Harlem Heritage aims to show visitors the soul of the borough. The Harlem Civil Rights Multimedia tour takes tourists to landmarks associated with Malcolm X, James Baldwin and Martin Luther King. The Renaissance tour walks you to Prohibition-era speakeasies, clubs and one-time residences of artists, writers and musicians.

★ Justin Ferate

1-212 223 2777/www.justinsnewyork.com. **Tours** phone or check website for schedule & meeting locations. **Tickets** $20. **No credit cards.**

This venerated historian wrote the book on Gotham walking tours. No, really – the city commissioned him to write the NYC tour-guide licensing exam, which he designed to educate and assess would-be guides. In addition to a regular roster of tours covering everything from midtown murals to Brooklyn's Green-Wood Cemetery and the quaint attractions of Bronx's City Island, Ferate leads a free 90-minute trek through Grand Central every Friday at 12.30pm.

Municipal Art Society Tours

1-212 935 3960/recorded information 1-212 439 1049/www.mas.org. **Tours** phone or check website for schedule & meeting locations. **Tickets** $15 (reservations may be required for some tours). **No credit cards.**

The Municipal Art Society (MAS) organises bus and walking tours in New York and further afield. Many – like 42nd Street Deco – are led by architects, designers, and writers and reflect the society's focus on contemporary architecture, urban planning and historic preservation. There's also a guided walk through Grand Central Terminal on Wednesdays at 12.30pm (suggested donation $10). Private tours are available by appointment.

SIGHTS

Downtown

Show us the money – and where to spend it.

The southern tip of Manhattan has always been the city's financial, legal and political powerhouse. It's where New York began, and where the 19th-century influx of immigrants injected the city with new energy. Yet with much of it off the Big Apple's orderly grid, Downtown doesn't conform to standard.

Downtown's landscape shifts from block to block. In the **Financial District**, gleaming towers rub shoulders with 18th-century landmarks; **Tribeca**'s haute dining spots are only a short hop from **Chinatown**'s frenetic food markets; and around the corner from the clubs of the **Meatpacking District**, impeccably dressed matrons tend to the delicate gardens of their **West Village** brownstones. And change is a constant force. The counterculture that erupted in **Greenwich Village** and the **Lower East Side** has largely been consigned to history, but iconoclastic art, music and retail can still be found. Still, the relentless gentrification and development has been a mixed blessing, and may finally be slowing in the face of a weakening economy.

Maps pp402-403	Restaurants &
Hotels p152	Cafés p178
	Bars p213

THE FINANCIAL DISTRICT

Battery Park

Subway J, M, Z to Broad Street; R, W to Whitehall Street; 1 to South Ferry; 4, 5 to Bowling Green.

It's easy to forget Manhattan is an island – what with all those pesky skyscrapers obscuring your view of the water. Until, that is, you reach the southern tip, where salty ocean breezes are reminders of the millions of immigrants who travelled on steamers in search of prosperity, liberty and a new home. This is where they landed, after passing through Ellis Island's immigration and quarantine centres.

Built to defend against attacks by the British in the War of 1812 (though it never saw military action), the sandstone fort of **Castle Clinton**, has been an aquarium, immigration centre and opera house; it now serves as a visitors' centre and ticket booth for **Statue of Liberty** and **Ellis Island** tours (*see p65*), as well as an intimate, open-air setting for concerts. Still, there's more than history here. In summer, visitors strolling the statue-lined Battery Park promenade can peer out at a harbour filled with jet-skiers and sailing boats. The park hosts a wide variety of events, and is a key venue of the annual **River to River Festival** (*see p263*) – a summertime celebration of downtown culture and the largest free arts festival in the city.

As you join the throngs making their way to Lady Liberty, you'll head south-east along the shore, where several ferry terminals jut into the harbour. Among them is the **Whitehall Ferry Terminal**, the boarding place for the famous **Staten Island Ferry** (*see p59*). Constructed in 1907, the terminal was severely damaged by

Island Hopping

A disused island army base is enjoying a second lease of life.

It's only a scant 800 yards from Lower Manhattan, just a seven-minute ride on a free ferry, but **Governors Island** (*listings p65*) feels like it's miles away. The verdant commons and stately red brick buildings recall not gritty Manhattan but an Ivy League campus by way of a colonial New England village.

In 1637, so the story goes, a Dutchman 'paid' the native Lenape tribe two axe heads, some beads and a few nails for ownership of the tiny island. In 1664, the British put the dampers on any plans the Dutch might have had when they took possession of it, along with the rest of New Amsterdam. Although it continued to change hands over the next decade, the British finally gained full control for 'the benefit and accommodation of His Majesty's Governors', and changed the name from Noten Eylant (or Nutten Island, for its wealth of nut trees) to Governors Island.

The island's strategic location, in the middle of New York Harbor, cemented its future as a military outpost, and for more than 200 years it was off limits to the public. All that changed in the mid 1990s, when the US Coast Guard decided to give up the high cost of island life and decamp. The island sat in limbo for several years, but it finally opened to summer visitors in 2006.

The 172-acre isle still retains a significant chunk of its military-era construction, including Fort Jay, started in 1776, and Castle Williams, completed in 1812 and for years used as a prison. And the 22-acre area containing the forts and historical officers' residences is now a national landmark, meaning that redevelopment is out of the question. The National Park Service, which jointly runs the island with the city and state, also organises free historical walking tours, during which you'll learn about the former army base's chequered past.

But there are also now many other reasons to visit. As well as providing a peaceful setting for biking (bring your own on the ferry, or rent from Bike & Roll, www.bikeandroll.com/newyork, once you've arrived), the island has started hosting concert series, art exhibitions and theatre performances (see www.govisland.com for a schedule). And further attractions are in the pipeline. In 2007, a team of internationally known design firms, including West 8 and Diller Scofidio + Renfro, was chosen to design a new park and promenade on the island. Their vision featured hills created from recycled materials, providing new viewpoints for panoramas of New York Harbor. The project is due to break ground at the end of 2009.

Sports Museum of America.

fire in 1991, but was completely rebuilt in 2005. More than 65,000 passengers take the free, 25-minute journey to the Staten Island shore each day; most are commuters but many are tourists, taking advantage of the unparalleled views of the Manhattan skyline and the Statue of Liberty. In the years before the Brooklyn Bridge was built, the **Battery Maritime Building** (11 South Street, between Broad & Whitehall Streets) served as a terminal for the ferry services between Manhattan and Brooklyn. Now it's the launch point for a free ferry to tranquil **Governors Island** on summer weekends (*see p63* **Island hopping**).

Just north of Battery Park you'll find the triangular **Bowling Green**, the city's oldest park and a popular lunchtime spot for Financial District workers; it's also the front lawn of the Alexander Hamilton Custom House, now home to the **National Museum of the American Indian** (*see right*), and abuts the new **Sports Museum of America** (*see right*). On its northern side, sculptor Arturo DiModica's muscular bronze bull embodies the potent capitalism of the Financial District. Constant rubbing by stockbrokers has smoothed the steer's nether regions to a bright finish.

Other interesting historical sites are close by: the rectory of the **Shrine of St Elizabeth Ann Seton** (7 State Street, between Pearl & Whitehall Streets, 1-212 269 6865, www.seton shrine.org), a 1790 Federal building dedicated to the first American-born saint, and the **Fraunces Tavern Museum** (*see right*), a restoration of the alehouse where George Washington toasted victory against the British.

The **New York Vietnam Veterans Memorial** (55 Water Street, between Coenties Slip & Hanover Square) stands one block to the east. Erected in 1985 and recently refreshed with a new plaza, it features the Walk of Honor – a pathway inscribed with the names of the 1,741 New Yorkers who lost their lives fighting in the conflict – and a touching monument etched with excerpts from letters, diary entries and poems written during the war. The newest memorial in the area is the **British Memorial Garden** at Hanover Square, William Street at Pearl Street. Completed in summer 2007, the garden commemorates the 67 Britons who died in New York on 9/11, and features hand-carved stone from Scotland, plants from Prince Charles's estate and iron bollards from London.

Nearby, the **Stone Street Historic District** is built around one of Manhattan's oldest roads, a cobblestone lane closed to traffic. Office workers and tourists now frequent its restaurants and bars, including the boisterous **Ulysses** (95 Pearl Street, at Stone Street, 1-212 482 0400) and **Stone Street Tavern** (52 Stone Street, near Broad Street, 1-212 785 5658).

Fraunces Tavern Museum

2nd & 3rd floors, 54 Pearl Street, at Broad Street (1-212 425 1778/www.fraunces tavern museum.org). Subway J, M, Z to Broad Street; 4, 5 to Bowling Green. **Open** noon-5pm Mon-Sat. **Admission** $4; $3 reductions; free under-7s. **No credit cards. Map** p402 E33.

This 18th-century tavern was favoured by General George Washington, and was the site of his famous farewell to the troops at the Revolution's close.

During the mid to late 1780s, the building housed the fledgling nation's departments of war, foreign affairs and treasury. In 1904, it became a repository for artefacts collected by the Sons of the Revolution in the State of New York. Highlights include a portrait gallery devoted to Washington, and the Long Room, the public dining room where the future President made his emotional leave-taking; relics include one of Washington's false teeth. There are also various temporary exhibitions and the tavern and restaurant (1-212 968 1776) serve hearty fare at lunch and dinner from Monday to Saturday.

★ FREE Governors Island

1-212 440 2202/www.govisland.com. R, W to Whitehall Street; 1 to South Ferry; 4, 5 to Bowling Green; then take ferry from Battery Maritime Building at Slip no.7. **Open** *Late May-mid Oct 10am-5pm Fri; 10am-7pm Sat, Sun. See p63 Island Hopping.*

FREE National Museum of the American Indian

George Gustav Heye Center, Alexander Hamilton Custom House, 1 Bowling Green, between State & Whitehall Streets (1-212 514 3700/www.nmai. si.edu). Subway R, W to Whitehall Street; 1 to South Ferry; 4, 5 to Bowling Green. **Open** 10am-5pm Mon-Wed, Fri-Sun; 10am-8pm Thur. **Admission** free. **Map** p402 E33.

This branch of the Smithsonian displays its collection around the grand rotunda of the 1907 Custom House, at the bottom of Broadway (which, many moons ago, began as an Indian trail). Although New York's first inhabitants are long gone, the life and culture of Native Americans is presented in rotating exhibitions – from intricately woven fibre Pomo baskets to ceremonial costumes – along with contemporary artwork and native dances in the Diker Pavilion for Native Arts & Culture.

Sports Museum of America

26 Broadway, at Beaver Street (1-212 747 0900/ www.sportsmuseum.com). Subway 4, 5 to Bowling Green. **Open** 9am-7pm daily. **Admission** $27; $20-$24 reductions; free under-4s. **Credit** AmEx, DC, Disc, MC, V.

This three-storey paean to sports opened across from Bowling Green in spring 2008. Numerous galleries are devoted to basketball, baseball, soccer, golf, hockey and other pastimes, and feature a plethora of historic memorabilia – Jesse Owens's diary from the 1936 Berlin Olympics, a football used in Super Bowl I, Lou Gehrig's Yankees jersey, childhood mementos from racing legend Jeff Gordon and tennis star Billie Jean King. The museum is also the new permanent home of the International Women's Sports Hall of Fame and college football's Heisman Trophy. Other attractions include an interactive cycle ride that allows you to time yourself against Tour de France champions; the virtual 'Goalie's Nightmare' which sends a computer-generated hockey puck speeding faceward at 110mph; and the Indy 500 course simulator, where the floor rumbles beneath your feet and a surround-sound system blasts the roar of engines. ▶ *For more on sports in New York, see p336.*

★ Statue of Liberty & Ellis Island Immigration Museum

1-212 363 3200/www.nps.gov/stli/ and www.ellis island.com. R, W to Whitehall Street; 1 to South Ferry; 4, 5 to Bowling Green; then take Statue of

SIGHTS

Liberty ferry (1-877 523 9849/www.statue cruises.com), departing every 20mins from gangway 4 or 5 in southernmost Battery Park.
Open ferry runs 8.30am-4.30pm daily. Purchase tickets at Castle Clinton in Battery Park.
Admission $12; $5-$10 reductions; free under-4s. **Credit** AmEx, DC, MC, V.
For the Statue of Liberty, *see p67 Profile.*
A half-mile across the harbour from Liberty Island is the 32-acre Ellis Island, gateway for over 12 million people who entered the country between 1892 and 1954. In the Immigration Museum (a former check-in depot), three floors of photos, interviews, interactive displays and exhibits pay tribute to the hopeful souls who made the voyage, and the nation they helped transform. Visitors can also search the museum's registry database and print copies of an ancestor's records. The $6 audio tour, narrated by Tom Brokaw, is informative and inspiring.

Ground Zero & Battery Park City

Subway A, C to Broadway-Nassau Street; E to World Trade Center; J, M, Z, 2, 3, 4, 5 to Fulton Street; R, W, 1 to Rector Street; 1 to South Ferry; 4, 5 to Bowling Green.

The streets around the former site of the World Trade Center have been drawing the bereaved and the curious since that harrowing day in September 2001. The worst attack on US soil took nearly 3,000 lives and left a gaping hole where one of the most recognisable American icons, the Twin Towers, had once helped to define the New York skyline. But these days, there's not much to see.

Construction on the new World Trade Center complex – due to include five office buildings, a park, a performing arts centre and a transit hub designed by Santiago Calatrava – has been plagued by in-fighting, missed deadlines and budget overruns. It's now unlikely that either the Freedom Tower (the development's 1,776-foot centrepiece) or the proposed World Trade Center museum and memorial will be completed by their 2011 target date, while Calatrava's designs for the PATH train station have been scaled back. There is a glimmer of good news: in May 2008, the Freedom Tower's steel framework rose 15 feet above street level when new sections were attached to the building's base.

To the east of Ground Zero, bargain hunters can sift through a seemingly endless stock of designer duds at discount bazaar **Century 21** (*see p233*). And just to the west of Ground Zero, the city-within-a-city **World Financial Center** (*see p68*) offers a surprisingly pleasant walk-through in the heart of one of New York's most intense commercial sectors.

West of the World Financial Center is **Battery Park City**, a 92-acre planned community devised in the 1950s to replace decaying shipping piers with new apartments, green spaces and schools. It's a manmade addition to the island, built on soil and rocks excavated from the World Trade Center construction site and sediment dredged from New York Harbor. Home to roughly 10,000 people, the self-contained neighbourhood was devastated after the 9/11 attacks, and nearly half of its residents moved away, although the area has been improved with new commercial development drawn by economic incentives and staggering riverfront views. Still, the most impressive aspects of BPC are its esplanade, a favoured route for bikers, skaters and joggers, and the strolling park (officially called Nelson A Rockefeller Park), both of which run along the Hudson River north of the Financial Center and connect to Battery Park at the south.

Close by the marina is the 1997 Police Memorial (Liberty Street, at South End Avenue), a granite pool and fountain that symbolically trace the lifespan of a police officer through the use of moving water, with names of the fallen etched into the wall. The **Irish Hunger Memorial** (Vesey Street, at North End Avenue) is here too, paying silent tribute to those who suffered during the famine from 1845 to 1852. Designed by artist Brian Tolle and landscape architect Gail Wittwer-Laird, the quarter-acre memorial incorporates vegetation, soil and stones from Ireland's various counties, and is also home to a reproduction of a 19th-century Irish cottage.

Although the neighbourhood doesn't have the sprawling greenery of some other parts of the city, Rockefeller Park's North Lawn, adjacent to the top-rated Stuyvesant High School, attracts sun worshippers, kite fliers and soccer players in the warm-weather months. The park also contains basketball and handball courts and an excellent children's playground.

Situated between Battery Park City and Battery Park are the inventively designed South Cove, with its quays and island; Teardrop Park, a two-acre space designed to evoke the Hudson River Valley; and Robert F Wagner Jr Park, where an observation deck offers fabulous views of both the harbour and the Verrazano-Narrows Bridge. The **Museum of Jewish Heritage** (*see p68*), Gotham's memorial to the Holocaust, is tucked amid the green; the entire park area is dotted with sculptures, including Tom Otterness's whimsical *The Real World* and Louise Bourgeois's *Eyes,* which watch over the Hudson from the lawn of Wagner Park. Across the street at the **Skyscraper Museum** (*see p68*), you can learn about the buildings that have created the city's iconic skyline and explore the World Trade Center Dossier, a moving exhibit about the fallen towers. The

SIGHTS

Profile Statue of Liberty

The long and storied history of New York's first lady.

Although she no longer greets new arrivals, the **Statue of Liberty** (listings p65) is still New York's, if not America's, most iconic sight. The sole occupant of Liberty Island, she stands 305 feet tall from her base to the tip of her gold-leaf torch. Up close, you can really appreciate how huge she truly is: her nose is four and a half feet long.

Lady Liberty was intended as a gift from France on America's 100th birthday. Frédéric Auguste Bartholdi, the statue's designer, was inspired by the ancient Colossus at Rhodes, although it was said that the face was modelled on that of his mother – and the body on that of his mistress. Bartholdi had initially planned a giant lighthouse-statue to stand sentry at the mouth of the Suez Canal, then under

VITAL STATS
There are 345 steps from her bottom to her top; she weighs 204 tons and has a 35-foot waist.

construction. But when the Egyptians were unreceptive, Bartholdi turned to New York Harbor. And so the proposed *Egypt Bringing Light to Asia* was reborn as *Liberty Enlightening the World*, the current statue's official title, as the French raised millions of francs to fund this expression of friendship for their ally from the Revolutionary War.

Construction began in Paris in 1874, with Gustave Eiffel (of Tower fame) crafting the skeletal iron framework. However, the French desire that she should be completed in time for America's centennial proved ill-fated: only the arm and torch were completed in time. The celebrated limb was exhibited at the Centennial Exhibition in Philadelphia and then spent six years on show in Madison Square Park; the head, meanwhile, was first displayed at the 1878 Paris Exposition.

In 1884, the statue was finally completed – only to be taken apart into hundreds of pieces to be shipped to New York, where it was placed on its pedestal and unveiled by President Grover Cleveland in 1886. It served as a lighthouse until 1902 and as the welcoming sign for millions of immigrants. These 'tired… poor… huddled masses' were evoked in Emma Lazarus's poem 'The New Colossus', written in 1883 to raise funds for the pedestal and engraved inside the statue in 1903.

You can now tour the interior (1-866 782 8834), viewing it through a glass ceiling to the accompaniment of a video system and a vigilant park ranger. The crown is off-limits for security reasons, but the panoramic views of New York City and the Harbor from the observation deck are sensational.

SIGHTS

Battery Park City Authority (1-212 417 2000, www.batteryparkcity.org) website lists events and has a useful map of the area.

Museum of Jewish Heritage: A Living Memorial to the Holocaust

Robert F Wagner Jr Park, 36 Battery Place, at First Place (1-646 437 4200/www.mjhnyc.org). Subway 1 to South Ferry; 4, 5 to Bowling Green. **Open** 10am-5.45pm Mon,Tue, Thur, Sun; 10am-8pm Wed; 10am-3pm Fri, eve of Jewish hols (until 5pm in summer). **Admission** $10; $5-$7 reductions; free under-12s. Free to all 4-8pm Wed. **Credit** AmEx, DC, MC, V. **Map** p402 E34.
This museum explores Jewish life before, during and after the Nazi genocide. The permanent collection includes documentary films, thousands of photos and 800 artefacts, many donated by Holocaust survivors and their families, while the Memorial Garden features English artist Andy Goldsworthy's *Garden of Stones,* 18 fire-hollowed boulders embedded with dwarf oak saplings. In spring 2009, the museum will open two new ongoing exhibits: one on Leo Frank, whose 1915 lynching by a Georgia mob led to the founding of the Anti-Defamation League, and another on Jewish refugee professors who found work at historically black colleges.

Skyscraper Museum

39 Battery Place, between Little West Street & 1st Place (1-212 968 1961/www.skyscraper.org). Subway 4, 5 to Bowling Green. **Open** noon-6pm Wed-Sun. **Admission** $5; $2.50 reductions. **Map** p402 E34.
The only institution of its kind in the world, this modest space explores high-rise buildings as objects of design, products of technology, real-estate investments and places of work and residence. Recent exhibits have covered architectural fantasies of the early 20th century, and charted the progress of the new World Trade Center complex and Burj Dubai, a massive cloudbuster in the United Arab Emirates that will be the world's tallest building when it's completed in 2009. From March to October, 'China Prophecy' examines Shanghai as a model of 21st-century urban development, through photography, architectural renderings and computer animations.
▶ *For more on the history of New York's skyscrapers, see p38.*

FREE World Financial Center & Winter Garden

From Liberty to Vesey Streets, between the Hudson River & West Street (1-212 417 7000/ www.worldfinancialcenter.com). Subway A, C to Broadway-Nassau Street; E to World Trade Center; J, M, Z, 2, 3, 4, 5 to Fulton Street. **Map** p402 D32.
Completed in 1988, Cesar Pelli's four glass and granite postmodern office towers, each crowned with a different geometric form, surround an upscale retail area and a series of restaurant-lined plazas that ring the marina. The Winter Garden hosts numerous film screenings, concerts and public art displays, as well as unique events such as the annual Bang on A Can Marathon in early June, when hundreds of innovative musicians (past performers have included John Cage, John Zorn, Steve Reich and Thurston Moore) participate in a non-stop, freeform celebration of contemporary classical music.

Wall Street

Subway J, M, Z to Broad Street; R, W, 1 to Rector Street; 2, 3, 4, 5 to Wall Street.

Since the city's earliest days as a fur-trading post, wheeling and dealing has been New York's main activity, and commerce the backbone of its prosperity. The southern point of Manhattan quickly evolved into the Financial District because, in the days before telecommunications, banks established their headquarters near the city's active port. Although the neighbourhood is bisected vertically by the ever-bustling Broadway, it's the east-west **Wall Street** (or 'the Street' in trader lingo) that's synonymous with the world's greatest den of capitalism.
Wall Street, which took its name from a defensive wooden wall built in 1653 to mark the northern limit of New Amsterdam, is big on legend despite being less than a mile long – blunted by Broadway on its western end, it spans only about half the width of Manhattan. It's at this western intersection that you'll find the Gothic Revival spire of **Trinity Church** (89 Broadway, at Wall Street, 1-212 602 0800, www.trinitywallstreet.org). The original burned down in 1776, and a second was demolished in 1839; the current version became the island's tallest structure when it was completed in 1846. Inside is the Trinity Church Museum, which displays historic diaries, photographs, sermons and burial records; adjacent Trinity Churchyard is the final resting place for notable New Yorkers such as Founding Father Alexander Hamilton, business tycoon John Jacob Astor and steamboat inventor Robert Fulton. **St Paul's Chapel** (*see p69*), the church's older satellite, is one of the finest Georgian structures in the US.
A block east of Trinity Church, at 26 Wall Street, is the **Federal Hall National Memorial**, a rather august Greek Revival building and – in a previous incarnation – the site of George Washington's first inauguration. It was along this stretch that corporate America made its first audacious architectural statements; a walk eastwards offers much evidence of what money can buy. Structures include **40 Wall Street** (between Nassau &

SIGHTS

William Streets), which battled the Chrysler Building in 1929 for the title of world's tallest building (the Empire State trounced them both in 1931), and the former **Merchants' Exchange** at 55 Wall Street (between Hanover & William Streets), with its stacked rows of Ionic and Corinthian columns, giant doors and a remarkable ballroom. Back around the corner is the **Equitable Building** (120 Broadway, between Cedar & Pine Streets), whose greedy use of vertical space helped instigate the zoning laws that now govern skyscrapers; stand across the street from the building to get the best view. Nearby is the **Federal Reserve Bank** (see below), with its huge gold vault.

The nerve centre of the US economy is the **New York Stock Exchange** (11 Wall Street, between Broad & New Streets). For security reasons, the Exchange is no longer open to the public, but the street outside offers an endless pageant of brokers, traders and their minions. For a lesson on Wall Street's influence over the years, visit the **Museum of American Finance** (see below) in its new home. A few blocks from the East River end of Wall Street, on Old Slip, is the **New York City Police Museum** (see right).

FREE Federal Reserve Bank

33 Liberty Street, between Nassau & William Streets (1-212 720 6130/www.newyorkfed.org). Subway 2, 3, 4, 5 to Wall Street. **Open** 9am-5pm Mon-Fri. **Tours** every hr on the half-hour (last tour 2.30pm); must be arranged at least 1 wk in advance (phone for reservations); tickets are sent by mail. **Admission** free. **Map** p402 E33.
Descend 50ft below street level and you'll find roughly a quarter of the world's gold (more than $100 billion dollars' worth), stored in a gigantic vault that rests on the solid bedrock of Manhattan Island. Visitors learn about the precious metal's history and the role of the New York Fed in its safeguarding.

Museum of American Finance

48 Wall Street, at William Street (1-212 908 4110/www.financialhistory.org). Subway 2, 3, 4, 5 to Wall Street; 1 to Rector Street. **Open** 10am-4pm Tue-Sat. **Admission** $8; $5 reductions; free under-6s. **Credit** AmEx, DC, MC, V. **Map** p402 E33.
In 2007, this pecuniary institution packed up its loot and moved into the old headquarters of the Bank of New York, founded by Secretary of the Treasury Alexander Hamilton. The permanent collection in the august Banking Hall traces the history of Wall Street and America's financial markets, with displays including a crisp $10,000 bill, a bearer bond made out to President George Washington, ticker tape from the morning of the stock-market crash of 1929, and a curvaceous couch made of $30,000 worth of nickels. The museum also serves as a de facto visitors' centre for the New York Stock Exchange,

closed to the public since 9/11, with videos of the Exchange floor and a Teaching Ticker that explains what each abbreviation, numeral and colour mean.

New York City Police Museum

100 Old Slip, between South & Water Streets (1-212 480 3100/www.nycpolicemuseum.org). Subway J, M, Z to Broad Street; 2, 3, 4, 5 to Wall Street. **Open** Sept-May 10am-5pm Mon-Sat. June-Aug 10am-5pm Mon-Sat; noon-5pm Sun. **Admission** *Suggested donation* $7; $5 reductions; free under-6s; $15 family. **No credit cards. Map** p402 F33.
The NYPD's tribute to 165 years of service features exhibits on its history and the tools of its trade, including vintage uniforms, squad cars and firearms. More notorious artefacts are also on view, including a gun used by one of Al Capone's minions in the 1928 murder of Frankie Yale. Critics have accused the institution of whitewashing police brutality and other scandals, although visitors can participate in a simulated police gunfight and determine if the shooting was warranted. The museum's most recent addition, 'Policing a Changed City', looks at the force's evolving role in a post-9/11 New York.

FREE St Paul's Chapel

209 Broadway, between Fulton & Vesey Streets (1-212 233 4164/www.saintpaulschapel.org). Subway A, C to Broadway-Nassau Street; J, M, Z, 2, 3, 4, 5 to Fulton Street. **Open** 10am-6pm Mon-Sat; 9am-4pm Sun. **Map** p402 E32.
The oldest building in New York still in continuous use (it dates from 1766 and was one of the few to survive the great fire ten years later), St Paul's is one of the nation's most valued Georgian structures. Extraordinarily, it suffered only minimal damage during 9/11; in the months following, it served as a makeshift refuge for exhausted rescue workers. The fence outside the landmark building became a focal point for flowers, photos and impromptu memorials to the tragedy, some of which remain.

South Street Seaport

Subway A, C to Broadway-Nassau Street; J, M, Z, 2, 3, 4, 5 to Fulton Street.

New York's fortunes originally rolled in on the swells that crash into its deep-water harbour. The city was perfectly situated for trade with Europe and, after 1825, goods from the Western Territories arrived via the Erie Canal and the Hudson River. By 1892, New York was also the point of entry for millions of immigrants, so its character was shaped not only by commodities but also the waves of new workers that arrived at its docks. The **South Street Seaport** is the best place to appreciate this port heritage.

If you enter the Seaport area from Water Street, the first thing you're likely to spot is the whitewashed **Titanic Memorial Lighthouse**. It was originally erected on top of the Seaman's Church Institute (Coenties Slip & South Street) in 1913, the year after the great ship sank, but was moved to its current location at the intersection of Pearl and Fulton Street in 1976. Check out the magnificent views of the Brooklyn Bridge from this corner of the locale.

When New York's role as a vital shipping hub diminished during the 20th century, the South Street Seaport area fell into disuse, but a massive redevelopment project in the mid 1980s saw old buildings converted into restaurants, bars, national chain stores and the **South Street Seaport Museum** (*see right*). The public spaces, including pedestrianised sections of both Fulton and Front Streets, are a favourite with sightseers and street performers, but it's only recently that New Yorkers have begun to rediscover the area, attracted by the arrival of cool cafés and bars such as **Jack's Stir Brew Coffee** (222 Front Street, between Beekman Street & Peck Slip, 1-212 227 7631) and sleek wine bar **Bin No. 220** (*see p213*). Free summer concerts, held during the River to River Festival (*see p263*), also appeal. Over at 11 Fulton Street, **Fulton Market** has gourmet food stalls and seafood restaurants.

Pier 17 once supported the famous Fulton Fish Market, a bustling, early morning trading centre dating back to the mid 1800s. However, in 2006, the market relocated to a larger facility in the Hunts Point area of the Bronx (*see p142*),

making it the second-largest fish market in the world. Interest in Pier 17, little more than a picturesque mall by day and an after-work watering hole by night, had dwindled since the 1980s, but a variety of proposals for mixed-use developments have recently been submitted in hopes of spurring a second renaissance.

South Street Seaport Museum

Visitors' centre, 12 Fulton Street, at South Street (1-212 748 8786/www.southstreetseaport museum.org). Subway A, C to Broadway-Nassau Street; J, M, Z, 2, 3, 4, 5 to Fulton Street. **Open** *Apr-Dec* 10am-6pm Tue-Sun. *Jan-Mar* 10am-5pm Fri-Sun. **Admission** $10; $5-$8 reductions; free under-5s. **Credit** AmEx, DC, MC, V. **Map** p402 F32.

Set in 11 blocks along the East River, this museum is an amalgam of galleries, historic ships, 19th-century buildings and a visitors' centre. Wander around the rebuilt streets and pop in to see an exhibition on marine life and history before climbing aboard the four-masted 1911 barque *Peking* or the 1930 tug, *WO Decker*. Planned exhibitions for 2009 include 'New Amsterdam, The Island at the Center of the World' (from September; *see also p21* **An Englishman in New York**). The seaport is generally thick with tourists, but it's a lively place to spend an afternoon, especially if you're with children.

▶ *See also p249 for details of the museum's gift shop, Bowne & Co. It's a working recreation of an 1870s-style letterpress printers.*

South Street Seaport. *See p69.*

CIVIC CENTER & CITY HALL

Subway J, M, Z to Chambers Street; R, W to City Hall; 2, 3 to Park Place; 4, 5, 6 to Brooklyn Bridge-City Hall.

The business of running New York takes place in the grand buildings of the **Civic Center**, an area that formed the budding city's northern boundary in the 1700s. City Hall Park was renovated just before the millennium, and pretty landscaping and abundant benches make it a popular lunching spot for local office workers.

At the park's southern end a granite 'time wheel' tracks the park's history. Like the steps of City Hall, the park has been the site of countless press conferences and protests. Mayor Rudy Giuliani attempted to close the steps to such activities, but a federal district judge declared the ban unconstitutional in April 2000.

At the northern end of the park, **City Hall** (*see p72*) houses the mayor's office and the chambers of the City Council, and is usually buzzing with VIP comings and goings. When City Hall was completed in 1812, its architects were so confident that the city would grow no further north that they didn't bother to put any marble on its northern side. The building, a beautiful blend of Federalist form and French Renaissance detail, is open to tours. Facing City Hall, the larger, golden-statue-topped Municipal Building contains other civic offices, including the marriage bureau.

Facing the park from the west is Cass Gilbert's famous **Woolworth Building** (233 Broadway, between Barclay Street & Park Place), the tallest building in the world when it opened in 1913. The neo-Gothic skyscraper's grand spires, gargoyles, vaulted ceilings and church-like interior earned it the moniker 'the Cathedral of Commerce'. Shoddy renovations lessened the building's glamour over the decades, but it's now in the midst of a multi-million dollar makeover.

The houses of crime and punishment are also located in the **Civic Center** near Foley Square, once a pond and later the site of the city's most notorious 19th-century slum (Five Points). These days, you'll find the State Supreme Court in the **New York County Courthouse** (60 Centre Street, at Pearl Street), a hexagonal Roman Revival building; the beautiful rotunda is decorated with a mural entitled *Law Through the Ages*. The **United States Courthouse** (40 Centre Street, between Duane & Pearl Streets) is a Corinthian temple crowned with a golden pyramid.

Next to City Hall, on Chambers Street, is the 1872 Old New York County Courthouse; it's popularly known as the **Tweed Courthouse**, a symbol of the runaway corruption of mid-19th-century municipal government. William 'Boss' Tweed (*see p25*), leader of the political machine Tammany Hall, famously pocketed some $10 million of the building's huge $14 million construction budget. What he didn't

SIGHTS

SIGHTS

steal bought a beautiful edifice, with exquisite Italianate detailing. These days, it houses the city's Department of Education, but it's also open for tours (1-212 639 9675, www.nyc.gov).

The **Criminal Courts Building & Manhattan Detention Complex** (100 Centre Street, between Leonard & White Streets) is still known as 'the Tombs', a nod to the original 1838 Egyptian Revival building – or, depending on who you ask, to its current grimness. Certainly, there's no denying that the hall's great granite slabs and looming towers are downright Kafkaesque. Each of the courts is open to the public on weekdays from 9am to 5pm. Your best bet for legal drama is the Criminal Courts; if you can't slip into a trial, you can at least observe legal eagles and their clients, or see the pleas at the Arraignment Court (until 1am).

The story behind the building's renaming is an interesting drama. Former mayor Giuliani declared it the Bernard B Kerik Complex in 2001, in honour of his own NYC Police Department Commissioner. But in July 2006, Kerik was disgraced after pleading guilty to accepting free home renovations and failing to report a hefty loan from a real-estate developer. Less than 48 hours after Kerik's court plea, new mayor Michael Bloomberg had workers remove Kerik's name between 1am and 3am, so that the new name would appear that same morning.

Nearby, the **African Burial Ground** (*see below*) was officially designated a National Monument by President Bush in 2006.

FREE African Burial Ground

Duane Street, between Broadway & Centre Streets, behind 290 Broadway (1-212 637 2019/www.nps.gov/afbg). Subway J, M, Z to Chambers Street; R, W to City Hall; 4, 5, 6 to Brooklyn Bridge-City Hall. **Open** 9am-5pm Mon-Fri. **Admission** free. **Map** p402 E31.
A major archaeological discovery, the African Burial Ground is a small remnant of a 6.6-acre unmarked gravesite where between 10,000 and 20,000 enslaved Africans – men, women and children – were buried. The burial ground, which closed in 1794, was unearthed during the construction of a federal office building in 1991 and designated a National Monument. In October 2007, a dedication ceremony was held for the newly erected stone memorial designed by architect Rodney Leon. The tall curved monument draws heavily on African architecture and contains a spiral path leading to an ancestral chamber. An interpretation centre is located inside the lobby of 290 Broadway.

FREE City Hall

City Hall Park, from Vesey to Chambers Streets, between Broadway & Park Row (1-212 639 9675/www.nyc.gov/designcommission). Subway J,

M, Z to Chambers Street; R, W to City Hall; 2, 3 to Park Place; 4, 5, 6 to Brooklyn Bridge-City Hall. **Open** *Tours* (individuals) noon Wed, 10am Thur; (groups) 10am Mon, Wed, Fri. **Admission** free. **Map** p402 E32.
Designed by French émigré Joseph François Mangin and native New Yorker John McComb, Jr, the fine, Federal-style City Hall was completed in 1812. Tours take in the rotunda, with its splendid coffered dome; the City Council Chamber; and the recently restored Governor's Room, which houses a collection of American 19th-century political portraits as well as historic furnishings (including George Washington's desk). Individuals can book (at least two days in advance) for the Thursday morning tour; alternatively, sign up at the Heritage Tourism Center at the southern end of City Hall Park on the east side of Broadway, at Barclay Street, for Wednesday's first-come, first-served tour at noon. Group tours should be booked at least one week in advance.

TRIBECA & SOHO

Subway A, C, E, 1 to Canal Street; C, E to Spring Street; N, R, W to Prince Street; 1 to Franklin Street, Houston Street.

In the 1960s and '70s, artists colonised the former industrial wasteland that was **Tribeca** (the Triangle Below Canal Street), squatting in its abandoned warehouses. Following the example of fellow creatives in neighbouring Soho, they eventually worked with the city to rezone and restore them. The preponderance of large, hulking former industrial buildings gives Tribeca an imposing profile, but fine small-scale cast-iron architecture still stands along White Street and the parallel thoroughfares.

Seeking luxury and privacy, many celebrities have settled in the area. Robert De Niro is the neighbourhood's best-known resident, and he's been the most active in raising its profile. In 1988, he founded the **Tribeca Film Center** (375 Greenwich Street, at Franklin Street) with partner Jane Rosenthal in the old Martinson Coffee Building; as well as screening rooms and offices, it houses his **Tribeca Grill** (1-212 941 3900). A few blocks away, De Niro's **Tribeca Cinemas** (54 Varick Street, at Laight Street, 1-212 966 8163, www.tribeca cinemas.com) hosts premières and glitzy parties, when it isn't serving as a venue for the increasingly large and commercial **Tribeca Film Festival** (*see p261*). Then, in spring 2008, the actor unveiled the exclusive, 88-room **Greenwich Hotel** (*see p153*).

Upscale shops, such as an **Issey Miyake** boutique with a Frank Gehry-designed interior (119 Hudson Street, at North Moore Street, 1-212 226 0100), and haute eateries cater to the well-heeled locals. Top dining options include **Nobu**

Soho.

(105 Hudson Street, at Franklin Street, 1-212 334 4445); French fine-dining spot **Chanterelle** (2 Harrison Street, near Hudson Street, 1-212 966 6960); celebrity chef David Bouley's eponymous flagship **Bouley** (120 West Broadway, at Duane Street, 1-212 964 2525); and Bouley's Austrian restaurant **Danube** (30 Hudson Street, near Duane Street, 1-212 791 3771, closed Sun). **Bouley Bakery & Market** (130 West Broadway, between Duane & Reade Streets, 1-212 219 1011) offers some of the city's finest (and priciest) pastries and other foodstuffs.

Now a retail mecca of the highest order, **Soho** (the area South of Houston Street) was once a hardscrabble manufacturing zone with the derisive nickname Hell's Hundred Acres. In the 1960s, it was earmarked for destruction by over-zealous urban planner Robert Moses, but its signature cast-iron warehouses were saved by the artists who inhabited them. The **King and Queen of Greene Street** (respectively, 72-76 Greene Street, between Broome & Spring Streets, and 28-30 Greene Street, between Canal & Grand Streets) are both fine examples of the area's beloved architectural landmarks.

After landlords sniffed the potential for profits in converting old loft buildings, Soho morphed into a playground for the young, the beautiful and the rich. It can still be a pleasure to stroll around the cobblestone side streets on weekday mornings, but the large chain stores and sidewalk-encroaching street vendors along Broadway create a shopping-mall-at-Christmas crush on weekends. The commercialism and crowds have also pushed a number of exclusive shops to other areas (although you'll still find Prada, Miu Miu and Paul Smith, among others) and many of the galleries that made Soho an art capital in the 1970s and '80s have decamped to cheaper and now hipper neighbourhoods such as Chelsea, the Lower East Side and Williamsburg. Surprisingly, some garment factories remain in Soho, especially near the border with Chinatown on Canal Street, though many of the very same elegant buildings house design studios, magazine publishers and record labels. Soho is also the home of the **New York City Fire Museum** (*see below*).

Just west of West Broadway, tenement- and townhouse-lined streets contain remnants of the Italian community that once dominated the area. Elderly men and women stroll along Sullivan Street to **St Anthony of Padua Roman Catholic Church** (no.155, at W Houston Street), dedicated in 1888. You'll still find old-school neighbourhood flavour in local businesses such as **Joe's Dairy** (no.156, between Houston & Prince Streets, 1-212 677 8780, closed Sun & Mon), **Pino's Prime Meat Market** (no.149, between Houston & Prince Streets, 1-212 475 8134, closed Sun) and the **Vesuvio Bakery** (160 Prince Street, between Thompson Street & West Broadway, 1-212 925 8248), whose old-fashioned façade has appeared in dozens of commercials over the years.

New York City Fire Museum

278 Spring Street, between Hudson & Varick Streets (1-212 691 1303/www.nycfire museum.org). Subway C, E to Spring Street; 1 to Houston Street. **Open** *10am-5pm Tue-Sat; 10am-4pm Sun.* **Admission** *Suggested donation $5; $1-$2 reductions.* **Credit** *AmEx, DC, Disc, MC, V.* **Map** *p403 D30.*
An active firehouse from 1904 to 1959, this museum is filled with all manner of life-saving gadgetry, from late 18th-century hand-pumped fire engines to present-day equipment.

SIGHTS

SIGHTS

LITTLE ITALY & NOLITA

Subway B, D, F, V to Broadway-Lafayette Street; J, M, N, Q, R, W, Z, 6 to Canal Street; J, M, Z to Bowery; N, R, W to Prince Street; 6 to Spring Street.

Abandoning the dismal tenements of the Five Points district (in what is now Chinatown), immigrants from Naples and Sicily began moving to **Little Italy** in the 1880s. The locale once stretched from Canal to Houston Streets, between Lafayette Street and the Bowery, but these days a strong Italian presence can only truly be observed on the blocks immediately surrounding Mulberry Street. As families prospered in the 1950s, they moved to the outer boroughs and suburbs; the area now seems on the verge of being swallowed by an expanding Chinatown to the south and migrating boutiques from **Nolita** (North of Little Italy).

Another telling change in the 'hood: **St Patrick's Old Cathedral** (260-264 Mulberry Street, between Houston & Prince Streets) no longer holds services in Italian, but in English and Spanish. Completed in 1809 and restored after a fire in 1868, this was the city's premier Catholic church until it was demoted, upon consecration of the Fifth Avenue cathedral of the same name. But ethnic pride remains: Italian-Americans flood in from across the city during the 11-day **Feast of San Gennaro** (*see p266*). For more than 80 years, on the second Thursday in September, Mulberry Street is closed to traffic to make room for parades, musicians, performers and vendors proffering sausages and *zeppole* (sugar-dusted fritters filled with custard or jam). And on the final Saturday in September, a statue of San Gennaro is carried in a Grand Procession outside the Church of the Most Precious Blood (109 Mulberry Street, between Canal & Hester Streets).

Touristy cafés and restaurants line Mulberry Street between Broome and Canal Streets, but pockets of the past linger nearby. Long-time residents still buy mouth-wateringly fresh mozzarella from **DiPalo's Fine Foods** (200 Grand Street, at Mott Street, 1-212 226 1033), and sandwiches packed with salami and cheeses at the **Italian Food Center** (186 Grand Street, at Mulberry Street, 1-212 925 2954). Legend has it that the first pizzeria in New York was opened by Gennaro Lombardi on Spring Street in 1905. **Lombardi's** moved down the block in 1994 (32 Spring Street, at Mott Street, 1-212 941 7994), but still serves its signature clam pies. These days, the area's restaurants are largely undistinguished grills and pasta houses, but two reliable choices are **Il Cortile** (125 Mulberry Street, between Canal & Hester Streets, 1-212 226 6060) and **La Mela** (167 Mulberry Street, between Broome & Grand Streets, 1-212 431 9493). Drop in for dessert at **Caffè Roma** (385 Broome Street, at Mulberry Street, 1-212 226 8413), which opened in 1891.

Of course, Little Italy is also the site of several notorious **Mafia landmarks**. The brick-fronted store now occupied by a shoe boutique (247 Mulberry Street, between Prince & Spring Streets) was once the Ravenite Social Club, where Mafia kingpin John Gotti made his deals until his arrest in 1990. Mobster Joey Gallo was shot and killed in 1972 while celebrating his birthday at Umberto's Clam House, which has since moved around the corner to 178 Mulberry Street, at Broome Street (1-212 431 7545). And several key sequences from *The Godfather* were filmed in the area, including the christening scene.

Nolita became a magnet for pricey boutiques and trendy eateries in the 1990s. Elizabeth, Mott and Mulberry Streets, between Houston and Spring Streets, in particular, are home to hip shops such as vintage clothier **Resurrection** (217 Mott Street, at Spring St, 1-212 625 1374, www.resurrectionvintage.com), menswear store **Groupe 16sur20** (267 Elizabeth Street, at Houston Street, 1-212 343 0007) and chic shoe label **Sigerson Morrison** (28 Prince Street, at Mott Street, 1-212 219 3893), known for its pixieish styles. An international cast of pretty young things still gravitates to eateries such as Japanese-fusion joint **Bond St** (6 Bond Street, at Lafayette Street, 1-212 777 2500) and rustic Italian **Peasant** (194 Elizabeth Street, at Spring Street, 1-212 965 9511, closed Mon & Sun).

CHINATOWN

Subway J, M, N, Q, R, W, Z, 6 to Canal Street.

Take a walk in the area south of Broome Street and west of Broadway, and you'll feel as though you've entered a different continent. You won't hear much English spoken along the crowded streets of **Chinatown**, which are lined with fish-, fruit- and vegetable-stocked stands and, especially along Canal Street, vendors selling bootleg CDs and DVDs (this is a bargain-hunter's paradise, but be warned that many of the goods are being sold illegally). Some of its residents eventually decamp to one of the four other Chinatowns in the city (two each in Queens and Brooklyn). However, a steady flow of new arrivals keeps this hub full to bursting, with thousands of both legal and illegal residents packed into the area surrounding East Canal Street and making this among the largest Chinese communities outside Asia. The busy streets get even wilder during the **Chinese New Year** festivities in February (*see p267*).

The markets on Canal Street sell some of the best and most affordable seafood and fresh produce in the city – you'll see buckets of live eels and crabs, square watermelons and piles of hairy rambutans. Street vendors sell satisfying snacks such as pork buns and sweet egg pancakes by the bagful. Need to quench your thirst? Many purveyors proffer fresh coconut milk, simply hacking the top of the coconut and plunging a straw inside the meaty interior. Mott Street, between Kenmare and Worth Streets, is lined with restaurants representing the cuisine of virtually every province of mainland China and Hong Kong; the Bowery, East Broadway and Division Street are just as diverse. Adding to the mix are myriad Indonesian, Malaysian, Thai and Vietnamese eateries and stores.

A statue of the legendary Chinese philosopher marks **Confucius Plaza**, at the corner of the Bowery and Division Street. In Columbus Park, at Bayard and Mulberry Streets, elderly men and women gather around card tables to play mahjong and dominoes (you can hear the clacking tiles from across the street), while more agile youngsters practise martial arts. The **Museum of Chinese in America** (*see below*), which just moved into larger premises on Centre Street, hosts shows and events that explore the Chinese immigrant experience in the western hemisphere. The **Eastern States Buddhist Temple of America** (64 Mott Street, between Bayard & Canal Streets, 1-212 966 6229), founded in 1962, is one of the country's oldest extant Chinese Buddhist temples.

For a different perspective on the area's culture, visit **Chinatown Fair** at the southern end of Mott Street, a noisy, dingy amusement arcade where some of the East Coast's best Dance Dance Revolution players congregate. Older 'kids' hit Chinatown to eat and drink at **Joe's Shanghai** (9 Pell Street, between Bowery & Mott Street, 1-212 233 8888), known for its soup dumplings, boiled pillows of dough filled with pork and broth; **Jing Fong** (20 Elizabeth Street, between Bowery & Canal Streets, 1-212 964 5256), a massive banquet hall that's a classic destination for dim sum; and **Happy Ending** (302 Broome Street, between Eldridge & Forsyth Streets, 1-212 334 9676), a hip nightspot for denizens of every ethnicity and sexuality. The bar occupies a former massage parlour, and its name is an unabashed nod to its erotically charged roots.

Museum of Chinese in America

211-215 Centre Street, between Grand & Howard Streets (1-212 619 4785/www.mocanyc.org). Subway J, M, Z, N, Q, R, W, 6 to Canal Street. **Open** noon-5pm Mon, Thur, Fri; noon-9pm Tue; 10am-5pm Sat, Sun. **Admission** call for details. **No credit cards**.

INSIDE TRACK
CHINATOWN

Wing Fat Shopping is a strange little subterranean mall, with its entrance at Chatham Square (no.8, to the right of the betting parlour). In a previous incarnation, the site was rumoured to have been a stop on the Underground Railroad a quarter-century before the Chinese began populating this area in the 1880s.

MOCA's former space on Mulberry Street closed in February 2008; the museum is scheduled into more spacious premises on Centre Street in early 2009. Designed by Vietnam Veterans Memorial architect Maya Lin, the building incorporates organic elements such as bronze walls, reclaimed wood floors and a giant skylight that illuminates its two-floor atrium. The Chinese-American experience is the main focus of the permanent collection, but the additional gallery space allows for more contemporary programming – including a survey of contemporary Chinese-American artists and a series of short films set in Chinatown. In autumn 2009, 'Archaeology of Change' tracks Chinatown's gentrification by spotlighting five erstwhile landmarks (including the museum itself, the former Grand Machinery Exchange).

LOWER EAST SIDE

Subway B, D to Grand Street; F to East Broadway; F, J, M, Z to Delancey-Essex Streets; F, V to Lower East Side-Second Avenue; J, M, Z to Bowery.

The **Lower East Side**, a roughly defined area south of Houston Street and west of the East River, is the latest Manhattan neighbourhood to be radically altered by the forces of gentrification. In the 19th century, tenement buildings were constructed here to house the growing number of German, Irish, Jewish and Italian immigrants. The appalling conditions of these overcrowded, unsanitary slums were captured by photographer and writer Jacob Riis in *How the Other Half Lives* in 1890; its publication spurred activists and prompted the introduction of more humane building codes. The dwellings have since been converted or demolished, but you can see how newcomers once lived by visiting the recreated apartments of the **Lower East Side Tenement Museum** (*see p77*).

This was once the focal point of Jewish culture in New York. Between 1870 and 1920, hundreds of synagogues and religious schools thrived alongside Yiddish newspapers, social-

Lower East Side.

reform societies and kosher bakeries. Vaudeville and classic Yiddish theatre also prospered here – the Marx Brothers, Eddie Cantor and George Gershwin all once lived in the district. Today, the Yiddish theatres are long gone and most of the synagogues founded by Eastern European immigrants in the 19th century have been repurposed or sit empty. Even longtime holdout Streit's Matzo sold its 82-year-old factory on Rivington Street in 2007.

Still, a few vestiges of the neighbourhood's Jewish roots remain. The **Eldridge Street Synagogue** (*see p80*), which recently underwent extensive renovation, has a small but vital congregation. On the southern edge of Chinatown, the **First Shearith Israel Graveyard** (55-57 St James Place, between James & Oliver Streets) is the burial ground of the country's first Jewish community; some gravestones date from 1683, including those of Spanish and Portuguese Jews who fled the Inquisition. And the **Forward Building** (175 E Broadway, at Canal Street) was once the headquarters of the *Jewish Daily Forward*, a Yiddish-language paper that had a peak circulation of 275,000 in the 1920s. It's now home to multi-million-dollar condominiums.

Those looking for a taste of the old Jewish Lower East Side should grab a table at Katz's **Delicatessen** (*see p186*). Opened in 1888, the kosher deli continues to serve some of the best pastrami in New York (and was the site of Meg Ryan's famous 'orgasm' scene in *When Harry Met Sally…*). Lox lovers are devoted to **Russ & Daughters** (*see p249*), serving its famous

herring, caviar and smoked salmon since 1914, while half-sour aficionados visit **Guss' Pickles** (*see p249*), a relic of the area's once-flourishing pickle district.

By the 1980s, when young artists and musicians began moving in, the area was a patchwork of Asian, Latino and Jewish enclaves. Hipster bars and music venues sprang up on and around Ludlow Street, creating an annex to the East Village. That scene still survives, but rents have risen dramatically and some stalwarts, such as Tonic and Luna Lounge, have closed their doors. Check who's playing at **Arlene's Grocery** (95 Stanton Street, between Ludlow & Orchard Streets, 1-212 995 1652), the **Bowery Ballroom** (*see p319*) or **Cake Shop** (*see p319*). The radical-political tradition lives on at **ABC No Rio** (156 Rivington Street, between Clinton & Suffolk Streets, 1-212 254 3697). The activist collective's **SOS: Sunday Open Series** was first established in 1980, when squatters took over an abandoned ground-floor space; it now houses a gallery, studios and performance area.

These days, visual art is the main draw. In 2007, the **New Museum of Contemporary Art** (*see p80*) decamped here from Chelsea, opening a $50 million building on the Bowery. Dozens of storefront galleries have opened in the vicinity, including **Rivington Arms** (*see p270*), **Reena Spaulings Fine Art** (*see p270*) and **Participant Inc** (253 E Houston Street, between Norfolk & Suffolk Streets, 1-212 254 4334, www.participantinc.org, closed Mon & Tue), a space for experimental work. The **Woodward Gallery** (133 Eldridge Street, between Broome & Delancey Streets, 1-212 966 3411, www.woodwardgallery.net, closed Mon & Sun) displays the old-guard avant-garde (Haring, Hockney, Basquiat), while Chelsea migrant **Envoy** (131 Chrystie Street, between Broome & Delancey Streets, 1-212 226 4555, www.envoygallery.com) has a reputation for attracting young New York artists on the verge of discovery. On the last Sunday of the month, the Lower East Side Business Improvement District sponsors a free tour of LES galleries, starting from the **Lower East Side Visitor Center** (261 Broome Street, between Allen & Orchard Streets, 1-212 226 9010).

Although the **Orchard Street** bargain district – a row of stores selling utilitarian goods such as socks, sportswear and luggage beloved of hagglers – persists, the strip is at the centre of a proliferation of small indie shops, including boutique **Suite Orchard** (*see p239*), eccentric menswear shop **THECAST** (*see p239*), stylist Nikki Fontanella's cool clothing store-cum-bar the **Dressing Room** (*see p237*), and vintage jewellery trove **Doyle & Doyle**

(189 Orchard Street, between East Houston & Stanton Streets, 1-212 677 9991, closed Mon, *see p243*). But more mainstream commercial gloss is encroaching on the area in the form of high-rise hotels and apartment buildings, as well as an outpost of rapidly expanding natural superstore chain **Whole Foods** (95 E Houston Street, between Bowery & Chrystie Street, 1-212 20 1320). The National Trust for Historic Preservation recently designated the Lower East Side one of America's 11 most endangered historic places; as the area continues to transform, groups such as the Lower East Side Conservancy are working to preserve its unique character.

▶ *For more on shopping in New York, see p226-258.*

Lower East Side Tenement Museum

Visitors' centre: 108 Orchard Street, at Delancey Street (1-212 982 8420/www.tenement.org). Subway F to Delancey Street; F, J, M, Z to Delancey-Essex Streets. **Open** *Tours every* 20mins 11.30am-4.30pm Mon; every 20mins 11.30am-5.30pm Tue-Fri; every 15mins 11am-5pm Sat, Sun. **Admission** $17; $13 reductions. **Credit** AmEx, DC, Disc, MC, V. **Map** p403 G30.

This fascinating museum – actually a series of restored tenement apartments at 97 Orchard Street – is accessible only by guided tour. Tickets are purchased at the visitors' centre at 108 Orchard Street and tours often sell out, so it's wise to book ahead. Costumed interpreters recount the daily lives of individual immigrant clans that called the building home over the decades. 'Getting By' visits the Sicilian Baldizzi family resident in apartment no.5 in the 1930s, while 'Piecing it Together' pays a call on the Russian Rogarshevsky family, mourning the loss of patriarch Abraham, a garment worker who died of tuberculosis in 1918. In summer 2008, the museum opened its first new tour in six years: 'The Moores: An Irish Family in America', which revisits its Dublin family who lived in the building in 1869 (*see p81* **Kitchen sink drama**). From April to December, the museum also offers walking tours of the Lower East Side.

City Secrets Weegee's Apartment

The notorious crime snapper lived in suitably insalubrious digs.

Born Usher Fellig in the Ukraine in 1899, legendary crime photographer Weegee was an immigrant child who grew up on the Lower East Side. His name had been unceremoniously changed to Arthur when his family arrived at Ellis Island in 1910. And then, by the late 1930s, he had adopted his third moniker, after colleagues gave him the phonetic nickname of Weegee thanks to his uncanny knack for arriving at fresh crime scenes as if he'd consulted a Ouija board. In fact, Weegee had been alerted by the police radios that he kept by his bed and in his car, which was fitted out as a mobile office.

From 1934 to 1947, his most fertile period, Weegee lived in a cramped one-room apartment on 5 Centre Market Place, at Grand Street, just above the John Jovino Gun Shop (which has since moved around the corner to Grand Street). Rumour has it that he bagged his first crime-scene shots just outside his own front door. The pictures he took of the locale, including seedy tableaux of cross-sections of society at the defunct Sammy's Bowery Follies (formerly at 267 Bowery, between E Houston & Stanton Streets), capture a gritty downtown cityscape that has all but disappeared.

Sammy's Bowery Follies.

SIGHTS

Walk Bridging Two Hip 'Hoods

Get the best of both worlds via the Williamsburg Bridge.

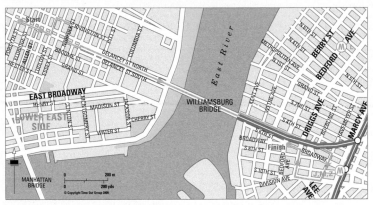

When you've had your fill of the Lower East Side's boutiques, bars and galleries, cross the river for more of the same on the other side of the East River. Manhattan's Lower East Side and Williamsburgh in Brooklyn are two of the city's most happening neighbourhoods right now – and they're linked by the Williamsburgh Bridge.

Kick off your stroll on Delancey and Forsyth Streets. There's no sleep 'til Brooklyn, so look up at the Jesus mural on the outside of the **Iglesia Adventista Delancey** (126 Forsyth Street, at Delancey Street) for divine inspiration – or at least a chuckle at Christ's goofy grin.

You'll want to stock up for your inter-borough walkabout. Head four blocks east to Ludlow Street and hang a left, then a right towards **Economy Candy** (108 Rivington Street, between Essex & Ludlow Streets, 1-212 254 1531). Where we're going, we can't take giant Elvis Pez dispensers, but you'll find other portable morsels such as Swedish Fish.

Swing back to Delancey by way of Norfolk Street and turn east. The mouth of the Williamsburg Bridge – completed

SIGHTS

in 1903 and at that time the longest suspension bridge in the world – is that big, red-metal gateway ahead. Leffert Lefferts Buck, the bridge's chief engineer, also built an ill-fated 'honeymoon' bridge at Niagara Falls, which collapsed into the falls when a run of ice came down from Lake Erie. But don't let that stop you. Hoof it uphill on the two-way bike-and footpath straight up the centre.

You'll soon reach a fork in the path and a sign reading 'City of New York Williams u gh', missing a couple letters, but complete with vestigial h and a few dozen layers of graffiti. Swing right; you'll soon be even with the subway tracks, so wave to the J train passengers on one side while you take in a great Financial District skyline vista on the other. People-watch on your way across; and then, at the midway point, cross to the north-side walkway to mix up the view, gaining an eyeful of the crumbling landmark **Domino Sugar Factory** before it's converted to luxury condos.

Strolling down towards land again, check out the vibrant graffiti decorating South 5th Street below. Then find George Washington's statue, standing guard over a small park (Roebling Street, between South 4th & 5th Streets) and an army of

empty benches. A compass underfoot points to the historical army encampment Valley Forge, 90 miles away.

Go south on Havemeyer Street, crossing below the elevated J train. A right onto Division Avenue puts you smack in the middle of a Hasidic neighbourhood. Stop in the **Smilowitz Heimishe Bake Shop** (167 Division Avenue, between Driggs Avenue & Roebling Street, 1-718 782 2955, closed Sat, phone for reduced summer hours), where you'll face the impossible choice between the delicate, culturally appropriate *hamantaschen* (filled, triangular pastries) or delectable chocolate croissants.

Hang a right at Driggs Avenue, taking in the well-preserved wrought-iron and brick architecture. You'll recognise Broadway by the aroma of porterhouse wafting from New York's steak shrine, **Peter Luger** (178 Broadway at Driggs Avenue, 1-718 387 7400; *see also p211*). No reservations? Console yourself with a drink next door at former stogie den **Velvet** (174 Broadway, between Bedford & Driggs Avenues, 1-718 302 4427, www.velvetbrooklyn.com). If you've downed too many cocktails to stumble back across the bridge, have someone point you to the Marcy Avenue J-train stop; you can be on your way back to Manhattan in minutes.

SIGHTS

Museum at Eldridge Street (Eldridge Street Synagogue)

12 Eldridge Street, between Canal & Division Streets (1-212 219 0302/www.eldridgestreet.org). Subway F to East Broadway. **Open** 10am-4pm Mon-Thur, Sun. **Admission** $10; $6-$8 reductions; free under-5s. **Credit** AmEx, DC, Disc, MC, V. **Map** p40 F31.

Established in 1887, the Eldridge Street Synagogue was among the earliest temples founded in America by the new wave of Eastern European Jews. For its first 50 years, the Moorish Revival *shul* had a congregation of thousands and doubled as a mutual-aid society for new arrivals in need of financial assistance, healthcare and employment. As the Lower East Side's Jewish population assimilated and immigration quotas were enforced, however, the synagogue fell into disrepair; by the 1950s, the badly damaged main sanctuary was closed, the congregation numbers had dwindled and services were moved into a smaller downstairs sanctuary.

Following a 20-year, $20 million facelift that rejuvenated its 70ft vaulted ceilings, ornate brass fixtures and breathtaking stained-glass rose windows, the decayed house of worship was reborn in December 2007, having been lovingly restored. The synagogue still only has a modest congregation, but guided tours of the magnificent main sanctuary and women's balcony take visitors back to its glory days.

★ New Museum of Contemporary Art

235 Bowery, between Prince & Stanton Streets (1-212 219 1222/www.newmuseum.org). Subway F, V Lower East Side-Second Avenue. **Open** noon-6pm Wed, Sat, Sun; noon-10pm Thur, Fri. **Admission** $12; $6-$8 reductions; free under-18s. Free to all 7-10pm Thur. **Credit** DC, MC, V. **Map** p403 F29.

The first new art museum ever constructed from the ground up below 14th Street, and the only museum in NYC devoted entirely to contemporary art, the aptly named New Museum opened in December 2007 and marks a major contribution to the continuing revitalisation of downtown Manhattan. The bold seven-storey building – a stack of zinc-clad, luminous boxes housing a series of fluid, skylit

galleries, a theatre and café – was designed by the cutting-edge Tokyo architectural firm Sejima + Nishizawa/SANAA. The focus is on emerging media and surveys of important but under-recognised artists, further evidence of a pioneering spirit.

EAST VILLAGE

Subway B, D, F, V to Broadway-Lafayette Street; L to First Avenue or Third Avenue; 6 to Astor Place or Bleecker Street.

Originally part of the Lower East Side, the **East Village** developed its distinct identity as a countercultural hotbed in the 1960s. The seeds had been planted as early as the turn of the century, however, when anarchists such as Emma Goldman and Johann Most plotted revolution in a 1st Street salon owned by Julius Schwab. By the dawning of the Age of Aquarius, rock clubs thrived on almost every corner; among them were the now-demolished Fillmore East, on Second Avenue, between 6th and 7th Streets, and the **Dom** (23 St Marks Place, between Second & Third Avenues), where the Velvet Underground often headlined (the building is now a condo). In the '70s, the neighbourhood took a dive as drugs and crime prevailed – but that didn't stop the influx of artists and punk rockers. In the early '80s, East Village galleries were among the first to display the work of groundbreaking artists Jean-Michel Basquiat and Keith Haring.

The blocks east of Broadway between Houston and 14th Streets have lost some of their edge, but remnants of their spirited past endure. Punks, yuppies, hippies, homeboys, vagrants and trust-fund kids have overrun the neighbourhood's former tenements, and indie record stores, bargain restaurants and grungy watering holes still line First and Second Avenues (although in decreasing numbers). For a quintessential old-school East Village experience, grab a stool at **Mars Bar** (25 E 1st Street, at Second Avenue, 1-212 473 9842), a graffiti-plastered hole-in-the-wall frequented by a rowdy punk and hardcore crowd.

Providing a sharp contrast to the radical associations of its more recent past, the **Merchant's House Museum** (*see p83*) on E 4th Street is a perfectly preserved specimen of upper-class domestic life in the 1800s. A short walk north brings you to the East Village's unofficial cultural centre: **St Mark's Church in-the-Bowery** (131 E 10th Street, at Second Avenue, 1-212 674 6377). Built in 1799, the Federal-style church sits on the site of Peter Stuyvesant's farm; the old guy himself, one of New York's first governors, is buried in the adjacent cemetery. Regular services are still held, as are exhibitions and performances from

Kitchen Sink Drama

The Tenement Museum explores the Irish immigrant experience.

In the spring of 1869, Bridget and Joseph Moore huddled over a tiny white coffin in the parlour of no.14, 97 Orchard Street. The couple – who struggled to pay the $8 rent on the modest fourth-floor apartment – were devastated by the sudden death of Agnes, their five-month-old daughter.

Or so believe staffers at the **Lower East Side Tenement Museum** (*see p77*), who pored over church records, birth certificates, newspapers, naturalisation papers and census documents to assemble a new tour entitled 'The Moores: An Irish Family in America'.

All Tenement Museum tours explore re-created residences at 97 Orchard, but 'The Moores' reaches the furthest back in time. Despite the passage of the years, researchers managed to uncover a wealth of details, including the fact that Agnes died from malnutrition and tuberculosis – most likely due to contaminated milk. Visitors discover that it was a common cause of infant mortality through a recording of 'The Swill Milk Song' that plays in an adjacent multimedia room: 'Like poison, 'tis sure to kill/As a thousand tongues can tell.'

Other period melodies recorded by Mick Moloney for the tour include 'No Irish Need Apply' from 1865, and 'Thousands Are Sailing', a traditional Gaelic lamentation for friends and relatives who departed for America.

Adorned with colourful rugs and knick-knacks, well-preserved furniture and religious artefacts, the refurbished abode may surprise tour-goers with its cheerful appearance. '97 Orchard was only six years old at this time,' explains museum research manager David Favaloro. 'The building was home to mostly artisans, shopkeepers and professionals – certainly not the poorest of the poor.' No.14 was still without running water or electricity, however, and the Moores would have been forced to share backyard outhouses with their neighbours.

While the Tenement Museum has explored the struggles and triumphs of the working-class Jews, Italians and Poles who called the Lower East Side home, this is the first time it has addressed the Irish immigrant experience. (The neighbourhood was predominantly German-speaking in the 19th century.) 'We ultimately decided on the Moores because they had an incredibly compelling story,' says Favaloro. 'And the focus on disease still has relevance today, as new immigrants face 21st-century healthcare problems.'

SIGHTS

INSIDE TRACK
GUSS' PICKLES

A feud rages on between rival pickle companies, both claiming to be the original **Guss'**. The current owner of the Lower East Side shop, now at 85 Orchard Street, claims to be the true keeper of the pickle flame, which was lit by Russian emigré Izzy Guss in 1920. However, a former business associate of the founding family, who's now based in Long Island and sells through Chelsea Market (see p87), says he holds the authentic recipe. A case of sour cukes?

arts groups such as the experimental **Ontological Theater** (1-212 533 4650).

St Marks Place (8th Street, between Lafayette Street & Avenue A) was once the East Village's main drag. From the 1950s to the '70s, the lane was a hotbed of artists, writers, radicals and musicians, including WH Auden, Abbie Hoffman, Lenny Bruce, Joni Mitchell and GG Allin; the cover of Led Zeppelin's 1975 album *Physical Graffiti* depicts the apartment buildings at nos.96 and 98. St Marks is still packed until the wee hours, but these days, it's with crowds of college students and tourists browsing for bargain T-shirts, used CDs and pot paraphernalia. Since tattooing became legal again in New York City in 1997 (it had been banned in 1961), a number of parlours have opened; among them is the famous **Fun City** (94 St Marks Place, between First Avenue & Avenue A, 1-212 353 8282), whose awning advertises cappuccino and tattoos.

Cutting between Broadway and Fourth Avenue south of E 8th Street, **Astor Place** is always swarming with young skateboarders and other modern-day street urchins. It's also the site of the **Cooper Union**; comprising schools of art, architecture and engineering, it bears the distinction of being the only free private college in the United States. During the 19th century, Astor Place marked the boundary between the slums to the east and some of the city's most fashionable homes. **Colonnade Row** (428-434 Lafayette Street, between Astor Place & E 4th Street) faces the distinguished Astor Public Library building, which theatre legend Joseph Papp rescued from demolition in the 1960s. Today, the old library is the **Public Theater** (see p353), a platform for first-run American plays and the headquarters of the **Shakespeare in the Park** festival (see p263), held in Central Park, and trendy music venue **Joe's Pub** (see p320).

Below Astor Place, Third Avenue (one block east of Lafayette Street) becomes the Bowery. For decades, the street languished as a seedy flophouse strip and the home of missionary organisations catering to the down and out. Recently, however, it has become increasingly sanitised, and has been invaded by high-rise condo buildings, ritzy restaurants and clubs, and the posh new **Bowery Hotel** (see p154).

As part of this gentrification, even the hallowed CBGB got the boot. Once host to legends such as the Ramones, Talking Heads and Patti Smith, and the unofficial home of US punk, the club shuttered in October 2006; owner Hilly Kristal died of cancer in August 2007. In its place is the second downtown boutique from swanky menswear designer **John Varvatos** (315 Bowery, at Bleecker Street, 1-212 358 0315), while growing music-photography chain **Morrison Hotel Gallery** (no.313, 1-212 677 2253) filled the void left by the CBGB Gallery next door. Both the new venues have kept mementos from the club, while other East Village bars and clubs carry on the cheap-beer-and-loud-music formula. Try the **Mercury Lounge** (see p322) and the **Bowery Poetry Club** (see p319), which has its roots in the poetry-slam scene but also regularly offers jazz, folk, hip hop and improv theatre.

Elsewhere in the neighbourhood, East 7th Street is a Ukrainian stronghold, of which the focal point is the Byzantine **St George's Ukrainian Catholic Church** at no.30. The **Ukrainian Museum** (222 E 6th Street, between Second & Third Avenues, 1-212 228 0110, closed Mon & Tue) houses artwork, artefacts and photos from the region. One block over, there's often a long line of beefy fraternity types waiting to enter **McSorley's Old Ale House** (15 E 7th Street, between Second & Third Avenues, 1-212 473 9148). Festooned with aged photos, yellowed newspaper articles and dusty memorabilia, the 155-year-old Irish tavern is purportedly the oldest continually operating pub in New York. (It still serves just one kind of beer – its own brew, available in light and dark formulas.) Representing a different corner of the globe, **Curry Row** (East 6th Street, between First & Second Avenues) is lined with Indian restaurants popular with budget-minded diners.

Alphabet City (which gets its name from its key avenues, A, B, C and D) stretches towards the East River. Once an edgy Puerto Rican neighbourhood with links to the drug trade, it has largely been overtaken by young professionals. Avenue C is also known as Loisaida Avenue, a rough approximation of 'Lower East Side' when pronounced with a

Spanish accent. Two churches on 4th Street are built in the Spanish colonial style: **San Isidro y San Leandro** (345 E 4th Street, between Avenues C & D) and **Iglesia Pentecostal Camino Damasco** (289 E 4th Street, between Avenues B & C). The **Nuyorican Poets Café** (*see p280*), a clubhouse for espresso-drinking wordsmiths since 1974, is known for its poetry slams, in which performers do lyric battle before a score-keeping audience.

Dating from 1837, **Tompkins Square Park** (from 7th to 10th Streets, between Avenues A & B), honours Daniel D Tompkins, governor of New York from 1807 to 1817, and vice-president during the tenure of the Monroe administration. Over the years, this 10.5-acre park has been a site for demonstrations and rioting. The last major uprising was in the early 1990s, when the city evicted squatters from the park and renovated it to suit the area's newly affluent residents. Along with dozens of 150-year-old elm trees (some of the oldest in the city), it boasts lovely landscaping, basketball courts, three playgrounds and two dog runs. Despite the drastic changes in and around the park over the past two decades, this is a place where bongo beaters, acoustic guitarists, punky squatters, khaki-wearing yuppies and the homeless all mingle.

North of Tompkins Square, around First Avenue and 11th Street, are remnants of earlier communities: discount fabric dealers, Italian cheese shops, Polish butchers and two great Italian coffee and cannoli houses: **De Robertis** (176 First Avenue, between 10th & 11th Streets, 1-212 674 7137, closed Mon) and **Veniero's Pasticceria & Caffè** (342 E 11th Street, at First Avenue, 1-212 674 7264).

Merchant's House Museum

29 E 4th Street, between Lafayette Street & Bowery (1-212 777 1089/www.merchants house.org). Subway B, D, F, V to Broadway-Lafayette Street; 6 to Bleecker Street. **Open** noon-5pm Mon, Thur-Sun. **Admission** $8; $5 reductions; free under-12s. **Credit** AmEx, DC, MC, V. **Map** p403 F29.

Merchant's House Museum, the city's only fully preserved 19th-century family home, is an elegant, late Federal-Greek Revival property kitted out with the same furnishings and decorations that it contained when it was inhabited from 1835 by hardware tycoon Seabury Tredwell and his family. Three years after Tredwell's eighth daughter died in 1933, it opened as a museum. You can peruse the house at your own pace (using the museum's printed guide) or book a group tour at least three weeks in advance.

GREENWICH VILLAGE

Subway A, B, C, D, E, F, V to W 4th Street; L, N, Q, R, W, 4, 5, 6 to 14th Street-Union Square; N, R, W to 8th Street-NYU; 1 to Christopher St-Sheridan Square.

Stretching from Houston Street to 14th Street, between Broadway and Sixth Avenue, **Greenwich Village** has inspired bohemians

SIGHTS

**INSIDE TRACK
ASTOR PLACE**

Astor Place is marked by a steel cube that has sat on a traffic island by the entrance to the 6 train since 1968. With a little elbow grease, the cube, whose proper title is *Alamo*, will spin on its axis.

SIGHTS

for almost a century. Now that it has become one of the most expensive (and exclusive) neighbourhoods in the city, you need a lot more than a struggling artist's or writer's income to inhabit its leafy streets. However, it's still a fine place for idle wandering, candlelit dining in out-of-the-way restaurants, and hopping between bars and cabaret venues.

The hippies who tuned out in **Washington Square Park** are always there in spirit and often in person, along with a disparate cast of characters that takes in chess hustlers, students and hip hop kids. Generation-Y skateboarders clatter near the base of the Washington Arch, a modestly sized replica of Paris's Arc de Triomphe, built in 1895 to honour George Washington. The park hums with musicians and street artists, but the once-ubiquitous pot dealers have largely disappeared thanks to the NYC Police Department's surveillance cameras. And now the 9.75-acre Village landmark is the subject of a different kind of controversy.

The NYC Parks Department has begun work on a $16 million redesign of the park, funded by the city, the Tisch family and NYU. While some aspects of the plan can't be faulted (refurbishing the dilapidated restrooms, for example), community activists have strongly protested the plan, fearing that others – such as altering the central plaza – will ruin the park's bohemian flavour. One of the more contested parts of the proposal is the transformation of the iconic fountain from a theatre-in-the-round to an ornamental showpiece – one with a spray so strong that no one could sit in or around it. Other aspects call for the removal of numerous mature trees and a reduction in the size of the central plaza so significant that an estimated 5,000 fewer people will be able to gather in it. The first phase of construction is set to be completed in spring 2009 but, in late 2008, the fate of the park had yet to be determined.

In the 1830s, the wealthy began building handsome townhouses around the square. A few of those properties are still privately owned and occupied, but many others have become part of the ever-expanding NYU campus. The university also owns the Washington Mews, a row of charming 19th-century former stables that line a tiny cobblestoned alley just to the north of the park between Fifth Avenue and University Place. Several famed literary figures, including Henry James, Herman Melville and Mark Twain, lived on or near the square. In 1871, the local creative community founded the **Salmagundi Club** (*see right*), America's oldest artists' club; it's now situated north of Washington Square on Fifth Avenue.

Greenwich Village continues to change with the times, for better and for worse. In the 1960s, Eighth Street was the closest New York got to San Francisco's Haight Street. Although it's currently a long procession of piercing parlours, punky boutiques and shoe stores, Jimi Hendrix's **Electric Lady Studios** is still at 52 W 8th Street, between Fifth & Sixth Avenues. Once the dingy but colourful stomping ground of Beat poets and folk and jazz musicians, the well-trafficked strip of Bleecker Street, between La Guardia Place and Sixth Avenue, is now an overcrowded stretch of poster shops, cheap restaurants and music venues for the college crowd. Storied hangouts such as Le Figaro Café (184 Bleecker Street, at MacDougal Street), Kerouac's favourite, are no more.

The famed Village Gate jazz club at the corner of Bleecker and Thompson Streets – which welcomed performances by Miles Davis, Nina Simone and John Cage – closed in 1993. However, in summer 2008, **(Le) Poisson Rouge** (*see p322*) opened on the site with a similar mission to present diverse genres under one roof. Just up the street on La Guardia Place is the **AIA Center for Architecture** (*see below*), which hosts temporary exhibitions on plans and projects in the city.

Not far from here, in the triangle formed by Sixth Avenue, Greenwich Avenue and 10th Street, you'll see the Gothic-style **Jefferson Market Library** (a branch of the New York Public Library). The lovely flower-filled garden facing Greenwich Avenue once held the art deco Women's House of Detention, which was torn down in 1974. Mae West did a little time there in 1926, on obscenity charges stemming from her Broadway show *Sex*.

FREE **AIA Center for Architecture**

536 La Guardia Place, between Bleecker & W 3rd Streets (1-212 683 0023/www.aiany.org). Subway A, B, C, D, E, F, V to W 4th Street. **Open** 9am-8pm Mon-Fri; 11am-5pm Sat. **Admission** free. **Map** p403 E29.

Designed by architect Andrew Berman, this three-storey building is a fitting home for architectural

---

INSIDE TRACK
DYLAN'S VILLAGE

Bob Dylan lived at and owned 94 MacDougal Street (on a row of historic brownstones near Bleecker Street) through much of the 1960s, performing in Washington Square Park and at clubs such as Cafe Wha? on MacDougal Street, between Bleecker and West 3rd Streets.

debate: the sweeping, light-filled design is a physical manifestation of AIA's goal of promoting transparency in both its access and programming. Berman cut away large slabs of flooring at the street and basement levels, converting underground spaces into bright, museum-quality galleries. He also installed a glass-enclosed library and conference room on the first floor, and a children's gallery and workshop on the mezzanine level. The building was New York's first public space to use an energy-efficient geothermal system. Water from two 1,260ft wells is piped through the building to help heat and cool it.

▶ *For more on New York City's architecture, see pp38-47.*

FREE **Salmagundi Club**

47 Fifth Avenue, at 12th Street (1-212 255 7740/www.salmagundi.org). Subway L, N, Q, R, W, 4, 5, 6 to 14th Street-Union Square. **Open** *Exhibitions* 1-5pm daily; phone for details. **Admission** free. **Map** p402 E28.
America's oldest artists' club, founded as the New York Sketch Club in 1871, is set in a landmark building and hosts exhibitions, lectures, classes and art auctions.

THE WEST VILLAGE & THE MEATPACKING DISTRICT

Subway A, C, E, L to 14th Street; 1 to Christopher St-Sheridan Square; 1, 2, 3 to 14th Street.

In the early 20th century, the **West Village** was largely a working-class Italian neighbourhood. These days, it's home to numerous celebrities (including Sarah Jessica Parker and Matthew Broderick), but a low-key, everyone-knows-everyone feel remains. It may not have the buzzy vibe of the East Village, but it has held on to much of its picturesque charm.

The area west of Sixth Avenue to the Hudson River, from 14th Street to Houston Street, possesses the quirky geographical features that moulded the Village's character. Only here could W 10th Street cross W 4th Street, and Waverly Place cross… Waverly Place. The West Village's layout doesn't follow the regular grid pattern but rather the original horse paths that settlers used to navigate it.

Locals and visitors crowd bistros along Seventh Avenue and Hudson Street and patronise the increasingly high-rent shops on this stretch of Bleecker Street, including three Marc Jacobs boutiques and three Ralph Lauren outposts. Detour to Christopher Street for Kyung Lee's brace of chic indie-designer boutiques, **Albertine** (no.13, at Gay Street, 1-212 924 8515) and **Claudine** (no.19, between Gay Street & Waverly Place, 1-212 414 4234).

The neighbourhood's bohemian population may have dwindled years ago, but a few old landmarks remain. Solemnly raise a glass in the **White Horse Tavern** (567 Hudson Street, at 11th Street, 1-212 989 3956), where poet Dylan Thomas went on his last drinking binge before his death in 1953. On and just off Seventh Avenue South are jazz and cabaret clubs, including the **Village Vanguard** (*see p329*).

The West Village is also a longstanding gay mecca, although the young gay scene has mostly moved north to Chelsea and Hell's Kitchen. The **Stonewall Inn** (*see p312*), on Christopher Street, is next to the original, the site of the 1969 rebellion that marked the birth of the modern gay-liberation movement. Inside Christopher Park, which faces the Inn, is George Segal's *Gay Pride*, plaster sculptures of two same-sex couples that commemorates the street's role in gay history. Along Christopher Street from Sheridan Square to the Hudson River pier, most of the area's shops, bars and restaurants are out, loud and proud. The Hudson riverfront features grass-covered piers, food vendors and picnic tables.

The north-west corridor of the West Village is known as the **Meatpacking District**, dating to its origins as a wholesale meat market in the 1930s. Until the 1990s, it was also a haunt for prostitutes, many of them transsexual. In recent years, however, following the arrival of pioneering fashion store **Jeffrey New York** (*see p229*), more designer flagships have moved in, including Diane von Furstenberg, Alexander McQueen and Stella McCartney. Frequent mentions on *Sex and the City,* along with the arrival of swanky **Hotel Gansevoort** (*see p158*) in 2004, cemented the area's reputation, although most of the meatpacking factories have since closed. A profusion of self-consciously hip eateries such as **Pastis** (9 Ninth Avenue, at Little W 12th Street, 1-212 929 4844) remain; nightclubs such as **Cielo** (*see p296*) and **APT** (*see p299*) draw a young crowd after dark.

SIGHTS

Midtown

Brave the crush for bright lights and dazzling sights.

The area from 14th to 59th Streets is iconic New York: jutting skyscrapers, crowded pavements and a yellow river of cabs streaming down the congested avenues. It doesn't hurt that some of the city's most recognisable landmarks are located here, from the Empire State Building to Rockefeller Center. But there's a lot more to Midtown than glistening towers and high-octane commerce. It contains the city's most concentrated contemporary gallery district (**Chelsea**), its hottest gay enclaves (Chelsea and **Hell's Kitchen**), some of its swankiest shops (**Fifth Avenue**) and, of course, the majority of its major theatres (on **Broadway**, especially around Times Square). There are even a few serene spots where you can retreat from the jostling crowds and traffic – the area's green quotient is being boosted, as Bryant and Madison Square Parks are joined by the long-anticipated first leg of the High Line park.

Maps pp404-405	Restaurants &
Hotels p160	Cafés p193
	Bars p220

CHELSEA

Subway A, C, E, 1, 2, 3 to 14th Street; C, E, 1 to 23rd Street; L to Eighth Avenue; 1 to 18th Street or 28th Street.

Formerly a working-class Irish neighbourhood, the corridor between 14th and 29th Streets west of Sixth Avenue emerged as the nexus of New York's queer life in the 1990s. Rising housing costs and the protean nature of New York's cultural landscape has seen its role slowly supplanted by Hell's Kitchen to the north (just as Chelsea once overtook the West Village), but the locale is still home to a large number of gay bars (*see p311*) as well as numerous restaurants, clothing stores and sex shops catering to the once-ubiquitous 'Chelsea boys'.

The neighbourhood's far-west warehouse district is still known for velvet-roped nightclubs such as **Marquee** (*see p297*) and **Cain** (544 W 27th Street, between Tenth & Eleventh Avenues, 1-212 947 8000, closed Mon, Tue, Sun), but it's become more residential in recent years. The plan to turn a defunct train track, known as the High Line, into a 1.5-mile promenade and urban park has been slow to bear fruit (*see p90* **High Point**); however, the first section is set to open by early 2009. The weekend flea markets tucked between buildings along 25th Street, between Sixth Avenue and Broadway, have shrunk in recent years (casualties of development), but you'll still find a heady assortment of clothes, furnishings, cameras and knick-knacks at the rummage-worthy **Antiques Garage** (*see p96*).

The nearby **Chelsea Hotel** (*see p160*) has been a magnet for creative types since it first opened in 1884; Mark Twain was an early guest. The list of former residents reads like a *Who's Who* of New York's arts heritage: Dylan Thomas, Arthur Miller, Quentin Crisp, Leonard Cohen, Bob Dylan, Joni Mitchell and Rufus Wainwright, to name a few. In the 1960s, it was the stomping ground of Andy Warhol's coterie of Superstars, and the location of his 1966 film

SIGHTS

The Chelsea Girls. The Chelsea gained punk-rock notoriety on 12 October 1978, when Sex Pistol Sid Vicious stabbed girlfriend Nancy Spungen to death in Room 100. Under new corporate management, the hotel has lost a measure of its boho glamour, but you can still stop by for a peek at the lobby artwork and a glimpse of the ghosts said to haunt its halls. The majority of the 250-room building is given over to apartments, but a number of traditional (if modest) hotel rooms are available.

Chelsea also provides a variety of impressive cultural offerings. The **Joyce Theater** (*see p357*) is a brilliantly renovated art deco cinema that presents better-known contemporary dance troupes, while the **Dance Theater Workshop** (*see p359*) performs at the Bessie Schönberg Theater. You'll find an astounding array of traditional Himalayan art and artefacts at the **Rubin Museum of Art** (*see below*), but if your tastes lean more towards the esoteric, check out pioneering arts centre the **Kitchen** (*see p360*).

To get a glimpse of how Chelsea looked back when it was first developed in the 1880s, stroll by **Cushman Row** (406-418 W 20th Street, between Ninth & Tenth Avenues) in the Chelsea Historic District. Just to the north is the block-long **General Theological Seminary of the Episcopal Church** (440 W 21st Street, between Ninth & Tenth Avenues, 1-212 243 5150, www.gts.edu), where the verdant garden courtyard (closed Sun) is a hidden oasis of tranquillity. The seminary's land was part of the estate known as Chelsea, owned by poet Clement Clarke Moore, author of *A Visit from St Nicholas* (more commonly known today as *'Twas the Night Before Christmas*).

Housed in a former Nabisco factory on Ninth Avenue, where the first Oreo cookie was made in 1912, the **Chelsea Market** (75 Ninth Avenue, between 15th & 16th Streets, www.chelseamarket.com) is a conglomeration of 18 structures built between the 1890s and the 1930s. The ground-floor food arcade offers artisanal bread, wine, imported Italian foods and freshly made ice-cream, among other treats; be sure to stop by Fat Witch for a free brownie sample. The upper floors house several major media companies, including Oxygen and the Food Network, where popular culinary shows such as *30 Minute Meals with Rachael Ray* are taped.

In the 1980s, many of New York's galleries left Soho for the western edge of Chelsea, from West 20th Street to West 29th Street, between Tenth and Eleventh Avenues (*see pp270-274*). Internationally recognised spaces such as **Mary Boone Gallery**, **Gagosian Gallery** and **PaceWildenstein**, as well as numerous less famous names, attract swarms of art lovers. The crowds are at their biggest at weekends and on Thursday nights, when many host free wine and cheese receptions. Not far from here, the Fashion Institute of Technology, at 27th Street, counts Calvin Klein, Carolina Herrera and Michael Kors among its alumni. The school's **Museum at FIT** (*see below*), a block away, mounts free exhibitions.

You can watch the sun go down from one of the spectacular Hudson River piers, which were once terminals for the world's grand ocean liners. Many city piers remain in a state of ruin, but the four between 17th and 23rd Streets have been transformed into mega sports centre **Chelsea Piers** (*see p342*). When you're down by the river, the **Starrett-Lehigh Building** (601 W 26th Street, at Eleventh Avenue) comes into view. The stunning 1929 structure was left in disrepair until the dot-com boom of the late 1990s, when media companies, photographers and designers snatched up its loft-like spaces.

FREE Museum at FIT

Building E, Seventh Avenue, at 27th Street (1-212 217 4558/www.fitnyc.edu/museum). Subway 1 to 28th Street. **Open** noon-8pm Tue-Fri; 10am-5pm Sat. **Admission** free. **Map** p404 D26.
The Fashion Institute of Technology owns one of the largest and most impressive collections of clothing, textiles and accessories in the world, including some 50,000 costumes and fabrics dating from the fifth century to the present. Overseen by fashion historian Valerie Steele, the museum showcases a selection from the permanent collection, as well as temporary exhibitions focusing on individual designers or the role fashion plays in society.

Rubin Museum of Art

150 W 17th Street, at Seventh Avenues (1-212 620 5000/www.rmanyc.org). Subway A, C, E to 14th Street; L to Eighth Avenue; 1 to 18th Street. **Open** 11am-5pm Mon, Thur; 11am-7pm Wed; 11am-10pm Fri; 11am-6pm Sat, Sun. **Admission** $10; $7 reductions; free under-12s. Free to all 7-10pm Fri. **Credit** AmEx, DC, Disc, MC, V. **Map** p403 D27.

INSIDE TRACK
LONDON TERRACE

Not all of Chelsea's celebrities live in the Chelsea Hotel. Occupying a full city block in Chelsea (23rd Street, between Ninth & Tenth Avenues), **London Terrace** is a distinctive 1920s Tudor-style apartment complex that's home to some rather famous names; among them are Debbie Harry, *Vanity Fair* photographer Annie Leibovitz, former First Daughter Chelsea Clinton and *Desperate Housewives* star Teri Hatcher.

SIGHTS

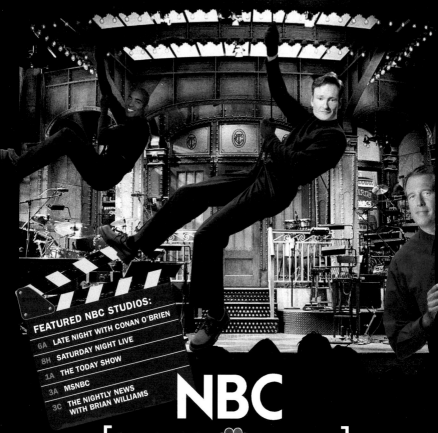

Opened in 2004, this six-storey museum (once home to Barneys New York) houses Donald and Shelley Rubin's impressive collection of Himalayan art and artefacts, as well as large-scale temporary exhibitions. Through 13 July 2009, 'Patron and Painter: Situ Panchen and the Revival of the Encampment Style' explores an important Tibetan painting tradition established in the 16th century.

FLATIRON DISTRICT & UNION SQUARE

Subway F, V to 14th Street; L, N, Q, R, W, 4, 5, 6 to 14th Street-Union Square; L to Sixth Avenue; N, R, W, 6 to 23rd Street or 28th Street.

Taking its name from the distinctive wedge-shaped Flatiron Building, this district extends from 14th to 29th Streets, between Sixth and Lexington Avenues. Initially, the locale was predominantly commercial, home to numerous toy manufacturers and photography studios. It's still not uncommon to see models and actors strolling to and from their shoots. However, in the 1980s, the district became more residential, as buyers were drawn to its 19th-century brownstones and early 20th-century industrial architecture. Clusters of restaurants and shops soon followed. By the turn of the millennium, many internet start-ups had moved to the area, earning it the nickname 'Silicon Alley'.

The Flatiron District has two major public spaces. Opened in 1847, **Madison Square Park** (from 23rd to 26th Streets, between Fifth & Madison Avenues, www.madisonsquarepark. org) is the more modest of the two. Originally favoured by the locale's genteel residents, it was eventually the site of several unfortunate and unsavoury events (*see p93* **Profile**), but got a much-needed makeover in 2001.

Cultural events now brighten the calendar. Organised by the Madison Square Park Conservancy, Mad Sq Art is a year-round 'gallery without walls', featuring sculptural, video and installation exhibitions from big-name artists such as Sol LeWitt, Roxy Paine and William Wegman. Summer, meanwhile, brings a series of concerts, readings and kids' events to the park. A further lure is celebrity chef Danny Meyer's **Shake Shack** (south side of Madison Square Park, near 23rd Street, at Madison Avenue, 1-212 889 6600), which attracts crowds in the summer months as area workers clamour for tasty burgers. The queues can be daunting, but New Yorkers are willing to wait for the chance to eat alfresco surrounded by lush foliage and dazzling artwork.

At the southern end of Madison Square lies the **Flatiron Building** (175 Fifth Avenue, between 22nd & 23rd Streets). The world's first steel-frame skyscraper, the 22-storey Beaux

Arts edifice is clad conspicuously in white limestone and terracotta, but it's the unique triangular shape that has drawn sightseers since it opened in 1902. Urban legend has it that a popular 1920s catchphrase originated at this corner of 23rd Street – police would give the '23 skidoo' to ne'er-do-wells trying to peek at ladies' petticoats as the unique wind currents that swirled around the building blew up their dresses. Speaking of rampant libidos, the nearby **Museum of Sex** (*see p91*) houses an impressive collection of salacious ephemera.

In the 19th century, the neighbourhood went by the moniker of Ladies' Mile, thanks to the ritzy department stores that once lined Broadway and Sixth Avenue. These retail palaces attracted the 'carriage trade', wealthy women who bought the latest imported fashions and household goods. By 1914, most of the department stores had moved north, leaving their proud cast-iron buildings behind. Today, the area is peppered with chain clothing stores, bookshops and tasteful home-furnishing shops such as **ABC Carpet & Home** (*see p254*).

The Flatiron District's other major public space, **Union Square** (from 14th to 17th Streets, between Union Square East & Union Square West) is named after neither the Union of the Civil War nor the labour rallies that once took place here, but simply for the union of Broadway and Bowery Lane (now Fourth Avenue). Even so, it does have its radical roots: from the 1920s until the early '60s, it was a favourite spot for tub-thumping political oratory. Following 9/11, the park became a focal point for the city's outpouring of grief. Today, it's best known as the home of the **Union Square Greenmarket** (*see p91*). The square is flanked by a variety of large businesses, including the W New York-Union Square hotel, a Virgin Megastore and a Barnes & Noble bookstore that hosts an excellent programme of author events (*see p278*).

INSIDE TRACK
METRONOME

It's not uncommon to see passers-by perplexed by the **Metronome**, a massive sculptural installation attached to 1 Union Square South that bellows steam and generates a barrage of numbers on a digital readout. Although they appear strange, they're not random numbers – the 15-digit display is actually a clock indicating the time relative to midnight. There's a detailed explanation at the website of Kristin Jones and Andrew Ginzel, the artists responsible; see www.jonesginzel.com.

SIGHTS

High Point

The inspiring revival of a defunct train track into a new park.

At any other construction project, piles of dirt wouldn't be reasons to celebrate. But up on the High Line, a public park project designed to revive a disused elevated freight-train track, they represent rebirth. In summer 2008, truckloads of soil started filling the dozens of planting beds that line the 1.5-mile walkway, between Gansevoort Street in the Meatpacking District and 34th Street in Midtown. Then, in the autumn, grasses, perennials, shrubs and trees were gradually sunk into topsoil. 'It's exciting to think that some of the plants that thrived up there in the first place will be back there again,' says Melissa Fisher, the staff horticulturist for non-profit community group Friends of the High Line (FHL).

Ever since the last train delivery on the elevated but now-defunct West Side Line in the early 1980s, this 22-block-long, three-storeys-high ribbon of rail on the far west side had been abandoned, an urban afterthought made lush by natural forces. 'The combination of nature atop this industrial artefact is amazing,' says Robert Hammond, co-founder of FHL. 'When you go up now, it's different from

how it looked when we first saw it ten years ago, but it's still special.'

The project's progress has been slow going at times, the first section of the park, which runs from Gansevoort Street to West 20th Street, will be open for walkers by early 2009. The second section, which extends to 30th Street, should be ready by the end of the year. According to Fisher, visitors will be able to stroll through lawns, meadows and woodlands, while taking in gorgeous views of the city.

What's more, the Whitney Museum of American Art has signed on to build a satellite museum, designed by Renzo Piano, at the southern end of the High Line. Construction is slated to begin in 2009 with a projected opening three years later. 'Having the Whitney anchor one side of the park ensures our art-oriented identity as well as being a park,' says FHL co-founder Josh David. 'Artists and local gallery owners were extremely supportive of the project from the beginning. They really understood the aesthetic and creative vision and got us off to a strong start within the local community.'

Museum of Sex

*233 Fifth Avenue, at 27th Street (1-212 689 6337/
www.mosex.org). Subway N, R, W, 6 to 28th
Street.* **Open** 11am-6.30pm Mon-Fri, Sun; 11am-
8pm Sat. **Admission** $14.50; $13.50 reductions.
Under-18s must be accompanied by an adult.
Credit AmEx, DC, MC, V. **Map** p404 E26.
For an institution devoted to erotica, this Midtown
museum is on the conservative side, ironic considering it's in NYC's former Tenderloin district, which
was chock-a-block with dance halls and brothels in
the 1800s. The museum offers a tastefully presented collection of vintage girlie magazines, Victorian-
era vibrators, blue movies and Real Dolls, plus
rotating exhibits on prostitution, fetishism, homo-
sexuality, masturbation and other semi-taboo topics.

Union Square Greenmarket

*From 16th to 17th Streets, between Union
Square East & Union Square West (1-212 788
7476/www.cenyc.org). Subway L, N, Q, R, W, 4,
5, 6 to 14th Street-Union Square.* **Open** 8am-
6pm Mon, Wed, Fri, Sat. **Map** p403 E27.
Shop elbow-to-elbow with top chefs for all manner
of locally grown produce, handmade breads, preserves and desserts. Between Thanksgiving and
Christmas, the adjacent Union Square Holiday
Market features knitwear, toys, candles and jewellery by local artisans. *Photo p92.*
▶ *For more food specialists in the city, see p246.*

GRAMERCY PARK & MURRAY HILL

*Subway L, N, Q, R, W, 4, 5, 6 to 14th Street-
Union Square; L to Sixth Avenue; N, R, W, 6 to
23rd Street or 28th Street; S, 4, 5, 6, 7 to 42nd
Street-Grand Central; 6 to 33rd Street.*

A key to **Gramercy Park**, the tranquil, gated
square at the bottom of Lexington Avenue
(between 20th & 21st Streets), is one of the most
sought-after treasures in all the five boroughs.
For the most part, only residents of the beautiful
surrounding townhouses and apartment
buildings have keys to the park, which was
developed in the 1830s to resemble a London
square; however, guests of the Gramercy Park
Hotel (*see p162*) also have park privileges.
The park is flanked by two private clubs;
members of both also also have access to the
square. One is the **Players Club** (16 Gramercy
Park South, between Park Avenue South &
Irving Place), housed in an 1845 brownstone
formerly owned by Edwin Booth (19th-century
actor and brother of John Wilkes Booth,
Abraham Lincoln's assassin). Next door at
no.15 is the Gothic Revival Samuel Tilden
House, which houses the **National Arts Club**
(1-212 475 3424, www.nationalartsclub.org,
closed Sat, Sun & July, Aug), the members of

which often donate their work in lieu of annual
dues. The busts of famous writers (Shakespeare,
Dante) along the façade were chosen to reflect
Tilden's library, which, along with his fortune,
helped create the New York Public Library.
Leading south from the park to 14th Street,
Irving Place is named after author Washington
Irving. Near the corner of 15th Street sits the
Fillmore New York at Irving Plaza (*see
p319*), a music venue. At the corner of Park
Avenue South and 17th Street is the final base
of the once-omnipotent Tammany Hall political
machine (*see p25*). Built in 1929, the building
now houses the New York Film Academy.
A few blocks away is the **Theodore
Roosevelt Birthplace** (*see p92*), a national
historic site that comprises a small museum
and several recreated rooms. Not far from here,
the low, fortress-like 69th **Regiment Armory**
(68 Lexington Avenue, between 25th & 26th
Streets), now used by the New York National
Guard, hosted a sensational 1913 art showcase,
which introduced Americans to Cubism,
Fauvism and Dadaism. The tradition continues
at the annual **Armory Show** (*see p260*).
The largely residential area bordered by
23rd and 30th Streets, Park Avenue and the
East River is known as **Kips Bay** after Jacobus
Henderson Kip, whose farm covered the area in
the 17th century. Third Avenue is the district's
main thoroughfare, and a locus of restaurants
representing a variety of eastern cuisines,
including Afghan, Tibetan and Turkish. The
two-block stretch of Lexington Avenue between
27th and 29th Streets is often called 'Curry Hill',
a play on nearby Murray Hill, because of the
plethora of Indian restaurants that line it.
Murray Hill itself spans 30th to 40th Streets,
between Third and Fifth Avenues. Townhouses
of the rich and powerful were once clustered
around Madison and Park Avenues. However,
while it's still a fashionable neighbourhood, now
populated mostly by upwardly-mobiles fresh
out of university, only a few streets retain the
elegance that made the locale so distinctive. One
such sight is **Sniffen Court** (150-158 E 36th
Street, between Lexington & Third Avenues), an
unspoiled row of 1864 carriage houses located
within earshot of the Queens Midtown Tunnel's
ceaseless traffic. The **Morgan Library &
Museum** (*see below*), also on 36th Street, houses
some 350,000 rare books, manuscripts, prints,
and silver and copper collectibles. If you're
more interested in contemporary European
culture, visit the nearby **Scandinavia House
– The Nordic Center in America** (*see p92*).

Morgan Library & Museum

*225 Madison Avenue, at 36th Street (1-212
685 0008/www.themorgan.org). Subway 6 to
33rd Street.* **Open** 10.30am-5pm Tue-Thur;

Union Square Greenmarket. *See p91.*

10.30am-9pm Fri; 10am-6pm Sat; 11am-6pm Sun.
Admission $12; $8 reductions; free under-12s.
Credit AmEx, DC, MC, V. **Map** p404 E25.
This Madison Avenue institution began as the private library of savvy financier J Pierpont Morgan, and is his artistic gift to the city. Building on the collection Morgan amassed in his lifetime, the museum houses first-rate works on paper, including drawings by Michelangelo, Rembrandt and Picasso; three Gutenberg Bibles; a copy of *Frankenstein* annotated by Mary Shelley; manuscripts by Dickens, Poe, Twain, Steinbeck and Wilde; sheet music handwritten by Beethoven and Mozart; and an original edition of Dickens' *A Christmas Carol* that's displayed every Yuletide. In 2006, a massive renovation and expansion orchestrated by Renzo Piano brought more natural light into the building and doubled the available exhibition space.

Planned exhibitions in 2009 include 'The Modern Stage: Set Design 1900-1970' (17 Apr-28 Aug), charting the impact of European trends on America, followed in the autumn by 'Reading Jane Austen', with letters, story outlines, journals and the only surviving manuscript of her novel *Lady Susan*.

Scandinavia House – The Nordic Center in America
58 Park Avenue, between 37th & 38th Streets (1-212 879 9779/www.scandinaviahouse.org). Subway S, 4, 5, 6, 7 to 42nd Street-Grand Central. **Open** noon-6pm Tue-Sat. **Admission** *Suggested donation* $3; $2 reductions. **Credit** AmEx, DC, MC, V. **Map** p404 E24.
One of city's top cultural centres, the Scandinavia House serves as a lifeline between the US and the five Nordic nations (Denmark, Finland, Iceland, Norway and Sweden), and offers a full schedule of film screenings, lectures and art and design exhibitions. The in-house AQ Café is a popular lunch spot with an innovative Swedish menu and on Saturdays, kids can play with Lego sets, read Norse fairy tales and crawl around volcanoes and ice caves in the Heimbold Family Children's Center.

Theodore Roosevelt Birthplace
28 E 20th Street, between Broadway & Park Avenue South (1-212 260 1616/ www.nps.gov/thrb). Subway 6 to 23rd Street. **Open** 9am-5pm Tue-Sat. **Tours** hourly 10am-4pm Tue-Sat. **Admission** $3; free under-18s.
No credit cards. Map p403 E27.
The brownstone where the 26th President of the United States was born, and where he lived until he was 14 years old, was demolished in 1916. But it was recreated after his death in 1919, complete with authentic period furniture (some collected and restored from the original house), personal effects and a trophy room.

HERALD SQUARE & THE GARMENT DISTRICT
Subway A, C, E, 1, 2, 3 to 34th Street-Penn Station; B, D, F, N, Q, R, V, W to 34th Street-Herald Square.

Seventh Avenue, aka Fashion Avenue, is the main drag of the **Garment District** (roughly from 34th to 40th Streets, between Broadway & Eighth Avenue) and where designers – along

Profile Madison Square Park

The troubled past and happier present of a New York gem.

Back in the 19th century, Madison Square Park was a highly desirable address. Leonard Jerome, Winston Churchill's grandfather, resided in a magnificent but since-demolished mansion at Madison Avenue and 26th Street, and high-society novelist Edith Wharton also made her home in the neighbourhood.

However, in time, Madison Square Park's fortunes fell, as a succession of unfortunate and unsavoury events turned its reputation downhill. After the violent Draft Riots of 1863, tens of thousands of Federal troops were bivouacked in the park. Ten years later, on 23 December 1873, PT Barnum's Hippodrome burned to the ground just north of the park taking Grace Chapel and two adjacent buildings with it. And then, in 1906, noted architect Stanford White was murdered atop one of his creations, the second Madison Square Garden.

By the 1990s, the park had become a decaying no-go zone given over to drug dealers and the homeless. But thanks to several million dollars of private money, it was transformed at the turn of the 21st century into a verdant oasis, and has since reclaimed its place in the heart of the city. This reversal of fortune has been largely down to the efforts of the Madison Square Conservancy, a non-profit group that's created a cultural programme in a bid to tempt people into the park while keeping crime out of it.

In summer, the park hosts a series of summer concerts, literary readings and kids' events. But the undoubted centrepiece of the initiative is **Mad Sq Art**, a 'gallery without walls' featuring four exhibitions a year by internationally known

SIGHTS

artists. From large-scale sculpture to site-specific installations in a variety of media, the works aim to give a fresh perspective on the park: in autumn 2008, Tadashi Kawamata populated it with handmade tree huts; and in spring 2009, New York-based performance artist Shannon Plumb premieres her video performances, featuring footage she filmed on-site over the course of almost a year. Still, it's not the first time that the green space has been the site of dramatic displays: for six years from 1876, the park was home to the arm and torch of the Statue of Liberty.

For more on the park, see www.madisonsquarepark.org.

WHERE TO EAT
Head to the park's **Shake Shack** (*see p197*), Danny Meyer's posh take on a refreshment stand.

with their seamstresses, fitters and assistants – feed America's multi-billion-dollar clothing industry. Delivery trucks and workers pushing racks of clothes clog streets, lined with wholesale trimming, button and fabric shops. The scene is particularly busy on 38th and 39th Streets.

Taking up an entire city block, from 34th Street to 35th Street, between Broadway and Seventh Avenue, is the legendary **Macy's** (*see p229*). With one million square feet of selling space spread across nine floors, it's the biggest and busiest department store in the world. Each Thanksgiving, the shopping mecca sponsors the world-famous Macy's Thanksgiving Day Parade, which passes by its entrance along Broadway. Facing Macy's, at the intersection of Broadway, 34th Street and Sixth Avenue, is **Herald Square**, named after a long-gone newspaper, the *New York Herald*. To the south, at Sixth Avenue and 33rd Street, the Manhattan Mall merely replicates the predictable downscale mall experience and is best avoided.

The area's lower section is known as **Greeley Square** after editor and reformer Horace Greeley, owner of the *Herald*'s rival, the *New York Tribune* (the two papers merged in 1924). Once grungy, the square now offers bistro chairs and rest areas for weary walkers. To the east, the many restaurants, spas and

karaoke bars of **Koreatown** line 32nd Street, between Broadway and Fifth Avenue.

Located not in Madison Square but on Seventh Avenue, between 31st and 33rd Streets, **Madison Square Garden** (*see p337*) is home for the Knicks, the Liberty and Rangers, and has welcomed rock icons from Elvis to Madonna as well as the Barnum & Bailey Circus and other big events. The massive arena is actually the fourth building to bear that name (the first two were appropriately located in the square after which they're named) and opened on Valentine's Day 1968, replacing the grand old Pennsylvania Station razed four years earlier. This brutal act of architectural vandalism spurred the creation of the city's Landmarks Preservation Commission, which has saved countless other edifices from a similar fate.

Beneath Madison Square Garden stands the current **Penn Station**, a claustrophobic catacomb of corridors serving 600,000 Amtrak, Long Island Railroad and New Jersey Transit passengers daily and the busiest train station in America. A proposal to relocate the station across the street to the 24-hour **General Post Office** (formally known as the James A Farley Post Office Building; 421 Eighth Avenue, between 31st & 33rd Streets), was championed by the late Senator Patrick Moynihan, but stalled when Amtrak declined to move their operations.

Koreatown.

THE THEATER DISTRICT & HELL'S KITCHEN

Subway A, C, E to 42nd Street-Port Authority; N, Q, R, S, W, 1, 2, 3, 7 to 42nd Street-Times Square.

If Midtown is a snapshot of iconic New York, then the junction of Broadway, Seventh Avenue and 42nd Street is an extreme close-up. Glaring neon signs and giant advertising screens keep 'the crossroads of the world' illuminated 24 hours a day, and draw a constant deluge of tourists. Stop in at the **Times Square Information Center** (1560 Broadway, between 46th & 47th Streets, 1-212 869 1890, www.timessquarenyc.org) for assistance.

Originally called Longacre Square, **Times Square** was renamed after the *New York Times* moved here in the early 1900s. The first electrified billboard graced the district in 1904, on the side of a bank at 46th and Broadway. The same year, the inaugural New Year's Eve party in Times Square doubled as the *Times'* housewarming party in its new HQ. More than 300,000 still gather here to watch a glittery mirrorball descend every 31 December.

The paper left the building only a decade after it had arrived (it now occupies a new $84-million tower on Eighth Avenue, between 40th

and 41st Streets). However, it retained ownership of its old headquarters until the 1960s, and erected the world's first scrolling electric news 'zipper' in 1928. The readout, now sponsored by Dow Jones, has trumpeted breaking stories from the stock-market crash of 1929 to the 2001 World Trade Center attacks.

In addition to being the world's largest billboard, Times Square is also the gateway to the **Theater District**, the zone between 42nd Street and 53rd Street, from Sixth Avenue to Ninth Avenue, where extravagant dramatic shows are put on six days a week (Monday is the traditional night off). While numerous off-Broadway theatres stage first-rate productions in the area, only 39 showhouses are officially Broadway theatres. The distinction is based on size rather than location or quality – Broadway theatres must have more than 500 seats.

The Theater District's transformation from the cradle of New York's sex industry began in 1984, when the city condemned properties along 42nd Street ('the Deuce'), between Seventh and Eighth Avenues. A change in zoning laws meant adult-oriented venues such as sleaze palace **Show World** (669 Eighth Avenue, between 42nd & 43rd Streets) must now subsist on X-rated videos rather than live 'dance' shows; the square's sex trade is now relegated to short stretches of Seventh and Eighth Avenues, just north and south of 42nd Street.

The transformation into a family-friendly theme park kicked into overdrive in 1997, when Disney renovated the New Amsterdam Theatre on 42nd Street to debut its stage version of *The Lion King*. Critics railed against the 'Disneyfication' of Times Square, but tourist dollars have kept commercialism galloping apace. The streets to the west of Eighth Avenue are filled with eateries catering to theatre-goers, especially along **Restaurant Row** (46th Street, between Eighth & Ninth Avenues).

The area's office buildings are filled with entertainment companies: recording studios, record labels, theatrical agencies and screening rooms. The **Brill Building** (1619 Broadway, at 49th Street) has long been the home of music publishers and producers; such luminaries as

SIGHTS

INSIDE TRACK
THE NAKED COWBOY

Dwarfed by the billboards but modest in scale only, the Naked Cowboy can often be seen wandering through Times Square, singing to tourists while clad only in underwear, boots and a ten-gallon hat. He's actually a thirtysomething Cincinnatian named Robert Burck.

Walk Antiques Roadshow

Trawling for bargains at Midtown's flea markets.

Junk-hounds can spend the day blissfully rummaging at the city's best-known weekend flea markets – and get some exercise into the bargain. Start at the one with the best deals: the **Annex/Hell's Kitchen Flea Market** (39th Street, between Ninth & Tenth Avenues, 1-212 243 5343), has 30-plus vendors selling such diverse stock as cameo lockets, Texas ties, gold candelabras, novelty owls and enough tattered bridal veils to keep Miss Havisham single for life. Some prices are steep ($64 for a retro cookie jar – really?), but haggling is encouraged. And if you're in the market for a fur stole, there will be at least half a dozen foxes (faces intact) from which to choose. (Tip: if it's about to rain, hop on the $1 Annex Market shuttle from Hell's Kitchen to the Antiques Garage; *see below*.)

Take a right on Ninth Avenue, ignoring the vendors bottlenecking the strip with their bootleg movies and toy-box rejects, to our recommended brunch spot. Recipient of *Time Out New York* magazine's 2008 Eat Out Award for Best Manhattan Diner, the **Skylight Diner** (402 W 34th Street, at Ninth Avenue, 1-212 244 0395) slaps together a mean fried-egg sandwich at an even meaner price ($2.25!).

From here, head east on 31st Street to Seventh Avenue, pausing on the corner to gaze up at the hulking **monastery of St John the Baptist** (210 W 31st Street). At odds with its Midtown location, it's run by Capuchin Franciscan friars; if it's Sunday, you can hear their bells for blocks. Continue down Seventh till you hit 25th Street, then hang a left. The **City Quilter** (133 W 25th Street, between Sixth & Seventh Avenues, 1-212 807 0390, www.cityquilter.com) specialises in fabrics and NYC-themed prints, such as quaint brownstones and Judie Rothermel skylines.

Now behold the flea-market mothership that is the **Antiques Garage** (112 W 25th Street, between Sixth & Seventh Avenues, 1-212 243 5343), where, every Saturday and Sunday, the cantankerous sellers push their retro wares (late-1980s karate magazines, Ross Perot campaign pins, bowling shoes, pillbox hats) in a two-storey parking garage. Dealer Michael Stolbach's booth, located on the ground floor, is especially worth seeking out: he trades in outsider art and old microgenre photos, such as 'African-American: Civil War' and 'Gay Interest: Affectionate Men'.

Jerry Lieber, Mike Stoller and Carole King wrote and auditioned their hits here. Both visiting rock royalty and aspiring musicians drool over the selection of new and vintage guitars (as well as other instruments) on **Music Row** (48th Street, between Sixth & Seventh Avenues), while eager tweens congregate under the windows of the second-floor MTV studios (1515 Broadway, at 45th Street), hoping for a wave from a big-name drop-in guest.

Glitzy attractions strive to outdo one another in hopes of snaring the tourist throngs and their wide-eyed progeny. **Madame Tussauds New York** (*see p98*), a Gothamised version of the London-born wax museum chain, sits next to **Ripley's Believe It Or Not! Odditorium** (*see p98*), which recently returned to the locale after a 35-year absence. On Broadway, the noisy **ESPN Zone** (1472 Broadway, at 42nd Street, 1-212 921 3776) offers hundreds of video games and enormous TVs showing sporting events; the vast **Toys 'R' Us** (1514 Broadway, at 44th Street, 1-800 869 7787, www.toysrustimes square.com) boasts a 60-foot indoor Ferris wheel and a two-floor Barbie emporium.

For more refined entertainments, head further uptown. Open since 1891, **Carnegie Hall** (*see p330*) has staged legendary shows by the likes of Judy Garland, Miles Davis and Yo-Yo Ma. Nearby is the famous **Carnegie Deli** (854 Seventh Avenue, at 55th Street, 1-212 757 2245), home to five-inch-tall pastrami and corned beef sandwiches. **ABC Television Studios**, at 7 Times Square, entices dozens of early-morning risers hoping to catch a glimpse of the *Good Morning America* crew.

Just west of Times Square, though a million miles away in character, is **Hell's Kitchen**. Irish immigrants scraped by here during the 19th century, followed by Italians, Greeks, Puerto Ricans, Dominicans and other ethnic groups. The neighbourhood maintained a tough crime-ridden veneer well into the 1970s, when, in an effort to invite gentrification, local activists renamed it Clinton after one-time mayor DeWitt Clinton (the new name never really took). Today, the neighbourhood is emerging as the city's new queer mecca. Gay men frequent nightspots such as **Therapy** and **Vlada** (*for both, see p313*); theatregoers and locals of every persuasion sup at in-spot eateries such as Mario Batali's **Esca** (402 W 43rd Street, at Ninth Avenue, 1-212 564 7272).

The desolate extreme West Side is dominated by the massive, black-glass **Jacob K Javits Convention Center** (Eleventh Avenue, between 34th & 39th Streets), home to a never-ending schedule of large-scale trade shows. At press time, the **Intrepid** (*see p98*), a retired aircraft carrier-cum-naval museum, returned to Pier 86 after a 25-month overhaul.

Hardened bargain-hunters may want to check out charity thrift emporium **Goodwill** across the way (103 W 25th Street, between Sixth & Seventh Avenues, 1-646 638 1725) or continue east to the **West 25th Street Market** (W 25th Street, between Fifth & Sixth Avenues, 1-212 243 5343). This flea spot is open all weekend, but the pickings are slim – and raunchy. Steer clear of the back alley, all rusty tools and bins of pornos, and head for the rows in front, where you may score killer vinyl for just a few dollars.

Cut across Broadway and rest your limbs in lovely **Madison Square Park** – where you can avail yourself of New York City's gleaming new pay toilet for 25¢. Revived, head down 24th and back to Sixth. Onward south, you'll see the **Chelsea Antique Collectible Flea Market** (Sixth Avenue, at 17th Street, 1-212 627 0667). The market is small but features such keepsakes as accordioned licence plates and mounds of ghetto-fab gold chains. Head east on 17th Street to Union Square where, as well as a cornucopia of foodstuffs in the **Greenmarket** (*see p91*) on Saturdays, you'll find young artists decamped nearby shilling handmade shadowboxes, haunting pinhole-camera prints and sweet-smelling soaps.

SIGHTS

INSIDE TRACK
MIDTOWN WI-FI

If you're travelling with a laptop, you'll have no trouble getting online in Midtown. You can surf alfresco for free in **Bryant Park** or **Madison Square Park**. Or if it's chilly, pop into the periodicals room of the **New York Public Library** (see p100), or foodie haven **Chelsea Market** (see p87), both have gratis Wi-Fi access.

The **Circle Line Terminal** is also in this neck of the woods, at Pier 83.

★ Intrepid Sea-Air-Space Museum

USS Intrepid, Pier 86, Twelfth Avenue & 46th Street (1-877 957 7447/www.intrepidmuseum. org). Subway A, C, E to 42nd Street-Port Authority, then M42 bus to Twelfth Avenue or 15min walk. **Open** *Apr-Sept* 10am-5pm Mon-Fri; 10am-6pm Sat, Sun. *Oct-Mar* 10am-5pm Tue-Sun. **Admission** $19.50; $7.50-$15.50 reductions; free under-2s. **Credit** AmEx, DC, Disc, MC, V. **Map** p404 B23.

Commissioned in 1943, this 27,000-ton, 898ft aircraft carrier survived torpedoes and kamikaze attacks during World War II, served during Vietnam and the Cuban Missile Crisis, and recovered two space capsules for NASA. The 'Fighting I' was finally decommissioned in 1974, but real-estate mogul Zachary Fisher saved it from the scrap yard by resurrecting it as an educational institution. On its flight deck and portside aircraft elevator are stationed top-notch examples of American military might, including a Navy F-14 Tomcat, an A-12 Blackbird spy plane and a fully restored Army AH-1G Cobra gunship helicopter. (Foreign powers are represented by a British F-1 Scimitar, a French Entendard IV-M and a Polish MiG-21.) In October 2006, the Intrepid began a two-year, $8 million renovation that allowed the anchor chain room, general berthing quarters and machine shop to be opened to the public for the first time.

Madame Tussauds New York

234 W 42nd Street, between Seventh & Eighth Avenues (1-800 246 8872/www.nycwax.com). Subway A, C, E to 42nd Street-Port Authority; N, Q, R, S, W, 1, 2, 3, 7 to 42nd Street-Times Square. **Open** 10am-8pm Mon-Thur, Sun; 10am-10pm Fri, Sat. **Admission** $29; $23-$26 reductions; free under-3s. **Credit** AmEx, DC, MC, V. **Map** p404 D24.

Even if you can't get a table at Nobu, you can always rub shoulders with the stars – or their paraffin doppelgangers, anyway – at this popular tourist attraction. A new crop of freshly waxed victims debuts every few months.

Ripley's Believe It or Not! Odditorium

234 W 42nd Street, between Seventh & Eighth Avenues (1-212 398 3133/www.ripleysnew york.com). Subway A, C, E to 42nd Street-Port Authority; N, Q, R, S, W, 1, 2, 3, 7 to 42nd Street-Times Square. **Open** 9am-1am daily (last entry midnight). **Admission** $24.95; $18.95-$21.95 reductions; free under-4s. **Credit** AmEx, DC, MC, V. **Map** p404 D24.

Times Square might be a little whitewashed these days, but you can get a feel for the old freak show at this repository of the eerie and uncanny. Items on display include a two-headed goat, a 3,000lb meteorite, medieval torture devices and the largest collection of shrunken heads in the developed world.

FIFTH AVENUE & AROUND

Subway B, D, F, N, Q, R, V, W to 34th Street-Herald Square; B, D, F, V to 42nd Street-Bryant Park or 47-50th Streets-Rockefeller Center; E, V to Fifth Avenue-53rd Street; N, Q, R, S, W, 1, 2, 3, 7 to 42nd Street-Times Square; 7 to Fifth Avenue.

The stretch of Fifth Avenue between Rockefeller Center and Central Park South showcases retail palaces bearing names that were famous long before the concept of branding was developed. Bracketed by **Saks Fifth Avenue** (49th to 50th Streets; see p229) and **Bergdorf Goodman** (at 58th Street; see p226), tenants include Chanel, Gucci, Prada and Tiffany & Co. This is the centre of high-end shopping in New York, worth a look even if you don't have the cash to splash.

Fifth Avenue is crowned by Grand Army Plaza at 59th Street, presided over by a gilded statue of General William Tecumseh Sherman. To the west stands the elegant **Plaza Hotel** building, where literary moppet Eloise was famously ensconced. Recently renovated, it's been mostly converted into condo units, but some rooms remain; see p167. To the north lies the luxe **Pierre Hotel** (see p152). From here, you can access **Central Park** (see p104).

Fifth Avenue is the main route for the city's many public processions: the **St Patrick's Day Parade** (see p260), the **LGBT Pride March** (see p307) and many others. Even without floats or marching bands, the sidewalks are always teeming with gawking tourists, fashion victims and society matrons. The most famous skyscraper in the world also has its entrance on Fifth Avenue: the **Empire State Building** (see p100), located smack-bang in the centre of Midtown and visible from almost anywhere in the city.

A pair of impassive stone lions, dubbed Patience and Fortitude by Mayor Fiorello La

Guardia during the Great Depression, guard the steps of the humanities and social sciences collection of the **New York Public Library** (*see p100*), a beautiful Beaux Arts building at 41st Street. You can't check anything out, but researchers pore over tomes in the top-floor Rose Main Reading Room, a hushed sanctuary of 23-foot tables and matching oak chairs. Just behind the library is **Bryant Park**, a well-manicured lawn that hosts a dizzying schedule of free entertainment during the summer (*see p261*).

The luxury **Bryant Park Hotel** (*see p168*) occupies the former American Radiator Building on 40th Street. Designed by architect Raymond Hood in the mid 1920s and recently renovated, the structure is faced with near-black brick and trimmed in gold leaf. Alexander Woollcott, Dorothy Parker and her 'vicious circle' held court and traded barbs at the nearby **Algonquin** (*see p168*); the lobby is still a great place to meet for a drink. Just north of the park, on Sixth Avenue, is the always thought-provoking **International Center of Photography** (*see p100*).

Step off Fifth Avenue into **Rockefeller Center** (*see p101*) and you'll find yourself in a 'city within a city', an interlacing complex of 19 buildings housing corporate offices, retail space and the popular Rockefeller Plaza. After plans for an expansion of the Metropolitan Opera on the site fell through in 1929, John D Rockefeller Jr set about creating the complex to house radio and television corporations. Designed by Raymond Hood and many other prominent architects, Rock Center grew over the decades, with each new building conforming to the original master plan and art deco design.

As you stroll through the Channel Gardens from Fifth Avenue, the magnificent General Electric Building gradually appears above you. The sunken plaza in the complex is the winter home of an oft-packed ice rink; an enormous Christmas tree looms above it each holiday season. The plaza is the most visible entrance to the restaurants and shops in the underground passages that link the buildings. It's also home to art auction house **Christie's** (20 Rockefeller Plaza, 49th Street, between Fifth & Sixth Avenues, 1-212 636 2000, www.christies.com, closed Sat, Sun); pop into the lobby to admire a mural by conceptualist Sol LeWitt. On weekday mornings, a (mainly tourist-filled) crowd gathers at the NBC network's glass-walled, ground-level studio (where the *Today* show is shot), at the south-west corner of Rockefeller Plaza and 49th Street.

When it opened on Sixth Avenue (at 50th Street) in 1932, **Radio City Music Hall** (*see p323*) was designed as a showcase for high-end variety acts, but the death of vaudeville led to a quick transition into what was then the world's largest movie house. Today, the art deco jewel hosts concerts and traditional Christmas and Easter shows featuring renowned precision dance troupe the Rockettes. Visitors can get a peek backstage, and meet one of the high-kicking dancers, on the Stage Door tour (11am-3pm daily; $17, $10-$14 reductions).

Facing Rockefeller Center is the beautiful **St Patrick's Cathedral** (*see p102*). Famous couples from F Scott and Zelda Fitzgerald to Liza Minnelli and David Gest have tied the knot here; funeral services for such notables as Andy Warhol and Joe DiMaggio have been held in its confines. A few blocks north is a clutch of museums, including the **Museum of Modern Art** (MoMa; *see p100*), the **American Folk Art Museum** (*see below*) and the **Paley Center for Media** (*see p101*).

American Folk Art Museum

45 W 53rd Street, between Fifth & Sixth Avenues (1-212 265 1040/www.folkart museum.org). Subway E, V to Fifth Avenue-53rd Street. **Open** 10.30am-5.30pm Tue-Thur, Sat, Sun; 10.30am-7.30pm Fri. **Admission** $9; $7 reductions; free under-12s. Free to all 5.30-7.30pm Fri. **Credit** AmEx, DC, Disc, MC, V. **Map** p404 E22.

MoMA's next-door neighbour celebrates outsider art and traditional crafts such as pottery, quilting, woodwork and jewellery design. The planned exhibitions for 2009 include 'Up Close: Henry Darger' (until June) and 'The Treasure of Ulysses Davis' (21 Apr-6 Sept), a celebration of the late African-American sculptor's work, including a series of carved busts of US presidents. The museum's original Lincoln Center location is now home to a satellite gallery and gift shop, where 'Textural Rhythms, Constructing the Jazz Tradition: Contemporary American Quilts' will be on display 24 March-23 August.

Other locations 2 Lincoln Square, Columbus Avenue, between 65th & 66th Streets, Upper West Side (1-212 595 9533).

INSIDE TRACK
THE ROARING TWENTIES

Swing Street, or 52nd Street between Fifth and Sixth Avenues, is a row of 1920s speakeasies that thrived during the Jazz Age. The only venue still open from that era is the **'21' Club** (21 W 52nd Street, between Fifth & Sixth Avenues, 1-212 582 7200, closed Sat, Sun mid June-Aug). The bar buzzes at night; the restaurant is a popular power-lunch spot.

SIGHTS

★ Empire State Building

350 Fifth Avenue, between 33rd & 34th Streets
(1-212 736 3100/www.esbnyc.com). Subway B,
D, F, N, Q, R, V, W to 34th Street-Herald
Square. **Open** 8am-2am daily (last lift at 1.15am).
Admission *86th floor* $18; $13-$16 reductions;
free under-5s. *102nd floor* add $15. **Credit**
AmEx, DC, Disc, MC, V. **Map** p404 E25.

Financed by General Motors executive John J
Raskob at the height of New York's skyscraper race,
the Empire State sprang up in a mere 14 months,
weeks ahead of schedule and $5 million under budget. Since its opening in 1931, it's been immortalised
in countless photos and films, from the original *King
Kong* to *Sleepless in Seattle.* Following the destruction of the World Trade Center in 2001, the 1,250ft
tower resumed its title as New York's tallest building; the nocturnal colour scheme of the tower lights
often honours holidays, charities or special events.

The enclosed observatory on the 102nd floor is
the city's highest lookout point, but the panoramic
deck on the 86th floor, 1,050 feet above the street, is
roomier. From here, you can enjoy views of all five
boroughs and five neighbouring states (when the
skies are clear, of course); at sunset, you can glimpse
an elongated urban shadow cast from Manhattan all
the way across the river to Queens. Parents with
young children might want to set aside time for the
New York Skyride, a simulated aerial tour of the
city, making 'unscheduled' detours to Coney Island,
FAO Schwarz and the New York subway system.

In recent years, the building has suffered from an
outdated infrastructure and low occupancy rates. In
2008, a $500 million renovation effort – including a
re-creation of the original gold-leaf-on-canvas ceilings and art deco-inspired uniforms for workers –
was started in a bid to attract higher-profile tenants.

International Center of Photography

1133 Sixth Avenue, at 43rd Street (1-212 857
9700/www.icp.org). Subway B, D, F, V to 42nd
Street-Bryant Park; N, Q, R, S, W, 1, 2, 3, 7 to
42nd Street-Times Square. **Open** 10am-6pm
Tue-Thur, Sat, Sun; 10am-8pm Fri. **Admission**
$12; $8 reductions; free under-12s. Pay what you
wish 5-8pm Fri. **Credit** AmEx, DC, Disc, MC, V.
Map p404 D24.

INSIDE TRACK
EMPIRE STATE DELAYS

The queue to get up the **Empire State
Building** can take up to two hours on
busy days; we recommend buying tickets
online to save time, and visiting late at
night, when most sightseers have turned
in. Alternatively, springing for an express
pass ($45) allows you to cut to the front.

Since 1974, the ICP has served as a pre-eminent
library, school and museum devoted to the photographic image. Photojournalism remains a vital
facet of the centre's programme, which also includes
contemporary photos and video. Recent shows in the
two-floor exhibition space have focused on the work
of W Eugene Smith, Bill Woods and Susan Meiselas,
as well as images from the Spanish Civil War.

★ Museum of Modern Art (MoMA)

11 W 53rd Street, between Fifth & Sixth
Avenues (1-212 708 9400/www.moma.org).
Subway E, V to Fifth Avenue-53rd Street. **Open**
10.30am-5.30pm Mon, Wed, Thur, Sat, Sun;
10.30am-8pm Fri. **Admission** (incl admission
to film programmes) $20; $12-$16 reductions;
free under-16s. Free to all 4-8pm Fri. **Credit**
AmEx, DC, MC, V. **Map** p404 E23.

After a two-year redesign by Japanese architect
Yoshio Taniguchi, MoMA reopened in 2004
with almost double the space to display some of
the most impressive artworks from the 19th, 20th
and 21st centuries. The museum's permanent collection now encompasses six curatorial departments:
Architecture & Design, Drawings, Film, Media,
Painting & Sculpture, Photography, and Prints
& Illustrated Books. Highlights include Picasso's
Les Demoiselles d'Avignon and Dali's *The
Persistence of Memory,* as well as masterpieces by
Giacometti, Hopper, Matisse, Monet, O'Keefe,
Pollock, Rothko, Warhol and many others. One
of MoMA's best-known holdings, Van Gogh's
The Starry Night, returns from a stint at the Van
Gogh Museum in Amsterdam in late June 2009.
Outside, the Philip Johnson-designed Abby Aldrich
Rockefeller Sculpture Garden, which houses works
by Calder, Rodin and Moore, overlooks the Modern,
a sleek high-end restaurant and bar run by superstar restaurateur Danny Meyer; for a more
reasonably priced, but equally impressive, dining
experience, try the Bar Room at the Modern.

Planned exhibitions for 2009 include 'Into the
Sunset: Photography's Image of the American West'
(29 Mar-8 June), retrospectives devoted to multimedia artist Aernout Mik (5 May-28 July) and Belgian
painter and printmaker James Ensor (28 June-
1 Sept); 'In & Out of Amsterdam, 1960-1975' (15
July-5 Oct), nearly 120 prints, posters, drawings,
installations and video pieces exploring the Dutch
city's role as an international art capital; and a major
gallery exhibition and film series devoted to filmmaker Tim Burton (15 Nov-15 Mar 2010).

▶ *For the affiliated P.S.1 Contemporary Art
Center in Queens, see p136.*

★ FREE New York Public Library

455 Fifth Avenue, at 42nd Street (1-212 930
0830/www.nypl.org). Subway B, D, F, V to 42nd
Street-Bryant Park; 7 to Fifth Avenue. **Open**
11am-7.30pm Tue, Wed; 10am-6pm Thur-Sat.
Admission free. **Map** p404 E24.

Museum of Modern Art (MoMA).

While the New York Public Library system consists of 89 individual branches, it's this austere Beaux Arts building in Bryant Park – home to 75 miles of shelves housing a massive humanities and social sciences archive – that most readily comes to mind. The library's free tours (at 11am and 2pm) stop at the beautifully renovated Rose Main Reading Room and the Bill Blass Public Catalog Room. The programme of special exhibitions rivals those of the city's finest museums; 2009 offerings include 'Between Collaboration and Resistance: French Literary Life Under Nazi Occupation' (3 Apr-25 July) and 'Voltaire's Candide: The 1759 Editions' from autumn through winter.

► *For readings at the library, see p279.*

Paley Center for Media
25 W 52nd Street, between Fifth & Sixth Avenues (1-212 621 6600/www.paleycenter.org). Subway B, D, F, V to 47-50th Streets-Rockefeller Center; E, V to Fifth Avenue-53rd Street. **Open** noon-6pm Tue-Sun; noon-8pm Thur. **Admission** $10; $5-$8 reductions. **No credit cards. Map** p404 E23.

A nirvana for telly addicts and pop-culture junkies, the Paley Center (formerly the Museum of Television & Radio) houses an immense archive of more than 100,000 radio and TV shows. Head to the fourth-floor library to search the system for your favourite episode of *Star Trek* or *Seinfeld*, then walk down one flight to your assigned console. (The radio listening room operates in the same fashion.) A theatre on the concourse level is the site of frequent screenings, premières and high-profile panel discussions.

★ Rockefeller Center
From 48th to 51st Streets, between Fifth & Sixth Avenues (tours 1-212 664 3700/7174/Top of the Rock 1-877 692 7625/www.rockefeller center.com). Subway B, D, F, V to 47-50th Streets-Rockefeller Center. **Open** 7am-11pm daily. *Tours* every 2 hrs 11am-5pm Mon-Sat; 11am-3pm Sun. *Observation deck* 8am-midnight daily (last lift at 11.15pm). **Admission** *Rockefeller Center tours* $12; $10 reductions (under-6s not admitted). *NBC Studio tours* $18.50; $15.50 reductions (under-6s not admitted). *Observation deck* $20; $13-$18 reductions; free under-6s. **Credit** AmEx, DC, Disc, MC, V. **Map** p404 E23.

Constructed under the aegis of industrialist John D Rockefeller in the 1930s, this art deco city-within-a-city is inhabited by NBC, Simon & Schuster, McGraw-Hill and other media giants, as well as Radio City Music Hall, Christie's auction house, and an underground shopping arcade. Guided tours of the entire complex are available daily, and there's a separate NBC Studio tour (call the number above or see website for details).

Public art installations are often on display outside 30 Rockefeller Plaza (past works have featured large-scale pieces by Louise Bourgeois, Jeff Koons and Anish Kapoor), but the most breathtaking sights are those seen from the 70th-floor Top of the Rock observation deck (combined tour/observation deck tickets are available). In the cold-weather months, the Plaza's sunken courtyard – eternally guarded by a bronze statue of Prometheus – transforms into a picturesque ice skating rink (*see p344*).

SIGHTS

St Patrick's Cathedral.

★ FREE St Patrick's Cathedral

Fifth Avenue, between 50th & 51st Streets (1-212 753 2261/www.saintpatrickscathedral.org). Subway B, D, F to 47-50th Streets-Rockefeller Center; E, V to Fifth Avenue-53rd Street. **Open** 7am-8.30pm daily. **Admission** free. **Map** p404 E23.

The largest Catholic church in America, St Patrick's, begun in 1858, counts presidents, business leaders and movie stars among its past and present parishioners. The Gothic-style façade features intricate white-marble spires, but equally impressive is the interior, including the Louis Tiffany-designed altar, solid bronze baldachin, and the rose window by stained-glass master Charles Connick.

▶ *Further uptown is another awe-inspiring Catholic house of worship, the Cathedral of St John the Divine; see p117.*

MIDTOWN EAST

Subway E, V to Lexington Avenue-53rd Street; S, 4, 5, 6, 7 to 42nd Street-Grand Central; 6 to 51st Street.

Shopping, dining and entertainment options wane east of Fifth Avenue in the 40s and 50s. However, this area is home to a number of iconic landmarks, and its busy side-streets are lined with large, imposing buildings. What the area lacks in street-level attractions it makes up for with a dizzying array of world-class architecture.

The 1913 **Grand Central Terminal** (*see p103*) is the city's most spectacular point of arrival, although it only welcomes commuter trains from Connecticut and upstate New York. Looming behind the station, the **MetLife Building** (formerly the Pan Am Building) was once the world's largest office tower. On Park Avenue is the famed **Waldorf-Astoria** hotel (*see p170*), formerly located on Fifth Avenue but rebuilt here in 1931 after the original was demolished to make way for the Empire State Building. Other must-see buildings in the vicinity include **Lever House** (390 Park Avenue, between 53rd & 54th Streets), the **Seagram Building** (375 Park Avenue, between 52nd & 53rd Streets), the **Citicorp Center** (from 53rd Street to 54th Street, between Lexington & Third Avenues) and the stunning art deco skyscraper that anchors the corner of Lexington Avenue and 51st Street, formerly the **General Electric Building** (and before that, the RCA Victor Building). A Chippendale crown tops the **Sony Building** (550 Madison Avenue, between 55th & 56th Streets), Philip Johnson's postmodern icon.

Along the river to the east lies **Tudor City**, a high-rise version of England's Hampton Court Palace. The pioneering 1925 residential development features a charming park, perfect for a respite from the rush of traffic. The neighbourhood is dominated by the **United Nations Headquarters** (*see p103*), with its sculpture-heavy grounds and famous glass-walled Secretariat building. Most of the grounds are off limits, but across First Avenue is Dag Hammarskjöld Plaza (47th Street, between First & Second Avenues), named for the former UN secretary general. Here, you can stroll through a lovely garden honouring Katharine Hepburn; the actress used to live nearby in Turtle Bay Gardens, a stretch of townhouses on 48th and 49th Streets, between Second and Third Avenues. On the other side of 47th Street is the Japan Society, with equally peaceful surroundings (*see right*).

E 42nd Street has even more architectural distinction, including the Romanesque Revival hall of the former Bowery Savings Bank (no.110) and the art deco details of the Chanin Building (no.122). Completed in 1930 by architect William Van Alen, the gleaming Chrysler Building (at Lexington Avenue) is a pinnacle of art deco architecture, paying homage to the automobile with vast radiator-cap eagles in lieu of traditional gargoyles and a brickwork relief sculpture of racing cars complete with chrome hubcaps. The Daily News Building (no.220), another art deco gem designed by Raymond Hood, was immortalised in the *Superman* films. Although the namesake tabloid no longer has its offices here (it moved to 33rd Street in the 1990s), the lobby still houses its giant globe and weather instruments.

FREE Grand Central Terminal

From 42nd to 44th Streets, between Vanderbilt & Lexington Avenues (tours 1-212 340 2347/ www.grandcentralterminal.com). Subway S, 4, 5, 6, 7 to 42nd Street-Grand Central. Map p404 E24.

Each day, the world's most famous station sees more than 400,000 visitors shuffle through its Beaux Arts threshold; only 125,000 of them are commuters. After its 1998 renovation, the terminal metamorphosed from a mere transport hub into a destination in itself, with decent shopping and first-rate drinking and dining options such as the Campbell Apartment

---

INSIDE TRACK
GRAND CENTRAL TERMINAL

The archway just outside the **Grand Central Oyster Bar & Restaurant** in Grand Central Terminal creates an interesting acoustical trick. Stand in one corner and whisper a message to a friend standing diagonally across from you. Because of the unique design of the low ceramic arches, it will sound as if you're next to each other.

---

lounge (off the West Balcony, 1-212 953 0409) and the Grand Central Oyster Bar & Restaurant (Lower Concourse, 1-212 490 6650, closed Sun).

Don't forget to look up when you're in the station's 80,000-square-foot main concourse. French painter Paul Helleu's astronomical mural depicts the Mediterranean sky complete with 2,500 stars (some of which are illuminated). Various tour options are available (see website for details); we recommend veteran guide Justin Ferate's free 90-minute walking tour of Grand Central and its environs on Fridays at 12.30pm (*see p61*).

▶ *For trains from Grand Central, see p373.*

Japan Society

333 E 47th Street, between First & Second Avenues (1-212 832 1155/www.japansociety.org). Subway E, V to Lexington Avenue-53rd Street; 6 to 51st Street. Open *Gallery* 11am-6pm Tue-Thur; 11am-9pm Fri; 11am-5pm Sat, Sun. Admission $12; $10 reductions; free under-16s. Free to all 6-9pm Fri. Credit AmEx, DC, Disc, MC, V. Map p404 F23.

In a serene setting, complete with waterfall and bamboo garden, the Japan Society celebrated its 100th birthday in 2007. In addition to a gallery for temporary exhibitions (such as 'KRAZY! The Delirious World of Anime + Manga + Video Games', from 13 March to 14 June 2009), the Society offers a range of performing arts, lectures and special events. The film centre is a major showcase for Japanese cinema in the US.

United Nations Headquarters

UN Plaza, First Avenue, between 42nd & 48th Streets (tours 1-212 963 8687/www.un.org/ tours). Subway S, 4, 5, 6, 7 to 42nd Street-Grand Central. Tours 9.45am-4.45pm Mon-Fri. Admission $13.50; $7.50-$9 reductions (under-5s not admitted). Credit AmEx, DC, MC, V. Map p404 G24.

Step inside this 18-acre complex and you'll no longer be in New York City – the UN is technically international territory under the jurisdiction of member countries. The Secretariat building, designed by Le Courbusier, is off limits, but 45-minute public tours pay a visit to the Security Council Chamber and General Assembly Hall, and highlight stunning artwork donated by member nations – a Venetian mosaic of Norman Rockwell's *The Golden Rule*, Yevgeny Vuchetich's *Let Us Beat Swords Into Plowshares* (donated by the Soviet Union in 1957), a stained-glass window by Marc Chagall memorialising Secretary-General Dag Hammarskjöld, and the Japanese Peace Bell, rung on the first day of spring and at the start of each session of the General Assembly. Visitors can sup from the vast international buffet in the Delegates Dining Room (fourth floor, 1-212 963 7626), which is open to the public 11.30am-2.30pm during the week (advance reservations are required).

SIGHTS

Uptown

Where high culture meets ghetto fabulous.

In the 19th century, the area above 57th Street was a bucolic getaway for locals living at the southern tip of the island. Today, much of the area above 57th Street still feels serene, thanks largely to Central Park and the presence of a number of New York's premier cultural institutions.

Although many of Manhattan's super-rich have migrated downtown, there's still an air of old money on the Upper East Side, where exclusive streets are kept clean by hose-wielding house staff while socialites drift in and out of Madison Avenue's designer flagships. Across the park, the formerly edgy Upper West Side is now an equally wealthy and far more fashionable address. Further north is Harlem: once a dangerous no-go area for visitors, it's now increasingly diverse, offering dynamic nightlife.

Map pp405-409	**Bars** p222
Hotels p171	**Shops** p226
Restaurants p202	

CENTRAL PARK

Numerous subway stations on multiple lines.

In 1853, the newly formed Central Park Commission chose landscape designer Frederick Law Olmsted and architect Calvert Vaux to turn a vast tract of rocky swampland into a rambling oasis of lush greenery. Inspired by the great parks of London and Paris, the Commission imagined a place that would provide city dwellers with respite from the crowded streets. It was a noble thought, but one that required the eviction of 1,600 mostly poor or immigrant inhabitants, including residents of Seneca Village, the city's oldest African-American settlement. Still, clear the area they did: when it opened in 1859, it became the first man-made public park in the US.

Although it suffered from neglect at various points in the 20th century (most recently in the 1970s, when it gained a reputation as a dangerous spot after dark), the park has been returned to its green glory thanks to the Central Park Conservancy. This not-for-profit civic group was formed in 1980, since when it's been instrumental in the park's restoration and maintenance.

Come summer, kites, Frisbees and soccer balls seem to fly every which way across **Sheep Meadow**, the designated quiet zone that begins at 66th Street. Sheep did indeed graze here until 1934, but they've since been replaced by sunbathers improving their tans and scoping out the throngs. The hungry and affluent can repair to the glitzy **Tavern on the Green** (Central Park West, at 67th Street, 1-212 873 3200), which sets up a grand outdoor café in the summer. However, picnicking alfresco, or snacking on a hot dog from one of the park's food vendors, is a most popular option. East of Sheep Meadow, between 66th and 72nd Streets, is the **Mall**, where you'll find volleyball courts and plenty of in-line skaters. And just east of the Mall's Naumburg Bandshell is Rumsey Playfield – site of the annual **Central Park SummerStage** series (*see p261*), an eclectic roster of free and benefit concerts.

Central Park.

A short stroll to about 64th Street brings you to the **Friedsam Memorial Carousel**, still a bargain at $2 a ride (for hours, *see p293*). At 65th is the old **Dairy** (*see p106*), which now houses the Central Park Conservancy's information centre. Nearby **Central Park Zoo** (*see p106*), between 63rd & 66th Streets, is another sure-fire hit with children; for more park activities for kids, *see p293*. And if you're here in winter, consider lacing up at the **Wollman Rink** (midpark, at 62nd Street; *see also p343*), which offers a picture-postcard view of the fancy hotels surrounding the park.

One of the most popular meeting places in the park is north of here: the grand **Bethesda Fountain & Terrace**, near the midpoint of the 72nd Street Transverse Road. When it was completed in 1869, the ornate passageway that connects the plaza around the fountain to the elm-lined promenade to the south boasted a stunning Minton tile ceiling. In the 1980s, after decades of weathering, the intricately patterned clay tiles were put into storage, but they were restored to their original splendour as part of a $7 million facelift in 2007. *Angel of the Waters*, the sculpture in the centre of the fountain, was created by Emma Stebbins, the first woman to be granted a major public art commission in New York.

To the west of the fountain, near the W 72nd Street entrance, sits **Strawberry Fields**, which memorialise John Lennon, who lived in the nearby Dakota Building. Also called the International Garden of Peace, it features a mosaic of the word 'imagine', donated by the Italian city of Naples. More than 160 species of flowers and plants from all over the world bloom here , strawberries among them. Just north of the fountain, meanwhile, is the **Loeb Boathouse** (midpark, at 75th Street). From here, you can take a rowing boat or a gondola out on the lake, which is crossed by the elegant Bow Bridge. The views afforded by the nearby **Central Park Boathouse Restaurant** (midpark, at 75th Street, 1-212 517 2233) make it a lovely place for brunch or drinks.

INSIDE TRACK
CENTRAL PARK PICNICS

If you're planning a Central Park picnic, the branch of gourmet grocer **Dean & DeLuca** at 1150 Madison Avenue (at 85th Street, 1-212 717 0800, deandeluca.com) is a high-quality (but expensive) option. Another good bet is the well-stocked **Grace's Market Place** (1237 Third Avenue, between 71st & 72nd Streets, 1-212 737 0600).

Further north is the popular **Belvedere Castle**, a restored Victorian building that sits atop the park's second-highest peak. Besides offering excellent views, it also houses the **Henry Luce Nature Observatory** (*see below*). The nearby Delacorte Theater hosts **Shakespeare in the Park** (*see p263*), a summer run of free open-air performances of plays by the Bard and others. And further north still sits the **Great Lawn** (midpark, between 79th & 85th Streets), a sprawling stretch of grass that doubles as a rallying point for political protests and a concert spot for just about any act that can attract six-figure audiences. The Metropolitan Opera and the New York Philharmonic perform here during the summer; at other times, it's favoured by seriously competitive soccer, baseball and softball teams.

In the mid 1990s, the **Reservoir** (midpark, between 85th & 96th Streets) was renamed in honour of the late Jacqueline Kennedy Onassis, who used to jog around it. Whether you prefer a running or walking pace, a turn here commands great views of the surrounding skyscrapers; in spring the cherry trees that ring the reservoir path and the bridle path below it make it particularly lovely.

Next to the Harlem Meer, in the northern reaches of the park, is the **Charles A Dana Discovery Center** (*see below*), which has a roster of activities.

Central Park Zoo

830 Fifth Avenue, between 63rd & 66th Streets (1-212 439 6500/www.wcs.org). Subway N, R, W to Fifth Avenue-59th Street. **Open** *Apr-Oct* 10am-5pm Mon-Fri; 10am-5.30pm Sat, Sun. *Nov-Mar* 10am-4.30pm daily. **Admission** $8; $3-$4 reductions; free under-3s (under-16s must be accompanied by an adult). **Credit** AmEx, DC, Disc, MC, V. **Map** p405 E21.

A collection of animals has been kept in Central Park since the 1860s. But in its current form, Central Park Zoo dates only from 1988. Around 130 species inhabit its 6.5-acre corner of the park, polar bears and penguins among them, and a new habitat dedicated to the endangered snow leopard is expected to open in spring 2009. The Tisch Children's Zoo houses more than 30 species that enjoy being petted, and the roving characters on the George Delacorte Musical Clock delight hoardes of children every half-hour.

FREE Charles A Dana Discovery Center

Park entrance on Malcolm X Boulevard (Lenox Avenue), at 110th Street (1-212 860 1370/www.centralparknyc.org). Subway 2, 3 to 110th Street-Central Park North. **Open** 10am-5pm Tue-Sun. **Admission** free. **Map** p406 E15.

Stop by the Dana Center for weekend family workshops, environmental and cultural exhibits, and outdoor performances on the plaza next to the Harlem Meer. From April to October, the centre lends out fishing rods and bait to those aged 16 and over with photo ID.

FREE Dairy

Park entrance on Fifth Avenue, at 65th Street (1-212 794 6564/www.centralparknyc.org). Subway N, R, W to Fifth Avenue-59th Street. **Open** 10am-5pm Tue-Sun. **Admission** free. **Map** p405 D21.

Built in 1872 to show city kids where milk comes from (cows, in this case), the Dairy is now the Central Park Conservancy's information centre. It contains interactive exhibits, videos explaining the park's history and a gift shop.

FREE Henry Luce Nature Observatory

Belvedere Castle, midpark, off the 79th Street Transverse Road (1-212 772 0210). Subway B, C to 81st Street-Museum of Natural History. **Open** 10am-5pm Tue-Sun. **Admission** free. **Map** p405 D19.

During the spring and autumn hawk migrations, park rangers discuss the various birds of prey found in the park and help visitors spot raptors from the castle roof. You can also borrow binoculars, maps and bird identification guides from here.

UPPER EAST SIDE

Subway F to Lexington Avenue-63rd Street; 4, 5, 6 to 86th Street; 6 to 68th Street-Hunter College, 77th Street, 96th Street or 103rd Street.

Gorgeous pre-war apartments owned by blue-blooded socialites, soigné restaurants filled with the Botoxed-ladies-who-lunch set, the deluxe boutiques of international designers… this is the prevailing image of the Upper East Side, and you'll see a lot of supporting evidence on Fifth, Madison and Park Avenues. Encouraged by the opening of Central Park in the late 19th century, the city's more affluent residents began building mansions on Fifth Avenue. By the start of the 20th century, even the superwealthy had warmed to the idea of giving up their large homes for smaller quarters provided they were near the park, which resulted in the construction of many new apartment blocks and hotels. Working-class folks later settled around Second and Third Avenues, following construction of an elevated East Side train line, but affluence remained the dominant characteristic.

Architecturally speaking, the overall look of the neighbourhood remains remarkably homogeneous. Along the expanse known as

Cooper-Hewitt, National Design Museum. *See p108.*

the **Gold Coast** – Fifth, Madison and Park Avenues, from 61st to 81st Streets – you'll see the great old mansions, many now foreign consulates. Some wonderful old carriage houses adorn 63rd and 64th Streets; close by, the 1916 limestone structure at 820 Fifth Avenue (at 63rd Street) was one of the earliest luxury apartment buildings on the avenue, and still has just one residence per floor. Wrapping around the corner of Madison Avenue at 45 East 66th Street, another flamboyant survivor (1906-08) features terracotta ornamentation that would befit a Gothic cathedral. (Andy Warhol lived a few doors up at no.57 from 1974 to 1987.) And further north, Stanford White designed 998 Fifth Avenue (at 81st Street) in the image of an Italian Renaissance palazzo.

Philanthropic gestures made by the moneyed classes over the past 130-odd years have helped create an impressive cluster of art collections, museums and cultural institutions. Indeed, Fifth Avenue from 82nd to 104th Streets is known as **Museum Mile**, and for good reason: it's lined by the **Metropolitan Museum of Art** (*see p110*); the Frank Lloyd Wright-designed **Solomon R Guggenheim Museum** (*see p111*); the **Cooper-Hewitt, National Design Museum** (*see p108*), housed in Andrew Carnegie's former mansion; the **Jewish Museum** (*see p110*); the **Museum of the City of New York** (*see p110*); and the **National Academy Museum** (1083 Fifth Avenue, at 89th Street, 1-212 369 4880,

www.nationalacademy.org), with a collection that includes works by Louise Bourgeois, Jasper Johns and Robert Rauschenberg. Although technically in Spanish Harlem, **El Museo del Barrio** (*see p109*) is also on the strip.

The museums don't end on Fifth Avenue. Elsewhere in the culture-soaked neighbourhood sit the **Asia Society & Museum** (*see p108*), the **China Institute** (*see p108*), the **Frick Collection** (*see p109*), the **Neue Galerie** (*see p111*) and the **Whitney Museum of American Art** (*see p111*). The **Goethe-Institut New York/German Cultural Center** (1014 Fifth Avenue, at 82nd Street, 1-212 439 8700, www.goethe.de/ins/us/ney) has had to transfer its screenings and exhibitions to other venues due to problems with fire regulations, but its library remains open (closed Mon, Sun).

Madison Avenue is New York's world-class ultra-luxe shopping strip. Between 57th and 86th Streets, it's packed with top designer

---

INSIDE TRACK
COOPER-HEWITT GARDENS

Admission to the **Cooper-Hewitt** (*see p108*) buys you access to the peaceful grassy garden behind the building, where you can linger over refreshments bought from the café.

---

names: Euro suspects such as Gucci, Prada and Chloé, and Americans including Donna Karan, multiple Ralph Lauren outposts and Tom Ford's eponymous menswear line (no.845, at 70th Street, 1-212 359 0300, www.tomford.com, closed Sun). Fashionable department store **Barneys New York** (*see p226*) is stocked with unusual designer finds and features witty, sometimes audacious, window displays. If you're shopping in the 70s, or visiting the museums, it's worth making the detour to Lexington for 1925 lunchroom/soda fountain the **Lexington Candy Shop** (*see p203*).

Asia Society & Museum

725 Park Avenue, at 70th Street (1-212 288 6400/www.asiasociety.org). Subway 6 to 68th Street-Hunter College. **Open** 11am-6pm Tue-Thur, Sat, Sun; 11am-9pm Fri. **Admission** $10; $5-$7 reductions; free under-15s (must be accompanied by an adult). Free to all 6-9pm Fri. **Credit** AmEx, DC, MC, V. **Map** p405 E20.

The Asia Society sponsors study missions and conferences while promoting public programmes in the US and abroad. The headquarters' striking galleries host exhibitions of art from dozens of countries and time periods (from ancient India and medieval Persia to contemporary Japan); some are assembled from public and private collections, including the permanent Mr and Mrs John D Rockefeller III collection of Asian art. A spacious, atrium-like café, with a pan-Asian menu, and a beautifully stocked gift shop, help make the society a one-stop destination for anyone with even a passing interest in Asian culture.

China Institute

125 E 65th Street, between Park & Lexington Avenues (1-212 744 8181/www.china institute.org). Subway F to Lexington Avenue-63rd Street; 6 to 68th Street-Hunter College. **Open** 10am-5pm Mon, Wed, Fri, Sat; 10am-8pm Tue, Thur. **Admission** $7; $4 reductions; free under-12s. Free to all 6-8pm Tue, Thur. **Credit** AmEx, DC, MC, V. **Map** p405 E21.

Consisting of just two small galleries, the China Institute is somewhat overshadowed by the nearby

Asia Society. But its rotating exhibitions – photographs of modern Beijing, for example, or high-profile collections on loan from Chinese institutions – are compelling. The institute offers lectures and courses on myriad subjects such as calligraphy, contemporary fashion design and traditional dance.

★ Cooper-Hewitt, National Design Museum

2 E 91st Street, at Fifth Avenue (1-212 849 8400/ www.cooperhewitt.org). Subway 4, 5, 6 to 86th Street. **Open** 10am-5pm Mon-Thur; 10am-9pm Fri; 10am-6pm Sat; noon-6pm Sun. **Admission** $15; $10 reductions; free under-12s. **Credit** AmEx, DC, Disc, MC, V. **Map** p406 E18.

Founded in 1897 by the Hewitt sisters, granddaughters of industrialist Peter Cooper, the only museum in the US solely dedicated to design (both historic

City Secrets The Poshest Rec Room

See an art lover's hidden sporting side.

One of the most fascinating features of the **Frick Collection** (*see right*) is hidden behind an unmarked door off a subterranean corridor. 'If you stand in the Oval Room, you're directly over a beautifully preserved 1914 bowling alley in our basement – it contains a snooker table as well as two lanes for bowling,'

says the museum's spokesperson, Heidi Rosenau. The area is closed to the public because of building code rules, but you can still get an idea of Henry Clay Frick's affluent lifestyle – the place retains the feel of a private residence through minimal labelling and the open display of sculptures and decorative objects.

Museum of the City of New York. *See p110.*

and modern) has been part of the Smithsonian since the 1960s. In 1976, it took up residence in the former home of steel magnate Andrew Carnegie: it's worth a look for the impressive mansion as much as for the roster of temporary exhibitions, which include an always-interesting series in which works are selected from the permanent collection by a prominent artist or designer. The gift shop is stocked with international design objects (some very affordable) as well as the appropriate books. An extensive renovation is planned over the next few years to expand the gallery space and create a new library, but the museum will remain open throughout 2009.

Planned exhibitions for 2009 include: 'Wall Stories: Children's Wallpaper and Books' (until 5 Apr), on the relationship between the two media; and 'Fashioning Felt' (6 Mar-7 Sept), examining new uses of this ancient material in fashion, architecture, home furnishings and other fields. *Photo p107.*

El Museo del Barrio

1230 Fifth Avenue, between 104th & 105th Streets (1-212 831 7272/www.elmuseo.org). *Subway 6 to 103rd Street.* **Open** 11am-5pm Wed-Sun. **Admission** $6; $4 reductions; free under-12s. Seniors free Thur. **Credit** AmEx, DC, MC, V. **Map** p406 E16.

Located in Spanish Harlem (aka El Barrio), El Museo del Barrio is dedicated to the work of Latino artists who reside in the US, as well as Latin American masters. The 8,000-piece collection ranges from pre-Columbian artefacts to contemporary installations, but the galleries are closed for renovation until

autumn 2009 (the theatre and workshop space remains open). The refurbishment includes the addition of a pan-Latin café.

★ Frick Collection

1 E 70th Street, between Fifth & Madison Avenues (1-212 288 0700/www.frick.org). *Subway 6 to 68th Street-Hunter College.* **Open** 10am-6pm Tue-Sat; 11am-5pm Sun. **Admission** $15; $5-$10 reductions (under-10s not admitted). *Voluntary donation* 11am-1pm Sun. **Credit** AmEx, DC, Disc, MC, V. **Map** p405 E20.

Industrialist and collector Henry Clay Frick commissioned this opulent mansion with a view to leaving his legacy to the public. Designed by Carrère & Hastings (the firm behind the New York Public Library) and built in 1914, the building was inspired by 18th-century British and French architecture.

In an effort to preserve the feel of a private residence, labelling is minimal, but you can opt for a free audio guide or pay $1 for a booklet. Works spanning the 14th to the 19th centuries include masterpieces by Rembrandt, Vermeer, Gainsborough and Bellini, exquisite period furniture, porcelain and other decorative objects. Aficionados of 18th-century French art will find two rooms especially enchanting: the panels of the Boucher Room (1750-52) depict children engaged in adult occupations, while the Fragonard Room contains the artist's series *The Progress of Love* – four of the paintings were commissioned (and rejected) by Louis XV's mistress Madame Du Barry. The interior fountain court is a serene spot in which to rest your feet. *See also left* **City secrets.**

Jewish Museum

1109 Fifth Avenue, at 92nd Street (1-212 423 3200/www.thejewishmuseum.org). Subway 4, 5 to 86th Street; 6 to 96th Street. **Open** 11am-5.45pm Mon-Wed, Sat, Sun; 11am-8pm Thur. Closed on Jewish holidays. **Admission** $12; $7.50-$10 reductions; free under-12s. Free to all Sat. **Credit** AmEx, DC, MC, V. **Map** p405 E18.

The former home of the financier, collector and Jewish leader Felix Warburg, the Jewish Museum's magnificent French Gothic-style mansion was given an exterior spruce-up for its 100th birthday in 2008. Inside, those with an interest in Jewish culture will find a far-reaching collection of more than 28,000 works of art, artefacts and media installations which are all arranged thematically in a two-floor permanent exhibit: entitled 'Culture and Continuity: The Jewish Journey', it traces the evolution of Judaism from antiquity to the present day. The excellent temporary shows, covering such diverse themes as the discovery of the Dead Sea Scrolls and abstract expressionism, appeal to a broad audience.

Planned exhibitions for 2009 include: 'Chagall and the Artists of the Russian Jewish Theater, 1919-1949' (until 22 Mar), featuring more than 200 works of art and ephemera, including massive murals created by Chagall for Yiddish-language company GOSET; 'Reclaimed: Paintings from the Collection of Jacques Goudstikker' (15 Mar-2 Aug), a selection of works that were stolen from the 1930s Amsterdam art dealer by the Nazis and restored to his heir by the Dutch government in 2006.

★ Metropolitan Museum of Art

1000 Fifth Avenue, at 82nd Street (1-212 535 7710/www.metmuseum.org). Subway 4, 5, 6 to 86th Street. **Open** 9.30am-5.30pm Tue-Thur, Sun; 9.30am-9pm Fri, Sat. **Admission** suggested donation (incl same-day admission to the Cloisters) $20; $10-$15 reductions; free under-12s. **Credit** AmEx, DC, Disc, MC, V. **Map** p405 E19.

See p112 **Profile**. For the Cloisters, which houses the Met's medieval art collection, *see p122*.

Planned exhibitions for 2009 at the Met include: 'Pierre Bonnard: The Late Interiors' (until 19 Apr); 'The Pictures Generation, 1974-1984' (21 Apr-2 Aug), a ground-breaking assemblage of works by the group of influential New York artists who explored how pictures shape as well as depict reality; 'Francis Bacon: A Centenary Retrospective' (20 May-16 Aug), a major overview in celebration of the 100th anniversary of the artist's birth, including previously unseen works; 'African and Oceanic Art from the Barbier-Mueller Museum, Geneva' (2 June-27 Sept), with more than 30 highlights from this wide-ranging collection; and Afghanistan: Hidden Treasures from the National Museum, Kabul' (23 June-20 Sept), a cache of art from this ancient crossroads of trade routes, dating from the Bronze Age to the Kushan period.

Museum of the City of New York

1220 Fifth Avenue, between 103rd & 104th Streets (1-212 534 1672/www.mcny.org). Subway 6 to 103rd Street. **Open** 10am-5pm Tue-Sun. **Admission** suggested donation $9;

Neue Galerie.

$5 reductions; $20 family. **Credit** AmEx, DC, Disc, MC, V. **Map** p405 E16.

Located at the northern end of Museum Mile, this institution contains a wealth of city history, organised into contemporary themed displays. As well as temporary exhibitions on such themes as 'Catholics in New York', there are permanent exhibits devoted to the city's maritime heritage, architecture and even interiors: six rooms, among them an original 1906 Park Avenue drawing room sumptuously decorated in the style of the Sala Della Zodiaco in the Ducal Palace, Mantua, chart New York living spaces from 1680 to 1906. Elsewhere, 'Perform' explores the evolution and quirks of the theatre industry through artefacts, photographs and video – sit in old seats salvaged from the demolished 1918 Henry Miller's Theatre and watch actors talk about the scene.

The museum's extensive toy collection comprises playthings from the colonial era to the present: toy trains, lead soldiers and battered teddy bears share shelf space with Kewpie dolls (created by a New York artist); Brooklyn-born photographer Arthur Leipzig's shots of the city's children at play in the 1940s are also on display. Lavishly appointed dolls' houses include the amazing Stettheimer Dollhouse: it was created in the '20s by Carrie Stettheimer, whose artist friends reinterpreted their masterpieces in miniature to hang on the walls. Look closely and you'll even spy a tiny version of Marcel Duchamp's famous *Nude Descending a Staircase*. Don't miss the museum's *Timescapes*, a 25-minute multimedia film that tells NYC's story from 1624 to the present, shown free with admission every half-hour. The expansive front terrace, with its tables and refreshment stand, is a good spot to recharge. *Photos pp108-109.*

▶ *There's more New York history at Lower East Side Tenement Museum (see p77), Ellis Island Immigration Museum (see p65) and Museum of Bronx History (see p146), among others.*

Neue Galerie

1048 Fifth Avenue, at 86th Street (1-212 628 6200/www.neuegalerie.org). Subway 4, 5, 6 to 86th Street. **Open** 11am-6pm Mon, Thur, Sat, Sun; 11am-9pm Fri. **Admission** $15; $10 reductions. Under-16s must be accompanied by an adult; under-12s not admitted. **Credit** AmEx, DC, MC, V. **Map** p405 E18.

The elegant Neue Galerie is devoted entirely to late 19th- and early 20th-century German and Austrian fine and decorative arts. The creation of the late art dealer Serge Sabarsky and cosmetics mogul Ronald S Lauder, it has the largest concentration of works by Gustav Klimt and Egon Schiele outside Vienna. There's also a bookstore, a small design shop and the civilised Café Sabarsky, serving updated Austrian cuisine and ravishing Viennese pastries.

▶ *For more German culture, check the events operated by the Goethe Institut; see p107.*

★ Solomon R Guggenheim Museum

1071 Fifth Avenue, at 89th Street (1-212 423 3500/www.guggenheim.org). Subway 4, 5, 6 to 86th Street. **Open** 10am-5.45pm Mon-Wed, Sat, Sun; 10am-7.45pm Fri. **Admission** $18; $15 reductions; free under-12s. Pay what you wish 5.45-7.15pm Fri. **Credit** AmEx, DC, MC, V. **Map** p406 E18.

The Guggenheim is as famous for its landmark building, designed by Frank Lloyd Wright and restored for its 50th birthday in 2009, as it is for its impressive collection and daring temporary shows. The museum owns Peggy Guggenheim's trove of cubist, surrealist and abstract expressionist works, along with the Panza di Biumo Collection of American minimalist and conceptual art from the 1960s and '70s. As well as works by Manet, Picasso, Chagall and Bourgeois, it includes the largest collection of Kandinskys in the US. In 1992, the addition of a ten-storey tower provided space for a sculpture gallery (with park views), an auditorium and a café.

Planned exhibitions for 2009 include: 'The Third Mind: American Artists Contemplate Asia, 1860-1989' (until 19 Apr), a major show exploring the impact of Asian art and concepts; 'Frank Lloyd Wright' (15 May-23 Aug), an examination of the architect's vision in the 50th anniversary year of his death and his most famous building's birth; and a retrospective of Kandinsky (18 Sept-10 Jan 2010).

▶ *For more on the Guggenheim's architecture, see p44.*

★ Whitney Museum of American Art

945 Madison Avenue, at 75th Street (1-212 570 3600/www.whitney.org). Subway 6 to 77th Street. **Open** 11am-6pm Wed, Thur, Sat, Sun; 1-9pm Fri. **Admission** $15; $10 reductions; free under-12s. Pay what you wish 6-9pm Fri. **Credit** AmEx, DC, MC, V. **Map** p405 E20.

Like the Guggenheim, the Whitney is set apart by its unique architecture: it's a Marcel Breuer-designed granite cube with an all-seeing upper-storey 'eye' window. When sculptor and art patron Gertrude Vanderbilt Whitney opened the museum in 1931, she dedicated it to living American artists. Today, the Whitney holds 18,000 pieces by around 2,700 artists, including Alexander Calder, Willem de Kooning, Edward Hopper (the museum owns his entire collection), Jasper Johns, Louise Nevelson, Georgia O'Keeffe and Claes Oldenburg. Still, the museum's reputation rests mainly on its temporary shows – particularly the Whitney Biennial, the exhibition everyone loves to hate. Held in even-numbered years, the Biennial is the most prestigious and controversial assessment of contemporary art in America. The pay-what-you-wish Whitney After Hours on Friday nights from 6-9pm includes events and live music. In 2008 Renzo Piano released initial designs for a Chelsea Whitney along the new High Line park (*see p90* **High Point**).

SIGHTS

Profile Metropolitan Museum of Art

The mother of all Manhattan museums is an essential stop on any itinerary.

Occupying 13 acres of Central Park, the Metropolitan Museum of Art (*listings p110*), which opened in 1880, is impressive in terms both of quality and scale. Added in 1895 by McKim Mead and White, the neoclassical façade is daunting. However, the museum is surprisingly easy to negotiate, particularly if you come early on a weekday and avoid the crowds.

The steep $20 admission price is only a suggested donation (a dollar will gain you entrance without reproachful glares), but it does include access to the Met's blockbuster temporary shows plus, for those with boundless energy, same-day admission to the Cloisters in Inwood (*see p122*). It would take many visits to cover all of the Met's two million square feet of gallery space, and you should focus on particular collections to save time.

Philippe de Montebello, the Met's longest-serving director, has retired after 31 years. His replacement – scholarly, 46-year-old British-born tapestries curator Thomas Campbell – takes up the reins in 2009, but the appointment is seen as one that will provide continuity rather than radical change.

COLLECTIONS

In the ground floor's north wing sit the collection of **Egyptian Art** (all gallery names are given in bold here) and the glass-walled atrium housing the Temple of Dendur, moved en masse from its original Nileside setting and now overlooking a reflective pool. Antiquity is also well-represented on the southern wing of the ground floor by the halls housing **Greek and Roman Art**, which reopened in 2007 after receiving an elegant makeover. Keep an eye out for the famous 'New

York kouros' one of the earliest free-standing marble statues from Greece.

Turning west brings you to the **Arts of Africa, Oceania and the Americas** collection; it was donated by Nelson Rockefeller as a memorial to his son Michael, who disappeared while visiting New Guinea in 1961. A wider-ranging bequest, the two-storey **Robert Lehman Wing** can be found at the western end of the floor. This eclectic collection is housed in a recreation of his townhouse and features Bellini's masterful

Madonna and Child as well as an array of Ingres paintings, Tiepolo drawings, the odd Rembrandt portrait, Venetian glass and Impressionist works.

Rounding out the ground floor highlights is the **American Wing** on the northwest corner. Its Engelhard Court reopens in spring 2009 as part of the wing's current revamp. Now more a sculpture court than an interior garden, it houses large-scale 19th-century works in bronze and marble – and one of its three fountains is by Tiffany.

From the Great Hall where you originally entered, a grand staircase brings you to the first floor. Veer left – pausing for the **Drawings, Prints and Photographs** galleries, which often hold small yet intriguing temporary exhibitions – and you'll come to the galleries housing **19th Century European Paintings and Sculpture**. These contain some of the Met's most popular rooms, particularly the two-room Monet holdings and a colony of Van Goghs that includes his oft-reproduced *Irises*. This Impressionist hall of fame gives way to – yes, you guessed it – the post-Impressionist section, which includes Modigliani, Matisse, Picasso and Seurat (look out for his pointillist masterpiece *Circus Sideshow*) as well as American masters of the period such as Sargent and Whistler.

The museum's nearby cache of **Modern Art** – which includes works by Pollock, de Kooning and Rothko, to name a few – was boosted in 2006 by a gift of a 63-piece collection of abstract expressionists from collector Muriel Newman, and the Met recently acquired 20 works by New York photographer Diane Arbus.

Retrace your steps westward and you'll reach the **European Paintings** galleries, which hold an amazing reserve of old masters. The Dutch section boasts five Vermeers, the largest collection of that master in the world, and a haunting Rembrandt self-portrait; the jewel of the French rooms is David's riveting *The Death of Socrates*; and the Spanish rooms are highlighted by El Grecos and Velázquez's stately *Portrait of Juan de Pareja*.

At the northern wing of the floor, you'll find the sprawling collection of **Asian Art**. It's easy to lose yourself among the Chinese lacquer, Japanese figurines and Indian sculpture, but be sure to check out the ceiling of the Jain Meeting Hall in the southeast Asian gallery. If you're still on your feet, give them a deserved rest in the Astor Court, a tranquil recreation of a Ming Dynasty garden, or head up to the Iris & B Gerald Cantor Roof Garden (open late May-late October). And don't miss the programme of temporary exhibitions; for details, see p110.

SIGHTS

WHERE TO EAT
Options are many and varied: try the casual **Cafeteria** on the ground floor; the smarter **Balcony Café** on second; or the **Cantor Roof Garden**.

Planned exhibitions for 2009 include: shows devoted to the work of Jenny Holzer (12 Mar-31 May) and Dan Graham (opens 25 June); 'Georgia O'Keefe: Abstraction' (17 Sept-17 Jan), the first show to focus on this aspect of O'Keefe's work across her career.

Yorkville

Not much remains of the old German and Hungarian immigrant communities that once filled Yorkville, the Upper East Side neighbourhood between Third Avenue and the East River, with delicatessens, beer halls and restaurants. However, one such flashback is the 73-year-old **Heidelberg** (1648 Second Avenue, between 85th & 86th Streets, 1-212 628 2332, www.heidelbergrestaurant.com), where dirndl-wearing waitresses serve up steins of Spaten and platters of sausages from the wurst-meisters at butcher shop Schaller & Weber a couple of doors up. However, the atmosphere becomes noticeably less rarefied as you walk east from the park, with grand edifices giving way to bland modern apartment blocks and walk-up tenements. Second Avenue in the 70s and 80s throbs with rowdy pick-up bars frequented by preppy, twentysomething crowds.

One elegant exception to this scene is **Gracie Mansion** (*see right*), at the eastern end of 88th Street. The only Federal-style mansion in Manhattan, it's served as New York's official mayoral residence since 1942 – although the current mayor, billionaire Michael Bloomberg, famously eschewed this traditional address in favour of his own Beaux Arts mansion at 17 E 79th Street (between Fifth & Madison Avenues). Although Gracie Mansion is fenced off, much of the exterior can be seen from surrounding **Carl Schurz Park**; you can buy provisions for a picnic in this undulating, shady green patch, or on the adjacent East River Promenade, at sprawling Italian gourmet food shop **Agata & Valentina** (1505 First Avenue, at 79th Street, 1-212 452 0690, www.agatavalentina.com).

One block from Gracie Mansion, the **Henderson Place Historic District** (at East End Avenue, between 86th & 87th Streets) contains two dozen handsome Queen Anne row houses, commissioned by furrier and noted real-estate developer John C Henderson. Twenty-four of the 32 houses remain, with the original turrets, double stoops and slate roofs. Although the city is home to an estimated 600,000 Muslims, the hugely dramatic **Islamic Cultural Center** (1711 Third Avenue, at 96th Street, 1-212 722 5234), built in 1990, was New York's first major mosque.

Gracie Mansion

Carl Schurz Park, 88th Street, at East End Avenue (1-212 570 4751). Subway 4, 5, 6 to 86th Street. **Tours** *Mar-mid Nov* 10am, 11am, 1pm, 2pm Wed. Closed mid Nov-Feb. **Admission** $7; $4 reductions; free students, under-12s. Reservations required; same-day reservations not permitted. **No credit cards**. **Map** p406 G18.
The green-shuttered yellow edifice, was built in 1799 by wealthy Scottish merchant Archibald Gracie as a country house. Today, the stately house is the focal point of tranquil Carl Schurz Park, named in honour of the German immigrant who became a newspaper editor and US senator. In 2002, Gracie Mansion's living quarters were opened up to public tours (lasting 45 minutes) for the first time in 60 years.

UPPER WEST SIDE

Subway A, B, C, D, 1 to 59th Street-Columbus Circle; B, C to 81st Street-Museum of Natural History; 1, 2, 3 to 72nd Street; 1, 2, 3 to 96th Street.

With a population that's more established than Downtown's but more bohemian than the Upper East Side's, this four-mile-long stretch west of Central Park is culturally rich and cosmopolitan. As on the Upper East Side, New Yorkers were drawn here during the late 19th century after the completion of Central Park, the opening of local subway lines and Columbia University's relocation to Morningside Heights. In the 20th century, central Europeans found refuge here, and Puerto Ricans settled along Amsterdam and Columbus Avenues in the 1960s. These days, new real-estate is reducing eye-level evidence of old immigrant life, and the neighbourhood's intellectual, politically liberal spirit has waned a little as apartment prices have risen. Sections of Riverside Drive, West End Avenue and Central Park West continue to rival the grandeur of the East Side's Fifth and Park Avenues.

The gateway to the Upper West Side is **Columbus Circle**, where Broadway meets 59th Street, Eighth Avenue, Central Park South and Central Park West – a rare rotary in a city of right angles. The architecture around it could make anyone's head spin. At the entrance to Central Park, a 700-ton statue of Christopher Columbus, goes almost unnoticed under the **Time Warner Center** across the street, which houses offices, apartments, hotel lodgings and **Jazz at Lincoln Center**'s stunning Frederick P Rose Hall (*see p326*). The first seven levels of the enormous glass complex are filled with high-end retailers and gourmet restaurants. The **Museum of Arts & Design** recently opened its new digs in a landmark building on the south side of the circle, itself the subject of a controversial redesign (*see p115* **Full circle**).

SIGHTS

The Upper West Side's seat of culture is **Lincoln Center** (*see p330*), a complex of concert halls and auditoriums built in the 1960s and the home of the New York Philharmonic, the New York City Ballet, the Metropolitan Opera and a host of other notable arts organisations. The big circular fountain in the central plaza is a popular gathering spot – especially in summer, when amateur dancers converge on it to dance alfresco at **Midsummer Night Swing** (*see p263*). The centre is in the middle of an overhaul that includes a redesign of public spaces, refurbishment of the various halls and new facilities (for more on this, *see p330*). Nearby is the **New York Public Library for the Performing Arts**, (40 Lincoln Center Plaza, at 65th Street, 1-212 870 1630, www.nypl.org, closed Sun); alongside its vast collection of films, letters, manuscripts, videos and sound recordings, it's also a venue for concerts and lectures.

Around Sherman and Verdi Squares (from 70th to 73rd Streets, where Broadway and Amsterdam Avenue intersect), classic early 20th-century buildings stand cheek-by-jowl with newer, often mundane high-rises. The jewel is the 1904 **Ansonia Hotel** (2109 Broadway, between 73rd & 74th Streets). Over the years, Enrico Caruso, Babe Ruth and Igor Stravinsky have lived in this Beaux Arts masterpiece; it was also the site of the Continental Baths, the gay bathhouse and cabaret where Bette Midler got her start and Plato's Retreat, a swinging '70s sex club.

On Broadway, the crowded 72nd Street subway station, which opened in 1904, is notable for its Beaux Arts entrance. The rococo **Beacon Theatre** (*see p317*), originally a 1920s movie palace, is now one of the city's premier mid-size concert venues, presenting an eclectic menu of music, African-American regional theatre and headliner comedy events in its rolling programme.

Full Circle

The Museum of Arts & Design crafts a new home.

For more than 20 years, the Museum of Arts & Design (*see p117*) was plagued by growing pains. 'The old building was really inadequate for our needs,' says chief curator David McFadden of the institution's former 53rd Street location, which opened in 1986. 'We never had a lecture hall or classrooms. If we wanted to put on a public programme, we had to repurpose gallery space.' But now, after an 18-month, $90-million overhaul, the museum is ensconced at new premises in the ten-storey 2 Columbus Circle building, complete with a 150-seat auditorium, classrooms, a restaurant and four floors of galleries.

Founded in 1956 as the Museum of Contemporary Crafts, the enterprise brings together objects in a wide range of media with a strong focus on materials and process. Other New York institutions address design but MAD, explains McFadden, 'looks at how things are made, not just the final product.' In the new building, visitors can watch resident artists create works in new on-site studios. And curators are now able to display some of the 2,000-piece permanent collection for the first time, including porcelain ware by Cindy Sherman, stained glass by Judith Schaechter and Robert Arneson's mural *Alice House Wall*.

Although the Columbus Circle location was ideal, the building itself – nicknamed the 'Lollipop Building', because of the Candyland-like columns that lined its base – was not. Originally designed in 1964 by Radio City Music Hall architect Edward Durell Stone to house the Gallery of Modern Art, 2 Columbus Circle was a windowless monolith that had sat empty since 1998. 'It was dark, gloomy and confusing. And it was bisected by all these random mezzanines – it was almost surrealistic,' says McFadden. Updating Stone's design, architect Brad Cloepfil levelled off each floor and 'unzipped the building', carving vertical and horizontal sections out of the concrete exterior.

The redesign was met with protests by pro-preservation forces, whose number included writer Tom Wolfe, artist Frank Stella and *New York Times* critic Herbert Muschamp. However, the museum's arrival may prove the capstone to Columbus Circle's renaissance, which began in 2003 with the opening of the Time Warner Center, the Shops at Columbus Circle and Jazz at Lincoln Center – followed by a massive renovation of the picturesque roundabout itself in 2005. Says McFadden, 'It feels like the Circle is finally whole again.'

SIGHTS

When Central Park was completed, magnificently tall residential buildings rose up along Central Park West to take advantage of the views. The first of these great apartment blocks was the **Dakota** (at 72nd Street), so named because its location was considered remote when it was built in 1884. The fortress-like building is known as the setting for *Rosemary's Baby* and the site of John Lennon's murder in 1980 (Yoko Ono still lives here); other residents have included Judy Garland, Rudolph Nureyev, Lauren Bacall and Boris Karloff but not Billy Joel, who was turned away by the co-op board when he tried to buy an apartment. You might recognise **55 Central Park West** (at 66th Street) from the movie *Ghostbusters*. Built in 1930, it was the first art deco building on the block. Heading north on Central Park West, you'll spy the massive twin-towered **San Remo Apartments** (at 74th Street), which also date from 1930.

A few blocks north, the **New-York Historical Society** (*see p117*) is the city's oldest museum, built in 1804. Across the street, at the glorious **American Museum of Natural History** (*see right*), dinosaur skeletons, a permanent rainforest exhibit and an IMAX theatre lure adults and school groups. Perhaps most popular is the museum's newest wing, the amazing glass-enclosed **Rose Center for Earth & Space**, which includes the totally retooled Hayden Planetarium.

The sizeable cluster of classic groceries and restaurants lining the avenues of the locale's northern end is where the Upper West Side shops, drinks and eats. To see West Siders in their natural habitat, get in line at the perpetually jammed smoked fish counter at gourmet market **Zabar's** (*see p247*). **Café Lalo** (201 W 83rd Street, between Amsterdam Avenue & Broadway, 1-212 496 6031) is famous for its lavish desserts; **H&H Bagels** (2239 Broadway, at 80th Street, 1-212 595 8003, open 24hrs) is the city's largest bagel purveyor; and the legendary (if scruffy) restaurant and deli **Barney Greengrass**, 'the Sturgeon King' (541 Amsterdam Avenue, at 86th Street, 1-212 724 4707, closed Mon) has specialised in smoked fish, knishes and what may be the city's best chopped liver since 1908.

Designed by Central Park's Frederick Law Olmsted, **Riverside Park** is a sinuous stretch of riverbank that starts at 72nd Street and ends at 158th Street, between Riverside Drive and the Hudson River. The stretch of park below 72nd Street, called Riverside Park South, includes a pier and beautiful patches of grass with park benches, and is a particularly peaceful city retreat. You'll probably see yachts, along with several houseboats, berthed at the 79th Street Boat Basin; in the summertime, there's an open-

air café in the adjacent park, where New Yorkers unwind with a beer and watch the sun set over the Hudson River. Several sites provide havens for quiet reflection. The **Soldiers' and Sailors' Monument** (89th Street, at Riverside Drive), built in 1902 by French sculptor Paul EM DuBoy, honours Union soldiers who died in the Civil War, and a 1908 memorial (100th Street, at Riverside Drive) pays tribute to fallen firemen.

★ American Museum of Natural History/Rose Center for Earth & Space

Central Park West, at 79th Street (1-212 769 5100/www.amnh.org). Subway B, C to 81st Street-Museum of Natural History. **Open** 10am-5.45pm daily. **Admission** suggested donation $15; $8.50-$11 reductions; free under-2s. **Credit** AmEx, DC, Disc, MC, V. **Map** p405 C/D19.

Home to the largest and arguably most fabulous collection of dinosaur fossils in the world, the American Museum of Natural History's fourth-floor dino halls have been blowing minds for decades. The thrills begin when you cross the threshold of the Theodore Roosevelt Rotunda, where you're confronted with a towering barosaurus rearing high on its hind legs to protect its young from an attacking allosaurus – an impressive welcome to the largest museum of its kind in the world. Roughly 80% of the bones on display were dug out of the ground by Indiana Jones types. But during the museum's mid 1990s renovation, several specimens were remodelled to incorporate discoveries made during the intervening years. The Tyrannosaurus rex, for instance, was once believed to have walked upright, Godzilla-style; it now stalks prey with its head lowered and tail raised parallel to the ground.

The rest of the museum is equally dramatic. The Hall of Human Origins, which opened in 2007, boasts a fine display of our old cousins, the Neanderthals. The Hall of Biodiversity examines world ecosystems and environmental preservation, and a life-size model of a blue whale hangs from the cavernous ceiling of the Hall of Ocean Life. The impressive Hall of Meteorites was brushed up and reorganised in 2003. The space's focal point is Ahnighito, the largest iron meteor on display anywhere in the world, weighing in at 34 tons (more than 30,000kg).

The spectacular $210 million Rose Center for Earth & Space – dazzling to come upon at night – is a giant silvery globe where you can discover the universe via 3-D shows in the Hayden Planetarium and light shows in the Big Bang Theater. An IMAX theatre screens larger-than-life nature programmes, and you can always learn something new from the innovative temporary exhibitions, an easily accessible research library (with vast photo and print archives), several cool gift shops and friendly, helpful staff.

Museum of Arts & Design

2 Columbus Circle, at Broadway (1-212 299 7777/www.madmuseum.org). Subway A, B, C, D, 1 to 59th Street-Columbus Circle. **Open** 11am-6pm Wed, Fri-Sun; 11am-8pm Thur. **Admission** $15; $12 reductions. **Credit** AmEx, DC, Disc, MC, V. **Map** p404 C22.

Formerly the American Craft Museum, this is the country's leading museum of contemporary crafts in clay, cloth, glass, metal and wood. The ninth-floor restaurant has an excellent view of Central Park. *See also p115* **Full circle**.

Planned exhibitions for 2009 include: 'Elegant Armor: The Art of Jewelry' (on view until 31 May 2009); 'Wood Working', a sampling of wood used in a wide variety of functional and artistic endeavours (17 June-13 Sept 2009); and 'Slash: Paper Under the Knife' (Oct 2009-Jan 2010).

New-York Historical Society

170 Central Park West, between 76th & 77th Streets (1-212 873 3400/www.ny history.org). Subway B, C to 81st Street-Museum of Natural History. **Open** 10am-6pm Tue-Thur, Sat; 11am-5.45pm Sun; 10am-8pm Fri. **Admission** $10; $6-$7 reductions; free under-12s. Free to all 6-8pm Fri. **Credit** AmEx, DC, MC, V. **Map** p405 D20.

Founded in 1804, New York's oldest museum was one of America's first cultural and educational institutions. Highlights in the vast Henry Luce III Center for the Study of American Culture include George Washington's Valley Forge camp cot, a complete series of the extant watercolours from Audubon's *Birds of America* and the world's single largest collection of Tiffany lamps.

MORNINGSIDE HEIGHTS

Subway 1, B, C to 110th Street-Cathedral Parkway; 1 to 116th Street or 125th Street.

Morningside Heights runs from 110th Street (also known west of Central Park as Cathedral Parkway) to 125th Street, between Morningside Park and the Hudson River. The Cathedral Church of St John the Divine and the campus of Columbia University exert considerable influence over the surrounding neighbourhood.

One of the oldest universities in the US, **Columbia** was initially chartered in 1754 as King's College (the name changed after the Revolutionary War). It moved to its present location in 1897. If you wander into Columbia's campus entrance at 116th Street, you won't fail to miss the impressive **Low Memorial Building** modelled on Rome's Pantheon. The former library, completed in 1897, is now an administrative building.

Thanks to the large student population of Columbia and its sister school, Barnard College,

the area has an academic feel, with bookshops, inexpensive restaurants and coffeehouses lining Broadway between 110th and 116th Streets. Better – and healthier – fare can be found across the street at **Community Food & Juice** (2893 Broadway, between 112th & 113th Streets, 1-212 665 2800). Neighbourhood standby **Mondel Chocolates** (2913 Broadway, at 114th Street, 1-212 864 2111, closed Sun) was the chocolatier of choice for the late Katharine Hepburn.

The **Cathedral Church of St John the Divine** (*see below*) is the seat of the Episcopal Diocese of New York. Known affectionately by locals as St John the Unfinished, the enormous cathedral (already larger than Paris's Notre Dame) will undergo hammering and chiselling well into this century. Just behind is the green expanse of **Morningside Park** (from 110th to 123rd Streets, between Morningside Avenue & Morningside Drive) and across the street is the **Hungarian Pastry Shop** (1030 Amsterdam Avenue, between 110th & 111th Streets, 1-212 866 4230), a great place for coffee, dessert and engaging graduate students in esoteric discussions as they procrastinate over their theses.

North of Columbia, **General Grant National Memorial** (aka Grant's Tomb), the mausoleum of former president Ulysses S Grant, is also located in the park. Across the street stands the towering Gothic-style **Riverside Church** (490 Riverside Drive, at 120th Street, 1-212 870 6700, www.the riversidechurchny.org), built in 1930. The tower contains the world's largest carillon: 74 bells, played every Sunday at 10.30am.

★ Cathedral Church of St John the Divine

1047 Amsterdam Avenue, at 112th Street (1-212 316 7540/www.stjohndivine.org). Subway B, C, 1 to 110th Street-Cathedral

---

INSIDE TRACK
BICYCLE BLESSINGS

In late April, visitors to the **Cathedral of St John the Divine** (*see above*) might think they've stepped into a massive spinning class: more than 100 cyclists assemble in the venerated house of worship for the annual Blessing of the Bicycles. 'Everybody brings their stories and experiences from the street,' says Reverend Thomas Miller. 'Every once in a while, someone will tell me a story about feeling blessed because they narrowly averted a crash.'

SIGHTS

SIGHTS

Parkway. **Open** 8am-6pm Mon-Sat; 8am-7pm Sat. **Admission** suggested donation $5; $4 reductions. **Credit** DC, Disc, MC, V. **Map** p406 C15.

Construction on 'St John the Unfinished' began in 1892 in Romanesque style, was put on hold for a Gothic Revival redesign in 1911, then ground to a halt in 1941, when the US entered World War II. It resumed in earnest in 1979, but a fire in 2001 destroyed the church's gift shop and damaged two 17th-century Italian tapestries, further delaying completion. In addition to Sunday services, the cathedral hosts concerts and tours. It bills itself as a place for all people – and it means it. Annual events include both winter and summer solstice celebrations, and the Blessing of the Animals during the Feast of St Francis, which draws pets and their people from all over the city.

INSIDE TRACK
TOM'S RESTAURANT

Tom's Restaurant (2880 Broadway, at 112th Street, 1-212 864 6137) will be familiar to *Seinfeld* fans. Although the interior doesn't resemble the show's diner, the exterior doubled as Monk's Café in the long-running sitcom. But long before Jerry et al decamped to its confines, it also inspired Suzanne Vega to write 'Tom's Diner'.

FREE **General Grant National Memorial**

Riverside Drive, at 122nd Street (1-212 666 1640). Subway 1 to 125th Street. **Open** 9am-5pm daily. **Admission** free. **Map** p407 B14.

'Who's buried in Grant's Tomb?' Groucho Marx used to ask on his quiz show. No one, as it turns out – the crypts of Civil War hero and 18th president Ulysses S Grant and his wife, Julia, are in full aboveground view. Note: the memorial is closed on Thanksgiving, Christmas and New Year's Day.

HARLEM

In the mythical melting pot that New Yorkers often use to define their city, **Harlem** has long been an integral yet uneasy ingredient. During the Jazz Age, America's most iconic black neighbourhood lured whites to its celebrated nightclubs, only to deter downtowners in the 1960s and '70s with the urban decay and crime of which it became emblematic. Duke Ellington's famous invitation to 'Take the A Train' uptown had lost its appeal, and many visitors (and many native New Yorkers) decline it even today.

The loss is theirs. Although the area isn't spilling over with sights, it boasts exuberant gospel choirs in historic churches, soul food restaurants serving down-home and upscale fare, markets purveying African cloths and Afro-centric T-shirts, and a rejuvenated nightlife and jazz scene. Few of the city's

Harlem.

arteries pulsate like the main drag of 125th Street, where street preachers and mix-tape hawkers vie for the attentions of the human parade. Harlem's buildings maintain the city's eclectic architectural heritage, as a stroll along broad avenues such as Adam Clayton Powell Jr Boulevard (Seventh Avenue) or down the sidestreets off Convent Avenue readily attest.

The village of Harlem, named by Dutch colonists after their native Haarlem, was annexed by the City of New York in 1873. The extension of elevated railroads the following decade brought eager developers who overbuilt in the suddenly accessible suburb. The consequent housing glut led to cheap rents, and Jewish, Italian and Irish immigrants escaping the tenements of the Lower East Side grabbed them up.

Around the turn of the 20th century, blacks joined the procession into Harlem, their ranks swelled by the great migration from the Deep South. By 1914, the black population of Harlem had risen well above 50,000; by the 1920s, Harlem was predominately black and the country's most populous African-American community. This prominence soon attracted some of black America's greatest artists: writers such as Langston Hughes and Zora Neale Hurston and musicians including Ellington, Louis Armstrong and Cab Calloway, an unprecedented cultural gathering known as the Harlem Renaissance. White New York took notice, venturing uptown – where the enforcement of Prohibition was lax – to enjoy the Cotton Club, Connie's Inn, Smalls Paradise, and the Savoy Ballroom, which supplied the beat for the city that never sleeps.

The Depression killed the Harlem Renaissance; it also wounded Harlem. By the 1960s, the community had been ravaged by middle-class flight and municipal neglect. Businesses closed, racial tensions ran high, and the looting during the 1977 blackout was among the worst the city had seen. However, as New York's economic standing improved in the mid-'90s, investment began slowly spilling into Harlem, spawning new businesses – and gentrification. There's been an infusion of wealth here in the past decade, visible in the new businesses along 125th Street as well as the phalanxes of renovated brownstones that beckon the middle class (white and black). Today, this moneyed influx's co-existence with Harlem's longstanding residents can be tense but it is seldom volatile.

Harlem rises up from the top of Central Park at 110th Street and extends north as far as 155th Street, though the hood's southern boundary on the West Side is marked by 125th Street. On the East Side, Spanish Harlem begins on 96th Street before petering out before 125th Street. Visitors practising the same common sense they would elsewhere have nothing to fear and will be amply rewarded by one of New York's most distinctive neighbourhoods.

West Harlem

Subway 2, 3 to 125th Street or 135th Street.

Harlem's main artery, **125th Street** ('the one-two-five'), beats loudest in West Harlem. Start at the crossroads: the mammoth **Harlem USA Mall** (300 W 125th Street, between Adam Clayton Powell Jr Boulevard/Seventh Avenue & Frederick Douglass Boulevard/Eighth Avenue, www.harlem-usa.com). The mall is a block east of a Magic Johnson multiplex movie theatre (2309 Frederick Douglass Boulevard/Eighth Avenue, at 124th Street, 1-212 665 6923) and the well-stocked **Hue-Man Bookstore** (*see p230*), specialising in African-American titles, plus the usual retail megastores. Across the street is the celebrated **Apollo Theater** (*see p316*), which hosts occasional concerts, a syndicated TV show and the classic Amateur Night every Wednesday. A block east is the highly regarded **Studio Museum in Harlem** (*see p121*).

Harlem's rich history is preserved in the archives of the **Schomburg Center for Research in Black Culture** (*see below*). This branch of the New York Public Library contains more than five million documents, artefacts, films and prints relating to the cultures of peoples of African descent, with a strong emphasis on the African-American experience. Nearby, the **Abyssinian Baptist Church** (*see right*) is celebrated for its history, political activism and rousing gospel choir.

While most tourists wind up at **Sylvia's** (328 Malcolm X Boulevard/Lenox Avenue, between 126th & 127th Streets, 1-212 996 0660), Harlem's best-known soul-food specialist, Harlemites in the know head for **Amy Ruth's** (113 W 116th Street, between Malcolm X Boulevard/Lenox Avenue & Adam Clayton Powell Jr Boulevard/Seventh Avenue, 1-212 280 8779). Each dish is named after a prominent African-American New Yorker; try the Terry Rivers, honey-dipped fried chicken. Heading east on West 116th Street, brings you to 'Little Senegal' a strip of West African markets and restaurants, of which **Le Baobab** (no.120, 1-212 864 4700) is the best.

Retrace your steps east, past the silver-domed **Masjid Malcolm Shabazz** (no.102, 1-212 662 2200), the mosque of Malcolm X's ministry, to the **Malcolm Shabazz Harlem Market** (no.52, 1-212 987 8131), an outdoor bazaar that buzzes with vendors, most from West Africa, selling clothes, jewellery, sculpture and other goods from covered stalls.

No visit to Harlem is complete without a visit to one of the nightspots devoted to the jazz that made the neighbourhood world renowned. The **Lenox Lounge** (*see p223*) is where Billie Holiday sang, John Coltrane played, the young Malcolm X hustled and James Baldwin held court. The Art Deco lounge (tastefully restored in 1999) has served as a backdrop in numerous films, such as *Malcolm X* and the 2000 remake of *Shaft*. **Showman's Bar** (375 W 125th Street, between St Nicholas & Morningside Avenues, 1-212 864 8941, closed Sun), is another mecca for jazz lovers, while on West 118th Street, **Minton's Playhouse** (*see p328*), once dubbed 'the black jazz capital of the world' by Miles Davis, reopened in 2006 after being shuttered for 30 years.

FREE Abyssinian Baptist Church

132 Odell Clark Place (138th Street), between Malcolm X Boulevard (Lenox Avenue) & Adam Clayton Powell Jr Boulevard (Seventh Avenue) (1-212 862 7474/www.abyssinian.org). Subway 2, 3 to 135th Street. **Open** 9am-9pm daily. **Admission** free. **Map** p407 E11.
From the staid gingerbread Gothic exterior, you'd never suspect the energy that charges the Abyssinian when the gospel choir rocks the church every Sunday (9am, 11am – get there early, and don't wear shorts or flip-flops). A cauldron of community activism since its Ethiopian elders moved it uptown in the 1920s, the church was under the leadership of legendary civil rights crusader Adam Clayton Powell Jr in the 1930s (there's a modest exhibit about him inside). Today, the pulpit belongs to the Rev Calvin Butts, who carries on the flame. Check the website for other events (which include a new Mid-Week Manna, at 7pm on Wednesdays).

FREE Schomburg Center for Research in Black Culture

515 Malcolm X Boulevard (Lenox Avenue), at 135th Street (1-212 491 2200). Subway 2, 3 to 135th Street. **Open** noon-8pm Mon-Wed; noon-6pm Thur, Fri; 10am-6pm Sat. **Admission** free. **Map** p407 D12.
An extraordinary trove of vintage literature and historical memorabilia relating to black culture and the African diaspora is housed in this institution, which was first founded in 1926 by its curator, bibliophile Arturo Alfonso Schomburg. The centre also hosts jazz concerts, films, lectures and tours.

★ Studio Museum in Harlem

144 W 125th Street, between Malcolm X Boulevard (Lenox Avenue) & Adam Clayton Powell Jr Boulevard (Seventh Avenue) (1-212 864 4500/www.studiomuseum.org). Subway 2, 3 to 125th Street. **Open** noon-6pm Wed-Fri, Sun; 10am-6pm Sat. Guided tours by appointment. **Admission** suggested donation $7; $3 reductions; free under-12s. Free to all Sun. **No credit cards. Map** p407 D13.
The first black fine arts museum in the country when it opened in 1968, the Studio Museum has become one of the jewels in the crown of the

art scene of the African diaspora. Under the leadership of director Lowery Stokes Sims (formerly of the Met) and chief curator Thelma Golden (formerly of the Whitney), this favourite presents shows in a variety of media by black artists from around the world.

Mount Morris & Strivers' Row

Subway 2, 3 to 125th Street or 135th Street.

Although subject to gentrification, Harlem's historic districts have done an impressive job maintaining their architectural identity. The **Mount Morris Historic District** (from 119th to 124th Streets, between Malcolm X Boulevard/Lenox Avenue & Mount Morris Park West) contains charming brownstones and a collection of religious buildings in a variety of architectural styles. These days, new boutiques, restaurants and pavement cafés dot the walk down the double-wide **Malcolm X Boulevard** (Lenox Avenue).

Another area of Harlem with a rich and varied historic past is **Strivers' Row**, also known as the St Nicholas Historic District. Running from 138th to 139th Streets, between Adam Clayton Powell Jr Boulevard (Seventh Avenue) and Frederick Douglass Boulevard (Eighth Avenue), these blocks of majestic houses were developed in 1891 by David H King Jr and designed by three different architects, including Stanford White. The two streets are home to three harmonious rows of brick townhouses, so well preserved that the alleyway sign advising you to 'walk your horses' is still visible.

Strivers' Row became a prime address for blacks, whose 'striving' for betterment gives it its name. Now, more upwardly mobile strivers are moving in alongside stylish boutiques such as **N** (114 W 116th Street, between Malcolm X Boulevard/Lenox Avenue & Adam Clayton Powell Jr Boulevard/Seventh Avenue, 1-212 961 1036, www.nharlem newyork.com, closed Mon), which sells contemporary clothing and accessories, some by African-American designers.

INSIDE TRACK
LONDEL'S SUPPER CLUB

Up around Strivers' Row, stop for a bite at **Londel's Supper Club** (2620 Frederick Douglass Boulevard/Eighth Avenue, between 139th & 140th Streets, 1-212 234 0601, closed Mon). Owned by former police officer Londel Davis, it serves some of the best blackened catfish in town.

East Harlem

Subway 6 to 110th Street; 6 to 116th Street.

East of Fifth Avenue is **East Harlem**, sometimes called Spanish Harlem but better known to its primarily Puerto Rican residents as El Barrio. North of 96th Street and east of Madison Avenue, El Barrio moves to a different beat. Its main east-west cross-street, East 116th Street, shows signs of a recent influx of Mexican immigrants. From 96th to 106th Streets, a little touch of East Village-style bohemia can be detected in such places as **Camaradas El Barrio** (2241 First Avenue, at 115th Street, 1-212 348 2703), a Puerto Rican tapas bar whose wooden benches, exposed brick and modest gallery create a casual hang for kicking back over a pitcher of sangria or taking in a salsa show. The **Graffiti Hall of Fame** (106th Street, between Madison & Park Avenues) celebrates old- and new-school taggers in a schoolyard. Be sure to check out **El Museo del Barrio** (*see p109*), Spanish Harlem's community museum.

Hamilton Heights

Subway 1 to 145th Street; A, B, C, D to 145th Street.

Named after Alexander Hamilton, who owned a farm and estate here in 1802, Hamilton Heights extends from 125th Street to the Trinity Cemetery at 155th Street, between Riverside Drive and St Nicholas Avenue. The former factory neighbourhood developed after the West Side elevated train was built in the early 20th century. Today, it's notable for the elegant turn-of-the-20th-century row houses in the Hamilton Heights Historic District, centred on the side streets off scenic **Convent Avenue** between 140th and 145th Streets – just beyond the Gothic Revival-style campus of the City College of New York (Convent Avenue, at 138th Street). There's not much going on in the neighbourhood after dark, with the notable exception of **St Nick's Pub** (*see p223*), a subterranean jazz hotspot where you can hear live music pumping every night. Monday's jam session is legendary.

WASHINGTON HEIGHTS & INWOOD

Subway 1 to 157th Street; A, C, 1 to 168th St; A to 190th Street.

The area from West 155th Street to Dyckman (200th) Street is called **Washington Heights**; venture north of that and you're in **Inwood**,

SIGHTS

Manhattan's northernmost neighbourhood, where the Harlem and Hudson Rivers converge. An ever-growing number of artists and young families are relocating to these parts, attracted by the spacious art deco buildings, big parks, hilly streets and (comparatively) low rents.

Washington Heights' main attraction is the **Morris-Jumel Mansion** (*see p123*), a stunning Palladian-style mansion that served as a swanky headquarters for George Washington during the autumn of 1776, but the small and often overlooked **Hispanic Society of America** (*see p123*), featuring a surprising collection of masterworks, is the real gem here.

Since the 1920s, waves of immigrants have settled in Washington Heights. In the post-World War II era, many German-Jewish refugees (among them Henry Kissinger, Dr Ruth Westheimer and Max Frankel, a former executive editor of *The New York Times*) moved to the western edge of the locale. Broadway once housed a sizeable Greek population – opera singer Maria Callas lived here in her youth. But in the last few decades, the southern and eastern parts of the area have become predominantly Spanish-speaking due to a large population of Dominican settlers.

A trek along Fort Washington Avenue, from about 173rd Street to Fort Tryon Park, puts you in the heart of what is now called **Hudson Heights** – the posh area of Washington Heights.

Start at the **George Washington Bridge**, the city's only bridge across the Hudson River. A pedestrian walkway (also a popular route for cyclists) allows for dazzling Manhattan views. Under the bridge on the New York side is a diminutive lighthouse. To see it up close, look for the footpath on the west side of the interchange on the Henry Hudson Parkway at about 170th Street. If you need to refuel, stop off at the lovely **New Leaf Café** (1 Margaret Corbin Drive, near Park Drive, 1-212 568 5323, closed Mon) within the Frederick Law Olmsted-designed Fort Tryon Park.

At the northern edge of the park is the **Cloisters** (*see right*), a museum built in 1938

using segments of five medieval cloisters shipped from Europe by the Rockefeller clan. It houses the Metropolitan Museum of Art's permanent medieval art collection, including the exquisite Unicorn Tapestries (c1500).

Inwood stretches from Dyckman Street up to 218th Street, the last residential block in Manhattan. Dyckman buzzes with streetlife and nightclubs from river to river, but, north of that, the island narrows considerably and the parks along the western shoreline culminate in the seclusion of **Inwood Hill Park**, another Frederick Law Olmsted legacy. Some believe that this is the location of the legendary 1626 transaction between Peter Minuit and the Native American Lenapes for the purchase of a strip of land called Manahatta – a plaque at the south-west corner of the ballpark near 214th Street marks the purported spot. The 196-acre refuge contains the island's last swathes of virgin forest and salt marsh. Today, with a bit of imagination, you can hike over the hilly terrain, liberally scattered with massive glacier-deposited boulders (called erratics), and picture Manhattan as it was before development. In recent years, the city's Parks Department has used the densely wooded area as a fledging spot for newly hatched bald eagles.

★ Cloisters
Fort Tryon Park, Fort Washington Avenue, at Margaret Corbin Plaza (1-212 923 3700/ www.metmuseum.org). Subway A to 190th

---

INSIDE TRACK
GW BRIDGE LIGHTHOUSE

Those who know Hildegarde Swift's book *The Little Red Lighthouse and the Great Gray Bridge* will recognise the lighthouse under the George Washington Bridge immediately. When the 1921 landmark was no longer needed, after the bridge was completed, fans of the book rallied against plans to put it up for auction.

Cloisters.

Street, then M4 bus or follow Margaret Corbin
Drive north, for about the length of 5 city blocks,
to the museum. **Open** Mar-Oct 9.30am-5.15pm
Tue-Sun. Nov-Feb 9.30am-4.45pm Tue-Sun.
Admission suggested donation (incl admission
to Metropolitan Museum of Art on the same day)
$20; $10-$15 reductions; free under-12s (must be
accompanied by an adult). **Credit** AmEx, DC,
Disc, MC, V. **Map** p409 B3.
Set in a lovely park overlooking the Hudson River,
the Cloisters houses the Met's medieval art and
architecture collections. A path winds through the
peaceful grounds to a castle that seems to have
survived from the Middle Ages. It was built a mere
71 years ago, using pieces of five medieval French
cloisters. The collection itself is an inspired trove of
Romanesque, Gothic and Baroque treasures brought
from Europe and assembled together in a manner
that somehow manages not to clash. Be sure to
check out the famous Unicorn Tapestries, the 12th-
century Fuentidueña Chapel and the Annunciation
Triptych by Robert Campin.

FREE Hispanic Society of America

Audubon Terrace, Broadway, between 155th &
156th Streets (1-212 926 2234/www.hispanic
society.org). Subway 1 to 157th Street. **Open**
10am-4.30pm Tue-Sat. **Admission** free.
Map p408 B9.
Though few people who pass this way seem aware
of it, the Hispanic Society boasts the largest
assemblage of Spanish art and manuscripts outside
Spain. Goya's masterful Duchess of Alba greets
you as you enter, while several haunting El Greco
portraits can be found on the second floor. The
collection is dominated by religious artefacts,
including 16th-century tombs from the monastery
of San Francisco in Cuéllar, Spain. Also on display
are decorative art objects and thousands of
black and white photographs that document life
in Spain and Latin America from the mid 19th
century to the present.

Morris-Jumel Mansion

65 Jumel Terrace, between 160th & 162nd
Streets (1-212 923 8008/www.morrisjumel.org).
Subway C to 163rd Street-Amsterdam Avenue.
Open 10am-4pm Wed-Sun. **Admission** $4; $3
reductions; free under-12s. **No credit cards.**
Map p408 C8.
Built in 1765, Manhattan's only surviving pre-
Revolutionary manse was originally the heart of a
130-acre estate that stretched from river to river
(on the grounds, a stone marker points south with
the legend 'new york, 11 miles'). George Washington
planned the Battle of Harlem Heights here in 1776,
after the British colonel Roger Morris moved out.
The handsome 18th-century Palladian-style villa
offers fantastic views. Its former driveway is now
Sylvan Terrace, which boasts the single longest continuous stretch (one block in total) of old wooden
houses in all of Manhattan.
► Other 18th-century buildings open to visitors
include the Fraunces Tavern Museum (see p64)
and the Van Cortlandt House Museum (see p146).

Brooklyn

The second borough is the first stop for hipsters.

Not long ago, the only tourists in Brooklyn were those who'd missed their Manhattan subway stop. However, in recent years, the second borough has become a destination in its own right. Boutique hotels are springing up everywhere, the music scene is thriving, and Gray Line are even running tours of the area. The borough is about to get even more attention – of the wrong kind, some residents fear – as the 21st location for MTV's seminal house-sharing reality show *The Real World*.

Progress has been in Brooklyn's lifeblood since Europeans first settled here in the early 1600s. Originally the Dutch settlement of Breuckelen, it was an independent city from 1834 until 1898. Today, the borough, which would be America's fourth-largest city if it were still independent, is home to numerous diverse communities: Russian enclaves in Brighton Beach and Polish residents in Greenpoint, the Italians in Bensonhurst and Chinese expats in Sunset Park, and both Arab and Puerto Rican immigrants in Cobble Hill. Almost 40 per cent of its denizens were born outside the US.

Map pp410-411	**Bars** p224
Hotels p174	**Shops** p226
Restaurants p207	

NEW DEVELOPMENTS

From the arty punks of Bushwick to the Bugaboo-pushing mums of Windsor Terrace, Brooklynites identify themselves by and take great pride in their respective neighbourhoods. It's this precarious small-town-in-a-big-city vibe that gets residents up in arms about impending developments, of which there are many. The **Williamsburg-Greenpoint** waterfront projects have caused controversy, with their multiple skyline-view-blocking highrises. Then there's the job-generating, invasive **Atlantic Yards**, a real-estate venture designed by Frank Gehry that will include more highrises, commercial space for big-box retailers, and a stadium for the New Jersey Nets basketball team (which will be renamed to reflect the move, slated for 2010-11). Many people have been uprooted through eminent domain seizures as part of the $4-billion project; community activist groups are fighting developer Bruce Ratner and his biggest proponent, Mayor Bloomberg, tooth and nail. *See also p338* **Fields of dreams**.

For more on what the borough has to offer, contact the **Brooklyn Tourism & Visitor Center** (Brooklyn Borough Hall, 209 Joralemon Street, between Court & Adams Streets, 1-718 802 3846, www.visitbrooklyn.org).

BROOKLYN HEIGHTS & DUMBO

Subway A, C, F to Jay Street-Borough Hall; A, C, G to Hoyt-Schermerhorn; M, R to Court Street; 2, 3, 4, 5 to Borough Hall.

Home to well-to-do families, prominent bankers and lawyers lured by its proximity to Wall Street, **Brooklyn Heights** is where you'll find

Brooklyn Heights Promenade.

the idyllic brownstoned, tree-lined streets of Brooklyn legend. Thanks to the area's historic district status, you'll find well-preserved, picturesque Greek Revival and Italianate row houses dating from the 1820s. Take a stroll down the gorgeous tree-lined streets – particularly Cranberry, Hicks, Pierrepont and Willow – to see the area at its best.

Both Henry and Montague Streets are crammed with shops, restaurants and bars. At the end of Montague, the **Brooklyn Heights Promenade** offers spectacular waterfront views of Manhattan, especially on the Fourth of July, when the Macy's firework display lights up the entire harbour sky. And just a short jaunt away is the venerable **Brooklyn Bridge** (*see p127*) a marvel of 19th-century engineering that became an important symbol of progress. If time permits, it's well worth taking a stroll or bike ride along the pedestrian walkway.

For those interested in history of the underground variety, the **New York Transit Museum** (*see p127*) is a must. There are more remnants of bygone Breuckelen at the **Brooklyn Historical Society** building (*see p127*), which, when completed in 1881, was the first structure in New York to feature locally produced terracotta on its façade. The grand **Borough Hall** (209 Joralemon Street, at Court Street, www.brooklyn-usa.org), the seat of local government, stands as a monument to Brooklyn's past incarnation as an entirely independent municipality. Completed in 1851 but only later crowned with a Victorian cupola, the Greek Revival edifice was renovated in the

late 1980s. The building is linked to the **New York State Supreme Court** (360 Adams Street, between Joralemon Street & Tech Place) by **Cadman Plaza** (from Prospect Street to Tech Place, between Cadman Plaza East & Cadman Plaza West). Close by, at the junction of Court and Remsen Streets, you can buy fresh produce and flowers on Tuesdays, Thursdays and Saturdays throughout most of the year.

The warehouses in the once-gritty waterfront neighbourhood of **Dumbo** (Down Under the Manhattan Bridge Overpass) were originally colonised by artists seeking cheap live/work spaces. These days, the area is bursting with million-dollar apartments and high-end design shops, but the spectacular views – taking in the Statue of Liberty, the lower Manhattan skyline and the Brooklyn and Manhattan Bridges – remain the same. One good vantage point is below the Brooklyn Bridge at the **Fulton Ferry Landing**, which juts out over

INSIDE TRACK
ALMONDINE

The salty, fluffy pretzel roll at chocolatier extraordinaire Jacques Torres's Dumbo patisserie **Almondine** (85 Water Street, between Main & Dock Streets, 1-718 797 5026) is a foodie cult favourite and only available in limited quantities. If you want to sample a bite, and you should, it's wise to get there early.

the East River at Old Fulton and Water Streets and is close to two lovely refurbished parks: **Empire-Fulton Ferry State Park** and **Brooklyn Bridge Park** (riverside, between the Manhattan & Brooklyn Bridges).

Also at the water's edge is a dock for the **New York Water Taxi** (1-212 742 1969, www.nywatertaxi.com), an affordable and picturesque way to travel from Manhattan to Williamsburg, Red Hook and points between. Along the same pier is the **Brooklyn Ice Cream Factory** (Fulton Ferry Landing, 1 Water Street, 1-718 246 3963, closed Mon Oct-Apr), located in a 1920s fireboat house and surely one of the best ice-cream spots in NYC. Next door, docked at the pier, is one of the borough's great cultural jewels: **Bargemusic** (1-718 624 2083), a 100-foot steel barge that was built in 1899 but has staged year-round chamber music concerts for the last 30 years.

The artists who flocked to the area en masse in the 1970s and '80s maintain a presence in the local galleries, most of which support the work

of emerging talent. Among them are **Smack Mellon** (92 Plymouth Street, at Washington Street, 1-718 834 8761, closed Mon & Tue) and **Wessel + O'Connor Fine Art** (111 Front Street, Suite 200, between Washington & Adams Streets, 1-718 596 1700, closed Mon, Tue & Sun Sept-June, and Mon, Sat & Sun July, Aug). The **Dumbo Arts Center** (30 Washington Street, between Plymouth & Water Streets, 1-718 694 0831, closed Mon & Tue) promotes artists through its gallery and sponsorship of the **Art Under the Bridge** festival (see p266), held in the autumn.

The area is also becoming a performing arts hotspot. You can catch anything from puppet theatre to Lou Reed in concert at **St Ann's Warehouse** (see p353). Another artsy venue with even more diverse programming – think vaudeville, burlesque and the Bunker, a well-known minimal techno night – is the **Galapagos Art Space** (16 Main Street, between Plymouth & Water Streets, 1-718 222 8500; see p320), which recently relocated from its Williamsburg birthplace to a gleaming, LEED-certified green space.

If you can't make it out to Bensonhurst, a prime Italo-Brooklyn neighbourhood, but still want an authentic New York pizza, line up for one of the city's best coal-fired pies at the famous **Grimaldi's** (19 Old Fulton Street, between Front & Water Streets, 1-718 858 4300). Across the street is the original building of the *Brooklyn Daily Eagle*, where Walt Whitman worked until he was fired for his lefty political leanings. Whitman printed the first ten pages of *Leaves of Grass* here; it's now home to luxury condos.

Eating options are multifarious. For jumbo lump crab-cake and goat's cheese gnocchi, head to **Five Front** (5 Front Street, 1-718 625 5559, closed Tue), tucked under the Brooklyn Bridge. Right at the waterfront, **Bubby's** (1 Main Street, at Water Street, 1-718 222 0666, closed Mon-Wed) offers comfort food in a cavernous, kid-friendly setting. **Superfine** (126 Front Street, 1-718 243 9005, closed Mon; *see p311*) is a trendy, gay-friendly restaurant and bar that serves a great Sunday brunch. And the always-packed **Jacques Torres Chocolate** shop (*see p248*) offers fabulous cocoa and premium chocolates, made on-site (watch through a glass window).

★ FREE Brooklyn Bridge

Subway A, C to High Street; J, M, Z to Chambers Street; 4, 5, 6 to Brooklyn Bridge-City Hall. **Map** p411 S8, S9.
Even if your trip to New York doesn't include a romp in the boroughs, you should try to make it halfway there by walking to the centre of the Brooklyn Bridge along its wide, wood-planked promenade. Stretching across the river's 1,595-foot span, the bridge was constructed in response to the harsh winter of 1867 when the East River froze over, severing connection between Manhattan and what was then the nation's third most populous city. It was the vision of German-born civil engineer John Augustus Roebling, who died before it was completed in 1893. When it opened, the 5,989ft-long structure was the world's longest bridge, and the first bridge in the world to use steel suspension cables. From it, you'll enjoy striking views of the Statue of Liberty and New York Harbor.
▶ *See p78 Walk, for another way into Brooklyn.*

Brooklyn Historical Society

128 Pierrepont Street, at Clinton Street, Brooklyn Heights (1-718 222 4111/www.brooklyn history.org). Subway A, C, F to Jay Street-Borough Hall; M, R to Court Street; 2, 3, 4, 5 to Borough Hall. **Open** noon-5pm Wed-Sun. **Admission** $6; $4 reductions; free under-12s. **Credit** AmEx, DC, MC, V. **Map** p411 S9.
Founded in 1863, the BHS is located in a landmark four-storey Queen Anne-style building and houses numerous permanent and ongoing exhibits, including 'It Happened in Brooklyn', highlighting local links to crucial moments in American history. A major photo and research library – featuring historic maps and newspapers, notable family histories, and archives from the area's abolitionist movement – is accessible by appointment.

New York Transit Museum

Corner of Boerum Place & Schermerhorn Street, Brooklyn Heights (1-718 694 1600/www.mta. info/mta/museum). Subway A, C, G to Hoyt-Schermerhorn. **Open** 10am-4pm Tue-Fri; noon-5pm Sat, Sun. **Admission** $5; $3 reductions; free under-3s; free seniors Wed. **Credit** AmEx, DC, MC, V. **Map** p410 S10.
Visitors can learn about the complex engineering and construction feats that helped establish the city's century-old subway system in this museum, located in an authentic 1930s subway station. The Transit Museum also allows visitors to climb aboard an exceptional collection of vintage subway and El ('Elevated') cars and explore a working signal tower. Exhibitions cover the history of the city's rapid transit system as well as current topics.
Other locations New York Transit Museum Gallery Annex & Store, Grand Central Terminal, adjacent to stationmaster's office, Main Concourse (*see p103*; 1-212 878 0106).

BOERUM HILL, CARROLL GARDENS & COBBLE HILL

Subway A, C, F to Jay Street; F, G to Bergen Street, Carroll Street; 2, 3, 4, 5, M, N, R, W to Court Street-Borough Hall.

A convenient if annoying real estate agents' contraction for these blurred-boundaried 'hoods, BoCoCa is a prime example of gentrification at work. Gone are the bodegas and cheap shoe shops along the stretch of Smith Street that runs from Atlantic Avenue to the Carroll Street subway stop; it's now known as the area's Restaurant Row. Among the strip's hottest spots are the classic bistro **Bar Tabac** (no.128, at Dean Street, Boerum Hill, 1-718 923 0918); New American favourites the **Grocery** (no.288, between Sackett & Union Streets, Carroll Gardens, 1-718 596 3335, closed Mon, Sun); and **Chestnut** (no.271, between DeGraw & Sackett Streets, Carroll Gardens, 1-718 243 0049, closed Mon). Get on-trend women's clothing at **Bird** (no.220, at Butler Street, Cobble Hill, 1-718 797 3774) and **Dear Fieldbinder** (no.198, between Sackett & Warren Streets, Carroll Gardens, 1-718 852 3620).

Head east to Boerum Hill's **Atlantic Avenue** for a slew of antique and modern furniture stores. Among the best are **City Foundry**, an industrial-chic furniture store

SIGHTS

SIGHTS

(no.365, between Bond & Hoyt Streets, 1-718 923 1786, closed Mon, Tue); and the ultramodern **Rico** (no.384, between Bond & Hoyt Streets, 1-718 797 2077). Browse upscale indie women's fashion at **Butter** (no.389, between Bond & Hoyt Streets, 1-718 260 9033) and its more affordable sister store **Eva Gentry Consignment** (no.371, between Hoyt & Bond Streets, 1-718 522 3522), then get a scoop of organic ice-cream in a compostable cup at **Blue Marble Ice Cream** (no.420, between Bond & Nevins Streets, 1-718 858 1100).

The mile-long stretch of Atlantic Avenue between Henry and Nevins Streets was once crowded with Middle Eastern restaurants and markets, though gentrification has also taken its toll. One stalwart is the **Sahadi Importing Company** (no.187, between Clinton & Court Streets, Cobble Hill, 1-718 624 4550, closed Sun), a neighbourhood institution that sells olives, spices, cheeses, nuts and other gourmet treats, and attracts fans from around the city.

Further south, you'll cross into the still predominantly Italian-American **Carroll Gardens**. Pick up a prosciutto loaf from the **Caputo Bakery** (no.329, between Sackett & Union Streets, 1-718 875 6871) or an aged soppressata salami from **Esposito & Sons** (no.357, between President & Union Streets, 1-718 875 6863); then relax in **Carroll Park** (from President to Carroll Streets, between Court & Smith Streets) and watch the old-timers play *bocce* (lawn bowling). Walk over the Brooklyn-Queens Expressway to **Cobble Hill**'s industrial waterfront and the corner building housing Mexican bistro **Alma**. The rooftop dining area has great views of the East River and lower Manhattan.

This quaint neighbourhood, to the west of Boerum Hill and Carroll Gardens, has a small-town feel. Less restaurant-heavy than Smith Street (though that's slowly changing), shady **Court Street** is dotted with cafés and shops, such as local fave **Book Court** (no.163, between Pacific & Dean Streets, Cobble Hill, 1-718 875 3677). Be sure to stop by the hugely charming **Sweet Melissa** (no.276, between Butler & Douglass Streets, 1-718 855 3410), which serves lunch, pastries and afternoon tea in a pretty back garden.

RED HOOK

Subway F, G to Smith-9th Streets, then B77 bus.

To the south-west of Cobble Hill and Carroll Gardens, the rough-and-tumble industrial locale of **Red Hook** had long avoided urban renewal. However, in recent years, the arrival of luxury condos and gourmet mega-grocer **Fairway** (1-718 694 6868, www.fairwaymarket.com) on Van

---

INSIDE TRACK
CHEYENNE DINER

The latest addition to Red Hook is the transplanted **Cheyenne Diner**, one of the city's few surviving 1940s railcar-style eateries, forced to close when its Midtown spot was targeted for development. Thanks to the campaigning efforts of Michael Perlman, a conservationist on a mission to save the city's diners, it was sold for a paltry $7,500, and, at time of writing, was about to make the journey across the river to Reed Street, where it will be elevated to overlook the water.

Brunt Street has given the impression that gentrification is fast arriving.

Luckily for its protective and obsessed residents, the Hook still feels like a well-kept secret, tucked away on a peninsula. While the area continues to evolve (a vast outpost of Swedish furniture superstore IKEA opened in June 2008), its time-warp charm is still evident, and its decaying piers make a moody backdrop for massive cranes, empty warehouses and trucks clattering over cobblestone streets. The lack of public transport has prevented it from becoming Williamsburg, the sequel. From the Smith-9th Streets subway stop, it's either a long walk or a transfer to the B77 bus, although the **New York Water Taxi** (1-212 742 1969, www.nywatertaxi.com) has improved the situation a little by adding stops to the Beard Street Pier behind Fairway.

Urban adventurers are rewarded with a trip out here. The area offers singular views of New York Harbor from **Valentino Pier**, and has an eclectic selection of artists' studios, bars and eateries. Retro bar and grill **Hope & Anchor** (347 Van Brunt Street, at Wolcott Street, 1-718 237 0276) opened in 2002, when the stretch was still a culinary wasteland. Similarly pioneering was the **Good Fork** (391 Van Brunt Street, near Coffey Street, 1-718 643 6636, closed Mon), now a local institution, which blends traditional Korean flavours into its trendy American cooking.

To check out the work of local artists, look for the word 'Gallery' hand-scrawled on the doors of the **Kentler International Drawing Space** (353 Van Brunt Street, between Wolcott & Dikeman Streets, 1-718 875 2098, closed Mon-Wed), or, at weekends, visit the **Brooklyn Waterfront Artists Coalition**'s 25,000-square-foot exhibition space (499 Van Brunt Street, at Beard Street Pier, 1-718 596 2507, www.bwac.org, closed Mon-Fri) in a Civil

War-era warehouse on the pier just south of Fairway. BWAC hosts large group shows in the spring and autumn. For more information on events and developments in Red Hook, visit **B61 Productions** (www.b61productions.com).

PARK SLOPE & PROSPECT HEIGHTS

Subway (Park Slope) F to 7th Avenue, 15th Street-Prospect Park; F, M, R to Fourth Ave-9th Street; M, R to Union Street. (Prospect Heights) B, Q, Franklin Avenue S to Prospect Park; 2, 3 to Eastern Parkway-Brooklyn Museum, Grand Army Plaza; M, R to 25th Street.

Bustling with lively children, baby buggies and the parents who cart them around, **Park Slope** houses hip, young families in Victorian brownstones and feeds them organically from the nation's oldest working food cooperative (only open to members). The neighbourhood's intellectual, progressive-mindedness and lefty political heritage is palpable; local residents include Hollywood actors (Jennifer Connelly, John Turturro and Steve Buscemi, among others) and famous authors (Paul Auster, Jonathan Safran Foer).

Fifth Avenue is the prime locale for restaurants and hip bars. Locals flock to the beloved, always-packed Venetian mainstay **al di là** (248 Fifth Avenue, at Carroll Street, 1-718 783 4565); late-night favourites **Blue Ribbon Brooklyn** (*see p210*) and **Blue Ribbon Sushi** (no.278, between 1st Street & Garfield Place, 1-718 840 0408), part of a New York mini-chain; and family-friendly Peruvian sensation **Coco Roco** (no.392, between 6th & 7th Streets, 1-718 965 3376). Innovative boutiques can be found all along Fifth Avenue too, including eco-friendly home furnisher **3r Living** (no.276, between Garfield Place & 1st Place, 1-718 832 0951); **Matter** (227 5th Avenue, at President Street, 1-718 230 1150, closed Mon), offering design objects, jewellery, books and a mini art gallery; cool urban gear depot **Brooklyn Industries** (no.206, at Union Street, 1-718 789 2764); and **Beacon's Closet** (no.220, at Union Street, 1-718 230 1630), which buys and sells vintage clothing.

Park Slope's lesbian community is one of the Big Apple's strongest. You can explore Sapphic lore at the **Lesbian Herstory Archives** (*see p308*), then do field research at **Cattyshack** (*see p314*) or **Ginger's Bar** (*see p314*). Both welcome boys, but Park Slope's gay gents usually occupy **Excelsior** (390 5th Avenue, 1-718 832 1599), a low-key bar with a vibrant jukebox and lush back garden. And whether you're straight or gay, boy or girl, you'll want to go off the beaten path to clubby bar **Union**

Hall (*see p224*), which has its own indoor *bocce* courts and a live music space downstairs.

The western edge of Prospect Park is a section of the landmarked **Park Slope Historic District**. Brownstones and several fine examples of Romanesque Revival and Queen Anne residences grace these streets. Particularly charming are the brick edifices that line Carroll Street, Montgomery Place and Berkeley Place. Fans of writer-director Noah Baumbach, who grew up in these parts, may recognise the locale from 2005 hit *The Squid and the Whale*, much of which was set here.

Central Park may be bigger and far more famous, but **Prospect Park** (main entrance at Grand Army Plaza, Prospect Heights, 1-718 965 8999, www.prospectpark.org) has a more rustic quality. By taking a short stroll into its lush green expanse, you may forget you're in the midst of a bustling metropolis. This masterpiece, which designers Frederick Law Olmsted and Calvert Vaux said was more in line with their vision than Central Park (their previous project), is a great spot for bird-watching, especially with a little guidance from the **Prospect Park Audubon Center at the Boathouse** (park entrance on Ocean Avenue, at Lincoln Road, Prospect Heights, 1-718 287 3400, closed Mon-Wed Apr-mid Dec, Mon-Fri mid Jan-Mar).

Alternatively, you can pretend you've left the city altogether by boating or hiking amid the waterfalls, pools and wildlife habitats of the **Ravine District** (park entrances on Prospect Park West, at 3rd, 9th & 15th Streets, Park Slope). The rolling green park was created with equestrians in mind; you can saddle a horse at the nearby **Kensington Stables** (*see p344*) or hop on a bike and pedal alongside rollerbladers and runners. Children enjoy riding the handcarved horses at the park's antique carousel (Flatbush Avenue, at Empire Boulevard) and seeing real animals in the **Prospect Park Zoo** (park entrance on Flatbush Avenue, near Ocean Avenue, Prospect Heights, 1-718 399 7339). A 15-minute walk from Prospect Park is the verdant necropolis of **Green-Wood Cemetery** (*see p130* **Walk**).

Near the main entrance to Prospect Park sits the massive Civil War memorial arch at **Grand Army Plaza** (intersection of Flatbush Avenue, Eastern Parkway & Prospect Park West) and the central branch of the **Brooklyn Public Library** (Grand Army Plaza, Prospect Heights, 1-718 230 2100, closed Sun). The library's central Brooklyn Collection includes thousands of artefacts and photos tracing the borough's history. Around the corner are the tranquil **Brooklyn Botanic Garden** (*see p131*) and also the **Brooklyn Museum** (*see p131*), which has a renowned Egyptology collection. In the

SIGHTS

Walk Tombs with a View

Mix with the great and the good at Brooklyn's landmark cemetery.

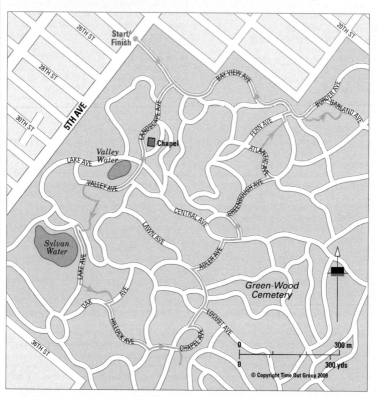

A century ago, Brooklyn's **Green-Wood Cemetery** (*see p131*) vied with Niagara Falls as New York State's greatest tourist attraction. Established in 1838, it's filled with Victorian mausoleums, cherubs and gargoyles, but these winding paths, rolling hills and natural ponds all served as the model for Central Park. It's still a beautiful place to spend a few hours paying your respects to the celebrated and notorious – among them Jean-Michel Basquiat, Leonard Bernstein and Mae West – who lie beneath this 428-acre outdoor museum.

Start your walk at the Gothic main gate (Fifth Avenue at 25th Street, Sunset Park, Brooklyn). The spectacular, soaring arches are carved from New Jersey brownstone. That chirping you hear comes from monk

parakeets that escaped a shipment to JFK in the 1960s and have nested here ever since.

Bear right and walk down **Landscape Avenue** to the chapel. Built in 1911, it was designed by Warren & Wetmore, the same firm behind Grand Central Terminal. Outside, with the creepy Receiving Tomb on your left (where bodies were stored when the ground was too frozen to dig), head to the corner of Lake Avenue. Graves here belong to Clifton and William Prentiss, brothers who fought on opposite sides of the Civil War. They were both mortally wounded on the same day in 1865 (and treated by a nurse named Walt Whitman).

Follow the pond on Waterside Path to **Valley Avenue**. The monument with the jug on top is the grave of John Eberhard Faber (who first put erasers on pencils). Make a left up Hill Side Path. The grave with the carved figure staring up at scenes from the deceased's life belongs to John Matthews, inventor of the soda fountain.

Cut across the grass and follow **Bluff Side Path** to the stairs down to Sylvan Water. Turn left on Lake, stopping by the tomb of Leonard Jerome, namesake of the Bronx's Jerome Avenue and grandfather of Winston Churchill. Make a left on **Ravine Path**. Up the steep incline, stop at the headstone marked 'Aloi' for a nice view of the Statue of Liberty. At the end of the path, make a right on Oak Avenue (turn around – that green bust is the grave of newspaperman Horace Greeley) and take your first left onto Hillock Avenue.

Make a left on **Landscape Avenue** and you'll find Bill 'The Butcher' Poole (think *Gangs of New York*), behind the huge tree on your left. Otherwise, head up Chapel Avenue and turn right on Thorn Path to the grave of Samuel Morse, inventor of the telegraph. Double back and make a right on **Chapel Avenue**. Walk around the immense Steinway family mausoleum and bear right. Make a right on Locust Avenue and pay your respects to disgraced power-monger Boss Tweed (left side), or stay on Chapel past Forest and Vista Avenues and make a right on Alder Avenue.

Next, make a right on Central Avenue and then a left on Sycamore Avenue. Then turn on Greenbough Avenue (you'll pass Henry Raymond, the founder of *The New York Times*), left on Atlantic Avenue and right on Warrior Path. Take the path to the end and climb the staircase to the **Civil War Soldiers' Monument**. The bench behind it has sweet views and it's also the site of the first and largest major battle of the Revolutionary War.

Follow Battle Path to the end, turn left on Garland Avenue. When you're even with the big tree, turn right. You're looking at the grave of Dodgers owner Charles Ebbets and, up the hill behind, the highest point in Brooklyn. Go straight on Garland, left on Border Avenue and right down Battle Avenue to the corner of Bay View Avenue. You'll pass the obelisk honouring the victims of the 1876 Brooklyn Theatre Fire on your way back to the main gate.

past few years, the museum has also hosted hugely successful exhibits of major contemporary artists such as Takashi Murakami, Annie Leibovitz and William Wegman, all of which drew sell-out crowds.

Brooklyn Botanic Garden

1000 Washington Avenue, at Eastern Parkway, Prospect Heights (1-718 623 7200/www.bbg.org). Subway B, Q, Franklin Avenue S to Prospect Park; 2, 3 to Eastern Parkway-Brooklyn Museum. **Open** *Mar-Oct* 8am-6pm Tue-Fri; 10am-6pm Sat, Sun. *Nov-Feb* 8am-4.30pm Tue-Fri; 10am-4.30pm Sat, Sun. **Admission** $8; $4 reductions; free under-12s. Free to all Tue; 10am-noon Sat; Sat, Sun mid Nov-Feb. **Credit** DC, MC, V. **Map** p410 U11.

This 52-acre haven of luscious greenery was founded in 1910. In April, when Sakura Matsuri, the annual Cherry Blossom Festival, takes place, prize buds and Japanese culture are in full bloom. The restored Eastern Parkway entrance and the Osborne Garden – an Italian-style formal garden – are also well worth a peek.

▶ *See p261 for details of the annual Cherry Blossom Festival.*

★ Brooklyn Museum

200 Eastern Parkway, at Washington Avenue, Prospect Heights (1-718 638 5000/www.brooklyn museum.org). Subway 2, 3 to Eastern Parkway-Brooklyn Museum. **Open** 10am-5pm Wed-Fri; 11am-6pm Sat, Sun; 11am-11pm 1st Sat of mth (except Sept). **Admission** $8; $4 reductions; free under-12s. Free to all 5-11pm 1st Sat of mth (except Sept). **Credit** AmEx, DC, MC, V. **Map** p410 U11.

Brooklyn's premier institution is a tranquil alternative to Manhattan's bigger-name spaces; it's rarely crowded. Among the museum's many assets is a rich, 4,000-piece Egyptian collection, which includes a gilded-ebony statue of Amenhotep III and, on a ceiling, a large-scale rendering of an ancient map of the cosmos, as well as a mummy preserved in its original coffin. Masterworks by Cézanne, Monet and Degas, part of an impressive European art collection, are displayed in the museum's recently renovated, skylighted Beaux-Arts Court. On the fifth floor, American paintings and sculptures include native son Thomas Cole's *The Pic-Nic* and Louis Rémy Mignot's *Niagara*. Don't miss the renowned Pacific Island and African galleries (this was the first American museum to display African objects as art).

★ FREE Green-Wood Cemetery

Fifth Avenue, at 25th Street, Sunset Park (1-718 768 7300/www.green-wood.com). Subway M, R to 25th Street. **Open** 8am-5pm daily (phone or check website for summer hours). **Admission** free. **Map** p410 S13. *See p130* **Walk**.

SIGHTS

Williamsburg.

WILLIAMSBURG

Subway L to Bedford Avenue.

With a thriving gallery scene and an abundance of funky bars and shops, Williamsburg channels the East Village (just one stop away on the L train) in its heyday. Yet Youtube parodies, such as the over-dramatic series *The Burg* and *Hipster Olympics* ('A battle of apathetic grandeur'), signal that the area and its denizens have tipped over into hipster cliché.

Bedford Avenue is the neighbourhood's main thoroughfare. By day, the epicentre of the strip is the **Bedford MiniMall** (no.218, between North 4th & 5th Streets) – you won't find a Gap or Starbucks here (yet), but you will be able to contemplate a beer selection that will make your head spin at **Spuyten Duyvil Grocery** (1-718 384 1520), browse an exceptionally edited selection of books and magazines at **Spoonbill & Sugartown, Booksellers** (1-718 387-7322) and drink some of the best iced coffee around at the **Verb Café** (1-718 599 0977). The café scene on Bedford is still growing, with newcomers such as the foodie **Blackbird Parlour** (no.197, at North 6th Street, 1-718 599-2707) and organic haven **Ella Café** (no.177, between North 7th & 8th Streets, 1-718 218 8079), while New York institution **Peter Luger** (*see p208*) grills what some carnivores consider to be the best steak in

the city. Wash down your meal with a to-die-for whiskey milkshake at **Relish**, housed in a refurbished railcar (225 Wythe Ave, at North 3rd Street, 1-718 963 4546).

You'll find chic shops along North 6th Street, particularly between Wythe and Kent Avenues. Among them are the designer co-op **5-in-1** (no.60, 1-718 384 1990, closed Tue-Thur), housed in a former railcar factory, and **Built By Wendy** (no.46, 1-718 384 2882), which offers retro-flavoured basics and cool tees for both sexes, plus killer canvas totes. The 'hood also has 40 art galleries (for our pick of the best, *see p275*), which all stay open late on the second Friday of every month. Pick up the free gallery guide *Wagmag* at local shops and cafés or visit www.wagmag.org for listings.

Famously, Williamsburg is also band central. From twee emo to stoner psychedelica, local rock bands and touring indie darlings play at **Music Hall of Williamsburg** (*see p322*), **Pete's Candy Store** (*see p323*) and **Warsaw** (261 Driggs Avenue, at Eckford Street, 1-718 387 0505, closed Mon), which doubles as the Polish National Home. Formerly a community swimming hole, **McCarren Park Pool** (at Lorimer Street and Driggs Avenue, www.thepoolparties.com) is now a distinctive outdoor concert venue hosting local and national acts, as well as other events such as June's **Renegade Craft Fair** (www.renegadecraft.com).

SIGHTS

On a very different note, the admission price to the **City Reliquary** (370 Metropolitan Avenue, near Havemeyer Street, 1-718 782 4842, closed Mon-Fri) tips you off to its nostalgic bent. A trifling 50 cents gets you into the weekends-only mini-museum of remnants of New York history: architectural salvage from renovated landmarks such as the Carlyle Hotel, old subway tokens and kitschy Statue of Liberty memorabilia. It also hosts themed temporary exhibitions.

Long before the trendsetters invaded, Williamsburg's waterfront location made it ideal for industry. When the Erie Canal linked the Atlantic Ocean to the Great Lakes in 1825, the area became a bustling port. Companies such as Pfizer and Domino Sugar started here, but businesses had begun to abandon the area's huge industrial spaces by the late 20th century. A sign of the area's rapid gentrification, the Domino refinery finally closed in 2004, though its signature sign is still a local landmark. The beloved **Brooklyn Brewery** (79 North 11th Street, between Berry Street & Wythe Avenue, 1-718 486 7422, www.brooklynbrewery.com) took up residence in a former ironworks. Visit during the happy 'hour' (Fridays 6-11pm) for $3 drafts or take a tour on Saturdays and Sundays from noon to 6pm.

FORT GREENE

Subway B, M, Q, R to DeKalb Avenue; B, Q, 2, 3, 4, 5 to Atlantic Avenue; C to Lafayette Avenue; D, M, N, R to Pacific Street; G to Fulton Street, Clinton-Washington Avenues.

With its stately Victorian brownstones and other grand buildings, Fort Greene has undergone a major revival over the past decade. It has long been a centre of African-American life and business – Spike Lee, Branford Marsalis and Chris Rock have all lived here. **Fort Greene Park** (from Myrtle to DeKalb Avenues, between St Edwards Street & Washington Park) was conceived in 1846 at the behest of poet Walt Whitman (then editor of the *Brooklyn Daily Eagle*); its masterplan was fully realised by the omnipresent Olmsted and Vaux in 1867. At the centre of the park stands the Prison Ship Martyrs Monument, erected in 1909 in memory of 11,000 American prisoners who died on British ships that were anchored nearby during the Revolutionary War.

Despite the implications of its name, the 34-storey **Williamsburgh Savings Bank**, located at the corner of Atlantic and Flatbush Avenues, is in Fort Greene, not Williamsburg. The 512-foot structure is the tallest in the borough and, with its four-sided clocktower, doubtlessly the most recognisable feature of the

City Reliquary.

Brooklyn skyline. The 1927 building has now been renamed One Hanson Place, and converted into (what else?) luxury condominiums.

Though originally founded in Brooklyn Heights, the **Brooklyn Academy of Music** (*see p330*) moved to its current site on Fort Greene's southern border in 1901. America's oldest operating performing arts centre, BAM was the home of the Metropolitan Opera until 1921; today, it's known for ambitious cultural performances of all varieties that draw big audiences from throughout the metropolitan area. Also famous – if for different reasons – is the cheesecake at **Junior's Restaurant** (386 Flatbush Avenue, at DeKalb Avenue, 1-718 852 5257), just a few blocks away.

Every Sunday, meandering Brooklynites hit the **Brownstoner's Brooklyn Flea** (Bishop Loughlin Memorial High School, entrance on Lafayette Avenue, between Clermont and Vanderbilt Avenues, http://brownstoner.com/brooklynflea) to browse handmade indie crafts, artisanal chocolate and perhaps less actual junk than some flea-loving cheapskates would like. In addition to some funky shops, a slew of popular restaurants can be found on or near **DeKalb Avenue**, including the South African **i-Shebeen Madiba** (no.195, at Carlton Avenue, 1-718 855 9190); lively bistro **Chez Oskar** (no.211, at Adelphi Street, 1-718 852 6250); and Francophilic favourite **iCi** (no.246, at Vanderbilt Avenue, 1-718 789 2778, closed Mon). Don't miss nearby **Stuart & Wright** (85 Lafayette Avenue, between South Elliott Place & South Portland Avenue, 1-718 797 0011), which stocks beautiful (if pricey) men's and women's clothing by local designers.

CONEY ISLAND & BRIGHTON BEACH

Subway B, Q to Brighton Beach; D, F, N, Q to Coney Island-Stillwell Avenue; F to Neptune Avenue; F, Q to West 8th Street-NY Aquarium.

Is it curtains for Coney? Summer 2008 was tipped as decayed amusement park Astroland's final season, before the stomach-turning rides, freak shows and funnel cake vendors are bulldozed into oblivion to make way for luxury beachside condos and a rumoured Disney-type destination. But we've heard that before; and as of late 2008, its seedy charms were still intact.

If nothing else, the proposed demise of this New York institution has been good PR: NYC's Parks Department estimates that five million more people visited Coney after reports that its days were numbered. The old-timers remember Coney Island in its heyday: an expanse of rides, hot-dog stands, a six-storey hotel shaped like an elephant and amusement parks (Dreamland, Luna Park, Steeplechase and Astroland, the only survivor). By 1966, nearly everything was gone, due to the wrecking ball, fire and a long, steady economic downturn.

In 2005 a developer bought about half of the area's entertainment district (including Astroland's 3.3 acres) and is looking to pour some $2 billion into its rejuvenation – calling for new hotels, restaurants, shops, arcades and cinemas on the site. However, municipal planners have vowed to protect the amusement district as much as possible, and a few of the attractions are protected landmarks (including the vintage wooden rollercoaster, the Cyclone, built in 1926, and the 1918 Wonder Wheel). For the latest news, visit www.coneyisland.com. In the meantime, it's safe to say that the only truly

INSIDE TRACK
M&I INTERNATIONAL FOODS

There are many Russian restaurants in and around Brighton Beach. But you can also buy interesting pickled foodstuffs to take home with you at the enormous **M&I International Foods** (249 Brighton Beach Avenue, 1-718 615 1011). Before you buy, you can taste the goods in advance at the upstairs café.

uncontroversial improvement to Coney Island is the seaside **KeySpan Park**, which opened in 2001. Home to the **Brooklyn Cyclones** (*see p339*), a minor-league baseball affiliate of the New York Mets, the park has brought professional baseball back to the borough.

Near here, the **New York Aquarium** (*see p285*) is the nation's oldest marine preserve and home to more than 350 aquatic species, including the California sea lions that perform daily at the outdoor, 1,600-seat Aquatheater. Don't forget to look up: various local artists have focused their energy on adding some colour to the signage.

The always captivating **Sideshows by the Seashore** is put on by **Coney Island USA** (1208 Surf Avenue, at W 12th Street, Coney Island, 1-718 372 5159, www.coneyisland.com), an organisation that keeps the torch burning for 20th-century-style attractions. These include legendary freaks such as human pincushion Scott Baker (aka the Twisted Shockmeister) and the heavily tattooed Insectavora, who eats flames and climbs the dangerous Ladder of Swords. The **Mermaid Parade** (*see p263*) and **Nathan's Famous Fourth of July Hot Dog Eating Contest** (held every year since 1916; *see p264*) are two quirky summertime rituals at Coney. Another popular annual event, since 2001, is the **Village Voice Siren Music Festival** (http://siren. villagevoice.com/siren) in July, which provides a platform for emerging bands. And on Friday evenings throughout the summer, the local fireworks display is the perfect nightcap to a day of sandy adventures.

If you head left on the boardwalk from Coney Island, a short walk brings you to **Brighton Beach**, New York's Little Odessa. Groups of Russian expats (the display of big hair and garish fashion is jaw-dropping) crowd semi-outdoor eateries such as **Tatiana** (3152 Brighton 6th Street, at the Boardwalk, 1-718 891 5151), where you can sup on borscht and smoked fish – but be wary if the waiter steers you towards expensive generic vodka. A better, if less picturesquely placed, bet is **Primorski** (282 Brighton Beach Avenue, 1-718 891 3111), north of the seafront.

As you walk along the main thoroughfare, catching snatches of Russian conversation over the clatter of the elevated train, you can almost forget you're not in the mother country. You can't go far without finding a **Caviar Kiosk** (like the one at 506 Brighton Beach Avenue, selling small cans of black caviar at $14.95. End the day where you started: by night, Tatiana morphs into a glitzy club, featuring artistes like Magdalina, 'the Russian Pamela Anderson'. If that doesn't convince you the Cold War is over, nothing will.

SIGHTS

Queens

Sup from the melting pot in this multiculti borough.

Already New York City's largest borough, Queens is expected to surpass Brooklyn as its most populous by the end of the decade. Even so, it lacks the iconic aura of its brasher southern neighbour. Most visitors know Queens from its airports (around 200,000 people pass though every day via JFK or La Guardia) or curmudgeonly TV characters, yet the borough is actually the country's most diverse urban area, with almost half its 2.2 million residents hailing from one of nearly 150 different nations. Not for nothing is the elevated 7 subway nicknamed the 'International Express'.

This ethnic diversity is best sampled at its restaurants. Astoria has tavernas and Brazilian *churrascarias*; Jackson Heights offers Indian, Thai and South American hotspots; and Flushing boasts the city's second largest Chinatown and countless Korean barbecues.

| Map p412 | Restaurants & |
| Bars p224 | Cafés p212 |

LONG ISLAND CITY

Subway E, V (V weekdays only) to 23rd Street-Ely Avenue; G to 21st Street-Jackson Avenue; 7 to Vernon Boulevard-Jackson Avenue, or 45th Road-Court House Square.

Just across the East River, Long Island City has been touted as the 'next Williamsburg' (the hipster Brooklyn enclave; *see p132*) for so long that countless other 'hoods have since claimed and passed on the mantle. In truth, its proximity and easy access – via subway, tunnel and bridge – to Midtown have made LIC more attractive to upscale professionals, who've moved into the modern apartment towers rising on the waterfront, than to hipsters or would-be artists. Nevertheless, the neighbourhood boasts one of the city's most adventurous museums and a burgeoning art scene.

If you're here in the warmer months, begin with a wave to Manhattan from **Watertaxi Beach** (Borden Avenue, at 2nd Street, www.watertaxibeach.com, open early May-mid Oct,

weather permitting), a man-made beach with a perpetual volleyball game ongoing. If you'd prefer a more sedate setting for gazing at Midtown, try **Gantry Plaza State Park** (48th Avenue, at Center Boulevard), named after the hulking 19th-century railroad gantries that once transferred cargo from ships to trains. Both are directly across the East River from the United Nations, giving postcard-worthy views of the skyline. Further dining options in the area include the **Waterfront Crabhouse** (2-03 Borden Avenue, at 2nd Street, 1-718 729 4862), an old-time saloon and oyster bar in an 1880s brick building, and, signalling LIC's recent culinary upgrade, **Tournesol** (50-12 Vernon Boulevard, at 50th Avenue, 1-718 472 4355), an engaging and highly affordable bistro.

A few blocks east, on Jackson Avenue, stands the **P.S.1 Contemporary Art Center** (*see p136*), a progressive museum affiliated with MoMA that highlights the work of the up-and-coming and the already-here. From July to September, it also becomes the city's dance hub with **P.S.1 Warm Up** (*see p300*). Close by,

P.S.1 Contemporary Art Center

and in complete contrast, a well-preserved block of 19th-century houses constitutes the **Hunters Point Historic District** (45th Avenue, between 21st & 23rd Streets).

★ P.S.1 Contemporary Art Center

22-25 Jackson Avenue, at 46th Avenue, Long Island City (1-718 784 2084/www.ps1.org). Subway E, V (V weekdays only) to 23rd Street-Ely Avenue; G to 21st Street-Jackson Avenue; 7 to 45th Road-Court House Square. **Open** noon-6pm Mon-Thur, Sun. **Admission** *Suggested donation $5; $2 reductions.* **Credit** AmEx, DC, MC, V. **Map** p412 V5.

In a distinctive Romanesque Revival building (a former public school), P.S.1 mounts cutting-edge shows and hosts an acclaimed international studio programme. The freewheeling contemporary art space is a veritable treasure hunt, with artwork in every corner from the stairwells to the roof. P.S.1 became an affiliate of MoMA in 1999, and sometimes stages collaborative exhibitions. Reflecting the museum's global outlook, it's focused in recent years on such luminaries as Janet Cardiff and Olafur Eliasson.

ASTORIA

Subway G, R, V to Steinway Street; N, W to Broadway, or Astoria-Ditmars Boulevard.

The N and W trains chug north to Astoria, a lively, traditionally Greek neighbourhood that in the last few decades has seen an influx of Brazilians, Bangladeshis, Eastern Europeans, Colombians and Egyptians; they've been joined by post-grads sharing row-house digs. A short downhill hike from Broadway subway station brings you to the **Isamu Noguchi Garden Museum** (*see p137*), which shows works by the visionary sculptor. Nearby is the **Socrates Sculpture Park** (Broadway, at Vernon Boulevard, www.socratessculpturepark.org), a riverfront art space that hosts regular concerts and movie screenings in July and August.

At the end of the subway line (Astoria-Ditmars Boulevard), walk west to **Astoria Park** (from Astoria Park South to Ditmars Boulevard, between Shore Boulevard & 19th Street) for its dramatic views of two bridges: the **Triborough Bridge**, Robert Moses's automotive labyrinth connecting Queens, the Bronx and Manhattan; and the 1916 **Hell Gate Bridge**, a single-arch steel tour de force and template for the Sydney Harbour Bridge.

Still New York's Greek-American stronghold, Astoria is well known for Hellenic eateries specialising in impeccably grilled seafood. **Elias Corner** (24-02 31st Street, at 24th Street, 1-718 932 1510) serves meze and a catch of the day in a breezy Aegean setting, while **Athens Café** (32-07 30th Avenue, between 32nd & 33rd Streets, 1-718 626 2164) is the neighbourhood's social nexus and a terrific place to stop for Greek coffee and pastries. One of the city's last central European beer gardens, **Bohemian Hall & Beer Garden** (29-19 24th Avenue, at 29th Street, 1-718 274 4925), offers Czech-style dining and drinking. Arrive early on weekends to nab a picnic table in the expansive, linden tree-shaded yard (open late May-Oct).

South of Astoria Boulevard, you can try a shisha – a (legal) hookah pipe – with thick Turkish coffee in the cafés of 'Little Egypt' along Steinway Street. Over at **Steinway & Sons** (1 Steinway Place, between 19th Avenue & 38th Street, 1-718 721 2600), take a tour of the still-thriving red-brick 1871 piano factory; call for a schedule.

★ Isamu Noguchi Garden Museum

9-01 33rd Road, between Vernon Boulevard & 10th Street, Astoria (1-718 204 7088/ www.noguchi.org). Subway N, W to Broadway, then bus Q104 to 11th Street; 7 to Vernon Boulevard-Jackson Avenue, then Q103 bus to 10th Street. **Open** 10am-5pm Wed-Fri; 11am-6pm Sat, Sun. **Admission** $10; $5 reductions; free under-12s. Voluntary donation 1st Fri of the mth. No pushchairs. **No credit cards. Map** p412 V3.
The former studio of Japanese-American sculptor Isamu Noguchi (1904-88), who moved to Queens to be nearer the quarries that supplied the granite and marble for his works, this museum is a monument to the artist's exquisitely harmonious sensibility. Thirteen indoor galleries showcase his organic, undulating work in granite, marble, bronze and wood and move seamlessly into the adjoining gardens with fountains and small footpaths. Particularly intriguing is the room devoted to his akari works (light fixtures encased by inventive paper shades). A shuttle service from Manhattan is available on weekends; call or check online for more details. *Photo p139.*

Museum of the Moving Image

35th Avenue, at 36th Street, Astoria (1-718 784 0077/www.movingimage.us). Subway G, R, V to Steinway Street. **Open** 11am-5pm Wed, Thur; 11am-8pm Fri; 11am-6.30pm Sat, Sun. **Admission** $10; $5-$7.50 reductions; free under-5s. Free to all 4-6.30pm Fri. No pushchairs. **Credit** AmEx, DC, MC, V. **Map** p412 W4. Closed until winter 2009/10.
Only 15 minutes from Midtown, the Museum of the Moving Image is one of the city's most dynamic institutions. Rubbing elbows with Kaufman Astoria Studios, it offers daily film and video programming

alongside displays of famous movie props, including the chariot driven by Charlton Heston in *Ben-Hur* and the Yoda puppet used in *The Empire Strikes Back*. It's currently closed for a massive renovation that includes a three-storey extension, but it's set to reopen in winter 2009-10 with a state-of-the-art 264-seat cinema, a smaller screening room, an education centre and expanded gallery spaces.
▶ *For the museum's itinerant programme of movie screenings, see p303.*

JACKSON HEIGHTS

Subway E, F, G, R, V to Jackson Heights-Roosevelt Avenue; 7 to 74th Street-Broadway.

Dizzying even by Queens standards, Jackson Heights' multiculturalism puts the sanitised display at Disney's Epcot to shame. **Little India** greets you at the subway exit and finds its focus at the art deco **Eagle Theater** (73-07 37th Road, at Broadway, 1-718 205 2800, www.eaglemovietheater.com), which presents the latest Bollywood blockbusters (subtitles in English). You can probably find the soundtrack just next door at **Today's Music** (73-09 37th Road, at Broadway, 1-718 429 7179), which also carries an array of bhangra. Colourful saris can be had at **India Sari Palace** (37-07 74th Street, at 37th Avenue, 1-718 426 2700) and bracelets and other trinkets at **Mita Jewelers** (37-30 74th Street, between 37th Avenue & 37th Road, 1-718 507 1555), but the main draw is culinary. The unofficial headquarters of the Indian expat community, **Jackson Diner** (37-47 74th Street, between Roosevelt & 37th Avenues, 1-718 672 1232) serves up sumptuous curries and Hindi soaps on Zee TV.

Along with adjoining Elmhurst, Jackson Heights has also welcomed successive waves of Latin American immigrants. Mexicans, Colombians and Argentinians are old-school in these parts: get a taste of Buenos Aires at the exuberant, *fútbol*-themed **Boca Junior Argentinian Steakhouse** (81-08 Queens Boulevard, at 51st Avenue, Elmhurst, 1-718 429 2077), or stop by **Chibcha** (79-05 Roosevelt Avenue, at 79th Street, Jackson Heights, 1-718 429 9033), a colourful Colombian spot with enormous plates of beef and rice, and merengue bands. The Thai contingent is reflected in several fine restaurants: **Arunee** (37-68 79th Street, between Roosevelt & 37th Avenues, 1-718 205 5559) doesn't hold back with the spices – or the volume on the Thai music videos.

The neighbourhood claims a roughly 30-square-block landmark district of mock Tudor and neo-Gothic-style co-op apartment buildings, with attached houses, tree-dotted lawns and park-like courtyards. There are good examples of these 1920s beauties on 70th Street, between

INSIDE TRACK
5 POINTZ

After a visit to P.S.1 Contemporary Art Center, cross the street for a rougher display of urban art: the graffiti-covered **5 Pointz** (on Jackson Avenue, between Crane & Davis Streets). There's no art inside, but the façade of the block-long converted warehouse, visible from the 7 train, offers an ever-evolving tableau of brilliant hues and different tagging styles from throughout the five boroughs.

SIGHTS

Queens of the Silver Screen

This workaday borough was once a movie-business hub – and may be again.

Despite the presence of the **Museum of the Moving Image** (*see p137*), set to reopen in winter 2009/10, modern-day Queens is an unlikely place to encounter celebrity glamour. However, the past was a very different story. In the 1920s, Astoria was a huge star in the celluloid universe, the professional base of both heartthrobs (Rudolph Valentino, Claudette Colbert) and wisecrackers (Groucho Marx, WC Fields).

Taking advantage of its proximity to talent-laden Broadway, Famous Players-Lasky (later Paramount Pictures) opened its first studios in 1920 on 36th Street in Astoria and quickly became one of the major forces of the Silent Era. Portions of Valentino's blockbuster *The Sheikh* (1921) were filmed here, as were three of DW Griffith's last films (including 1925 *Sally of the Sawdust*, Fields' first feature-length effort). With the introduction of sound, the studio produced the Marx Brothers' *Animal Crackers* (1930) and *The Cocoanuts* (1929), and talking debuts from Edward G Robinson, Tallulah Bankhead and Colbert.

However, with the arrival of 'talkies', Hollywood became the movie capital, its warm and reliable weather proving a big attraction to the industry. After Paramount moved west, the Army's Signal Corps Pictorial Service moved into the largely vacated studios in 1942, using it as a location for its propaganda films until 1971. After several years of neglect, the studios were declared a National Historic Landmark in 1976; six years later developer George S Kaufman bought

them and created **Kaufman Astoria Studios** (www.kaufmanastoria.com).

Having been used for films such as *The Age of Innocence* and *Scent of a Woman*, and for TV shows including *Law & Order*, Kaufman Astoria Studios are still going strong today. Woody Allen recently used the facility for *Whatever Works*, his next offering starring Larry David, and the American version of BBC hit *Life on Mars* was also shot here. Augmented by recent tax breaks from both city and state, this resurgence has fuelled plans for the studio's expansion; at the time of writing, it was preparing to break ground on a $20-million building across the street with an 18,000-square-foot soundstage.

Long Island City's **Silvercup Studios** (www.silvercupstudios.com), the borough's other film and TV production company, can also boast an impressive recent output: *Gangs of New York*, *The Devil Wears Prada*, *Sex and the City* (both the small- and big-screen versions), *The Sopranos, 30 Rock* and new privileged-Manhattan-teen series *Gossip Girl* have all emanated from this former bakery, which boasts a landmark mounted sign that's visible from Queensboro Plaza. And like Kaufman Astoria, it's also expanding. At press time, construction of a massive $1 billion complex on the East River had been stalled by the logistics of removing a major generator south of the Queensboro Bridge, but it's expected to go ahead eventually. Just more evidence that Queens, former kingpin of the Silent Era, is once again ready to make some noise.

Kaufman Astoria Studios.

SIGHTS

Isamu Noguchi Garden Museum. *See p137.*

34th Avenue and Northern Boulevard, and on 34th Avenue, between 76th and 77th Streets, and between 80th and 81st Streets.

FLUSHING

Subway 7 to Main Street, 103rd Street-Corona Plaza, 111th Street, or Willets Point-Shea Stadium.

Egalitarian Dutchmen staked their claim to 'Vlissingen' in the 1600s and were shortly joined by pacifist Friends, or Quakers, seeking religious freedom in the New World. These liberal settlers promulgated the Flushing Remonstrance, a groundbreaking 1657 edict extending 'the law of love, peace and liberty' to Jews and Muslims. It's now regarded as a forerunner of the United States Constitution's First Amendment.

The plain wooden **Friends Meeting House** (137-16 Northern Boulevard, between Main & Union Streets), built in 1694, creates a startling juxtaposition to the prosperous Chinatown that rings its weathered wooden walls. The neighbourhood still boasts hundreds of temples and churches used by immigrants from Korea, China and south Asia. Off Main Street, **St George's Church** (135-32 38th Avenue, between Prince & Main Streets, 1-718 359 1171), an Episcopalian steeple chartered by King George III, was once a dominant site, but now competes for attention with restaurants and shops. The interior is worth a brief visit if only to see the two examples of Queens-made Tiffany stained glass and to hear church

services in Caribbean-accented English, Chinese and Spanish. Ambitious explorers will want to make the jaunt south to the **Hindu Temple Society** (4557 Bowne Street, between Holly & 45th Avenues, 1-718 460 8484), a Ganesh temple whose ornate exterior was hand-carved in India.

The restaurants and dumpling stalls of Flushing's **Chinatown** are another way to commune with the divine. Teenagers tend to love the unique bubble tea – sweet, milky tea loaded with tapioca balls – that you can find in cafés such as doughnut-serving **Sago** (39-02 Main Street, at 39th Avenue, 1-718 353 2899) or tea specialists **Ten Ren** (135-18 Roosevelt Avenue, between Main & Prince Streets, 1-718 461 9305). For weekend brunch, try dim sum at **Gala Manor** (37-02 Main Street, at 37th Avenue, 1-718 888 9293) or Malaysian delicacies at **Sentosa** (39-07 Prince Street, between Roosevelt & 39th Avenues, 1-718 886 6331).

Flushing Town Hall (137-135 Northern Boulevard, at Linden Place, 1-718 463 7700, www.flushingtownhall.org, closed Mon), built during the Civil War in the highly fanciful Romanesque Revival style, showcases local arts groups, and hosts jazz concerts, chamber music and multimedia exhibits. Here you can catch the **Queens Jazz Trail** (1-718 463 7700, www.flushingtownhall.org), a monthly trolley tour of the homes of jazz legends from the borough (Count Basie, Ella Fitzgerald, Dizzy Gillespie, Billie Holiday, John Coltrane et al). The centrepiece is the **Louis Armstrong House** in Corona (*see p140*), a modest brick home in a working-class community that 'Satchmo' never abandoned.

INSIDE TRACK
59TH STREET BRIDGE

Hop aboard the 7 subway and you'll be treated to a view of the Manhattan skyline through the elegant spans of the **59th Street Bridge** (aka Queensboro Bridge), completed in 1909. Although nowhere near as famous as the Brooklyn Bridge, it has come to represent New York in everything from F Scott Fitzgerald's *The Great Gatsby* to Woody Allen's *Manhattan*, the opening credits of *Taxi* to Simon & Garfunkel's 'The 59th Street Bridge Song (Feelin' Groovy)'.

The most visited site in Queens is rambling **Flushing Meadows-Corona Park** (*see below*), where the 1939 and 1964/5 World's Fairs were held. Larger than Central Park, it's home to the **Queens Zoo**, where natural environments include a lush parrot habitat; **Queens Theatre in the Park**, an indoor amphitheatre designed by Philip Johnson; the **New York Hall of Science** (*see below*), an acclaimed interactive museum; the **Queens Botanical Garden**, a 39-acre cavalcade of greenery; and the **Queens Museum of Art** (*see below*), which exhibits increasingly avant-garde shows that tie art to the local immigrant experience – fittingly enough for the building that was the first home of the United Nations. Also here are **Citi Field**, the new home to the Mets baseball team (*see p338* **Fields of dreams**); and the USTA (United States Tennis Association) National Tennis Center. The US Open (*see p342*) raises a racket at summer's end, but the general public can play here during the other 11 months of the year.

★ FREE Flushing Meadows-Corona Park

From 111th Street to Van Wyck Expressway, between Flushing Bay & Grand Central Parkway (1-718 760 6565/Queens Zoo 1-718 220 5100/ www.queenszoo.com). Subway 7 to Willets Point-Shea Stadium.

Most Manhattanites only venture out to these parts to catch a Mets game or tennis at the US Open, but visitors will also be enticed by the 1964/5 World's Fair sculptures, particularly the iconic 140-foot-high Unisphere, a mammoth steel globe that was the symbol of the fair (and site of the apocalyptic battle scene between humans and aliens in the first *Men in Black* movie). Also visible are the remnants of the New York State Pavilion, erected by Philip Johnson for the fair. Measuring 350 feet by 250 feet, this now-eerie plaza is bordered by 16 100-ft steel columns.

Louis Armstrong House

34-56 107th Street, between 34th & 37th Avenues, Corona (1-718 478 8274/www.satchmo.net). Subway 7 to 103rd Street-Corona Plaza. **Open** 10am-5pm Tue-Fri; noon-5pm Sat, Sun. *Tours hourly 10am-5pm Tue-Fri; hourly noon-5pm Sat, Sun.* **Admission** $8; $6 reductions; free under-4s. **Credit** ($15 minimum) DC, MC, V.

Pilgrims to the two-storey house where the great 'Satchmo' lived from 1943 until his death in 1971 will find a shrine to the revolutionary trumpet player – as well as his wife's passion for wallpaper. Her decorative attentions extended to the interiors of cupboards, closets – even bathroom cabinets. The 45-minute tour is enhanced by audiotapes of Louis that give much insight into the tranquil domesticity he sought in the then suburban neighbourhood – a far cry from the glamorous life he could have led.
▶ *For more on jazz in New York City, see p325.*

New York Hall of Science

47-01 111th Street, at 47th Avenue, Flushing Meadows-Corona Park (1-718 699 0005/ www.nyscience.org). Subway 7 to 111th Street. **Open** *July, Aug* 9.30am-5pm Mon-Fri; 10am-6pm Sat, Sun. *Sept-June* 9.30am-2pm Mon-Thur; 9.30am-5pm Fri; 10am-6pm Sat, Sun. **Admission** $11; $8 reductions. *Sept-June* free 2-5pm Fri, 10-11am Sun. *Science playground* (open Mar-Dec) extra $4. **Credit** AmEx, DC, Disc, MC, V.

The fun-for-all-ages New York Hall of Science, built for the 1964/5 World's Fair and recently expanded, demystifies its subject matter through colourful hands-on exhibits, with topics such as 'Marvellous Molecules' and 'The Realm of the Atom'. Children can burn off excess energy – and learn a thing or two – in the 30,000 sq ft outdoor science playground, which manages to entertain while it educates.

Queens Museum of Art

New York City Building, park entrance on 49th Avenue, at 111th Street, Flushing Meadows-Corona Park (1-718 592 9700/www.queens museum.org). Subway 7 to 111th Street, then walk south on 111th Street, turning left on to 49th Avenue; continue into the park & over Grand Central Parkway Bridge. **Open** 10am-5pm Wed-Fri; noon-5pm Sat, Sun. **Admission** *Suggested donation* $5; $2.50 reductions. **No credit cards**.

In the grounds of the 1939 and 1964/5 World's Fairs, the QMA holds one of the city's most amazing sights: the Panorama of the City of New York a 9,335-square-foot, 895,000-building scale model (one inch equals 100 feet) of all five boroughs. A new lighting system mimics the arc of the sun as it passes over NYC, yet despite periodic updates of the model, one part of the Panorama remains decidedly untouched – the Twin Towers still stand proudly (albeit one twelve-hundredth of their actual size). Contemporary and visiting exhibits have grown more bold and inventive in recent years, garnering increasing acclaim.

The Bronx

Art deco landmarks, creative enclaves… and wild animals?

The only New York borough that's physically attached to the mainland of America, the Bronx seems much further from Manhattan to most visitors – and, indeed, most Manhattanites – than it really is. Much of this perceived distance is down to the South Bronx's global reputation for urban strife, and it isn't helped by the fact that the borough's two biggest visitor attractions – Yankee Stadium and the Bronx Zoo – are generally covered in quick trips in and out. This is a shame, for the Bronx also glistens with the art deco gems of the Grand Concourse, cooks up a storm with its own Little Italy in Belmont, enchants the city's nature-deprived urbanites with its world-class New York Botanical Garden, and boasts one of the most up-and-coming art scenes in the city in the rejuvenated South Bronx.

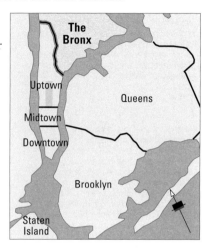

THE BRONX IN BRIEF

The Bronx was settled in the 1630s by the family of Jonas Bronck, a Swedish farmer who had a 500-acre homestead in what is now the south-eastern Morrisania section. The area became known as 'the Broncks' farm; although the spelling was altered, the name stuck. The area was originally part of Westchester County but, like the other boroughs, it was incorporated into New York City in 1898.

Like Queens and Brooklyn, the Bronx in the early 20th century drew much of its population from the ever-expanding pools of Irish, German, Italian and Eastern European Jewish immigrants who flocked to the area for its cheap rents and open spaces. After World War II, as the borough grew more urbanised, the descendants of the European immigrants moved out to the suburbs of Long Island and Westchester, and fresh waves of newcomers, hailing from the Caribbean, Latin America, Africa, Albania and Russia, took their places.

From the late 1940s until the early '70s the Bronx probably witnessed more upheaval than the other areas of the city combined, bearing the brunt of city planner Robert Moses's

drastic remaking of the city. Thousands of residents saw their old apartment buildings razed to make room for the Whitestone and Throgs Neck Bridges, the east-to-west Cross Bronx Expressway and the north-to-south Bruckner Boulevard extension of the New England Thruway. Many areas fell into neglect, a condition exacerbated by the economic and social downturns that plagued the entire city in the 1960s and '70s. The local community felt cut off, forgotten and left to rot, and with good reason. It's only in recent years that the area has started to come alive once more.

THE SOUTH BRONX

Subway 4 to 161st Street-Yankee Stadium; 6 to Hunts Point Avenue, 138th Street-Third Avenue.

In the 1960s and '70s, the **South Bronx** was so ravaged by post-war 'white flight' and community displacement from the construction of the Cross Bronx Expressway that the neighbourhood became virtually synonymous with urban blight. Crime was rife and arson

INSIDE TRACK
BRONX CULTURE TROLLEY

Those wanting a closer look at the up-and-coming South Bronx arts scene should hop on the **Bronx Culture Trolley** (1-718 931 9500 ext 33, www.bronxarts.org), a free shuttle that visits the area's most happening galleries, performance spaces and museums. It runs on the first Wednesday evening of the month, with no service in January or September.

became widespread, as landlords discovered that renovating decayed property was far less lucrative than simply burning it down to collect insurance. During a World Series game at Yankee Stadium in 1977, TV cameras caught a building on fire just blocks away. 'Ladies and gentlemen,' commentator Howard Cosell told the world, 'the Bronx is burning.'

These days, the South Bronx is rising from the ashes. In 2006, Mayor Bloomberg announced the South Bronx Initiative, aiming to revitalise the area, while eco-sensitive organisations such as Sustainable South Bronx (www.ssbx.org) are converting vacant lots into green spaces such as **Barretto Point Park** (between Tiffany & Barretto Streets) and **Hunts Point Riverside Park** (at the foot of Lafayette Avenue on the Bronx River). In 2005, after much delay, Hunts Point became the new home for the city's **Fulton Fish Market** (1-718 378 2356, www.newfultonfishmarket.com), which moved from its long-time Seaport site to a large modern facility.

The area has also seen an influx of young professional refugees from overpriced Manhattan and Brooklyn: new condos are sprouting up, old warehouses are being redeveloped, once-crumbling tenements are being refurbished and, inevitably, chain stores are moving in. Young families have been snapping up the renovated townhouses on Alexander Avenue and furnishing them from the thoroughfare's rejuvenated antiques stores, while industrial lofts on Bruckner Boulevard have become homes to creatives. Yet despite developers' hopes for 'SoBro,' the area has not quite turned into the Next Big Thing. Yet.

Hunts Point is also becoming a creative live-work hub. In 1994, a group of artists and community leaders converted an industrial building into the **Point** (940 Garrison Avenue, at Manida Street, 1-718 542 4139, www.thepoint.org), a predominantly Latino performance space and gallery specialising in photography. The Point also leads lively

walking tours (phone for reservations) that explore the history of locally born music, such as mambo and hip hop. The nearby **Bronx Academy of Arts & Dance** (BAAD; 2nd Floor, 841 Barretto Street, between Garrison & Lafayette Avenues, 1-718 842 5223, www.bronxacademyofartsanddance.org) provides a platform for dance, theatre and visual arts events – including annual festival Out Like That!, celebrating works by lesbian, gay, bisexual and transgender artists – and more than a dozen painters and sculptors work in the academy's studios.

Another artistic South Bronx hotbed can be found further south-west in **Mott Haven**. Here, the **Haven Art Gallery** (50 Bruckner Boulevard, between Alexander & Willis Avenues, 1-718 585 5753, www.havenarts.org) features photojournalism exhibits, large-scale installations and spoken-word performances, while the **Bruckner Bar & Grill** (1 Bruckner Boulevard, at Third Avenue, 1-718 665 2001) lures locals (and curious Manhattanites) with exquisite burgers served in English muffins and occasional poetry readings.

Of course, the vast majority of visitors to the South Bronx are just stopping long enough to take in a baseball game at **Yankee Stadium**, at 161st Street and River Avenue. Some of baseball's most famous legends made history on its diamond, from Babe Ruth to Derek Jeter. But in April 2009, the Yankees will vacate 'the House that Ruth Built' and move to their new home, a brand-new $1.3 billion stadium across the street (*see p337* **Fields of Dreams**). **Monument Park**, which celebrates the exploits of past Yankee heroes, will move to the new site and can be visited, along with the clubhouse and the dugout, as part of a tour ($20 adults, $15 reductions; phone to check) when there isn't a day game.

GRAND CONCOURSE

Subway B, D to 167th Street; B, D, 4 to Kingsbridge Road; 4 to 161st Street-Yankee Stadium.

A few blocks east of Yankee Stadium runs the four-and-a-half-mile **Grand Concourse**, which begins at 138th Street in the South Bronx and ends at Mosholu Parkway just shy of Van Cortlandt Park (*see p145*). Once the most prestigious drag in the Bronx, it's still an absolute must for lovers of art deco. Engineer Louis Risse designed the boulevard in 1892, modelling it after Paris's Champs-Elysées; it was first opened to traffic in 1909, but it wasn't until the arrival of a new subway line that rapid development along the Concourse arrived in the deco style so popular at the time. For its centennial, the boulevard received a modest facelift with new trees and flowers, streetlights, bike lanes and cobblestone sidewalks.

Starting at 161st Street and heading south, look for the permanent street plaques that make up the **Bronx Walk of Fame**, honouring famous Bronxites from Stanley Kubrick to Colin Powell and hip hop 'godfather' Afrika Bambaataa. Heading north, the buildings date mostly from the 1920s to the early '40s, and display the country's largest array of art deco housing. Erected in 1937 at the corner of 161st Street, **888 Grand Concourse** has a large concave entrance of gilded mosaic and is topped by a curvy metallic marquee. Inside, the mirrored lobby's central fountain and sunburst-patterned floor could rival those of any hotel on Miami Beach's Ocean Drive.

The grandest building on the Concourse is the landmark **Andrew Freedman Home**, a 1924 French-inspired limestone palazzo between McClennan and 166th Streets. Freedman, a millionaire subway contractor, left the bulk of his $7 million fortune with instructions to build a poorhouse for the rich – that is, those who had lost their fortunes and were suffering an impecunious old age. It now shelters the Family Preservation Center (FPC), a community-based social service agency. Across the street, the **Bronx Museum of the Arts** (*see below*), established in 1971 in a former synagogue, exhibits socially conscious, contemporary works largely by Bronx-based artists.

A few blocks north, at 1150 Grand Concourse at McClellan Place, is a 1937 art deco jewel notable for the colourful marine-themed mosaic flanking its doors; pause inside the lobby for a glimpse of its two large murals depicting pastoral scenes, which are in sharp contrast with the locale. Near the intersection of Fordham Road, keep an eye out for the Italian rococo exterior of the **Paradise Theater** (2403 Grand Concourse, between Elm Place & E 188th Street), once the largest cinema in the city and now a landmark.

North to Kingsbridge Road sits the **Edgar Allan Poe Cottage** (*see p144*), a small wooden farmhouse where the writer lived from 1846 to 1849. Moved to the Grand Concourse from its original spot on Fordham Road in 1913, the museum has period furniture and details about Poe and his work.

★ Bronx Museum of the Arts
1040 Grand Concourse, at 165th Street (1-718 681 6000/www.bxma.org). Subway B, D to 167th Street Grand Concourse; 4 to 161st Street-Yankee Stadium. **Open** noon-6pm Thur-Mon; noon-8pm Fri. **Admission** $5; $3 reductions. Free to all Fri. **Credit** AmEx, DC, Disc, MC, V. Founded in 1971 and featuring more than 800 works, this multicultural art museum shines a spotlight on 20th- and 21st-century artists that are either Bronx-based or of African, Asian or Latino ancestry. In 2009, the museum will mark the centennial of the Grand Concourse with a year-long exhibit devoted to the boulevard's history.

Bronx Museum of the Arts.

New York Botanical Garden.

Edgar Allan Poe Cottage

*2640 Grand Concourse, at Kingsbridge Road
(1-718 881 8900/www.bronxhistoricalsociety.
org). Subway B, D, 4 to Kingsbridge Road.*
Open 10am-4pm Sat; 1-5pm Sun. **Admission**
$5; $3 reductions. **No credit cards**.
Pay homage to Poe in the very house where he wrote
literary gems including *Annabel Lee* and *The Bells*.
At the time of writing, the cottage was undergoing
a major renovation and is not expected to reopen
until 2010, with a brand-new visitors' centre, whose
sloping shingle roof is supposed to resemble the
wings of the bird from the poet's famous *The Raven*.

BELMONT & BRONX PARK

*Subway B, D, 4 to Fordham Road, then Bx12
bus to Arthur Avenue.*

Originally settled in the late 19th century by
Italian immigrants hired to landscape nearby
Bronx Zoo, **Belmont** is centred on Arthur

INSIDE TRACK
BOTANICAL GARDEN TRAVEL

If you're heading to the Botanical Garden
from Manhattan, look into special tickets
on Metro-North's Harlem line train
from Grand Central Terminal – they
may include admission to the garden
itself. Check www.mta.info for details.

Avenue, lined with delis, bakeries, restaurants
and stores selling T-shirts proclaiming the
locale to be New York's 'real Little Italy'. Still
celebrating masses in Italian, neo-classical **Our
Lady of Mt Carmel Church** (627 E 187th
Street, at Hughes Avenue, 1-718 295 3770) has
been serving the community for more than a
century. You can get a quick survey of Italian-
American history and culture from the modest
exhibits at the **Enrico Fermi Cultural
Center** (in the Belmont Branch Library, 610 E
186th Street, between Arthur & Hughes
Avenues, 1-718 933 6410, closed Sun).

Food, however, is the area's real draw.
Arthur Avenue Retail Market (2344 Arthur
Avenue, between Crescent Avenue & E 186th
Street, closed Sun) is a covered market built in
the 1940s when Mayor Fiorello La Guardia
campaigned to get the pushcarts off the street.
Inside, you'll find **Mike's Deli** (1-718 295 5033),
where you can try the trademark *schiacciata*
sandwich of grilled vegetables. For a full meal,
try old-school, red-sauce joints such as **Mario's**
(2342 Arthur Avenue, between Crescent Avenue
& E 186th Street, 1-718 584 1188, closed Sun),
featured in several *Sopranos* episodes and Mario
Puzo's novel *The Godfather*; **Dominick's** (2335
Arthur Avenue, between Crescent Avenue & E
186th Street, 1-718 733 2807, closed Mon), where
there are no menus (your waiter will guide you
course-by-course through your meal); or the no-
frills but charming **Roberto's** (603 Crescent
Avenue, between Hughes & Arthur Avenue,
1-718 733 9503, closed Sun).

steamy Jungle World, a re-creation of an Asian rain-forest inside a 37,000sq ft building. The super-popular Congo Gorilla Forest has turned 6.5 acres into a dramatic Central African rainforest habitat. A glass-enclosed tunnel winds through the forest, allowing visitors to get close to the dozens of primate families in residence, including 26 majestic western lowland gorillas. For those who prefer cats, Tiger Mountain has six adult Siberian tigers that look particularly regal on snowy days. Recent additions at the zoo include African wild dogs, an aquatic aviary and a butterfly garden, featuring 1,000 colourful flutterers. For visitors who want a bird's-eye view, the Skyfari, an aerial tram ride over the zoo itself, is excellent.

▶ *For other zoos, see p106, p129 and p140.*

New York Botanical Garden

Bronx River Parkway, at Fordham Road (1-718 817 8700/www.nybg.org). Subway B, D to Bedford Park Boulevard, then take the Bx26 bus to Garden gate; or Metro-North (Harlem Line local) from Grand Central Terminal to Botanical Garden. **Open** 10am-6pm Tue-Sun. **Admission** $20; $7-$18 reductions; free under-2s. *Grounds only* $6; $1-$3 reductions. Free to all Wed, 10am-noon Sat. **Credit** AmEx, DC, MC, V.

The serene 250 acres of the New York Botanical Garden comprise 50 gardens and plant collections, including the Rockefeller Rose Garden, the Everett Children's Adventure Garden and the last 50 original acres of a forest that once covered all of New York City. In spring, the gardens are frothy with pastel blossoms, as clusters of lilac, cherry, magnolia and crab apple trees burst into bloom, followed in autumn by vivid foliage in the oak and maple groves. On a rainy day, stay warm and sheltered inside the Enid A Haupt Conservatory, a striking glass-walled greenhouse – the nation's largest – built in 1902. It offers seasonal exhibits, as well as the World of Plants, a series of environmental galleries that takes you on an eco-tour through tropical rainforests, deserts and a palm-tree oasis.

If you're not too stuffed to continue, Belmont is in easy walking distance of **Bronx Park**, home to two of the borough's most celebrated attractions. Make your way east along 187th Street, then south along Southern Boulevard, and you'll come to the **Bronx Zoo** (*see below*). Opened in 1899 by Theodore Roosevelt, it's the largest urban zoo in the US at 265 acres. A 15-minute walk north of the zoo – and still in Bronx Park – brings you to the serene 250 acres of the **New York Botanical Garden** (*see below*), which offers respite from cars and concrete in the form of 50 different gardens.

★ Bronx Zoo/Wildlife Conservation Society

Bronx River Parkway, at Fordham Road (1-718 367 1010/www.bronxzoo.org). Subway 2 to Pelham Parkway, then walk two blocks, turn left at Boston Road and bear right to the zoo's Bronxdale entrance; or Metro-North's Harlem Line to Fordham, then take the Bx9 bus south to the zoo entrance, or the Bx12 bus east to Southern Boulevard, & walk east to the zoo entrance. **Open** *Apr-Oct* 10am-5pm Mon-Fri; 10am-5.30pm Sat, Sun. *Nov-Mar* 10am-4.30pm daily. **Admission** $15; $11-$13 reductions. Pay-what-you-wish Wed. Some rides & exhibitions cost extra. **Credit** AmEx, DC, Disc, MC, V.

Home to more than 4,500 creatures, the zoo shuns cages in favour of indoor and outdoor environments that mimic the natural habitats of its mammals, birds and reptiles. Nearly 100 species, including monkeys, leopards and tapirs, live inside the lush,

RIVERDALE & VAN CORTLANDT PARK

Subway D to Norwood-205th Street; 1 to 242nd Street-Van Cortlandt Park.

Riverdale, along the north-west coast of the Bronx, reflects the borough's suburban past; its huge homes perch on narrow, winding streets that meander toward the Hudson River. The only one you can actually visit is **Wave Hill House** (*see p146*), an 1843 stone mansion set on a former private estate that is now both a cultural and environmental centre. The nearby, 1,146-acre **Van Cortlandt Park** (entrance on Broadway, at 242nd Street) often hosts cricket teams largely made up of West and East

Indians. You can hike through a 100-year-old forest, play golf on the nation's first municipal course or rent horses at stables in the park.

The oldest building in the Bronx is **Van Cortlandt House Museum** (*see below*), a pre-Revolutionary Georgian building built in 1748 and commandeered by both sides during the Revolutionary War. Abutting the park is **Woodlawn Cemetery**, the resting place for such notable souls as Herman Melville, Duke Ellington, Miles Davis, FW Woolworth and Fiorello La Guardia. To help you pay your respects, maps are available at the visitors' entrance at Webster Avenue and E 233rd Street. About five blocks south on Bainbridge Avenue, history buffs will also enjoy stopping in at the Bronx Historical Society's **Museum of Bronx History** (*see below*), set in a lovely 1758 stone farmhouse.

Museum of Bronx History

Valentine-Varian House, 3266 Bainbridge Avenue, between Van Cortlandt Avenue & E 208th Street (1-718 881 8900/www.bronx historicalsociety.org). Subway D to Norwood-205th Street. **Open** 10am-4pm Sat; 1-5pm Sun. **Admission** $3; $2 reductions. **No credit cards.** Operated by the Bronx County Historical Society, the museum's collection of documents and photographs is displayed in the Valentine-Varian House, a Federal-style fieldstone residence built in 1758. ▶ *The society also offers historical tours of the Bronx neighbourhoods.*

Van Cortlandt House Museum

Van Cortlandt Park, entrance on Broadway, at 246th Street (1-718 543 3344/www.van cortlandthouse.org). Subway 1 to 242nd Street-Van Cortlandt Park. **Open** 10am-3pm Tue-Fri; 11am-4pm Sat, Sun. **Admission** $5; $3 reductions; free under-12s. Free to all Wed. **Credit** ($11 minimum) DC, MC, V. A one-time wheat plantation that has since been turned into a colonial museum, Van Cortlandt House was alternately used as headquarters by George Washington and British General Sir William Howe during the Revolutionary War.

INSIDE TRACK
RIVERDALE PARK

Van Cortlandt Park is an appealing place for a stroll, but it's also worth crossing Riverdale to the less celebrated, Hudson River-hugging **Riverdale Park** to wander or cycle its quiet pathways. You can enter this swath of forest preserve along Palisade Avenue, between 232nd and 254th Streets.

Wave Hill House

W 249th Street, at Independence Avenue (1-718 549 3200/www.wavehill.org). Metro-North (Hudson Line local) from Grand Central Terminal to Riverdale. **Open** *mid Apr-mid Oct* 9am-5.30pm Tue-Sun. *Mid Oct-mid Apr* 9am-4.30pm Tue-Sun. **Admission** $6; $2-$3 reductions; free under-6s. Free to all 9am-noon Sat; all day Tue Jan-Apr, July, Aug, Nov, Dec; 9am-noon Tue May, June, Sept, Oct. **No credit cards**.
Laze around in these 28 lush acres overlooking the Hudson River at Wave Hill, a Georgian Revival house that was home to Mark Twain, Teddy Roosevelt and conductor Arturo Toscanini. It's now a spectacular nature preserve and conservation centre, where you can see art exhibits and dance and music performances. The cultivated gardens and woodlands afford excellent views of the river, especially at sunset. The in-house art gallery shows nature-themed exhibits, and the organisation presents year-round concerts, performances and other events.

PELHAM BAY PARK

Subway 6 to Pelham Bay Park.

Pelham Bay Park, in the borough's northeastern corner, is NYC's biggest park, once home to the Siwonay Indians. Take a car or a bike if you want to explore the 2,765 acres; pick up a map at the Ranger Nature Center, near the entrance on Bruckner Boulevard at Wilkinson Avenue. The **Bartow-Pell Mansion Museum** (*see below*), in the park's south-eastern quarter, overlooks Long Island Sound. The park's 13 miles of coastline skirt the Hutchinson River to the west and the Long Island Sound and Eastchester Bay to the east. In summer, locals hit sandy **Orchard Beach**; set up in the 1930s, this 'Riviera of New York' is that rare beast – a Robert Moses creation not universally lamented.

Bartow-Pell Mansion Museum

895 Shore Road North, at Pelham Bay Park (1-718 885 1461/www.bartowpellmansion museum.org). Subway 6 to Pelham Bay Park, then take the Bee-Line bus 45 (ask driver to stop at the Bartow-Pell Mansion; bus does not run on Sun), or take a cab from the subway station. **Open** noon-4pm Wed, Sat, Sun. **Admission** $8; $6 reductions; free under-6s. **Credit** AmEx, DC, MC, V.
Operating as a museum since 1946, this stunning estate dates from 1654, when Thomas Pell bought the land from the Siwonay Indians. It was Robert Bartow, publisher and Pell descendant, who added the 1842 Greek Revival stone mansion, which faces a reflecting pool ringed by gardens.
▶ *Just east of Pelham Bay Park lies City Island, a quasi-New England fishing village in New York City (see p365).*

Staten Island

The ferry is famous – but the destination itself is worth a look.

A recent marketing campaign hailed Staten Island as a slice of Small Town USA in the big city. Certainly, the largely suburban borough has the city's lowest population (470,000), and a study by the Citizens Committee for Children of New York asserted that its lower crime rates, good schools and accessible health care make it the best part of the city in which to bring up kids. But Staten Island isn't simply an idyll out of a John Cougar Mellencamp song. Worsening traffic and gentrification are both local concerns, with *The New York Times* singling out St George, Tompkinsville and Stapleton as a new 'Bohemia by the Bay'. Diversity is also growing, with soaring Mexican, Hindu and Sri Lankan populations. And with a cast of characters including both controversial district Congressman Vito Fossella and the elusive Ninja Burglar, you've got all the elements for an afternoon soap.

In its early days, Staten Island was an isolated community, anonymous until Henry Hudson sailed in and christened it *Staaten Eylandt* (Dutch for 'State's Island') in 1609. Early settlers were driven out by Native Americans, the island's first inhabitants, but the Dutch took hold in 1661, establishing shipping and manufacturing enclaves on the northern shore, and farms and hamlets in the south. It became one of the five boroughs in 1898 but remained a backwater until 1964, when the Verrazano-Narrows Bridge joined the island to Brooklyn's Bay Ridge neighbourhood. Many say that's when small-town Staten Island truly vanished.

Still, many quaint aspects remain – not least the free **Staten Island Ferry** (*see p59*), which links the southern tip of Manhattan with the island's St George terminal. The building offers panoramic views of lower Manhattan's skyline through floor-to-ceiling glass, and recently became home to 400 tropical fish in two 14-foot, 2,244-gallon saltwater tanks. A new outdoor promenade with shops, restaurants and an IMAX theatre is still in development, but promises easier access to many attractions

including *Postcards*, a memorial to the 253 Staten Islanders lost on 9/11, and the **Richmond County Savings Bank Ballpark**, home to four-time minor league champions the Staten Island Yankees.

Across the street, look for the distinctive clocktower of **Borough Hall** (10 Richmond Terrace) and step inside for a peek at the Works Progress Administration murals depicting local history. Also worth a look is the Spanish baroque-styled lobby of the restored 1920s vaudeville venue **St George Theatre** (35 Hyatt Street, at Central Avenue, 1-718 442 2900, www.stgeorgetheatre.com), two blocks inland. The **Staten Island Museum** (75 Stuyvesant Place, at Wall Street, 1-718 727 1135, www.staten islandmuseum.org) lies two blocks north.

Continuing north, then west along Richmond Terrace to Westervelt Avenue, and then uphill two blocks to St Marks Place, you'll come upon the landmark **St George-New Brighton Historic District**, full of Queen Anne and Colonial Revival buildings from the early 1830s. An artsy crowd favours **Bay Street** for the offbeat **Cargo Café** (120 Bay Street, 1-718 876

0539, http://cargocafe.com) and two **Every Thing Goes** shops (1-718 273 7139, www.etg stores.com, closed Mon & Sun), run by a local hippie commune.

The bustle subsides inland. A short bus ride west along Richmond Terrace, you could spend an entire day looking around the 83-acre **Snug Harbor Cultural Center** (*see p149*) and the **Staten Island Zoo** (*see p149*), adjacent to the Clove Lakes Park, boasts a rainforest and one of the East Coast's largest reptile collections.

Both buses and the single-line Staten Island Railroad depart from St George for destinations along the eastern half of the island. Along Hylan Boulevard is photographer **Alice Austen's house** (*see below*), a 15-minute bus ride east of the ferry. At the east end of Bay Street, **Fort Wadsworth** (*see below*) is one of the oldest military sites in the nation. From here, you can take in views of the Verrazano bridge and downtown Manhattan from one of NYC's highest points. Further along the eastern coast runs the two-mile **FDR Boardwalk**: the fourth longest in the world, it runs by South Beach, a sandy strip that's great for picnicking, fishing, beach volleyball and swimming.

If you're seeking a more spiritual calm, head to the centre of the island to the **Jacques Marchais Museum of Tibetan Art** (*see p149*), a reproduction of a Himalayan mountain temple. Nearby, guides in period garb offer tours of **Historic Richmond Town** (*see p149*), the island's one-time county seat. A stone's throw away, **High Rock Park** (*see below*) is the entry point for more than 30 miles of hiking trails, part of the 2,800-acre **Greenbelt** (www.sigreenbelt.org).

Opportunities for good, clean fun abound on the island's south-eastern coast (a 40-minute ride on the S78 bus), where you can swim, picnic and fish at **Wolfe's Pond Park** (Cornelia Avenue, at Hylan Boulevard, 1-718 984 8266). To the west, **Sandy Ground Historical Society** (1538 Woodrow Road, at Bloomingdale Road, 1-718-317-5796, closed Mon) celebrates the history of America's first settlement of free blacks. A little further south, **Conference House** (*see below*), site of a failed attempt at peace between American and British in 1776, is now a museum of colonial life.

The island is growing greener. **Fresh Kills Park**, 2,200 acres of land that once served as New York's garbage dump, is slated to become the city's largest park – three times the size of Central Park. While the project's completion is 30 years away, the Parks Department currently offers tours of the site twice a month (see www.nycparks.org). The finished park will include a sports stadium, cycling trails and a monument to the World Trade Center on the site where its wreckage rested after 9/11.

Alice Austen House
2 Hylan Boulevard, between Bay & Edgewater Streets (1-718 816 4506/www.aliceausten.org). From the Staten Island Ferry, take the S51 bus to Hylan Boulevard. **Open** *Mar-Dec* noon-5pm Thur-Sun. **Admission** *Suggested donation $2.* **No credit cards.**
Alice Austen's beautiful turn-of-the-19th-century photographs are the highlight at this 18th-century cottage: there are no fewer than 3,000 of Austen's glass negative photos here. The restored house and grounds often host concerts and events, and offers breathtaking harbour views.

Conference House (Billopp House)
7455 Hylan Boulevard, at Craig Avenue (1-718 984 0415/www.theconferencehouse.org). From the Staten Island Ferry, take the S78 bus to Craig Avenue. **Open** *Apr-mid Dec* 1-4pm Fri-Sun. **Admission** $3; $2 reductions. **No credit cards.**
In 1776, Britain's Lord Howe parlayed with John Adams and Benjamin Franklin in this 17th-century house, the only surviving pre-Revolutionary manor in the city, while trying to stop the American Revolution. Tours point out 18th-century furnishings, decor and daily objects such as quill pens and cookware. The lovely grounds command a terrific view over Raritan Bay, and provide a picturesque setting for free concerts and events.

FREE Fort Wadsworth
East end of Bay Street (1-718 354 4500). From the Staten Island Ferry, take the S51 bus to Fort Wadsworth on weekdays, Von Briesen Park on weekends. **Open** dawn-dusk daily. *Visitors' Center* 10am-5pm Wed-Sun. *Tours* phone for schedule. **Admission** free.
Explore the fortifications that guarded NYC for almost 200 years at Ford Wadsworth, which was occupied by a blockhouse as far back as the 17th century. You can take one of several themed tours, such as the popular evening lantern-light events.

FREE High Rock Park
200 Nevada Avenue, at Rockland Avenue (1-718 667 2165/www.sigreenbelt.org). From the Staten Island Ferry, take the S62 bus to Manor Road, then the S54 bus to Nevada Avenue. **Open** dawn-dusk daily. *Greenbelt Nature Center Visitors' Center (700 Rockland Avenue, at Brielle Avenue, 1-718 351 3450)* 10am-5pm Tue-Sun. **Admission** free.
At the 90-acre High Rock Park, visitors can hike the mile-long Swamp Trail, climb Todt Hill or explore trails through forests, meadows and wetlands.

★ Historic Richmond Town
441 Clarke Avenue, between Richmond Road & St Patrick's Place (1-718 351 1611/www.historic richmondtown.org). From the Staten Island

Ford Wadsworth

Ferry, take the S74 bus to St Patrick's Place. **Open** *Sept-June* 1-5pm Wed-Sun. *July, Aug* 11am-5pm Wed-Fri; 1-5pm Sat, Sun. Closed 1st wk Jan. **Admission** $5; $3.50-$4 reductions; free under-5s. **No credit cards**.
This colonial-era 'living museum' includes residences, public buildings and the oldest schoolhouse in the nation; it dates back to 1695. Tours and activities, from pumpkin picking to quilting, are available.

Jacques Marchais Museum of Tibetan Art
338 Lighthouse Avenue, off Richmond Road (1-718 987 3500/www.tibetanmuseum.org). From the Staten Island Ferry, take the S74 bus to Lighthouse Avenue. **Open** 1-5pm Wed-Sun. **Admission** $5; $3 reductions; free under-6s. **Credit** AmEx, DC, MC, V.
This tiny museum contains a formidable Buddhist altar, tranquil meditation gardens and the largest collection of Tibetan art outside that region. The museum also hosts meditation workshops and t'ai chi classes; a Tibetan festival is held every October.

Staten Island Zoo
614 Broadway, between Glenwood Place & Colonial Court (1-718 442 3100/www.staten islandzoo.org). From the Staten Island Ferry, take the S48 bus to Broadway. **Open** 10am-4.45pm daily. **Admission** $7; $4-$5 reductions; free under-3s. Free to all 2-4.45pm Wed (suggested donation $2). **Credit** AmEx, DC, Disc, MC, V.
Home of 'Staten Island Chuck', NYC's very own furry Groundhog Day forecaster, also holds one of the East Coast's largest reptile and amphibian collections.
▶ *For other zoos see p106, p129, p140 and p145.*

Snug Harbor Cultural Center

1000 Richmond Terrace, between Snug Harbor Road & Tysen Avenue (1-718 448 2500/tickets 1-718 815 7684/www.snug-harbor.org). From the Staten Island Ferry, take bus S40 bus to the north gate (tell the bus driver).
Stately Greek Revival structures form the nucleus of this former sailors' retirement home. Dating from 1833, the centre was converted into a visual- and performing arts complex that includes two art spaces, a botanical garden and a children's museum; the **Noble Maritime Collection**, which holds various artworks by John A Noble (1-718 447 6490, www.noble-maritime.org, closed Mon-Wed); plus a 400-seat auditorium and the city's oldest concert venue.

FREE Art Lab
1-718 447 8667/www.artlab.info. **Open** 9am-8pm Mon-Thur; 9am-5pm Fri-Sun. **Admission** free.
This non-profit space runs classes in fine arts, crafts and photography for kids and adults. The gallery shows the work of a different local artist each month.

Newhouse Center for Contemporary Art
1-718 448 2500/www.newhousecenter.org. **Open** 10am-5pm Tue-Sun. **Admission** $3; $2 reductions. **Credit** AmEx, DC, MC, V.
Staten Island's premier venue for contemporary art holds two or three annual exhibits from leading international sculptors, painters and mixed-media artists in its 15,000sq ft gallery.

FREE Staten Island Botanical Garden
1-718 273 8200/www.sibg.org. **Open** dawn-dusk daily. **Admission** *Chinese Scholar's Garden* $5; $4 reductions. *Grounds & other gardens* free. **Credit** AmEx, DC, MC, V.
Stroll through more than 20 themed gardens, including the traditional Chinese Scholar's Garden, with its pavilions, meandering paths and delicate footbridges, and the medieval-style Secret Garden, complete with 38-foot-high castle and a maze.

Staten Island Children's Museum
1-718 273 2060/www.statenislandkids.org. **Open** *Sept-late June* noon-5pm Tue-Fri; 10am-5pm Sat, Sun. *Late June-Aug* 10am-5pm Tue-Sun. **Admission** $5. **Credit** AmEx, DC, MC, V.
This museum's hands-on exhibits, workshops and after-school programmes entertain kids of all ages.

SIGHTS

Consume

Hotels

Take your pick of bedrooms in the city that never sleeps.

Although prices can be high, New York has never been short of accommodation options. A recent surge in development hasn't just hit the expected neighbourhoods (Tribeca, Midtown, the Upper West Side), but also previously under-served areas like the Lower East Side and Brooklyn. New shingles include **Hotel Le Bleu**, a stylish addition to otherwise sedate Park Slope, and the **Thompson Lower East Side**, which joins 60 Thompson, 6 Columbus and Gild Hall in Thompson's growing NYC empire. On the Upper East Side, meanwhile, the **Pierre**, grande

dame of the city's hotel scene, was due to reopen following a massive $100 million renovation as this guide went to press.

Want to splurge? Check into the ultra-exclusive **Greenwich Hotel**, Robert De Niro's latest Tribeca venture. But if you've got Frette tastes on an Ikea budget, a new wave of chic hostel-style lodgings offer modest accommodation with a bit of boutique gloss (*see p165* **Cheap Chic Sleep**).

CONSUME

PRICES AND INFORMATION

Rates can vary wildly within a single property, and the prices quoted here – obtained from the hotels – reflect that disparity. Unless indicated, the prices given are for a double room, from the cheapest in low season to the most expensive in high season. Of course, the prices quoted here are not guaranteed, but they offer a good indication of the hotel's average rack rates – what you would pay if you walked in off the street and asked for a room. Special deals are often available, and you can frequently shave more off the price by booking on the hotel's website. Reservation agencies are able to offer reduced rates by pre-booking blocks of rooms. Try **www.hotels.com**, **www.priceline.com**, **www.expedia.com**, **www.lastminute.com** or the New York-based **Quikbook** (1-212 779 7666, 1-800 789 9887, www.quikbook.com).

Thousands of B&B rooms are available. However, in the absence of a central organisation, they can be hard to find.

> ❶ Red numbers given in this chapter correspond to the location of each hotel on the street maps. *See pp403-412.*

New York Habitat (1-212 255 8018, www.nyhabitat.com) arranges a variety of services, from B&Bs to short-term furnished apartment rentals, while **City Sonnet** (1-212 614 3034, www.citysonnet.com) is an artist-run agency specialising in downtown locations. Expect to pay at least $135 for a room. Many B&Bs are unhosted, and breakfast is usually continental (if it's served at all), but the vibe is likely to be more personal than in a hotel. For a longer visit, it can be cheaper and more convenient to rent a place of your own. For gay-friendly B&Bs (where straight guests are often welcome too), *see p308.*

Downtown

FINANCIAL DISTRICT

Expensive

Gild Hall
15 Gold Street, at Platt Street, New York, NY 10038 (1-212 232 7700/www.thompson hotels.com). Subway A, C to Broadway-Nassau Street; J, M, Z, 2, 3, 4, 5 to Fulton Street. **Rates** $289-$699 double. **Rooms** 126. **Credit** AmEx, DC, Disc, MC, V. **Map** p402 F32 ❶

Thompson Hotels brings its luxury aesthetic to the Financial District; the group took over this small boutique property, formerly the Wall Street District Hotel, in 2008. The lodge-like lobby is breathtaking, with wood accents, leather sofas, a faux antler chandelier and photographs by the late society lensman Slim Aarons. A split-level library and champagne bar are further enticements. Rooms are more modestly sized, but fitted out with sleek custom-made wood furnishings, high-definition flat screens, 400-thread-count Sfera linens and minibars stocked by gourmet grocer Dean & DeLuca. For something more substantial, repair to the Libertine, a modern spin on a traditional British tavern devised by celebrity chef Todd English.
Bar. Business centre. Concierge. Disabled-adapted rooms. Gyms (3). Internet (wireless; free). No smoking floors. Parking ($45). Restaurant. Room service. TV: pay movies.
Other locations *See below* 60 Thompson.

TRIBECA & SOHO

Deluxe

★ Greenwich Hotel
377 Greenwich Street, between Franklin & North Moore Streets, New York, NY 10013 (1-212 941 8900/www.thegreenwichhotel.com). Subway 1 to Franklin Street. **Rates** $625-$825 double. **Rooms** 88. **Credit** AmEx, DC, Disc, MC, V. **Map** p402 D31 ❷
Well-heeled travellers love Robert de Niro's lavish Tribeca bolthole, which opened to much fanfare in April 2008. It's so exclusive, there's no sign at the entrance. Even the more modest courtyard rooms have hardwood floors, plush sofas, walk-in showers and French doors that open on to the private patio. Design elements include rustic factory beams in the lobby's ceiling and the lumber from a 250-year-old Japanese farmhouse that shelters the downstairs Shibui Spa, housing a shiatsu massage room and lantern-lit swimming pool. When hunger hits, stroll over to chef Agostino Sciandri's Ago restaurant for light fare or a full meal (the 22-ounce *bistecca alla Fiorentina* is the house speciality). *Photos pp154-155. Bar. Internet (wireless; free). Pool (1 indoor). Restaurant. Spa.*
▶ *For more details of Robert de Niro's Tribeca empire, see p72.*

Mercer
147 Mercer Street, at Prince Street, New York, NY 10012 (1-212 966 6060/1-888 918 6060/ www.mercerhotel.com). Subway N, R, W to Prince Street. **Rates** $595-$820 double. **Rooms** 75. **Credit** AmEx, DC, Disc, MC, V. **Map** p403 E29 ❸
Opened in 2001 by red-hot hotelier André Balazs, Soho's first luxury boutique hotel still has ample flourishes to keep it a notch above nearby competitors, which may be why celebs like Marc Jacobs and

Mischa Barton favour it. The lobby, appointed with oversized white couches and chairs, and shelves lined with colourful books, acts as a bar, library and lounge – exclusive to hotel guests. The loft-like rooms are large by New York standards and feature furniture by Christian Liagre, enormous washrooms and Face Stockholm products. The restaurant, Mercer Kitchen, serves Jean-Georges Vongerichten's stylish version of casual American cuisine. Secreted two levels down, the Submercer lounge recently reopened after five years.
Bars (2). Concierge. Disabled-adapted rooms. Internet (wireless; free). No smoking rooms. Parking ($55). Restaurant. Room service.

Expensive

Duane Street Hotel
130 Duane Street, at Church Street, New York, NY 10013 (1-212 964 4600/www.duanestreet hotel.com). Subway A, C, 1, 2, 3 to Chambers Street. **Rates** $319-$420 double. **Rooms** 45. **Credit** AmEx, DC, Disc, MC, V. **Map** p402 E31 ❹
Hersha Hospitality – which also operates Hotel 373 in Manhattan (373 Fifth Avenue, at 35th Street, 1-212 213 3388, www.hotel373.com) and Nu Hotel in Brooklyn (*see p174*) – opened this boutique accommodation in 2007 and, after a somewhat rocky start, seems to have got back on track with improved customer service and better soundproofing. The small, understated rooms are accented with a warm colour palette and dark mahogany floors, and feature plasma-screen TVs and slate-and-marble bathrooms with glass-enclosed, rain-style showers. The intimate vibe is continued at 'beca, the hotel's 40-seat restaurant, where Chef Kristiaan Ueno cooks up Asian and Mediterranean cuisine. *Photo p158. Bar. Business centre. Concierge. Internet (wireless; free). No smoking. Parking ($25). Restaurant. Room service.*

60 Thompson
60 Thompson Street, between Broome & Spring Streets, New York, NY 10012 (1-212 431 0400/ 1-877 431 0400/www.60thompson.com). Subway

CONSUME

Greenwich Hotel. See p153.

C, E to Spring Street. **Rates** $399-$819 double.
Rooms 97. **Credit** AmEx, DC, Disc, MC, V.
Map p403 E30 ⑤
Designed by high-profile interior decorator Thomas
O'Brien, this stylish hotel has been luring chic
jet-setters since it opened in 2001. Don't be surprised
if you have to walk through a photo shoot when you
enter – it's a popular backdrop with the fashion
crowd. A60, the exclusive guests-only rooftop bar,
offers commanding city views and its Moroccan-
inspired decor is particularly magazine-spread-
worthy. The modern rooms are dotted with pampering details like pure down duvets and pillows
and the acclaimed restaurant Kittichai serves a
sumptuous spread of creative Thai cuisine beside a
pool filled with floating orchids. In warmer months,
be sure to request a table on the pavement terrace.
Bars (2). Concierge. Disabled-adapted rooms.
Gym. Internet (wireless; free). No smoking floors.
Parking ($55). Restaurant. Room service. TV:
DVD/pay movies.

INSIDE TRACK
THE KEMPS ARRIVE

A highly anticipated addition to Soho's
hotel scene is the **Crosby Street Hotel**,
the first US outpost from the London-
based Firmdale group (www.firmdale.
com), owned by Tim and Kit Kemp.
Due to open in May 2009, the hotel will
have 86 bedrooms and suites, plus a
restaurant and bar with garden.

Other locations Gild Hall (*see p152*);
Thompson Lower East Side, 190 Allen Street,
between Houston & Stanton, New York, NY
10002 (1-212 460 5300); 6 Columbus, 6 Columbus
Circle, Upper West Side, New York, NY 10019
(1-212 204 3000).

SoHo Grand Hotel
*310 West Broadway, between Canal & Grand
Streets, New York, NY 10013 (1-212 965 3000/
1-800 965 3000/www.sohogrand.com). Subway
A, C, E, 1 to Canal Street.* **Rates** $359-$609
double. **Rooms** 365. **Credit** AmEx, DC, Disc,
MC, V. **Map** p403 E30 ⑥
Fittingly, this Soho property makes good use
of industrial materials like poured concrete, cast
iron and bottle glass (used for the staircase). Built
in 1996, the Bill Sofield-designed rooms (including
two spacious penthouse lofts) are in a restrained
palette of greys and beiges accented by natural
materials. (The tranquil vibe is fortified by luxe
Frette Egyptian cotton bedding and robes and
Malin+Goetz bath products. Bizarrely, you can also
boost your soothing in-room experience by request-
ing a gold fish for the duration of your stay.) There
are free bicycles if you want to explore the area;
alternatively, hole up, order a cocktail in the Grand
Bar and Lounge, or dine on haute macaroni and
cheese in the Gallery.
*Bars (2). Business centre. Concierge. Disabled-
adapted rooms. Gym. Internet (wireless; $9.95/day).
No smoking floors. Restaurants (3). Room service.*
Other locations Tribeca Grand Hotel, 2 Sixth
Avenue, between Walker & White Streets,
Tribeca, New York, NY 10013 (1-877 519 6600).

Moderate

★ Cosmopolitan

95 West Broadway, at Chambers Street, New York, NY 10007 (1-212 566 1900/1-888 895 9400/www.cosmohotel.com). Subway A, C, 1, 2, 3 to Chambers Street. **Rates** $215-$300 double. **Rooms** 150. **Credit** AmEx, DC, MC, V. **Map** p402 E31 ❼

Despite the name, you won't find froufrou cocktails at this well-maintained hotel in two adjacent 1850s buildings – or even a bar in which to drink them. The Cosmopolitan is geared towards travellers with little need for extras. Open continuously since the mid 19th century, it remains a tourist favourite for its address, clean rooms and reasonable rates. *Internet (wireless; free). No smoking.*

LITTLE ITALY & NOLITA

Moderate

SoHotel

341 Broome Street, between Elizabeth Street & Bowery, New York, NY 10013 (1-212 226 1482/www.sohotel-ny.com). Subway J, M, Z to Bowery; 6 to Spring Street. **Rates** $119-$239 double. **Rooms** 100. **Credit** AmEx, DC, Disc, MC, V. **Map** p403 F30 ❽

This modest hotel at the nexus of Chinatown, Little Italy and Nolita has a rich history befitting its storied locale – General George Washington and his troops took command of the city on this spot in 1783, and in previous incarnations, the hotel hosted financier William Waldorf Astor and boxing legend Gentleman Jim Corbett, among other colourful guests. Today, the rooms are small and basic, and amenities largely non-existent. But charming touches like large framed paintings, hardwood floors, stucco walls and vaulted ceilings place the SoHotel a rung above similar establishments. Complimentary morning coffee is served in the lobby. *Internet (wireless; free). No smoking rooms.*

LOWER EAST SIDE

Expensive

Blue Moon

100 Orchard Street, between Delancey & Broome Streets, New York, NY 10002 (1-212 533 9080/www.bluemoon-nyc.com). Subway F to Delancey Street. **Rates** $340-$1,050 double. **Rooms** 22. **Credit** AmEx, DC, Disc, MC, V. **Map** p403 F30 ❾

This eight-storey, 22-room hotel housed in a former 19th-century tenement eschews chic modernism in favour of old-world charm. (Owner Randy Settenbrino incorporated historic newspaper clippings, ads and photos he discovered during renovation into the decor, complementing original wood mouldings, art nouveau fixtures and wrought-iron beds.) Amenities are limited, but Orchard Street and the surrounding thoroughfares offer dozens of boutiques, restaurants, bars and clubs. Some rooms come with views of the nearby Williamsburg Bridge. *Concierge. Internet (wireless; free). No smoking.*
▶ *There's more history next door at the Lower East Side Tenement Museum; see p77.*

CONSUME

Bowery Hotel

335 Bowery, at E 3rd Street, New York, NY 10003 (1-212 505 9100/www.thebowery hotel.com). Subway B, D, F, V to Broadway-Lafayette Street; 6 to Bleecker Street. **Rates** $425-$1,200 double. **Rooms** 135. **Credit** AmEx, DC, Disc, MC, V. **Map** p403 F29 ➓

This fanciful boutique hotel from Eric Goode and Sean MacPherson (the team behind ultra-exclusive restaurant the Waverly Inn, as well as the Maritime Hotel and the Jane; *see p160*) is the capstone in the gentrification of the Bowery. Shunning minimalism, the duo have created plush rooms that pair old-world touches (oriental rugs, wood-beamed ceilings, marble washstands) with modern amenities (Wi-Fi, flat-screen TVs, DVD library). Floor-to-ceiling windows offer stunning views of the neighbourhood's historic tenements and two years after the Bowery opened its doors, city scene-seekers continue to line up to eat (Italian restaurant Gemma), drink (Lobby Bar) and sleep here. If you're lucky enough to pop in during a lull, cosy up by the fire in the wood-panelled lobby.

Bars (2). Concierge. Disabled-adapted rooms. Internet (wireless; free). No smoking rooms. Parking ($45). Restaurant. Room service. TV: DVD/pay movies.

★ Hotel on Rivington

107 Rivington Street, between Essex & Ludlow Streets, New York, NY 10002 (1-212 475 2600/ www.hotelonrivington.com). Subway F to Delancey Street; J, M, Z to Delancey-Essex Streets. **Rates** $389-$595 double. **Rooms** 110. **Credit** AmEx, DC, Disc, MC, V. **Map** p403 G29 ⓫

Floor-to-ceiling windows are a theme throughout this 20-storey posh palace: the second-floor lobby overlooks the storefronts of Rivington Street, and every chic-but-simple room (by Parisian designer India Mahdavi) has an unobstructed city view. Even Thor, the eclectic restaurant now run by Stanton Social executive chef Jesi Solomon, has a 21ft glass ceiling. To make the most of the potential for exhibitionism, get your tresses tamed at the onsite Ricardo Rojas Salon before slipping into a banquette at 105 Riv, the wildly popular street-level bar.

Bars (2). Concierge. Gym. Internet (wireless; free). No smoking floors. Parking ($50). Restaurant.

Moderate

★ Off Soho Suites Hotel

11 Rivington Street, between Bowery & Chrystie Street, New York, NY 10002 (1-212 979 9808/ 1-800 633 7646/www.offsoho.com). Subway B, D to Grand Street; F, V to Lower East Side-Second Avenue; J, M, Z to Bowery. **Rates** $179-$399 double. **Rooms** 38. **Credit** AmEx, DC, MC, V. **Map** p403 F30 ⓬

These no-frills suites became a great deal more popular after the hip restaurant Freemans (*see p185*)

opened at the end of the alley across the street a few years ago. The rates are decent value for the now-thriving Lower East Side location and the spartan but spacious rooms accommodate either two or four guests (the latter have an added sleeper sofa). Budget travellers can save money by using the in-room kitchenettes and washing their clothes in the basement coin-operated laundry.

Concierge. Disabled-adapted rooms. Gym. Internet (wireless; free). No smoking rooms.

EAST VILLAGE

Moderate

Hotel East Houston

151 E Houston Street, at Eldridge Street, New York, NY 10002 (1-212 777 0012/www.hoteleast houston.com). Subway F, V to Lower East Side-Second Avenue. **Rates** $249-$299 double. **Rooms** 42. **Credit** AmEx, DC, Disc, MC, V. **Map** p403 G29 ⓭

Opened in autumn 2007, this six-storey building continues the Lower East Side's boutique hotel boom with rooms dressed up in rococo-inspired wallpaper and a rich colour palette of golds, chocolate and pomegranate. As enticing as the living quarters are – complete with flat-screen, high-definition TVs – you'll want to spend much of your time soaking up the sun (and views) on the rooftop patio.

Business centre. Concierge. Disabled-adapted rooms. Internet (high-speed, wireless; free). No smoking. TV: DVD/pay movies.

Budget

East Village Bed & Coffee

110 Avenue C, between 7th & 8th Streets, New York, NY 10009 (1-212 533 4175/www.bedandcoffee.com). Subway F, V to Lower East Side-Second Avenue; L to First Avenue. **Rates** $105-$140 double. **Rooms** 9. **Credit** AmEx, DC, MC, V. **Map** p403 G28 ⓮

Popular with European travellers, this East Village B&B (minus the breakfast) embodies quirky downtown culture. Each of the nine guest rooms has a unique theme: for example, the 'Black and White Room' or the 'Treehouse' (not as outlandish as it sounds, with an ivory and olive colour scheme, animal-print linens and a whitewashed brick wall). Owner Anne Edris encourages guests to mingle in the communal areas, which include fully equipped kitchens and three loft-like living rooms (bathrooms are also shared). When the weather's nice, sip your complimentary morning java in the private garden.

Internet (wireless; free). No smoking (except in garden).

Other locations Second Home on Second Avenue, 221 Second Avenue, between 13th & 14th Streets, East Village, New York, NY 10003 (1-212 677 3161).

CONSUME

Hotel 17

225 E 17th Street, between Second & Third Avenues, New York, NY 10003 (1-212 475 2845/www.hotel17ny.com). Subway L to Third Avenue; N, Q, R, W, 4, 5, 6 to 14th Street-Union Square. **Rates** $99-$240 double. **Rooms** 125. **Credit** DC, MC, V. **Map** p403 F27 **⑮**

Shabby chic is the best way to describe this East Village hotel, located a few blocks from Union Square. Past the minuscule but well-appointed lobby, the rooms are a study in contrast, as antique dressers are paired with paisley bedspreads and mismatched vintage wallpaper. In most cases, bathrooms are shared between two to four rooms, but they're kept immaculately clean. Over the years, the building has been featured in numerous fashion mag layouts and films – including Woody Allen's *Manhattan Murder Mystery* – and has put up Madonna, and, more recently, transsexual downtown diva Amanda Lepore. Who knows who you might bump into on your way to the loo? *Concierge. Internet (wireless; free). No smoking floors. Room service. TV: DVD.*

Duane Street Hotel. *See p153.*

CONSUME

★ St Marks Hotel

*2 St Marks Place, at Third Avenue, New York,
NY 10003 (1-212 674 0100/www.stmarkshotel.
net). Subway 6 to Astor Place.* **Rates** $140-$170
double. **Rooms** 64. **No credit cards.**
Map p403 F28 ⑯

Nestled among the tattoo parlours, sushi joints and
piercing shops of St Marks Place, this small hotel
received a much needed facelift in 2007; its modest
rooms, which have double beds and private baths,
are now bright, warm and understated (if somewhat
bland) and offer Wi-Fi and flat-screen TVs. Note that
the hotel is in a pre-war building with no lifts.
*Bar. Concierge. Internet (wireless; $10/day).
No smoking rooms. Restaurant. TV: DVD.*
▶ *St Marks is within stumbling distance of
dozens of hot East Village bars and restaurants;
see p215 and p184 respectively.*

Hostels

Bowery's Whitehouse Hotel of New York

*340 Bowery, between 2nd & 3rd Streets, New
York, NY 10012 (1-212 477 5623/www.white
househotelofny.com). Subway B, D, F, V to
Broadway-Lafayette Street; 6 to Bleecker Street.*
Rates $53.90-$56.50 double. **Rooms** 200. **Credit**
AmEx, DC, Disc, MC, V. **Map** p403 F29 ⑰

Even as the Bowery becomes progressively
upscale, with new pricey restaurants and clubs
popping up almost weekly, the unapologetically
budget Whitehouse remains steadfastly bare-
bones. Built in 1919 as housing for railroad workers, the renovated hostel offers curfew-free access
to semi-private cubicles at unbelievably low rates.
(Be warned, though, that the ceilings are an open
latticework, so noisy neighbours may interrupt
your slumber.) Towels and linens are provided, and
a microwave and large-screen TV are available
in the lounge.
Internet (wireless; $5/day). No smoking.

GREENWICH VILLAGE

Moderate

Washington Square Hotel

*103 Waverly Place, between MacDougal Street
& Sixth Avenue, New York, NY 10011 (1-212
777 9515/1-800 222 0418/www.washington
squarehotel.com). Subway A, B, C, D, E, F, V
to W 4th Street.* **Rates** $215-$235 double.
Rooms 155. **Credit** AmEx, DC, MC, V.
Map p403 E28 ⑱

This quintessential Greenwich Village hotel has
been a haven for writers and artists for decades, and
also has something of a rock 'n' roll past: Bob Dylan
and Joan Baez both lived here way back when they
sang for change in nearby Washington Square Park.
Today, the century-old hotel remains popular with

travellers wanting to soak up Village life. The deluxe
rooms come with art deco furnishings and leather
headboards, and the cosy bar-lounge serves afternoon tea and light fare. Rates include a continental
breakfast – or you can splurge on the Sunday jazz
brunch at North Square, the hotel's restaurant.
*Bars (2). Disabled-adapted rooms. Gym. Internet
(wireless; free, lobby only). No smoking.
Restaurant.*

Budget

Larchmont Hotel

*27 W 11th Street, between Fifth & Sixth
Avenues, New York, NY 10011 (1-212 989
9333/www.larchmonthotel.com). Subway F, V
to 14th Street; L to Sixth Avenue.* **Rates** $119-
$149 double. **Rooms** 66. **Credit** AmEx, DC, MC,
V. **Map** p403 E28 ⑲

Housed in a 1910 Beaux Arts building, the attractive, affordable Larchmont may be the best value in
Greenwich Village. The decor (wicker furniture, floral bedspreads) recalls the *The Golden Girls*, but with
prices this reasonable, you can accept low marks for
style. All the bathrooms are shared, but rooms come
with a washbasin, bathrobe and slippers.
Internet (wireless; free). No smoking.

WEST VILLAGE & MEATPACKING DISTRICT

Deluxe

★ Hotel Gansevoort

*18 Ninth Avenue, at 13th Street, New York,
NY 10014 (1-212 206 6700/1-877 426 7386/
www.hotelgansevoort.com). Subway A, C, E to
14th Street; L to Eighth Avenue.* **Rates** $635-
$675 double. **Rooms** 186. **Credit** AmEx, DC,
Disc, MC, V. **Map** p403 C28 ⑳

It's hard to miss this commanding hotel – a soaring
14-floor contemporary structure that stands out
against the cobbled streets and warehouse storefronts of the Meatpacking District. Designed by
Stephen B Jacobs, the five-year-old luxury property
gets strong marks for style. Guests enter through
the world's tallest revolving door into a lobby featuring four 18ft light boxes that change colour
throughout the evening. The sleek rooms offer a
more muted colour scheme, but are fitted with plush
feather beds and photography from local artists.
(The roomy marble bathrooms are stocked with
Cutler toiletries.) The roof garden has a pool with
underwater music and 360-degree views of the city
and Jeffrey Chodorow's glossy Japanese eaterie Ono
has private dining huts and a robatayaki bar – all
behind a red velvet rope. For R&R, there's a subterranean spa and a rooftop bar, Plunge.
*Bars (3). Business centre. Gym. Internet
(wireless; free). Pool (1 outdoor). Restaurant.
Room service. Spa.*

CONSUME

Moderate

Abingdon Guest House

*21 Eighth Avenue, between Jane & W 12th
Streets, New York, NY 10014 (1-212 243
5384/www.abingdonguesthouse.com). Subway A,
C, E to 14th Street; L to Eighth Avenue.* **Rates**
$189-$305 double. **Rooms** 9. **Credit** AmEx, DC,
Disc, MC, V. **Map** p403 D28 ㉑

A charming option for those who want to be close
to the Meatpacking District but can't afford the
Gansevoort (*see p159*). Rooms in the converted townhouse are done up in plush fabrics, antique furnishings (many with four-posters) and have private baths.
Internet (wireless; free). No smoking.

Budget

★ Jane

*113 Jane Street, at West Street, New York, NY
10014 (1-212 924 6700/www.thejanenyc.com).
Subway A, C, E to 14th Street; L to Eighth
Avenue.* **Rates** $99 single, $250 double.
Rooms 208. **Credit** AmEx, DC, Disc, MC, V.
Map p403 D28 ㉒

If you're prone to seasickness, you might want to steer
clear of the Jane, where standard rooms are done up
like ship's cabins to reflect the building's maritime
history. Quarters are small and most share bathrooms
but guests have access to the pool and rooftop bar –
as well as yacht-worthy views of the Hudson.
Bar. Internet (wireless; free). No smoking rooms.
▶ *See also p165 Cheap Chic Sleep.*

Midtown

CHELSEA

Expensive

Inn on 23rd Street

*131 W 23rd Street, between Sixth & Seventh
Avenues, New York, NY 10011 (1-212 463 0330/
www.innon23rd.com). Subway F, V, 1 to 23rd
Street.* **Rates** $249-$399 double. **Rooms** 14.
Credit AmEx, DC, Disc, MC, V. **Map** p404 D26 ㉓

**THE BEST
OLD NEW YORK STYLE**

For landmark luxury
Plaza. *See p167.*

For literary history
Algonquin Hotel. *See p168.*

For Victoriana revived
Blue Moon. *See p155.*

This Chelsea gem, a renovated 19th-century
townhouse, offers the charm of a traditional
bed and breakfast with amenities (a lift,
pillowtop mattresses, private bathrooms, white-
noise machines). Owners and innkeepers Annette
and Barry Fisherman have styled each of the 14
bedrooms with a unique theme, such as Maritime,
Bamboo and 1940s.
*Concierge. Disabled-adapted rooms. Internet
(wireless; free). No smoking. TV: DVD.*

★ Maritime Hotel

*363 W 16th Street, between Eighth & Ninth
Avenues, New York, NY 10011 (1-212 242
4300/www.themaritimehotel.com). Subway
A, C, E to 14th Street; L to Eighth Avenue.*
Rates $375-$435 double. **Map** p403 C27 ㉔

What are porthole windows doing on a hotel in
Chelsea? Well, it's not *all* a gimmick – the building
was once the headquarters of the Maritime Union,
so in 2002, owners Eric Goode and Sean MacPherson
created the Maritime Hotel by blending the look of
a luxury yacht with a chic 1960s aesthetic. The
lobby is a bit dark, but the retro stylish rooms,
modelled after ship's cabins, are much more eye-
catching (each has one large porthole window and
lots of glossy teak panelling). For more space, book
one of the two penthouses, which have their own
private terrace and outdoor shower. Onsite eating
and drinking options include Matsuri, a gorgeous
Japanese restaurant; La Bottega, an Italian trattoria
with a lantern-festooned patio; Cabana, an airy
rooftop bar; and Hiro, a buzzing basement lounge.
*Bars (3). Business centre. Concierge. Disabled-
adapted rooms. Gym. Internet (wireless; free).
No smoking floors. Restaurants (2). Room
service. TV: DVD/pay movies.*

Moderate

Hotel Chelsea (aka Chelsea Hotel)

*222 W 23rd Street, between Seventh & Eighth
Avenues, New York, NY 10011 (1-212 243
3700/www.hotelchelsea.com). Subway C, E, 1 to
23rd Street.* **Rates** $200-$700 double. **Rooms** 400.
Credit AmEx, DC, Disc, MC, V. **Map** p404 D26 ㉕

Built in 1884, the Chelsea has a long and infamous
past: writer (and noted sot) Dylan Thomas slipped
into a fatal coma here in 1953, *Lost Weekend* author
Charles R Jackson committed suicide in his room
in 1968, and Nancy Spungen was allegedly
murdered in Room 100 by Sex Pistol boyfriend Sid
Vicious, a decade later. Rooms are generally large
with high ceilings, but certain amenities, like flat-
panel TVs, washer-dryers and marble fireplaces,
vary. Make no mistake, you're paying for the
hotel's sordid (if not grungy) past – the rooms
aren't exactly gleaming.
*Concierge. Disabled-adapted rooms. Internet
(wireless; free). No smoking rooms. TV:
pay movies.*

Jane.

Budget

Chelsea Lodge

318 W 20th Street, between Eighth & Ninth Avenues, New York, NY 10011 (1-212 243 4499/www.chelsealodge.com). Subway C, E to 23rd Street. **Rates** $129-$150 double. **Rooms** 26. **Credit** AmEx, DC, MC, V. **Map** p403 D27 ㉖

If Martha Stewart decorated a log cabin, it would probably end up looking something like this inn, housed in a landmark brownstone just blocks from the Chelsea gallery district. All of the rooms (including the four suites down the block at 334 West 20th Street) come with TVs, showers and air-conditioning. Although most are fairly small, the accommodation is so incredibly charming that reservations fill up quickly. Note: there's no sign outside.

Concierge. Disabled-adapted rooms. Internet (wireless; free). No smoking. TV: DVD.

Hostels

Chelsea Center

313 W 29th Street, between Eighth & Ninth Avenues, New York, NY 10001 (1-212 643 0214/www.chelseacenterhostel.com). Subway A, C, E to 34th Street-Penn Station; 1 to 28th Street. **Rates** $35 per person in dorm. **Rooms** 20 dorm beds. **Map** p404 D25 ㉗

Relive your student days in this formerly women-only residence with shared rooms and a communal kitchen and living area. Bathrooms are clean, and there's a patio garden with a big table for socialising. Only one room has air-conditioning, but on the plus side, rates include breakfast.

Internet (wireless; free). No smoking rooms.

FLATIRON DISTRICT & UNION SQUARE

Moderate

Hotel Thirty Thirty

30 E 30th Street, between Madison Avenue & Park Avenue South, New York, NY 10016 (1-212 689 1900/1-800 804 4480/www.thirty thirty-nyc.com). Subway 6 to 28th Street. **Rates** $119-$425 double. **Rooms** 252. **Credit** AmEx, DC, Disc, MC, V. **Map** p404 E25 ㉘

Before it became a smart hotel, Thirty Thirty was a residence for single women, and 60 tenants still live here. Ambient music sets the tone in the spare, very fashionable, block-long lobby. Rooms are small but sleek and complemented by clean lines and textured fabrics. Executive-floor rooms are slightly larger, with nifty workspaces and slate bathrooms thrown into the mix. The hotel's restaurant, Zana's, serves upmarket Mediterranean fare and there's an evening cocktail bar.

Bar. Concierge. Disabled-adapted rooms. Internet (high-speed; $10/day). No smoking rooms. Parking ($30). Restaurant.

Budget

Gershwin Hotel

7 E 27th Street, between Fifth & Madison Avenues, New York, NY 10016 (1-212 545 8000/www.gershwinhotel.com). Subway N, R, W, 6 to 28th Street. **Rates** $30-$60 per person in 4- to 8-bed dorm; $109-$145 for 1-3 people in private room. **Rooms** 60 beds in dorms; 135 private. **Credit** AmEx, DC, MC, V. **Map** p404 E26 ㉙
Works by Lichtenstein line the hallways, and an original Warhol soup can painting hangs in the lobby of this pop art-themed budget hotel. Rooms are less than pristine – especially the hostel-style dorms – but the rates are extremely reasonable for a location just off Fifth Avenue. There are also four suites – the one with screen-printed walls and a sitting room is a favourite of regular guests.
Concierge. Disabled-adapted rooms. Internet (wireless; $10). No smoking floors.
▶ *See also p165 Cheap Chic Sleep.*

GRAMERCY PARK & MURRAY HILL

Deluxe

Gramercy Park Hotel

2 Lexington Avenue, at 21st Street, New York, NY 10010 (1-212 475 4320/www.gramercypark hotel.com). Subway 6 to 23rd Street. **Rates** $545-$645 double. **Rooms** 185. **Credit** AmEx, DC, Disc, MC, V. **Map** p404 E23 ㉚
New Yorkers held their collective breath when hotelier Ian Schrager announced he was revamping the Gramercy Park Hotel, a 1924 gem that had hosted everyone from Humphrey Bogart to David Bowie. They needn't have worried: the redesigned lobby, unveiled in 2006, retains the Boho spirit with its stuccoed walls, ruby-red banquettes, an enormous Venetian chandelier and working fireplace, and artwork from Cy Twombly, Andy Warhol, Richard Prince and Julian Schnabel (the hotel's art director). The eclectic elegance continues in the spacious rooms, which include tapestry-covered chairs, hand-tufted rugs, mahogany English drinking cabinets and a Pre-Raphaelite colour palate of deep reds and blues. Guests can lounge on the private roof deck, get a facial at the in-house Aerospa, or sip cocktails at the Schnabel-designed Rose and Jade bars.
Bars (3). Business centre. Concierge. Disabled-adapted rooms. Gym. Internet (wireless; $15/day). No smoking floors. Parking ($55). Restaurant. Room service. Spa. TV: DVD/pay movies.

Expensive

Hotel Chandler

12 E 31st Street, between Fifth & Madison Avenues, New York, New York, NY 10016 (1-212 889 6363/www.hotelchandler.com). Subway 6

to 33rd Street. **Rates** $250-$500 double. **Rooms** 127. **Credit** AmEx, DC, Disc, MC, V. **Map** p404 E25 ㉛
Though modest in size, rooms at this delightful hotel are style conscious, with black and white photographs of New York streetscapes on the walls, chequered carpeting, and Frette robes and Aveda products in the bathrooms. The in-house Bar 12:31 offers cocktails and light nibbles.
Bar. Disabled-adapted room. Gym. Internet (wireless; free). No smoking floors. Parking ($40). Room service.

Moderate

Marcel at Gramercy

201 E 24th Street, at Third Avenue, New York, NY 10010 (1-212 696 3800/www.nychotels.com). Subway 6 to 23rd Street. **Rates** $227-$347 double. **Rooms** 135. **Credit** AmEx, DC, Disc, MC, V. **Map** p404 F26 ㉜
Revamped in early 2008, this fashionable Gramercy Park hotel has a hip aesthetic that extends from the lobby, with its marble concierge desk, sprawling leather banquette and in-house library, to the medium-sized rooms, which offer a sleek black and pewter palette, rain-head showers and Frette linens. Complimentary breakfast is served in the tenth floor guest lounge, where you'll also find desktop computers equipped with free high-speed internet access. For something more substantial, the hotel's new Bar Milano – run by chefs Eric Kleinman and Steve Connaughton (of 'inoteca and Lupa fame, respectively) – serves inventive takes on classic Italian fare until 2am, while master mixologist Tony Abou-Ganim oversees the adjacent 26-seat bar.
Bar. Business centre. Concierge. Disabled-adapted rooms. Internet (wireless; $12/day). No smoking floors. Parking ($28). Restaurant. Room service. TV: pay movies.
Other locations Ameritania Hotel, 230 W 54th Street, at Broadway, Theater District, New York, NY 10019 (1-888 664 6835); Amsterdam Court, 226 W 50th Street, between Broadway & Eighth Avenue, Theater District, New York, NY 10019 (1-888 664 6835); Bentley, 500 E 62nd Street, at York Avenue, New York, NY 10065 (1-888 664 6835); Moderne, 243 W 55th Street, between Broadway & Eighth Avenue, Theater District, New York, NY 10019 (1-888 664 6835).

INSIDE TRACK
GRAMERCY PARK

The **Gramercy Park Hotel**'s (*see p162*) greatest amenity is a free key to nearby Gramercy Park (*see p91*) – one of the most exclusive outdoor spaces in the city.

CONSUME

Budget

★ **Carlton Arms Hotel**

160 E 25th Street, at Third Avenue, New York,
NY 10010 (1-212 679 0680/www.carlton
arms.com). Subway 6 to 23rd Street. **Rates**
$110-$130 double. **Rooms** 54. **Credit** DC, MC,
V. **Map** p404 F26 ⓸

The Carlton Arms Art Project started in the late
1970s, when a small group of creative types brought
fresh paint and new ideas to a run-down shelter.
Today, the site is a Bohemian backpackers' paradise
and a live-in gallery, every room, bathroom and
hallway festooned with outré artwork. (Themed
quarters include the Money Room and a tribute to a
traditional English cottage.) Discounts are offered for
students, overseas guests and week-long stays. Most
guests share baths; tack on $15 for a private toilet.
Rooms get booked early, so reserve well in advance.
Concierge. Internet (shared terminal; $2/10mins).
▶ *See also p165 Cheap Chic Sleep.*

Murray Hill Inn

143 E 30th Street, between Lexington & Third
Avenues (1-212 683 6900/www.nyinns.com).
Subway 6 to 28th Street. **Rates** from $89 double
with shared bath; from $129 single/double with
private bath. **Rooms** 45. **Credit** AmEx, DC,
MC, V. **Map** p404 F25 ⓸

Although many of its rooms now have private
bathrooms, this Euro-style inn sacrifices creature
comforts for economy. But with the Empire State
Building and Madison Square Park nearby, you'll
soon forget you're roughing it. Discounted rates are
available for returning guests and families of NYU
students. Be sure to book well in advance, or try the
sister locations listed below.
Concierge. Internet (wireless; $6.95/day).
Other locations Amsterdam Inn, 340
Amsterdam Avenue, at 76th Street, Upper West
Side, New York, NY 10024 (1-212 579 7500);
Central Park Hostel (*see p173*); Union Square
Inn, 209 E 14th Street, between Second & Third
Avenues, East Village, New York, NY 10003 (1-
212 614 0500).

HERALD SQUARE & GARMENT DISTRICT

Moderate

★ **Hotel Metro**

45 W 35th Street, between Fifth & Sixth Avenues,
New York, NY 10001 (1-212 947 2500/1-800
356 3870/www.hotelmetronyc.com). Subway B,
D, F, N, Q, R, V, W to 34th Street-Herald Square.
Rates $275-$365 double. **Rooms** 179. **Credit**
AmEx, DC, MC, V. **Map** p404 E25 ⓸

Renovated in 2006, the Metro offers good service, a
chic retro vibe and close proximity to the shopping
meccas of Herald Square. Black and white portraits

of Hollywood legends adorn the lobby, and the tiny
rooms are clean. Take in views of the Empire State
Building from the rooftop bar of Metro Grill.
Bar. Business centre. Concierge. Disabled-adapted
rooms. Gym. Internet (wireless; free). No smoking
floors. Parking ($27). Restaurant. Room service.
TV: pay movies.

Hotel Pennsylvania

401 Seventh Avenue, between 32nd & 33rd
Streets, New York, NY 10001 (1-212 736 5000/
1-800 223 8585/www.hotelpenn.com). Subway A,
C, E, 1, 2, 3 to 34th Street-Penn Station. **Rates**
$226-$366 double. **Rooms** 1,700. **Credit** AmEx,
DC, Disc, MC, V. **Map** p404 D25 ⓸

One of the city's largest and most popular hotels, the
Pennsylvania offers reasonable rates and a convenient location (directly opposite Penn Station and
Madison Square Garden, and mere blocks from
Macy's and the Empire State Building). After a $7
million renovation in 2008, the rooms are still fairly
modest, but offer pleasant respite from the hubbub
outside. The host hotel for the annual Westminster
Kennel Club Dog Show, the Penn is also happy to
accommodate pets: canines get doggie treats at
check-in, and owners receive a copy of *Fido-Friendly*
magazine. Kitties are welcome too.
Business centre. Concierge. Disabled-adapted
rooms. Gym. Internet (wireless; $10/day).
Parking ($40). Restaurants (2). Room service.
TV: pay movies.

Budget

Americana Inn

69 W 38th Street, at Sixth Avenue, New York,
NY 10018 (1-212 840 6700/www.newyork
hotel.com). Subway B, D, F, N, Q, R, V, W to
34th Street-Herald Square; B, D, F, V to 42nd
Street. **Rates** $145-$190 double. **Rooms** 54.
Credit AmEx, DC, MC, V. **Map** p404 E24 ⓸

This budget hotel has a speakeasy feel: the signage
is discreet and you'll have to ring the doorbell to
enter. But what the Americana might lack in ambience (with its linoleum floors and fluorescent lighting), it makes up for in location (a rhinestone's throw
from the Theater District) and reasonable prices.
And although all bathrooms are shared, rooms come
with a mini-sink and large walk-in closets.
Disabled-adapted rooms. Internet (wireless;
$1/10mins). No smoking.

THEATER DISTRICT & HELL'S KITCHEN

Expensive

Dream Hotel

210 W 55th Street, between Broadway & Seventh
Avenue, New York, NY 10019 (1-212 247 2000/
1-866 437 3266/www.dreamny.com). Subway N,

CONSUME

Q, R, W to 57th Street. **Rates** $275-$575 double.
Rooms 230. **Credit** AmEx, DC, Disc, MC, V.
Map p405 D22 ㊳

Vikram Chatwal, the mastermind behind the Time
and Night hotels (*see p166*), turned the old Majestic
Hotel into a luxury lodge with a trippy slumber-
land theme. The lobby sums up the whimsical
aesthetic: walls are cloaked in Paul Smith-style
stripes, a crystal boat dangles from the ceiling and
an enormous gold statue of Catherine the Great
stands guard. Rooms are more streamlined, with
white walls, satin headboards and an ethereal
blue backlight that glows under the bed. Luxurious
touches include feather duvet-topped beds, plasma
TVs and an iPod loaded with ambient music.
Diners can choose between Amalia, whose
Mediterranean menu was overseen by Dos
Caminos chef Ivy Stark, or the more popular Italian
ristorante Serafina, sporting a Fellini-esque
interior crafted by New Yorker David Rockwell. If
the lush surroundings can't help you unwind, book
an appointment at the Ayurvedic spa, conceived by
none other than New Age guru Deepak Chopra.
Ava, the rooftop bar, wows drinkers with its
panoramic views of the city.
*Bars (3). Concierge. Gym. Internet (high speed;
$9.95/day). No smoking. Parking ($40).
Restaurants (2). Room service. Spa. TV.*

Flatotel

*135 W 52nd Street, between Sixth & Seventh
Avenues, New York, NY 10019 (1-212 703
9400/www.flatotel.com). Subway N, R, W to 49th
Street; 1 to 50th Street.* **Rates** $310-$440 double.
Rooms 272. **Credit** AmEx, DC, Disc, MC, V.
Map p404 D23 ㊳

Upon entering, the Flatotel seems to have a hip
swagger: techno beats pump through the granite
lobby, where dimly lit nooks and cowhide couches
are filled with guests drinking cocktails. Rooms are
less cutting edge, but as the hotel's name suggests,
feel more like apartments than temporary lodgings,
with kitchenettes and spacious bathrooms. A slew
of reality television shows, including *America's Next
Top Model*, has been filmed in the penthouse suites.
The in-house restaurant, Moda, serves Italian-
inspired fare; in temperate weather, catch a breeze
with your cocktail in the restaurant's alfresco atrium. For private imbibing, call the martini butler,
who will mix the drink in your room.
*Bar. Business centre. Concierge. Disabled-adapted
rooms. Gym. Internet (wireless; free). No smoking
floors. Parking ($30). Restaurant. Room service.*

Hotel 41

*206 W 41st Street, between Seventh & Eighth
Avenues, New York, NY 10036 (1-212 703
8600/www.hotel41.com). Subway N, Q, R, S,
W, 1, 2, 3, 7 to 42nd Street-Times Square.*
Rates $289-$330 double. **Rooms** 47. **Credit**
AmEx, DC, Disc, MC, V. **Map** p404 D24 ㊵

Although its look is cool – especially for the Theater
District – this seven-storey boutique hotel is decid-
edly warm and inviting: reading lamps extend from
dark-wood headboards, and triple-glazed windows
filter out the cacophony from the streets below.
Averaging 100-125sq ft, standard rooms are tiny
even by New York standards, but suites have
Jacuzzis and private terrace views of Times Square.
Bar 41 serves breakfast, lunch and dinner.
*Bar-restaurant. Disabled-adapted room. Internet
(free). No smoking floors. Parking ($32-$42).
Room service.*

Hudson

*356 W 58th Street, between Eighth & Ninth
Avenues, New York, NY 10019 (1-212 554
6000/www.hudsonhotel.com). Subway A, B, C,
D, 1 to 59th Street-Columbus Circle.* **Rates**
$329-$659 double. **Rooms** 804. **Credit** AmEx,
DC, Disc, MC, V. **Map** p405 C22 ㊶

The Philippe Starck-designed Hudson – the third
New York palace in the international Morgans Hotel
Group – might have dinky rooms, but it certainly
gets points for looks. The property boasts a private
courtyard shaded with enormous potted trees, a roof
terrace that overlooks the Hudson River and sleek,
panelled rooms that evoke the interior of a classic
luxury liner. The glass-ceilinged lobby (with imported English ivy), the Hudson Cafeteria and the three
onsite bars are all crawling with beautiful people.
*Bars (4). Business centre. Concierge. Disabled-
adapted rooms. Gym. Internet (wireless; $10/day).
No smoking rooms. Restaurant. Room service.*
Other locations Morgans, 237 Madison
Avenue, between 37th & 38th Streets, Murray
Hill, New York, NY 10016 (1-212 686 0300/1-800
334 3408); Royalton, 44 W 44th Street, between
Fifth & Sixth Avenues, Midtown, New York,
NY 10036 (1-212 869 4400/1-800 635 9013).

★ London NYC

*151 W 54th Street, between Sixth & Seventh
Avenues, New York, NY 10019 (1-866 690
2029/www.thelondonnyc.com). Subway B, D,
E to Seventh Avenue.* **Rates** $299-$549 double.
Rooms 562. **Credit** AmEx, DC, Disc, MC, V.
Map p405 D22 ㊷

Formerly the Rihga Royal Hotel, this 54-storey high-
rise was completely overhauled in a contemporary
English style (by David Collins, the designer behind
some of London's most fashionable bars and restaurants) and reopened as the chic London NYC in early
2007. Space is the biggest luxury here: the 500sq ft
London Suites offer long curvaceous banquettes
(the coffee tables adjust to dining-table heights),
mammoth leather desks with ample storage, and living quarters and bedrooms divided by mirrored
French doors (with flat-screen TVs in both). If the
London is out of your price range, you can always
pop in for a look-see: the inviting lobby is done up as
a grand London residence. It's also the site of two

Cheap Chic Sleep

Some of Manhattan's smallest hotel rooms have prices to match.

Facing an ailing economy and increasingly style-savvy travellers, New York hoteliers are devising inventive takes on budget accommodation. Artsy, inexpensive inns aren't new to the Big Apple: young visitors have been flocking to the **Gershwin** (*see p162*) and **Carlton Arms** (*see p163* for years. However, a new breed of smart boarding houses and 'hostels' is embracing a trendier aesthetic, offering thoughtful perks to make up for limited floorspace.

Midtown's **Pod Hotel** (*see p171*), opened in 2007 by Mercer Hotel co-owners Richard Born and Ira Drukier, offers bunk-bed rooms from just $89 a night (double- and queen-bed rooms start at $129). Appealing to modern tastes and technological requirements, the minimalist, IKEA-style rooms are equipped with iPod stations, LCD-screen TVs and free Wi-Fi. And although a third of the Pod's 347 quarters have shared bathroom facilities, in-room monitors indicate when the bathrooms are vacant. Manager David Bernstein says the hotel is targeting the 19- to 35-year-old demographic, but that they 'get everyone from grandmas to teenagers'.

Just steps from Bryant Park and Times Square, **RoomMate Grace Hotel** (*see p167*) is more extravagant. But 220-square-foot quad-occupancy rooms with bunk beds and private baths can still be had for $275 a night, not bad when split four ways (larger 'petite' rooms with one queen-sized bed start at $279). As well as flat-screen TVs and mini-fridges, the sleek chambers include free Wi-Fi and – a rare hotel perk – complimentary local calls. Guests can also order cocktails at the poolside bar or take advantage of the hotel gym and in-room massage service.

Taking the modern boarding-house theme a step further is the **Jane** (*see p160*). Opened in autumn 2008, the 200-room 'micro-hotel' offers 50-square-foot, nautical-themed cabins with single beds from just $99. Although there's barely enough space to stand, the air-conditioned wood-panelled rooms come with under-bed storage, free Wi-Fi, iPod docks and wall-mounted 23-inch flatscreen TVs.

The Jane's maritime theme wasn't chosen at random. Opened in 1907 as the American Seaman's Friend Society Sailors Home, the building housed crewmen on layover; *Titanic* survivors were also sheltered there after the luxury liner sank in 1912. The 14-storey landmark had fallen on hard times until the arrival of Sean MacPherson and Eric Goode, the duo behind the upscale Bowery and Maritime Hotels.

'When I came to New York in the early '80s, I'd stay at these funky little places that were dirt-cheap, and I'd meet all these cool artists and musicians,' says MacPherson. 'Now hotels are so expensive you can't get that experience any more. I guess this is a way to rectify a situation that I helped to create.'

To foster a communal spirit, MacPherson and Goode converted the main ballroom – at one time the Jane Street Theater, birthplace of *Hedwig and the Angry Inch* – into a giant living room. '[We're] redefining "single occupancy",' says MacPherson. 'We allow an idiosyncratic mix of people to come and enjoy New York without sinking everything into their hotel room.'

RoomMate Grace Hotel.

CONSUME

THE BEST
RELAXATION ZONES

For holistic indulgence
Dream Hotel. See p163.

For green peace
Gramercy Park Hotel. See p162.

For bathroom bliss
Mercer. See p153.

eateries from Britain's favourite foul-mouthed chef: Gordon Ramsay at the London and the less formal (and less expensive) Maze, as well as a stylish bar.
Bar. Business centre. Concierge. Disabled-adapted rooms. Gym. Internet (wireless; free). No smoking floors. Parking ($55). Restaurants (2). Room service. Spa. TV: pay movies.

Night Hotel
132 W 45th Street, between Sixth & Seventh Avenues, New York, NY 10036 (1-212 835 9600/www.nighthotelny.com). Subway N, Q, R, S, W, 1, 2, 3, 7 to 42nd Street-Times Square. **Rates** $230-$589 double. **Rooms** 72. **Credit** AmEx, DC, Disc, MC, V. **Map** p404 D24 ❸
At this night-themed boutique property from Vikram Chatwal (of Dream Hotel and Time; *see p163 & below*), guests see the city through the romantic lens of 'modern Gothic Gotham'. A nightcrawler's roost, the hotel's stylish black and white motif extends beyond the loungey lobby to the sultry and hand-some rooms. The Addams Family would love it.
Bar. Concierge. Disabled-adapted rooms. Internet (wireless; $10/day). No smoking floors. Parking ($55). Restaurant. Room service. TV: DVD/ pay movies.

Time
224 W 49th Street, between Broadway & Eighth Avenue, New York, NY 10019 (1-212 320 2900/1-877 846 3692/www.thetimeny.com). Subway C, E, 1 to 50th Street; N, R, W to 49th Street. **Rates** $349-$559 double. **Rooms** 193. **Credit** AmEx, DC, Disc, MC, V. **Map** p404 D23 ❹
Ever wondered what it would be like to feel, taste and smell colour? Adam Tihany, who also designed sister properties Night and Dream Hotels (*see above & p163*), worked with the idea of stimulating the senses through a single primary colour (guest rooms are furnished in either red, yellow or blue). Expect to find your room replete with matching duvets, jellybeans and reading material, as well as a chro-matically inspired scent.
Bar. Concierge. Disabled-adapted rooms. Gym. Internet (high-speed; $11/day). No smoking. Parking ($25). Restaurant. Room service. TV: pay movies.

W New York-Times Square
1567 Broadway, at 47th Street, New York, NY 10036 (1-212 930 7400/1-888 627 8680/www. whotels.com). Subway N, R, W to 49th Street; 1 to 50th Street. **Rates** $300-$579 double. **Rooms** 507. **Credit** AmEx, DC, Disc, MC, V. **Map** p404 D23 ❹
'Whatever, whenever' is the motto of this upmarket boutique chain with five Big Apple locations (a sixth, W New York – Downtown, is expected to open near Wall Street in late 2009), and staff are at the ready to gratify your every whim. Glamour is the watchword of the Times Square branch: a waterfall gushes in the street-level entrance (reception is on the seventh floor). To your right, the Living Room is a sprawl of white leather seating. Every private room features a floating-glass desk and a sleek bathroom stocked with Bliss spa products (the Lexington Avenue outpost has a Bliss spa too), but it's the bed-to-ceiling headboard mirror and sexy room service menu that really get the mind racing. Steve Hanson's Blue Fin serves a combination of stellar sushi and superb cocktails.
Bars (2). Business centre. Concierge. Disabled-adapted rooms. Gym. Internet (wireless; $17/day). No smoking floors. Parking ($55). Restaurant. Room service. TV: DVD.
Other locations W New York, 541 Lexington Avenue, between 49th & 50th Streets, New York, NY 10022 (1-212 755 1200); W New York – The Court, 130 East 39th Street, between Lexington & Park Avenues, New York, NY 10016 (1-212 685 1100); W New York – The Tuscany, 120 East 39th Street, between Lexington & Park Avenues, New York, NY 10016 (1-212 686 1600); W Union Square, 201 Park Avenue South, at E 17th Street, New York, NY 10003 (1-212 253 9119).

Warwick New York Hotel
65 W 54th Street, at Sixth Avenue, New York, NY 10019 (1-212 247 2700/1-800 223 4099/ www.warwickhotels.com). Subway E, V to Fifth Avenue-53rd Street; F to 57th Street. **Rates** $305-$475 double. **Rooms** 426. **Credit** AmEx, DC, MC, V. **Map** p405 E22 ❹
You'd never know it from its dated façade, but the grand Warwick was frequented by Elvis Presley and the Beatles during their tours, and the top-floor suite with wraparound balcony was once Cary Grant's home. (Built by newspaper baron William Randolph Hearst in 1926, the Warwick is listed by the National Trust for Historic Preservation.) Rooms are exceptionally large by midtown standards, and have feminine touches such as floral curtains and bedspreads. Check out the historical-themed 1930s wall paintings by illustra-tor Dean Cornwell in the refurbished Murals on 54 restaurant – they contain images considered obscene at the time (such as an Indian's bare but-tocks), which Cornwell included in revenge over a payment dispute.

Bars (2). Business centre. Concierge. Disabled-adapted rooms. Gym. Internet (wireless; $13/day). No smoking. Parking ($40). Restaurant. Room service. TV: DVD/pay movies.

Moderate

414 Hotel
414 W 46th Street, between Ninth & Tenth Avenues, New York, NY 10036 (1-212 399 0006/www.414hotel.com). Subway A, C, E to 42nd Street-Port Authority. **Rates** $209-$229 double. **Rooms** 22. **Credit** AmEx, DC, MC, V. **Map** p404 C23 ❹
This small hotel's shockingly affordable rates and reclusive location make it feel like a secret you've been lucky to stumble upon. Immaculate rooms are tastefully appointed with suede headboards, vases full of colourful roses and framed black and white photos of the city. There's a glowing fireplace and computer in the lobby and a leafy courtyard outside.
Business centre. Concierge. Disabled-adapted rooms. Internet (wireless; free). No smoking. Room service.

Hotel Edison
228 W 47th Street, at Broadway, New York, NY 10036 (1-212 840 5000/1-800 637 7070/ www.edisonhotelnyc.com). Subway N, R, W to 49th Street; 1 to 50th Street. **Rates** $195-$265 double. **Rooms** 800. **Credit** AmEx, DC, Disc, MC, V. **Map** p404 D23 ❹
Theatre lovers – many of the blue-haired variety – flock to this 1931 art deco hotel for its affordable rates and proximity to the Broadway show palaces. Rooms are a standard size but decidedly spruce. Café Edison, a classic diner just off the lobby, is a long-time favourite of Broadway actors and their fans – Neil Simon was so smitten that he put it in one of his plays.
Bar. Business centre. Concierge. Disabled-adapted rooms. Gym. Internet (wireless; $10/day). No smoking. Restaurant. Room service. TV: pay movies.

RoomMate Grace Hotel
125 West 45th Street, between Sixth & Seventh Avenues, New York, NY 10036 (1-212 354 2323/www.room-matehotels.com). Subway N, Q, R, S, W, 1, 2, 3, 7 to 42nd Street-Times Square. **Rates** $279-$600 double; $275-$525 quad bunk. **Rooms** 139. **Credit** AmEx, DC, Disc, MC, V. **Map** p404 D23 ❹
In 2008 the Spanish RoomMate chain took over André Balazs' Hotel QT but maintained the celebrity hotelier's budget-boutique vibe. Although modestly furnished, the minimalist rooms come with Egyptian cotton linens, 25-inch flat-screen TVs and bathrooms with rainfall-style showers. Prices are commensurate with the sleek, chic aesthetic but if you're travelling with a posse, quad-bunk rooms,

which can comfortably sleep four, offer a more economical option. If you need to spread out, take a dip in the hotel pool.
Bar. Concierge, Gym. Internet (wireless; free). No smoking rooms. Pool (1 indoor). TV: DVD/pay movies.
▶ *See also p165 Cheap Chic Sleep.*

Hostels

Big Apple Hostel
119 W 45th Street, between Sixth & Seventh Avenues, New York, NY 10036 (1-212 302 2603/www.bigapplehostel.com). Subway B, D, F, V to 42nd Street-Bryant Park; N, Q, R, S, W, 1, 2, 3, 7 to 42nd Street-Times Square. **Rates** $45-$60 per person in dorm; $250 private room. **Rooms** 112 dorm beds; 11 private. **Credit** DC, MC, V. **Map** p404 D23 ❺
Long popular with backpackers, this bare-bones hostel is lacking in frills, but dorms are spotless and cheap for the location. The Big Apple puts you just steps from the Theater District and Times Square. If you want to get away from the masses, though, you can take refuge in the breezy back patio, equipped with a grill for summer barbecues. Linens are provided, but remember to pack a towel.
Internet (wireless; free). No smoking.

FIFTH AVENUE & AROUND

Deluxe

Plaza
768 Fifth Avenue, at Central Park South, New York, NY 10019 (1-212 759 3000/1-800 759 3000/www.fairmont.com/theplaza). Subway N, R, W to Fifth Avenue-59th Street. **Rates** $595-$1,145 double. **Rooms** 282. **Credit** AmEx, DC, Disc, MC, V. **Map** p405 E22 ❺
This landmark French Renaissance-style building dating from 1907 reopened in spring 2008 after a two-year, $400 million renovation. Although 152 rooms were converted into private condo units, guests can still check in to one of 282 elegantly appointed quarters complete with Louis XV-inspired furnishings and white-glove butler service. The opulent vibe extends into the bathrooms, which feature 24 carat gold-plated sinks and fixtures. The property's legendary public spaces – the Palm Court restaurant, the restored Oak Room and Oak Bar, and Grand Ballroom (the setting for Truman Capote's famed Black and White Ball in 1966) – have been designated as landmarks and preserved for the public. The onsite Caudalie Vinothérapie Spa is the French grape-based skincare line's first US outpost.
Bars (2). Concierge. Disabled-adapted rooms. Gym. Internet (wireless; $15/day). No smoking rooms. Parking ($65). Restaurants (2). Room service. Spa. TV: DVD/pay movies.

CONSUME

Expensive

Algonquin Hotel

59 W 44th Street, between Fifth & Sixth Avenues, New York, NY 10036 (1-212 840 6800/www.thealgonquin.net). Subway B, D, F, V to 42nd Street-Bryant Park; 7 to Fifth Avenue. **Rates** $299-$700 double. **Rooms** 174. **Credit** AmEx, DC, Disc, MC, V. **Map** p404 E24 ⑫

The lobby of this 1902 landmark hotel with a strong literary past (Alexander Woollcott and Dorothy Parker swapped bon mots in the famous Round Table Room) is decked out with upholstered chairs, antique lamps and large paintings of Jazz Age greats. Although modern amenities like flat-screen TVs and free Wi-Fi are standard, there's a strong sense of old New York in the rooms furnished with dark mahogany dressers and intricately patterned carpets and bedspreads. Even the hallway wallpaper is covered with cartoons by Robert Mankoff from *The New Yorker* (to commemorate Harold Ross, who secured funding for the magazine over long meetings at the Algonquin Round Table). The lobby still buzzes with a buttoned-up after-work crowd looking to wet their whistle in style and on Mondays, you can catch readings by local authors.
Bar. Concierge. Disabled-adapted rooms. Gym. Internet (wireless; free). No smoking. Parking ($30). Restaurant. Room service. TV: pay movies.
▶ *See p281 for details of the cabaret performances in the Oak Room (Tuesday through Saturday evenings).*

Bryant Park Hotel

40 W 40th Street, between Fifth & Sixth Avenues, New York, NY 10018 (1-212 869 0100/www.bryantparkhotel.com). Subway B, D, F, V to 42nd Street-Bryant Park; 7 to Fifth Avenue. **Rates** $349-$725 double. **Rooms** 128. **Credit** AmEx, DC, MC, V. **Map** p404 E24 ⑬

This hotel has seen a lot more action since Koi, the East Coast branch of the splashy Los Angeles restaurant, opened in 2005. Ian Schrager's partner Philip Pilevsky converted the 1924 American Radiator Building into his first New York property and now the Bryant Park has all the right accessories to lure a modish crowd: a gorgeous 70-seat screening room with red velour chairs and built-in desks, 20 park view suites with private terraces and, thanks to the hotel's close proximity to Bryant Park, a well-heeled clientele during Fashion Week. And yet, even with Bose Wave radios, flat-screen TVs, Tibetan rugs and travertine marble bathrooms, the rooms can feel somewhat stark. However, you can always head downstairs for a cocktail in the vaulted Cellar Bar to redress the balance.
Bar. Concierge. Disabled-adapted rooms. Gym. Internet (wireless; $9.95/day). No smoking floors. Parking ($45). Restaurant.

Le Parker Meridien

118 W 57th Street, between Sixth & Seventh Avenues (1-212 245 5000/1-800 543 4300/ www.parkermeridien.com). Subway F to 57th Street. **Rates** $370-$680 double. **Rooms** 730. **Credit** AmEx, DC, Disc, MC, V. **Map** p405 D22 ⑭

Given its cathedral ceilings, Damien Hirst painting and swanky bar, you might never want to leave the lobby of this haven a few doors down from Carnegie Hall. But when you finally venture up to your room (via lifts that screen Charlie Chaplin shorts and *Tom & Jerry* cartoons) you'll find a streamlined chamber outfitted with simple wood furnishings and Aeron desk chairs. Request north-facing quarters and you'll get a magnificent view of Central Park. No need to feel guilty if you overindulge at the excellent retro-style Burger Joint (hidden behind a curtain in the lobby) – just work off the calories at Gravity, the hotel's 15,000sq ft gym, or in the rooftop pool.
Bar. Business centre. Concierge. Disabled-adapted rooms. Gym. Internet (wireless; $15/day). No smoking floors. Parking ($50). Pool. Restaurants (3). Room service. Spa. TV: DVD/pay movies.

MIDTOWN EAST

Deluxe

★ Four Seasons

57 E 57th Street, between Madison & Park Avenues, New York, NY 10022 (1-212 758 5700/1-800 332 3442/www.fourseasons.com). Subway N, R, W to Lexington Avenue-59th Street; 4, 5, 6 to 59th Street. **Rates** $795-$1,150 double. **Rooms** 368. **Credit** AmEx, DC, Disc, MC, V. **Map** p405 E22 ⑮

One of New York's most opulent hotels, the Four Seasons hasn't slipped a notch in its two decades in business. Everybody who's anybody, from music-industry executives to politicians, continue to drop in for a bit of New York luxury. Renowned architect IM Pei came out of retirement to craft its sharp geometric look (in neutral cream and honey tones), and the rooms – which include deep-soak tubs and furnished terraces – are among the largest in the city. (The three-bedroom Royal Suite measures 2,000sq ft.) At 682 feet (52 storeys), the Four Seasons is New York's tallest hotel and from the

---

INSIDE TRACK
BEDTIME READING

More than 6,000 books were handpicked from indie fave the Strand Book Store (*see p231*) to match the theme of the rooms they adorn at the **Library Hotel** (*see p169*).

Algonquin Hotel.

higher floors, the views of the city are superb. But it's the pampering that keeps the elite coming back. The hotel is known for catering to guests' every need; your 4am hot fudge sundae is only a room-service call away.

Bars (2). Business centre. Concierge. Disabled-adapted rooms. Gym. Internet (high-speed; $10/day). No smoking floors. Parking ($60). Restaurants (2). Room service. Spa. TV: DVD/pay movies.

Expensive

Hotel Elysée

60 E 54th Street, between Madison & Park Avenues, New York, NY 10022 (1-212 753 1066/www.elyseehotel.com). Subway E, V to Lexington Avenue-53rd Street; 6 to 51st Street. **Rates** $295-$605 double. **Rooms** 103. **Credit** AmEx, DC, Disc, MC, V. **Map** p405 E22 ⑤⑥

The Hotel Elysée is a well-preserved piece of New York's Jazz Age: quarters are appointed with a touch of romance (period fabrics, antique furniture) and some rooms have coloured-glass conservatories and terraces. Elysée is popular with publishers and literary types, who convene over complimentary wine and cheese in the evening. Downstairs is the Monkey Bar, a 70-year-old nightspot that has been given a modern makeover and an Asian-fusion menu. Guests receive free passes to the New York Sports Club, five blocks away.

Bar. Internet (wireless; free). No smoking. Restaurant.

Library Hotel

299 Madison Avenue, at 41st Street, New York, NY 10017 (1-212 983 4500/www.libraryhotel. com). Subway S, 4, 5, 6, 7 to 42nd Street-Grand Central; 7 to Fifth Avenue. **Rates** $275-$679 double. **Rooms** 60. **Credit** AmEx, DC, MC, V. **Map** p404 E24 ⑤⑦

Even before you enter this literary-themed boutique hotel, you'll see quotations from famous authors inscribed in the pavement. The books, and the rooms they occupy, are organised according to the Dewey decimal system: each of the hotel's ten floors are allocated one of the ten categories of the DDC (Literature, Philosophy, The Arts, etc) and each room contains a collection of books and artwork pertaining to a subject within its category (Botany, Fairy Tales and Political Science, to name a few). Rates include breakfast, evening wine and cheese gatherings in the second-floor Reading Room, a host of in-room amenities such as Belgian chocolates, DVDs and a selection of newspapers, and access to the mahogany-lined writer's den (which has a lovely tiny terrace and a glowing fireplace). The hotel's restaurant Madison & Vine, is just off the lobby. The Library's sister property, Hotel Giraffe, embodies modern European style 15 blocks south. *Photos pp170-171.*

Bar. Business centre. Concierge. Disabled-adapted rooms. Internet (wireless; free). No smoking. Restaurant. Room service.

Other locations Hotel Giraffe, 365 Park Avenue South, at 26th Street, Flatiron District, New York, NY 10016 (1-212 685 7700/1-877 296 0009).

New York Palace Hotel

455 Madison Avenue, between 50th & 51st Streets, New York, NY 10022 (1-212 888 7000/1-800 697 2522/www.newyorkpalace.com). Subway E, V to Fifth Avenue-53rd Street. **Rates** $345-$650 double. **Rooms** 899. **Credit** AmEx, DC, Disc, MC, V. **Map** p404 E23 🟢

With its red carpet, twinkling lights and fancy tea parties, the Palace conforms to the classic luxury hotel fantasy – it's hard to believe it was once owned by noted miser (and jailbird) Leona Helmsley. Designed by McKim, Mead & White, the cluster of mansions now holds nearly 900 rooms decorated in an art deco or neoclassical style. Triplex suites have a top-tier terrace, solarium and private rooftop garden. The famous restaurant Le Cirque 2000 is no longer here (it's now in its third incarnation further uptown as Le Cirque), but you can dine at the elegant Istana Restaurant, or sip a manhattan in the extravagant new restaurant and lounge, Gilt.

Bars (2). Business centre. Concierge. Disabled-adapted rooms. Gym. Internet (wireless; $15/day). No smoking floors. Parking ($50). Restaurants (2). Room service. Spa. TV: DVD/pay movies.

Roger Smith

501 Lexington Avenue, between 47th & 48th Streets, New York, NY 10017 (1-212 755 1400/1-800 445 0277/www.rogersmith.com).

Subway E, V to Lexington Avenue-53rd Street; 6 to 51st Street. **Rates** $299-$499 double. **Rooms** 136. **Credit** AmEx, DC, Disc, MC, V. **Map** p404 F23 🟢

The spacious chambers at this arty spot make it a good option for families with a little cash to spare. Each room is decorated with unique furnishings and colourful wallpaper. The Roger Smith Gallery hosts rotating exhibitions, and a few interesting pieces by artist James Knowles (whose family owns the hotel) adorn the lobby.

Bar. Concierge. Internet (wireless; free). No smoking floors. Restaurant. Room service. TV: DVD.

Waldorf-Astoria

301 Park Avenue, at 50th Street, New York, NY 10022 (1-212 355 3000/1-800 925 3673/ www.waldorfastoria.com). Subway E, V to Lexington Avenue-53rd Street; 6 to 51st Street. **Rates** $300-$500 double. **Rooms** 1,400. **Credit** AmEx, DC, Disc, MC, V. **Map** p404 E23 🟢

First built in 1893, the Waldorf-Astoria was the city's largest hotel before it was demolished to make way for the Empire State Building. The current art deco Waldorf opened in 1931 and now has protected status as a historic hotel – past guests include Princess Grace, Sophia Loren and a long list of US presidents. The rooms, with wingback chairs, love seats, rich colours and layered fabrics, feel as if they were dec-

Library Hotel. *See p169.*

orated by Upper East Side socialites of yore. Those socialites would feel right at home at the exclusive Louis Vuitton-owned Guerlain Spa, due to open as this guide went to press. Double-check your attire before entering the hotel – you won't be allowed in if you're wearing a baseball cap and ripped jeans. *Bars (4). Business centre. Concierge. Disabled-adapted rooms. Gym. Internet (high-speed; $15/day). No smoking floors. Parking ($50). Restaurants (4). Room service. Spa. TV: pay movies.*

Budget

Pod Hotel

230 E 51st Street, at Third Avenue, New York, NY 10022 (1-212 355 0300/www.thepodhotel. com). Subway E to Lexington Avenue-53rd; 6 to 51st Street. **Rates** $129-$249 double. **Rooms** 347. **Credit** AmEx, DC, MC, V. **Map** p404 F23 ⑥⓵
This surprisingly stylish East Side hotel opened in early 2007, offering tiny but futuristic rooms that are well suited to people who favour convenience and value over elbow room. The 100sq ft single-bed 'pods' offer a nominal decor and under-bed dressers; baths are shared. The outdoor Pod Café is roomy enough, though, and serves organic yogurt and baked goods from Balthazar Bakery .
Bar. Concierge. Disabled-adapted rooms. Internet (wireless; free). No smoking rooms. Restaurant.
▶ *See also p165 Cheap Chic Sleep.*

Uptown

UPPER EAST SIDE

Expensive

Wales Hotel

1295 Madison Avenue, at 92nd Street, New York, NY 10128 (1-212 876 6000/www.wales hotel.com). Subway 4, 5, 6 to 86th Street; 6 to 96th Street. **Rates** $300-$500 double. **Rooms** 88. **Credit** AmEx, DC, Disc, MC, V. **Map** p406 E18 ⑥⓶
Purpose-built as a hotel in the early 1900s, the ten-storey Wales is a comfortable, convenient choice for a culture jaunt due to its proximity to Museum Mile. Tucked in the quietly affluent Carnegie Hill neighbourhood just above Madison Avenue's prime retail stretch, it's also well placed for an upmarket shopping spree. Standard double rooms are small, but high ceilings, large windows (with the original Edwardian frames) and an unfussy contemporary-classic style prevents them from seeming cramped; some of the suites are the size of many New Yorkers' apartments. At time of writing, the hotel was still undergoing a rolling renovation; by publication, all quarters should be redecorated with designer wallpaper, sleek new bathrooms and HD TVs. Higher-floor rooms on the east side have Central Park views, but all guests can enjoy it on the large roof terrace. Unusually,

CONSUME

Harlem Flophouse. *See p174.*

breakfast is included, and two onsite restaurants (the well-reviewed but pricey italian Joanna's and good-quality mini-chain Sarabeth's) provide plenty of choice for further meals or snacks.
Bar. Concierge. Disabled-adapted rooms. Internet (wireless; $10/day). Gym. No smoking floors. Parking ($49). Restaurants (2). Room service. TV: pay movies.

UPPER WEST SIDE
Expensive

On the Ave Hotel
222 W 77th Street, between Broadway & Amsterdam Avenue, New York, NY 10024

(1-212 362 1100/1-800 497 6028/www.ontheave-nyc.com). Subway 1 to 79th Street. **Rates** $300-$350 double. **Rooms** 281. **Credit** AmEx, DC, Disc, MC, V. **Map** p405 C19 ⑨
Given the affluent area, it's hardly surprising that On the Ave's rooms are stylish, with industrial-style bathroom sinks, HD TVs, ergonomic Herman Miller chairs, plus down comforters and Egyptian cotton sheets that make you want to stay in bed all day. Penthouse suites have fantastic balcony views of Central Park, but all guests have access to the verdant Adirondack balcony on the 16th floor. Although there's no shortage of restaurants in the locale, the hotel has two new eateries worth checking out: Fatty Crab and West Branch (the latest outing from celebrity chef Tom Valenti).

Bar. Business centre. Concierge. Disabled-adapted rooms. Gym. Internet (wireless; $12.95/day). No smoking. Parking ($50). Restaurants (2). Room service. TV: DVD/pay movies.
▶ See p161 for On the Ave's Citylife Hotel Group sibling Hotel Thirty Thirty.

Moderate

Country Inn the City
270 W 77th Street, between Broadway & West End Avenue, New York, NY 10024 (1-212 580 4183/www.countryinnthecity.com). Subway 1 to 79th Street. **Rates** $250-$375 double. **Rooms** 4. **No credit cards. Map** p405 C19 ㉔
The name of this charming B&B on the West Side is pretty accurate. Four-poster beds, flagons of brandy and moose heads in the hallways make this intimate inn a special retreat in the middle of the city. Note that they do not accept walk-ins.
Internet (wireless; free). No smoking.

Hotel Beacon
2130 Broadway, between 74th & 75th Streets, New York, NY 10023 (1-212 787 1100/1-800 572 4969/www.beaconhotel.com). Subway 1, 2, 3 to 72nd Street. **Rates** $220-$320 double. **Rooms** 259. **Credit** AmEx, DC, Disc, MC, V. **Map** p405 C20 ㉕
The Beacon offers very good value in a desirable neighbourhood that's only a short walk from Central and Riverside Parks. Rooms are clean and spacious, and include stylish marble bathrooms. The classic diner Viand Café downstairs has plenty of cheap eats.
Business centre. Concierge. Disabled-adapted rooms. Internet (wireless; $10/day). No smoking floors. TV: pay movies.

Hotel Belleclaire
250 W 77th Street, at Broadway, New York, NY 10024 (1-212 362 7700/www.hotelbelle claire.com). Subway 1 to 79th Street. **Rates** $189-$329 double. **Rooms** 197. **Credit** AmEx, DC, MC, V. **Map** p405 C19 ㉖
Housed in a landmark building near Lincoln Center, Central Park and Columbus Circle, the sleek Belleclaire is a steal for savvy travellers. The recently renovated rooms feature goose-down comforters, sleek padded headboards and mod lighting fixtures. Each room is equipped with a fridge – perfect for chilling your protein shake while you're hitting the state-of-the-art fitness centre.
Concierge. Disabled-adapted rooms. Gym. Internet (wireless; free). No smoking. Room service.

Marrakech
2688 Broadway, at 103rd Street, New York, NY 10025 (1-212 222 2954/www.marrakechhotel nyc.com). Subway 1 to 103rd Street. **Rates** $129-$399 double. **Rooms** 125. **Credit** AmEx, DC, Disc, MC, V. **Map** p406 C16 ㉗

Formerly the Hotel Malibu, nightclub and restaurant designer Lionel Ohayon (Crobar, Koi) was enlisted to turn this Upper West Side accommodation into a Manhattan take on Morocco. Rooms are warm-toned with diffused lighting and North African decorative touches, such as colourful embroidered cushions. Frills are limited, and there's no lift, but twentysomethings will appreciate the lively Morningside Heights scene nearby.
Bar. Business centre. Concierge. Internet (wireless; free). No smoking. TV: pay movies.

Hostels

Central Park Hostel
19 W 103rd Street, at Central Park West, New York, NY 10025 (1-212 678 0491/www.central parkhostel.com). Subway B, C to 103rd Street. **Rates** $34-$38 bed in dorm; $119-$179 private room with shared bath; $129-$179 studio. **Rooms** 202 beds in dorms; 21 private rooms; 7 studios. **No credit cards. Map** p406 D16 ㉖
Housed in a renovated brownstone, this tidy hostel offers dorm-style rooms that sleep four, six or eight people; private chambers with two beds and newly refurbished studio apartments with private bathrooms are also available. Credit cards are not accepted as payment, but are required to hold reservations.
Internet (wireless; free). No smoking.

Hostelling International New York
891 Amsterdam Avenue, at 103rd Street, New York, NY 10025 (1-212 932 2300/www.hinew york.org). Subway 1 to 103rd Street. **Rates** $29-$45 per person in dorm rooms; $135 family rooms; $150 private room with bath. **Rooms** 672 beds in dorms; 3 family rooms; 2 private rooms. **Credit** AmEx, DC, Disc, MC, V. **Map** p406 C16 ㉖
This budget lodging is actually the city's only 'real' hostel (a not-for-profit accommodation that belongs to the International Youth Hostel Federation), but it's also one of the most architecturally stunning. The gabled, Gothic-inspired brick and stone building spans the length of an entire city block, and is much admired by locals as well as those staying

CONSUME

THE BEST HOTEL POOLS

For laps over Central Park
Le Parker Meridien. See p168.

For rooftop cocktails
Hotel Gansevoort. See p159.

For lounging on a budget
RoomMate Grace Hotel. See p167.

there. The interior is somewhat institutional and the immaculate rooms are admittedly rather spare, but at least they're air-conditioned, and there is a shared kitchen and a large backyard. Linens and towels are free of charge. International travellers can pick up phone cards, MetroCards, souvenirs and sundries in the in-house shop.
Business centre. Disabled-adapted rooms. Internet (wireless; free). No smoking.

Jazz on the Park Hostel
36 W 106th Street, between Central Park West & Manhattan Avenue, New York, NY 10025 (1-212 932 1600/www.jazzonthepark.com). Subway B, C to 103rd Street. **Rates** $20-$65 per person in 2- to 12-bed dorm; $125-$200 private room with bath. **Beds** 310. **Credit** DC, MC, V. **Map** p406 D16 ⑦

Jazz on the Park might be the trendiest hostel in the city – the lounge is kitted out like a space-age techno club, and has a piano and pool table. But some visitors have been known to complain about the customer service, so make sure to double-check your room type and check-in date before you arrive. In summer, the back patio hosts a weekly barbecue. Linens, towels and a continental breakfast are complimentary, lockers come with a surcharge. Note that ISIC card holders receive a two per cent discount on room rates except at Jazz on Lenox and there's a 14-day maximum stay condition in place. *Internet (wireless; free). No smoking.*
Other locations Jazz on the Town Hostel, 307 E 14th Street, between First & Second Avenues, East Village, New York, NY 10003 (1-212 228 2780); Jazz on the City, 201 W 95th Street, at Amsterdam Avenue, Upper West Side, New York, NY 10025 (1-212 678 0323); Jazz on the Villa, 12 W 129th Street, at Fifth Avenue, Harlem, New York, NY 10027 (1-212 722 6252); Jazz on Lenox, 104 W 128th Street, at Malcolm X Boulevard (Lenox Avenue), Harlem, New York, NY 10027 (1-212 222 5773).

West End Studios
850 West End Avenue, at 102nd Street, New York, NY 10025 (1-212 749 7104/www.westend studios.com). Subway 1 to 103rd Street. **Rates** $23-$27 per person in 4- to 6-bed dorm; $34-$65 private room. **Beds** 85. **No credit cards.** **Map** p406 D16 ⑦

This six-storey elevator building on the Upper West Side is a long way from most tourist destinations (although it's within walking distance of Columbia University and Central Park), but visitors enjoy art deco-inspired rooms that are a cut above typical hostel offerings. Fresh linens daily, TVs and alarm clocks all come as standard. The hotel has a basement laundry facility and a front desk that's open 24/7, so you can come and go as you please.
Concierge. Internet (wireless; $10/day). No smoking.

HARLEM
Moderate

102Brownstone
102 W 118th Street, between Malcolm X Boulevard (Lenox Avenue) & Adam Clayton Powell Jr Boulevard (Seventh Avenue), New York, NY 10026 (1-212 662 4223/www.102 brownstone.com). Subway 2, 3 to 116th Street. **Rates** $175-$275. **Rooms** 6. **Credit** AmEx, DC, MC, V. **Map** p407 D14 ⑦

Located near Marcus Garvey Park on a landmark, tree-lined street, 102Brownstone features six substantial suites, all renovated and individually themed by lively proprietor Lizette Lanoue, who owns and lives in the 1892 Greek Revival row house with her husband. (We love the tranquil Zen and dreamy Luna quarters.) Lanoue aims to be unobtrusive and to make guests feel as though they are in their own apartment – an apartment with a Jacuzzi, that is. *Internet (wireless; free). No smoking. TV: DVD.*

Budget

★ Harlem Flophouse
242 W 123rd Street, between Adam Clayton Powell Jr Boulevard (Seventh Avenue) & Frederick Douglass Boulevard, New York, NY 10027 (1-212 662 0678/www.harlemflop house.com). Subway A, B, C, D to 125th Street. **Rates** $100-$175 single/double with shared bath. **Rooms** 4. **Credit** DC, MC, V. **Map** p407 D14 ⑦

The dark-wood interior, moody lighting and lilting jazz music make Rene Calvo's Harlem inn feel more like a 1930s speakeasy than a 21st-century B&B. The airy suites, named for Harlem Renaissance figures such as Chester Himes and Cozy Cole, have restored tin ceilings, glamorous chandeliers and working sinks in antique cabinets. *Photos p172. Concierge. Internet (wireless; free). No smoking.*

Brooklyn

BOERUM HILL, CARROLL GARDENS & COBBLE HILL
Moderate

Nu Hotel
85 Smith Street, between Atlantic Avenue & State Street, Brooklyn, NY 11201 (1-718 852 8585/www.nuhotelbrooklyn.com). Subway F to Bergen Street; A, C, 2, 3, 4, 5 to Jay Street-Borough Hall. **Rates** $199-$459 double. **Rooms** 93. **Credit** AmEx, DC, Disc, MC, V. **Map** p410 T10 ⑦

This area of Brooklyn has been a top dining, drinking and shopping destination for years, but prior to the opening of this five-storey boutique hotel in

CONSUME

Break for the Borough

Brooklyn starts to welcome guests in a slew of new hotels.

Although Brooklyn's growing attractions (adventurous art, music and theatre scenes, some first-rate restaurants) have been luring visitors for a few years, it hasn't been seen as a base for tourists – until now. As ever-rising rents push young creative types out of Manhattan, and formerly diverse areas are homogenised by national chains, visitors in search of New York's bohemian spirit may find the atmosphere they crave across the East River.

'Brooklyn is Manhattan's Left Bank,' says Robert Gaeta, a fourth-generation Brooklynite and manager of Park Slope's **Hotel Le Bleu** (*see p176*). What's more, he notes, 'You can still get an authentic taste of old New York here. There's a lot of cultural diversity; the neighbourhoods are still very unique.'

When the **New York Marriott Brooklyn** (333 Adams Street, near Willoughby Street, 1-718 246 7000, www.marriott. com) opened in 1998, it was the borough's first new hotel in 68 years. But in recent years, attendance at the borough's tourist sites has increased by five per cent; hoteliers have caught on, sparking a boom in construction. Over the next two years, Brooklyn is set to gain 2,000 hotel rooms, according to the Brooklyn Tourism office.

Now that apartments in Williamsburg and Dumbo are fetching millions of dollars, it was inevitable that boutique hotels would follow and the good news is that prices compare favourably to those on the island. The first two opened in late 2007: Hotel Le Bleu offers 48 rooms, many with breathtaking views of the Manhattan skyline, while Williamsburg's 54-room **Hotel Le Jolie** (*see p176*) allows indie music fans the chance to spend the night in the hotspot after a gig.

Summer 2008 saw the arrival of the 93-room **Nu Hotel** (*see p174*) on the edge of Brooklyn Heights. So far, the property is seeing a diverse cross-section of guests, according to general manager Bertrand Nelson. 'We've had people in the film business, bands, athletes and lots of Europeans. When I ask people what brings them to Brooklyn, they reply, "Oh, we heard this is the place to see now".'

Early in 2009, look for the 200-room **Aloft Hotel** (www.alofthotels.com) – a spin-off of the W hotel chain. And, a little further off, **Hotel Indigo** (www.v3hotels.com) is slated to open in 2010, adding 170 more rooms to downtown Brooklyn. All in all, there'll be plenty of choice for overnighters in this fast-improving part of town.

CONSUME

Hotel Le Bleu.

summer 2008, visitors had to hoof it back to Manhattan at the end of the night. Now they can choose from three types of loft-style rooms, all of which offer 32-inch flat-screen TVs, minimalist decor and roomy Aveda-stocked bathrooms with chalkboards (for creative musings or housekeeping requests, one imagines). Nu Suites feature a cosy bed nook with hammocks and a sitting area, while Nu Queen Suites come with bunk beds for children and modular furniture. The hotel is LEED-certified green, equipped with cork floors, organic sheets, bike storage and furnishings crafted from sustainable teak.

Bar. Business centre. Concierge. Disabled-adapted rooms. Gym. Internet (wireless; free). No smoking. Parking ($25). TV: pay movies.
▶ *See also p175 Break for the Borough.*

PARK SLOPE

Moderate

Bed & Breakfast on the Park

113 Prospect Park West, between 6th & 7th Streets, Brooklyn, NY 11215 (1-718 499 6115/ www.bbnyc.com). Subway F to Seventh Avenue. **Rates** $175-$365 double. **Rooms** 7. **Credit** DC, MC, V. **Map** p410 T12 ⑦

Staying at this 1895 brownstone, which faces lush Prospect Park, is like taking up residence in the pages of Edith Wharton's *The Age of Innocence*. The parlour floor is crammed with antique furniture, and guest rooms are furnished with love seats and canopy beds swathed in French linens. The Lady Liberty room boasts a rooftop garden and an antique bath tub.

Business centre. Concierge. Internet (wireless; free). No smoking. TV: pay movies.

Hotel Le Bleu

370 Fourth Avenue, at 5th Street, Brooklyn, NY 11215 (1-718 625 1500/www.hotellebleu. com). Subway F, M, R to 9th Street-Fourth Avenue; R to Union Street. **Rates** $280-$330 double. **Rooms** 48. **Credit** AmEx, DC, MC, V. **Map** p410 T10 ⑦

The Manhattanisation of Park Slope hit new heights in November 2007, when Andres Escobar's steel and glass hotel popped up on industrial Fourth Avenue. Couples will find the open shower design a plus; more conventional draws include 42-inch plasma TVs, goose-down comforters, iPod docking stations and free Wi-Fi in every room. If you're not keen on wandering the somewhat desolate avenue for sustenance, the two-floor Vue restaurant serves up intercontinental cuisine and views of the Manhattan skyline.

Bar. Concierge. Disabled-adapted rooms. Internet (wireless; free). No smoking. Parking (free). Restaurant. Room service. TV: DVD/pay movies.
▶ *See also p175 Break for the Borough.*

WILLIAMSBURG

Moderate

Hotel Le Jolie

235 Meeker Avenue, at Jackson Street, Brooklyn, NY 11211 (1-718 625 2100/www.hotelle jolie.com). Subway G, L to Metropolitan Avenue. **Rates** $209-$289 double. **Rooms** 54. **Credit** AmEx, DC, Disc, MC, V. **Map** p411 V8 ⑦

Williamsburg is finally grown up enough to earn a fresh, modern-looking hotel – too bad it's right on top of the Brooklyn-Queens Expressway. Inside, though, 54 well-maintained rooms offer king-size beds (fitted with allergen-free goose-down comforters and Egyptian cotton sheets), ergonomic Aeron desk chairs and 42-inch flat-screen TVs.

Business centre. Concierge. Disabled-adapted rooms. Internet (wireless; free). No smoking. Parking (free). Room service. TV: pay movies.
▶ *See also p175 Break for the Borough.*

OTHER AREAS

Budget

Akwaaba Mansion

347 MacDonough Street, between Lewis & Stuyvesant Avenues, Bedford-Stuyvesant, Brooklyn, NY 11233 (1-718 455 5958/www. akwaaba.com). Subway A, C to Utica Avenue. **Rates** $160-$175 double. **Rooms** 4. **Credit** AmEx, DC, Disc, MC, V. **Map** p410 W10 ⑦

Akwaaba means 'welcome' in Ghanaian, a fitting name for this gorgeous restored 1860s mansion with 14ft ceilings, ornate fireplaces, a wide screened-in porch and secluded flower garden. The rooms are decorated with African artefacts and textiles and all feature private lavatories. (The Black Memorabilia room sports a king-sized bed and Jacuzzi for two.) A hearty Southern-style breakfast and complimentary afternoon tea are served in the dining room or on the porch.

Concierge. Internet (wireless; free). No smoking.

Awesome Bed & Breakfast

136 Lawrence Street, between Fulton & Willoughby Streets, Downtown Brooklyn, NY 11201 (1-718 858 4859/www.awesome-bed-and-breakfast.com). Subway A, C, F to Jay Street-Borough Hall; M, R to Lawrence Street; 2, 3 to Hoyt Street. **Rates** $140-$160 double; $180-$195 triple/quad. **Rooms** 6. **Credit** AmEx, DC, MC, V. **Map** p410 T10 ⑦

'Awesome' isn't normally a word used to describe an outer-borough B&B, but these colourful rooms offer eye-popping details like giant daisies and purple drapes. The Dragon Palace room, for instance, features a dragon mural and Chinese furnishings. The bathrooms, though communal, are equally snazzy; complimentary breakfast is delivered to your door.

No smoking.

CONSUME

Restaurants & Cafés

Let the feasting begin.

Times are tough in New York. Given the current economic climate, plus high food and fuel prices, you'd think that the restaurant business would be feeling the pinch. But in Gotham, that doesn't appear to be the case – at least not yet. Restaurants and bars are continuing to open at a boom-time rate, nurturing New Yorkers' insatiable appetite for something new and great.

The sheer number and variety of restaurants in New York City – one count says more than 16,000 in Manhattan alone, from high-end food palaces to neighbourhood holes-in-the-wall – means that even residents need never eat at the same place twice. And the fierce competition for your cash means that restaurateurs are always thinking of creative ways to appeal to your tastebuds.

THE SCENE IN 2009

As much as its denizens value the variety of the Big Apple's edible offerings, there's one thing that may turn them on even more: the scene. New Yorkers are slaves to fashion, and if a restaurant is hot, chances are they'll want in. This year's hands-down most illustrious entrant to the list of impossible-to-get-into places is **Momofuku Ko**, which may be the most challenging reservation New Yorkers have ever tried to score. The 13-seat spot, from pork bun wunderkind David Chang, requires diners to snare reservations online – a new day opens for booking each morning – at www.momofuku.com. Suffice to say that it's the most sought-after table (or in this case, chef's counter in town), but, luckily, Chang has two other excellent options: **Momofuku Ssäm Bar** (*see p189*) and **Noodle Bar**.

For visitors craving a more traditional splurge that you might stand a fighting chance of accessing, French chef Alain Ducasse has returned to NYC with his third attempt at winning diners' palates. And the third time seems to have been lucky: with **Adour Alain Ducasse** (*see p199*) at the St Regis New York, the famed toque combines elegant French fare

with a formidable wine list. Elsewhere, the Upper West Side has recently become the new home to three notable fine dining destinations: the plush **Eighty One** (*see p206*), from former Sea Grill chef Ed Brown; **Dovetail** (*see p204*), a New American project from Compass's John Frasier; and **Bar Boulud**, a wine-and-charcuterie outfit from celebrated Lyonnais chef Daniel Boulud (*see p203* **Daniel**).

But it's not just new destinations that have captured local imaginations. The closing of beloved Meatpacking District spot Florent led to a flurry of media coverage, plenty of *bon voyage* celebrations and weeks of booked-solid reservations for regulars who couldn't bear to see the groundbreaker go. Happily, many old-timers are still holding on, including venerable fixtures such as the **Grand Central Oyster Bar** (*see p202*) and 1980s icons such as the **Odeon** (*see p180*), while several once-faded (or shuttered) classics – the **'21' Club** (*see p201*), the **Russian Tea Room** (*see p201*) – have been resurrected. And new traditions are always being made. Newcomers such as cosy locavore gastropub **Back Forty** (*see p186*) and off-the-beaten-track **Trestle on Tenth**

❶ Blue numbers given in this chapter correspond to the location of each restaurant and café on the street maps. *See pp402-412*.

About the reviews
The reviews in this chapter are adapted from the annual Time Out Eating & Drinking New York Guide *($9.99.*

CONSUME

INSIDE TRACK
TIPPING

Tipping etiquette can be a nightmare if you don't know what you are doing. However, things are simple here. Few restaurants add service to the bill for parties under six ; it's customary to give between 15 and 20 per cent. The easiest way to figure out the amount is to double the sales tax. Bartenders also get tipped – $1 a drink should ensure friendly pours.

(*see p194*) are giving diners restaurants with which they can forge new relationships. In New York, a return customer is really the best thing for which any restaurant can ask.

Elsewhere, the meat mania that has swept town over the last few years continues. Joining the new-style steakhouses and burger joints, the latest wave of carnivorous eateries is in the form of regional-biased barbecue joints (*see p210* **Give us a 'cue**). And, moving far from fashion, the city retains a vast collection of restaurants serving authentic, keenly priced eats from around the globe. In Manhattan, there are cheek-by-jowl Asian restaurants in **Chinatown**, while the stretch of West 32nd Street between Fifth Avenue and Broadway is lined with Korean eateries. Further afield, **Harlem** offers soul food and African cooking, while Queens offers Greek fare (in **Astoria**) and Indian cuisine (in **Jackson Heights**).

The essentials

Snagging reservations for popular places can be difficult, so be sure to call ahead. Super-trendy spots can be fully booked weeks in advance, although the majority require only a few days' notice (or less). Most restaurants fill up between 7pm and 9pm, and it's harder to bag a table on weekends than weekdays. If you don't mind eating early (5pm) or late (after 10pm), your chances of getting in to a hotspot will improve greatly. Alternatively, you can try to nab a reservation by calling at 5pm on the day you want to dine and hoping for a last-minute cancellation. Dress codes are rarely enforced, but some ultra-fancy eateries require men to don a jacket and tie. If in doubt, call ahead and ask, but note that you can never really overdress in this town.

Note that prices given for main courses in this chapter are averages. We've used the **$** symbol to indicate operations offering particularly good value: restaurants with main courses for around $10 or less, plus cafés and sandwich stops.

DOWNTOWN
Financial District

$ Financier Pâtisserie
62 Stone Street, between Hanover Square & Mill Lane (1-212 344 5600/www.financier pastries.com). Subway 2, 3 to Wall Street. **Open** 7am-8pm Mon-Fri; 8.30am-6.30pm Sat. **Average sandwich** $7. **Credit** AmEx, DC, MC, V. **Map** p402 F33 ❶ Café
Tucked down a cobblestone street, this sweet gem offers tasty café fare to office workers, tourists and locals seeking a pleasant alternative to the Financial District's ubiquitous pubs and delis. Savoury items, including hot pressed sandwiches (try the croque-monsieur), fresh salads, tarts and quiches are all delicious. But the pastries are where Financier excels, including classic éclairs, opera cake, and miniature *financiers*, which are free with each coffee. **Other locations** 35 Cedar Street, at William Street, Financial District (1-212 952 3838); 3-4 World Financial Center, Financial District (1-212 786 3220).

$ Jack's Stir Brew Coffee
222 Front Street, between Beekman Street & Peck Slip (1-212 227 7631/www.jacksstir brew.com). Subway A, C to Broadway-Nassau Street. **Open** 6am-7pm daily. **Average coffee** $2. **No credit cards. Map** p402 F32 ❷ Café
Java fiends convene at this award-winning caffeine spot that offers organic, shade-grown beans and a

Ed's Lobster Bar. *See p181.*

homey vibe. Coffee is served by chatty, quick-to-grin espresso artisans with a knack for oddball concoctions, such as the super-silky Mountie latte, infused with maple syrup.

Tribeca & Soho

★ Balthazar

80 Spring Street, between Broadway & Crosby Street (1-212 965 1414/www.balthazarny.com). Subway N, R, W to Prince Street; 6 to Spring Street. **Open** 7.30-11am, noon-5pm, 6pm-12.30am Mon-Fri; 10am-4pm, 6pm-midnight Sat; 10am-4pm, 5.30-11pm Sun. **Main course** $24. **Credit** AmEx, DC, Disc, MC, V. **Map** p403 E30 ❸ **French**

Not only is the iconic Balthazar still trendy, but the kitchen rarely makes a false step. At dinner, the place is perennially packed with rail-thin lookers dressed to the nines. But the bread is great, the food is good, and the service is surprisingly friendly. The $110 three-tiered seafood platter casts the most impressive shadow of any dish in town, the roasted chicken on mashed potatoes for two, *délicieux*. Don't hate the patrons because they're beautiful; just join them.

Bouley Bakery & Market

130 West Broadway, at Duane Street (1-212 608 5829/www.davidbouley.com). Subway A, C, E, 1, 2, 3 to Chambers Street. **Open** *Bakery* 7.30am-10pm Mon-Thur; 7.30am-7.30pm Fri-Sun. *Upstairs* 5.30-11pm Mon-Thur; 5.30-11.30pm Fri; 11am-3pm, 5.30-11.30pm Sat; 11am-4pm Sun.

Average sandwich $9. **Main course** $18. **Credit** AmEx, DC, Disc, MC, V. **Map** p402 E31 ❹ **American creative/café**

Chef David Bouley's casual tri-level enterprise, across the street from the upscale Bouley, has a handful of identities: a basement houses a small meat and fish counter, a cheese cellar and takeout options, and the street-level pâtisserie is filled with heavenly loaves, soups and elegant pre-made sandwiches. The real surprises, however, are upstairs, beginning with the six-seat sushi bar. The rest of the upstairs menu – mostly French, with some small Asian twists – is a bargain, and every dish could pass muster at Bouley proper for twice the price.

Other locations Bouley, 120 West Broadway, at Duane Street, Tribeca (1-212 964 2525).

▶ *See p246 for other top city bakeries.*

Landmarc Tribeca

179 West Broadway, between Leonard & Worth Streets (1-212 343 3883/www.anvilny.com). Subway 1 to Franklin Street. **Open** noon-2am Mon-Fri; 9am-2am Sat, Sun. **Main course** $26. **Credit** AmEx, DC, Disc, MC, V. **Map** p402 E31 ❺ **Eclectic**

This downtown dining destination quickly distinguished itself among Tribeca restaurants by serving heady bistro dishes (bone marrow, crispy sweetbreads) until 2am, and stocking the wine list with reasonably priced half bottles. Chef-owner Marc Murphy focuses on the tried-and-true: frisée aux lardons, boudin noir and several types of mussels. Metal beams and exposed brick add an

CONSUME

La Esquina. See p183.

CONSUME

unfinished edge to the elegant bi-level space. Those who have little restraint when it comes to sweets will appreciate the dessert menu: miniature portions cost just $4 a pop and a tasting of six goes for $16. **Other locations** Landmarc at the Time Warner Center, 3rd floor, 10 Columbus Circle, at Eighth Avenue, Upper West Side (1-212 823 6123).

★ Megu

62 Thomas Street, between Church Street & West Broadway (1-212 964 7777/www.megunyc. com). Subway A, C, 1, 2, 3 to Chambers Street. **Open** 11.30am-2.30pm, 5.30-10.15pm Mon-Wed; 11.15am-2.30pm, 5.30-11.15pm Thur, Fri; 5.30-11.15pm Sat; 5.30-10.15pm Sun. **Main course** $30. **Umami tasting menu** $80-$150. **Credit** AmEx, Disc, DC, MC, V. **Map** p402 E31 ⑥ Japanese

Since the day this awe-inspiring temple of Japanese cuisine opened in 2004, diners have criticised its overblown prices and unwieldy, complicated menu. But critics often forget to mention that this is one of the most thrilling meals you'll find in New York. Spring for one of the tasting menus: a parade of ingenious little bites and surprising presentations. Megu is equally serious about sushi. Three simple, glistening pieces delivered at the end of the meal are as breathtaking and as pleasurable as any you've had.

Other locations 845 UN Plaza, Trump World Tower, First Avenue, between 47th & 48th Streets, Midtown East (1-212 964 7777).

Nobu

105 Hudson Street, at Franklin Street (1-212 219 0500/www.noburestaurants.com). Subway 1 to Franklin Street. **Open** 11.45am-2.15pm, 5.45-10.15pm Mon-Fri; 5.45-10.15pm Sat, Sun. **Average sushi dinner** $32. **Omakase tasting menu** from $100. **Credit** AmEx, DC, Disc, MC, V. **Map** p402 E31 ⑦ Japanese

Since opening in 1994, the original Nobu has promised impeccable fish and serious stargazing – and it still delivers both: luscious fluke sashimi with crunchy, salty bits of dried miso at your table, Martha Stewart at the next. While chef Nobu Matsuhisa and his partners have taken Nobu worldwide (and opened a showy outpost on 57th Street), they've left this Tribeca mainstay in its slightly weathered but beloved form.

Other locations Nobu Fifty Seven, 40 W 57th Street, between Fifth & Sixth Avenues, Fifth Avenue & Around (1-212 757 3000).

Odeon

145 West Broadway, between Duane & Thomas Streets (1-212 233 0507/www.theodeon restaurant.com). Subway A, C, 1, 2, 3 to Chambers Street. **Open** 11.45am-1am Mon-Wed; 11.45am-2am Thur, Fri; 10am-2am Sat, Sun. **Main course** $22. **Credit** AmEx, DC, Disc, MC, V. **Map** p402 E31 ⑧ French

The Odeon has been part of the downtown scene for so long that it's hard to remember a time when Tribeca wasn't home to the iconic bistro. It's still a great destination for drinks, and diners can't go wrong with the tried-and-true standards: French onion soup blanketed with bubbling gruyère, crunchy fried calamari made to be dipped in tartar and spicy chipotle sauces, and steak au poivre with fries. The final hint of 1980s-style decadence: a wonderfully nostalgic caramelised banana tart.

★ Savoy

70 Prince Street, at Crosby Street (1-212 219 8570/www.savoynyc.com). Subway N, R, W to Prince Street; 6 to Spring Street. **Open** noon-10.30pm Mon-Thur; noon-11pm Fri, Sat; 6-10pm Sun. **Main course** $28. **Credit** AmEx, DC, MC, V. **Map** p403 E29 ➒ American creative
Chef Peter Hoffman maintains his reputation as one of the godfathers of the local foods movement at this comfortable Soho stalwart, outfitted with a wood-burning fireplace (in use during colder months) and a congenial, semicircular bar. Hoffman makes daily pilgrimages to the Union Square Greenmarket to assemble Savoy's farm-forward, aggressively seasonal menus, which can include flaky halibut, perched over a verdant fava bean purée, or duck, vibrantly pink within and sporting a slightly crunchy, salted crust.
► *See p91 for the Union Square Greenmarket.*

$ 'Wichcraft

397 Greenwich Street, at Beach Street (1-212 780 0577/www.wichcraftnyc.com). Subway 1 to Franklin Street. **Open** 7am-8.30pm Mon-Fri; 10am-6pm Sat, Sun. **Average sandwich** $8. **Credit** AmEx, DC, Disc, MC, V. **Map** p402 D31 ➓ Café
The panini craze has not yet passed; witness long lines of lunchers at Tom Colicchio's sophisticated sandwich shop. Breakfast sandwiches (available all day) play it straight, as does the corned beef with Swiss cheese and mustard seed sauce. But you can catch a heady whiff of Craft and Craftbar in the sandwich of marinated white anchovies, soft-cooked egg, roasted onion and frisée on country bread. End with a peanut butter cream'wich.
Other locations throughout the city.

Little Italy & Nolita

$ Café Habana

17 Prince Street, at Elizabeth Street (1-212 625 2001/www.ecoeatery.com). Subway N, R, W to Prince Street; 6 to Spring Street. **Open** 9am-midnight daily. **Main course** $10. **Credit** AmEx, DC, MC, V. **Map** p403 F29 ⓫ Cuban
The fashionable people milling around Nolita at all hours don't look like they eat, but they do – here. They storm this chrome corner fixture for the sexy scene and the addictive grilled corn: golden ears doused in fresh mayo, chargrilled and generously sprinkled with chili powder and grated cotija cheese. Staples include a Cuban sandwich of roasted pork, ham, melted Swiss and sliced pickles, and crisp beer-battered catfish with spicy mayo. For dessert, try

the *cajeta* (caramel) flan. Locals love the takeout annex next door (open May-Oct), where they get that corn-on-a-stick to go.
Other locations 757 Fulton Street, at South Portland Avenue, Fort Greene, Brooklyn (1-718 858 9500).

Ed's Lobster Bar

222 Lafayette Street, between Kenmare & Spring Streets (1-212 343 3236/www.lobsterbarnyc. com). Subway B, D, F, V to Broadway-Lafayette Street. **Open** noon-3pm, 5-11pm Tue-Thur; noon-3pm, 5pm-midnight Fri; noon-midnight Sat; noon-9pm Sun. **Main course** $21. **Credit** AmEx, DC, MC, V. **Map** p403 E30 ⓬ Seafood
Chef Ed McFarland (Pearl Oyster Bar) takes on the city's shellfish shack formula – pioneered at his old stomping ground – at this tiny Soho spot. If you secure a place at the 30-seat marble bar or one of the few tables in the whitewashed eaterie, expect superlative raw-bar eats, delicately fried clams and

Prize Bites

Our selection of 2008 award winners.

Every year, *Time Out New York* recognises the best of the city's thousands of restaurants. The opinions of our culinary experts are combined with votes from *TONY* readers to form a list of outstanding eateries. Below are some of the winners from the 2008 awards.

BEST VEGETARIAN RESTAURANT
Blossom. *See p193.*

BEST NEW COFFEEHOUSE
Irving Farm Coffee Company. *See p191.*

BEST PLACE TO BE SEEN
Waverly Inn. *See p193.*

BEST BARBECUE
Hill Country. *See p193.*

BEST MEAL IN A TOURIST DISTRICT
Omido. *See p199.*

BEST DOWNMARKET OFFSHOOT FROM AN UPMARKET CHEF
Back Forty. *See p186.*

BEST JUSTIFICATION OF INGREDIENTS WORSHIP
Eighty One. *See p206.*

CONSUME

lobster served every which way: steamed, grilled, broiled, chilled, stuffed into a pie and the crowd favourite, the lobster roll. Here, it's a buttered bun stuffed with premium chunks of meat and just a light coating of mayo. *Photos pp178-179.*

★ La Esquina
106 Kenmare Street, at Cleveland Place (1-646 613 7100/www.esquinanyc.com). Subway 6 to Spring Street. **Open** *Taqueria* 8am-5am Mon-Fri; noon-5am Sat, Sun. *Café* noon-midnight daily. *Restaurant* 6pm-midnight daily. **Main course** $21. **Credit** AmEx, DC, MC, V. **Map** p403 E30 ⑬ Mexican
This cabbie-pit-stop-turned-taco-stand has a hidden passageway to an elaborate underground grotto and restaurant. There are three dining and drinking areas: first, a street-level taqueria, serving a short-order menu of fish tacos and Mexican tortas. Around the corner is a 30-seat café, its shelves stocked with books and old vinyl. Lastly, there's a dungeonesque restaurant and lounge accessible through a back door of the taqueria (to enter, you have to confirm that you have a reservation). It's worth the hassle: a world of Mexican murals, fine tequilas, *huitlacoche* quesadillas and crab tostadas awaits. *Photo p180.*

Lombardi's
32 Spring Street, between Mott & Mulberry Streets (1-212 941 7994/www.firstpizza.com). Subway 6 to Spring Street. **Open** 11.30am-11pm Mon-Thur, Sun; 11.30am-midnight Fri, Sat. **Large pizza** $19.50. **No credit cards. Map** p403 F30 ⑭ Pizza
Lombardi's is the city's oldest pizzeria, established in 1905, and offering pies at their best – made in a coal-fired oven and with a chewy, thin crust. The pepperoni is fantastic, as are the killer meatballs. The setting is classic pizza parlour, with wooden booths and red and white checked tablecloths. It's hard to vouch for how the pizzas tasted a century ago, but we can safely attest that today, Lombardi's bakes a hot contender for the best pie in the city.
▶ *Grimaldi's in Brooklyn is also good for old-school pizza; see p211.*

Peasant
194 Elizabeth Street, between Prince & Spring Streets (1-212 965 9511/www.peasantnyc.com). Subway B, D, F, V to Broadway-Lafayette Street; 6 to Bleecker Street. **Open** 6-11pm Tue-Sat; 6-10pm Sun. **Main course** $27. **Credit** AmEx, DC, MC, V. **Map** p403 E29 ⑮ Italian
The dining room at Peasant, one of downtown's most celebrated Italian restaurants, is equal parts rustic and urban chic. Cement floors and metal chairs give the place an unfinished edge, while the gaping brick oven and lengthy wooden bar provide the telltale old-world notes. Dishes that emerge from the fire are particularly good, including gooey speck-wrapped bocconcini (mozzarella), which arrive at the table bubbly and molten.

THE BEST
CLASSIC NEW YORK NOSH

For a burger
Corner Bistro. *See p191.*

For a pizza
Grimaldi's. *See p211.*

For pastrami on rye
Katz's Delicatessen. *See p185.*

Public
210 Elizabeth Street, between Prince & Spring Streets (1-212 343 7011/www.public-nyc.com). Subway N, R, W to Prince Street; 6 to Spring Street. **Open** 6-11.30pm Mon-Thur; 6pm-midnight Fri; 11am-3.30pm, 6pm-midnight Sat, Sun. **Main course** $25. **Credit** AmEx, DC, Disc, MC, V. **Map** p403 E29 ⑯ Eclectic
This sceney designer restaurant inside a former bakery brings a touch of the Meatpacking District to Nolita. Moodily lit and industrially chic, its two conjoined spaces showcase a sleek mix of concrete, exposed brick and wood panelling. The mastermind behind Public's globally-inspired cuisine is British-trained Brad Farmerie, whose travels have left a cosmopolitan mark on his culinary concoctions. Reflecting pan-Pacific, Middle Eastern and Southeast Asian influences, the clipboard menu offers creative dishes such as grilled kangaroo on a coriander falafel; snail and oxtail ravioli; and pan-seared Tasmanian sea trout, all poetically presented and paired with interesting wines.

Chinatown

$ Doyers Vietnamese Restaurant
11 Doyers Street, between Bowery & Pell Street (1-212 513 1521). Subway J, M, Z, N, Q, R, W, 6 to Canal Street. **Open** 11am-10pm Mon-Thur, Sun; 11am-11pm Fri, Sat. **Main course** $8. **Credit** AmEx. **Map** p402 F31 ⑰ Vietnamese
Hidden in a basement on a zigzagging Chinatown alley, this bare-bones joint features a menu that requires (and rewards) exploration. The long appetisers list includes sweet-and-smoky sugarcane wrapped with grilled shrimp, and a delicious Vietnamese crêpe crammed with shrimp and pork. In the winter, hot-pot soups (served on a tabletop stove) feature the same exceptional broth base and come packed with vegetables, no matter the add-in.

★ Golden Bridge Restaurant
50 Bowery, between Bayard & Canal Streets (1-212 227 8831). Subway B, D to Grand Street; J, M, Z, N, Q, R, W, 6 to Canal Street. **Open** 9am-midnight daily. **Average dim sum** $3. **Credit** DC, MC, V. **Map** p402 F31 ⑱ Chinese

CONSUME

CONSUME

Peking Duck House.

In this dim sum house, carts patrol a spacious dining room that overlooks the Manhattan Bridge. Flag one of them down to procure fresh Cantonese standards such as clams in black bean sauce and pillowy pork buns, plus more unusual items including an egg tart with a soft taro crust. Look for the elusive cart with the mysterious wooden bucket; it's filled with sweetened tofu. Watch out for the weekday special, when all dim sum cost $2.25 each.

$ Jing Fong

20 Elizabeth Street, between Bayard & Canal Street (1-212 964 5256). Subway J, M, Z, N, Q, R, W, 6 to Canal Street. **Open** 9.30am-10pm daily. **Main course** $10. **Credit** AmEx, DC, MC, V. **Map** p402 F31 ⑲ Chinese

For some, Jing Fong might be intimidating: it's marked by giant escalators, a vast dining room and walkie-talkie-toting waiters marshalling diners. But it has remarkable dim sum. The shrimp shumai with glass noodles is exceptional, while the freshness and originality of the more mundane offerings keep people coming back for more.

Peking Duck House

28 Mott Street, between Mosco & Pell Streets (1-212 227 1810/www.pekingduckhousenyc.com). Subway J, M, Z, N, Q, R, W, 6 to Canal Street. **Open** 11.30am-10pm Mon-Thur, Sun; 11.30am-11pm Fri, Sat. **Main course** $15. **Credit** AmEx, DC, MC, V. **Map** p402 F31 ⑳ Chinese

Your waiter parades the roasted duck past your party before placing it on the centre show table. A chef brandishes his knives dramatically, then slices the aromatic, crisp-skinned, succulent meat with great flair. Folks at other tables drool with envy. (Don't they know that this establishment doesn't require you to order the speciality in advance? Pity.) Select the 'three-way' and your duck will yield the main course, a vegetable stir-fry with leftover bits of meat and a cabbage soup made with the remaining bone.

Lower East Side

Clinton Street Baking Company

4 Clinton Street, between E Houston & Stanton Streets (1-646 602 6263/www.clintonstreet baking.com). Subway F to Delancey Street; J, M, Z to Delancey-Essex Streets. **Open** 8am-4pm, 6-11pm Mon-Fri; 10am-4pm, 6-11pm Sat; 10am-4pm Sun. **Main course** $16. **Credit** (evenings only) AmEx, DC, MC, V. **Map** p403 G29 ㉑ Café

The warm buttermilk biscuits and fluffy plate-size pancakes at this pioneering little eaterie are reason enough to face the brunch-time crowds. If you want to avoid the onslaught, the homey LES spot is just as reliable at both lunch and dinner, when locals drop in for fish tacos and a daily $10 beer-and-burger special from 6pm to 8pm: eight ounces of Black Angus topped with Swiss cheese and caramelised onions, served with a Brooklyn Lager.

Although the menu claims French-African influences, the best items come straight from the bistro, like steak frites, dripping with juices and a side of aggressively seasoned fries.

Freemans
2 Freeman Alley, off Rivington Street, between Bowery & Chrystie Street (1-212 420 0012/ www.freemansrestaurant.com). Subway F, V to Lower East Side-Second Avenue; J, M, Z to Bowery. **Open** 11am-4pm, 6-11.30pm daily. **Main course** $19. **Credit** AmEx, DC, Disc, MC, V. **Map** p403 F29 ㉔ **American**
Up at the end of a graffiti-marked alley, Freemans' colonial tavern-meets-hunting lodge style, has found a welcome home with retro-loving Lower East Siders. Garage-sale oil paintings and moose antlers serve as backdrops to a curved zinc bar, while the menu recalls a simpler time – devils on horseback (prunes stuffed with Stilton cheese and wrapped in bacon); rum-soaked ribs, the meat falling off the bone with a gentle nudge of the fork; and stiff cocktails that'll get you good and sauced.

'Inoteca
98 Rivington Street, at Ludlow Street (1-212 614 0473/www.inotecanyc.com). Subway F to Delancey Street; J, M, Z to Delancey-Essex Streets. **Open** noon-3am Mon-Fri; 10am-3am Sat, Sun. **Average small plate** $9. **Credit** AmEx, DC, MC, V. **Map** p403 G29 ㉕ **Italian**
Spending time in this close-packed wine and snacks haven is a bit like visiting a small trattoria in Italy: friends gather together to share great food and good, well-priced wine in a room that is abuzz with life and chatter. The truffled egg toast remains the signature dish. But salads and antipasti – tender grilled calamari with borlotti beans and fennel, and dense, delicious meatballs – are perfect with a bottle from the small producer Italian wine list.

Katz's Delicatessen
205 E Houston Street, at Ludlow Street (1-212 254-2246/www.katzdeli.com). Subway F, V to Lower East Side-Second Avenue. **Open** 8am-10pm Mon, Tue, Sun; 8am-11pm Wed, Thur;

$ Congee Village
100 Allen Street, between Broome & Delancey Streets (1-212 941 1818/www.congeevillage restaurants.com). Subway F to Delancey Street; J, M, Z to Delancey-Essex Streets. **Open** 10.30am-12.30am Mon-Thur, Sun; 10.30am-2am Fri, Sat. **Main course** $12. **Credit** AmEx, DC, MC, V. **Map** p403 F30 ㉒ **Chinese**
If you've never indulged in the starchy comfort of congee, this is a good place to be initiated. The rice porridge, cooked to bubbling in a clay pot over a slow fire, is best early in the day; pick a chunky version, such as the treasure-laden seafood or sliced fish. Blue clams in black bean sauce are pulled out of the wok at precisely the moment of maximum tenderness, while crabs are impeccably fresh. Service is brisk, but on a typical night, it's easy to see why: the queue winds out the door.

Les Enfants Terribles
37 Canal Street, at Ludlow Street (1-212 777 7518/www.lesenfantsterriblesnyc.com). Subway F to East Broadway. **Open** 10am-midnight daily. **Main course** $18. **Credit** AmEx. **Map** p403 G30 ㉓ **African**
A lively hangout, Les Enfants Terribles serves up good food to patrons who enjoy the positive nightlife vibe while lounging in the worn-in brown leather banquettes. From framed wall photos, Picasso looks on at the bohemian hang, which revels in its own artiness and is echoed by the suave waitstaff.

> ### INSIDE TRACK
> ### LIGHTING UP
>
> A strict city-wide smoking ban means smokers have to slip outside for a post-prandial cigarette these days. The only legal indoor places to smoke are either venues that largely cater to cigar smokers (and actually sell cigars and cigarettes; *see p224*) or spaces that have created areas specifically for smokers, and that somehow pass legal muster.

CONSUME

THE BEST
LATE-NIGHT EATS

For decadent fondue-dipping
Bourgeois Pig. *See p186.*

For a booze-soaking hot dog
Crif Dogs. *See p187.*

For all-hours American classics
Empire Diner. *See p194.*

8am-3am Fri, Sat. **Average sandwich** $15.
Credit AmEx, DC, Disc, MC, V. **Map** p403 F29
❷⑥ **American**
This cavernous old dining hall is a repository of living history. Arrive at 11am on a Sunday morning, and the line may be out the door. Grab a ticket and approach the long counter. First, a hot dog. The weenies here are without peer; crisp-skinned, all-beef dogs that are worth the $3.10 tag. Then shuffle down and order your legendarily shareable sandwich. The pastrami is simply da best. Everything tastes better with a glass of the hoppy house lager; if you're on the wagon, make it a Dr Brown's soda.
▶ *See p76 for more local kosher nosh.*

Oliva

161 E Houston Street, at Allen Street (1-212 228 4143/www.olivanyc.com). Subway F, V to Lower East Side-Second Avenue. **Open** 5.30pm-midnight Mon-Thur; 5.30pm-1am Fri; 11am-1am Sat, Sun. **Main course** $16. **Tapas** $8. **Credit** AmEx. **Map** p403 F29 ❷⑦ **Spanish**
With a Cuban salsa band playing most nights of the week, this spirited sangria and tapas eatery often gets as loud as the corner of Houston and Allen outside. Oliva primarily peddles traditional tapas, from a fat wedge of tortilla and warm or ham-flecked croquettes to plump olives. A few Basque-tinged bites are also on offer: the tastiest is the txangurro, crab bulging with tarragon and a dash of cognac. The buzzy, tightly packed room is lined with wooden tables spray-painted with images of red bulls. ¡Olé!

Le Père Pinard

175 Ludlow Street, between E Houston & Stanton Streets (1-212 777 4917/www.lepere pinard.com). Subway F, V to Lower East Side-Second Avenue. **Open** 5pm-midnight Mon-Wed; 5pm-1am Thur; 5pm-2am Fri, Sat; 5pm-11am Sun. **Main course** $23. **Credit** AmEx. **Map** p403 F29 ❷⑧ **French**
See p207 **Secret gardens**.

★ Stanton Social

99 Stanton Street, between Ludlow & Orchard Streets (1-212 995 0099/www.thestanton social.com). Subway F, V to Lower East Side-

Second Avenue. **Open** 5pm-2am Mon-Wed; 5pm-3am Thur, Fri; 11.30am-3am Sat; 11.30am-2am Sun. **Average small plate** $15. **Credit** AmEx, DC, Disc, MC, V. **Map** p403 G29 ❷⑨ **Eclectic**
Plenty of trendy spots have opened on the Lower East Side, but none with as much eye candy as this. Gorgeous chandeliers, lizard-skin banquettes and retro rounded booths only hint at the 1940s-inspired elegance of the three-level restaurant. Not that the decor steals the show. Chris Santos has created 40 shareable, international plates, all of which receive special treatment. French onion soup comes in dumpling form; red snapper tacos are covered with an irresistibly fiery mango and avocado salsa.

East Village

Back Forty

190 Avenue B, between 11th & 12th Streets (1-212 388 1990/www.backfortynyc.com). Subway L to First Avenue. **Open** 6-11pm Mon-Thur; 6pm-midnight Fri, Sat; noon-3.30, 6-10pm Sun. **Main course** $15. **Credit** AmEx, DC, MC, V. **Map** p403 G28 ❸⓪ **American**
Chef-restaurateur Peter Hoffman (Savoy) is behind this East Village seasonal-eats tavern, where farmhouse chic prevails in the decor and on the menu. The offerings vary, but the veggies consistently shine: in season, baby cauliflower gratin with leeks and gruyère is explosively flavourful, and you'll rarely taste better brussels sprouts (marinated in shallot butter and dotted with dried cherries). Though some mains are middling (a lobster and crab roll is a little stringy), the creamy stout float is one of many reasons you'll be coming back.

Bourgeois Pig

111 E 7th Street, between First Avenue & Avenue A (1-212 475 2246/www.thepigny.com). Subway F, V to Lower East Side-Second Avenue; 6 to Astor Place. **Open** 5pm-2am Mon-Thur, Sun; 5pm-3am Fri, Sat. **Average fondue** $24. **Credit** AmEx, DC, MC, V. **Map** p403 F28 ❸① **Wine bar**
There's nothing bourgeois about the industrial metal steps down to this wine and fondue spot. But inside, ornate mirrors and antique chairs give the tiny red-lit space a decidedly decadent feel. Trendy locals snack on tasty *bruschetta* or bubbling cheese fondue – the raclette is extremely good – served with heaps of assorted breads, crudités and fresh fruit for dipping. The brief wine list is well chosen and prices are halved during the daily happy hour (3-7pm) and all night on Mondays and Tuesdays. *Photos pp190-191.*
Other locations Bourgeois Pig West, 124 MacDougal Street, between W 3rd & Bleecker Streets, Greenwich Village (1-212 254 0575).

$ Caracas Arepa Bar

91 E 7th Street, between First Avenue & Avenue A (1-212 228 5062/www.caracasarepabar.com). Subway F, V to Lower East Side-Second Avenue;

6 to Astor Place. **Open** noon-11pm Tue-Sat; noon-10pm Sun. **Arepa** $4. **Credit** AmEx, DC, Disc, MC, V. **Map** p403 F28 ❷ **Venezuelan**
This endearing spot, with flower-patterned, vinyl-covered tables, zaps you straight to Caracas. The secret is in the *arepas* themselves: each patty is made from scratch daily. The pita-like pockets are stuffed with a choice of 18 fillings, such as chicken and avocado or mushrooms with tofu. Top off your snack with a *cocada*, a thick and creamy milkshake made with freshly grated coconut and cinnamon.

Caravan of Dreams

405 E 6th Street, between First Avenue & Avenue A (1-212 254 1613/www.caravan ofdreams.net). Subway L to First Avenue, 6 to Astor Place. **Open** 11am-11pm Mon-Fri; 11am-midnight Sat. **Main course** $20. **Credit** AmEx, DC, MC, V. **Map** p403 F28 ❸ **Vegetarian**
This longtime East Village hangout offers both regular meat-free dishes – grilled seitan nachos, black-bean chili, stir-fries – and 'live foods' made from uncooked fruits, vegetables, nuts and seeds. Live 'hummus' with a twist (whipped from cold-processed tahini and raw almonds instead of the usual chickpeas) can be scooped up with pressed flaxseed 'chips'; the live Love Boat pairs almond-Brazil nut 'meatballs' with mango chutney and cool marinara sauce on a napa cabbage leaf. Naturally, there are loads of salads and some macrobiotically-balanced rice and seaweed combos.

ChikaLicious

203 E 10th Street, between First & Second Avenues (1-212 995 9511/www.chikalicious.com). Subway L to Third Avenue; 6 to Astor Place. **Open** 3-10.45pm Thur-Sun. **Dessert prix fixe** $12. **Credit** AmEx, DC, MC, V. **Map** p403 F28 ❹ **Café**
Pastry Chef Chika Tillman, the chick with a whisk, gives diners a voyeuristic thrill as she preps, pipes and plates her desserts in expert fashion. A multi-course 'meal' may include an amuse-bouche such as coconut sorbet in a little pool of chocolate-infused tea gelée. The main course might be a warm chocolate tart with pink-peppercorn ice-cream, a mocha and hazelnut trifle or a delicious fromage blanc cheesecake. It all ends with darling petit fours. As if you needed them.

$ Crif Dogs

113 St Marks Place, between First Avenue & Avenue A (1-212 614 2728). Subway L to First Avenue; 6 to Astor Place. **Open** noon-2am Mon-Fri; noon-4am Fri, Sat; noon-midnight Sun. **Average hot dog** $4. **Credit** AmEx, DC, MC, V. **Map** p403 F28 ❺ **American**
Crif's snappy deep-fried or grilled dogs have a cult following among tube-steak aficionados, who swarm the St Mark's Place joint at all hours for combos such as the Spicy Redneck (bacon-wrapped and covered in chili, coleslaw and jalapeños) and the Chihuahua (bacon-wrapped with sour cream and avocado).

Back Forty.

Gnocco Cucina & Tradizione

*337 E 10th Street, between Avenues A & B
(1-212 677 1913/www.gnocco.com). Subway L
to First Avenue.* **Open** 5pm-midnight Mon-Fri;
noon-midnight Sat, Sun. **Main course** $15.
Credit AmEx. **Map** p403 G28 **36** **Italian**
See p207 **Secret gardens**.

★ Momofuku Ssäm Bar

*207 Second Avenue, at 13th Street (1-212 254
3500/www.momofuku.com). Subway L to First
or Third Avenues; L, N, Q, R, W, 4, 5, 6 to 14th
Street-Union Square.* **Open** 11am-midnight
Mon-Thur, Sun; 11am-2am Fri, Sat. **Main
course** $16. **Credit** AmEx, DC, MC, V.
Map p403 F27 **37** **Korean**
At chef David Chang's second restaurant, waiters
hustle to noisy rock music in the 50-seat space,
which feels expansive compared with its Noodle Bar
predecessor's crowded counter dining. If you do opt
to sit at the counter, however, you can watch chefs
behind it create concoctions including the wonderfully fatty pork-belly steamed bun with hoisin sauce
and cucumbers, and the house *ssäm* (Korean for
'wrap'), which might be the finest burrito in the city.
Other locations Momofuku Ko, 163 First
Avenue, at 10th Street, East Village (no phone);
Momofuku Noodle Bar, 171 First Avenue,
between 10th & 11th Streets, East Village
(1-212 777 7773).

$ Podunk

*231 E 5th Street, between Second & Third
Avenues (1-212 677 7722). Subway F to Lower
East Side-Second Avenue; 6 to Astor Place.*
Open 11am-9pm Tue-Sun. **Average pastry**
$4. **No credit cards. Map** p403 F28 **38** **Café**
Step through the creaky screened door and out of
Manhattan. In her round granny glasses and ban-
danna, Elspeth, the Minnesotan owner, brings a mellow rural vibe to her knick-knacked tea shop. She
offers more than 85 types of tea (try spicy ginger-
verbena or iced strawberry-hibiscus); and 22 'informal tea meals' featuring freshly baked vanilla
cupcakes, lemon-ginger cookies and cranberry-
pecan scones. While away the afternoon in an
Adirondack chair or gather a dozen of your best
friends for a private tea party.

Veselka

*144 Second Avenue, at 9th Street (1-212 228
9682/www.veselka.com). Subway L to Third
Avenue; 6 to Astor Place.* **Open** 24hrs daily.
Main course $15. **Credit** AmEx, DC,
MC, V. **Map** p403 F28 **39** **Eastern European**
When you need food to soak up the mess of drinks
you've consumed in the East Village, Veselka is a
dream come true: a relatively inexpensive Eastern
European restaurant with plenty of seats and open
24 hours a day. Hearty appetites can get a platter
of classic Ukrainian grub: goulash, *kielbasa*, beef

Stroganoff or *bigos* stew. Save room for the sweet
stuff too: they've got pies, cakes, egg creams and
milkshakes – plus Ukrainian poppy seed cake and
kutya (traditional pudding made with
berries, raisins, walnuts, poppy seeds and honey).
▶ *For more on Ukrainian culture in the East
Village, see p82.*

Greenwich Village

Blue Hill

*75 Washington Place, between Washington
Square West & Sixth Avenue (1-212 539 1776
www.bluehillnyc.com). Subway A, B, C, D, E, F,
V to W 4th Street.* **Open** 5.30-11pm Mon-Sat;
5.30-10pm Sun. **Main course** $28. **Credit**
AmEx, DC, MC, V. **Map** p403 E28 **40** **American**
More than a mere crusader for sustainability, Dan
Barber is also one of the most talented cooks in town,
building his menu around whatever's at its peak on
his Westchester farm (home to a sibling restaurant).
During fresh pea season, bright green infuses every
inch of the menu, from a velvety spring pea soup to
sous-vide duck breast as soft as sushi fanned over
a slivered bed of sugar snap peas. Once among the
most sedate restaurants in the Village, this subterranean jewel has become one of the most raucous.

BondSt

*6 Bond Street, between Broadway & Lafayette
Street (1-212 777 2500). Subway B, D, F, V to
Broadway-Lafayette; 6 to Bleecker Street.* **Open**
6pm-midnight Mon, Sun; 6pm-1.30am Tue-Sat.
Average roll $10. **Omakase** $40-$120. **Credit**
AmEx, DC, MC, V. **Map** p403 E29 **41** **Japanese**
The sleek, minimalist decor and pretty crowd make
BondSt's dining rooms seem like a bento box full of
Prada, but the Japanese-fusion menu proves that
there's some substance behind the style here.
Though the quality of the sushi and sashimi is surprisingly middling, the small plates adeptly show
off the kitchen's skill, especially in dishes such as
scallop carpaccio, where tarragon-touched fish discs
sit atop citrusy ice shavings. Desserts such as
sake crème brûlée demonstrate that the creativity
doesn't stop with the savoury bites.

Il Buco

*47 Bond Street, between Lafayette Street &
Bowery (1-212 533 1932/www.ilbuco.com).
Subway B, D, F, V to Broadway-Lafayette Street;
6 to Bleecker Street.* **Open** 6pm-midnight Mon;
noon-3.30pm, 6pm-midnight Tue-Thur; noon-
3.30pm, 6pm-1am Fri, Sat; 5pm-midnight Sun.
Main course $28. **Credit** AmEx, DC, MC, V.
Map p403 F29 **42** **Italian**
The old-world charm of well-worn communal
tables, dangling copper cookware and flickering
lamps may help explain why a ten-year-old restaurant is still tough to get into on a Saturday night.
Seasonal produce shapes the menu of chef Ed Witt

CONSUME

(Daniel, River Café). *Primi* include wood-grilled, balsamic-glazed quail over organic beans, and a thin-crust pizza with fresh porcini, shallots and aged Asturian goat's cheese. Roasted suckling pig snuggled into soft polenta gets a kick from wild fennel and sautéed chicory and you can dunk the warm country bread in Umbrian olive oils produced exclusively for Il Buco.

Five Points

31 Great Jones Street, between Lafayette Street & Bowery (1-212 253 5700/www.fivepoints restaurant.com). Subway B, D, F, V to Broadway-Lafayette Street; 6 to Bleecker Street. **Open** noon-3pm, 5.30pm-midnight Mon-Fri; 11am-3pm, 6pm-midnight Sat; 11am-3pm, 5.30-10pm Sun. **Main course** $23. **Credit** AmEx, DC, MC, V. **Map** p403 F29 ⑬ **American**
Five Points is one of those rare places where grown-ups and scenesters, romantics and power brokers can all coexist happily. The vaguely country-style dining room bustles nightly the way a great neighbourhood restaurant should. Chef-owner Marc Meyer's ever-changing seasonal menu might include a side dish of roasted corn, a salad of fresh figs, or scallops with deliciously sweet corn chowder. Happy hour is not to be missed: from 5pm to 6pm on weeknights, martinis are $5 and oysters are just two bucks each.

$ Peanut Butter & Co

240 Sullivan Street, between Bleecker & W 3rd Streets (1-212 677 3995/www.ilovepeanut butter.com). Subway A, B, C, D, E, F, V to W 4th Street. **Open** 11am-9pm Mon-Thur, Sun; 11am-10pm Fri, Sat. **Sandwich** $6. **Credit** AmEx, DC, Disc, MC, V. **Map** p403 E29 ⑭ **Café**
The staff at PB & Co grinds peanuts daily to create childhood throwbacks such as the popular Elvis – the King's infamous favourite of peanut butter, bacon, banana and honey, grilled. The cold cinnamon-raisin-flavoured peanut butter sandwich with vanilla cream cheese and tart apple slices is good taste and texture rolled into one. Death by Peanut Butter is a landslide of ice-cream, Peanut Butter Cap'n Crunch and peanut butter chips. Heaven.

West Village & Meatpacking District

Bar Blanc

142 W 10th Street, between Greenwich Avenue & Waverly Place (1-212 255 2330/www.bar blanc.com). Subway A, C, E, B, D, F, V to W 4th Street. **Open** 5.30-11pm Tue-Sun. **Main course** $26. **Credit** AmEx, DC, MC, V. **Map** p403 D28 ⑮ **French**
Cooked up by a trio of Bouley alums, Bar Blanc is true to its name: there's a white marble bar, the brick walls are sheathed in white plaster, and the seats are a snowy vinyl. But chef Cesar Ramirez's rich and

classic food is anything but stark. An appetiser of pan-seared jumbo scallops is coated in orange-zest confit, and slow-cooked entrées, such as fettuccine with mustard-braised rabbit and roasted tomatoes, reflect the workings of a chef who takes his time. Service can be equally slow, but excellent desserts, such as the roasted pineapple in basil oil, make waiting a pleasure.
▶ *For Bouley Bakery itself, see p179.*

Barbuto

775 Washington Street, between Jane & W 12th Streets (1-212 924 9700/www.barbutonyc.com). Subway A, C, E to 14th Street; L to Eighth Avenue. **Open** noon-11pm Mon-Wed; noon-midnight Thur-Sat; noon-10pm Sun. **Main course** $18. **Credit** AmEx, DC, Disc, MC, V. **Map** p403 C28 ⑯ **Italian**
The raw, cement-floored space that once held the coffee and cocktail bar Braque has become a serious restaurant. Owner Fabrizio Ferri (who runs the Industria Superstudio complex) has teamed with chef Jonathan Waxman to create a season-driven kitchen. The earthy cooking is top-notch: marvellously light calamari comes in lemon-garlic sauce; *chitarra all'aia* mixes pasta with walnuts, garlic, olive oil and Parmesan; fried Vermont veal is faultless. In the summer, the garage doors go up and the crowd of stylists, assistants, yuppies and West Village whatevers mob the corner from breakfast until last call.

Bobo

181 W 10th Street, at Seventh Avenue South (1-212 488 2626/www.bobonewyork.com). Subway

Bourgeois Pig. *See p186.*

1 to Christopher Street. **Open** 6-11pm Mon-Wed;
6pm-midnight Thur, Fri; noon-3pm, 6pm-
midnight Sat; noon-3pm, 6-11pm Sun. **Main
course** $25. **Credit** AmEx, DC, MC, V.
Map p403 D28 ❹ **French**
See p207 **Secret gardens**.

Casa
*72 Bedford Street, at Commerce Street (1-212
366 9410/www.casarestaurant.com). Subway 1
to Christopher Street-Sheridan Square.* **Open**
6-11pm Mon-Thur; 6pm-midnight Fri; 10am-3pm,
6pm-midnight Sat; 10am-3pm, 6-11pm Sun. **Main
course** $19. **Credit** AmEx, DC, MC, V. **Map**
p403 D29 ❹ **Brazilian**
Sure, you'll find *feijoada* and several trusty steak
platters, but Casa is one of the few Brazilian restaurants in Manhattan to venture successfully into the
regional cuisines of Bahia and Minas Gerais. A
youthful crowd of Villagers dotted with expats fills
the narrow, white-walled single room to sample the
cheese bread and appetisers such as the lime-
infused *lula frita* (calamari). Entrées explore the
entire country, but it's the Bahian stews cooked in
palm oil – such as the sultry *moqueca de frutos do
mar* (seafood) and *xinxim de galinha* (chicken) –
that underscore just how far you are from 'Little
Brasil's' 46th Street.

★ $ Corner Bistro
*331 W 4th Street, at Jane Street (1-212 242
9502). Subway A, C, E to 14th Street; L to
Eighth Avenue.* **Open** 11.30am-4am Mon-Sat;
noon-4am Sun. **Average burger** $5. **No
credit cards**. **Map** p403 D28 ❹ **American**

There's only one reason to come to this legendary
pub: it serves up the city's best burgers – and beer
is just $2.50 a mug (well, that makes two reasons).
The patties here are cheap, delish and no-frills,
served on a flimsy paper plate. To get one, you may
have to queue for a good hour, especially on
weekend nights. Fortunately, the game is on the
tube, and a jukebox covers everything from
Calexico to Coltrane.

EN Japanese Brasserie
*435 Hudson Street, at Leroy Street (1-212 647
9196/www.enjb.com). Subway 1 to Houston
Street.* **Open** 5.30-11pm Mon-Thur, Sun; 5.30pm-
midnight Fri, Sat. **Main course** $15. **Credit**
AmEx, DC, Disc, MC, V. **Map** p403 D29 ❺
Japanese
Sibling restaurateurs Bunkei and Reika Yo give us
a sense of Japanese living in this multi-level space.
On the ground floor are tatami-style rooms; on the
mezzanine are recreations of a living room, dining
room and library of a Japanese home from the Meiji
era. But the main dining room is where the action is.
Chef Koji Nakano offers hand-made miso paste, tofu
and yuba in dishes such as Berkshire pork belly
braised in sansho miso; and foie gras and poached
daikon steak with white miso vinegar. Try the sake
and shochu flights (or wonderful cocktails) for an
authentic Asian buzz.

$ Irving Farm Coffee Company
*56 Seventh Avenue, between 13th & 14th Streets
(1-212 475 5200/www.irvingfarm.com). Subway
F, V, 1, 2, 3 to 14th Street; L to Sixth Avenue.*
Open 7am-7pm Mon-Fri; 8am-8pm Sat, Sun.

Craftsteak.

Average coffee $2. **Credit** AmEx, DC, Disc, MC, V. **Map** p403 D27 ⑤ **Café**

The beans are roasted upstate, but there's a downtown vibe at this West Village coffee bar. Espresso – dutifully short, wonderfully dark – is the poison of choice for workforce warriors frequenting the shop; more leisurely joe pros opt for a steamy cappuccino topped with a dense thicket of foam. Globe lamps illuminate a sweets-stocked case, and the lively staff percolates at first mention of a double shot.

Moustache

90 Bedford Street, between Barrow & Grove Streets (1-212 229 2220). Subway 1 to Christopher Street-Sheridan Square. **Open** noon-midnight daily. **Main course** $13. **No credit cards. Map** p403 D29 ⑤ **Middle Eastern**

Located on a leafy, brownstone-lined West Village street, this beloved cheap-eats haven serves some of the city's best Middle Eastern food. The small, exposed brick dining room packs in a neighbourhood crowd nightly – it's not unusual to see a line outside this no-reservations spot. But it's worth the wait. The freshly baked pitas, still puffed up with hot air when served, are perfect for scooping up the smoky baba ghanoush. More elaborate offerings include *ouzi*: rice, chicken, vegetables and raisins cooked in filo.

Other locations 265 E 10th Street, between First Avenue & Avenue A, East Village (1-212 228 2022).

Pearl Oyster Bar

18 Cornelia Street, between Bleecker & W 4th Streets (1-212 691 8211/www.pearloyster bar.com). Subway A, C, E, B, D, F, V to W 4th Street. **Open** noon-2.30pm, 6-11pm Mon-Fri; 6-11pm Sat. **Main course** $24. **Credit** DC, MC, V. **Map** p403 D29 ⑤ **Seafood**

There's a good reason this convivial, no-reservations, New England-style fish joint always has a queue – the food is outstanding. The lemon-scented lobster roll, sweet meat laced with mayonnaise on a butter-enriched bun, is better than you could have imagined. More sophisticated dishes fare equally well: a bouillabaisse is a briny lobster broth packed with mussels, cod, scallops and clams, with an aioli-smothered crouton balanced on top – great value at $20. Finally, a restaurant worthy of its hype.

▶ *See p181 for more quality from Ed McFarland.*

$ 'sNice

45 Eighth Avenue, at W 4th Street (1-212 645 0310). Subway A, C, E to 14th Street; L to Eighth Avenue. **Open** 7.30am-10pm Mon-Fri; 8am-10pm Sat, Sun. **Average sandwich** $8. **No credit cards. Map** p403 D28 ⑤ **Café**

'Snice is nice – if you're looking for is a cosy joint, where you can read a paper, do a little laptopping, and enjoy cheap, simple and satisfying veggie fare. Far roomier than it appears from its corner windows, the exposed-brick café has what may well be the largest menu in the city, covered with carefully wrought descriptions of each burrito, sandwich and salad. Standouts include the quinoa salad with mixed greens and avocado dressing, and the brie, pear and rocket baguette dressed with raspberry mustard.

Other locations 315 Fifth Avenue, at 3rd Street, Park Slope, Brooklyn (1-718 788 2121).

★ Spotted Pig

314 W 11th Street, at Greenwich Street (1-212 620 0393/www.thespottedpig.com). Subway A, C, E to 14th Street; L to Eighth Avenue. **Open** noon-2am Mon-Fri; 11am-2am Sat, Sun. **Main course** $15. **Credit** AmEx, DC, MC, V. **Map** p403 D28 ⑤ **Eclectic**

Yes, this West Village spot is still hopping – and even after opening more seating upstairs, a wait is always expected. Some might credit the big names involved (Mario Batali consults and April Bloomfield, of London's River Café, is in the kitchen). The burger is a must-order: a top-secret blend of ground beef grilled rare (unless otherwise specified) and covered with gobs of pungent roquefort. It arrives plated with a tower of crispy shoestring fries tossed with rosemary. But the kitchen saves the best treat for dessert: a delectable slice of moist orange and bourbon chocolate cake.

Waverly Inn

16 Bank Street, at Waverly Place (no phone). Subway A, C, E, 1, 2, 3 to 14th Street; L to Eighth Avenue. **Open** 5-10pm Mon-Thur; 5-11pm Fri, Sat; 11.30am-3pm, 5-10pm Sun. **Main course** $24. **Credit** AmEx, DC, MC, V. **Map** p403 D28 ⑤⑥ **American**
Eric Goode and Sean MacPherson (both of the Bowery and Maritime Hotels), along with *Vanity Fair* editor-in-chief Graydon Carter, have breathed new life into this West Village mainstay. They've kept the uneven wooden floors, low ceilings and ivy-covered patio, and added a dose of panache – velvet curtains and a mural by artist Edward Sorel. The casual menu consists of bistro bites and comfort food staples. The city may not need another tuna tartare, but the version here is fantastic. Reservations are currently handled only via a private number, although you can try booking a table in person.

MIDTOWN
Chelsea

Blossom

187 Ninth Avenue, between 21st & 22nd Streets (1-212 627 1144/www.blossomnyc.com). Subway C, E to 23rd Street. **Open** 5-10pm Mon-Thur; 12.45-2.30pm, 5-10pm Fri-Sun. **Main course** $17. **Credit** AmEx, DC, Disc, MC, V. **Map** p404 C26 ⑤⑦ **Vegetarian**
For cautious carnivores, Blossom offers one big surprise: all the eggless pastas and mock meats actually taste pretty good. For vegans, it's a candlelit godsend. Guiltily dreaming of veal scaloppine? Try

THE BEST
WEEKEND BRUNCH

For French toast in wonderland
Alice's Tea Cup. *See p204.*

For the Downtown crowd
Balthazar. *See p178.*

For breakfast in Brooklyn
Diner. *See p210.*

the pan-seared seitan cutlets, tender wheat gluten served with basil mashed potatoes, swiss chard, a white wine caper sauce and artichokes.

Buddakan

75 Ninth Avenue, between 15th & 16th Streets (1-212 989 6699/www.buddakannyc.com). Subway A, C, E to 14th Street; L to Eighth Avenue. **Open** 5.30-10.45pm Mon, Sun; 5.30-11.45pm Tue, Wed; 5.30pm-12.45am Thur-Sat. **Main course** $25. **Credit** AmEx, DC, MC, V. **Map** p403 C27 ⑤⑧ **Chinese**
When Stephen Starr first opened this stately pleasure dome in 2006, New Yorkers flocked to gawk at the fake tapestries and Buddha statues; the grand staircase leading down to the 'Chinoiserie', an enormous golden-hued dining hall centred on a long communal table; and the gigantic chandeliers suspended from its 35ft ceiling. While the hordes still turn out, many have discovered the real value of Buddakan lies in its gastronomy. A sensual appetiser of devilled tuna tartare insists on slow consumption, while a Szechuan rib-eye steak has just the right piquancy. By the end of the evening, Starr's real surprise is the reasonableness of the bill.

Cookshop

156 Tenth Avenue, at 20th Street (1-212 924 4440/www.cookshopny.com). Subway C, E to 23rd Street. **Open** 11.30am-3pm, 5.30-11.30pm Mon-Fri; 11am-3pm, 5.30-11.30pm Sat; 11am-3pm, 5.30-10pm Sun. **Main course** $24. **Credit** AmEx, DC, MC, V. **Map** p403 C27 ⑤⑨ **American**
Vicki Freeman and chef-husband-co-owner Marc Meyer want Cookshop to be a platform for sustainable ingredients from independent farmers. True to the restaurant's mission, the ingredients are consistently top-notch, and the menu changes daily. While organic ingredients alone don't guarantee a great meal, Meyer knows how to let the natural flavours speak for themselves, and Cookshop scores points for getting the house-made ice-cream to taste as good as Ben & Jerry's.

Craftsteak

85 Tenth Avenue, between 15th & 16th Streets (1-212 400 6699/www.craftrestaurant.com). Subway A, C, E to 14th Street; L to Eighth Avenue. **Open** 5.30-10pm Mon-Thur, Sun; 5.30-11pm Fri, Sat. **Main course** $45. **Credit** AmEx, DC, MC, V. **Map** p403 C27 ⑥⓿ **Steakhouse**
Prices here run steep even by steakhouse standards, but Tom Colicchio has methodically honed the grand, modern Craftsteak into one of the better steakhouses in New York. His pro-choice formula from the original Craft takes a beefy turn in preparation style (corn versus grass-fed, Wagyu versus 42-day-ageing) and in sides (30 options). Most of the dozens of starters are unusual, as is Colicchio's preferred steak-cooking method: roasted, rather than grilled, which helps accentuate the beautifully

CONSUME

marbled Wagyu, but can make pedestrian cuts taste like pricey pot roast. Regardless, pleasant culinary and aesthetic distractions abound.

Other locations Craft, 43 E 19th Street, between Broadway & Park Avenue South (1-212 780 0880); Craftbar, 900 Broadway, at 20th Street (1-212 461 4300); both Flatiron District.

▶ *For Tom Colicchio's 'Wichcraft, see p181.*

Del Posto

85 Tenth Avenue, between 15th & 16th Streets (1-212 497 8090/www.delposto.com). Subway A, C, E to 14th Street; L to Eighth Avenue. **Open** 5.30-11pm Mon, Tue; noon-2pm, 5.30-11pm Wed-Fri; 4.30-11pm Sat; 4.30-10pm Sun. **Main course** $29. **Credit** AmEx, DC, MC, V. **Map** p403 C27
61 Italian

With four-star ambitions and prices to match, Mario Batali's Del Posto set the bar awfully high when it opened in 2005, but the cavernous restaurant has become nothing less than the city's top destination for refined, upscale Italian cuisine. The clubby dining room, serenaded nightly by a twinkling grand piano, feels like the lobby of a very opulent grand hotel. The kitchen, under the stewardship of long-time Batali protégé Mark Ladner, challenges its French competition in butter consumption. The most show-stopping dishes, intended for sharing, include hunks of lamb and veal and pitch-perfect risotto for two.

Empire Diner

210 Tenth Avenue, at 22nd Street (1-212 243 2736/www.empire-diner.com). Subway C, E to 23rd Street. **Open** 24hrs daily. **Main course** $17. **Credit** DC, MC, V. **Map** p404 C26 **62**
American

It's 3am – do you know where your middle-of-the-night grub is? This Fodero-style diner is a longtime Chelsea fave. It looks like a classic – gleaming stainless steel walls and rotating stools – but few other hash houses have candlelight, pavement café tables and a pianist playing dinner music. Fewer still attempt dishes such as sesame noodles with chicken, and linguine with smoked salmon, watercress and garlic. The more standard platters are terrific – a juicy blue-cheese steak burger, for instance – and desserts live up to diner standards, especially a thick chocolate pudding.

RUB

208 W 23rd Street, between Seventh & Eighth Avenues (1-212 524 4300/www.rubbbq.net). Subway C, E to 23rd Street. **Open** 11.30am-11pm Mon-Thur; 11.30am-midnight Fri, Sat; 11.30am-10pm Sun. **Main course** $16. **Credit** AmEx, DC, Disc, MC, V. **Map** p404 D26 **63** Barbecue
The name stands for 'Righteous Urban Barbecue', and that's not all that's cocky about this 'cue joint. RUB takes no reservations and doesn't apologise – even for the paper plates and paper towels. The

message: our barbecue is so good, nothing else matters. Paul Kirk, a seven-time world barbecue champion, is the man behind the mission, and while the grub ain't flawless by Kansas City Barbecue Society standards, less discerning eaters will find much to praise. Ribs are lean and tender, and the details are just right: Wonder Bread comes with each platter, and sides include baked beans studded with bits of brisket.

★ Tia Pol

205 Tenth Avenue, between 22nd & 23rd Streets (1-212 675 8805/www.tiapol.com). Subway C, E to 23rd Street. **Open** 5.30-11pm Mon; 11am-3pm, 5.30-11pm Tue-Thur; 11am-3pm, 5.30pm-midnight Fri; 11am-3pm, 6pm-midnight Sat; 11am-3pm, 6-10pm Sun. **Average small plate** $8. **Credit** AmEx, DC, MC, V. **Map** p404 C26
64 Spanish

Reaching crowd capacity at this tapas spot isn't tough: it's as slender as the white asparagus that garnishes some of its dishes. Seating is on high stools, with spill-over at the bustling bar, where handsome diners stand cheek by jowl while guzzling fruity sangria. The memorable menu is one part classical, two parts wholly original: munch on superb renditions from the tapas canon – springy squid 'en su tinta' (in its own ink); patatas bravas topped with spicy aioli – and then delve into eclectic treats that are eyebrow-raising on paper and delicious on the tongue, such as chorizo with bittersweet chocolate.

Trestle on Tenth

242 Tenth Avenue, at 24th Street (1-212 645-5659/www.trestleontenth.com). Subway C, E to 23rd Street. **Open** 5.30-10.30pm Tue-Thur; 5.30-11pm Fri, Sat; 5.30-10pm Sun. **Main course** $24. **Credit** AmEx, DC, Disc, MC, V. **Map** p404 C26
65 American creative

Once the High Line is finished, the hordes are sure to drop from its trestles to find sustenance here. But at the time of writing, this airy bar, brick-lined dining room and cosy back garden were for those in the know. The exquisitely prepared modern American cuisine gets its nouvelle accents from Swiss owner-chef Ralf Kuettel. Among the appetisers are oysters drizzled in a tarragon mignonette and an unearthly pork shoulder crépinette with sautéed spinach. Mains, such as the crisp chicken paillard and the coriander-studded hanger steak, are enhanced by a side of gratinéed dumplings. Be sure to sample the changing wine selection.

▶ *For more on the High Line, see p90.*

Flatiron District & Union Square

Casa Mono/Bar Jamón

Casa Mono: 52 Irving Place, at E 17th Street. Bar Jamón: 125 E 17th Street, at Irving Place (1-212 253 2773/www.casamononyc.com). Subway L to Third Avenue; N, Q, R, W, 4, 5, 6 to 14th Street-Union Square. **Open** *Casa Mono* noon-midnight daily. *Bar Jamón* 5pm-2am Mon-Fri; noon-2am Sat, Sun. **Average small plate** $12. **Credit** AmEx, DC, MC, V. **Map** p403 F27 ⑯ **Spanish**

Offal-loving consulting chef Mario Batali and protégé Andy Nusser go where many standard Manhattan tapas restaurants fear to tread: cock's combs with cèpes, pig's feet with caper aioli and sweetbreads dusted with almond flour and fried. Non-organ lovers should try the juicy skirt steak atop onion marmalade, soft crab with black truffle aioli, or the fried duck egg, a delicately flavoured breakfast-meets-dinner dish topping a mound of sautéed fingerling potatoes and salt-cured tuna loin. For a cheaper option, head to the attached Bar Jamón, serving a more casual menu of treasured Ibérico hams, bocaditos and Spanish cheeses.

City Bakery

3 W 18th Street, between Fifth & Sixth Avenues (1-212 366 1414/www.thecitybakery.com). Subway L, N, Q, R, W, 4, 5, 6 to 14th Street-Union Square. **Open** 7.30am-7pm Mon-Fri; 7.30am-6pm Sat; 9am-5.30pm Sun. **Salad bar** $12.50 per pound. **Credit** AmEx, DC, MC, V. **Map** p403 E27 ⑰ **Café**

Pastry genius Maury Rubin's loft-size City Bakery is jammed with shoppers loading up on unusual salad bar choices (grilled pineapple with ancho chile or beansprouts with smoked tofu). There's also a small selection of soups, pizzas and hot dishes. But never mind all that: the thick, incredibly rich hot chocolate with fat house-made marshmallows is heaven in a cup (replaced by fruit-infused lemonade in the summer), and the moist 'melted' chocolate-chip cookies are divinely decadent.

★ Hill Country

30 W 26th Street, between Broadway & Sixth Avenue (1-212 255 4544/www.hillcountry ny.com). Subway N, R, W to 28th Street. **Open** noon-10pm Mon-Wed; noon-11pm Thur-Sat; 11am-10pm Sun. **Average pound of meat** $18. **Credit** AmEx, DC, Disc, MC, V. **Map** p404 E26 ⑱ **Barbecue**

The guys behind Hill Country are about as Texan as Bloomberg in a stetson, but the cooking is an authentic, world-class take on the restaurant's namesake region, including sausage imported from Lockhart, Texas, barbecue stalwart Kreuz market and two options for brisket: go for the 'moist' (read: fatty) version. Beef shoulder emerges from the smoker in 20-pound slabs, and show-stealing tips-on pork ribs are hefty with just enough fat to imbue proper flavour. Desserts, such as jelly-filled cupcakes with peanut butter frosting, live out some kind of *Leave It to Beaver* fantasy, but June Cleaver wouldn't approve of the two dozen tequilas and bourbons.

Pure Food & Wine

54 Irving Place, between 17th & 18th Streets (1-212 477 1010/www.purefoodandwine.com). Subway L, N, Q, R, W, 4, 5, 6 to 14th Street-Union Square. **Open** 5.30-11pm daily. **Main course** $23. **Credit** AmEx, DC, MC, V. **Map** p403 F27 ⑲ **Vegetarian**

The dishes delivered to your table – whether out in the leafy patio or inside the ambient dining room – are minor miracles, not only because they look gorgeous and taste terrific, but because they come from a kitchen that lacks a stove. Everything at Pure is raw and vegan – from the pad thai appetiser to the lasagne, a rich stack of courgette, pesto and creamy

CONSUME

Profile Danny Meyer

The top tastemaker's influence goes beyond his celebrated tables.

CONSUME

Gotham's ultra-competitive restaurant climate has given rise to an aggressive breed of chef/self-promoter prone to dominating the highest-profile echelons of the city's dining culture. It's a wonder, then, that arguably the most successful restaurateur in the metropolis's recent culinary history also has a reputation for being a maddeningly, unshakeably nice guy: Danny Meyer, the big city restaurant king with Midwestern values.

A St Louis, Missouri, native whose first entry into the New York dining scene was as an assistant manager, Meyer opened his first restaurant in 1985. The **Union Square Café** (*see p197*), which helped put Greenmarket dining on the map, remains one of the toughest spots to score a table. Since that first success, Meyer's empire has flourished to include restaurants, from the similarly market-driven **Gramercy Tavern** (*see p197*) to the **Modern** (*see p197*), the fine-dining establishment at the MoMA, and the barbecue-and-jazz haven **Blue Smoke** (*see p197*). He's also helped raise the profile of regional American cooking with the **Big Apple Barbecue Block Party** (www.bigapplebbq.org), a weekend-long event that draws in 'cuers from far and wide.

However, Meyer's contribution to the city doesn't revolve around food alone. What the community-oriented restaurateur did for Union Square, he's recently done for **Madison Square Park** (*see p93*), playing a key role in cleaning up the once-crime-ridden green space – it's now hugged by several of his restaurants, among them **Eleven Madison Park** (11 Madison Avenue, 1-212 889 0905), **Tabla** (*see p197*), and **Shake Shack** (*see p197*). And, affirming his influence, New York is becoming populated with spin-off establishments from Meyer's acolytes: for example, Andrew Boggs and Stephanie Schneider's **Huckleberry Bar** (*see p224*) in Boerum Hill; and Emily Isaac's **Trois Pommes Patisserie** in Park Slope. 'I am incredibly happy to see so many of my staff succeeding – it's a lot of fun,' Meyer recently told *Time Out New York*. Aw, what a nice guy.

THREE TO TRY
Tuna filet mignon at the **Union Square Café**.

The burger – *any* burger – at **Shake Shack**.

Memphis baby-back ribs at **Blue Smoke**.

'cheese' made from cashews. Wines, most organic, are top-notch, as are the desserts, especially the confoundingly fudgy chocolate layer cake.

$ Shake Shack

Madison Square Park, 23rd Street, at Madison Avenue (1-212 889 6600/www.shakeshack nyc.com). Subway N, R, W, 6 to 23rd Street. **Open** 11am-11pm daily. **Average burger** $6. **Credit** AmEx, DC, MC, V. **Map** p404 E26 ⓐ **American**

With Shake Shack, Danny Meyer (Union Square Café, Gramercy Tavern) takes American fast food to new heights. The zinc-clad, modernist concession stand dispenses superb burgers, hot dogs and shakes to Madison Square Park visitors. Sirloin and brisket are ground daily for excellent beefy patties, and the savoury franks are served Chicago-style on poppy seed buns with a 'salad' of toppings and a sprinkle of celery salt. Shakes are rich and creamy; there's beer and wine to boot. Expect long queues (and waits). **Other locations** 366 Columbus Avenue, at 77th Street, Upper West Side (1-646 747 8770).

Tabla

11 Madison Avenue, at 25th Street (1-212 889 0667/www.tablany.com). Subway N, R, W, 6 to 23rd Street. **Open** noon-2pm, 5.30-10pm Mon-Wed; noon-2pm, 5.30-10.30pm Thur, Fri; 5.30-10.30pm Sat; 5-9pm Sun. **3-course prix fixe** $35 lunch, $64 dinner. **Credit** AmEx, DC, Disc, MC, V. **Map** p404 E26 ⓐ **Indian**

Ascend the giant wooden staircase from the packed Bread Bar to a dome-shaped dining room where men and women in designer duds dine on upscale Indian food with a Western influence. Chef Floyd Cardoz mixes fennel seed with familiar rosemary and tarragon to create tastes that are at once unique and recognisable. Greenmarket foods such as watermelon are used in curries, and foie gras may be paired with plums in the summer and apples in the fall. Expect fresh seafood spiced with Indian flavours like coconut curry all year round on Tabla's ever-changing tasting menus. **Other locations** Tabla Bread Bar, 11 Madison Avenue, at 25th Street, Flatiron District (1-212 889 0667).

★ Union Square Café

21 E 16th Street, between Fifth Avenue & Union Square West (1-212 243 4020/www.union squarecafe.com). Subway L, N, Q, R, W, 4, 5, 6 to 14th Street-Union Square. **Open** noon-10pm Mon-Thur, Sun; 5.30-11pm Fri, Sat. **Main course** $30. **Credit** AmEx, DC, Disc, MC, V. **Map** p403 E27 ⓐ **American**

The Union Square Café's art collection and floor-to-ceiling murals have been here as long as the tuna filet mignon has been on the menu. That 1980s throwback, served with a pale green heap of wasabi mashed potatoes, remains hugely popular despite

being more dated than a John Hughes movie. Novelty is not what keeps this New York classic packed year after year. Danny Meyer's first New York restaurant – a pioneer in greenmarket cooking – remains one of the city's most relaxed fine dining establishments.

▶ *See p91 for more on the Union Square Greenmarket.*

Gramercy Park & Murray Hill

★ Artisanal

2 Park Avenue, at 32nd Street (1-212 725 8585/www.artisanalbistro.com). Subway 6 to 33rd Street. **Open** 11.45pm-10pm Mon-Fri; 11am-10pm Sat, Sun. **Main course** $22. **Credit** AmEx, DC, Disc, MC, V. **Map** p404 E25 ⓐ **French**

As New York's bistros veer towards uniformity, Terrance Brennan's high-ceilinged deco gem makes its mark with an all-out homage to fromage. Skip the appetisers and open with fondue, which comes in three varieties. Familiar bistro fare awaits with such entrées as steak frites and a delectable glazed Scottish salmon, but the curd gets the last word with the cheese and wine pairings. These flights of three cheeses – chosen by region, style or theme (for example, each one produced in a monastery) – are matched with three wines (or beers or even sakes) for a sumptuous and intriguing finale.

Blue Smoke

116 E 27th Street, between Park Avenue South & Lexington Avenue (1-212 447 7733/www.blue smoke.com). Subway 6 to 28th Street. **Open** 11.30am-10pm Mon, Sun; 11.30am-11pm Tue-Thur; 11.30am-1am Fri, Sat. **Main course** $20. **Credit** AmEx, DC, Disc, MC, V. **Map** p404 E26 ⓐ **Barbecue**

St Louis native Danny Meyer's barbecue joint tops the short list of Manhattan's best 'cue contenders. Chef Kenny Callaghan knows his wet sauces and dry rubs: the menu includes traditional Texas salt and pepper beef ribs, Memphis baby backs and Kansas City spare ribs. The atmosphere is sports-heavy and includes a prominent bourbon bar and galvanised metal buckets for your bones.

★ Gramercy Tavern

42 E 20th Street, between Broadway & Park Avenue South (1-212 477 0777/www.gramercy tavern.com). Subway N, R, W, 6 to 23rd Street. **Open** noon-2pm, 5.30-10pm Mon-Thur; noon-2pm, 5.30-11pm Fri; 5.30-11pm Sat; 5.30-10pm Sun. **3-course prix fixe** $82. **Credit** AmEx, DC, Disc, MC, V. **Map** p403 E27 ⓐ **American creative**

The 2007 handoff from founding chef Tom Colicchio to Michael Anthony carried the rarity of a papal succession, yet the farmhouse-style setting, with its decorative brambles, pine cones and intoxicating

CONSUME

Les Halles.

smell from the grill, is still here. Colicchio and his hearty, meat-heavy fare are not, however, and it's delicate constructions of vegetables and fish that dominate now.

Les Halles

411 Park Avenue South, between 28th & 29th Streets (1-212 679 4111/www.leshalles.net). Subway 6 to 28th Street. **Open** 7.30am-midnight daily. **Main course** $19. **Credit** AmEx, DC, Disc, MC, V. **Map** p404 E26 ⑦ **French**

Though Anthony Bourdain is just the 'chef-at-large' at Les Halles these days, his meat-oriented philosophy still permeates the place, from the butcher shop inside the restaurant to the steak knives that appear at every place setting. With classic French fare including steak tartare and crêpes suzette prepared tableside for a largely out-of-towner crowd, this is practically a theme-park restaurant – the theme

---

INSIDE TRACK
DIY BBQ

Many of the Asian barbecue joints on the block-long strip of 32nd Street known as Koreatown give you the option of cooking your own meat on a gas grill built into the table, although you can also ask the server to do it for you.

---

being simply that animals are delicious. Steaks, sausages and chops done in over a dozen different ways are solid, but the kitchen's efforts lack a certain joie de vivre.

Other locations 15 John Street, between Broadway & Nassau Street, Financial District (1-212 285 8585).

Herald Square & Garment District

$ Mandoo Bar

2 W 32nd Street, between Fifth Avenue & Broadway (1-212 279 3075). Subway B, D, F, V, N, Q, R, W to 34th Street-Herald Square. **Open** 11am-11pm daily. **Main course** $10. **Credit** AmEx, DC, MC, V. **Map** p404 E25 ⑦ **Korean**

If the two ladies painstakingly filling and crimping dough squares in the front window don't give it away, we will – this wood-wrapped industrial-style spot elevates *mandoo*, Korean dumplings, above mere appetiser status. Six varieties of the tasty morsels are offered here, filled with such delights as subtly piquant kimchi, juicy pork, succulent shrimp and vegetables. Try them miniaturised as in 'baby mandoo', swimming in a soothing beef broth or atop springy, soupy ramen noodles.

New York Kom Tang Kalbi House

32 W 32nd Street, between Fifth Avenue & Broadway (1-212 947 8482). Subway B, D, F, V, N, Q, R, W to 34th Street-Herald Square. **Open** 24hrs Mon-Sat. **Main course** $15. **Credit** AmEx, DC, MC, V. **Map** p404 E25 ⑦ **Korean**

Tender *kalbi* (barbecued short ribs) are indeed the stars here; their signature smoky flavour comes from being cooked over *soot bul* (wood chips). The city's oldest Korean restaurant also makes crisp, seafood-laden *haemool pajun* (pancakes); sweet, juicy *yuk hwe* (raw beef salad); and garlicky *bulgogi*. *Kom tang*, or 'bear soup', is a milky beef broth that's deep and soothing.

Theater District & Hell's Kitchen

Breeze

661 Ninth Avenue, between 45th & 46th Streets (1-212 262 7777/www.breezenyc.com). Subway A, C, E to 42nd Street-Port Authority. **Open** 11.30am-11.30pm Mon-Thur, Sun; noon-midnight Fri, Sat. **Main course** $16. **Credit** AmEx, DC, MC, V. **Map** p404 C23 ⑦ **Thai**

With a progressive look – tangerine walls, triangular mirrors, menus printed on DVDs – and a refined menu, Breeze sails past the other Hell's Kitchen contenders, combining French techniques and Thai cuisine to spellbinding effect. Addictive fried dumplings filled with wild mushrooms and caramelised onions are topped with a delectable soy-black truffle foam. Nearly as tasty is the smoky grilled salmon, which comes glazed in a zesty fire-roasted chili-orange sauce.

Daisy May's BBQ USA

623 Eleventh Avenue, at 46th Street (1-212 977 1500/www.daisymaysbbq.com). Subway A, C, E to 42nd Street-Port Authority. **Open** 11am-9pm Mon; 11am-10pm Tue-Fri; noon-10pm Sat; noon-9pm Sun. **Main course** $16. **Credit** AmEx, DC, Disc, MC, V. **Map** p404 B23 ⑩ **Barbecue**
Southerners know that the best barbecue comes from run-down shacks in the worst parts of town – so don't let the location of Daisy May's BBQ USA, on a desolate stretch of Eleventh Avenue deter you: despite a few missteps (the pulled pork is over-stewed in its own sauce), this is the real down-home deal, a masterful barbecue survey. The Kansas City sweet and sticky pork ribs are meaty and just tender enough, while the creamed corn tastes like ballpark nachos – and that's a good thing.
▶ *See also p 210 Give Us a 'Cue.*

Omido

1695 Broadway, between 53rd & 54th Streets (1-212 247 8110/www.hungryperson-sysco.com/omido). Subway B, D, E to Seventh Avenue. **Open** 11.30am-11.45pm Mon-Fri; 5-11.45pm Sat, Sun. **Main course** $25. **Credit** AmEx, DC, MC, V. **Map** p405 D22 ⑪ **Japanese**
As this 'hood isn't generally known for top-notch dining, you may be surprised to find one of the best sushi dens in the city. The centrepiece of the dark-wood-appointed, AvroKO-designed space is the glistening case of jewel-like dishes. Foie gras atop a salmon, tuna and yellowtail roll elevates the already rich fish to a buttery supremacy, and a sashimi platter groans with an alluring landscape of seafood. Don't leave without sampling the Hoji blancmange, a roasted green tea custard.

Midtown

Abboccato

138 W 55th Street, between Sixth & Seventh Avenues (1-212 265 4000). Subway F, N, Q, R, W to 57th Street. **Open** 7.30-10.30am, noon-3pm, 5.30-10pm Mon; 7.30-10.30am, noon-3pm, 5.30-11pm Tue-Sat; 7.30-10.30am, 4-10pm Sun. **Main courses** $28. **Credit** AmEx, DC, Disc, MC, V. **Map** p405 D22 ⑫ **Italian**
When he sends out authentic Greek food at his nearby restaurant Molyvos (871 Seventh Avenue, between 55th & 56th Streets, 1-212 582 7500), executive chef Jim Botsacos is only telling half the story: his father's. Now, as chef-partner at Abboccato ('touch of sweetness') he pays tribute to his Italian mother. Each dish is associated with a region of Italy, such as Umbrian-style quail and octopus with Sicilian oregano. To make his carbonara taste like the real thing, Botsacos uses more flavourful duck eggs. His *vaniglia e cioccolato*, meanwhile, combines

Adour Alain Ducasse.

two classic dishes into one: vanilla-scented veal cheeks and wild boar stewed in red wine, spices and chocolate. It's dinner and dessert rolled into one.

★ Adour Alain Ducasse

St Regis New York, 2 E 55th Street, at Fifth Avenue (1-212 710 2277/www.adour-stregis.com). Subway E, V to Fifth Avenue-53rd Street; F to 57th Street. **Open** 5.30-10.30pm Mon-Thur, Sun; 5.30-11pm Fri, Sat. **Main course** $40. **Credit** AmEx, DC, Disc, MC, V. **Map** p405 D22 ⑬ **French**
Legendary chef-restaurateur Alain Ducasse teamed with the final toque at his defunct Essex House restaurant to open this temple of fine dining (and drinking) in the former L'Espinasse space. Here, wine is the muse (the list includes 70 under-$50 selections among its 1,800-strong list), and chef Tony Esnault's menu is equally decadent. Entrées, such as a sumptuous tenderloin and short ribs anointed with foie gras-truffle jus, are rich without being heavy. Ditto the desserts, which include a chocolate 'sorbet' – a cold chocolate core ringed by a coating of pudding, coffee granita, vanilla cream and, in a Ducasse-worthy flourish, a gold-leafed chocolate disc.

Anthos

36 W 52nd Street, between Fifth & Sixth Avenues (1-212 582 6900). Subway B, D, F, V to 47-50th Streets-Rockefeller Center.

Deals on Meals

Dine at some of the city's top restaurants for a fraction of the price.

Travellers to New York City generally require expense accounts if they wish to partake in the metropolis's epicurean treasures. However, bargain prix fixe menus, usually offered at lunchtime, allow diners to sample the work of New York's top chefs without causing serious damage to their wallets. Although **New York City Restaurant Week** (*see p263*) takes place twice a year, with notable restaurants offering special three-course meals for far less than the regular price (usually around $25 for lunch and $35 for dinner), some restaurants offer fixed-price deals year-round.

If it's fine dining you're seeking, try **Jean Georges** (*see p206*). A $28 two-course lunch in the main dining room (each additional plate costs $12) allows for sampling of some Vongerichten classics – such as the devastatingly silky brûléed foie gras – without having to commit to the $98 three-course dinner. The more casual **Nougatine**, the café at Jean Georges, offers a $24.07 three-course weekday lunch. Lovers of Mediterranean cuisine

might prefer haute Greek destination **Anthos** (*see p199*), the most formal of chef Michael Psilakis' restaurants, for a $28 three-course prix-fixe lunch that usually includes the signature lamb burger and sheep's milk ricotta dumplings.

For the full-on tourist experience, try the $35 prix fixe lunch at the **Russian Tea Room** (*see p201*): featuring the famous borscht, it's a budget-con way to soak in the gilded-era atmosphere. Nearby, underrated Midtown Italian eaterie **Abboccato** (*see p199*) has one of the city's best deals in its gothic dining room, offering three courses for $28 at lunch and $35 for dinner. One of our favourite dishes is the veal Milanese with watercress, red onions and tomato confit.

Another great dinnertime deal is the $38 three-course Sunday Supper at **Dovetail** (*see p204*). Chef John Fraser's eclectic gem offers three courses for the price of one à la carte entrée – if it's on the menu, try the veal short rib gnocchi. You might find that the bargain makes the food taste that much better.

Russian Tea Room.

CONSUME

Open noon-2.45pm, 5-10.30pm Mon-Thur; noon-2.45pm, 5-11pm Fri; 5-11pm Sat. **Main courses** $35. **Credit** AmEx, DC, MC, V. **Map** p404 E23
❸❹ **Greek**
At this haute Greek spot from chef Michael Psilakis, the setting is lush – big front windows, curved ceiling, cherry blossom prints (anthos means 'blossom') – but the focus is squarely on the cuisine. A master of seafood, Psilakis shows it best in his *crudo*: vibrant bites of fish with Greek touches like blood-red tuna topped with mastic oil and yellowtail paired with fennel pollen and ouzo-marinated cherries. For dessert, expect Greek standards with a twist.

★ Bar Room at the Modern

9 W 53rd Street, between Fifth & Sixth Avenues (1-212 333 1220/www.themodernnyc.com). Subway E, V to Fifth Avenue-53rd Street. **Open** noon-2.15pm, 6-9.30pm Mon-Thur; noon-2.15pm, 5.30-10.30pm Fri; 5.30-10.30pm Sat. **Main course** $16. **Credit** AmEx, DC, Disc, MC, V. **Map** p405 E22 ❻❺ **American creative**
Those who can't afford to drop a pay cheque at chef Gabriel Kreuther's formal MoMA dining room, the Modern, should drop into the equally stunning and less pricey Bar Room (which shares the same kitchen). From the 30 savoury dishes on the menu (which features several small and medium size plates), standouts include Arctic char tartare. Desserts come courtesy of pastry chef Marc Aumont, and the wine list is extensive to say the least.
▶ *For MoMA itself, see p100.*

Carnegie Deli

854 Seventh Avenue, at 55th Street (1-212 757 2245/www.carnegiedeli.com). Subway B, D, E to Seventh Avenue; N, Q, R, W to 57th Street. **Open** 6.30am-4am daily. **Average sandwich** $15. **No credit cards**. **Map** p405 D22
❽❻ **American**
If the Carnegie Deli didn't invent schmaltz, it certainly perfected it. All of the gargantuan sandwiches have punny names: Bacon Whoopee (BLT with chicken salad), Carnegie Haul (pastrami, tongue and salami). A waiter sings the deli's virtues in a corny video loop, and more than 600 celebrity glossies crowd the walls. This sexagenarian legend is a time capsule of the bygone Borscht Belt-era when shtick could make up for cramped quarters, surly waiters and shabby tables – and tourists still eat it up. But when you're craving a deli classic, you can't do much better than the Carnegie's obscenely stuffed pastrami and corned beef sandwiches on rye.

Russian Tea Room

150 W 57th Street, between Sixth & Seventh Avenues (1-212 581 7100). Subway F, N, Q, R, W to 57th Street. **Open** 11.30am-3pm, 4.45-11.15pm Mon-Fri; 11am-3pm, 4.45-10pm Sat, Sun. **Main course** $35. **Credit** AmEx, DC, MC, V. **Map** p405 D22 ❺❼ **Russian**

The reborn socialite centre has never looked – or tasted – better. Nostalgia buffs will be happy to hear that nothing's happened to the gilded-bird friezes or the famously tacky crystal-bear aquarium but the food, thankfully, has not been frozen in time. Chef Gary Robins modernises the menu, looking to former Soviet republics for inspiration. He makes the best borscht in the city, and goes more exotic with entrées such as cocoa-dusted seared venison with truffle-scented *tvorog* (cheese) dumplings. The pleasure doesn't come cheap, however.

★ Town

Chambers Hotel, 15 W 56th Street, between Fifth & Sixth Avenues (1-212 582 4445/www.townnyc.com). Subway E, V to Fifth Avenue-53rd Street; N, R, W to Fifth Avenue-59th Street. **Open** 7-10.30am, noon-2.30pm, 5.30-10.30pm Mon-Fri; 7-10.30am, 5.30-10.30pm Sat; 7-10.30am, 11am-2.30pm, 5.30-9pm Sun. **Main course** $30. **6-course tasting menu** $75. **Credit** AmEx, DC, Disc, MC, V. **Map** p405 E22 ❻❽ **American creative**
A hot, sexy restaurant can easily become old news – especially when it gains a popular sibling (Country, Carlton Hotel, 90 Madison Avenue, at 29th Street, 1-212 889 7100). Town, however, has been gracefully transformed from It spot into a timeless classic. The dining room is at once cavernous and warm: soaring ceilings mimic those of a concert hall, while plush banquettes, soft lighting and muted acoustics bring the space back to earth. Geoffrey Zakarian's kitchen plays with similar contradictions, sending out hyper-styled, borderline fussy dishes; as a result, the best ones are also the simplest – such as a phenomenal Flintstones-size venison chop or a simple slice of rosy roasted lamb.

'21' Club

21 W 52nd Street, between Fifth & Sixth Avenues (1-212 582 7200/www.21club.com). Subway B, D, F to 47-50th Streets-Rockefeller Center; E, V to Fifth Avenue-53rd Street. **Open** noon-10pm Mon-Thur; noon-11pm Fri; 5.30-11pm Sat. **Main course** $39. **Credit** AmEx, DC, Disc, MC, V. **Map** p404 E23 ❻❾ **American**
After more than 75 years, this clubby sanctum for the powerful remains true to its past while thriving in the present. Chef Erik Blauberg creates contemporary seasonal fare such as crisped black sea bass in champagne sauce. For '21 Classics', Blauberg ransacked the '21' archives and revived dishes that are part of culinary history; steak Diane, flambéed tableside, was on the restaurant's first menu. The famous burger is a bargain at $29 ($26 at lunch), its mix of ground lean meats getting a flavour boost from duck fat. Act like a magnate and sip an after-dinner drink in the front lounge, where original Remingtons line the walls.

CONSUME

Midtown East

Aja

1066 First Avenue, at 58th Street (1-212 888 8008/www.ajaasiancuisine.com). Subway N, R, W to Lexington Avenue-59th Street; 4, 5, 6 to 59th Street. **Open** 5pm-midnight Mon-Thur, Sun; 5pm-1am Fri, Sat. **Main course** $20. **Credit** AmEx, DC, Disc, MC, V. **Map** p405 F22
90 **Pan-Asian**

Surrounded by glittering stone walls and exposed beams and watched by an eight-foot-tall Buddha, well-dressed eaters chat away at this sceney Pan-Asian spot. Servers are in a rush to get you out of the door and the prices are steep, but the plates are bountiful and the sushi here is so creamy and fresh it melts in your mouth. The Peking duck, large enough to feed a table of four, is a mound of crisp skin and moist meat with a side of warm moo shu pancakes and a salty-tangy sauce for DIY-style eating.

Other locations 432 Sixth Avenue, between 9th & 10th Streets, Greenwich Village (1-212 253 7100).

★ Grand Central Oyster Bar & Restaurant

Grand Central Terminal, Lower Concourse, 42nd Street, at Park Avenue (1-212 490 6650/ www.oysterbarny.com). Subway S, 4, 5, 6, 7 to 42nd Street-Grand Central. **Open** 11.30am-9.30pm Mon-Fri; noon-9.30pm Sat. **Main course** $25. **Credit** AmEx, DC, Disc, MC, V. **Map** p404 E24 **91** **Seafood**

At the legendary 96-year-old Grand Central Oyster Bar, located in the epic and gorgeous hub that shares its name, the surly countermen at the mile-long bar (the best seats in the house) are part of the charm. Avoid the more complicated fish concoctions and play it safe with a reliably awe-inspiring platter of iced, just-shucked oysters (there can be a whopping three-dozen varieties to choose from at any given time, from Baja to Plymouth Rock). As long as the station is abuzz and the oysters good – they are – the other dishes are really beside the point.
▶ *For more on the iconic transport hub, see p103.*

Sparks Steak House

210 E 46th Street, between Second & Third Avenues (1-212 687 4855/www.sparkssteak house.com). Subway S, 4, 5, 6, 7 to 42nd Street-Grand Central. **Open** noon-11pm Mon-Thur; noon-11.30pm Fri; 5-11.30pm Sat. **Main course** $40. **Credit** AmEx, DC, Disc, MC, V. **Map** p404 F23 **92** **Steakhouse**

Sparks used to be a mob hangout. Now the delightfully old-school, panelled dining room is just mobbed. Even with a reservation, you may wait for an hour at the cramped bar. It's worth it, however – especially when a starter of plump broiled shrimp with garlicky lemon butter reaches your table. The signature sirloin is a lean 16-ounce hunk of prime

Anthos. *See p199.*

with heft, chew and a salty, lightly charred exterior. When your fork slides through a velvety wedge of chocolate mousse cake, you'll feel sorry for Gambino crime boss Paul Castellano, who was famously whacked as he approached the entrance one night in 1985: he died before enjoying his meal.

UPTOWN

Upper East Side

Café Sabarsky

Neue Galerie, 1048 Fifth Avenue, at 86th Street (1-212 288 0665/www.cafesabarsky.com). Subway 4, 5, 6 to 86th Street. **Open** 9am-6pm Mon, Wed; 9am-9pm Thur-Sun. **Main course** $19. **Credit** AmEx, DC, MC, V. **Map** p406 E18 **93** **Austrian/café**

Purveyor of indulgent pastries and whipped cream-topped *einspänner* coffee for Neue Galerie patrons by day, this sophisticated, high-ceilinged room becomes an upscale restaurant four nights a week. Appetisers are most adventurous – the creaminess of the *spaetzle* is a perfect base for sweetcorn, tarragon and wild mushrooms – while main course specials such as the Wiener schnitzel tartly garnished with lingonberries are capable yet ultimately feel like the calm before the Sturm und Drang of dessert. Try the Klimt torte, which masterfully alternates layers of hazelnut cake with chocolate.

CONSUME

The revolving door off Park Avenue and the grandiose interior, with neo-classical columns and velvet seats, announce it: this is fine dining. The cuisine at Daniel Boulud's flagship, which is rooted in French technique with au courant flourishes like fusion elements and an emphasis on local produce, is refined without blowing you away – though it has its moments. Cooked pluots are a smart acidic counterpoint to seared foie gras. Vermont veal cooked three ways aptly showcases crisp sweetbreads, rare tenderloin and braised cheeks. For desserts, the pastry chef's creations are as whimsical as they are delicious.
Other locations Café Boulud, 20 E 76th Street, between Fifth & Madison Avenues, Upper East Side (1-212 772 2600); Bar Boulud, 1900 Broadway, between 63rd & 64th Streets, Upper West Side (1-212 595 0303).

Etats-Unis
242 E 81st Street, between Second & Third Avenues (1-212 517 8826/www.etatsunis restaurant.com). Subway 6 to 77th Street. **Open** 6-10.30pm daily. **Main course** $34. **Credit** AmEx, DC, MC, V. **Map** p405 F19 **96 American creative**
With simple wood floors and an open kitchen, this spot evokes a cosy neighbourhood bistro – albeit one with Michelin-star-quality food and prices to match. A daily-changing menu makes the most of the finest in-season produce and free-range meats (in summer, this can be anything from roasted artichoke hearts with plump day-boat scallops to pork chops topped by peach chutney); and the execution is impeccable, whether it be in the perfectly cooked filet mignon or the well-seasoned shrimp. Yet what shines above all is the date pudding with rum sauce: this decadent dessert is one of the finest in New York.

$ Lexington Candy Shop
1226 Lexington Avenue, at 83rd Street (1-212 288 0057/www.lexingtoncandyshop.net). Subway 4, 5, 6 to 86th Street. **Open** 7am-7pm Mon-Sat; 9am-6pm Sun. **Main course** $9. **Credit** AmEx, DC, Disc, MC, V. **Map** p405 E19 **97 American**
You won't see much candy for sale at Lexington Candy Shop. Instead, you'll find a wonderfully preserved retro diner (it was founded in 1925), its long

Central Park Boathouse Restaurant
Central Park Lake, park entrance on Fifth Avenue, at 72nd Street (1-212 517 2233/ www.thecentralparkboathouse.com). Subway 6 to 68th Street-Hunter College. **Open** *Apr-Nov* noon-4pm, 5.30-9pm Mon-Fri; 9am-4pm, 6-9pm Sat, Sun. *Dec-Mar* noon-4pm Mon-Fri; 9.30am-4pm Sat, Sun. **Main course** $37. **Credit** AmEx, DC, MC, V. **Map** p405 D20 **94 Seafood**
Central Park Boathouse's lakeside setting is just serene enough to offset the somewhat stiff service and hefty prices. The Field Greens salad is a gorgeous sculpture of tomatoes, cucumbers, red onion, olives and large, rectangular chunks of feta cheese. Crab cakes, more crab than cake, are worth every penny. Allow yourself to linger over mascarpone cheesecake before taking the restaurant's trolley through the park back to civilisation. Paying for location is par for the course in New York routine; here, it's well worth it.

Daniel
60 E 65th Street, between Madison & Park Avenues (1-212 288 0033/www.danielnyc.com). Subway F to Lexington Avenue-63rd Street; 6 to 68th Street-Hunter College. **Open** 5.45-11pm Mon-Thur; 5.30-11pm Fri, Sat. **3-course prix fixe** $105. **Credit** AmEx, DC, MC, V. **Map** p405 E21 **95 French**

CONSUME

INSIDE TRACK
CENTRAL PARK VIEWS

If you don't want to fork out for an expensive meal, you can enjoy virtually the same view of the lake commanded by the **Central Park Boathouse** (*see left*) over drinks, cheese plates and other appetisers in the adjacent outdoor bar.

INSIDE TRACK
BAKERY BARGAINS

Several celebrated chefs have more casual eateries where you can sample their talents for far less than the cost of their fine-dining establishments, such as Thomas (Per Se) Keller's **Bouchon Bakery** (see p204) and David Bouley's upstairs dining room at **Bouley Bakery & Market** (see p178).

counter lined with chatty locals on their lunch hours, tucking into burgers and chocolate malteds. If you come for breakfast, order the doorstop slabs of French toast. *Photos p205.*

Park Avenue Summer

100 E 63rd Street, between Park & Lexington Avenues (1-212 644 1900/www.parkavenyc.com/ summer). Subway F to Lexington Avenue-63rd Street. **Open** 11.30am-3pm, 5.30-10pm Mon-Thur; 11.30am-3pm, 5.30-11pm Fri; 11am-3pm, 5.30-11pm Sat; 11am-3pm, 5-9pm Sun. **Main course** $34. **Credit** AmEx, DC, Disc, MC, V. **Map** p405 E21 ➒ **American creative**
Manager Roger Morlock, chef Craig Koketsu and design firm AvroKO have conceived an ode to seasonal dining: the design, the uniforms and the very name (yes, it will be Park Avenue Autumn, Winter and Spring too) will rotate along with the menu. 'Summer' means sunny wall panels and ample clusters of flowers to go with the warm-weather foods. Appetisers showcase produce (baby beet salad, corn soup) and seafood (peekytoe crab salad, fluke sashimi), often mixing both with winning results. A seared John Dory fillet is brought to life by an audaciously rich combo of truffles (both slices and oil) and egg (poached with a fried brioche crust). Pastry chef Richard Leach, a James Beard Award winner, dazzles with his moist chocolate cake and whipped mascarpone.

Upper West Side

$ Alice's Tea Cup

102 W 73rd Street, at Columbus Avenue (1-212 799 3006/www.alicesteacup.com). Subway B, C, 1, 2, 3 to 72nd Street. **Open** 8am-8pm daily. **Sandwich** $8. **Credit** AmEx, DC, Disc, MC, V. **Map** p405 C20 ➒ **Café**
Wander into this sequestered basement and you'll be transported to a story land inspired by Lewis Carroll. First, pass through the quirky gift-boutique-cum-bakeshop, where you can browse Wonderland-themed knick-knacks along with dense, delicious scones and muffins. Proceed further in (not easy on weekends) and you'll discover a sweet room serving big brunch plates (sandwiches, salads, eggs) and

the full teatime monty ($30). It's a fairy tale indeed, except for the service, which can be slow.
Other locations 156 E 64th Street, between Third & Lexington Avenues, Upper East Side (1-212 486 9200); 220 E 81st Street, between Second & Third Avenues, Upper East Side (1-212 734 4832).

Bouchon Bakery

3rd Floor, Time Warner Center, 10 Columbus Circle, at Broadway (1-212 823 9366/www. bouchonbakery.com). Subway A, B, C, D, 1 to 59th Street-Columbus Circle. **Open** 11.30am-9pm Mon-Sat; 11.30am-7pm Sun. **Main course** $15. **Credit** AmEx, DC, MC, V. **Map** p405 D22 ➓ **Café**
The appeal is obvious: sample Thomas Keller's food for far less than it costs at Per Se, where the tasting menu is now a whopping $275 per person. The reality is that you will have to eat in an open café setting in the middle of a mall, under a giant Samsung sign, and choose from a limited selection of sandwiches, salads, quiches and spreadable entrées (pâté, foie gras and so on). That said, this is a great place for lunch. The servers are friendly and the sandwiches are impeccably plated – though portions can be small.
▶ *See p205 for Per Se review and listing.*

Café Luxembourg

200 W 70th Street, between Amsterdam & West End Avenues (1-212 873 7411/www.cafe luxembourg.com). Subway B, C, 1, 2, 3 to 72nd Street. **Open** 8am-midnight Mon-Fri; 9am-midnight Sat, Sun. **Main course** $31. **Credit** AmEx, DC, MC, V. **Map** p405 C20 ➓ **French**
Café Luxembourg isn't trying to be anything other than what it is – a comfortable neighbourhood bistro successfully executing traditional French-American fare. With prices in this range, you might expect more flair but this restaurant's signature offering isn't on the menu, it's in the casual comfort created by the fusion of simple decor, attentive, unfussy service and uncomplicated food expertly prepared. Seasonal starters and desserts punctuate a short menu of steak frites, grilled fish and crème brûlée. It all adds up to an atmosphere of relaxed elegance that keeps the neighbourhood regulars (celebrities and ordinary Joes alike) coming back.

★ Dovetail

103 W 77th Street, at Columbus Avenue (1-212 362 3800). Subway B, C to 81st Street-Museum of Natural History; 1 to 79th Street. **Open** 5.30-11pm Mon-Sat; 5.30-10pm Sun. **Main course** $32. **Credit** AmEx, DC, Disc, MC, V. **Map** p405 C19 ➓ **American**
This upscale gem joins a small class of UWS restaurants that justify a special trip uptown. Though the earth-toned look smacks of a hotel restaurant and service is dispassionate, the successful menu from chef John Fraser has a rich,

CONSUME

Lexington Candy Shop. *See p203*.

CONSUME

seasonal emphasis. Foie gras and butter infuse many dishes (monkfish, pillowy veal short rib gnocchi), and meat, such as a charred sirloin accompanied by beef cheek lasagne layered with paper-thin slices of turnips, is equally hearty.

Eighty One
45 W 81st Street, between Central Park West & Columbus Avenue (1-212 873 8181/www. 81nyc.com). Subway B, C to 81st Street-Museum of Natural History. **Open** 5-10.30pm Mon-Thur, Sun; 5-11.30pm Fri, Sat. **Main course** $37. **Credit** AmEx, DC, MC, V. **Map** p405 C19 ⓾ American
Chef Ed Brown presides over this grand, white-columned eatery. Despite clumsy service and an awkward menu breakdown, the meals here excel. If it swims, it wins: silken scallop and foie gras are united in wonton skin 'ravioli'; halibut is surrounded by clams and bathed in a vibrant parsley-tinged sauce. A profusion of luxe ingredients translate to a pricey meal, but it proves a worthy splurge in a neighbourhood that is slowly earning its fine-dining cred, one restaurant at a time.

Gennaro
665 Amsterdam Avenue, between 92nd & 93rd Streets (1-212 665 5348). Subway 1, 2, 3 to 96th Street. **Open** 5-10.30pm Mon-Thur, Sun; 5-11pm Fri, Sat. **Main course** $12. **No credit cards**. **Map** p406 C17 ⓾ Italian
Normally, a per-person minimum (of $20) might make you bristle, but at this wildly popular neighbourhood restaurant it's just an excuse to order dessert – or wine. The antipasti platter for two is a meal in itself, and the best thing on a very nice menu. Roughly double the cost of the other dishes, it contains more than double the amount of food. The daily-changing starter plate is likely to include rock shrimp, caponata, prosciutto, roasted peppers, bruschetta, mozzarella, portobello mushrooms, grilled aubergine and a seafood salad – which puts you in the perfect position to skip the pasta and meat and go straight to tiramisu or flourless choco-late-hazelnut cake.

Jean Georges
Trump International Hotel & Tower, 1 Central Park West, at Columbus Circle (1-212 299 3900/ www.jean-georges.com). Subway A, C, B, D, 1 to 59th Street-Columbus Circle. **Open** noon-2.30pm, 5.30-11pm Mon-Thur; 5.15-11pm Fri, Sat. **4-course prix fixe** $98; **7-course prix fixe** $148. **Credit** AmEx, DC, MC, V. **Map** p405 D22 ⓾ French
Unlike so many of its vaunted peers, Jean Georges has avoided becoming a shadow of itself because the cooking still has the power to take your breath away. A foie gras terrine starter is legendary for a reason: every bite of the velvety pâté that harbours roasted strawberries on a round of brioche (all coated in a

thin brûlée shell) is worth savouring. Inventive themed dessert quartets from pastry chef Johnny Iuzzini include 'summer', featuring an uncannily ripe-tasting red plum sorbet and a saline palate cleanser of sliced nectarines, crunchy pistachios and briny goat's cheese. The more casual, on-site Nougatine café is a less expensive option.

★ Per Se
4th Floor, Time Warner Center, 10 Columbus Circle, at Broadway (1-212 823 9335/www.perse ny.com). Subway A, B, C, D, 1 to 59th Street-Columbus Circle. **Open** 5.30-10pm Mon-Thur; 11.30am-1.30pm, 5.30-10.30pm Fri-Sun. **Tasting menu** $275/$305. **Credit** AmEx, DC, MC, V. **Map** p405 D22 ⓾ French
Expectations are high at Per Se – and that goes both ways. You're expected to come when they'll have you and fork over a fee if you cancel. You're expected to wear the right clothes, pay a non-negotiable service charge and pretend you aren't eating in a shopping mall. The restaurant, in turn, is expected to deliver one hell of a tasting menu. And it does. Dish after dish is flawless, beginning with Thomas Keller's signature salmon tartare cone and luxe oysters and caviar starter. Have you tasted steak with mash or chocolate brownies with coffee ice-cream? Probably. Have you had them this good? Unlikely. Worth every penny.

Telepan
72 W 69th Street, at Columbus Avenue (1-212 580 4300/www.telepan-ny.com). Subway B, C to 72nd Street; 1 to 66th Street-Lincoln Center. **Open** 5-11pm Mon, Tue; 11.30am-2.30pm, 5-11pm Wed, Thur; 11.30am-2.30pm, 5-11.30pm Fri, Sat; 11am-2.30pm, 5-10.30pm Sun. **Main course** $28. **Credit** AmEx, DC, Disc, MC, V. **Map** p405 C21 ⓾ American
Every New York neighbourhood has its designated local foods champion, and on the Upper West Side, Bill Telepan is it. His restaurant, with agrarian-themed art on the walls, is a paean to what's in season. A gratifying appetiser of a runny egg perched on top of a fried green tomato slice and farmhouse cheddar cheese is all country simplicity, as is a main course of juicy and generously salted roasted chicken, which comes with egg noodles and wild mushrooms.

Harlem

★ Amy Ruth's
113 W 116th Street, between Malcolm X Blvd (Lenox Avenue) & Adam Clayton Powell Jr Blvd (Seventh Avenue) (1-212 280 8779/ www.amyruthsharlem.com). Subway 2, 3 to 116th Street. **Open** 7.30am-11pm Mon-Thur, Sun; 24hrs Fri, Sat. **Main course** $13. **Credit** AmEx, DC, Disc, MC, V. **Map** p407 D14 ⓾ American regional

Secret Gardens

Grab a table at these under-appreciated alfresco spots before the word gets out.

In summer, the heat is on to nab a seat in the crowded outdoor spaces of popular restaurants. But it is possible to escape the hordes and find a peaceful place in the sun, if you know where to look.

Though the brownstone digs at **Bobo** (*see p190*) are stunning, as is chef Patrick Connolly's greenmarket menu, the trellis-embellished garden is even lovelier. Sip the eponymous house cocktail (prosecco with Aperol over ice) while watching a lemon tree wave in the wind. Reservations are recommended, so call ahead.

You'll find a wooden patio and a backyard filled with enough foliage to fool you into thinking you're in the countryside at the **Farm on Adderley** (*see p210*). Get a table beneath the stringed lights, then tuck into pork chops with sweet potato gnocchi and poached egg-topped grilled asparagus.

The recently overhauled tiled back garden at Gallic Lower East Sider **Le Père Pinard** (*see p186*) is adorned with white latticework fencing, string lights and both hanging plants and hanging bikes. Sup on plump mussels and pâtés made in-house;

arrive early to enjoy lingering sunlight and a three-course prix fixe for $17.

Pre- or post-P.S.1, swing by retro-themed **Lounge 47** (*see p225*) and saunter into its sunny, pebble-strewn bamboo garden. The verdant hideaway is heaven for long, lazy afternoons of imbibing (try the cooling LIC Iced Tea – a peachy version of the classic Long Island variety) and chomping hamburgers painted with spicy chipotle mayo.

Royalty and serfs alike are welcome at the **Queen's Hideaway** (*see p211*), where an idyllic, vine-covered, crayon-hued courtyard seems designed for unhurried dining sessions. Sample chef-owner Liza Queen's eclectic edibles, including sweet pea flan or beer-battered shark, and close the evening with a fat slice of fruit pie.

Escape the East Village hubbub at **Gnocco Cucina & Tradizione** (*see p189*), an Italian stalwart with a subdued, secluded stone backyard filled with foliage and blossoms. Order a reasonably priced bottle of prosecco ($32) and dive into crisp pizzas, tender pastas and the restaurant's namesake: savoury fritters with paper-thin prosciutto, salami and *capocollo*.

CONSUME

Farm on Adderley.

Fette Sau. *See p210.*

Portraits of jazz giants hang on the walls of this perpetually packed two-storey Harlem fave. A bottle of Frank's RedHot dresses every table – a sign of the soul food goodness to come. Indeed, the richly battered catfish or the fried chicken and waffles platters (many named for famous African-Americans, including Rev Al Sharpton and Doug E Fresh), served with your choice of white or dark meat, go down peppery-sweet with a splash of the hot stuff. Titanic helpings of cinnamon-crusted peach cobbler and thickly iced red velvet cake lend the menu a grandmotherly touch.

▶ For more on food in West Harlem, see p120.

$ Le Baobab
120 W 116th Street, between Adam Clayton Powell Jr Blvd (Seventh Avenue) & Malcolm X Blvd (Lenox Avenue) (1-212 864 4700). Subway 2, 3 to 116th Street. **Open** noon-2am daily. **Main course** $11. **No credit cards**. **Map** p407 D14 ⑩⑨ African
With its elegant beige-painted dining room, decorated with burgundy chairs and portraits of African-Americans, Le Baobab is a stately restaurant that doesn't forget its Senegalese roots. *Thiebou diene* consists of generous chunks of market-fresh fish stewed in tomato sauce with carrots, aubergine, cabbage and cassava, all spooned over plump, nutty rice. *Soupou kanja*, a savoury lamb stew flavoured with fish and thickened with okra and palm oil, is both rich and complex. For dessert, *thiakry*, couscous mixed with vanilla-enriched sour cream and bits of fruit, is as comforting as tapioca pudding.

$ Charles' Southern Style Kitchen
2837-2841 Frederick Douglass Blvd (Eighth Avenue), between 151st & 152nd Streets (1-212 926 4313). Subway B, D to 155th Street. **Open** 7am-2am Mon-Sat; 8am-9pm Sun. **Main course** $9. **Prix fixe buffet** $14. **Credit** DC, MC, V. **Map** p408 D10 ⑩ American regional
Charles Gabriel grew up cooking for 19 siblings in North Carolina, so he knows Southern cooking. His Harlem kitchen launches a multilateral assault on the arteries, offering breakfast, fried seafood, takeout fare and an eat-in buffet. He whips up four specials a day – a hit parade of soulful grub, such as pan-fried chicken, barbecued ribs, meaty oxtails, flash-fried whiting, and pork chops smothered in peppery brown gravy.

Melba's
300 W 114th Street, at Frederick Douglass Blvd (Eighth Avenue) (1-212 864 7777/www.melba srestaurant.com). Subway B, C to 116th Street. **Open** 5-11pm Tue-Thur; 5pm-midnight Fri, Sat; 10am-3pm, 5-10pm Sun. **Main course** $14. **Credit** AmEx, DC, MC, V. **Map** p406 D15 ⑪ American regional
When it was opened in 2005 by the niece of the woman behind legendary Sylvia's, Melba's was heralded both for its neo-soul sensibility and as an

emblem of a Harlem Renaissance developing along lower Frederick Douglass Boulevard. Though praise for its chicken and waffles from Bobby Flay on the Food Network followed, the dish turns out to be surprisingly dry and uninspired; it's the 'neo' aspect of the soul menu that is most successful. Spring rolls filled with black-eyed peas and collard greens are a small revelation, while braising the short ribs with wine brings out a mellow quality that accentuates their tenderness.

BROOKLYN

Al di là
248 Fifth Avenue, at Carroll Street, Park Slope (1-718 783 4565/www.aldilatrattoria.com). Subway M, R to Union Street. **Open** 6-10.30pm Mon, Wed, Thur; 6-11pm Fri; 5.30-10.30pm Sat; 5-10pm Sun. **Main course** $16. **Credit** DC, MC, V. **Map** p410 T11 ⑫ Italian
Aspiring restaurateurs along Fifth Avenue in Park Slope should study this convivial place on the corner: eight-year-old Al di là, which remains unsurpassed in the locale. Affable owner Emiliano Coppa orchestrates the inevitable wait (due to the no-reservations policy) with panache. Coppa's wife, co-owner and chef Anna Klinger, produces Northern Italian dishes with a Venetian slant. It would be hard to improve upon her braised rabbit with black olives atop polenta, and even simple pastas, such as the homemade tagliatelle al ragù, are superb.
Other locations al di là vino, 607 Carroll Street, at Fifth Avenue, Park Slope, Brooklyn (1-718 783 4565).

Blue Ribbon Brooklyn
280 Fifth Avenue, between Garfield Place & 1st Street, Park Slope (1-718 840 0404/www.blue ribbonrestaurants.com). Subway M, R to Union Street. **Open** 5pm-midnight Mon-Thur; 5pm-2am Fri; 4pm-2am Sat, Sun. **Main course** $23. **Credit** AmEx, DC, MC, V. **Map** p410 T11 ⑬ American creative
With the success of the Soho original, the French-trained brothers Bromberg opened this night owl draw in Brooklyn, offering up a clever mix of down-home cooking and haute cuisine, all available into

---

THE BEST
RESTAURANT VIEWS

For park life
Central Park Boathouse. *See p203.*

For the Manhattan skyline
River Café. *See p212.*

For food as exquisite as the views
Per Se. *See p206.*

CONSUME

the wee hours of the morning. A heaping plate of crispy fried chicken shares the menu with a tender duck club sandwich layered between homemade raisin bread and one of the best cheeseburgers around. The super-fresh raw bar boasts oysters, clams, head-on prawns and lobster.
Other locations throughout the city.

Diner

85 Broadway, at Berry Street, Williamsburg (1-718 486 3077/www.dinernyc.com). Subway J, M, Z to Marcy Avenue; L to Bedford Avenue. **Open** 11am-midnight Mon-Thur, Sun; 11am-1am Fri, Sat. **Main course** $20. **Credit** AmEx, DC, MC, V. **Map** p411 U8 ⑭ **American**
A former greasy spoon in a tricked-out 1920s dining car, Diner was an instant classic when it opened in 1999. Despite its location (off Bedford Avenue high street in the shadow of the Williamsburg Bridge), this neighbourhood icon's popularity has only grown with age. Locals steam up the windows in winter and smoke up the patios in summer over satisfying eats by former Savoy chef Caroline Fidanza. The number of salads (two) and burgers more than doubles when a waitress writes out the daily specials on the white paper tablecloth. Dishes such as beefsteak tomato salad, cucumber gazpacho, hanger steak and one-man cherry pies are gastro-diner originals.

Farm on Adderley

1108 Cortelyou Road, between Stratford & Westminster Roads, Ditmas Park (1-718 287 3101/www.thefarmonadderley.com). Subway Q to Cortelyou Road. **Open** 11am-3.30pm, 5.30-11pm daily. **Main course** $16. **Credit** AmEx, DC, Disc, MC, V. **American**
See p207 **Secret gardens**.

Fette Sau

354 Metropolitan Avenue, between Havemeyer & Roebling Streets, Williamsburg (1-718 963 3404). Subway L to Lorimer Street; G to Metropolitan Avenue. **Open** 5pm-2am Mon-Thur, Sun; 5pm-4am Fri, Sat. **Main course** $15. **Credit** DC, MC, V. **Map** p411 U8 ⑮ **Barbecue**
With a name that's German for 'fat pig', this hipster barbecue draw goes straight for your inner glutton. Joe and Kim Carroll have refurbished a former auto body shop, and the driveway and cement floors are now packed with picnic tables. A self-service 'cue station features glistening cuts of beef, lamb and pork by the pound. Stick to staples such as tender baby back ribs with a hint of smoke and a light rub of espresso and brown sugar, and the less orthodox pastrami. The sides and desserts, unfortunately, leave something to be desired, but the bar makes up for it with an encyclopedic bourbon menu and ten tap beers. *Photo p208.*

Give Us a 'Cue

Before you decide where to dine, bone up on the regional barbecue basics.

While there's never been a shortage of places for carnivores to indulge their taste for meat in New York, a spate of new barbecue spots has followed hot on the heels of the steakhouse revival. A cut above indiscriminate rib joints, many of these finger-lickin' good eateries have a regional bias. This whirlwind tour of Stateside styles will help you choose between the numerous excellent options.

NORTH CAROLINA
Carolina barbecue consists exclusively of pork. The pig is smoked for up to 14 hours over hickory and oak, then finished with a thin vinegar-based sauce and served on soft white bread. Find it at the **Smoke Joint** (*see p212*).

MEMPHIS
Like Carolina 'cue, Memphis meats highlight the hog, particularly pulled pork sandwiches and ribs. But while Memphis purists insist on pulling meat from the bone without the aid of a knife,

they don't discriminate between sauces and rubs. Find it at **Daisy May's BBQ USA** (*see p198*).

TEXAS
Lone Star style is (usually) all about the beef. Brisket, ribs and sausage are cooked over mesquite or live oak wood. But the crown jewel of this cow-worshipping 'cue is the brisket, sporting a light coating of rub or none at all. Texas barbecue shies away from heavy sauces, generally serving thinner, tangy mustard or chili-based lubes on the side. Find it at **Hill Country** (*see p195*) and **Blue Smoke** (*see p197*).

KANSAS CITY
The smoke kings marry the best of Texas (brisket, beef ribs and burnt ends), Memphis and North Carolina (pork sandwiches), but carve out their own niche with their KC sauce, a thick and sticky union of ketchup, butter, pepper, garlic and molasses. Find it at **RUB** (*see p194*).

CONSUME

Peter Luger.

CONSUME

★ Grimaldi's

*19 Old Fulton Street, between Front & Water
Streets Dumbo (1-718 858 4300/www.grimaldis.
com) Subway F to York Street.* **Open** 11.30am-
10.45pm Mon-Thur, Sun; 11.30am-11.45pm Fri;
noon-11.45am Sat. **Average pizza** $15. **No
credit cards. Map** p411 S9 **116 Pizza**
The tourist hordes haven't ruined Grimaldi's,
whose pedigree – going back to Patsy Grimaldi's
first job at his uncle's pizzeria in 1941 – assures it
guidebook coverage. The jukebox still honours
Frank Sinatra, and oh, the pizza: a thin crust covered with a mozzarella-to-sauce ratio that achieves
the Platonic ideal.

Marlow & Sons

*81 Broadway at Berry Street, Williamsburg
(1-718 384 1441/www.marlowandsons.com).
Subway J, M, Z to Marcy Avenue.* **Open**
11am-midnight daily. **Main course** $20.
Credit AmEx, DC, MC, V. **Map** p411 U8
117 American creative
Billyburgers craving fresh oysters and bold cocktails hightail it over to this popular eaterie, which
playfully serves as an old-time oyster bar, quaint
general store and daytime café. Seated in the
charming front-room shop, diners survey the stock
of gourmet olive oils and honeys while wolfing
down fresh-as-the-greenmarket salads, succulent
brick chicken and the creative crostini of the

moment (such as goat's cheese with flash-fried
strawberries). In the back room, an oyster shucker
cracks open the catch of the day, while the bar-
tender mixes the kind of potent drinks that helped
make the owners' earlier ventures (Bonita and next-
door Diner) successes.

★ Peter Luger

*178 Broadway, at Driggs Avenue, Williamsburg
(1-718 387 7400/www.peterluger.com). Subway
J, M, Z to Marcy Avenue.* **Open** 11.45am-10pm
Mon-Thur; 11.45am-11pm Fri, Sat; 12.45-10pm
Sun. **Steak for 2** $81. **No credit cards. Map** p411 U8 **118 Steakhouse**
Although a slew of Luger copycats have prospered
in the last several years, none have captured the elusive charm of this stucco walled, beer-hall style
eaterie, with its well-worn wooden floors and tables,
and waiters in waistcoats and bow ties. Excess is
the thing, be it the reasonably health-conscious
tomato salad (thick slices of tomato and onion with
an odd addition of steak sauce), the famous porterhouse for two, 44 ounces of sliced prime beef, or the
decent apple strudel, which comes with a bowl full
of *schlag* (whipped cream). Go for it all – it's a New
York experience that's worth having.

Queen's Hideaway

*222 Franklin Street, between Green & Huron
Streets, Greenpoint (1-718 383 2355/*

www.thequeenshideaway.com). Subway G to Greenpoint Avenue. **Open** 6-10.30pm Tue-Sat. **Main course** $16. **No credit cards. Map** p411 U6 **⑲ American**
See p207 **Secret gardens.**

River Café
1 Water Street at Old Fulton Street, Dumbo (1-718 522 5200/www.rivercafe.com). Subway F to York Street. **Open** noon-3pm, 5.30-11pm Mon-Sat; 11.30-3pm, 5.30-11pm Sun. **3-course prix fixe** $98; **6-course prix fixe** $125. **Credit** AmEx, DC, Disc, MC, V. **Map** p411 S9 **⑳ American**
Many people consider the River Café to be the best restaurant in Brooklyn, and it is probably the most expensive. The romantic waterside eaterie could easily skate by on its gorgeous views of downtown Manhattan, but chef Brad Steelman has created two exquisite prix-fixe menus: three courses (you choose) or six courses (he chooses). Stellar dishes include crisp oysters with smoked salmon and caviar, rack of lamb or lobster specials. For dessert, few can resist the chocolate marquise Brooklyn Bridge, shaped like its sparkling namesake.

Smoke Joint
87 South Elliott Place, between Fulton Street & Lafayette Avenue, Fort Greene (1-718 797 1011/www.thesmokejoint.com). Subway C to Lafayette Avenue; G to Fulton Street; B, M, Q, R to DeKalb Avenue. **Open** noon-10pm Mon-Thur, Sun; noon-11pm Fri, Sat. **Main course** $15. **Credit** AmEx, DC, Disc, MC, V. **Map** p410 T10 **㉑ Barbecue**
What sets apart this Fort Greene spot is its claim that it offers 'real New York barbecue'. But it doesn't stray far from the four basic 'cue groups: ribs, chicken, brisket and pork. 'Brooklyn wings' have plenty of smoky flavour, and the lean, slightly singed baby back ribs tasted of hickory, mesquite and maple woods. House sauces are especially addictive: piquant 'joint smoke' is cooked for six hours, and the vinegary 'holla-peña' is made with sambal spice. The space sports a honky-tonk look, with a bright orange paint job and enclosed porch.
▶ *See also p210* **Give us a 'Cue.**

QUEENS

★ Elias Corner
24-02 31st Street, at 24th Avenue, Astoria (1-718 932 1510). Subway N, W to Astoria-Ditmars Blvd. **Open** 4pm-midnight daily. **Main course** $25. **No credit cards. Map** p412 X3 **㉒ Greek**
It's not the simple blue-and-white Hellenic decor or the plastic fish on the walls that lure capacity crowds to this Astoria taverna each weekend. The glistening display of fresh seafood destined to be your dinner is what keeps diners coming. Elias's grilled fish is exceptional even in a neighbourhood

packed with Greek restaurants. Those in the know order the swordfish kebabs, fired up simply with green peppers, onions and tomatoes.

$ Jackson Diner
37-47 74th Street, between Roosevelt & 37th Avenues, Jackson Heights (1-718 672 1232/ www.jacksondiner.com). Subway E, F, V, G, R to Jackson Heights-Roosevelt Avenue; 7 to 74th Street-Broadway. **Open** 11.30am-10pm Mon-Thur, Sun; 11.30am-10.30pm Fri, Sat. **Main course** $13. **No credit cards. Map** p412 X5 **㉓ Indian**
Harried waiters and Formica-topped tables complete the diner experience at this weekend meet-and-eat headquarters for New York's Indian expat community. Watch Hindi soaps on Zee TV while enjoying *samosa chat* topped with chickpeas, yogurt, onion, tomato, and a sweet-spicy mix of tamarind and mint chutneys. Specials such as *murgh tikka makhanwala*, tender pieces of marinated chicken simmered in curry and cream, are fiery and flavourful – ask for mild if you're not immune to potent chilies.
▶ *For more on Little India, see p137.*

$ Sripraphai
64-13 39th Avenue, between 64th & 65th Streets, Woodside (1-718 899 9599/www. sripraphairestaurant.com). Subway 7 to 61st Street-Woodside. **Open** 11.30am-9.30pm Mon, Tue, Thur-Sun. **Main course** $10. **No credit cards. Map** p412 X5 **㉔ Thai**
It's not hard to find Thai food in New York these days. It's just hard to find Thai food like this. Every dish is distinctively spiced and traditional. Catfish salad offers fluffy, deep-fried minced fish with mint, coriander, chopped cashew and lemon juice. Green curry with beef is a thick, piquant broth filled with roasted Thai aubergine and spices. Although there are dining rooms on two levels and a garden (open in summer), be prepared for a short wait.

$ Zenon Taverna
34-10 31st Avenue, at 34th Street, Astoria (1-718 956 0133/www.zenontaverna.com). Subway N, W to Broadway. **Open** 11am-11pm daily. **Main course** $14. **No credit cards. Map** p412 W4 **㉕ Greek**
The faux stone entryway and murals of ancient ruins don't detract from the Mediterranean charm of this oasis that's been serving Greek and Cypriot food for more than 20 years. Large wedges of lemon arrive on most dishes, a final squeeze lending a refreshing splash of acidity to meats and fish alike. Generally it works, cutting the fattiness of plump *loukaniko* (pork sausages), seasoned to the hilt, and balancing the charred taste of incredibly tender grilled octopus. Filling sweets, such as *galaktopoureko* (syrupy layers of filo baked with custard cream), merit a taste, if your stomach isn't already bursting.

Bars

Welcome to the Big Tipple.

New York boasts an ever-growing embarrassment of bars, but finding them can be a challenge. One of the more notable trends in the city of late has been for unmarked, speakeasy-style watering holes; Death & Company and the Back Room are two key examples of the style. This retro theme has been furthered with the recent wave of old-timey drinking parlours that specialise in the hard stuff: even White Star, the latest from mixmaster Sasha Petraske, favours straight-up spirits.

Still, you'll of course find plenty of cocktails all over town, if that's your pleasure. Beers and wines, too. And if you prefer genuinely vintage establishments to the newer models, try venerable fixtures such as the eccentric Ear Inn, the art deco Lenox Lounge or the newly refurbished but otherwise old-school Oak Bar in the Plaza hotel (*see p167*), now a protected historic monument.

DOWNTOWN

Financial District

Bin No. 220

220 Front Street, between Beekman Street & Peck Slip (1-212 374 9463/www.bin220.com). Subway A, C to Broadway-Nassau; J, M, Z, 2, 3, 4, 5 to Fulton Street. **Open** 4pm-4am daily. **Average drink** $10. **Credit** AmEx, DC, MC, V. **Map** p402 F32 ❶
This sleek Italian-style wine bar, where banker types devour cured meats, cheeses and olive oil, offers refuge from the South Street Seaport tourist scene. Located on historic Front Street, the spot boasts cast-iron columns, a polished walnut bar and a nifty metal wine rack. Most patrons come for the selection of 60 wines (20 are available by the glass), but a well-stocked bar satisfies those who prefer the hard stuff.

Stone Street Tavern

52 Stone Street, between Coenties Alley & William Street (1-212 785 5658/www.stone streettavernnyc.com). Subway J, M, Z to Broad Street; 2, 3 to Wall Street. **Open** 11.30am-12.30am Mon, Sat, Sun; 11.30am-3am Tue-Fri. **Average drink** $7. **Credit** AmEx, DC, Disc, MC, V. **Map** p402 E33 ❷
Brokers' fresh-pressed shirts and shiny leather shoes rule at this alehouse, located on a quaint cobblestone block in the Financial District. After the markets close, the weathered wooden floors get further scuffed by martini sippers and Coors Light chuggers, whose boisterous gabbing competes with a circa-1996 soundtrack (hello, Cranberries!). Later on, the bar evolves into a more serene spot to grab a pint or lofty pub eats like cheese-crusted fries and a beer-battered grouper sandwich with tartar sauce.

Tribeca & Soho

★ B Flat

277 Church Street, between Franklin & White Streets (1-212 219 2970/www.b flat.info). Subway 1 to Franklin Street. **Open** 6pm-2am Mon-Thur; 6am-3am Fri, Sat. **Average drink** $12. **Credit** AmEx, DC, MC, V. **Map** p402 E31 ❸
Slink underground to this red-lit rathskeller for heady cocktails conjured by mixologists from cult favourite Angel's Share. While couples take to booths for Japanese nibbles (tuna tataki, fried oysters), the 'bar chefs' craft Far East-influenced potions. Gawk at their transparent shakers as they pour drinks like the Groovy (shiso-infused vodka and yuzu juice) or the Giant Steps (wasabi-infused vodka and sake).

 Green numbers given in this chapter correspond to the location of each bar as marked on the street maps. *See pp402-412.*

INSIDE TRACK ID

Don't forget to carry photo ID at all times, such as a passport. Even those who are well over the legal drinking age of 21 can get 'carded'.

Still peckish? Head upstairs to Tokyo Bar, where Japanese comfort food is served late.

Broome Street Bar

363 West Broadway, at Broome Street (1-212 925 2086). Subway C, E to Spring Street. **Open** 11am-1am Mon-Thur, Sun; 11am-2am Fri, Sat. **Average drink** $9. **Credit** DC, MC, V. **Map** p403 E30 ➍

The stained-glass visage of a young boy in a cap stares at passers by from this been-here-forever typical New York corner establishment (the current owners have operated the place for 36 years). Tourists from nearby hotels come to sup with locals at the bar with its chalkboard menus and numerous microbrews (we like the herbal Schneider Weisse). A small bar menu is available until 1am.

Ear Inn

326 Spring Street, between Greenwich & Washington Streets (1-212 226 9060/ www.earinn.com). Subway C, E to Spring Street; 1 to Houston Street. **Average drink** $6. **Credit** AmEx, DC, Disc, MC, V. **Map** p403 D30 ➎

When it opened in 1817, the historic Ear was popular with colourful characters ambling in from the docks of the Hudson. The basic decor (dark-wood bar, wobbly tables and chairs, retro ephemera) hasn't changed much since, and locals continue to pack the place thanks to its relaxed vibe and creaky charm. Basic fare (burgers, pasta, salads and the like) is also served.

▶ *See right City Secrets.*

Fanelli's Café

94 Prince Street, at Mercer Street (1-212 226 9412). Subway N, R, W to Prince Street. **Open** 10am-1.30am Mon-Thur, Sun; 10am-3.30am Fri, Sat. **Average drink** $5. **Credit** AmEx, DC, MC, V. **Map** p403 E29 ➏

On a lovely cobblestoned corner, this 1847 joint claims to be the second-oldest continuously operating bar and restaurant in the city. Prints of boxing legends and one of the city's best burgers add to the easy feel. The banter of locals and the merry clinking of pint glasses blesses the place with a soundtrack straight out of the old days. *Photo p216.*

MercBar

151 Mercer Street, between Houston and Prince Streets (1-212 966 2727/www.mercbar.com).

Subway B, D, F, V to Broadway-Lafayette Street; N, R, W to Prince Street; 6 to Bleecker Street. **Open** 5pm-1am Mon, Tue, Sun; 5pm-2am Wed; 5pm-2.30am Thur; 5pm-3.30am Fri, Sat. **Average drink** $11. **Credit** AmEx, DC, Disc, MC, V. **Map** p403 E29 ➐

If you're seeking some civilised company of the upwardly mobile variety, join the well-coiffed after-work crowd at MercBar. The lodge-like interior, dressed up with landscape paintings and a canoe suspended above the sleek mahogany bar, feels like a tony lakeside cabin. Bartenders stick with the get-away theme, mixing the signature Vacation (rum, cachaça, pineapple juice and 7-Up).

M1-5

52 Walker Street, between Broadway & Church Street (1-212 965 1701/www.m1-5.com). Subway J, M, Z, N, Q, R, W, 6 to Canal Street. **Open** 4pm-4am daily. **Average drink** $7. **Credit** AmEx, DC, Disc, MC, V. **Map** p402 E31 ➑

The name of this huge, red-walled hangout refers to Tribeca's zoning ordinance, which permits trendy restaurants to coexist with warehouses. The mixed-use concept also applies to M1-5's crowd: suited brokers shoot pool alongside baby-faced indie screenwriters. Both come out for the full, well-stocked bar specialising in stiff martinis.

Pegu Club

77 W Houston Street, at West Broadway (1-212 473 7348/www.peguclub.com). Subway B, D, F, V to Broadway-Lafayette Street; N, R to Prince Street. **Open** 5pm-2am Mon-Wed, Sun; 5pm-4am Thur-Sat. **Average drink** $12. **Credit** AmEx, DC, Disc, MC, V. **Map** p403 E29 ➒

Audrey Saunders, the drinks maven who turned Bemelmans Bar (*see p222*) into one of the city's most respected cocktail lounges, is behind this sleek liquid destination, inspired by a British officers' club in Burma. The beverage programme features classics culled from decades-old booze bibles (try the eponymous signature cocktail, made with gin, bitters and orange curaçao). An utterly civilised Asian-colonial air pervades the room.

Chinatown

Asia Roma

40 Mulberry Street, between Bayard & Mosco Streets (1-212 385 1133/www.asiaroma.com). Subway J, M, Z, N, Q, R, W, 6 to Canal Street. **Open** noon-2am Mon-Thur; noon-4am Fri; 5pm-4am Sat; 5pm-2am Sun. **Average drink** $8. **Credit** AmEx, DC, Disc, MC, V. **Map** p402 F31 ➓

A blue neon sign points karaoke lovers to this basement lounge, where groups of young revellers take to the stage to shamelessly belt out Mandarin pop songs along with sing-along standards from Tina Turner and Billy Idol. Hesitant newcomers can loosen up with a speciality cocktail procured from the upstairs bar. Harness liquid courage via a Zen martini – Absolut Citron infused with green tea.

Lower East Side

★ Back Room

102 Norfolk Street, between Delancey & Rivington Streets (1-212 228 5098). Subway F, V, J, M, Z to Delancey-Essex Streets. **Open** 7.30pm-4am Tue-Sat. **Average drink** $9. **Credit** AmEx, DC, MC, V. **Map** p403 G30 ⑪
For access to this ersatz speakeasy, look for a sign that reads The Lower East Side Toy Company. Pass through the gate, walk down an alleyway and up a set of stairs to find a dimly lit den fitted with a gleaming bar. Cocktails are poured into teacups, and bottled beer is brown-bagged before being served. A trick bookcase leads to the real 'back room', a VIP-only lounge.

Botanica

47 E Houston Street, between Mott & Mulberry Streets (1-212 343 7251). Subway B, D, F, V to Broadway-Lafayette Street; 6 to Bleecker Street. **Open** 5pm-4am Mon-Fri; 6pm-4am Sat, Sun. **Average drink** $5. **Credit** AmEx, DC, Disc, MC, V. **Map** p403 F29 ⑫
The thrift-store decor (mismatched chairs with sagging seats, statues of the Virgin Mary and a faux fireplace) makes for a charmingly shabby backdrop at this downtown dive, a favourite among laid-back creative types and the occasional gaggle of NYU students. Libations range from basic brews (eight on tap) to house cocktails like the Mean Bean martini, made with vodka and spicy green beans from Rick's Picks. DJs spin every night (except Monday), providing a sultry soundtrack for the singles lounging in the conversation-friendly back room.

East Side Company Bar

49 Essex Street, between Broome & Grand Streets (1-212 614 7408). Subway F to Delancey Street; J, M, Z to Delancey-Essex Streets. **Open** 7pm-4am Mon-Sat. **Average drink** $10. **Credit** AmEx, DC, Disc, MC, V. **Map** p403 G30 ⑬
If you can't get into mixologist Sasha Petraske's exclusive, reservation-only Milk & Honey (134

City Secrets House Spirits

Some locals at the Ear Inn may have outstayed their welcome.

There are few better places in which to enjoy a well-pulled pint and romanticise about the NYC of yore than the **Ear Inn** (*see p214*), on the ground floor of a three-storey, 19th-century house that's also served as a tobacconist and a bordello. And, apparently, not all of the spirits within are of the alcoholic kind.

Regulars believe that the Ear is haunted by the ghost of Mickey, a sailor killed outside the place long ago. But there are also thought to be up to 20 more

souls chilling in the rooms upstairs. That apartment, owned by Ear Inn proprietor Martin Sheridan, has been vacant for years: the last tenants were getting shaken awake by resident phantoms. 'Waitresses go upstairs to get something and they come back saying they'll never go up there again,' Sheridan says. 'But Mickey never hurts anyone. He just messes with the ladies and moves your pint of beer when you're not looking. He's a playful old bloody ghost.'

THE BEST
THEME SPOTS

For speakeasy chic
Back Room. *See p215.*

For cruise-ship comfort
Highline. *See p218.*

For gentlemen's-club cool
Union Hall. *See p224.*

Eldridge Street, between Broome & Delancey Streets, unlisted phone, www.mlkhny.com), you'll fare much better at one of his new Lower East Side spots: the phone numbers are readily available, and you can also walk in off the street. This snug space also has a 1940s-era vibe (leather booths, classic cocktails) as well as a few welcome additions, such as a raw bar.
▶ *Petraske also runs the White Star; see p217.*

Happy Ending Lounge
302 Broome Street, between Eldridge & Forsyth Streets (1-212 334 9676/www.happyending lounge.com). Subway B, D to Grand Street; J, M, Z to Bowery. **Open** 10pm-4am Tue; 7pm-4am Wed-Sat. **Average drink** $8. **Credit** AmEx, DC, MC, V. **Map** p403 F30 ⑭
Yes, the racy name of this downtown bar refers to that kind of happy ending – the two-storey space

was once home to a massage parlour that went all the way. Traces of that sordid past remain (see the shower knobs poking out from the walls), but these days the only lubricants on the premises are cocktails – try the spicy, frothy Mr Ginger, made with ginger ale and house-infused ginger vodka.

Loreley
7 Rivington Street, between Bowery & Chrystie Street (1-212 253 7077/www.loreleynyc.com). Subway J, M, Z to Bowery. **Open** noon-4am daily. **Average drink** $10. **Credit** AmEx, DC, Disc, MC, V. **Map** p403 F30 ⑮
Perhaps bar owner Michael Momm, aka DJ Foosh, wanted a place where he could spin to his heart's content. Maybe he missed the biergartens of his youth in Cologne. Whatever. Just rejoice that he opened Loreley. Twelve drafts and eight bottled varieties of Germany's finest brews are available, along with wines from the country's Loreley region and a full roster of spirits. Avoid drinking battery-acid-like schnapps straight and sample it in the Black German instead, a combination of blackberry schnapps, vodka and champagne served in a martini glass.

★ Schiller's Liquor Bar
131 Rivington Street, at Norfolk Street (1-212 260 4555/www.schillersny.com). Subway F to Delancey Street; J, M, Z to Delancey-Essex Streets. **Open** 8am-2am Mon, Tue; 8am-3am Wed-Fri; 10am-3am Sat; 10am-2am Sun.

Fanelli's Cafe. *See p214.*

CONSUME

Average drink $7. **Credit** AmEx, DC, MC, V.
Map p403 G29 ⑯
The drink menu famously hawks a down-to-earth
hierarchy of wines: Good, Decent, Cheap. Not one
of them will run to more than eight bucks a glass.
As at Keith McNally's other establishments,
Balthazar (*see p178*) and Pastis, folks pack in for
the scene, triple-parking at the bar, and elaborate
cocktails. Views are star-studded: sightings may
include Gandolfini and Wintour. Whether you're
downing white sangria or scarfing steak frites, you
can't help thinking that the vicar of vibe has tri-
umphed once again.

White Star
*21 Essex Street, between Canal & Hester
Streets (1-212 995 5464). Subway F to East
Broadway.* **Open** 6pm-3am daily. **Average
drink** $8. **Credit** AmEx, DC, Disc, MC, V.
Map p403 G30 ⑰
Sasha Petraske broke new ground when he opened
Milk & Honey, among the city's first serious cocktail parlours, in 2000. It follows, then, that it would
be Petraske who is driving a departure from the
trend, just as it reaches a fever pitch. At this tiny
bar, outfitted in grey wainscoting and hung with
the celestial Moroccan lamps for which it is named,
he pours spirits meant to be sipped – not mixed.
Libations like Kübler absinthe, amari and aperitivi
are available in short 35ml pours.

East Village

Blue Owl
*196 Second Avenue, between 12th & 13th Streets
(1-212 505 2583/www.blueowlnyc.com). Subway
L to First or Third Avenue.* **Open** 5pm-4am
daily. **Average drink** $10. **Credit** AmEx, DC,
MC, V. **Map** p403 F28 ⑱
Creatures of the night come to nest at this subterranean bar, where the lights are low, the patrons well
heeled and the drinks properly stiff. Stake out one
of the stylish pressed-tin tables, nibble on house-
marinated olives and sip a Blue Owl – a sultry mix
of Miller's gin, maraschino liqueur and lemon juice.

★ Death & Company
*433 E 6th Street, between First Avenue &
Avenue A (1-212 388 0882/www.deathand
company.com). Subway F, V to Lower East Side-
Second Avenue; 6 to Astor Place.* **Open** 6pm-
midnight daily. **Average drink** $13. **Credit**
AmEx, DC, MC, V. **Map** p403 F28 ⑲
The nattily-attired mixologists are deadly serious
about drinks at this pseudo speakeasy with Gothic
flair (don't be intimidated by the imposing wooden
door). Black walls and cushy booths combine with
chandeliers to set the luxuriously sombre mood.
Patrons bored by shot-and-beer bars can sample the
inventive cocktails as well as top-notch grub including bacon-swaddled filet mignon bites.

Grassroots Tavern
*20 St Marks Place, between Second & Third
Avenues (1-212 260 2876). Subway 6 to Astor
Place.* **Open** 4pm-4am daily. **Average drink** $4.
No credit cards. **Map** p403 F28 ⑳
One of the only honest dives on an otherwise
gimmicky stretch of St Marks Place, this bar lures
in-the-know East Villagers to its dark basement
digs. A weekday happy hour, from 4pm to 8pm,
entices with a dollar off already dirt-cheap pints
and two bucks off pitchers. The cut-rate prices
should free up some dough to sample some of the
dozen suds on tap.

International Bar
*120½ First Avenue, between St Marks Place
& E 7th Street (1-212 777 1643). Subway F,
V to Lower East Side-Second Avenue; L to
First Avenue.* **Open** 1pm-4am daily. **Average
drink** $3.50. **Credit** AmEx, DC, Disc, MC, V.
Map p403 F28 ㉑
The walls have been cleared of graffiti, but the
second coming of this legendary saloon stays
true to its dive bar roots (the original shuttered in
2005 after more than 40 years of business). A scuffed
mahogany bar and vintage film posters make up the
decor, and the jukebox is still killer (Black Flag, Nina
Simone). Liquor tops out at $6, taps like Stella and
Yuengling are $5 or less, and two-buck cans of
Schaefer can be paired with whiskey shots ($4 for
both). The cheap booze and grimy vibe foster the
feeling that I-Bar never left.

Shoolbred's
*197 Second Avenue, between 12th & 13th Streets
(1-212 529 0340/www.shoolbreds.com). Subway
L to Third Avenue; 6 to Astor Place.* **Open** 4pm-
2am daily. **Average drink** $8. **Credit** AmEx,
DC, Disc, MC, V. **Map** p403 F28 ㉒
This East Village bar owes its atmosphere to
co-owner and Tony Award-winning set designer
William Ivey Long, who filled the cosy pub with
stained-glass flourishes, an abundance of orchids,
cherrywood-panelled walls and Louise Bourgeois
lithographs. Despite frat bait like well-priced beer
(the house ale goes for just $5 a pint), there's little
spillover from the area's college-friendly bars.

CONSUME

INSIDE TRACK
HIGH TIMES

For stellar views with your booze, head
to one of the city's rooftop hotel bars.
Plunge at the **Hotel Gansevoort** (*see
p159*), Ava at **Dream Hotel** (*see p163*),
Cabana at the **Maritime Hotel** (*see
p160*) and A60 at **60 Thompson**
(guests and members only; *see p153*)
are all recommended.

Instead you'll find low-key tipplers conversing over fresh screwdrivers and greyhounds, made to order with an old-fashioned citrus press on the bar.

Solex
103 First Avenue, between 6th & 7th Streets (1-212 777 6677/www.solexnyc.com). Subway F, V to Lower East Side-Second Avenue; 6 to Astor Place. **Open** 6pm-2am daily. **Average drink** $8. **Credit** AmEx, DC, MC, V. **Map** p403 F28 ㉓
This Lilliputian hangout features a Scandinavian-sleek interior outfitted with translucent plastic ceiling panels. Climb into a chest-height chair in the company of stylish downtowners, and select from more than two dozen French reds and whites by the glass poured by tie-clad waiters. Hungry? The late-night kitchen turns out buttery, offbeat eats such as truffle-topped quiche and a beef Wellington 'éclair'.

Terroir
413 E 12th Street, between First Avenue & Avenue A (no phone/www.wineisterroir.com). Subway L to First Avenue; L, N, Q, R, W, 4, 5, 6 to 14th Street-Union Square. **Open** 5pm-2am Mon-Sat. **Average drink** $13. **No credit cards. Map** p403 F28 ㉔
Oeno-evangelist Paul Grieco preaches the powers of terroir – grapes that express a sense of place – at this tiny, sparse wine haunt. The super-knowledgable waitstaff aptly helps patrons navigate the 36 by-the-glass options, including a robust Le Bouchet cabernet franc. Equally compelling is the line-up of wine and beer cocktails, including the frothy Abby Flip (Ommegang Abbey Ale, coriander syrup, pomegranate molasses and egg) and restaurant-calibre small plates (sage-wrapped lamb sausages). Stellar sips and a menu to match: hallelujah!

Greenwich Village

124 Rabbit Club
124 MacDougal Street, between Bleecker & W 3rd Streets (1-212 254 0575/www.124rabbit club.com). Subway A, B, C, D, E, F, V to W 4th Street. **Open** 6pm-4am daily. **Average drink** $8. **No credit cards. Map** p403 E29 ㉕

THE BEST
VINTAGE LOOKS

For Victorian charm
Fanelli's Café. *See p214.*

For art deco designs
Lenox Lounge. *See p223.*

For faux-French sophistication
Schiller's Liquor Bar. *See p216.*

European suds get the speakeasy treatment at this murky, unmarked cellar that could double as an S&M dungeon. Coarse brick walls and votives sheathed in broken bottles welcome serious beer geeks whom you'll elbow aside for a seat at the brass bar. Once there, you can sample 70-odd imported quaffs, such as the tart Belgian ale Rodenbach. Be sure to visit the loo: appropriately, it features a re-creation of Brussels' legendary peeing-boy statue.

Vol de Nuit Bar (aka Belgian Beer Lounge)
148 W 4th Street, between Sixth Avenue & MacDougal Street (1-212 982 3388/ www.voldenuitbar.com). Subway A, B, C, D, E, F, V to W 4th Street. **Open** 4pm-midnight Mon-Thur, Sun; 4pm-2.30am Fri, Sat. **Credit** AmEx, DC, Disc, MC, V. **Map** p403 E29 ㉖
Duck through an unmarked doorway on a busy stretch of West 4th Street and find yourself in a red-walled Belgian bar that serves brews exclusively from the motherland. Clusters of European grad students knock back glasses of De Konick and La Chouffe – just two of 19 beers on tap and 26 by the bottle. Moules and frites, fittingly, are the only eats.

West Village & Meatpacking District

Brass Monkey
55 Little W 12th Street, between Washington Street & Tenth Avenue (1-212 675 6686/ www.brassmonkeynyc.com). Subway A, C, E to 14th St; L to Eighth Ave. **Open** 11.30am-4am

CONSUME

Flatiron Lounge. *See p221.*

daily. **Average drink** $7. **Credit** AmEx, DC, Disc, MC, V. **Map** p403 C28 ㉗

Though Meatpacking mayhem rages around this low-key pub, the Brass Monkey remains the eye of the nightlife storm. The attitude is relaxed and the decor is simple – just plain wooden chairs and tables. You won't find any hypersweet cocktails or tarted-up bar snacks, either: there's a rotating list of 20 drafts (including Hoegaarden, Chimay and Magic Hat), 60 bottled beers, and tavern fare like mussels, burgers and shepherd's pie.

★ 5 Ninth

5 Ninth Avenue, between Gansevoort & Little W 12th Street (1-212 929 9460/www.5ninth.com). Subway A, C, E to14th Street; L to Eighth Avenue. **Open** 6pm-3am daily. **Average drink** $12. **Credit** AmEx, DC, MC, V. **Map** p403 C28 ㉘

The bar at this rustic Meatpacking District restaurant, located in an 1848 brownstone, is flush with speakeasy charm. The space is all exposed beams and brick, and the main ingredients in the heady cocktails are Scotch, cognac and whiskey. The Weeski, for one, is a potent blend of whiskey, Lillet, Cointreau and orange bitters. A fireplace and one of the city's prettiest gardens add to the intimate atmosphere – a stylish beacon within the area's garish nightlife scene.

Highline

835 Washington Street, at Little West 12th Street (1-212 243 3339/www.nychighline.com). Subway A, C, E to 14th Street. **Open** 11.30am-

11.30pm daily. **Average drink** $12. **Credit** AmEx, DC, MC, V. **Map** p403 C28 ㉙

This three-level concoction of restaurant, bar and cocktail lounge-cum-cruise-ship offers an 'onboard' wining-and-dining experience. Decorations are full of travel references and include pink and purple fabric patterned after the Thai Airways logo. The Bed Lounge evokes cabin service: a chilled out area where you can lie back with a drink served on a tray next to your recliner. On the 'upper deck', munch on appetisers like pad thai-stuffed spring rolls.

▶ *See p89 for details of the new High Line park.*

Otheroom

143 Perry Street, between Greenwich & Washington Streets (1-212 645 9758/ www.theotheroom.com). Subway 1 to Christopher Street-Sheridan Square. **Open** 5pm-2am Mon, Sun; 5pm-4am Tue-Sat. **Average drink** $7. **No credit cards. Map** p403 D28 ㉚

This gallery moonlights as a lounge, where a sleek, civilised crowd drinks amid the work of up-and-coming artists. You won't find any hard liquor, but rather a (fittingly) well-curated selection of New World wines by the glass. Those more given to hops can choose among 50 microbrews (ten taps, 40 bottles) while mulling over the changing art display.

Other locations Anotheroom, 249 West Broadway, between Ericsson Place & Walker Street, Tribeca (1-212 226-1418); Room, 144 Sullivan Street, between Houston & Prince Streets, Soho (1-212 477-2102).

Lenox Lounge. *See p223.*

MIDTOWN

Chelsea

Half King

505 W 23rd Street, between Tenth & Eleventh Avenues (1-212 462 4300/www.thehalfking.com). Subway C, E to 23rd Street. **Open** 11am-4am Mon-Fri; 9am-4am Sat, Sun. **Average drink** $7. **Credit** DC, MC, V. **Map** p404 C26 ③①
Don't let their blasé appearance fool you – the creative types gathered at the Half King's yellow pine bar are probably as excited as you are to catch a glimpse of the part-owner, author Sebastian Junger. While you're waiting, order a draft like Widmer, a cloudy Hefeweizen or a specialty cocktail (we like the Parisian, made with Hendrick's Gin, sauvignon blanc and elderflower liquor).
▶ *Check out the Monday-night reading series, and see p280 for more on spoken word events.*

Honey

243 W 14th Street, between Seventh & Eighth Avenues (1-212 620 0077/www.honeyny.com). Subway A, C, E, 1, 2, 3 to 14th Street; L to Eighth Avenue. **Open** 5pm-2am Mon-Wed, Sun; 5pm-4am Thur, Fri; 8pm-4am Sat. **Average drink** $10. **Credit** AmEx, DC, Disc, MC, V. **Map** p403 D27 ③②
Head down the stairs from the street to this rathskeller to sip signature libations such as the Picasso Honey (honey liquor, gin and Cointreau,

with a honey-stick garnish) and devour bar snacks such as beer-battered shrimp. We prefer the cavernous, mahogany and brick room on chill weeknights; weekends find this hive positively buzzing.

Tillman's

165 W 26th Street, between Sixth & Seventh Avenues (1-212 627 8320/www.tillmansnyc.com). Subway F, V, 1 to 23rd Street. **Open** 5pm-2am Mon-Wed; 5pm-4am Thur, Fri; 8pm-4am Sat. **Average drink** $12. **Credit** AmEx, DC, MC, V. **Map** p404 D26 ③③
Sepia images of jazz, funk and soul legends line the walls at this warm, earth-toned cocktail emporium. Waitresses glide amid crescent-shaped leather booths, and it's likely that you'll hear Coltrane oozing from the speakers. Given the old-fashioned aesthetic, a classic cocktail is the way to go: try a well-crafted Negroni or a bracing Dark & Stormy (dark rum, ginger beer and lime juice).

Gramercy Park & Murray Hill

3Steps

322 Second Avenue, between 18th & 19th Streets (1-212 533 5336/www.3stepsnyc.com). Subway L to First or Third Avenue. **Open** 5pm-4am Mon-Sat. **Average drink** $8. **Credit** AmEx, DC, Disc, MC, V. **Map** p403 F27 ③④
Young professionals and first-daters gather at the butcher-block bar inside this subterranean Gramercy groggery. There, black-clad bartenders

muddle fruity and herbed cocktails – like the cucumber Cosmo – to order. The cut-rate happy hour (5-10pm Mon-Fri) fosters a loquacious crowd.

Flatiron District & Union Square

★ Flatiron Lounge

37 W 19th Street, between Fifth & Sixth Avenues (1-212 727 7741/www.flatironlounge.com). Subway F, V, N, R, W to 23rd Street. **Open** 5pm-2am Mon-Wed, Sun; 5pm-4am Thur-Sat. **Average drink** $13. **Credit** AmEx, DC, MC, V. **Map** p403 E27 ㉟

Red leather booths, mahogany tables and globe-shaped lamps amp up the vintage vibe at this art deco space. Co-owner Julie Reiner's notable mixology skills have made the bar a destination, and her Beijing Punch (jasmine-infused vodka and white peach purée) is not to be missed. The 30ft bar, built in 1927, stays packed well into the wee hours. *Photos pp 218-219.*

Revival

129 E 15th Street, between Irving Place & Third Avenue (1-212 253 8061). Subway L to Third Avenue; N, Q, R, W, 4, 5, 6 to 14th Street-Union Square. **Open** 4pm-4am daily. **Average drink** $7. **Credit** AmEx, DC, Disc, MC, V. **Map** p403 F27 ㊱

A favourite hang of both suits and scenesters, this townhouse boasts three TVs showing sports and *The Simpsons* on the ground floor, and a lounge with cushiony sofas and a small bar upstairs. The after-work happy hour ($1 off beer and $2 off booze, 4-7pm daily) is ideal for a cut-rate G&T or pint of Stella – but be prepared for a bit of a meat market.

230 Fifth

230 Fifth Avenue, between 26th & 27th Streets (1-212 725 4300/www.230-fifth.com). Subway N, R, W to 28th Street. **Open** 4pm-4am daily. **Average drink** $12. **Credit** AmEx, DC, MC, V. **Map** p404 E26 ㊲

This rooftop bar dazzles with truly spectacular views of the Manhattan skyline, but the glitzy indoor lounge – with its wraparound sofas and bold lighting – shouldn't be overlooked.

THE BEST HARD LIQUOR BARS

For vodka
Russian Samovar. *See p221.*

For whiskey
Dram Shop. *See p223.*

For a bit of everything
White Star. *See p217.*

Theater District

Inc Lounge

Time Hotel, 224 W 49th Street, at Broadway (1-212 320 2984). Subway N, R, W to 49th Street; 1 to 50th Street. **Open** 5pm-4am daily. **Average drink** $11. **Credit** AmEx, DC, Disc, MC, V. **Map** p404 D23 ㊳

Bar maven Ric Addison is behind this sleek second-floor lounge inside the Time Hotel. Lucite chandeliers, mermaid-patterned wallpaper from Scottish textile studio Timorous Beasties and seating upholstered in all manner of animal skin glam up the space, which is accessible via a Willy Wonka-esque glass elevator. Cocktails are the focus: order up a Gin & Sin (Bombay Sapphire, Chambord, lemon and lime juice) to pair with a house-made pizza.

Russian Samovar

256 W 52nd Street, between Broadway & Eighth Avenue (1-212 757 0168/www.russiansamovar. com). Subway C, E, 1 to 50th Street. **Open** noon-4am Mon-Sat; 5pm-4am Sun. **Average drink** $6. **Credit** AmEx, DC, Disc, MC, V. **Map** p404 D23 ㊴

At this Ruski haven, house-infused vodkas are the poison of choice. Impress friends by sampling the eye-opening pepper, or (for $15), choose three of more than 20 seasonal varieties, which can include raspberry, apple-cinnamon, ginger or tarragon. If you don't want to drink on an empty stomach, try a satisfying bowl of borscht or the toothsome beef Stroganoff. ► *For Russian treats of a more establishment nature, head to the Russian Tea Room; see p201.*

Midtown East

Azza

137 E 55th Street, at Lexington Avenue (1-212 755 7055/www.azzanyc.com). Subway 4, 5, 6 to 51st Street-Lexington Avenue. **Open** 10.30pm-4am Thur-Sat. **Average drink** $10. **Credit** AmEx, DC, MC, V. **Map** p405 E22 ㊵

Cushy sofas and sultry lanterns encourage hushed conversations and the occasional make-out session at this French-Moroccan lounge. World beats set the tone for the blissed-out crowd, and cocktails, like the Azzamore (strawberry vodka, triple sec, pomegranate juice and strawberry purée) or the Mint Tease (Citrus vodka, Cointreau, lemon-mint simple syrup and green tea) keep everyone friendly. Sporting types should head to the game room for gentlemanly pursuits such as blackjack.

Bookmarks Rooftop Lounge & Terrace

Library Hotel, 299 Madison Avenue, at 41st Street (1-212 204 5498/www.hospitalityholdings.com). Subway S, 4, 5, 6, 7 to 42nd Street-Grand Central; 7 to Fifth Avenue. **Open** 4pm-12.30am Mon-Sat. **Average drink** $13.50. **Credit** AmEx, DC, MC, V. **Map** p404 E24 ㊶

The fireplace, cosy sofas and club chairs at this rooftop bar suggest a decadent penthouse apartment. The enclosed greenhouse and the outdoor terrace (in less frigid weather) are both ideal perches for sipping luxurious cocktails – such as the Hemingway, made with rum, mint and champagne – and enjoying the multimillion-dollar view of Midtown's soaring skyscrapers.

★ Top of the Tower

Beekman Tower Hotel, 3 Mitchell Place, at First Avenue (1-212 980 4796/www.thetopof thetower.com). Subway E, V to Lexington Avenue-53rd Street; 6 to 51st Street. **Open** 7.30pm-1am Mon-Fri; 7.30pm-2am Sat, Sun. **Average drink** $16. **Credit** AmEx, DC, Disc, MC, V. **Map** p404 F23 ㊷

Sweeping views of Midtown and the East River are not the only draws at Top of the Tower, a swank lounge with two small outdoor terraces, perched on the 26th floor of this art deco landmark hotel. There's also live jazz piano (Thur-Sat) and signature cocktails like the chocolatey Gotham Martini.

UPTOWN

Upper East Side

Auction House

300 E 89th Street, between First & Second Avenues (1-212 427 4458). Subway 4, 5, 6 to 86th Street. **Open** 7.30pm-4am daily. **Average drink** $6. **Credit** AmEx, DC, MC, V. **Map** p406 F18 ㊸

Red velvet curtains, sofas and bordello-style wallpaper amp up the lusty vibe at this UES spot, presided over by a suggestive portrait of Adam, Eve and the infamous apple. Although there aren't any house specials, and the wine selection isn't very distinguished, the cosy atmosphere more than makes up for it.

★ Bemelmans Bar

The Carlyle, 35 E 76th Street, at Madison Avenue (1-212 744 1600/www.thecarlyle.com). Subway 6 to 77th Street. **Open** noon-1am Mon-Thur, Sun; noon-2am Fri, Sat. **Average drink** $19. **Credit** AmEx, DC, Disc, MC, V. **Map** p405 E20 ㊹

The Plaza may have Eloise, but the Carlyle has its own children's book connection – the wonderful 1947 murals of Central Park by *Madeline* creator Ludwig Bemelmans in this, the quintessential classy New York bar. Live music adds to the atmosphere most nights (a cover charge of $20-$25 applies from 9pm). ▶ *See p214 for Audrey Saunders' Pegu Club.*

Felice

1166 First Avenue, at 64th Street (1-212 593 2223/www.felicewinebar.com). Subway 6 to 68th Street-Hunter College. **Open** noon-midnight

INSIDE TRACK
SUBWAY INN

The ancient, dingy **Subway Inn**, located near Bloomingdale's (143 E 60th Street, between Lexington & Third Avenues, Upper East Side, 1-212 223 8929), is one of the city's most beloved boozers. Sadly, though, its days are numbered due to a planned development. Dive-bar aficionados should try to have a last tipple before it closes its doors.

daily. **Average drink** $14. **Credit** AmEx, DC, Disc, MC, V. **Map** p405 F21 ㊺

The mushrooming enoteca trend is creeping Uptown via this Tuscan wine bar on the Upper East Side. The smooth stone bar and communal table, lit by a chandelier crafted from roped-together glass jugs, host a rotating gaggle of grown-up *Gossip Girls* and their well-groomed men. Choose from 20 wines by the glass paired with antipasti and house-made pastas.

Upper West Side

Ding Dong Lounge

929 Columbus Avenue, between 105th Street & 106th Street (Duke Ellington Blvd) (1-212 663 2600/www.dingdonglounge.com). Subway B, C to 103rd Street. **Open** 4pm-4am daily. **Average drink** $6. **Credit** DC, MC, V. **Map** p406 C16 ㊻

Goth chandeliers and kick-ass music mark this dark dive as punk – with broadened horizons. The tap pulls, dispensing Stella Artois, Guinness and Bass, are sawn-off guitar necks, and the walls are covered with vintage concert posters (from Dylan to the Damned). The affable local clientele and mood-lit conversation nooks make it surprisingly accessible (even without a working knowledge of Dee Dee Ramone).

P&G

279 Amsterdam Avenue, at 73rd Street (1-212 874 8568). Subway 1, 2, 3 to 72nd Street. **Open** 10am-4am Mon-Sat; noon-4am Sun. **Average drink** $6. **No credit cards.** **Map** p405 C20 ㊼

When current proprietor Tom Chahalis' father and uncle first opened this place in 1942, an Austrian gentleman they had met on the boat over to America became a regular patron but couldn't cover his bar tabs. He wound up paying for his beer with art, which explains the Teutonic landscape murals on the walls and the soldier diorama tucked away behind a TV in one corner. Everything else is textbook dive, from the outside signage to the cheap drinks and classic rock jukebox.

Pudding Stones West

*635 Amsterdam Avenue, at 91st Street
(1-212 787 0501/www.puddingstones
winebar.com). Subway 1, 2, 3 to 96th Street.*
Open 4pm-4am Mon-Fri; 11am-4am Sat, Sun.
Average drink $15. **Credit** AmEx, DC, MC, V.
Map p406 C18 ⓭

The waitstaff has your comfort in mind at this
friendly candlelit bar. If you can't decide among the
43 wines by the glass, Pudding Stones (which gets
its name from the smooth, wide pebbles that cover
grounds of many vineyards) offers generous three-
pour flights of red, white or sparkling for $12-$14 –
delicious with a pot of garlicky, wine-soaked mussels. If you seem particularly oenophilic, the server
just might take you for a spin around the joint's
pride and joy: a temperature-controlled closet
stocked with 87 bottles.
Other locations 1457 Third Avenue, between
82nd & 83rd Streets, Upper East Side (1-212
717 5797).

Harlem

Lenox Lounge

*288 Malcolm X Boulevard (Lenox Avenue),
between 124th & 125th Streets (1-212 427
0253). Subway 2, 3 to 125th Street.* **Open**
noon-4am daily. **Average drink** $5 (cover
varies). **Credit** AmEx, DC, MC, V.
Map p407 D13 ⓭

This is where a street hustler named Malcolm
worked before he found religion and added an X to
his name. Now the famous Harlem lounge and jazz
club welcomes a mix of old-school cats, unobtrusive
booze hounds and jazz-loving tourists into its arms.
Settle into the gorgeously restored art deco bar at
the front, or retire to the music room at the back.
▶ *For more on music at the Lenox, see p327.*

★ St Nick's Pub

*773 St Nicholas Avenue, at 149th Street
(1-212 283 7132/www.stnicksjazzpub.net).
Subway A, B, C, D, 1 to 145th Street.* **Open**
8pm-4am daily. **Average drink** $7. **No credit
cards. Map** p408 C10 ⓭

St Nick's Pub has barely changed since the 1940s,
when Duke Ellington first urged taking the A train
up to Sugar Hill. The whitewashed walls, low ceiling and narrow passageway along the bar towards
the stage reinforce the basement feel, but St Nick's
is warmed by its neighbourhood vibe, cheap drinks
and random free eats. On Monday nights, when
the jam sessions kick in, you'll be glad you heeded
the Duke's advice. *Photo p220.*

BROOKLYN

Dram Shop

*339 9th Street, between Fifth & Sixth Avenues,
Park Slope (1-718 788 1444). Subway F to
Seventh Avenue.* **Open** 3pm-4am Mon-Fri;

Huckleberry Bar. See p224.

CONSUME

noon-4am Sat, Sun. **Average drink** $7. **Credit** AmEx, DC, Disc, MC, V. **Map** p410 T11 🟠 *See p225* **Dram Yankees!**.

Huckleberry Bar

588 Grand Street, between Leonard & Lorimer Streets, Williamsburg (1-718 218 8555/www.huckleberrybar.com). Subway L to Lorimer Street; G to Metropolitan Avenue. **Open** 4pm-4am Mon-Sat; 2-6pm Sun. **Average drink** $10. **Credit** AmEx, DC, MC, V. **Map** p411 V8 🟢
East Billyburg's upscaling continues at this baroque cocktail boutique from the Danny Meyer-pedigreed Stephanie Schneider (Gramercy Tavern; *see p197*) and Andrew Boggs (Union Square Café, *see p197*; Blue Smoke, *see p197*). Acquire an intimate table in the expansive, old-world room and ask the barkeeps to muddle a pitch-perfect classic vodka gimlet or a speciality tipple like the Edward Bulwer-Lytton, concocted with ginger-infused rum. *Photo p223.*

Jake Walk

282 Smith Street, at Sackett Street, Carroll Gardens (1-347 599 0294/www.thejake walk.com). Subway F, G to Carroll Street. **Open** 4pm-2am daily. **Average drink** $9. **Credit** AmEx, DC, MC, V. **Map** p410 S10 🟢
See p225 **Dram Yankees!**.

Sunny's

253 Conover Street, between Beard & Reed Streets, Red Hook (1-718 625 8211/www.sunnys redhook.com). Subway F, G to Smith-9th Streets, then take the B77 bus to Conover Street. **Open** 8pm-2am Wed; 8pm-4am Fri, Sat. **Average drink** $5. **No credit cards. Map** p410 R11 🟢
This unassuming wharfside tavern has been in the Balzano family since 1890. On weekends, the bar buzzes with middle-aged and new-generation bohemians (the latter distinguished by their PBR

**INSIDE TRACK
SMOKING**

Despite the strict citywide smoking ban, you can still indulge your habit in establishments that could prove a percentage of their income came from selling tobacco products when the ban was enforced. Among them are **Circa Tabac** (32 Watts Street, between Sixth Avenue & Thompson Street, Soho, 1-212 941 1781, www.circatabac.com) and **Hudson Bar & Books** cigar bar (636 Hudson Street, at Horatio Street, 1-212 229 2642, www.barandbooks.cz), which also has branches in Midtown and the Upper East Side.

---

cans), plus the odd salty dog (canines, not sailors). Despite the nautical overtones, you're more likely to hear bossa nova or bluegrass than sea chanteys.

★ Superfine

126 Front Street, between Pearl & Jay Streets, Dumbo (1-718 243 9005). Subway A, C to High Street; F to York Street. **Open** 11.30am-2am Tue-Thur; 11.30am-4am Fri; 3pm-4am Sat; 11am-2am Sun. **Average drink** $7. **Credit** AmEx, DC, Disc, MC, V. **Map** p411 T9 🟢
This loft-like restaurant lures thirsty locals from their Dumbo pads for drinks after dark. The hopping neodive is also a gallery for local artists – a fact that keeps Superfine's worn-in shabby-chic furniture occupied with bespectacled and paint-splattered types. You can also find the patrons tossing back mixed drinks by the pool table – which, in a fitting show of creativity, is covered in bright orange felt.
▶ *For more on Brooklyn's art scene, see p275.*

★ Union Hall

702 Union Street, between Fifth & Sixth Avenues, Park Slope (1-718 638 4400/ www.unionhallny.com). Subway M, R to Union Street. **Open** 4pm-4am Mon-Fri; noon-4am Sat, Sun. **Average drink** $5. **Credit** AmEx, DC, MC, V. **Map** p410 T11 🟢
Upstairs at Union Hall couples chomp on miniburgers and nip at microbrews in the gentlemen's club anteroom (decorated with Soviet-era globes, paintings of fez-capped men, fireplaces) – before battling it out on the clay bocce courts. Downstairs, in the taxidermy-filled basement, the stage hosts bands, comedians and offbeat events.

QUEENS

★ Bohemian Hall & Beer Garden

29-19 24th Avenue, between 29th & 30th Streets, Astoria (1-718 274 4925/www.bohemian hall.com). Subway N, W to Astoria Boulevard. **Open** 5pm-2am Mon-Fri; noon-3am Sat, Sun. **Average drink** $4. **Credit** DC, MC, V. **Map** p412 X3 🟢
Prost! This authentic Czech beer garden features plenty of mingle-friendly picnic tables, where you can sample cheap, robust platters of sausage, $5 Stolis and $4 Spaten Oktoberfests. Though the huge, tree-canopied garden is open year-round (in winter, the area is tented and heated), summer is prime time to soak up some rays over a pint.

LIC Bar

45-58 Vernon Boulevard, between 45th Road & 46th Avenue, Long Island City (1-718 786 5400/www.licbar.com). Subway 7 to Vernon Boulevard-Jackson Avenue. **Open** 4pm-2am Mon-Wed; 4pm-4am Thur, Fri; 1pm-4am Sat, Sun. **Average drink** $6. **Credit** AmEx, DC, Disc, MC, V. **Map** p412 V5 🟢

Dram Yankees!

Native whiskies come of age.

Historically, New York bar-goers have viewed American whiskey as a cheap way to get drunk. A rough-and-tumble liquor associated with trashy rock 'n' rollers and rueful country tunes – something you shoot, not sip. But just as artisanal American foods have caught on, a serious interest in native whiskey has followed, and a number of bars and restaurants focusing on American hard stuff have opened around the city.

'Whiskey' is a blanket term for a spirit distilled from fermented grain mash and aged in wooden barrels. The best-known type of American whiskey is bourbon, which by law must be distilled from at least 51 per cent corn and held in new, charred containers for two years or more. Then there's Tennessee whiskey (essentially, bourbon that's been filtered through charcoal), as well as corn, wheat, and rye whiskies, each with its own set of distilling regulations.

Those with an interest in sampling America's finest would do well to make a pilgrimage to Brooklyn, where several specialist bars have taken root. Park Slope's **Dram Shop** (*see p224*) offers more than 20 American small-batch and speciality whiskies, and co-owner Clay Mallow says he'll be expanding the American whiskey list, mostly because it's unexpectedly outselling Scotch. 'We were surprised,' says Mallow. 'American whiskey has really caught on.'

The obvious parallel to whiskey's rise is the city's thriving locavore (local food eaters') movement. Joe Carroll, who opened Williamsburg barbecue joint **Fette Sau** in 2007 (*see p211*), says that interest in US whiskey 'really began to take hold over the last five to eight years, as people became eager to get in touch with our own history and indigenous products.' The bar houses well over 50 varieties – including a handful of rare vintages that he finds at auctions.

The quality-to-cost ratio also plays a role. 'You can get a great glass of bourbon for far cheaper than a great glass of Scotch,' believes Mallow; and as if to prove his point, many of the varieties at the **Jake Walk** (*see p224*) go for $10 or less. At this Carroll Gardens bar, which opened its doors in spring 2008 by the team behind the Smith & Vine wine shop, co-owner and bartender Ari Form stocks his bar with 25 bourbons, 11 ryes and a handful of 'Others' (such as corn and wheat varieties). Be sure to sample the floral and smooth Hudson Manhattan Rye Whiskey ($16), the first rye whiskey produced in New York since Prohibition.

But cost isn't everything. Master mixologist and *Imbibe!* author David Wondrich thinks that while whiskey's popularity may in part be due to its affordable price tag, 'American whiskies – especially rye – can definitely achieve the flavour complexities of Scotch, and much of the market is moving towards boutique specialty varieties.'

As with anything that's in fashion, spirit trends tend to cycle. 'American whiskey is in at the moment; it's the "antivodka",' says Wondrich. But he feels that the amber spirit with a long history has far too much going for it to lay its popularity on a passing fad – it can be a true examplar of American artisanal traditions, with enough character to please even the most exacting sippers. We'll drink to that.

CONSUME

LIC's owners inherited the previous bar's brick, wood and tin ceiling fixtures, then brought in a laid-back attitude all their own – plus a much more extensive drink selection. They also added an outdoor patio and even order delivery from nearby restaurants, which makes it a convenient keep-the-party-going pit stop for music fans who migrate down the block after a boogie at the P.S.1 Warm Up (*see p300*).

Lounge 47

47-10 Vernon Boulevard, between 47th Avenue & 47th Road, Long Island City (1-718 937 2044). Subway 7 to Vernon Boulevard-Jackson Avenue. **Open** noon-1am Mon-Thur, Sun; noon-2am Fri, Sat. **Average drink** $7. **Credit** AmEx, DC, Disc, MC, V. **Map** p412 V5 ⑤

Just one subway stop into Queens is a bar decked out with 1960s and '70s furniture and Dutch vintage wallpaper. The reasonably priced cocktails, including the LIC Long Island iced tea, spruced up with a hit of peach nectar, and a full bar menu (with tasty panini) pull in folks from Silvercup Studios and P.S.1.
▶ *See p136 and p138 for P.S.1 and Silvercup Studios.*

Shops & Services

Welcome to the consumer capital of the world.

Financial circumstances mean that shopping is no longer the national pastime it once was, but New York City remains America's retail capital. As well as the famous department stores and global flagships, New York retains an impressive number of unusual, independently run businesses. Only time will tell how many survive in this turbulent economic era. Still, whatever you're looking for – big-name fashion or one-off items from obscure local designers, cut-price CDs or rare vinyl, fresh-from-the-studio home design or flea market bric-a-brac – you won't be disappointed.
The only pitfall is exhaustion if you attempt to cover too much ground. We recommend taking it slowly and arranging your retail excursions by neighbourhood; for a guide, *see p227* **Where to shop**.

THE SHOPPING SCENE

Though major markdowns are traditionally held at the end of each season, many of New York's best finds can be scored throughout the year from insider events. Barneys' ever-popular twice-yearly warehouse sales and designers' frequent sample sales all make excellent sources for reduced-price clothing from established and cutting-edge labels. To find out where the bargain fests are being held during any given week, consult the Seek section of *Time Out New York* or visit the website at www.timeoutnewyork.com. Otherwise, **Top Button** (www.topbutton.com) and the **SSS Sample Sales hotline** (1-212 947 8748, www.clothingline.com) also provide excellent discount resources.

While many shops in the city keep late hours most nights of the week, Thursday is generally the unofficial shop-after-work night, when most places remain open until at least 8pm. Stores downtown generally stay open an hour or so later than those uptown. Note that some of the shops listed in this chapter have more than one location; we have detailed up to three other branches below the review. For the bigger chains, check individual shop websites or consult the business pages in the telephone book for more addresses across the city.

Sales tax in the city is 8.375 per cent, though there are exemptions. For details, *see p380*.

General

DEPARTMENT STORES

★ Barneys New York

660 Madison Avenue, at 61st Street, Upper East Side (1-212 826 8900/www.barneys.com). Subway N, R, W to Fifth Avenue-59th Street; 4, 5, 6 to 59th Street. **Open** 10am-8pm Mon-Fri; 10am-7pm Sat; 11am-6pm Sun. **Credit** AmEx, DC, MC, V. **Map** p405 E22.

This bastion of style has a reputation for spotlighting less-ubiquitous designer labels compared with other upmarket department stores, and it also has its own quirky-classic line. Its funky, boutique-sized CO-OP branches (see website for locations) carry threads by up-and-comers, plus the latest hot denim lines. Every February and August, the Chelsea CO-OP hosts the Barneys Warehouse Sale, when prices are slashed by 50 to 80 per cent.

Other locations CO-OPs throughout the city.

Bergdorf Goodman

754 Fifth Avenue, at 57th Street, Midtown (1-212 753 7300/www.bergdorfgoodman.com). Subway E, V to Fifth Avenue-53rd Street; N, R, W to Fifth Avenue-59th Street. **Open** 10am-8pm Mon-Fri; 10am-7pm Sat; noon-6pm Sun. **Credit** AmEx, DC, MC, V. **Map** p405 E22.

If Barneys aims for a high-fashion crowd, then Bergdorf's is geared more towards an elegant, understated clientele – although its fifth floor is dedicated to younger, trend-driven labels. Known for its

CONSUME

designer clothes, luxury accessories and wide-ranging beauty department in the basement, it also stocks selected home goods and stationery. The men's store is across the street at 745 Fifth Avenue.

Bloomingdale's

1000 Third Avenue, at 59th Street, Upper East Side (1-212 705 2000/www.bloomingdales.com). Subway N, R, W to Lexington Avenue-59th Street; 4, 5, 6 to 59th Street. **Open** 10am-8.30pm Mon-Fri; 10am-7pm Sat; 11am-7pm Sun. **Credit** AmEx, DC, MC, V. **Map** p405 F22.

Ranking among the city's top tourist attractions, Bloomies is a gigantic, glitzy department store with everything from bags to beauty products, home furnishings to designer duds. The hipper, compact Soho outpost offers mainly young fashion, denim and cosmetics.

Other locations 504 Broadway, between Broome & Spring Streets, Soho (1-212 279 5900).

Henri Bendel

712 Fifth Avenue, at 56th Street, Midtown East (1-212 247 1100/www.henribendel.com). Subway E, V to Fifth Avenue-53rd Street; N, R, W to Fifth Avenue-59th Street. **Open** 10am-8pm Mon-Sat; noon-7pm Sun. **Credit** AmEx, DC, Disc, MC, V. **Map** p405 E22.

While the merchandise (a mix of mid-price and designer clothes, fashion accessories and big-brand cosmetics) and prices are comparable to those of other upscale stores, the goods at Bendel's somehow seem more desirable in this opulent atmosphere – and those darling brown-striped shopping bags don't hurt, either. Bendel's is the new home for celebrity hairdresser Frédéric Fekkai's flagship salon.

Where to Shop

New York's best shopping neighbourhoods in brief.

SOHO

Although it's been heavily commercialised, this once edgy, arty enclave still has some idiosyncratic survivors and numerous top-notch shops. Urban fashion abounds on Lafayette Street, while Broome Street is becoming a burgeoning enclave for chic home design.

NOLITA

This area has been colonised by indie designers, especially along Mott and Mulberry Streets.

LOWER EAST SIDE

Once the centre of the rag trade, this old Jewish neighbourhood was associated with bargain outlets and bagels. Now a bar- and boutique-rich patch, it's especially good for vintage, streetwear and eccentrically decorated shops selling the wares of New York designers. Orchard, Ludlow and Rivington Streets have the highest concentration of retail.

EAST VILLAGE

Although the shops are more scattered here than in the LES, you'll find a highly browsable mix of vintage clothing, streetwear, records, stylish home and children's goods.

WEST VILLAGE & MEATPACKING DISTRICT

On the other side of the island, the once-edgy wholesale meat market stretching south from 14th Street has become a high-end consumer playground, its warehouses populated by a clutch of daring international designers, including Stella McCartney, Alexander McQueen and Yigal Azrouël. The western strip of Bleecker Street is lined with a further cache of designer boutiques.

FIFTH AVENUE & UPPER EAST SIDE

Most of the city's famous department stores line up on Fifth Avenue between 42nd and 59th Street, where you'll also find a parade of big-name designer flagships and chain stores. The exceptions are Bloomingdale's and Barneys, which are both on the Upper East Side. Here, Madison Avenue has long been synonymous with the crème de la crème of international fashion.

BROOKLYN

Williamsburg, just one stop from Manhattan on the L train, is giving the Lower East Side a run for its money as the hip place to shop and hang out. As well as the main drag, Bedford Avenue, North 6th and Grand Streets are good hunting grounds for vintage clothes, funky, locally made fashion, arty interiors and record stores. Those who want to explore Brooklyn further will find more treasures in Cobble Hill and Boerum Hill (especially Court and Smith Streets and Atlantic Avenue) and Greenpoint (Franklin Avenue).

CONSUME

Jeffrey New York

449 W 14th Street, between Ninth & Tenth Avenues, Meatpacking District (1-212 206 1272/ www.jeffreynewyork.com). Subway A, C, E to 14th Street; L to Eighth Avenue. **Open** 10am-8pm Mon-Wed, Fri; 10am-9pm Thur; 10am-7pm Sat; 12.30-6pm Sun. **Credit** AmEx, DC, MC, V. **Map** p403 C27.

Jeffrey Kalinsky, a former Barneys shoe buyer, was a Meatpacking District pioneer when he opened his namesake store in 1999. Designer clothing abounds here – by Yves Saint Laurent, Halston, L'Wren Scott and young British star Christopher Kane, among others. But the centrepiece is without doubt the shoe salon, which features the work of Manolo Blahnik, Prada and Christian Louboutin, as well as newer names to watch.

Macy's

151 W 34th Street, between Broadway & Seventh Avenue, Garment District (1-212 695 4400/ www.macys.com). Subway B, D, F, N, Q, R, V, W to 34th Street-Herald Square; 1, 2, 3 to 34th Street-Penn Station. **Open** 10am-9.30pm Mon-Sat; 11am-8.30pm Sun. **Credit** AmEx, DC, Disc, MC, V. **Map** p404 D25.

It may not be as glamorous as New York's other famous stores, but for sheer breadth of stock, the 34th Street behemoth is hard to beat. You won't find exalted labels here, though – mid-priced fashion and designers' diffusion lines for all ages are its bread and butter, along with all the big beauty names. Among the largely mainstream refreshment options (McDonalds, Starbucks) is a Ben & Jerry's outpost.

▶ *There's also a branch of the Metropolitan Museum of Art gift store here; see p110.*

Saks Fifth Avenue

611 Fifth Avenue, at 50th Street, Midtown (1-212 753 4000/www.saksfifthavenue.com). Subway E, V to Fifth Avenue-53rd Street. **Open** 10am-8pm Mon-Sat; noon-6pm Sun. **Credit** AmEx, DC, Disc, MC, V. **Map** p404 E23.

Although Saks maintains a presence in 25 states, the Fifth Avenue location is the original, established in 1924 by New York retailers Horace Saks and Bernard Gimbel. The store features all the big names

in women's fashion, from Armani to Yves Saint Laurent, plus an excellent menswear department and a children's section. There are also fine household linens and an opulent beauty hall – although some might find the aggressive tactics of the sales staff a bit off-putting.

MALLS
Shops at Columbus Circle

Time Warner Center, 10 Columbus Circle, at 59th Street, Upper West Side (1-212 823 6300/www.shopsatcolumbuscircle.com). Subway A, B, C, D, 1 to 59th Street-Columbus Circle. **Open** 10am-9pm Mon-Sat; 11am-7pm Sun (hours vary for some shops, bars and restaurants). **Credit** varies. **Map** p405 D22.

Classier than your average mall, the retail contingent of the 2.8 million sq ft Time Warner Center features upscale stores such as Coach and Cole Haan for accessories and shoes, Bose home entertainment, the fancy kitchenware purveyor Williams-Sonoma and True Religion jeans, as well as national shopping centre staples J Crew, Crabtree & Evelyn and Borders. Some of the city's top restaurants, including Per Se (*see p206*) and a branch of Landmarc (*see p179*) have made it a dining destination that transcends the stigma of eating at the mall.

▶ *Next door is the new Museum of Arts & Design; see p117.*

Specialist

BOOKS & MAGAZINES

New York is so saturated with **Barnes & Noble** branches (www.barnesandnoble.com) that some neighbourhoods seem to have a megastore every few blocks. While the stock varies little from branch to branch, several feature readings by authors. **Borders**, a smaller national chain (www.borders.com), also provides under-one-roof browsing, as does **Shakespeare & Co** (www.shakeandco.com), an independent alternative with four stores. For details of shops and venues that host readings, *see pp278-280.* Weekly listings of such events can be found in *Time Out New York* magazine. For gay and lesbian bookstores, *see p307.*

General

Book Culture

536 W 112th Street, between Amsterdam Avenue & Broadway, Upper West Side (1-212 865 1588/www.bookculture.com). Subway 1 to 110th Street-Cathedral Parkway. **Open** 9am-10pm Mon-Fri; 10am-8pm Sat; 11am-7pm Sun. **Credit** AmEx, DC, Disc, MC, V. **Map** p406 C15.

CONSUME

Ostensibly catering to the Columbia University community, two-storey Book Culture lures bibliophiles uptown with stellar fiction and scholarly book collections, as well as its various discount tables sure to yield surprises. This is one of the more welcoming places to browse in the city.

McNally Jackson

52 Prince Street, between Lafayette & Mulberry Streets, Nolita (1-212 274 1160/www.mcnally jackson.com). Subway R, W to Prince Street; 6 to Spring Street. **Open** 10am-10pm Mon-Sat; 10am-9pm Sun. **Credit** AmEx, DC, Disc, MC, V. **Map** p403 F29.

The New York outpost of Canada's excellent and expanding chain, McNally Jackson (formerly McNally Robinson) has a good selection of novels, non-fiction titles and also magazines. A diverse range of writers present readings in the shop's comfortable café.

192 Books

192 Tenth Avenue, between 21st & 22nd Streets, Chelsea (1-212 255 4022/www.192books.com). Subway C, E to 23rd Street. **Open** noon-6pm Mon, Sun; noon-7pm Tue-Fri; 11am-7pm Sat. **Credit** AmEx, DC, MC, V. **Map** p404 C26.

In an era when many an indie bookshop has closed its doors, this youngster, open since 2003, is proving that quirky boutique booksellers can make it after all. Owned and 'curated' by art dealer Paula Cooper and her husband, editor Jack Macrae, 192 offers a strong selection of art books and literature, as well as books on gardening, history, politics, design, music and memoirs. Regular readings, signings and discussions, some featuring well-known writers, are further good reasons to drop by.

St Mark's Bookshop

31 Third Avenue, between 8th & 9th Streets, East Village (1-212 260 7853/www.stmarks bookshop.com). Subway R, W to 8th Street-NYU; 6 to Astor Place. **Open** 10am-midnight Mon-Sat; 11am-midnight Sun. **Credit** AmEx, DC, Disc, MC, V. **Map** p403 F28.

Students, academics and arty types gravitate to this East Village bookseller, which maintains strong inventories on cultural theory, graphic design, poetry and film studies, as well as numerous avant-garde journals and 'zines. The fiction section is one of the finest in the city.

▶ *The bookstore stages regular readings at the Solas bar; see p280.*

Specialist

Books of Wonder

18 W 18th Street, between Fifth & Sixth Avenues, Flatiron District (1-212 989 3270/ www.booksofwonder.com). Subway F, V to 14th Street; L to Sixth Avenue; 1 to 18th Street.

Open 10am-7pm Mon-Sat; 11am-6pm Sun. **Credit** AmEx, DC, Disc, MC, V. **Map** p403 E27.

Joining forces with the Cupcake Café, the city's only independent children's bookstore still features titles both new (signed copies, such as the latest in Eoin Colfer's *Artemis Fowl* series) and old (rare and out-of-print editions), plus foreign-language and reference titles, and a special collection of Oz books.

Forbidden Planet

840 Broadway, at 13th Street, Greenwich Village (1-212 475 6161/www.fpnyc.com). Subway L, N, Q, R, W, 4, 5, 6 to 14th Street-Union Square. **Open** 10am-10pm Mon, Tue, Sun; 9am-midnight Wed; 10am midnight Thur-Sat. **Credit** AmEx, DC, Disc, MC, V. **Map** p403 E27.

Embracing both pop-culture and the cult underground, the Planet takes comics seriously. You'll find graphic novels and film and TV tie-ins here too.

Hue-Man Bookstore & Café

2319 Frederick Douglass Boulevard (Eighth Avenue), between 124th & 125th Streets (1-212 665 7400/www.huemanbookstore.com). Subway A, B, C, D to 125th Street. **Open** 10am-8pm Mon-Sat; 11am-7pm Sun. **Credit** AmEx, DC, Disc, MC, V. **Map** p407 D13.

Focusing on African-American non-fiction and fiction, this superstore-sized Harlem indie also stocks bestsellers and general interest books.

▶ *For the readings here, see p279.*

City Secrets Cover Stories

The writers who pass through the doors of **Housing Works Bookstore Café** are a high-minded mix of the establishment and up-and-comers: Lydia Davis, Jonathan Lethem, Samantha Hunt and Dave Eggers, to name a few. This place has secrets aplenty – there's a sub-basement, lined with 100,000 books, where staffers have been known to get frisky between the covers and not only do celebs shop here (sightings include Winona Ryder, Keanu Reeves and Parker Posey), they donate their books, too. Volumes from Salman Rushdie, Woody Allen, Paul Giamatti, Gwyneth Paltrow (who inscribed her name on the sides) and Cindy Sherman have all graced the shelves, and you can tell what Peter Sarsgaard has been up to by what he brings in: war titles when he was filming *Jarhead* and natural-pregnancy books donated after the birth of his daughter, Ramona.

Strand Book Store.

CONSUME

Mysterious Bookshop

58 Warren Street, between Church Street & West Broadway, Financial District (1-212 587 1011/www.mysteriousbookshop.com). Subway A, C, 1, 2 to Chambers Street. **Open** 11am-7pm daily. **Credit** AmEx, DC, Disc, MC, V. **Map** p402 E32.

Devotees of mystery, crime and spy genres will know owner Otto Penzler, both as an editor and from his book recommendations on Amazon.com. His 30-year-old shop holds a wealth of paperbacks, hardbacks and autographed first editions.

Printed Matter

195 Tenth Avenue, between 21st & 22nd Streets, Chelsea (1-212 925 0325/http://printedmatter. org). Subway C, E to 23rd Street. **Credit** 6pm Tue, Wed; 11am-7pm Thur-Sat. **Credit** AmEx, DC, Disc, MC, V. **Map** p404 C26.

This non-profit organisation, which operates a public reading room as well as a shop, is exclusively devoted to artists' books – from David Shrigley's deceptively naive illustrations to provocative photographic self-portraits by Matthias Herrmann. Works by unknown and emerging artists share shelf space with those of veterans such as Yoko Ono.

Used & antiquarian

★ Housing Works Bookstore Café

126 Crosby Street, between Houston & Prince Streets, Soho (1-212 334 3324/www.housing worksubc.com). Subway B, D, F, V to Broadway-Lafayette Street; R, W to Prince Street; 6 to Bleecker Street. **Open** 10am-9pm Mon-Fri; noon-7pm Sat, Sun. **Credit** AmEx, DC, Disc MC, V. **Map** p403 E29.

Housing Works is an extraordinarily unusual and endearing place. The two-level space – which stocks a range of literary fiction, non-fiction, rare books and collectibles – is a peaceful spot for solo relaxation or for meeting friends over coffee or wine. All proceeds from the café go to providing support services for homeless people living with HIV/AIDS. The premises also host an interesting array of literary events.

Strand Book Store

828 Broadway, at 12th Street, Greenwich Village (1-212 473 1452/www.strandbooks.com). Subway L, N, Q, R, W, 4, 5, 6 to 14th Street-Union Square. **Open** 9.30am-10.30pm Mon-Sat; 11am-10.30pm Sun. **Credit** AmEx, DC, Disc, MC, V. **Map** p403 E28.

Boasting 18 miles of bookshelves, the Strand's mammoth collection of over two million discount volumes is made all the more daunting by its chaotic, towering shelves and surly staff. Reviewer discounts are in the basement, while rare volumes lurk upstairs. If you spend enough time here you can find just about anything from that out-of-print Victorian book of manners to the kitschiest in sci-fi pulp.

Other locations Strand Kiosk, Central Park, Fifth Avenue, at 60th Street, Upper East Side (1-646 284 5506).

CHILDREN

Fashion

Babesta

*66 West Broadway, between Murray &
Warren Streets, Tribeca (1-212 608
4522/www.babesta.com). Subway 1, 2, 3 to
Chambers Street.* **Open** 11am-7pm Mon-Fri;
noon-6pm Sat, Sun. **Credit** AmEx, DC, Disc,
MC, V. **Map** p402 E32.

Husband and wife team Aslan and Jenn Cattaui fill
their cosy 450sq ft store with the stuff kids love –
Junk Food concert tees, Uglydolls, Eazy Bean chairs
and vintage wear that'll make parents envious. The
shop mainly focuses on the under-six set, but there
are also pieces for older children from popular lines
such as Chaos Recycled.

Pink Olive

*439 E 9th Street, between First Avenue &
Avenue A, East Village (1-212 780 0036/
www.pinkoliveboutique.com). Subway L to First
Avenue.* **Open** 1-9pm Mon, Wed-Fri; noon-7pm
Sat; noon-6pm Sun. **Credit** AmEx, DC, Disc, MC,
V. **Map** p403 F28.

Owner Grace Kang was a buyer for Bloomingdale's
and Barneys, so it's no surprise that her 500sq ft
East Village store is filled to the brim with chic
clothes and accessories for kids. Look for items by
Wallcandy, Zid Zid and Blabla. The new Park Slope
site also offers home goods.
Other locations 167 Fifth Avenue, between
Lincoln & Berkeley Places, Park Slope, Brooklyn
(1-718 398 2016).

Toys

FAO Schwarz

*767 Fifth Avenue, at 58th Street, Midtown
(1-212 644 9400/www.fao.com). Subway N, R, W
to Lexington Avenue-59th Street; 4, 5, 6 to 59th
Street.* **Open** 10am-6pm Mon-Wed; 10am-7pm
Thur-Sat; 10am-8pm Sun. **Credit** AmEx, DC,
Disc, MC, V. **Map** p405 E22.

Giant stuffed animals, life-size Lego people, a full-
service ice-cream parlour, a motion-simulator ride,
plus a Madame Alexander Doll Factory, a Styled by
Me Barbie area and a Hot Wheels Factory where
kids can build their own toys – it all beckons at this
three-storey toy box. A Zutano clothing boutique
can be found on the lower level.

Homefront Kids

*Third Floor, 202 E 29th Street, between Second
& Third Avenues, Murray Hill (1-212 381 1966).
Subway 6 to 28th Street.* **Open** 10am-6pm Mon-
Sat; 11am-6pm Sun. **Credit** AmEx, DC, Disc, MC,
V. **Map** p404 F26.

Marion Sakow, a former schoolteacher, owns this
2,000sq ft toy emporium. To get to the goods –

everything from an artful French stamp set to
Tangoes Jr, a learning toy based on ancient Chinese
tangram puzzles – visitors must walk through her
family-owned hardware store and take a freight elevator to the third floor.

Kidding Around

*60 W 15th Street, between Fifth & Sixth
Avenues, Flatiron District (1-212 645 6337/
www.kiddingaround.us). Subway F, V to 14th
Street; L to Sixth Avenue.* **Open** 10am-7pm
Mon-Sat; 11am-6pm Sun. **Credit** AmEx, DC,
Disc, MC, V. **Map** p403 E27.

Grab costume dress-up sets and Groovy Girls goodies at this local favourite. You'll also find tons of
great playthings and clothing for kids.

ELECTRONICS & PHOTOGRAPHY

iPod junkies can get their fix 24/7 at the
Apple Store's Fifth Avenue open-all-hours
flagship (no.767, between 58th & 59th Streets,
1-212 336 1440, www.apple.com), which is
marked by a dramatic 32-foot glass entrance.
There are further branches at 103 Prince
Street, between Greene & Mercer Streets, in
Soho and 401 W 14th Street, at Ninth Avenue
in the Meatpacking District. All are equipped
with Genius Bars, offering technical help for
Mac users as well as repairs; well-regarded
Apple specialist **Tekserve** (119 W 23rd
Street, between Sixth & Seventh Avenue,
Chelsea, 1-212 929 3645) is another trusted
resource. For PCs, **New York Computer
Help** (1-212 599 0339, www.newyork
computerhelp.com) provides a free
diagnostic and repair ($85 per hour) at
two midtown locations.

Mobile phones can be rented on a weekly
or daily basis from **Roberts Rent-a-phone**
(1-800 964 2468, www.roberts-rent-a-
phone.com), which delivers to any US
address within 24 hours. However, it may
be cheaper to buy a phone (for as little as
$40) and a pay-as-you-go card from one of
the ubiquitous main service providers. For
more on mobile phones, *see p382.*

B&H

*420 Ninth Avenue, at 34th Street, Garment
District (1-212 444 5040/www.bhphoto
video.com). Subway A, C, E to 34th Street-Penn
Station.* **Open** 9am-7pm Mon-Thur; 9am-2pm Fri;
10am-5pm Sun. **Credit** AmEx, DC, Disc, MC, V.
Map p404 C25.

Whether you're a professional or a keen amateur,
B&H is the ultimate one-stop shop for all your photographic, video and audio needs (including professional audio equipment and discounted Bang &
Olufsen products).

CONSUME

FASHION

Designer

You'll find flagships for every big international designer – and more besides – on the Upper East Side's Madison and Fifth Avenues. There is also a growing number in Soho, Bleecker Street in the West Village and in the Meatpacking District.

Adam

678 Hudson Street, between 13th & 14th Streets, Meatpacking District (1-212 229 2838/www.shop adam.com). Subway A, C, E to 14th Street; L to Eighth Avenue. **Open** 11am-8pm Mon-Sat; noon-7pm Sun. **Credit** AmEx, DC, Disc, MC, V. **Map** p403 C27.

The former creative director for Oscar de la Renta, Adam Lippes used to sell his clean-cut designs for both genders through posh shops like Bendel's, Intermix and Saks. His eponymous shop brings together his signature collections under one elegant roof, saving a schlep around town.

Built by Wendy

7 Centre Market Place, at Grand Street, Soho (1-212 925 6538/www.builtbywendy.com). Subway B, D to Grand Street; N, Q, R, W, J, M, Z, 6 to Canal Street. **Open** noon-7pm Mon-Sat; noon-6pm Sun. **Credit** AmEx, DC, MC, V. **Map** p403 F30.

Chicago-bred designer and author Wendy Mullin started selling handmade clothes and guitar straps out of record stores in 1991. Today, her youthful men's and women's garb still maintains a homespun look and Midwestern vibe, via men's plaid flannel shirts and girlish dresses, as well as cool graphic T-shirts. Stylish rockers, take note: guitar straps are available in colourful canvas and ultrasuede. **Other locations** 46 N 6th Street, at Kent Avenue, Williamsburg, Brooklyn (1-718 384 2882).

Edit

1368 Lexington Avenue, between 90th & 91st Streets, Upper East Side (1-212 876 1368/ www.editfashion.com). Subway 4, 5, 6 to 86th Street. **Open** 10.30am-8pm Mon-Fri; 10am-6pm Sat, Sun. **Credit** AmEx, DC, Disc, MC, V. **Map** p406 E18.

Scanning the racks at this handsome bi-level townhouse, a short detour from Museum Mile, is akin to peeking into a socialite's closet. Luxe labels like Derek Lam and Marchesa mix with less expensive ones such as J Brand, Velvet and Nili Lotan.

Kirna Zabete

96 Greene Street, between Prince & Spring Streets, Soho (1-212 941 9656/www.kirnazabete.com). Subway C, E to Spring Street; R, W to Prince Street. **Open** 11am-7pm Mon-Sat; noon-6pm Sun. **Credit** AmEx, DC, MC, V. **Map** p403 E30.

The designers stocked at this ten-year-old bi-level boutique – big hitters like Balenciaga, Lanvin and Chloé and younger names such as Alexander Wang and David Szeto – may be exclusive, but the vibe in the simple space, with its painted floorboards and

CONSUME

Earnest Sewn. *See p238.*

www.treesforcities.org

Trees for Cities
Charity registration number 1032154

Travelling creates so
many lasting memories.

Make your trip mean
something for years to
come - not just for you
but for the environment
and for people living in
deprived urban areas.

Anyone can offset their
flights, but when your
plant trees with Trees for
Cities, you'll help create
a green space for an
urban community that
really needs it.

**Leave
Your
Mark**

Create a green future for cities.

white walls, is unintimidating. The laid-back air is reinforced by a selection of art books and fun gifts.

Lyell
173 Elizabeth Street, between Kenmare & Spring Streets, Nolita (1-212 966 8484/www.lyellnyc. com). Subway J, M, Z to Bowery; 6 to Spring Street. **Open** 11.30am-7pm daily. **Credit** AmEx, DC, Disc, MC, V. **Map** p403 F30.
Lyell creator Emma Fletcher's exquisite 1930s-inspired tea dresses and clean-lined silk blouses are all impeccably tailored in New York City; the line has been adopted by such stylish young stars as Zooey Deschanel and Michelle Williams.

Marc Jacobs
163 Mercer Street, between Houston & Prince Streets, Soho (1-212 343 1490/www.marcjacobs. com). Subway B, D, F, V to Broadway-Lafayette Street; R, W to Prince Street; 6 to Bleecker Street. **Open** 11am-7pm Mon-Sat; noon-6pm Sun. **Credit** AmEx, DC, Disc, MC, V. **Map** p403 E29.
Although Jacobs' popular Marc by Marc Jacobs diffusion line is eclipsing his main collection, these luxurious designs are impeccably tailored. The shop also stocks the designer's oft-copied bags, plus shoes for both sexes. A trio of shops on Bleecker Street in the West Village is devoted to the less expensive diffusion line (for women at no.403-405, at 11th Street; for men at no.382, between Charles and Perry Streets; for accessories at no.385, at Perry Street); a bijou mainline accessories outpost and a lovely children's shop have sprouted nearby at 301 and 298 W 4th Street.

Phillip Lim
115 Mercer Street, between Prince & Spring Streets, Soho (1-212 334 1160/www.31philliplim. com). Subway R, W to Prince Street; 6 to Spring Street. **Open** 11am-7pm Mon-Sat; noon-6pm Sun. **Credit** AmEx, DC, MC, V. **Map** p403 E29.
Since Phillip Lim debuted his collection in 2005, he has amassed a devoted international following for his simple yet strong silhouettes and beautifully constructed tailoring-with-a-twist. His first-ever boutique gathers together his award-winning womens- and menswear and accessories under one roof.

Tracy Reese
641 Hudson Street, between Gansevoort & Horatio Streets, Meatpacking District (1-212 807 0505/www.tracyreese.com). Subway A, C, E to 14th Street; L to Eighth Avenue. **Open** 11am-7pm Mon-Sat; noon-6pm Sun. **Credit** AmEx, DC, Disc, MC, V. **Map** p403 C28.
Fitted 1950s-inspired shapes, unusual prints and a dash of lacy, frilly or embroidered embellishment define Tracy Reese's ultra-feminine style. At her 2,200sq ft flagship you'll also find her younger, cheaper Plenty line and Plenty Frock!, which offers glam cocktail dresses from around $250.

Discount

★ Century 21
22 Cortlandt Street, between Broadway & Church Street, Financial District (1-212 227 9092/www.c21stores.com). Subway R, W to Cortlandt Street. **Open** 7.45am-9pm Mon-Wed; 7.45am-9.30pm Thur, Fri; 10am-9pm Sat; 11am-8pm Sun. **Credit** AmEx, DC, Disc, MC, V. **Map** p402 E32.
A Gucci men's suit for $300? A Marc Jacobs cashmere sweater for less than $200? Roberto Cavalli sunglasses for a scant $30? No, you're not dreaming – you're shopping at Century 21. The prized score is admittedly rare but the place is still intoxicating; savings range between 25% and 75% off regular store prices, making this a mecca for less-minted fashionistas.
Other locations 472 86th Street, between Fourth & Fifth Avenues, Bay Ridge, Brooklyn (1-718 748 3266).

Loehmann's
101 Seventh Avenue, at 16th Street, Chelsea (1-212 352 0856/www.loehmanns.com). Subway A, C, E to 14th Street; L to Eighth Avenue. **Open** 9am-9pm Mon-Sat; 11am-7pm Sun. **Credit** AmEx, DC, Disc, MC, V. **Map** p403 D27.
Plucking surplus stock, samples and cancelled orders from Seventh Avenue designers, founder Frieda Loehmann started this venerable discount emporium in 1921 in Williamsburg. Today, it's become a go-to spot for bargain hounds. Though often crowded and cramped, its five floors offer major markdowns on current and off-season clothes and accessories for the entire family, along with housewares. If you're unafraid to show some skin in the communal dressing room, make a beeline for the Back Room, where you can score posh European brands such as Valentino, Prada and Armani.
Other locations 2101 Broadway, between 73rd & 74th Streets (1-212 882 9990).

Samples for (eco)mpassion
2 Great Jones Street, between Broadway & Lafayette Street, East Village (1-212 777 0707/www.greenfinds.com). Subway B, D, F, V to Broadway-Lafayette Street; 6 to Bleecker Street.

INSIDE TRACK
SAMPLE SALES
Sales are usually held in the designers' shops, showrooms or rented loft spaces, and are known to get seriously heated. Typically, most sales lack changing rooms, so bring a courageous spirit with you (and plenty of cash) and remember to wear appropriate undergarments to avoid embarrassment.

Open noon-7pm Thur-Sun. **Credit** AmEx, DC, Disc, MC, V. **Map** p403 E29.

A marriage of founder Ike Rodriguez's defunct Find Outlet and his earth-conscious e-tailer, green finds.com, this charity-focused shop donates 5% of the proceeds to a different non-profit organisation each month. You can expect heavy discounts on wares from indie stars such as Lauren Moffatt and eco-designer Linda Loudermilk.

General

National chains J Crew, Banana Republic and Gap, offering good-value basics for both sexes, are all over town; at press time, European behemoths Zara, Mango and H&M were about to be joined by British fashion giant **Topshop** (478 Broadway, between Broome & Grand Streets, Soho, www.topshop.com). Hip boutique chains **Intermix** (www.intermixonline.com) and **Scoop** (www.scoopnyc.com) combine lofty labels with denim and 'it' accessories, while former coat specialist **Searle** (www.searlenyc.com) mixes its sophisticated own-label dresses, tailored separates and sheepskins with other designer pieces and fashion-driven accessories.

★ BBlessing

181 Orchard Street, between Houston & Stanton Streets, Lower East Side (1-212 378 8005/ www.bblessing.com). Subway F, V to Lower East Side-Second Avenue. **Open** 1-9pm Mon-Fri; noon-8pm Sat, Sun. **Credit** AmEx, DC, Disc, MC, V. **Map** p403 F29.

NYC Blue

Track down that elusive perfect pair of jeans.

In the retail wonderland that is New York, deciding where to shop for jeans is almost as mind-boggling as negotiating the wealth of styles. Department stores **Barneys** (*see p226*) and **Bloomingdale's** (*see p227*) have excellent ranges of 'premium' denim – and Bloomie's smaller Soho outpost is less daunting and hipper than its uptown parent. Ladies looking for on-trend jeans at lower prices should check out J Crew's younger sibling **Madewell** (486 Broadway, at Broome Street, Soho, 1-212 226 6954, www.madewell1937.com), which has a well-stocked denim section featuring several styles in a range of colours and washes for little more than $100. Elsewhere, though, here's our pick of the specialist spots:

Hard not to start with the daddy of them all. Red-tabbed 501s have been sported by such fashion icons as James Dean, Elvis and Marlon Brando. Today, the various NYC branches of the **Levi's Store** (*see p238*) offer riveted classics along with freshly minted well-priced goodies like eco-friendly skinny jeans ($69.50) for lasses and slim 507s (from $69.50) for lanky dudes.

One of only two stores of its kind in the world (the other is in Tokyo), Soho's **Diesel Denim Gallery** (*see p237*) houses limited-edition selvage so rarefied that it's on par with the boutique's cutting-edge art installations. Denim devotees flock to the minimally adorned spot to snap up hand-distressed pieces. Although

some styles cost $400, fans swear that the jeans' fit seems bespoke.

Also in Soho, denim behemoth **7 For All Mankind** (*see p240*) recently opened its first New York shop. The store features the line's complete collection – including women's, men's and kids' denim and sportswear, as well as handbags and accessories.

The Meatpacking District is home to a pair of independents. Established by former Paper Denim & Cloth designer Scott Morrison, culty jeans label **Earnest Sewn** (*see p238*) marries vintage American style with old-school workmanship. Each pair (from $180 and up) can take up to 18 hours to make, and boasts butt-boosting pockets and flattering seams. But if Morrison's denims don't fit the bill, you're not far from the **Jean Shop** (*see p238*). When you desire denim as singular as your fingerprint, this clothier specialises in hand-crafted, custom-finished jeans ($260-$600) made from top-notch Japanese selvage.

While most of the action happens downtown, the uptown crowd also gets in on the act at the **National Jean Company** (*see p239*). This spacious emporium houses an impressive 3,000 pairs of jeans from more than 20 brands in its 'denim library', including the usual suspects J Brand, James, Citizens and 7, plus the latest niche labels like New York's Raven Denim and the Current/Elliott line, designed by a pair of celebrity stylists.

CONSUME

Market NYC. See p238.

A collaboration between design collectives Surface to Air and Breakbeat Science (the name's double B is an homage to their first joint project, BBS Tokyo), this men's outpost has an interior that's as chic as the clothing within it. As well as a showcase for relaxed, high-end clothing from the likes of Rag & Bone, Raf Simons and the store's eponymous label, a selection of music, films, decorative objects and accessories make it a great stop for gifts.

Calypso Christiane Celle

815 Madison Avenue, between 68th & 69th Streets, Upper East Side (1-212 585 0310/ www.calypso-celle.com). Subway 6 to 68th Street-Hunter College. **Open** 10am-7pm Mon-Sat; noon-6pm Sun. **Credit** AmEx, DC, MC, V. **Map** p403 C28.

Christiane Celle has created a Calypso empire: as well as a string of boutiques stocking her own womenswear line – which embraces everything from colourful, girlish frocks to chunky knitwear – and select supplementary designers, she has a devoted home store (199 Lafayette Street, at Broome Street, Soho 1-212 925 6200). Bargain hunters should head for the Calypso outlet at 407 Broome Street, between Centre & Lafayette Streets, Soho (1-212 941 9700). **Other locations** throughout the city.

Dave's Quality Meat

7 E 3rd Street, between Bowery & Second Avenue, East Village (1-212 505 7551/ www.davesqualitymeat.com). Subway F, V to Lower East Side-Second Avenue. **Open** 11.30am-

7.30pm Mon-Sat; 11.30am-6.30pm Sun. **Credit** AmEx, DC, Disc, MC, V. **Map** p403 F29.

Dave Ortiz – formerly of ghetto urban threads label Zoo York – and professional skateboarder Chris Keefe stock a range of top-shelf streetwear in their wittily designed shop. As well as a line-up of the latest sneaks by adidas, Nike and Vans, DQM's graphic print tees and hoodies are displayed in the deli case.

Diesel Denim Gallery

68 Greene Street, between Broome & Spring Streets, Soho (1-212 966 5593/www.diesel.com). Subway: C, E to Spring Street; N, R, W to Prince Street. **Open** 11am-7pm Mon-Sat; noon-6pm Sun. **Credit** AmEx, DC, Disc, MC, V. **Map** p403 E30. *See p236* **NYC Blue.**

D/L Cerney

13 E 7th Street, between Second & Third Avenues, East Village (1-212 673 7033). Subway N, R, W to 8th Street-NYU; 6 to Astor Place. **Open** noon-8pm daily. **Credit** AmEx, DC, MC, V. **Map** p403 F28.

Duane Cerney and his wife Linda St John branched out of their vintage clothing business by creating their own nostalgic designs; now the D/L Cerney line forms the bulk of the stock in this narrow shop: neat, figure-skimming dresses and nipped-in jackets for women, gabardine shirts and dapper suits for men. Although the collection is made in New York, price points are reasonable: from around $250 for a dress and around $200 for a gent's jacket. The selection of mint-condition vintage accessories is a remnant of the shop's earlier incarnation.

Dressing Room

75A Orchard Street, between Broome & Grand Streets, Lower East Side (1-212 966 7330/ www.thedressingroomnyc.com). Subway B, D to Grand Street; F to Delancey Street. **Open** 1pm-midnight Sun, Tue, Wed; 1pm-2am Thur-Sat. **Credit** AmEx, DC, Disc, MC, V. **Map** p403 F30.
At first glance, the Dressing Room may look like any Lower East side lounge, thanks to a handsome wood bar, but stylist and designer Nikki Fontanella's quirky co-op-cum-watering-hole rewards the curious. The adjoining room displays designs by indie labels, which rotate every four months, while downstairs is a cache of vintage finds.

Earnest Sewn

821 Washington Street, between Gansevoort & Little W 12th Streets, Meatpacking District (1-212 242 3414/www.earnestsewn.com). Subway A, C, E to 14th Street; L to Eighth Avenue. **Open** 11am-7pm Mon-Fri, Sun; 11am-8pm Sat. **Credit** AmEx, DC, Disc, MC, V. **Map** p403 C28.
See p236 **NYC Blue.** *Photo p233.*
Other locations 90 Orchard Street, at Broome Street, Soho (1-212 979 5120).

5 in 1

60 North 6th Street, between Kent & Wythe Avenues, Williamsburg, Brooklyn (1-718 384 1990/www.studio5in1.com). Subway L to Bedford Avenue. **Open** noon-7pm Tue-Sat. **Credit** AmEx, DC, Disc, MC, V. **Map** p411 U7.
A designer co-op in a former railroad-car manufacturer, 5 in 1 houses edgy clothing and accessories from the likes of local up-and-comers Made Her Think (jewellery), Eventide (women's clothes) and graphic T-shirt company Obesity and Speed. Prices start at around $50 and go up to $500, but you can be sure that you're getting a unique item. In step with 5 in 1's artful wares, a gallery located in the back of the former factory space hosts rotating exhibitions.

Honey in the Rough

161 Rivington Street, between Clinton & Suffolk Streets, Lower East Side (1-212 228 6415/ www.honeyintherough.com). Subway F to Delancey Street; J, M, Z to Delancey-Essex Streets. **Open** noon-8pm Mon-Sat; noon-7pm Sun. **Credit** AmEx, DC, Disc, MC, V. **Map** p403 G29.
Looking for something sweet and charming? Hit this cosy, ultra-femme boutique. Owner Ashley Hanosh fills the well-worn spot with an excellent line-up of local indie labels including Mociun, Samantha Pleet and Eventide, alongside a carefully selected assemblage of accessories, some of which is exclusive to the shop, such as Japanese-Parisian designer Yukié Deuxpoints's art nouveau-inspired jewellery.

THECAST. *See p240.*

Jean Shop

435 W 14th Street, at Washington Street, Meatpacking District (1-212 366 5326/ www.worldjeanshop.com). Subway A,C,E to 14th Street; L to Eighth Avenue. **Open** 11am-7pm Mon-Sat; noon-6pm Sun. **Credit** AmEx, DC, MC, V. **Map** p403 C27.
See p236 **NYC Blue.**
Other locations 424 West Broadway, between Prince & Spring Streets, Soho (1-212 334 5822).

Levi's Store

25 W 14th Street, between Fifth & Sixth Avenues, Flatiron District (1-212 242 2128/ www.levistrauss.com). Subway F, V to 14th Street; L to Sixth Avenue. **Open** 10am-9pm Mon-Sat; 11am-8pm Sun. **Credit** AmEx, Disc, MC, V. **Map** p403 E27.
See p236 **NYC Blue.**
Other locations 536 Broadway, between Prince & Spring Streets, Soho (1-646 613 1847); 750 Lexington Avenue, between 59th & 60th Streets, Upper East Side (1-212 826 5957).

Market NYC

268 Mulberry Street, between Houston & Prince Streets, Nolita (1-212 580 8995/www.themarket nyc.com). Subway B, D, F, V to Broadway-Lafayette Street; N, R, W to Prince Street; 6 to Bleecker Street. **Open** 11am-7pm Sat, Sun. **No credit cards. Map** p403 F29.
Every weekend, independent clothing and accessories designers set up shop in the gymnasium of a church's youth centre (complete with basketball

noon-8pm Fri, Sat. **Credit** AmEx, DC, MC, V.
Map p403 E29.
The joint venture of one-time graffiti artists Stash
and Futura, Nort Recon carries everything from
tricked-out skateboards to parkas.

Oak

*28 Bond Street, between Bowery & Lafayette
Street, East Village (1-212 677 1293/www.oak
nyc.com). Subway B, D, F, V to Broadway-
Lafayette Street; 6 to Bleecker Street.* **Open**
11am-8pm Mon-Sat; 11am-7pm Sun. **Credit**
AmEx, DC, MC, V. **Map** p403 F29.
The culty Brooklyn mini-chain recently crossed the
river with this 3,000sq ft spot. Expect to find a
well-edited blend of men's and women's loot from
the likes of Filippa K, Unconditional and Hyden Yoo.
Other locations 208 N 8th Street, between
Driggs Avenue & Roebling Street, Williamsburg,
Brooklyn (1-718 782 0521).

Odin

*199 Lafayette Street, between Broome &
Kenmare Streets, Soho (1-212 966 0026/
www.odinnewyork.com). Subway 6 to Spring
Street.* **Open** 11am-8pm Mon-Sat; noon-7pm Sun.
Credit AmEx, DC, MC, V. **Map** p403 E30.
The Norse god Odin is often portrayed sporting an
eye patch and an array of shabby robes to complement his dour, bearded visage. That may have been
fashionable in medieval Scandinavia, but to make it
in NYC, he'd have to pick up some Robert Gellar,
Rag & Bone or Comme des Garçons from this
upscale men's boutique bearing his name. Tasteful
masculine jewellery and dapper shoes are also
available to those with a healthy cash flow.
Other locations 328 E 11th Street, between
First & Second Avenues (1-212 475 0666).

Opening Ceremony

*35 Howard Street, between Broadway &
Lafayette Street, Soho (1-212 219 2688/
www.openingceremony.us). Subway J, M, N, Q, R,
W, Z, 6 to Canal Street.* **Open** 11am-8pm Mon-
Sat; noon-7pm Sun. **Credit** AmEx, DC, MC, V.
Map p403 E30.
Opening Ceremony offers a stylish trip around the
world in a tri-level, warehouse-size space gussied up
with grape-coloured walls and crystal chandeliers.
The name references the Olympic Games, and each
year, the store assembles hip US designers, pitted
against the competition from abroad: until autumn
2009, Japan is the focus, with the likes of Hiromi
Tsuyoshi, Nude: Masahiko Maruyama and John
Lawrence Sullivan.

Reed Space

*151 Orchard Street, between Rivington &
Stanton Streets, Lower East Side (1-212 253
0588/www.thereedspace.com). Subway F, J,
M, Z to Essex Street-Delancey.* **Open** 1-7pm

hoop), giving punters the chance to buy a variety of
unique wares direct from the makers. *Photo p237.*

National Jean Company

*1375 Third Avenue, between 78th & 79th
Streets, Upper East Side (1-212 772 2392/
www.nationaljeancompany.com). Subway 6 to
77th Street.* **Open** 10am-9pm Mon-Fri; 10am-
8pm Sat; 11am-7pm Sun. **Credit** AmEx, Disc,
MC, V. **Map** p405 F19.
See p236 **NYC Blue.**

Nom de Guerre

*640 Broadway, at Bleecker Street, Greenwich
Village (1-212 253 2891/www.nomdeguerre.net).
Subway 6 to Bleecker Street.* **Open** noon-8pm
Mon-Sat, noon-7pm Sun. **Credit** AmEx, DC, MC,
V. **Map** p403 E29.
Fitting nicely in with its revolutionary name, this
upscale streetwear label's Noho flagship is designed
to resemble a bunker; the average shopper would
have to be sleuth-level perceptive to spot the faded
stencil on the sidewalk in front of the forbidding
caged metal staircase that leads down to the store.
A design collective founded by four New Yorkers,
the understated line has a rugged, utilitarian look,
encompassing upscale denim, military-inspired
jackets and classic shirts and knitwear.

Nort Recon

*359 Lafayette Street, between Bleecker &
Bond Streets, East Village (1-212 614 8502/
www.reconstore.com). Subway 6 to Bleecker
Street.* **Open** noon-7pm Mon-Thur, Sun;

CONSUME

Mon-Fri; noon-7pm Sat, Sun. **Credit** AmEx, DC, Disc, MC, V. **Map** p403 F29.

The brainchild of Staple Design, which has worked on product design and branding with the likes of Nike, Timberland and New Era, Reed Space displays a collection of local (Pegleg, 3Sixteen and Staple's own label among others) and international streetwear brands, plus art books, culture mags, music and DVDs in its super-cool shop.

7 For All Mankind

394 West Broadway between Broome and Spring Streets, Soho (1-212 226 8615/www.7forallman kind.com). Subway C, E to Spring Street; N, R, W to Prince Street. **Open** 11am-8pm Mon-Sat; noon-7pm Sun. **Credit** AmEx, MC, V. **Map** p403 E30. *See p236* **NYC Blue.**

Suite Orchard

145A Orchard Street, at Rivington Street, Lower East Side (1-212 533 4115/www.suite orchard.com). Subway F, V to Second Avenue-Lower East Side; J, M, Z to Delancey Street. **Open** noon-7pm Tue, Wed, Fri, Sun; noon-8pm Thur, Sat. **Credit** AmEx, DC, MC, V. **Map** p403 F29.

Fashion veterans and sisters Cindy and Sonia Huang worked at Diane von Furstenberg and Chloé, respectively, before joining forces to make their mark on the Lower East Side. Adorned with grey and white striped walls, the boudoir-inspired spot pays tribute to their well-honed aesthetic via gamine pieces from Alexander Wang, Sonia by Sonia Rykiel and European upstart Camilla Staerk, plus the siblings' own Soni & Cindy line.

TG-170

170 Ludlow Street, between Houston & Stanton Streets, Lower East Side (1-212 995 8660/ www.tg170.com). Subway F to Delancey Street; J, M, Z to Delancey-Essex Streets. **Open** noon-8pm daily. **Credit** AmEx, DC, MC, V. **Map** p403 G29.

Terri Gillis has an eye for emerging designers: she was the first to carry Built by Wendy. You'll still find her wares hanging in the expansive boutique, as well as pieces by New York's Lauren Moffatt and Alice Ritter.

THE BEST
RUMMAGING SPOTS

For designer bargains
Century 21. *See p235.*

For trash and treasures
Hell's Kitchen Flea Market. *See p254.*

For obscure LPs
Other Music. *See p256.*

THECAST

Lower Level, 119 Ludlow Street, between Rivington & Delancey Streets, Lower East Side (1-212 228 2020/www.thecast.com). Subway F, V to Second Avenue-Lower East Side. **Open** noon-8pm daily. **Credit** AmEx, DC, Disc, MC, V. **Map** p403 G30.

A chalkboard set next to an open metal hatch in the sidewalk in front of a nondescript hair salon is the only marker for the subterranean outpost of this idiosyncratic menswear label. Chuck Guarino and Ryan Turner launched THECAST with a collection of artful T-shirts in 2004; starting at $70, these are still central to a collection that spans well-cut jeans in premium denim to dapper suits and soft, silk-lined leather biker jackets, all displayed in an anarchically jumbled interior. *Photos pp238-239.*

Used & vintage

Allan & Suzi

416 Amsterdam Avenue, at 80th Street, Upper West Side (1-212 724 7445/www.allanand suzi.net). Subway 1 to 79th Street. **Open** 12.30-7pm Mon-Sat; noon-6pm Sun. **Credit** AmEx, DC, Disc, MC, V. **Map** p405 C19.

Models and celebs drop off worn-once Gaultiers, Muglers, Pradas and Manolos here. The platform shoe collection is flashback-inducing and incomparable, as is the selection of vintage jewellery.

Beacon's Closet

88 North 11th Street, between Berry Street & Wythe Avenue, Williamsburg, Brooklyn (1-718 486 0816/www.beaconscloset.com). Subway L to Bedford Avenue. **Open** noon-9pm Mon-Fri; 11am-8pm Sat, Sun. **Credit** AmEx, DC, Disc, MC, V. **Map** p411 U7.

Some vintage boutiques boast prices more akin to major fashion labels. Not so at this bustling Brooklyn favourite, where not only are the prices great, but so is the Williamsburg-appropriate clothing selection – from iconic T-shirts and party dresses to sneakers, leathers and denim, plus second-hand CDs.

Edith Machinist

104 Rivington Street, between Essex & Ludlow Streets, Lower East Side (1-212 979 9992). Subway F to Delancey Street; J, M, Z to Delancey-Essex Streets. **Open** 1-8pm Mon-Fri; noon-8pm Sat, Sun. **Credit** AmEx, DC, Disc, MC, V. **Map** p403 G29.

Check out one of the city's best collections of (mostly) fine leather bags, not to mention an army of shoes, at this slightly below-street-level shop. There's no trash here – only the cream of the vintage crop. The front rack displays men's vintage clothing.

Girls Love Shoes

29 Ludlow Street, between Canal & Hester Streets, Lower East Side (1-212 966 7463/

Profile Alexis Bittar

From 1980s club kid to Lucite master.

Brooklyn-born designer Alexis Bittar has come a long way since 1988, when he began hawking his handmade jewellery on the corner of Prince and Greene Streets in Soho. 'I was one of the first vendors there,' he says. 'It's now a bit of a zoo, but at the time there were only six of us.' These days, Bittar's business is a slicker operation with a Dumbo atelier and two shops in Manhattan, the second of which opened in 2008 (see p244).

Bittar's interest in fashion and design developed as a teenager, and seminal nightclubs like Danceteria and Area were a creative spur: 'It was an exciting mix of underground fashion, music and pure exhibitionism and I wanted to be a part of it,' he says. 'The easiest way to get involved was by dressing up and "giving a look" when you went to clubs.'

Bittar started selling vintage clothing and jewellery on St Marks Place in 1983. 'I was selling Bakelite jewellery for a while and was impressed with how people really valued the fact that it had been hand-carved.'

Suddenly, Bittar's obsession with both old and new had a head-on collision: 'I was in a store and came up with the idea of fusing the styles of Lalique glass with Bakelite, and using Lucite. It was just a thought, but I followed it through and started carving it by hand in my bedroom.' He started selling the fruits of his labour and slowly built a Lucite empire.

Today, he employs a staff of 160, but personally carves the prototype of each new piece in his collections. In the workshop, giant blocks of Lucite are whittled down by hand into chunky cuffs, teardrop earrings and knuckle-engulfing rings; all of the luminous, jewel-like colours and intricate patterns are hand painted, and embellishments like studs or crystals are manually applied to these wearable works of art.

CONSUME

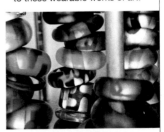

Airline flights are one of the biggest producers of the global warming gas CO_2. But with **The CarbonNeutral Company** you can make your travel a little greener.

Go to **www.carbonneutral.com** to calculate your flight emissions then 'neutralise' them through international projects which save exactly the same amount of carbon dioxide.

Contact us at **shop@carbonneutral.com** or call into the office on **0870 199 99 88** for more details.

CarbonNeutral®flights

www.glsnewyork.com). *Subway F to East Broadway; F to Delancey St; J, M, Z to Delancey-Essex Streets.* **Open** noon-7pm Tue-Sun. **Credit** AmEx, DC, Disc, MC, V. **Map** p403 G30.

Sisters Zia and Dana Zilprin have handpicked ladies' shoes – all aged to perfection – and arranged them by size on floor-to-ceiling racks. History buffs can find styles from every era beginning with the 1930s, reminding us of the trends we thought were forever banned. For those gals who lack footwear fetishes, the store also offers a handful of accessories. *Photos pp244-245.*

INA

15 Bleecker Street, between Bowery & Lafayette Street (1-212 228 8511/www.inanyc.com). Subway 6 to Bleecker Street; B, D, F, V to Broadway-Lafayette Street. **Open** noon-8pm Mon-Sat; noon-7pm Sun. **Credit** AmEx, DC, MC, V. **Map** p403 F29.

This string of consignment shops offers immaculate, on-trend items at a fraction of their original prices. This branch caters to both sexes; others (check the website) are for men or women only. **Other locations** throughout the city.

Marmalade

172 Ludlow Street, between Houston & Stanton Streets, Lower East Side (1-212 473 8070/www.marmaladevintage.com). Subway F, V to Lower East Side-Second Avenue. **Open** noon-9pm daily. **Credit** AmEx, DC, MC, V. **Map** p403 G29.

Containing a kaleidoscope of covetable colours and patterns, Marmalade has some of the hottest 1970s and '80s threads to be found below Houston Street, including a rainbow of retro shoes.

New & Almost New

166 Elizabeth Street, between Kenmare & Spring Streets, Nolita (1-212 226 6677/www.newand almostnew.com). Subway 6 to Spring Street; B, D to Grand Street. **Open** 12.30-6.30pm Mon-Sat; 1-5pm Sun. **Credit** AmEx, DC, Disc, MC, V. **Map** p403 F30.

Germophobe label lovers, rejoice, as 40% of the merchandise at this resale shop is brand new. Owner Maggie Chan hand selects every piece, ensuring its quality and authenticity. Among the merchandise hanging on the colour-coded racks are lofty labels such as Prada, Chanel and Hermès (prices from $15 to $600).

FASHION ACCESSORIES & SERVICES

Cleaning & repairs

There are numerous shoe-repair shops in most neighbourhoods, but if you want to be sure of top-notch treatment, try Leather Spa.

JJ Hat Center. *See p244.*

Acme Cleaners

508 Hudson Street, between Christopher & W 10th Streets, West Village (1-212 255 4702). Subway 1 to Christopher Street. **Open** 7am-7pm Mon-Fri; 8am-6pm Sat. **Credit** AmEx, DC, MC, V. **Map** p403 D29.

In an area populated by posh boutiques, this highly-regarded dry cleaner gets referrals from its fashionable neighbours. But the prices are still down to earth: from $4.50 for a top; $7 for a jacket or trousers.

Leather Spa

10 W 55th Street, between Fifth & Sixth Avenues, Midtown (1-212 262 4823/www.leather spa.com). Subway E, V to Fifth Avenue-53rd Street. **Open** 8am-7pm Mon-Fri; 10am-5pm Sat. **Credit** AmEx, DC, MC, V. **Map** p405 E22.

Recommended by glossy mags and posh shoe shops alike, the crème de la crème of cobblers can rejuvenate even the most faded footwear and handbags – at a price. As well as standard repairs (from $10 a for a women's reheel), a cleaning and reconditioning service is offered (from $35).

Clothing hire

Ilus

248 Elizabeth Street, between E Houston & Prince Streets, Nolita (1-646 454 1678/ www.ilus-nyc.com). Subway F, V to 2nd Avenue. **Open** noon-7pm Mon-Fri; noon-6pm Sat; noon-5pm Sun. **Credit** AmEx, DC, Disc, MC, V. **Map** p404 F29.

Need a special occasion outfit at short notice? At this glamorous dress hire boutique, you can rent a Marc Bouwer silk gown for $125 (retail $795), a Badgley Mischka Platinum strapless chiffon party frock for $100 ($650) or handmade jewels by Maggan Soderberg for $10. The standard rental period is three nights, but there are also extended options.

Hats

Hat Shop
120 Thompson Street, at Prince Street, Soho (1-212 219 1445/www.thehatshopnyc.com). Subway C, E to Spring Street. **Open** noon-7pm Mon-Sat; 1-6pm Sun. **Credit** AmEx, DC, MC, V. **Map** p403 E29.
Linda Pagan showcases the creations of 30 local milliners in her delightful little shop, from everyday classics in straw or felt to extravagant special occasion confections.

★ JJ Hat Center
310 Fifth Avenue, between 31st & 32nd Streets, Flatiron District (1-212 239 4368/ www.jjhatcenter.com). Subway B, D, F, N, Q, R, V, W to 34th Street. **Open** 9am-6pm Mon-Fri; 9.30am-5.30pm Sat. **Credit** AmEx, DC, Disc, MC, V. **Map** p404 E25.
Trad hats are back in the fashion spotlight, but this venerable shop, in business since 1911, is oblivious to passing trends. Dapper gents sporting the shop's wares will help you choose from more than 2,000 fedoras, pork pies, caps and other styles on display in the splendid, chandelier-illuminated, wood-panelled showroom. Prices start at $35 for a wool-blend cap. *Photo p243.*

Jewellery

Alexis Bittar
465 Broome Street, between Greene & Mercer Streets, Soho (1-212 625 8340/www.alexis bittar.com). Subway N, R, W to Prince Street; 6 to Spring Street. **Open** 11am-7pm Mon-Sat; noon-6pm Sun. **Credit** AmEx, DC, Disc, MC, V. **Map** p403 E30.
See p241 **Profile**.

Girls Love Shoes. *See p240.*

Other locations 353D Bleecker Street, between Charles & W 10th Streets, West Village (1-212 727 1093).

★ Doyle & Doyle
189 Orchard Street, between Houston & Stanton Streets, Lower East Side (1-212 677 9991 /www.doyledoyle.com). Subway F, V to Lower East Side-Second Avenue. **Open** 1-7pm Tue, Wed, Fri-Sun; 1-8pm Thur. **Credit** AmEx, DC, Disc, MC, V. **Map** p403 F29.
Whether your taste is art deco or nouveau, Victorian or Edwardian, gemologist sisters Pam and Elizabeth Doyle, who specialise in estate and antique jewellery, will have that one-of-a-kind item you're looking for, including engagement and eternity rings. The artfully displayed pieces within wall-mounted wooden framed cases are just a fraction of what's in stock.

Fragments
116 Prince Street, between Greene & Wooster Streets, Soho (1-212 334 9588/www.fragments. com). Subway B, D, F, V to Broadway-Lafayette Street; N, R, W to Prince Street. **Open** 11am-7pm Mon-Sat; noon-6pm Sun. **Credit** AmEx, DC, Disc, MC, V. **Map** p403 E29.
Over two decades, Fragments owner Janet Goldman has assembled a stable of more than 100 jewellery designers, who offer their creations to her before selling them to major stores such as Barneys.
Other locations 997 Madison Avenue, between 77th & 78th Streets, Upper East Side (1-212 537 5000).

CONSUME

Lingerie & underwear

Bloomingdale's has an encyclopedic lingerie department, while **Victoria's Secret** (www.victoriassecret.com) is the choice of the masses for inexpensive yet pretty unmentionables.

Bra Smyth

905 Madison Avenue, between 72nd & 73rd Streets, Upper East Side (1-212 772 9400/ www.brasmyth.com). Subway 6 to 77th Street. **Open** 10am-7pm Mon-Sat; noon-5pm Sun. **Credit** AmEx, DC, Disc, MC, V. **Map** p405 E20.
This shop stocks sizes to suit all cleavages, and the employees are so experienced that they can guess your bust measurements the second you walk in the door (they're usually right). Onsite seamstresses can alter your purchase for a customised fit.
Other locations 2177 Broadway, at 77th Street (1-212 721 5111).

★ Kiki de Montparnasse

79 Greene Street, between Broome & Spring Streets, Soho (1-212 965 8150/www.kikidm.com). Subway R, W to Prince Street; 6 to Spring Street. **Open** 11am-7pm Mon-Fri; noon-7pm Sat, Sun. **Credit** AmEx, DC, MC, V. **Map** p403 E30.
This erotic luxury boutique channels the spirit of its namesake, a 1920s sexual icon and Man Ray muse, with a posh array of tastefully provocative contemporary lingerie in satin and French lace, including such novelties as cotton tank tops with built-in

garters and knickers embroidered with saucy legends. Bedroom accoutrements, including molten crystal 'dilettos' and feather ticklers, give new meaning to the term 'satisfied customer'.

Na

51 Wooster Street, between Broome & Grand Streets, Soho (1-212 219 3450/www.nanew york.com). Subway A, C, E, N, R, Q, W to Canal Street. **Open** noon-7pm Tue-Sat. **Credit** AmEx, DC, MC, V. **Map** p403 E30.
'Art and underwear' reads the sign above the entrance to this basement shop; the curious who venture inside will find Japanese artist/designer and erstwhile DJ Na's collection of men's colourful hand-printed skivvies (boxers or briefs), adorned with everything from lipstick marks to her signature cowboy boots. Call before visiting, as opening hours can be erratic.

Luggage

Flight 001

96 Greenwich Avenue, between Jane & W 12th Streets, Meatpacking District (1-212 691 1001/ www.flight001.com). Subway A, C, E to 14th Street; L to Eighth Avenue. **Open** 11am-8.30pm Mon-Fri; 11am-8pm Sat; noon-6pm Sun. **Credit** AmEx, DC, Disc, MC, V. **Map** p403 D28.
As well as a tasteful selection of luggage by the likes of Mandarina Duck, Orla Kiely and Samsonite, this one-stop shop carries everything for the chic jet-setter, including fun travel products such as Redeye Pak in-flight survival kits, eye masks, emergency

totes that squash down to tennis ball size and 'essentials' such as expanding toilet tissue tablets and single-use packets of Woolite.

Other locations 58 5th Avenue, at Bergen Street, Park Slope, Brooklyn (1-718 789 1001); 132 Smith Street, at Dean Street, Cobble Hill, Brooklyn (1-718 243 0001).

Shoes

See also p240 **Girls Love Shoes.**

Chuckies

1073 Third Avenue, between 63rd & 64th Streets, Upper East Side (1-212 593 9898). Subway F to Lexington Avenue-63rd Street. **Open** 10.45am-7.45pm Mon-Fri; 10.45am-7.30pm Sat; 12.30-7pm Sun. **Credit** AmEx, DC, Disc, MC, V. **Map** p405 E21.

An alternative to the department stores, Chuckies carries high-profile labels for women, such as Prada, YSL, Jimmy Choo and Lanvin, in addition to up-and-comers such as Camilla Skovgaard, who has created fab footwear for Matthew Williamson and Pucci. **Other locations** 1169 Madison Avenue, between 85th & 86th Streets, Upper East Side (1-212 249 2254).

Moo Shoes

78 Orchard Street, between Broome & Grand Streets, Lower East Side (1-212 254 6512/ www.mooshoes.com). Subway F to Delancey Street; J, M, Z to Delancey-Essex Streets. **Open** 11.30am-7.30pm Mon-Sat; noon-6pm Sun. **Credit** AmEx, DC, Disc, MC, V. **Map** p403 G30.

Now that Stella McCartney has a range of cruelty-free footwear, non-leather options are more fashionable. Moo stocks a variety of brands for men and women, such as Vegetarian Shoes, Simple and NOVACAS, plus styles from independent designers such as Elizabeth Olsen, whose arty line of high heels and handbags is anything but hippyish.

Sigerson Morrison

987 Madison Avenue, between 76th & 77th Streets, Upper East Side (1-212 734 2100/ www.sigersonmorrison.com). Subway 6 to 77th Street. **Open** 10am-6pm Mon-Sat. **Credit** AmEx, DC, Disc, MC, V. **Map** p405 E19.

The culty downtown footwear brand recently hatched its first uptown depot. In the sleek white space, mirrored display cubes and glossy backlit shelves dish up sleek boots and pixie-like pointy-toed flats in colourful leathers or exotic skins. The Belle line is slightly cheaper.

Other locations 28 Prince Street, between Elizabeth & Mott Streets (1-212 219 3893).

Té Casan

382 West Broadway, between Broome & Spring Streets, Soho (1-212 584 8000/www.tecasan.

com). Subway C, E to Spring Street. **Open** 11am-8pm Mon-Sat; noon-7pm Sun. **Credit** AmEx, DC, Disc, MC, V. **Map** p403 E30.

A sprawling bi-level space dedicated to limited-edition collections from seven nascent labels for women. The store boasts a team of talented international designers who aren't big names yet, but who have worked for some of the top design houses. So while the style and quality are comparable to more celebrated makes, you won't see your purchase stomping all over town.

Trainers/sneakers

Alife Rivington Club

158 Rivington Street, between Clinton & Suffolk Streets, Lower East Side (1-212 375 8128/ www.rivingtonclub.com). Subway F to Delancey Street; J, M, Z to Delancey-Essex Streets. **Open** noon-7pm Mon-Sat; noon-6pm Sun. **Credit** AmEx, DC, MC, V. **Map** p403 G29.

To become a member of this 'club', you have to find it: there's no sign outside the shop. But if sneakers are your religion, seek it out you must. Alife is arguably the best spot in the city for exclusive or limited-edition kicks from Nike, Converse and adidas. T-shirts, jackets, hoodies and hats come courtesy of the in-house brand or in collaboration with Nike and Lacoste.

Classic Kicks

298 Elizabeth Street, between Houston & Bleecker Streets, East Village (1-212 979 9514/www.classickicks.com). Subway B, D, F, V to Broadway-Lafayette Street; 6 to Bleecker Street. **Open** noon-7pm Mon-Sat. **Credit** AmEx, DC, MC, V. **Map** p403 F29.

One of the more female-friendly sneaker shops, with a selection of smaller sizes, Classic Kicks stocks mainstream and rare styles by Nike, Converse, New Balance and Vans, to name a few, along with a decent selection of graphic tees and fitted hats.

FOOD & DRINK

Bakeries

Amy's Bread

672 Ninth Avenue, between 46th & 47th Streets, Hell's Kitchen (1-212 977 2670/www.amys bread.com). Subway C, E to 50th Street; N, R, W to 49th Street. **Open** 7.30am-11pm Mon-Fri; 8am-11pm Sat; 9am-6pm Sun. **Credit** AmEx, DC, Disc, MC, V. **Map** p404 C23.

Whether you want sweet (chocolate-chubbie cookies) or savoury (hefty French sourdough boules), Amy's never disappoints. The grilled cheese sandwich (made with chipotle peppers) is one of the best in the city.

Other locations Chelsea Market, 75 Ninth Avenue, between 15th & 16th Streets, Chelsea

CONSUME

(1-212 462 4338); 250 Bleecker Street, at Leroy Street, West Village (1-212 675 7802).

Billy's Bakery
184 Ninth Avenue, between 21st & 22nd Streets, Chelsea (1-212 647 9956/www.billysbakery nyc.com). Subway C, E to 23rd Street. **Open** 9am-11pm Mon-Thur, Sun; 9am-midnight Fri, Sat. **Credit** AmEx, DC, Disc, MC, V. **Map** p404 C26.
Amid super-sweet retro delights such as coconut cream pie, cupcakes, Hello Dollies (indulgent graham cracker treats) and Famous Chocolate Icebox Cake, you'll find friendly service in a setting that will remind you of grandma's kitchen – or, at least, it will if your grandmother was Betty Crocker.

Magnolia Bakery
401 Bleecker Street, at 11th Street, West Village (1-212 462 2572). Subway 1 to Christopher Street. **Open** 9am-11.30pm Mon-Thur; 10am-12.30am Fri, Sat; 9am-11.30pm Sun. **Credit** AmEx, DC, Disc, MC, V. **Map** p403 D28.
Part sweet market, part meet market, Magnolia skyrocketed to fame after featuring on *Sex and the City*, and it's still oven-hot. The pastel-iced cupcakes are much vaunted, but you can also pick up other treats, including the custardy, Southern-style banana pudding (Brits: think trifle). Comfort food doesn't get much more classy.
Other locations 200 Columbus Avenue, at 69th Street, Upper West Side (1-212 724 8101).

Sullivan Street Bakery
533 W 47th Street, between Tenth & Eleventh Avenues, Hell's Kitchen (1-212 265 5580/ www.sullivanstreetbakery.com). Subway C, E to 50th Street. **Open** 8am-7pm Mon-Sat; 8am-4pm Sun **Credit** DC, MC, V. **Map** p404 C23.
Superlative Italian breads and thin-crust pizza to go make this bakery popular with lunch-breakers and celebrity chefs alike.

Drinks

Astor Wines & Spirits
399 Lafayette Street, at 4th Street, East Village (1-212 674 7500/www.astorwines.com). Subway 6 to Astor Place; N, R, W to 8th Street-NYU. **Open** 9am-9pm Mon-Sat; noon-6pm Sun. **Credit** AmEx, DC, Disc, MC, V. **Map** p403 F28.
An oenophile's delight, high-ceilinged, wide-aisled Astor Wines is a terrific place to browse for wines of every price range, vineyard and year. Sakes and spirits are also well represented, and you're quite likely to bump into a sommelier hunting on behalf of one of the classier restaurants.

Porto Rico Importing Co
201 Bleecker Street, between Sixth Avenue & MacDougal Street, Greenwich Village (1-212 477

5421/www.portorico.com). Subway A, B, C, D, E, F, V to W 4th Street. **Open** 8am-9pm Mon-Fri; 9am-9pm Sat; noon-7pm Sun. **Credit** AmEx, DC, Disc, MC, V. **Map** p403 E29.
This small, family-run store has earned a large following with a terrific range of coffees as well as its own prepared blends. Prices are reasonable and the selection of teas warrants exploration.
Other locations 107 Thompson Street, between Prince & Spring Streets, Soho (1-212 966 5758); 40½ St Marks Place, between First & Second Avenues, East Village (1-212 533 1982); 636 Grand Street, between Manhattan Avenue & Leonard Street, Williamsburg, Brooklyn (1-718 782 1200).

General

Dean & DeLuca
560 Broadway, at Prince Street, Soho (1-212 226 6800/www.deananddeluca.com). Subway N, R, W to Prince Street. **Open** 7am-8pm Mon-Fri; 8am-8pm Sat, Sun. **Credit** AmEx, DC, Disc, MC, V. **Map** p403 E29.
Dean & DeLuca's flagship store provides the most sophisticated (and pricey) selection of speciality food items in the city.
Other locations throughout the city.

Whole Foods
Concourse level, Time Warner Center, 10 Columbus Circle, at Broadway, Upper West Side (1-212 823 9600/www.wholefoodsmarket.com). Subway A, B, C, D, 1 to 59th Street-Columbus Circle. **Open** 8am-11pm daily. **Credit** AmEx, DC, Disc, MC, V. **Map** p405 D22.
You'll feel healthier just walking around looking at this veritable cornucopia of fresh food. As well as organic fruit and vegetables, groceries, breads and baked goods, you can pick up ready-made salads and hot meals, eco clothing and beauty products. It's all wonderful, but your wallet will suffer.
Other locations throughout the city.

Zabar's
2245 Broadway, at 80th Street, Upper West Side (1-212 787 2000/www.zabars.com). Subway 1 to

---

THE BEST
IN-STORE ATTRACTIONS

For imbibers
Dressing Room. *See p238.*

For art aficionados
BBlessing. *See p236.*

For Willy Wonka fantasies
Jacques Torres Chocolate. *See p248.*

CONSUME

79th Street. **Open** 8am-7.30pm Mon-Fri; 8am-8pm Sat; 9am-6pm Sun. **Credit** AmEx, DC, MC, V. **Map** p405 C19.

Zabar's is more than just a market – it's a genuine New York City landmark. It began in 1934 as a tiny storefront specialising in Jewish 'appetising' delicacies and has gradually expanded to take over half a block of prime Upper West Side real estate. What never ceases to surprise, however, is its reasonable prices – even for high-end foods. Besides the famous smoked fish and rafts of delicacies, Zabar's has fabulous bread, cheese, olives and coffee – and an entire floor dedicated to gadgets and homewares.

Markets

There are more than 40 open-air 'greenmarkets', sponsored by the city authorities, in various locations on different days. The largest and best known is at **Union Square**, where small producers of cheese, flowers, herbs, fruits and vegetables hawk their goods on Mondays, Wednesdays, Fridays and Saturdays (8am-6pm). Arrive early, before the prime stuff sells out. For other venues, check with the Council on the Environment of NYC (1-212 788 7476, www.cenyc.org/greenmarket). An indoor alternative, **Chelsea Market** (75 Ninth Avenue, at 16th Street, www.chelsea market.com, open 7am-9pm Mon-Sat; 10am-8pm Sun) is a one-stop gastronomic shopping playground occupying a whole block in a renovated Nabisco biscuit factory. It features a number of high-quality stores selling flowers, fish, fruit, baked goods, meat and liquors.

Specialist

Chinatown Ice Cream Factory

65 Bayard Street, between Mott & Elizabeth Streets, Lower East Side (1-212 608 4170/ www.chinatownicecreamfactory.com). Subway J, M, N, Q, R, W, Z, 6 to Canal Street. **Open** 11am-10pm daily. **No credit cards. Map** p402 F31.

Capping many a Chinatown feast, the 'factory' storefront serves up a wide array of ice-creams and sorbets, with flavours that are familiar to westerners (chocolate chip, vanilla) and Chinese tastebuds (red bean, black sesame, lychee), as well as several new experimental scoops (zen butter).

Jacques Torres Chocolate

350 Hudson Street, between Charlton & King Streets, entrance on King Street, Soho (1-212 414 2462/www.mrchocolate.com). Subway 1 to Houston Street. **Open** 9am-7pm Mon-Sat; 10am-6pm Sun. **Credit** AmEx, DC, MC, V. **Map** p403 D29.

Walk into Jacques Torres's glass-walled shop and café, and you'll be surrounded by a Willy Wonka-esque factory that turns raw cocoa beans

into luscious chocolate goodies before your eyes. As well as selling the usual assortments, truffles and bars (plus more unusual delicacies such as chocolate-covered cornflakes), the shop serves deliciously rich hot chocolate, steamed to order.

Other locations 66 Water Street, between Dock & Main Streets, Dumbo, Brooklyn (1-718 875 9772); 285 Amsterdam Avenue, between 73rd & 74th Streets, Upper West Side (no phone).

La Maison du Chocolat

1018 Madison Avenue, between 78th & 79th Streets, Upper East Side (1-212 744 7117/ www.lamaisonduchocolat.com). Subway 6 to 77th Street. **Open** 10am-7pm Mon-Sat; noon-6pm Sun. **Credit** AmEx, DC, MC, V. **Map** p405 E19.

This suave cocoa-brown boutique, the creation of Robert Linxe, packages luxe (and pricey) examples of edible Parisian perfection as if they were fine jewellery. The tea salon serves hot drinks, pastries and, of course, chocolates.

Other locations 30 Rockefeller Plaza, 49th Street, between Fifth & Sixth Avenues, Midtown (1-212 265 9404).

Murray's Cheese

254 Bleecker Street, between Sixth & Seventh Avenues, Greenwich Village (1-212 243 3289/ www.murrayscheese.com). Subway A, B, C, D, E, F, V to W 4th Street. **Open** 8am-8pm Mon-Sat; 10am-7pm Sun. **Credit** AmEx, DC, MC, V. **Map** p403 D29.

For the last word in curd, New Yorkers have been flocking to Murray's for almost a century to sniff out the best international and domestic cheeses. The helpful staff will guide you through the daunting 300-plus selection of stinky, runny, washed rind and aged cheesy comestibles.

Guss' Pickles

85-87 Orchard Street, between Broome & Grand Streets, Lower East Side (1-212 334 3616). Subway F to Delancey Street; J, M, Z to Delancey-Essex Streets. **Open** 10am-6pm Mon-Thur, Sun; 10am-4pm Fri. **Credit** AmEx, DC, MC, V. **Map** p403 G30.

A survivor of the Lower East Side's old pickle district, this shrine to the brine offers an array of sours and half-sours, pickled peppers, watermelon rinds and sauerkraut.

Russ & Daughters

179 E Houston Street, between Allen & Orchard Streets, Lower East Side (1-212 475 4880/ www.russanddaughters.com). Subway F, V to Lower East Side-Second Avenue. **Open** 9am-7pm Mon-Sat; 8am-5.30pm Sun. **Credit** AmEx, DC, Disc, MC, V. **Map** p403 F29.

Russ & Daughters, which has been open since 1914, sells eight kinds of smoked salmon and many Jewish-inflected Eastern European delectables, along with dried fruits, chocolates and caviar.

Yonah Schimmel Knish Bakery

137 E Houston Street, between First & Second Avenues, Lower East Side (1-212 477 2858/ www.yonahschimmel.com). Subway F, V to Lower East Side-Second Avenue. **Open** 9am-7pm Mon-Thur, Sun; 9am-9pm Fri, Sat. **Credit** AmEx, DC, Disc, MC, V. **Map** p403 F29.

Far more of a New York landmark than the neighbouring cinema of that name, this 'knishery' has been doling out its carborific goodies since 1910. Traditional potato, kasha and spinach knishes are most popular, but sweet potato and blueberry fillings are also available. The latkes (potato pancakes) are a city secret.

GIFTS & SOUVENIRS

Babeland

94 Rivington Street, between Ludlow & Orchard Streets, Lower East Side (1-212 375 1701/ www.babeland.com). Subway F, J, M, Z to Delancey. **Open** noon-10pm Mon-Wed, Sun; noon-11pm Thur-Sat. **Credit** AmEx, DC, MC, V. **Map** p403 G29.

At this friendly sex-toy boutique – run by women and skewed towards women – browsers are encouraged to handle all manner of buzzing, wriggling and bendable playthings, including the famed Rabbit Pearl vibrator. The shop also stocks a huge variety of condoms and hosts frank sex-ed classes on a variety of subjects.

Other locations 43 Mercer Street, between Broome & Grand Streets, Soho (1-212 966 2120); 462 Bergen Street, between Fifth & Flatbush Avenues, Park Slope, Brooklyn (1-718 638 3820).

★ Bowne & Co Stationers

South Street Seaport Museum, 211 Water Street, at Fulton Street, Financial District (1-212 748 8651). Subway A, C, J, M, Z to Broadway-Nassau Street. **Open** 10am-5pm Tue-Sun. **Credit** AmEx, DC, MC, V. **Map** p402 F32.

South Street Seaport Museum's re-creation of an 1870s-style print shop, Bowne & Co Stationers, holds the title of NYC's most venerable letterpress outpost. It's more than just a relic: the 19th-century platen presses – hand-set using antique type and powered by a treadle – offer an old-fashioned alternative to Word's latest font selection. What's more, you can watch the quaint machine imprint your calling cards using classic Crane & Co stationery (from $165). *Photo p250.*

Brooklyn Superhero Supply Company

372 Fifth Avenue, between 5th & 6th Streets, Park Slope, Brooklyn (1-718 499 9884/ www.superherosupplies.com). Subway F, R to 4th

Avenue-9th Street. **Open** 11am-5pm daily. **Credit** AmEx, DC, Disc, MC, V. **Map** p410 T11.

This mysterious shop – where you can buy such novelties as capes, X-ray goggles and gallon tins of Immortality – is actually a front (and money-earner) for the non-profit 826 NYC kids' writing centre (a chapter of the San Francisco centre founded by novelist Dave Eggers), hidden behind a concealed door.

★ Kiosk

95 Spring Street, between Broadway & Mercer Street, Soho (1-212 226 8601/www.kiosk kiosk.com). Subway 6 to Spring Street. **Open** 1-7pm Tue-Sat. **Credit** AmEx, DC, MC, V. **Map** p403 E30.

Don't be put off by the unprepossessing, graffiti-covered stairway that leads up to this gem of a shop. Alisa Grifo has collected an array of inexpensive items – mostly simple and functional but with a strong design aesthetic – from around the world, such as hairpins in a cool retro box from Mexico, Finnish liquorice, colourful net bags from Germany and a butterfly can-opener from Japan.

Pb&Caviar

88 Thomas Street, between West Broadway & Hudson Street, Tribeca (1-212 608 1112/ www.pbcaviar.com). Subway A, C, E, 1, 2, 3 to Chambers Street. **Open** 11am-7pm Tue-Sat;

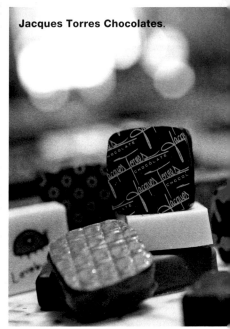

Jacques Torres Chocolates.

Bowne & Co Stationers. See p249.

CONSUME

11am-5pm Sun. **Credit** AmEx, DC, Disc, MC, V. **Map** p402 E31.

Shoppers of all ages will find something they want at Evin Cosby's (yes, that Cosby) carefully curated Tribeca boutique. She serves up a well-edited selection of women's and children's clothing, organic beauty products, fair-trade handmade toys and unique home decor.

Sustainable NYC

137 Avenue A, between 8th & 9th Streets, East Village (1-212 254 5400/www.sustainable-nyc.com). Subway L to First Avenue; 6 to Astor Place. **Open** noon-8pm Mon-Wed, Sun; 11am-10pm Thur-Sat. **Credit** AmEx, DC, Disc, MC, V. **Map** p403 G28.

Marked by a solar-powered sign, the gift-centric shop houses a wealth of eco-minded goods within its green walls: John Masters shampoos, fair-trade jewellery and sun-fuelled BlackBerry chargers.

HEALTH & BEAUTY

Complementary medicine

Body Central

Fifth Floor, 99 University Place, at 12th Street, Greenwich Village (1-212 677 5633/www.body centralnyc.com). Subway L, N, Q, R, W, 4, 5, 6 to 14th Street-Union Square. **Open** noon-9pm Mon, Wed; 8.30am-9pm Tue, Thur; 8.30am-2pm Fri. **Credit** AmEx, DC, MC, V. **Map** p403 E28.

Under the direction of Dr JoAnn Weinrib, Body Central offers a range of health and wellness services including chiropractic, massage, acupuncture and physical therapy.

Hairdressers & barbers

The styling superstars at **Frédéric Fekkai** (Fourth Floor, Henri Bendel, www.frederic fekkai.com; *see p227*) and **Sally Hershberger Downtown** (425 W 14th Street, between Ninth & Tenth Avenues, 1-212 206 8700, www.sallyhershberger.com, closed Sun, Mon) are top-notch, but they do tend to charge hair-raising prices.

Astor Place Hair Stylists

2 Astor Place, at Broadway, East Village (1-212 475 9854). Subway R, W to 8th Street-NYU; 6 to Astor Place. **Open** 8am-8pm Mon; 8am-10pm Tue-Sat; 9am-6pm Sun. **No credit cards.** **Map** p403 E28.

The army of barbers here does everything from neat trims to more complicated and creative shaved designs. You can't make an appointment; just take a number and wait outside with the crowd. Sunday mornings are usually quieter. Cuts start at $14; blow-dries, $25; dreads, $75.

Blow

342 W 14th Street, between Eighth & Ninth Avenues, Meatpacking District (1-212 989 6282/

www.blowny.com). Subway A, C, E to 14th Street.
Open 8am-8pm Mon-Fri; 10am-8pm Sat; noon-6pm Sun. **Credit** AmEx, DC, Disc, MC, V.
Map p403 C27.
Launched as a scissor-free 'blow-dry bar', this award-winning salon now offers cuts, colour and select beauty services as well as expertly executed blow-outs (from around $40).
Other locations Second Floor, 843 Lexington Avenue, between 64th & 65th Streets, Upper East Side (1-212 452 0246).

John Masters Organics

77 Sullivan Street, between Spring & Broome Streets, Soho (1-212 343 9590/www.john masters.com). Subway C, E to Spring Street; R, W to Prince Street. **Open** 11am-7pm Mon-Sat.
Credit AmEx, DC, MC, V. **Map** p403 E30.
A visit to this environmentally friendly salon – powered by wind energy – is like visiting an intoxicating botanical garden: the organic scalp treatment will send you into relaxed oblivion, and ammonia-free, herbal-based colour treatments will appeal to your inner purist. Cuts or colouring treatments start at $100, but even if you don't need a restyle it's worth stopping in for John Masters Organics chic apothecary line.

Mudhoney

148 Sullivan Street, between Houston & Prince Streets, Soho (1-212 533 1160/www.mudhoney hairsalon.com). Subway C, E to Spring Street; 1 to Houston Street. **Open** noon-8pm Tue-Fri; noon-6pm Sat, Sun. **No credit cards**.
Map p403 E29.
Looking for the perfect post-modern punk crop or an ironic mullet? Head for the city's premier rock 'n' roll salon, where the decor alone – a torture chair, lascivious stained-glass – is worth a visit. Cuts start at $80, and attract just as much attention as you want.
Other locations 7 Bond Street, between Broadway & Lafayette Street, East Village (1-212 228 8128); 85 Kenmare Street, between Mulberry & Lafayette Streets, Little Italy (1-212 472 7407).

Scott J

242 E 86th Street, between Second & Third Avenues, Upper East Side (1-212 496 3901/ www.scottj.com). Subway 4, 5, 6 to 86th Street.
Open 10am-10pm Mon, Tue, Sun; noon-11pm Wed; 9am-11pm Thur, Fri; 9am-10pm Sat.
Credit DC, MC, V. **Map** p406 F18.
This trio of laid-back Aveda salons has a stable of competent stylists in a wide range of price categories (haircuts from $55 for women; from $45 for men). Massages and other relaxing treatments are offered at the Upper East Side and Broadway locations.
Other locations 257 Columbus Avenue, at 72nd Street, Upper West Side (1-212 496 3904); Second Floor, 2929 Broadway, between 114th & 115th Street, Upper West Side (1-212 496 3902).

Opticians

A former flea market stall, **Fabulous Fanny's** (335 E 9th Street, between First & Second Avenues, 1-212 533 0637, www.fabulous fannys.com) has been the city's premier source of period frames for two decades, with more than 30,000 pairs of specs dating as far back as the 1700s.

Bond 07 by Selima

7 Bond Street, between Broadway & Lafayette Street, East Village (1-212 677 8487/www.selima optique.com). Subway B, D, F, V to Broadway-Lafayette Street; 6 to Bleecker Street. **Open** 11am-7pm Mon-Sat; noon-6pm Sun. **Credit** AmEx, DC, MC, V. **Map** p403 E29.
Eyewear designer Selima Salaun's spacious East Village shop stocks her full range of frames alongside a collection of vintage designer clothes, accessories and jewellery. Nostalgic styles, including square and curvy cat-eye 1950s-inspired shapes and 1970s-vibe large rounded frames, come in a variety of eye-catching colour combinations, and you can have your prescription filled on-site.
Other locations throughout the city.
▶ *The shop shares premises with an outpost of the Mudhoney hair salon; see left.*

Morgenthal Frederics

399 W Broadway, at Spring Street, Soho (1-212 966 0099/www.morgenthalfrederics.com). Subway C, E to Spring Street. **Open** 11am-8pm Mon-Fri; 11am-7pm Sat; noon-6pm Sun. **Credit** AmEx, DC, MC, V. **Map** p403 E30.
The house-designed, handmade frames displayed in Morgenthal Fredercis' David Rockwell-designed shops exude quality and subtly nostalgic style. Frames start from $325 for plastic, but the buffalo horn and gold ranges are more expensive; you can even have a pair accented with tiny diamonds for around $2,000.
Other locations throughout the city.

PHARMACIES

The fact that there's a **Duane Reade** pharmacy on almost every corner of Manhattan is lamented among chain-deriding locals; however, it's convenient if you need an aspirin pronto. Several branches, including the one at 250 W 57th Street, at Broadway (1-212 265 2101, www.duanereade.com), are open 24 hours. Competitor **Rite Aid** (with one of several 24-hour branches at 301 W 50th Street, at Eighth Avenue, 1-212 247 8736, www.riteaid.com) is also widespread.

J Leon Lascoff & Son

1209 Lexington Avenue, at 82nd Street, Upper East Side (1-212 288 9500). Subway 4, 5, 6 to

86th Street. **Open** 8.30am-6.30pm Mon-Fri; 9am-6pm Sat. **Credit** DC, MC, V. **Map** p405 F19.
Founded in 1899, Lascoff's moved to its 'new' location in 1931. The shop hasn't changed much since, and a collection of its original preparations and other artefacts are on display in the old-fashioned wooden cabinets, along with modern goods, which include DR Harris grooming products and Mason Pearson brushes, as well as more prosaic pharmaceutical necessities.

Shops

Bond No.9
9 Bond Street, between Broadway & Lafayette Street, East Village (1-212 228 1732/www.bond no9.com). Subway B, D, F, V to Broadway-Lafayette Street; 6 to Bleecker Street. **Open** 11am-8pm Mon-Fri; 10am-7pm Sat; noon-6pm Sun. **Credit** AmEx, DC, MC, V. **Map** p403 E29.
The collection of scents here pays olfactory homage to New York City. Choose from 34 'neighbourhoods' and 'sensibilities', including Wall Street, Park Avenue, Eau de Noho, even Chinatown (but don't worry, it smells of peach blossoms, gardenia and patchouli, not fish stands). The arty bottles and neat, colourful packaging are particularly gift friendly. **Other locations** 680 Madison Avenue, at 61st Street, Upper East Side (1-212 838 2780); 897 Madison Avenue, at 73rd Street, Upper East Side (1-212 794 4480); 399 Bleecker Street, at 11th Street, West Village (1-212 633 1641).

CB I Hate Perfume
93 Wythe Avenue, between North 10th & 11th Streets, Williamsburg, Brooklyn (1-718 384 6890/www.cbihateperfume.com). Subway L to

Bedford Avenue. **Open** noon-6pm Tue-Sat. **Credit** DC, MC, V. **Map** p411 U7.
Contrary to his shop's name, Christopher Brosius doesn't actually hate what he sells, he just despises the concept of mass-produced fragrances. Collaborate with him on a signature scent of your own (by appointment), or buy one of his ready-made scent 'experiences' such as Gathering Apples or At the Beach 1966.

Georgia
89A E Houston Street, between Elizabeth Street & Bowery, East Village (1-646 827 2428/ www.georgiany.com). Subway F, V to 2nd Avenue. **Open** noon-10pm daily. **Credit** AmEx, DC, MC, V. **Map** p403 F29.
This decadent, artfully dishevelled new beauty emporium combines top-of-the-line products (John Masters Organics, Côté Bastide, ERBE skincare), drugstore necessities and its own brand of glamorous staples such as hairbrushes and silk pillow covers, as well as lingerie by the likes of Huit and Eberjey. A tiny but full-service hair salon (just two seats) offers conditioning ($35), blowouts ($65), cuts (from $80) and more.

Kiehl's
109 Third Avenue, between 13th & 14th Streets, East Village (1-212 677 3171/www.kiehls.com). Subway L to Third Avenue; N, Q, R, W, 4, 5, 6 to 14th Street-Union Square. **Open** 10am-8pm Mon-Sat; 11am-6pm Sun. **Credit** AmEx, DC, Disc, MC, V. **Map** p403 F27.
The apothecary founded on this East Village site in 1851 has morphed into a major skincare brand widely sold in upscale department stores, but the products, in their minimal-frills packaging, are

CONSUME

Juvenex.

still good value and produce great results. The lip balms and thick-as-custard Creme de Corps are cult classics.

Other locations 150 Columbus Avenue, between 66th & 67th Streets, Upper West Side (1-212 799 3438).

Ricky's

590 Broadway, between Houston & Prince Streets, Soho (1-212 226 5552/www.rickys-nyc.com). Subway B, D, F, V to Broadway-Lafayette Street; R, W to Prince Street. **Open** 9am-9pm Mon-Fri, Sun; 9am-10pm Sat. **Credit** AmEx, DC, Disc, MC, V. **Map** p403 E29.

The quirky chain mixes false eyelashes, feather boas and body jewellery with drugstore essentials and upmarket haircare brands. Ricky's own line, Mattése, is also well worth a look.

Other locations throughout the city.

SPAS & SALONS

The city's top hotels come with spas to match: those at the **Plaza** (*see p167*) and **Waldorf-Astoria** (*see p170*) are especially recommended.

Cornelia Day Resort

Eighth Floor, 663 Fifth Avenue, between 52nd & 53rd Streets, Midtown (1-212 871 3050/www.cornelia.com). Subway E, V to Fifth Avenue; B, D, F, V to 47th-50th Street-Rockefeller Center. **Open** 9am-10pm Mon-Sat; 9am-9pm Sun. **Credit** AmEx, DC, MC, V. **Map** p404 E23.

The Romanian tradition of eating a teaspoon of honey begins many of the treatments at this massive, elegant oasis (where a 60-minute massage costs $175). Amenities include a rooftop garden and one of the city's only Watsu pools (the water is warmed to match your body's temperature, and a therapist massages your floating limbs). Clients are encouraged to spend an entire day unwinding in the bevy of rooms – including the healthy in-house café and the Relaxation Library, which offers comfy couches and cashmere blankets.

Homme Spa

465 Lexington Avenue, between 45th & 46th Streets, Midtown East (1-212 983 0033/www.hommespa.com). Subway S 4, 5, 6, 7, to 42nd Street-Grand Central. **Open** 11am-3am Mon-Fri; noon-midnight Sat, Sun. **Credit** AmEx, DC, Disc, MC, V. **Map** p404 F24.

The ingenious idea of prefacing a signature hot-towel massage with a spell in a recliner, watching TV sports is metrosexual nirvana. This bi-level, 15,000-square-foot midtown space (which offers services for women, too) includes a sealed steam area, a sauna, a spacious lounge and softly lit treatment rooms.

Iguazu Day Spa

350 Hudson Street, between Charlton & King Streets, Soho (1-212 647 0007/www.iguazudayspa.com). Subway 1 to Houston Street. **Open** 11am-8pm Mon-Sat; noon-6pm Sun. **Credit** AmEx, DC, Disc, MC, V. **Map** p403 D29.

Although it's helmed by Fabien Azoulay, a former manager at men-only spa Nickel, this small, pristine duplex caters to both sexes and offers everything from party-worthy blowouts and manicures to pore-suctioning backcials. The signature Pachamama Massage (75 minutes, $168) pairs hot stones, bamboo sticks and a host of yummy-smelling oils with a blend of massage techniques (shiatsu, deep-tissue and Swedish, plus Thai stretching).

Juvenex

Fifth Floor, 25 W 32nd Street, between Fifth Avenue & Broadway, Garment District (1-646 733 1330/www.juvenexspa.com). Subway B, D, F, N, Q, R, V, W to 34th Street. **Open** 24hrs daily. **Credit** AmEx, DC, MC, V. **Map** p404 E25.

An unassuming Koreatown building is home to this huge, soundproof, round-the-clock oasis. Shy gals take note: nudity is encouraged in the communal areas, full body scrubs are executed in shared, barely screened-off spaces, and the spa goes unisex after 7pm. The facilities are impressive, though: lolling in one of the igloo-like saunas, made from 20 tons of jade stones and infused with Chinese herbs, is said to increase metabolism, improve circulation and detox the body. A basic Purification Program costs $115.

Tattoos & piercings

Invisible NYC

148 Orchard Street, between Stanton & Rivington Streets, Lower East Side (1-212 228 1358/www.invisiblenyc.com). Subway F, V to Lower East Side-Second Avenue. **Open** 1-9pm daily. **No credit cards. Map** p403 F29.

At this tattoo salon specialising in large-scale Japanese body art, human canvases are adorned in the back and contemporary paintings are sold in the front gallery. The five inkers have waiting lists as long as six months, but the doodles are all custom-made, so your $180/hour artwork is guaranteed to be one of a kind.

HOUSE & HOME

Antiques

Among bargain-hungry New Yorkers, flea market rummaging is pursued with religious devotion. What better way to walk off that overstuffed omelette from brunch than to explore aisles of old vinyl records, unusual trinkets, vintage linens and funky furniture? *See also p96* **Walk**.

CONSUME

Brownstoner's Brooklyn Flea.

CONSUME

Antiques Garage
112 W 25th Street, between Sixth & Seventh Avenues, Chelsea (1-212 243 5343/www.annex markets.com). Subway F, V to 23rd Street. **Open** 9am-5pm Sat, Sun. **No credit cards.** **Map** p404 D26.
Designers (and the occasional dolled-down celebrity) hunt regularly – and early – at this flea market in a vacant parking garage. Specialities include old prints, vintage clothing, and other household paraphernalia.

Brownstoner's Brooklyn Flea
Bishop Loughlin Memorial High School, entrance on Lafayette Avenue, between Clermont & Vanderbilt Avenues, Fort Greene, Brooklyn (no phone/www.brownstoner.com/brooklynflea). G to Clinton-Washington Avenues. **Open** 10am-5pm Sun. **No credit cards.**
The city's newest rummaging spot, in this large Brooklyn schoolyard, has a great mix of bric-a-brac and antiques, vintage clothing, vinyl and new crafts. Refuel at stands selling Latin-American nosh and baked goods, and be sure to check out the elaborate façade of the Masonic temple across the street.

Hell's Kitchen Flea Market
39th Street, between Ninth & Tenth Avenues, Hell's Kitchen (1-212 243 5343/www.annex markets.com). Subway A, C, E to 34th Street-Penn Station. **Open** sunrise-sunset Sat, Sun. **No credit cards.** **Map** p404 C24.
The huge Annex Antiques Fair & Flea Market on 26th Street lost its lease to a property developer, and is now a much smaller affair, so many of the vendors packed up and moved to this stretch of road in Hell's Kitchen, where you'll find a mix of vintage clothing and textiles, furniture and other bric-a-brac miscellany.
▶ *For a tour of the area's flea markets, see p96.*

General

★ ABC Carpet & Home
888 Broadway, at 19th Street, Flatiron District (1-212 473 3000/www.abchome.com). Subway L, N, Q, R, W, 4, 5, 6 to 14th Street-Union Square. **Open** 10am-8pm Mon-Thur; 10am-6.30pm Fri; 11am-7pm Sat; noon-6.30pm Sun. **Credit** AmEx, DC, Disc, MC, V. **Map** p403 E27.
Most of ABC's 35,000-strong carpet range is housed in-shop across the street at no.881 – except the rarest rugs, which reside on the sixth floor of the main store. Once you've browsed everything from organic soap to hand-beaded lamp shades on the bazaar-style ground floor, stock up on booze-filled bonbons by French chocolatier Michel Cluizel. On the upper floors, furniture spans every style, from slick European minimalism to antique oriental and mid-century modern. The massive Bronx warehouse outlet offers discounted furnishings, but don't expect incredible bargains as prices are still steep.
Other locations ABC Carpet & Home Warehouse, 1055 Bronx River Avenue, between Bruckner Boulevard & Westchester Avenue, Bronx (1-718 842 8772).

Fishs Eddy

889 Broadway, at 19th Street, Flatiron District (1-212 420 9020/www.fishseddy.com). Subway N, R, W to 23rd Street. **Open** 10am-9pm Mon; 9am-9pm Tue-Sat; 10am-8pm Sun. **Credit** AmEx, DC, Disc, MC, V. **Map** p403 E27.

Penny-pinchers frequent this barn-like space for sturdy, vintage dishware and glasses, recycled from restaurants, ocean liners and hotels (plain white side plates are a mere 99¢). But there are plenty of affordable, freshly minted kitchen goods too. Add whimsy to mealtime with glasses adorned with flamingoes or pole-dancers ($5 and up), platters printed with the Brooklyn skyline ($16.95-$24.95) and Floor Plan dinnerware (from $7.95). NYC apartments have never been so cheap. *Photo p256.*

Matter

405 Broome Street, between Centre & Lafayette Streets, Soho (1-212 343 2600/www.matter matters.com). Subway 6 to Spring Street. **Open** noon-7pm Mon-Sat; noon-6pm Sun. **Credit** AmEx, DC, Disc, MC, V. **Map** p403 F30.

The Soho spin-off of Brooklyn design store Matter offers an eclectic international selection of furniture, home accessories and jewellery, including Iraqi-Brit architect Zaha Hadid's interlocking Nekton stools and hot duo FredriksonStallard's provocative cross-shaped clothes brushes. There are some great New York-centric gifts too: look out for metal manhole-cover coasters by Curios and Tel Aviv-based Johnathan Hopp's miniature porcelain buildings.

Other locations 227 5th Avenue, between President & Carroll Streets, Brooklyn (1-718 230 1150).

MoMA Design Store

44 W 53rd Street, between Fifth & Sixth Avenues, Midtown (1-212 767 1050/www.moma store.org). Subway E, V to Fifth Avenue-53rd Street. **Open** 9.30am-6.30pm Mon-Thur, Sat, Sun; 9.30am-9pm Fri. **Credit** AmEx, DC, MC, V. **Map** p405 E22.

A must for contemporary design fans, the museum's stand-alone retail arm assembles an impressive array of contemporary furnishings and gifts, including sculptural vases, clocks, kitchenware and gadgets. Downstairs at the Spring Street location, there's an outpost of minimalist Japanese lifestyle store Muji along with larger furniture. **Other locations** 81 Spring Street, at Crosby Street, Soho (1-646 613 1367).
▶ *For the museum itself, see p100.*

Moss

150 Greene Street, between Houston & Prince Streets, Soho (1-212 204 7100/www.moss online.com). Subway B, D, F, V to Broadway-Lafayette Street; N, R, W to Prince Street; 6 to Bleecker Street. **Open** 11am-7pm Mon-Sat; noon-6pm Sun. **Credit** AmEx, DC, Disc, MC, V. **Map** p403 E29.

Proprietor Murray Moss has curated what is perhaps the most impressive collection of high-design items in the city. Many of the streamlined clocks, curvy sofas and funky household items are kept protected under glass at this temple of contemporary home design. For creativity on a larger scale, stop by his 'museum' adjacent to the store.

Ochre

Broome Street, between Greene & Mercer Streets, Soho (1-212 414 4332/www.ochre.net). Subway R, W to Prince Street; 6 to Spring Street. **Open** 11am-7pm Mon-Sat; noon-6pm Sun. **Credit** AmEx, DC, MC, V. **Map** p403 E30.

This serene, quietly tasteful store is arranged like one of the neighbourhood's chic loft apartments, with delicate, handmade ceramics, organic skincare

CONSUME

CONSUME

Fishs Eddy. *See p255*.

products, decorative cushions, vintage Indian throws and curiosities like simple, spicy-scented cinnamon boxes displayed on a variety of vintage tables, chests and other furniture.

MUSIC & ENTERTAINMENT

CDs & records

Academy Annex
96 North 6th Street, between Berry Street & Wythe Avenue, Williamsburg, Brooklyn (1-718 218 8200/www.academyannex.com). Subway L to Bedford Avenue. **Open** noon-8pm Mon-Thur, Sun; noon-10pm Fri, Sat. **Credit** AmEx, DC, Disc, MC, V. **Map** p411 U7.
See p257 **Vinyl Solution**.

Big City Records
521 E 12th Street, between Avenues A & B (1-212 539 0208). Subway L to 1st Avenue. **Open** noon-8pm daily. **Credit** AmEx, DC, Disc, MC, V. **Map** p403 G28.
See p257 **Vinyl Solution**.

Fat Beats
Second Floor, 406 Sixth Avenue, between 8th & 9th Streets, Greenwich Village (1-212 673 3883/ www.fatbeats.com). Subway A, B, C, D, E, F, V to W 4th Street. **Open** noon-9pm Mon-Sat; noon-6pm Sun. **Credit** DC, MC, V. **Map** p403 D28.
Ground zero for headz seeking the latest or the most obscure in hip hop. Everyone – Beck, DJ Evil

Dee, DJ Premier, Q-Tip – shops at this tiny Greenwich Village shrine to vinyl for treasured hip hop, jazz, funk and reggae releases, underground magazines (like Wax Poetics) and cult flicks (such as Wild Style).

J&R Music World
23 Park Row, at Beekman Street, Financial District (1-212 238 9000/www.jr.com). Subway A, C to Broadway-Nassau. **Open** 9am-7.30pm Mon-Sat; 10.30am-6.30pm Sun. **Credit** AmEx, DC, Disc, MC, V. **Map** p402 E32.
Lurking within J&R's block-long electronics emporium, this music store is a godsend for world music lovers as well as seekers of the obscure. And if you can't find that rare tango or fado disc you were looking for, chances are the remainder bins will have something to alleviate the disappointment.

Jazz Record Center
Room 804, 236 W 26th Street, between Seventh & Eighth Avenues, Chelsea (1-212 675 4480/ www.jazzrecordcenter.com). Subway C, E to 23rd Street; 1 to 28th Street. **Open** 10am-6pm Mon-Sat. **Credit** DC, Disc, MC, V. **Map** p404 D26.
The city's best jazz store stocks current and out-of-print records, books, videos and other jazz-related merchandise.

Other Music
15 E 4th Street, between Broadway & Lafayette Street, East Village (1-212 477 8150/ www.othermusic.com). Subway R, W to 8th

Vinyl Solution

A pair of music insiders reveal the best places to score quality discs.

Best known as musicians in the Dap-Kings, the band that backs Sharon Jones (and has toured with Amy Winehouse), saxophonist Neal Sugarman and bass player Gabriel Roth have a history of soul. They're also the founders of Daptone Records, an indie label for soul, funk, gospel and Afrobeat artists that they started out of a Brooklyn basement studio in 2001. Not surprisingly, they each own an extensive record library. 'We're not obsessive about it,' Roth notes, 'but we're always looking for new music that we like.'

In Manhattan, Sugarman and Roth worship **Big City Records** (*see p256*), a shrine to soul and funk 45s and LPs. 'The guy who runs the place has amazing taste,' Sugarman says. What's more, Big City boasts an excellent discount trove that the pair frequently root around in. Says Roth: 'Don't neglect the dollar bins!'

'Almost every time I come in to **Academy Annex** (*see p256*), I buy a record,' Roth says. 'There's a good balance between organisation and chaos, they have a big new arrivals section and a lot of turnover.' For Sugarman, it's cut prices and multiple copies of unusual classics that attract him to the NYC chainlet's B-burg location. 'I've probably bought five copies of the Ohio Players' *First Impressions* LP because it was cheap enough that I could turn friends on to [it].'

Also in Williamsburg, the duo love **Sound Fix** (*see p258*), a small store and café with a slick, red interior ('You can get all jacked up on coffee and buy records here,' says Sugarman, admiringly). The pair like this spot for its broad collection of new vinyl compilations, such as the *Studio One Lovers* album that Roth picks out. 'This is a nice compilation of some sweet reggae,' he says. 'It has one of my favourite songs ever: "I'm Still Waiting".'

Away from Williamsburg but still in Brooklyn, Greenpoint's **Permanent Records** (*see p258*) is another favourite for its old-school, pretension-free vibe and knowledgeable staff. 'When I was growing up, this is how music stores used to be,' says Sugarman. 'It was a real social experience. They're just turning people on to albums, which is different from used-record stores where you have a bunch of diggers who are hoarding the stuff they're into.'

Permanent Records.

Sugarman (left) and Roth in **Academy Annex**.

CONSUME

Street-NYU; 6 to Astor Place. **Open** noon-9pm Mon-Fri; noon-8pm Sat; noon-7pm Sun. **Credit** AmEx, DC, Disc, MC, V. **Map** p403 E29.

This wee audio temple is dedicated to small-label, often imported new and used CDs and LPs across numerous genres, from American roots and indie to electronica, soul and 'La Decadanse' (lounge, Moog and slow-core soundtracks). Small concerts are occasionally held here.

Permanent Records

181 Franklin Street, between Green & Huron Streets, Greenpoint, Brooklyn (1-718 383 4083, www.permanentrecords.info). Subway G to Greenpoint Avenue. **Open** 11am-9pm Mon-Sat; 11am-8pm Sun. **Credit** AmEx, DC, Disc, MC, V. **Map** p411 U6.
See p257 **Vinyl Solution**.

Sound Fix

110 Bedford Avenue, at North 11th Street, Williamsburg, Brooklyn (1-718 388 8090, www.soundfixrecords.com). Subway L to Bedford Avenue. **Open** noon-9pm Mon-Sat; noon-8pm Sun. **Credit** AmEx, DC, MC, V. **Map** p411 U7.
See p257 **Vinyl Solution**.

Sounds

20 St Marks Place, between Second & Third Avenues, East Village (1-212 677 3444). Subway 6 to Astor Place. **Open** noon-8pm Wed, Thur; noon-9pm Fri-Sun. **No credit cards.** **Map** p403 F28.

Housed in two neighbouring storefronts, Sounds is the best bargain on the block for new and used music (up to 40% off retail price for the former). The shop specialises in all kinds of jazz and international recordings, both obscure and less so, and also has a good selection of rock and pop.

Musical instruments

Sam Ash Music

160 W 48th Street, between Sixth & Seventh Avenues, Theater District (1-212 719 2299/ www.samashmusic.com). Subway B, D, F, V to 47th-50th Streets-Rockefeller Center; N, R, W to 49th Street. **Open** 10am-8pm Mon-Sat; noon-6pm Sun. **Credit** AmEx, DC, Disc, MC, V. **Map** p404 D23.

This octogenarian musical instrument emporium dominates its midtown block with four contiguous shops. New, vintage and custom guitars of all varieties are available, along with amps, DJ equipment, drums, keyboards, recording equipment, turntables and an array of sheet music.
Other locations 2600 Flatbush Avenue, at Hendrickson Place, Flatlands, Brooklyn (1-718 951 3888); 113-25 Queens Boulevard, between 87th Avenue & 87th Road, Forest Hills, Queens (1-718 793 7983).

SPORTS & FITNESS

Blades, Board & Skate

659 Broadway, between Bleecker & Bond Streets, Greenwich Village (1-212 477 7350/www.blades. com). Subway B, D, F, V to Broadway-Lafayette Street; 6 to Bleecker Street. **Open** 10am-9pm Mon-Sat; 11am-7pm Sun. **Credit** AmEx, DC, Disc, MC, V. **Map** p403 E29.

The requisite clothing and accessories are sold here, alongside in-line skates, skate- and snowboards.
Other locations throughout the city.

Paragon Sporting Goods

867 Broadway, at 18th Street, Flatiron District (1-212 255 8036/www.paragonsports.com). Subway L, N, Q, R, W, 4, 5, 6 to 14th Street-Union Square. **Open** 10am-8pm Mon-Sat; 11.30am-7pm Sun. **Credit** AmEx, DC, Disc, MC, V. **Map** p403 E27.

Three floors of equipment and clothing for almost every activity, from the everyday (a slew of gym gear, sneaks and sunglasses) to the more niche (badminton, kayaking) make this the New York sports-gear mecca.

Shut Skates

158 Orchard Street, between Rivington & Stanton Streets, Lower East Side (1-212 420 1469/www.shutnyc.com). Subway F, V to Second Avenue. **Open** 1-7pm Mon-Fri; noon-7pm Sat, Sun. **Credit** AmEx, DC, MC, V. **Map** p403 G30.

Zoo York co-founder Rodney Smith resurrected his 1980s skateboard label Shut in his flagship location. In the polished, handsome space, the graffiti-style boards (priced from around $130) shine as both art and high-end equipment, alongside hats, shirts and other skating accessories.

TICKETS

While it's cheaper to buy tickets for performances directly from the venue, many of them don't offer this option, especially when it comes to booking online. The main booking agencies for concerts and other events are **Ticketmaster** (1-212 307 4100, www.ticketmaster.com) and **TicketWeb** (1-866 468 7619, www.ticketweb.com), while **Telecharge** 1-212 239 6200, www.tele charge.com) specialises in Broadway and Off Broadway shows.

TRAVELLERS' NEEDS

Got carried away in the shops? **XS Baggage** (1-718 301 5803, www.xsbaggage.com) will ship a single suitcase or multiple boxes to almost anywhere in the world, by air or sea. **Flight 001** (*see p245*) sells all manner of travel aids and accessories. For mobile phone rental and computer repairs, *see p232*.

Arts & Entertainment

Calendar

Join the crowd at these seasonal happenings.

New Yorkers rarely struggle to find something to celebrate. The venerable city-wide traditions are well known, but don't miss the neighbourhood shindigs: you can soak up the local vibe at quirky annual traditions such as Brooklyn's Mermaid Parade or East Village Beatnik bash Howl!, and take advantage of free summer concerts and outdoor films in the city's green spaces, such as Bryant, Central and Madison Square Parks.

For more festivals and events, check out the other chapters in the Arts & Entertainment section. Specific dates are given for 2009 where possible, but before you set out or plan a trip around an event, it's wise to call first as dates, times and locations are subject to change. For the latest listings, consult the Own This City section of *Time Out New York* magazine.

SPRING

Ringling Bros and Barnum & Bailey Circus Animal Walk

34th Street, from the Queens Midtown Tunnel to Madison Square Garden, Seventh Avenue, between 31st & 33rd Streets (1-212 307 7171/ www.ringling.com). **Date** Mar.

Midnight parades open and close the Ringling Bros and Barnum & Bailey circus's NYC run; true circus freaks make the trek to see elephants, horses and zebras march through the tunnel and on to the streets of Manhattan in this surreal spectacle.

Armory Show

Piers 92 & 94, Twelfth Avenue, at 55th Street, Hell's Kitchen (1-212 645 6440/www.thearmory show.com). Subway C, E to 50th Street. **Date** 4-8 Mar. **Map** p405 B22.

Named after its 1913 predecessor, which heralded the arrival of modern art in the US, this contemporary international art mart debuted in Gramercy Park's 69th Regiment Armory in 1999. Now held on the Hudson River, it recently expanded: the new 'Modern' section is held at Pier 92 and deals in older 20th century work.

St Patrick's Day Parade

Fifth Avenue, from 44th to 86th Streets (no phone/www.saintpatricksdayparade.com). **Date** 17 Mar.

Dating from 1762, this massive march is one of the city's longest-running annual traditions. If you feel like braving huge crowds and potentially nasty weather, you'll see thousands of green-clad merry-makers strutting to the sounds of pipe bands. Celebrations continue late into the night as the city's Irish bars teem with suds-swigging revellers.

New York Antiquarian Book Fair

Park Avenue Armory, Park Avenue, between 66th & 67th Streets, Upper East Side (1-212 777 5218/www.sanfordsmith.com). Subway 6 to 68th Street-Hunter College. **Date** early Apr. **Map** p405 E21.

If you are looking for a first edition of Voltaire's *Candide*, a 17th-century map of the world or a fragment of the Dead Sea Scrolls, then this annual expo of rare books, manuscripts, autographs, maps and ephemera is for you. Bibliophiles and collectors flock here by the hundreds to buy from around 200 international dealers. You may also find original Hollywood screenplays and shooting scripts.
► *For the city's best bookstores, see p229.*

Easter Parade

Fifth Avenue, from 49th to 57th Streets (1-212 484 1222). Subway E, V to Fifth Avenue-53rd Street. **Date** 12 Apr.

'Parade' is something of a misnomer for this little festival of creative-hat wearers. From 11am on Easter Sunday, Fifth Avenue becomes a car-free promenade of gussied-up crowds milling around and showing off their extravagant bonnets. Arrive early to secure a prime viewing spot near St Patrick's Cathedral, at 50th Street. After the event, head to Tavern on the Green (Central Park West, at 67th Street) for the Mad Hatter's Easter Bonnet Contest, where you'll see even more head-coverings.

★ Tribeca Film Festival
Date 22 Apr-3 May.
See p304.

Cherry Blossom Festival
For listing, see p131 Brooklyn Botanic Garden.
Date 2, 3 May.
The climax to the cherry blossom season, when the BBG's 220 trees are in flower, the annual *sakura matsuri* celebrates both the blooms and Japanese culture with concerts, traditional dance, sword demonstrations and tea ceremonies.

Bike New York: The Great Five Boro Bike Tour
Battery Park to Staten Island (1-212 932 2453/ www.bikenewyork.org). Subway A, C, J, M, Z, 1, 2, 3 to Chambers Street; R, W to City Hall; 4, 5, 6 to Brooklyn Bridge-City Hall, then bike to Battery Park. Date 3 May. Map p402 E34.
Thousands of cyclists take over the city for a 42-mile Tour de New York. (Pedestrians and motorists should plan on extra getting-around time on this date.) Advance registration is required if you want to take part. Event organisers suggest using the trains listed above, as some subway exits below Chambers Street may be closed to bike-toting cyclists for safety reasons, and bikes are not allowed at the South Ferry (1 train), Whitehall Street (R, W) and Bowling Green (4, 5) stations.
▶ *For more on cycling, see p341.*

Lower East Side Festival of the Arts
Theater for the New City, 155 First Avenue, between 9th & 10th Streets (1-212 254 1109/ www.theaterforthenewcity.net). Subway L to First Avenue; 6 to Astor Place. Date 22-24 May. Map p403 F28.
This celebration of artistic diversity features performances by dozens of theatrical troupes, poetry readings, films and family-friendly programming. It's run by the Theatre for the New City company, who have been performing political and community themed plays in the city since 1971.

Washington Square Outdoor Art Exhibit
Various streets surrounding Washington Square Park, Greenwich Village (1-212 982 6255/washingtonsquareoutdoorartexhibit.org). Subway A, B, C, D, E, F, V to W 4th Street; R, W to 8th Street-NYU. Date 23-25, 30, 31 May; 5-7, 12, 13 Sept.
Exhibitors here show off photography, sculpture, paintings and one-of-a-kind crafts. It's a great way for browsers and buyers alike to spend an afternoon.

Bryant Park Free Summer Season
Bryant Park, Sixth Avenue, at 42nd Street, Midtown (1-212 768 4242/www.bryantpark.org). Subway B, D, F, V to 42nd Street-Bryant Park; 7 to Fifth Avenue. Date late May-late Aug. Map p404 E24.
One of the highlights of the park's free entertainment season is the ever-popular Monday night alfresco movie series (from late June), but there's plenty of fun to be had in the daylight hours as well. You can catch Broadway musical numbers as part of the Broadway in Bryant Park series; *Good Morning America* mini-concerts featuring big-name acts for early risers; and a variety of readings, classes and public art projects.

Red Hook Waterfront Arts Festival
Various locations in Red Hook, Brooklyn (1-718 596 2507/www.bwac.org). Subway A, C, F to Jay Street-Borough Hall, then B61 bus to Van Brunt Street; F, G to Smith-9th Streets, then B77 bus to Van Brunt Street. Date late May/early June.
The Red Hook Waterfront Arts Festival is an evolving and environmentally aware neighbourhood cultural bash including dance, music and spoken word performances from local artists, along with the Brooklyn Waterfront Artists' Pier Show.

SOFA New York
Seventh Regiment Armory, 643 Park Avenue, at 67th Street, Upper East Side (1-800 563 7632/ www.sofaexpo.com). Subway 6 to 68th Street-Hunter College. Date late May-early June. Map p405 E21.
Browse this giant show of Sculptural Objects and Functional Art and you might find that perfect conversation piece for your home.

SUMMER

Met in the Parks
Date June.
See p333.

Central Park SummerStage
Rumsey Playfield, Central Park, entrance on Fifth Avenue, at 72nd Street (1-212 360 2777/ www.summerstage.org). Subway 6 to 68th Street-Hunter College. Date June-Aug. Map p405 E20.
Central Park SummerStage is a festival that breaks down the boundaries between artistic mediums. Rockers, orchestras, authors and dance companies take over the stage at this very popular, mostly free annual series. Show up early or plan to listen from outside the gates (not a bad option if you bring a blanket and snacks). Tickets are needed for some benefit shows and special events.

River to River Festival.

ARTS & ENTERTAINMENT

Shakespeare in the Park
Date June-Aug.
See p353.

★ River to River Festival
Various venues along the West Side & southern waterfronts of Manhattan (no phone/www. rivertorivernyc.org). **Date** June-Sept.
Lower Manhattan organisations come together to present more than 500 free events (including everything from walks to all manner of arts performances) in some of the city's coolest waterfront venues. Performers in 2008 included Sonic Youth, Jill Sobule and Ted Leo.

Museum Mile Festival
Fifth Avenue, from 82nd to 105th Streets, Upper East Side (1-212 606 2296/www. museummilefestival.org). **Date** early June.
Who says high culture has to carry high prices? For one day a year, nine of Fifth Avenue's esteemed institutions – including the Guggenheim, the Met, Cooper-Hewitt National Design Museum and the Museum of the City of New York – welcome people free of charge. Music, dance and children's activities outside turn it into a massive block party-style celebration.

National Puerto Rican Day Parade
Fifth Avenue, from 44th to 86th Streets (1-718 401 0404). **Date** early June.
Salsa music blares, and scantily clad revellers dance along the route or ride colourful floats at this free-wheeling celebration of the city's single largest Hispanic community.

Broadway Bares
Roseland Ballroom, 239 W 52nd Street, between Broadway & Eighth Avenue, Theater District (1-212 840 0770/www.broadwaycares.org). Subway 1 to 50th Street. **Date** mid June.
Map p404 D23.
Equal parts ingenious and unusual, this annual fundraiser for Broadway Cares/Equity Fights AIDS is your chance to see some of the Great White Way's hottest bodies sans costumes. Broadway Cares also hosts an annual auction of autographed teddy bears ('Broadway Bears') in February, and a show-tune-filled Easter Bonnet Competition in April, as well as theatre-themed events throughout the year.

Egg Rolls & Egg Creams Festival
Eldridge Street Synagogue, 12 Eldridge Street, between Canal & Division Streets, Lower East Side (1-212 219 0903/www.eldridgestreet.org). Subway B, D to Grand Street; F to East Broadway. **Date** mid June. **Map** p402 F31.
A block party celebrating the convergence of Jewish and Chinese traditions on the Lower East Side, with acrobats, yarmulke makers, Torah scribes, language lessons and, of course, plenty of the titular treats.

JVC Jazz Festival
Date last 2wks June.
See p325.

★ Mermaid Parade
Coney Island, Brooklyn (1-718 372 5159/ www.coneyisland.com). Subway D, F, N, Q to Coney Island-Stillwell Avenue. **Date** 20 June.
Decked-out mermaids and mermen of all shapes, sizes and ages share the parade route with elaborate, kitschy floats, come rain or shine. It's the wackiest summer solstice event you'll see, and draws a suitably diverse crowd. Check the website for details; the parade location varies each year. *Photos pp264-265.*

★ LGBT Pride March
From Fifth Avenue, at 52nd Street, to Christopher Street (1-212 807 7433/ www.nycpride.org). **Date** 28 June.
Downtown Manhattan becomes a sea of rainbow flags as lesbian, gay, bisexual and transgendered people from the city and beyond parade down Fifth Avenue in commemoration of the 1969 Stonewall Riots. After the march, there's a massive street fair and a dance on the West Side piers.

Summer Restaurant Week
Various locations (no phone/www.nycvisit.com/ restaurantweek). **Date** late June/early July.
Gastronomes take note: twice a year, for two weeks at a stretch, some of the city's finest restaurants dish out three-course prix-fixe lunches for around $24; some places also offer dinner for $35. For the full list of participating restaurants, visit the website. The whole thing is, not surprisingly, extremely popular and if you want to take advantage of the deal you're advised to make reservations well in advance.
▶ *See p200 Deals on Meals for other gourmet bargains to be had in the city.*

★ Midsummer Night Swing
Lincoln Center Plaza, Columbus Avenue, between 64th & 65th Streets, Upper West Side (1-212 875 5766/www.lincolncenter.org). Subway 1 to 66th Street-Lincoln Center. **Date** late June-mid July. **Map** p405 C21.
Lincoln Center's plaza is turned into a giant dance-floor as bands play salsa, Cajun, swing and other music. Each night is devoted to a different dance style; parties are preceded by lessons.

Celebrate Brooklyn! Performing Arts Festival
Prospect Park Bandshell, Prospect Park West, at 9th Street, Park Slope, Brooklyn (1-718 855 7882/www.celebratebrooklyn.org). Subway F to Seventh Avenue. **Date** late June-late Aug.
Map p410 T12.
A series of major outdoor events includes music, dance, film and spoken word acts. A $3 donation is requested, and admission charged for some shows.

ARTS & ENTERTAINMENT

Mermaid Parade. *See p263.*

New York Philharmonic Concerts in the Parks
Date July-Aug.
See p333.

★ P.S.1 Warm Up
For listing, see p136. P.S.1 Contemporary
Art Center. **Date** July-Sept.
Since 1997, this weekly Saturday afternoon bash (2-9pm) in the museum's courtyard has drawn fashionable types from all over the city to dance, drink beer and relax in a beach-like environment. Local and international DJs and bands provide the seriously diverse soundtrack.

Nathan's Famous Fourth of July Hot Dog Eating Contest
Outside Nathan's Famous, corner of Surf
& Stillwell Avenues, Coney Island, Brooklyn
(1-718 946 2202/www.nathansfamous.com).
Subway D, F, N, Q to Coney Island-Stillwell
Avenue. **Date** 4 July.
Liable to amuse and appal in equal measure, this annual Fourth of July event organised by the 93-year-old Coney Island hotdog vendor holds an undeniable fascination. Eaters gather from all over the world for the granddaddy of all pig-out contests. Maybe not suitable for the fastidious.

Macy's Fireworks Display
East River, location varies (1-212 494 4495).
Date 4 July.
This world-famous annual fireworks display is the city's star attraction on Independence Day. The pyrotechnics are launched from barges on the East River at around 9pm, so look for outdoor vantage points along the lower FDR Drive (which is closed to traffic for the event), the Brooklyn and Long Island City waterfronts, or on Roosevelt Island. Keep in mind, however, that spectators are packed like sardines at prime public spots, so many choose to keep their distance.

Bastille Day on 60th Street
60th Street, between Fifth & Lexington Avenues
(no phone/www.bastilledaynyc.com). Subway N,
R, W to Fifth Avenue-59th Street; 4, 5, 6 to 59th
Street. **Date** 14 July. **Map** p405 E22.
Francophiles flock to this festival on France's answer to the Fourth of July for cancan dancing, pommes frites, pétanque and all manner of other Gallic attractions.

Lincoln Center Out of Doors Festival
For listing, see p351 Lincoln Center. **Date** Aug.
Map p405 C21.
Free dance, music, theatre, opera and more make up the programme at this family-friendly and ambitious festival organised by Lincoln Center.

New York International Fringe Festival
Various locations (1-212 279 4488/
www.fringenyc.org). **Date** Aug.
Wacky and sometimes wonderful, Downtown's Fringe Festival shoehorns hundreds of performances into 16 theatre-crammed days.
▶ *See p355 for more information on*
Off-Off Broadway shows.

Harlem Week
Various Harlem locations (1-212 862 8477/
www.harlemdiscover.com). Subway B, C, 2, 3
to 135th Street. **Date** Aug.
Get into the groove at this massive street fair, which
serves up music, art and food along 135th Street. In
fact, 'week' is now a misnomer: concerts, film, dance,
fashion and sports events are on tap all month.

Central Park Zoo Chillout! Weekend
Central Park, entrance on Fifth Avenue, at 65th
Street (1-212 439 6500/www.centralparkzoo.org).
Subway N, R, W to Fifth Avenue-59th Street;
4, 5, 6 to 59th Street. **Date** early Aug. **Map**
p405 E21.
If you're roaming the city during the dog days of
August, especially with overheated children, this
two-day party is the perfect chilly antidote. The
weekend freeze-fest features penguin and polar-bear
shows, ice carvers, games and other frosty fun.

Spiegelworld
South Street Seaport, Pier 17, Fulton Street,
at South Street (1-212 279 4200/www.spiegel
world.com). Subway A, C to Broadway-Nassau
Street; J, M, Z, 2, 3, 4, 5 to Fulton Street. **Dates**
Aug-Nov. **Map** p402 F33.
Spiegelworld's collection of sumptuous tents, complete with an outdoor bar and a line-up of stellar performers, arrives on the waterfront for a few months
of rousing entertainment. The schedule is always
packed with a diverse array of performers, such as
burlesque, drag, family-friendly fare, artistic
activism and all kinds of music.

AUTUMN

Howl!
Various East Village locations (1-212 505 2225/
www.howlfestival.com). Date early Sept.
Taking its name from the seminal poem by long-
time neighbourhood resident Allen Ginsberg, this
buzzing five-day Beat and Boho fest is a grab bag
of art events, film screenings, poetry readings, performance art and much more.

West Indian-American Day Carnival
Eastern Parkway, from Utica Avenue to Grand
Army Plaza, Brooklyn (1-718 467 1797/www.
wiadca.org). Subway 2, 3 to Grand Army Plaza; 3,
4 to Crown Heights-Utica Avenue. **Date** 7 Sept.
The streets come alive with the jubilant clangour of
steel drum bands and the steady throb of calypso
and soca music at this colourful cultural celebration.
Mas bands – elaborately costumed marchers –
dance along the parade route, thousands move to the
beat on the pavement, and vendors sell Caribbean
crafts, clothing, souvenirs and food.

Broadway on Broadway
43rd Street, at Broadway, Theater District (1-
212 768 1560/www.broadwayonbroadway.com).
Subway N, Q, R, S, W, 1, 2, 3, 7 to 42nd Street-
Times Square. **Date** mid Sept. **Map** p404 D24.
At the start of each theatre season, Broadway's
biggest stars convene for one night in the middle of
Times Square to belt out show-stopping numbers.
The season's new productions mount sneak pre-
views, and it's all free.

INSIDE TRACK
DELACORTE THEATRE

Jet-lagged visitors are ideally placed to snag tickets to a star-studded show at summer's Shakespeare in the Park. Opt for a weekday and line up at the Delacorte Theater as early as 6am. Bring something to read, a blanket or folding chair if possible – plus local takeout menus so you can order food to be delivered from your mobile phone.

Feast of San Gennaro
Mulberry Street, from Canal to Houston Streets, Little Italy (1-212 768 9320/www.san gennaro.org). Subway B, D, F, V to Broadway-Lafayette Street; J, M, N, Q, R, W, Z, 6 to Canal Street. **Date** mid Sept. **Map** p404 F30.
This massive 11-day street fair stretches along the main drag of what's left of Little Italy. Come on opening and closing days to see the marching band of old-timers, or after dark, when sparkling lights arch over Mulberry Street and the smells of frying *zeppole* (custard- or jam-filled fritters) and sausages hang in the sultry air.

Art Under the Bridge Festival
Various locations in Dumbo, Brooklyn (1-718 694 0831/www.dumboartscenter.org). Subway A, C to High Street; F to York Street. **Date** late Sept.
Dumbo has been an artists' enclave for decades, and this weekend of art appreciation is hugely popular with the many local creative types. The festival progamme features concerts, forums, a short-film series and studio visits.

New York Film Festival
Date late Sept-mid Oct.
See p304.

Atlantic Antic
Atlantic Avenue, from Fourth Avenue to Hicks Street, Brooklyn (1-718 875 8993/www.atlanticave.org). Subway B, Q, 2, 3, 4, 5 to Atlantic Avenue; D, M, N, R to Pacific Street. **Date** early Oct.
Entertainment, ethnic food, kids' activities and the inimitable World Cheesecake-Eating Contest pack the avenue with wide-eyed punters at this monumental Brooklyn festival.

Open House New York
Various locations (1-917 583 2398/www.ohny.org). **Date** early Oct.
Get an insider's view – literally – of the city that even most locals haven't seen. More than 100 sites of architectural interest that are normally off-limits to the public throw open their doors and welcome curious visitors during a weekend of urban exploration. A range of lectures and an educational programme are also on offer all week.

Next Wave Festival
For listing, see p330 Brooklyn Academy of Music. **Date** early Oct-mid Dec.
The best of the best in the city's avant-garde music, dance, theatre and opera scenes are performed at this lengthy annual affair.

CMJ Music Marathon & FilmFest
Various locations (1-917 606 1908/www.cmj.com). **Date** late Oct.
The annual *College Music Journal* schmooze-fest draws thousands of fans and music-industry types to one of the best showcases for new rock, indie rock, hip hop and electronica acts. The FilmFest, which runs in tandem with the music blow-out, includes a wide range of feature and short films, many music-related, and pulls in a suitably hip crowd.

Village Halloween Parade
Sixth Avenue, from Spring to 21st Streets (no phone/www.halloween-nyc.com). **Date** 31 Oct.
The sidewalks at this iconic Village shindig are always packed beyond belief. For the best vantage point, don a costume and watch from inside the parade (line-up starts at 6.30pm on Sixth Avenue, at Spring Street; the parade kicks off at 7pm).

New York City Marathon
Staten Island side of the Verrazano-Narrows Bridge, to Tavern on the Green, in Central Park (1-212 423 2249/www.nycmarathon.org). **Date** 1 Nov.
Catch sight of 35,000 marathoners as they hotfoot it (or, alternatively, puff, pant and stagger) through all five boroughs over a 26.2-mile course. Scope out a spot somewhere in the middle to get a good view of the passing herd.

Macy's Thanksgiving Day Parade & Eve Balloon Blowup
Central Park West, at 77th Street to Macy's, Broadway, at 34th Street (1-212 494 4495/www.macysparade.com). **Date** 25, 26 Nov.
The stars of this nationally televised parade, at 9am on Thanksgiving Day, are the gigantic balloons, elaborate floats and good ol' Santa Claus. The evening before, New Yorkers brave the cold night air to watch the rubbery colossi take their shape at the inflation area (from 77th to 81st Streets, between Central Park West & Columbus Avenue).

Radio City Christmas Spectacular
For listing, see p323 Radio City Music Hall. **Date** Nov-early Jan.

The high-kicking Rockettes and an onstage nativity scene with live animals are the attractions at this (pricey) annual homage to the Yuletide season.

Christmas Tree-Lighting Ceremony
Rockefeller Center, Fifth Avenue, between 49th & 50th Streets (1-212 332 6868/www.rockefeller center.com). Subway B, D, F, V to 47th-50th Streets-Rockefeller Center. **Date** late Nov/early Dec. **Map** p404 E23.
The crowds can be overwhelming here, even if you stake out a place early. Those who brave them will witness celebrity appearances and pop-star performances. But there's plenty of time during the holiday season to marvel at the giant evergreen.

WINTER
Unsilent Night
Washington Square arch, Fifth Avenue, at Waverly Place, to Tompkins Square Park (no phone/www.unsilentnight.com). Subway A, B, C, E, D, F, V to W 4th Street. **Date** mid Dec.
Phil Kline's boom box chorale parade has become a bona fide holiday tradition: his luminous, shimmering wash of bell tones is one of the loveliest communal new music experiences you'll ever witness.

National Chorale Messiah Sing-In
Avery Fisher Hall, Lincoln Center, Columbus Avenue, at 65th Street (1-212 333 5333/www.lincolncenter.org or www.nationalchorale.org). Subway 1 to 66th Street-Lincoln Center. **Date** mid Dec. **Map** p405 C21.
Hallelujah! Chase those holiday blues away by joining with the National Chorale and hundreds of your fellow audience members in a rehearsal and performance of Handel's *Messiah*. No previous singing experience is necessary to take part, and you can buy the score on site, though picking one up early for advance perusal would certainly help novices.

New Year's Eve Ball Drop
Times Square, Theater District (1-212 768 1560/www.timessquarenyc.org). Subway N, Q, R, S, W, 1, 2, 3, 7 to 42nd Street-Times Square. **Date** 31 Dec. **Map** p404 D24.
Meet up with half a million others and watch the giant illuminated ball descend amid a blizzard of confetti and cheering. Expect freezing temperatures, densely packed crowds, absolutely no public conveniences – and very tight security.

New Year's Eve Fireworks
Naumburg Bandshell, middle of Central Park, at 72nd Street (1-212 310-6600/www.central parknyc.org). Subway B, C to 72nd Street; 6 to 68th Street-Hunter College. **Date** 31 Dec. **Map** p405 E20.

The fireworks explode at midnight, and there's a variety of evening festivities, including dancing and a costume contest. The best views are from Tavern on the Green (at 67th Street), Central Park West (at 72nd Street) and Fifth Avenue (at 90th Street).

New Year's Eve Midnight Run
Naumburg Bandshell, middle of Central Park, at 72nd Street (1-212 860 4455/www.nyrrc.org). Subway B, C to 72nd Street; 6 to 68th Street-Hunter College. **Date** 31 Dec. **Map** p405 E20.
If you have managed to stay sober, you can see in the new year with a four-mile jog through the park. There's also a masquerade parade, fireworks, prizes and a (booze-free) toast at the halfway mark.

New Year's Day Marathon Poetry Reading
For listing, see p280 Poetry Project. **Date** 1 Jan.
Some big-name Bohemians (Patti Smith, Richard Hell, Jim Carroll) step up to the mic during this all-day spoken-word spectacle.

Winter Antiques Show
Seventh Regiment Armory, 643 Park Avenue, between 66th & 67th Streets, Upper East Side (1-718 292 7392/www.winterantiquesshow.com). Subway 6 to 68th Street-Hunter College. **Date** late Jan. **Map** p405 E21.
One of the world's most prestigious antiques shows, this event brings together more than 70 American and international dealers for ten days.

Winter Restaurant Week
For listing, see p263 Summer Restaurant Week. **Date** late Jan/early Feb.
The Winter Restaurant Week provides yet another opportunity to sample delicious gourmet food at soup kitchen prices (well, almost).

Chinese New Year
Around Mott Street, Chinatown (1-212 966 0100). Subway J, M, N, Q, R, W, Z, 6 to Canal Street. **Date** late Jan/early Feb.
Gung hay fat choy!, the greeting goes. Chinatown bustles with colour and is charged with energy during the two weeks of the Lunar New Year. Festivities on hand include a staged fireworks display, a vivid dragon parade, various performances and a predictable wealth of delicious Chinese food.

Art Show
Seventh Regiment Armory, 643 Park Avenue, between 66th & 67th Streets, Upper East Side (1-212 488 5550/www.artdealers.org). Subway 6 to 68th Street-Hunter College. **Date** late Feb. **Map** p405 E21.
Whether you're a serious collector or just a casual art fan, this vast fair is a great chance to peruse some of the world's most impressive for-sale pieces dating from the 17th century to the present.

ARTS & ENTERTAINMENT

Art Galleries

See and be seen on a circuit that now stretches far beyond Manhattan.

Despite the growing popularity of international art fairs, New York City remains the *ne plus ultra* of all art scenes, drawing aficionados from all over the world to its ever-increasing selection of galleries. New spaces seem to open every day, both in high-profile areas and at more unusual locations such as bookstores, in shopfront windows – even private homes. There's no doubt that Chelsea still offers the greatest concentration of galleries in the city but these days the Lower East Side is rapidly gaining a reputation as the city's new art hotspot.

COMMERCIAL GALLERIES

In **Chelsea**'s sleek white cubes, you'll find group shows by up-and-comers, blockbuster exhibits from art-world celebrities as well as a slew of provocative work. However, dozens of venues have quite recently cropped up in the **Lower East Side**, close to the recently opened New Museum of Contemporary Art (*see p80*), many of which have riskier programmes than their uptown counterparts. **Soho** is also seeing a resurgence, with a scattering of galleries popping up in tandem with the Lower East Side boom. Distance from the Chelsea scene allows venues to execute riskier agendas, and some of the city's best work is shown in these galleries.

Uptown, the Museum Mile galleries cater to more traditional tastes and show the work of mid-career and established artists alongside the old masters, while the old-guard 57th Street crew turns out a continuous series of blue-chip shows. In Brooklyn, **Williamsburg** has a number of top-quality galleries around Bedford Avenue. Queens' artistic hotbed lies in **Long Island City**, where MoMA's scrappier sibling P.S.1 Contemporary Art Center (*see p136*) never fails to gratify the art pilgrims who venture there. Check www.licartists.org for events in the area.

Note that galleries are generally closed on Mondays, and many are open only on weekdays from May or June to early September – some

---

About the author
TJ Carlin *is Art Listings Editor of* Time Out New York *magazine, and also contributes to* Art Review.

close for the whole of August. We've listed summer hours for most venues, but it's always wise to call before heading out. *Time Out New York* magazine has the latest listings and reviews, and the Friday and Sunday editions of the *New York Times* feature art news and comment. For extensive listings, pick up the monthly *Gallery Guide* (www.galleryguide. org), free in many galleries or around $3 at newsstands across the city. Sites such as ArtCal (www.artcal.net) also list opening receptions.

Soho

Subway A, C, E, J, M, N, Q, R, W, Z, 1, 6 to Canal Street; B, D, F, V to Broadway-Lafayette Street; N, R, W to Prince Street; 6 to Spring Street.

★ Deitch Projects

18 Wooster Street, between Canal & Grand Streets (1-212 343 7300/www.deitch.com). **Open** noon-6pm Tue-Sat. **Map** p403 E30.
Jeffrey Deitch is an art-world impresario whose gallery features live spectacles, as well as large-scale, ambitious efforts by artists such as Yoko Ono and Michel Gondry. Some credit Deitch with initiating the art market craze as we know it today. **Other locations** 6 Grand Street, at Wooster Street, Soho (1-212 343 7300).

Gavin Brown

620 Greenwich Street, at Leroy Street (1-212 627 5258/www.gavinbrown.biz). **Open** *Sept-June* 10am-6pm Tue-Sat. *July, Aug* 10am-6pm Mon-Fri. **Map** p403 D29.

Brown always has his finger on the pulse. The London native has given starts to such art stars as Elizabeth Peyton, who had a solo show at the New Museum of Contemporary Art in autumn 2008. This informal gallery also showcases the creative output of Rob Pruitt and Peter Doig, among others.

★ Guild & Greyshkul
28 Wooster Street, between Canal & Grand Streets (1-212 625 9224/www.guildgreyshkul.com). **Open** *Sept-July* 11am-6pm Tue.-Sat. **Map** p403 E30.
Three up-and-coming artists, Sara and Johannes VanDerBeek (children of the late filmmaker Stan VanDerBeek) plus friend Anya Kielar, opened this studio and exhibition space on Wooster Street in 2003 with the aim of fostering intellectual exchange among their peers. The roster of artists is largely drawn from graduates of Columbia University's MFA programme.

Harris Lieberman
89 Vandam Street, between Greenwich & Hudson Streets (1-212 206 1290/www.harris lieberman.com). **Open** *Sept-June* 11am-6pm Tue-Sat. *July, Aug* 11am-6pm Tue-Fri. **Map** p403 D30.
This outpost near the Hudson was launched in 2005 by a husband-and-wife team, both long-time directors on the Chelsea scene. Their wide range of experience, coupled with a keen eye, translates to a young international stable.

Maccarone
630 Greenwich Street, at Morton Street (1-212 431 4977/www.maccarone.net). **Open** *Sept-June* 10am-6pm Tue-Sat. *July, Aug* 10am-6pm Mon-Fri. **Map** p403 D29.

INSIDE TRACK
DEITCH PROJECTS

If you're here in early September, don't miss **Deitch Projects'** (*see p268*) annual Art Parade. This procession of artist-made floats and performances wends it way down West Broadway in celebration of the beginning of the autumn gallery season.

The former Luhring Augustine director Michele Maccarone, an outspoken dealer and activist for artists, holds court in this 8,000sq ft space, where she dedicates herself to representing artists such as Nate Lowman, Corey McCorkle and Christian Jankowski.

Peter Blum
99 Wooster Street, between Prince & Spring Streets (1-212 343 0441/www.peterblum gallery.com). **Open** *Sept-July* 10am-6pm Tue-Fri; 11am-6pm Sat. **Map** p403 E30.
This elegant space is manned by a dealer with an impeccable eye and wide tastes. Past exhibitions have run the gamut from drawings by Robert Ryman and Alex Katz to terracotta funerary figures from West Africa and colourful quilts from the hands of noted African-American folk artist Rosie Lee Tompkins.

Team Gallery
83 Grand Street, between Greene & Wooster Streets (1-212 279 9219/www.teamgal.com). **Open** *Oct-May* 10am-6pm Tue-Sat. *June-Sept* 10am-6pm Mon-Fri. **Map** p403 E30.

ARTS & ENTERTAINMENT

Rivington Arms. *See p270.*

Andrea Rosen Gallery.

Gallery owner José Freire relocated from an überhip Chelsea address to this high-ceilinged space in 2006, indicating that downtown is the place to be. The gallery is host to such hotshots as Cory Arcangel and Ryan McGinley, and also represents more established artists including Ross Knight.

Lower East Side

Subway F to East Broadway or Delancey Street; F, V to Lower East Side-Second Avenue; J, M, Z to Delancey-Essex Streets.

★ CANADA
55 Chrystie Street, between Canal & Hester Streets (1-212 925 4631/www.canadanewyork. com). **Open** *Sept-mid Aug* noon-6pm Wed-Sun. **Map** p403 F30.
A trailblazer of the Chinatown/Lower East Side gallery phenomenon, CANADA opened its doors at the foot of the Manhattan Bridge in 2000. Its artist/curator/directors strive to support a wide range of work – from paintings and mixed-media installations to performance – by artists such as Devendra Banhart, Michael Mahalchick and Carrie Moyer. Expect an eclectic programme of events, such as book launches and experimental music shows, alongside the exhibitions.

★ Miguel Abreu Gallery
36 Orchard Street, between Canal & Hester Streets (1-212 995 1774/www.miguelabreu gallery.com). **Open** *Sept-July* 11am-6.30pm Wed-Sun. *Aug* by appointment only. **Map** p403 G30.

Since neighbouring project space Orchard closed in spring 2008, filmmaker Miguel Abreu has picked up the slack by hosting a highly intellectual series of performances, art theory seminars and film screenings. The gallery represents inspired artists such as Hans Bellmer, RH Quaytman and Eileen Quinlan.
▶ *See p76 for more on Orchard Street.*

Reena Spaulings Fine Art
165 East Broadway, at Rutgers Street (1-212 477 5006/www.reenaspaulings.com). **Open** *Sept-July* noon-6pm Thur-Sun. **Map** p402 G31.
What started as artist Emily Sundblad's storefront studio has, with help from critic and gallery co-founder John Kelsey, become a conceptual project: the space holds work by Spaulings, a fictional, collectively authored artist. Since 2004, the establishment has also held solo shows by US and European artists, including Seth Price, Jutta Koether and Josh Smith.

Rivington Arms
4 E 2nd Street, at Bowery (1-646 654 3213/ www.rivingtonarms.com). **Open** *Sept-July* 11am-6pm Tue-Fri; noon-6pm Sat, Sun. **Map** p403 F29.
This intimate storefront space, run by Melissa Bent and Mirabelle Marden (painter Brice Marden's daughter), has a fashionable following and tends to feature work by young, hip artists with a strong emphasis on painting and photography. *Photo p269.*

Chelsea

Subway A, C, E to 14th Street; C, E to 23rd Street; L to Eighth Avenue.

It can be hard to see even half the galleries in this neighbourhood in one day. The subway takes you only as far as Eighth Avenue, so you'll have to walk at least one long block west or take the M23 crosstown bus to reach the galleries.

★ Andrea Rosen Gallery

525 W 24th Street, between Tenth & Eleventh Avenues (1-212 627 6000/www.andrearosen gallery.com). **Open** *Sept-June* 10am-6pm Tue-Sat. *July, Aug* 10am-6pm Mon-Fri. **Map** p404 C26.
During the past 18 years, Andrea Rosen has established several major careers: the late Felix Gonzalez-Torres got his start here (the gallery now handles the artist's estate), as did Wolfgang Tillmans, Andrea Zittel and John Currin (who left for Gagosian in 2003). And there will probably be more to come – it also represents much-touted young sculptor David Altmejd. The work here is often characterised as formally beautiful and pleasing to the eye.

Andrew Kreps Gallery

525 W 22nd Street, between Tenth & Eleventh Avenues (1-212 741 8849/www.andrewkreps. com). **Open** *Sept-June* 10am-6pm Tue-Sat. *July, Aug* 10am-6pm Mon-Fri. **Map** p404 C26.
The radicals in Andrew Kreps's adventurous stable of artists include Ricci Albenda, Roe Ethridge, Robert Melee and Ruth Root.

Anton Kern Gallery

532 W 20th Street, between Tenth & Eleventh Avenues (1-212 367 9663/www.antonkern gallery.com). **Open** *Sept-June* 10am-6pm Tue-Sat. *July, Aug* 10am-6pm Mon-Fri. **Map** p403 C27.
The son of artist Georg Baselitz, Kern presents young American and European artists whose installations have provided the New York art scene with some of its most visionary shows. Kai Althoff, Sarah Jones and Jim Lambie have all been featured here.

★ Bellwether

134 Tenth Avenue, between 18th & 19th Streets (1-212 929 5959/www.bellwethergallery.com). **Open** *Sept-June* 10am-6pm Tue-Sat. *July, Aug* 11am-6pm Mon-Fri. **Map** p403 C27.
Becky Smith's popular gallery has been on a steady rise since its move from Brooklyn. Now one of the hottest spaces in Chelsea, Bellwether has been setting trends within the art world since 1999, and represents a list of promising talents including Anne Hardy, Daphne Fitzpatrick and Jansson Stegner.

★ D'Amelio Terras

525 W 22nd Street, between Tenth & Eleventh Avenues (1-212 352 9460/www.damelio terras.com). **Open** *Sept-May* 10am-6pm Tue-Sat. *June-Aug* 10am-6pm Mon-Fri. **Map** p404 B26.
D'Amelio Terras was one of the first spaces to set up shop in Chelsea, back in the 1990s. The gallery devotes the month of January to specially curated

examinations of post-war art in an effort to set the stage for and educate the public about the rest of its programme, which features museum-calibre artists such as Joanne Greenbaum, Matt Keegan and Cornelia Parker.

Daniel Reich Gallery

537A W 23rd Street, between Tenth & Eleventh Avenues (1-212 924 4949/www.danielreich gallery.com). **Open** *Sept-June* 11am-6pm Tue-Sat. *July, Aug* 11am-6pm Mon-Fri. **Map** p404 C26.
Young gallerist Daniel Reich exhibited works out of his tiny apartment before settling into this ground-floor space; he continues to use a room in the Chelsea Hotel as an outpost. Despite its white-cube setting, the gallery hosts a group of artists who think outside of the box, among them Christian Holstad, Susanne M Winterling and Futoshi Miyagi.

David Zwirner

519, 525 & 533 W 19th Street, between Tenth & Eleventh Avenues (1-212 727 2070/ www.davidzwirner.com). **Open** *Sept-June* 10am-6pm Tue-Sat. *July, Aug* 10am-6pm Mon-Fri. **Map** p403 C27.
German expatriate David Zwirner has assembled a head-turning array of international contemporary artists on his books that includes such luminaries as Marcel Dzama, Luc Tuymans, Chris Ofili, Neo Rauch and Lisa Yuskavage.

Friedrich Petzel Gallery

535 & 537 W 22nd Street, between Tenth & Eleventh Avenues (1-212 680 9467/www.petzel. com). **Open** *Sept-June* 10am-6pm Tue-Sat. *July, Aug* 10am-6pm Mon-Fri. **Map** p404 C26.
The Friedrich Petzel Gallery represents some of the brightest young stars on the international scene, so you can count on some intriguing shows. Sculptor Keith Edmier, photographer Dana Hoey, painter and filmmaker Sarah Morris and installation artists Jorge Pardo and Philippe Parreno all show here.

Gagosian Gallery

555 W 24th Street, between Tenth & Eleventh Avenues (1-212 741 1111/www.gagosian.com). **Open** *Sept-June* 10am-6pm Tue-Sat. *July-Aug* 10am-6pm Mon-Fri. **Map** p404 C26.
A massive figure on the international art scene, Larry Gagosian has hugely successful outposts in Los Angeles, London and Rome, as well as no fewer than three spaces scattered around New York City. His mammoth contribution to 24th Street's top-level galleries showcases work by such prominent art-world names as Richard Serra, Ellen Gallagher, Damien Hirst, Julian Schnabel, Georg Baselitz and Richard Artschwager.
Other locations 522 W 21st Street, between Tenth & Eleventh Avenues, Chelsea (1-212 741 1717); 980 Madison Avenue, at 76th Street, Upper East Side (1-212 744 2313).

ARTS & ENTERTAINMENT

Gladstone Gallery

515 W 24th Street, between Tenth & Eleventh Avenues (1-212 206 9300/www.gladstone gallery.com). **Open** *Sept-July* 10am-6pm Tue-Sat. *Aug* 10am-6pm Mon-Fri. **Map** p404 C26.
Gladstone is strictly blue-chip, focusing on such conceptualist and daring talents as Matthew Barney, Sarah Lucas and Anish Kapoor.

Greene Naftali

8th Floor, 508 W 26th Street, between Tenth & Eleventh Avenues (1-212 463 7770/www.greene naftaligallery.com). **Open** *Sept-June* 10am-6pm Tue-Sat. *July, Aug* 10am-6pm Mon-Fri. **Map** p404 C26.
You don't have to be an art lover to enjoy Greene Naftali, a gallery that's well worth visiting purely for its wonderful light and spectacular panorama. But the always-keen vision of Carol Greene outdoes even the gallery's eighth-floor view. Mavericks like sculptor Rachel Harrison and video artist Paul Chan put smiles on the faces of critics and punters alike.
▶ *While you're here, check out the striking Starrett-Lehigh Building down the road; see p91.*

John Connelly Presents

625 W 27th Street, between Eleventh & Twelfth Avenues (1-212 337 9563/www.johnconnelly presents.com). **Open** *Sept-June* 10am-6pm Tue-Sat. *July, Aug* 10am-6pm Mon-Fri. **Map** p404 B26.
Connelly, a long-time director of the Andrea Rosen Gallery, quickly earned a reputation as one of the most exciting young dealers around after he struck out on his own. In 2006, he and six other Chelsea gallerists moved their enterprises into a string of old loading dock bays along 27th Street, creating one of the hottest gallery-hopping blocks in the 'hood. Expect provocative works by emerging young artists, with an emphasis on installation.

Lehmann Maupin

540 W 26th Street, between Tenth & Eleventh Avenues (1-212 255 2923/www.lehmannmaupin. com). **Open** *Sept-June* 10am-6pm Tue-Sat. *July, Aug* 10am-6pm Mon-Fri. **Map** p404 C26.
Epic exhibitions in this Rem Koolhaas-designed former garage feature hip international artists – think Tracey Emin, Gilbert & George, Teresita Fernandez, Do-Ho Suh and Juergen Teller. It also recently opened an outpost in Manhattan's newest art neighbourhood, the Bowery.
Other locations 201 Chrystie Street, between Rivington & Stanton Streets, Lower East Side (1-212 254 0054).

Leo Koenig Inc

545 W 23rd Street, between Tenth & Eleventh Avenues (1-212 334 9255/www.leokoenig.com). **Open** *Sept-July* 10am-6pm Tue-Sat. **Map** p404 C26.
Koenig's father is Kasper Koenig, the internationally known curator and museum director, but Leo has been making a name for himself showcasing cutting-edge talents including Torben Giehler, Christian Schumann and Wendy White.

Luhring Augustine

531 W 24th Street, between Tenth & Eleventh Avenues (1-212 206 9100/www.luhring augustine.com). **Open** *Sept-June* 10am-6pm Tue-Sat. *July, Aug* 10am-5.30pm Mon-Fri. **Map** p404 C26.
Designed by Richard Gluckman, the area's architect of choice, this gallery features work from an impressive index of contemporary artists, such as British sculptor Rachel Whiteread, Swiss video star Pipilotti Rist and Americans Janine Antoni, Larry Clark and Gregory Crewdson.

Mary Boone Gallery

541 W 24th Street, between Tenth & Eleventh Avenues (1-212 752 2929/www.maryboone gallery.com). **Open** *Sept-June* 10am-6pm Tue-Sat. *July, Aug* by appointment only. **Map** p404 C26.
The gallery owner and art dealer Mary Boone made her name in the 1980s representing Julian Schnabel, Jean-Michel Basquiat and Francesco Clemente at her renowned Soho gallery. She later moved to Midtown and, in 2000, added this sweeping space in a former garage, showing established artists including David Salle, Barbara Kruger and Eric Fischl alongside up-and-comers such as Brian Alfred and Hilary Harkness.
Other locations 745 Fifth Avenue, between 57th & 58th Streets, Midtown (1-212 752 2929).

Matthew Marks Gallery

523 W 24th Street, between Tenth & Eleventh Avenues (1-212 243 0200/www.matthewmarks. com). **Open** *Sept-June* 11am-6pm Tue-Sat. *July-mid Aug* 11am-6pm Mon-Fri. **Map** p404 C26.
The Matthew Marks Gallery was a driving force behind Chelsea's transformation into one of the city's top art destinations and, with four outposts to its name, it remains one of the neighbourhood's powerhouses. The gallery showcases such internationally renowned talent as Robert Gober, Nan Goldin, Andreas Gursky, Ellsworth Kelly and Brice Marden.
Other locations 521 W 21st Street, 522 W 22st Street & 526 W 22nd Street, all between Tenth & Eleventh Avenues, Chelsea.

Metro Pictures

519 W 24th Street, between Tenth & Eleventh Avenues (1-212 206 7100/www.metropictures gallery.com). **Open** *Sept-June* 10am-6pm Tue-Sat. *July* 10am-6pm Mon-Fri. **Map** p404 C26.
Metro Pictures is best known for representing art-world superstar Cindy Sherman, along with such big contemporary names as multimedia artist Mike Kelley, Robert Longo (famous for his works produced using photography and charcoal) and the late German artist Martin Kippenberger.

Paula Cooper Gallery.

Paula Cooper Gallery

534 W 21st Street, between Tenth & Eleventh Avenues (1-212 255 1105/www.paulacooper gallery.com). **Open** *Sept-June* 10am-6pm Tue-Sat. *July, Aug* 10am-5pm Mon-Fri. **Map** p404 C26.
Cooper has built up an impressive art temple for worshippers of contemporary work, making its reputation on minimalist and conceptualist work (Andres Serrano, Carl Andre et al). You'll also see younger artists such as Kelley Walker and John Tremblay.
Other locations 521 W 21st Street, between Tenth & Eleventh Avenues, Chelsea (1-212 255 5247); 465 W 23rd Street, between Ninth & Tenth Avenues, Chelsea (1-212 255 1105).

Postmasters

459 W 19th Street, between Ninth & Tenth Avenues (1-212 727 3323/www.postmastersart. com). **Open** *Sept-June* 11am-6pm Tue-Sat. *July, Aug* by appointment only. **Map** p403 C27.

Run by savvy duo Magdalena Sawon and Tamas Banovich, Postmasters, displaying in a vast converted garage, emphasises technologically inflected art (most of which leans towards the conceptual) in the form of sculpture by David Herbert and Jack Risley, painting by Steve Mumford and David Diao and new media by artists such as Katarzyna Kozyra, Anthony Goicolea and Natalie Jeremijenko, among others. In addition, the gallery exhibits installations from the likes of Diana Cooper and Christian Schumann.

303 Gallery

525 W 22nd Street, between Tenth & Eleventh Avenues (1-212 255 1121/www.303gallery.com). **Open** *Sept-June* 10am-6pm Tue-Sat. *July, Aug* 10am-6pm Mon-Fri. **Map** p404 C26.
Rirkrit Tiravanija made his well-known Thai cooking sculpture debut at this gallery's old Soho location. Now relocated, the 303 currently represents

Doug Aitken, Stephen Shore, Thomas Demand and various other artists in the middle of their careers. Look out for 2009 exhibitions by Valentin Carron, Ceal Floyer and Laylah Ali.

Tracy Williams
313 W 4th Street, between Bank & W 12th Streets (1-212 229 2757/www.tracywilliams ltd.com). **Open** *Sept-June* 11am-6pm Tue-Sat. *July* 11am-6pm Mon-Fri. **Map** p403 D28.
Once senior vice president of contemporary art at both Sotheby's and Christie's, Williams opened a place of her own in her private 1840s townhouse during 2004. Visit the gallery on any opening night and you'll be rewarded with an alfresco jaunt in its charming back garden.

Zach Feuer/LFL
530 W 24th Street, between Tenth & Eleventh Avenues (1-212 989 7700/www.zachfeuer.com). **Open** *Oct-June* 10am-6pm Tue-Sat. *July-Sept* 10am-6pm Tue-Fri. **Map** p404 B26.
Feuer opened his first Chelsea space in 2000, when he was in his early twenties. Now in a new, more spacious location, with an emphasis on formal painting and sculpture, the gallery has amassed a roster of artists who are regularly exhibited in museums around the world. Look out for Phoebe Washburn's large-scale wood installations and works by hot painters Tal R and Dana Schutz.

57th Street & around

Subway E, V to Fifth Avenue-53rd Street; F to 57th Street; N, R, W to Fifth Avenue-59th Street.

Greenberg Van Doren Gallery
7th Floor, 730 Fifth Avenue, at 57th Street (1-212 445 0444/www.gvdgallery.com). **Open** *Sept-May* 10am-6pm Tue-Sat. *June-Aug* 10am-5pm Mon-Fri. **Map** p405 E22.
The uptown branch of this elegant gallery represents established artists James Brooks and Richard Diebenkorn, while the new downtown outpost, Eleven Rivington, focuses on emerging and international talent. Tim Davis and Benjamin Edwards are a few of the younger stars here.
Other locations 11 Rivington Street, between Bowery & Chrystie Street, Lower East Side (1-212 982 1930).

Marian Goodman Gallery
4th Floor, 24 W 57th Street, between Fifth & Sixth Avenues (1-212 977 7160/ www.mariangoodman.com). **Open** *Sept-June* 10am-6pm Tue-Sat. *July, Aug* 10am-6pm Mon-Fri. **Map** p405 E22.
This highly regarded space has an impressive host of renowned art-world names on its books. In particular, look out for John Baldessari, Christian

Boltanski, Maurizio Cattelan, Gabriel Orozco, Gerhard Richter, Thomas Struth and Jeff Wall, among many others.

McKee Gallery
4th Floor, 745 Fifth Avenue, between 57th & 58th Streets (1-212 688 5951/www.mckee gallery.com). **Open** *Sept-May* 10am-6pm Tue-Sat. *June, July* 10am-5pm Mon-Fri. *Aug* by appointment only. **Map** p405 E22.
McKee's major claim to fame is the estate of art legend Philip Guston. Need another reason to visit? You'll also find the work of Martin Puryear, Vija Celmins and the playful Jeanne Silverthorne in this extremely airy Midtown space.

Pace Wildenstein
2nd Floor, 32 E 57th Street, between Madison & Park Avenues (1-212 421 3292/www.pace wildenstein.com). **Open** *Sept-May* 9.30am-6pm Tue-Sat. *June-Aug* 9.30am-6pm Mon-Thur; 9.30am-4pm Fri. **Map** p405 E22.
To view shows by a few of the 20th century's most significant artists, head to this institution, where you'll find pieces by such notables as Chuck Close, Agnes Martin, Pablo Picasso, Elizabeth Murray and Kiki Smith. The Pace Prints division at this location exhibits works on paper by everyone from old masters to notable contemporaries (a stand-alone contemporary-only outpost recently opened in Chelsea). The gallery also deals in fine ethnic and world art.
Other locations 545 W 22nd Street (1-212 989 4258), 534 W 25th Street (1-212 929 7000), 521 W 26th Street (1-212 629 6100); all between Tenth & Eleventh Avenues, Chelsea.

Project
3rd Floor, 37 W 57th Street, between Fifth & Sixth Avenues (1-212 688 1585/www.elproyecto. com). **Open** *Sept-June* 10am-6pm Mon-Sat. *July, Aug* 10am-5pm Mon-Fri. **Map** p405 E22.
This gallery has been the darling of European critics and curators since it opened to a flurry of excitement in 1998, and its move from Harlem to Midtown in summer 2003 only increased its keen following among press and public alike. Expect Project to exhibit work by acclaimed young artists along the lines of Julie Mehretu, Peter Rostovsky and Stephen Vitiello.

★ Tibor de Nagy
12th Floor, 724 Fifth Avenue, between 56th & 57th Streets (1-212 262 5050/www.tibordenagy. com). **Open** *Sept-May* 10am-5.30pm Tue-Sat. *June-Aug* 10am-5.30pm Mon-Fri. **Map** p405 E22.
While this long-standing gallery presents contemporary work in several media, the real speciality here is painting, particularly landscapes, although there are a couple of worthwhile collagists among the coterie. Real standouts include Tom Burckhardt, and Jess and Sarah McEneaney.

ARTS & ENTERTAINMENT

Upper East Side

Subway 6 to 68th Street-Hunter College or 77th Street.

Knoedler & Company
19 E 70th Street, between Fifth & Madison Avenues (1-212 794 0550/www.knoedler gallery.com). **Open** *Sept-May* 9.30am-5.30pm Tue-Sat. *June-Aug* 9.30am-5pm Mon-Fri. **Map** p405 E20.
Opened in 1846, this is the oldest gallery in New York. It continues to uphold its formidable reputation by exhibiting museum-quality post-war work and excellent contemporary art from the likes of Lee Bontecou and John Walker.

L&M Arts
45 E 78th Street, at Madison Avenue (1-212 861 0020/www.lmgallery.com). **Open** *Sept-June* 10am-5.30pm Tue-Sat. *July, Aug* 10am-5pm Mon-Fri. **Map** p405 E19.
Here lies Yves Klein's United States headquarters, the estate of Joseph Cornell and a stable of artists (Sol LeWitt, Agnes Martin, Louise Bourgeois) that reads like a best-of list for the 20th century.

★ Zwirner & Wirth
32 E 69th Street, between Madison & Park Avenues (1-212 517 8677/www.zwirner andwirth.com). **Open** *Sept-June* 10am-6pm Tue-Sat. *July, Aug* 10am-6pm Mon-Fri. **Map** p405 E20.
Zwirner & Wirth, located in a stylishly renovated townhouse, exhibits a wide range of modern and contemporary masters along the lines of Dan Flavin, Martin Kippenberger and Bruce Nauman. The gallery combines the art know-how of New York gallerist David Zwirner and his London-based partner, gallerist Iwan Wirth.

Brooklyn

Brooklynite Gallery
334 Malcolm X Boulevard, between Bainbridge & Decatur Streets, Bedford-Stuyvesant (1-347 405 5976/www.brooklynitegallery.com). Subway A, C to Utica Avenue. **Open** 1-7pm Thur-Sat. **Map** p410 W10.
This pioneer in Bed-Stuy has a rad LED display above the entrance and a beautiful backyard with a building façade made entirely of recycled fridge doors. The gallery's programme, which concentrates on pop and street art from around the world, is equally compelling.
▶ *For more on Brooklyn's art scene, see p128.*

Jack the Pelican Presents
487 Driggs Avenue, between North 9th & 10th Streets, Williamsburg (1-718 782 0183/ www.jackthepelicanpresents.com). Subway L
to Bedford Avenue. **Open** noon-6pm Mon, Thur-Sun. **Map** p411 U7.
While many of partners Don Carroll and Matt Zalla's peers have jumped ship to the island, these two prove that Brooklyn can still keep it real. Jack the Pelican is known for a relaxed atmosphere (the space opens on to the sidewalk of one of Williamsburg's more popular streets) and offbeat art.

★ Pierogi
177 North 9th Street, between Bedford & Driggs Avenues, Williamsburg (1-718 599 2144/www. pierogi2000.com). Subway L to Bedford Avenue. **Open** 11am-6pm Tue-Sun; also by appointment. **Map** p411 U7.
Pierogi, one of Williamsburg's established galleries, presents the Flat Files, a series of drawers containing works on paper by some 800 artists. Don't pass up the chance to don the special white gloves and handle the archived artwork yourself.

NOT-FOR-PROFIT SPACES

apexart
291 Church Street, between Walker & White Streets, Tribeca (1-212 431 5270/www. apexart.org). Subway J, M, N, Q, R, W, Z, 6 to Canal Street; 1 to Franklin Street. **Open** *Sept-July* 11am-6pm Tue-Sat. **Map** p402 E31.
Founded in 1994 by artist Steven Rand, apexart gets its inspiration from the independent critics, curators and artists selected for its curatorial programme, which tends to dictate rather than follow prevailing fashions in the art world.

Artists Space
3rd Floor, 38 Greene Street, at Grand Street, Soho (1-212 226 3970/www.artistsspace.org). Subway A, C, E to Canal Street. **Open** *Sept-June* 11am-6pm Tue-Sat. *July* 11am-5pm Tue-Fri. **Map** p403 E30.
Open since 1972, this space exhibits a diverse crew of young artists working in all media. The organisation also plays host to one of the largest artist registries in the country.

INSIDE TRACK
BEYOND WILLIAMSBURG

Williamsburg is the uncontested hub of Brooklyn's art scene, but edgier spaces have recently started to spring up in other parts of the borough – there's a thriving street-art enclave in **Bushwick** (*see p276* **Off the streets**), for instance. For a printable map of the area's venues, see www.williamsburggallery association.com.

ARTS & ENTERTAINMENT

Off the Streets

An enclave of Brooklyn galleries brings street art inside.

Ever notice sneakers hanging from power lines? Look up in Brooklyn and you will. Legend has it that the inner-city practice once marked the territory of nearby drug dealers, signalled street deaths or possibly even celebrated lost virginity.

Growing up, Adam ('Ad') Deville and his identical twin Andrew ('Droo') were fascinated by these urban myths. In 1999, under the collaborative name Skewville, the Queens natives started decorating utility lines with their own handmade, two-dimensional plywood shoes. A decade later, they've flung more than 3,000 pairs on utility lines around the world – and such public-space-invading visual projects now have their own genre: 'street art'.

Recently, Ad's focus has moved indoors. In summer 2008, he and fiancée Ali Ha (aka fabric artist Pufferella) opened **Factory Fresh** (1053 Flushing Avenue, between Kickerbocker Avenue & Vandervoort Place, 1-917 682 6753, www.factoryfresh.net, closed Mon, Tue), a Brooklyn gallery that shows the work of street-art photographers, up-and-coming illustrators and, naturally, Skewville.

Deville's spot is the most recent addition to Bushwick's 'Gang of Four', a loose-knit community of like-minded art spaces within walking distance of the Morgan Avenue L train stop. Others include **English Kills** (114 Forrest Street, off Flushing Avenue, 1-718 366 7323, www.englishkillsartgallery.com, closed Mon-Fri), a hulking warehouse and studio that in 2008 hosted a blacklit installation from collage-artist prankster Judith Supine; and **Ad Hoc Art** (49 Bogart Street, at Grattan Street, 1-718 366 2466, www.adhocart.org, closed Mon, Tue), a heavily trafficked gallery that specialises in the new contemporary art movement and has a particular affinity with street artists such as wheatpaste master Swoon, urban-flower painter Michael DeFeo and spraypaint legend Lady Pink.

But the biggest similarity among the four is attitude: they're all welcoming to visitors. This is especially true at **Pocket Utopia** (1037 Flushing Avenue, between Morgan Avenue & Vandervoot Place, 1-917 400 3869, www.pocketutopia.com, closed Mon-Fri), an abandoned hair salon that's been converted into an experimental art nook by curator Austin Thomas and turned into the kind of jovially inviting place that describes itself as ideal for 'exhibiting, socialising… and eating egg rolls!' You'd be lucky to get crackers in Chelsea.

Factory Fresh.

ARTS & ENTERTAINMENT

Dorsky Gallery
11-03 45th Avenue, at 11th Street, Long Island City, Queens (1-718 937 6317/www.dorsky.org). Subway E, V (V weekdays only) to 23rd Street-Ely Avenue. **Open** *Sept-June* 11am-6pm Mon-Thur, Sun. *July, Aug* 9am-5pm Mon-Fri. **Map** p412 V5.
This slightly out-of-the-way nonprofit is well worth the trek; for over a decade the venue has been sponsoring shows by independent curators and putting on symposia and artists' talks events.

★ Drawing Center
35 Wooster Street, between Broome & Grand Streets, Soho (1-212 219 2166/www.drawing center.org). Subway A, C, E, J, M, N, Q, R, W, Z, 6 to Canal Street. **Open** *Sept-July* 10am-6pm Tue-Fri; 11am-6pm Sat.* **Map** p403 E30.
A stronghold of works on paper, this 30-year-old Soho standout assembles critically acclaimed programmes – including museum-calibre legends – but also mounts exhibitions drawn entirely from its curated flatfiles; these are open to submission by all, which guarantees hot young blood.

Momenta Art
359 Bedford Avenue, between South 4th & South 5th Streets, Williamsburg, Brooklyn (1-718 218 8058/www.momentaart.org). Subway L to Bedford Avenue. **Open** *Sept-June* noon-6pm Mon, Thur-Sun. **Map** p411 U8.
Momenta is housed in a tiny space, yet it conveys the importance of a serious Chelsea gallery. You'll find exhibitions from a cross-section of emerging artists – most of them will be conceptualists, all of them will be challenging the norms in one way or another.

SculptureCenter
44-19 Purves Street, at Jackson Avenue, Long Island City, Queens (1-718 361 1750/www. sculpture-center.org). Subway E, V to 23rd Street-Ely Avenue; G to Long Island City-Court Square; 7 to 45th Road-Court House Square. **Open** 11am-6pm Mon, Thur-Sun. **Map** p412 V5.
One of the best places to see work by blossoming and mid-career artists, SculptureCenter is known for its very broad definition of sculpture. The impressive steel and brick premises used to be a trolley repair shop; the redesign was executed by acclaimed architect Maya Lin in 2002.

Smack Mellon Gallery
92 Plymouth Street, between Washington & Main Streets, Dumbo, Brooklyn (1-718 834 8761/www. smackmellon.org). Subway A, C to High Street; F to York Street. **Open** noon-6pm Wed-Sun. **Map** p411 T9.
Avant-garde group shows fill this gallery's expansive waterfront digs in a 1910 boiler house. The renovated space has ample room for emerging and mid-career artists to exhibit work in all media.

★ White Columns
320 W 13th Street, between Hudson & W 4th Streets, entrance on Horatio Street, Meatpacking District (1-212 924 4212/www.whitecolumns. org). Subway A, C, E, 1, 2, 3 to 14th Street; L to Eighth Avenue. **Open** noon-6pm Tue-Sat. **Map** p403 D28.
British-born Matthew Higgs – artist, writer, former Turner Prize judge and now director and chief curator here at New York's oldest alternative art space – has been getting high marks for shaking things up. He has kept White Columns committed to under-represented artists, while also expanding the curatorial focus far beyond New York.

PHOTOGRAPHY

For a comprehensive overview of photography exhibitions, keep an eye out for the bi-monthly directory *Photograph* ($8 at galleries or online at www.photography-guide.com).

Howard Greenberg Gallery
41 E 57th Street, at Madison Avenue, Midtown East (1-212 334 0010/www.howardgreenberg. com). Subway N, R, W to Fifth Avenue-59th Street. **Open** *Sept-June* 10am-6pm Tue-Sat. *July, Aug* 10am-6pm Mon-Thur; 10am-5pm Fri. **Map** p405 E22.
Founded in 1981 and originally called Photofind, the Howard Greenberg Gallery was one of the first spaces to exhibit photojournalism and street photography. The gallery's collection includes countless images snapped by Berenice Abbott, Edward Steichen and Henri Cartier-Bresson.

Pace/MacGill
9th Floor, 32 E 57th Street, between Madison & Park Avenues, Midtown East (1-212 759 7999/www.pacemacgill.com). Subway N, R, W to Lexington Avenue-59th Street; 4, 5, 6 to 59th Street. **Open** *Sept-late June* 9.30am-5.30pm Tue-Fri; 10am-6pm Sat. *Late June-Aug* 9.30am-5.30pm Mon-Thur; 9.30am-4pm Fri. **Map** p405 E22.
Pace/MacGill shows work by such established names as Walker Evans, Robert Frank and Irving Penn, in addition to groundbreaking contemporaries like Chuck Close and Kiki Smith.

★ Yossi Milo
525 W 25th Street, between Tenth & Eleventh Avenues, Chelsea (1-212 414 0370/www.yossi milo.com). Subway C, E to 23rd Street; L to Eighth Avenue. **Open** *Sept-June* 10am-6pm Tue-Sat. *July, Aug* 10am-6pm Mon-Fri. **Map** p404 B26.
Yossi Milo's impressive roster of international camera talent encompasses emerging artists beginning to amass a following, as well as more established photographers. Look out for striking and innovative work by Tierney Gearon, Philippe Gronon and Pieter Hugo.

ARTS & ENTERTAINMENT

Books & Poetry

Listen to the literati – or take the mic yourself.

As you'd expect, major chains such as Barnes & Noble play a big role on New York City's thriving literary scene when it comes to author events. But if you're looking for events with more atmosphere, a number of smaller, independent happenings have sprung up in the past year. The FSG Reading Series benefits both from its roster of writers and its setting, while the St Mark's Bookshop Reading Series is also a good bet.

Of course, big events can also be rewarding and intimate. Amanda Stern's Happy Ending Series will be supplementing its residence at the tiny Happy Ending bar with a monthly spot at the larger Joe's Pub (*see p320*). And there's also the massive yet elegant New York Public Library, where Slavoj Žižek, Toni Morrison and others have shared their ideas. To find out who's reading where, check the listings in *Time Out New York* magazine.

AUTHOR APPEARANCES

Barnes & Noble
33 E 17th Street, between Broadway & Park Avenue South, Union Square (1-212 253 0810/ www.barnesandnoble.com). Subway L, N, Q, R, W, 4, 5, 6 to 14th Street-Union Square. **Admission** free. **Map** p403 E27.
Many an author touches down at Barnes & Noble's city-wide branches, and the Union Square flagship offers an especially varied schedule. In its Upstairs at the Square series, writers are paired with musicians: William Gibson appeared with Martha Wainwright, while Joseph O'Neill shared the bill with Aimee Mann. The Upper West Side branch (2289 Broadway, at 82nd Street, 1-212 362 8835) also hosts readings by the likes of multi-talented critic Daniel Mendelsohn and astute leftist Thomas Frank.
▶ *Preface a visit here with a spin around the fabled '18 miles of books' at the nearby Strand Book Store (see p231).*

Bluestockings
172 Allen Street, between Rivington & Stanton Streets, Lower East Side (1-212 777 6028/ www.bluestockings.com). Subway F, V to Lower

About the author
Michael Miller is the Books Editor of Time Out New York, *and also contributes to monthly literary review* The Believer.

East Side-Second Avenue. **Admission** free (suggested donation $5). **Credit** AmEx, DC, MC, V. **Map** p403 F29.
This progressive bookstore and café hosts frequent readings and discussions, often on feminist and lesbian themes. The list of previous readers includes graphic novelist Alison Bechdel, novelist Aoibheann Sweeney and political writer Michelle Goldberg.
▶ *For more gay and lesbian literature, see p307.*

BookCourt
163 Court Street, between Dean & Pacific Streets, Cobble Hill, Brooklyn (1-718 875 3677/ www.bookcourt.org). Subway D, M, N, R to Atlantic Ave-Pacific Street. **Admission** free. **Map** p410 S10.
This great local bookstore has a helpful staff and an impressive reading series. Past authors have included the likes of Jhumpa Lahiri, Heidi Julavits, Peter Cameron, Jennifer Egan and Jonathan Lethem.

Freebird
123 Columbia Street, between Degraw & Kane Streets, Cobble Hill, Brooklyn (1-718 643 8484/ www.freebirdbooks.com). Subway F, G to Bergen Street. **Admission** free. **Map** p410 S10.
Open on Thursday and Friday evenings and all day at weekends, the Freebird used-book store holds several literary events a month. Authors who've read here include Jonathan Ames, Kathryn Harrison and Nick Flynn.

ARTS & ENTERTAINMENT

★ FSG Reading Series
Russian Samovar, 256 West 52nd Street, between Eighth Avenue & Broadway, Theater District (1-212 757 0168). Subway C, E to 50th Street. **Admission $5. No credit cards. Map** p404 D23.
Farrar, Straus & Giroux has started a sporadic but excellent reading series above this Russian eaterie. Acerbic satirist Sam Lipsyte has shared the bill with crime novelist and scriptwriter Richard Price, who gave a sneak peak of *Lush Life*; *New Yorker* classical music critic and *The Rest Is Noise* author Alex Ross appeared with debut novelist Rivka Galchen, who gave a preview of *Atmospheric Disturbances*.

★ Happy Ending Series
Happy Ending, 302 Broome Street, between Eldridge & Forsyth Streets, Lower East Side (1-212 334 9676). Subway F, V to Delancey Street; J, M, Z to Delancey-Essex Streets. **Admission** free. **Map** p403 F30.
Held at a popular Lower East Side watering hole, Amanda Stern's convivial literary series is a great mix of authorial brilliance and endearing self-mockery. Readings from the likes of Ed Park, Fiona Maazel and Samantha Hunt are mixed with musical interludes.
▶ *Stern will be staging Happy Ending Series shows at Joe's Pub (see p320) from early 2009.*

★ Housing Works Bookstore Café
For listing, see p231. **Admission** free; book donations encouraged.
The emerging and the illustrious mingle at the mic (and in the audience) at this Soho bookstore and café, which has one of the best reading series in the city. All the profits from events go to homeless people living with HIV and AIDS. Authors run the gamut: recent visitors have included Paula Fox, Anne Carson, Gary Shteyngart and Jonathan Lethem.

Hue-Man Bookstore
For listing, see p230. **Admission** free.
This spacious Harlem bookstore holds frequent readings, as well as in-store appearances by authors such as Chris Abani and E Lynn Harris. The emphasis is on African-American writers and topics.

★ KGB Bar
2nd Floor, 85 E 4th Street, between Second & Third Avenues, East Village (1-212 505 3360/ www.kgbbar.com). Subway F, V to Lower East Side-Second Avenue; 6 to Astor Place. **Admission** free. **Map** p403 F29.
This dark and formerly smoky East Village hangout, with an old-school communist theme, runs several top-notch weekly series featuring NYC writers, poets, fantasy authors and others.

Littoral
Issue Project Room, Can Factory, 232 3rd Street, at Third Avenue, Brooklyn (1-718 330 0313/www.issueprojectroom.org). Subway F,

G to Carroll Street. **Admission** $5-$15. **No credit cards. Map** p410 T11.
The literary series at Littoral aims to mix boundary-pushing literature and avant-garde music. David Ohle and Joe Wenderoth are among the roster of recent readers.

McNally Jackson Bookstore
For listing, see p230. **Admission** free.
This excellent Canadian import invites a wide range of non-fiction writers and novelists – Kate Christensen, Adam Mansbach, Edward P Jones and Darcey Steinke, among others – to read in its comfortable café space.

New School
66 W 12th Street, between Fifth & Sixth Avenues, Greenwich Village (1-212 229 5353/ tickets 1-212 229 5488/www.newschool.edu). Subway F, V to 14th Street; L to Sixth Avenue. **Admission** free-$15. **Credit** AmEx, DC, MC, V. **Map** p403 E28.
Nathaniel Mackey, Denis Johnson and John Ashbery are a few of the writers who have participated in the university's wide-ranging schedule of readings. It's also worth looking out for political discussions and literary forums.

New York Public Library
Humanities & Social Sciences Library, Celeste Bartos Forum, 42nd Street, at Fifth Avenue, Midtown (1-212 930 0571/www.nypl.org/events). Subway F, V to 42nd Street. **Admission** free-$10. **No credit cards. Map** p404 E24.
This large, elegant space invites leading authors to discuss books and engage in lively literary debates with punters. Recent guests have included genocide historian Samantha Power, novelist-critic André Aciman and Toni Morrison.
▶ *For tours of the library itself, see p100.*

92nd Street Y
1395 Lexington Avenue, at 92nd Street, Upper East Side (1-212 415 5500/www.92y.org). Subway 6 to 96th Street. **Admission** $10-$40. **Credit** AmEx, DC, MC, V. **Map** p406 F17.
Big-name novelists, journalists and poets preside over some grand intellectual feasts here, with talks

ARTS & ENTERTAINMENT

by critic James Wood, as well as a reading series featuring the likes of Don DeLillo, Bernard-Henri Lévy and Judy Blume. The Biographers/Critics and Brunch events are also popular.

★ 192 Books
For listing, see p230. **Admission** free.
This lovely independent bookstore boasts a phenomenal reading series, bringing in top authors such as Rachel Kushner, Joan Didion and Harry Mathews to read from their works.

Poetry Project
St Mark's Church in-the-Bowery, 131 E 10th Street, at Second Avenue, East Village (1-212 674 0910/www.poetryproject.com). Subway L to First Avenue; 6 to Astor Place. **Admission** $8; $7 reductions. **No credit cards. Map** p403 F28.
The Project, housed in a beautiful old church, has hosted an amazing roster of poets since its inception in 1966, including creative luminaries such as Ted Berrigan, Richard Hell and Eileen Myles.

St Mark's Bookshop Reading Series
Solas Bar, 232 East 9th Street, between Second & Third Avenues, East Village (1-212 260 7853/ www.stmarksbookshop.com). Subway 6 to Astor Place; N, R to 8th Street. **Admission** free. **Map** p403 F28.

Nuyorican Poets Café.

The independent bookshop has a reading series with downtown spirit. Recent readers have included the legendary critic-novelist Gary Indiana, *Believer* editor and novelist Ed Park, musician-author LD Beghtol as well as the avant-garde theatre legend Richard Foreman.
▶ *For St Mark's Bookshop itself, see p230.*

SPOKEN WORD

Most spoken word events begin with a featured poet or two, before moving on to an open mic. If you'd like to take part, show up a little early and ask for the sign-up sheet. Feel free to express approval, but keep criticism to yourself. The **Ultimate NYC Poetry Calendar** (www.poetz.com/calendar) has listings.

Bowery Poetry Club
308 Bowery, between Bleecker & Houston Streets, East Village (1-212 614 0505/ www.bowerypoetry.com). Subway B, D, F, V to Broadway-Lafayette Street; 6 to Bleecker Street. **Admission** free-$10. **No credit cards. Map** p403 F29.
Celebrating the grand oral traditions and cyberific future of poetry, the funky BPC features a jam-packed programme of high-energy spoken word events, plus hip hop, burlesque, comedy, theatre and afternoon workshops. The Urbana Poetry Slam team leads an open mic on Tuesday nights.

Moth StorySLAM
1-212 742 0551/www.themoth.org. **Admission** $6. **No credit cards.**
Known for its big-name monthly storytelling shows, the Moth also sponsors open slams in various venues. Ten raconteurs get five minutes each to tell a favourite story (no notes allowed!) to a panel of judges.

Nuyorican Poets Café
236 E 3rd Street, between Avenues B & C, East Village (1-212 505 8183/www.nuyorican.org). Subway F, V to Lower East Side-Second Avenue. **Admission** $5-$15. **No credit cards. Map** p403 G29.
This 35-year-old East Village community arts centre is known for its long history of raucous slams, jam sessions and anything-goes open mics.

SOS: Sunday Open Series
ABC No Rio, 156 Rivington Street, between Clinton & Suffolk Streets, Lower East Side (1-212 254 3697/www.abcnorio.org). Subway F to Delancey Street; J, M, Z to Delancey-Essex Streets. **Admission** $3. **No credit cards. Map** p403 G29.
Community-based art centre ABC No Rio's long-running Sunday afternoon open mic promises a welcoming vibe, no time limits and 'no BS'.

Cabaret & Comedy

Crooners and stand-ups sit on either side of the same nightlife coin.

Although Bob Fosse's classic 1972 movie musical *Cabaret* depicts a world of racy decadence, the word itself now usually means something quite different. At a cabaret show, it's just the music that gets stripped down: reduced to its bare essence by a vocalist in a cosy club. The only slap is likely to be on a bass, the only tickle on the ivories of a piano.

Just as cabaret is rich and varied, so the comedy circuit offers a wealth of styles. Mainstream stand-ups compete with avant-garde improv troupes; the crowds range from respectful to raucous. As with cabaret, *Time Out New York* has weekly listings.

CABARET

Cabaret in New York today is a confluence of opposites: the heights of polish and the depths of amateurism; intense honesty and airy pretense; earnestness and camp. Singers of all stripes and abilities share the same crowded rooms, supplementing familiar tunes from the Great American Songbook with modern songs by the likes of Joni Mitchell and Tom Waits.

Manhattan's three fanciest cabarets are in tony hotels: the **Oak Room** (at the Algonquin), **Feinstein's** (at the Loews Regency) and the **Café Carlyle** (at, yes, the Carlyle). Local clubs such as **Don't Tell Mama** and the **Duplex** are casual, fun and less pricey, but the talent is often entry-level. The **Laurie Beechman Theater** falls between these two poles, as does the hopping **Metropolitan Room**.

Classic nightspots

Café Carlyle

Carlyle, 35 E 76th Street, at Madison Avenue, Upper East Side (1-212 744 1600/www. thecarlyle.com). Subway 6 to 77th Street. **Shows** 8.45pm Mon-Thur; 8.45pm, 10.45pm Fri, Sat. **Cover** $50-$125 (sometimes with compulsory dinner). **Credit** AmEx, DC, Disc, MC, V. **Map** p405 E20.

About the authors

Time Out New York's *Comedy Editor* **Jane Borden** *is also a performer, and a freelance joke-writer for* Saturday Night Live. *For cabaret writer* **Adam Feldman**, *see p345.*

With its airy murals by Marcel Vertes, this elegant boîte in the Carlyle hotel is the epitome of New York chic, attracting top-level singers such as Eartha Kitt, Barbara Cook and Judy Collins. Woody Allen often plays clarinet with Eddie Davis and his New Orleans Jazz Band on Monday nights.

▶ *To drink in the atmosphere at a lower price, Bemelmans Bar across the hall has an excellent pianist (Mon-Sat only).*

Feinstein's at the Loews Regency

Loews Regency Hotel, 540 Park Avenue, at 61st Street, Upper East Side (1-212 339 4095/www. feinsteinsattheregency.com). Subway N, R, W to Lexington Avenue-59th Street; 4, 5, 6 to 59th Street. **Shows** 8.30pm Tue-Thur; 8pm, 10pm Fri, Sat. **Cover** $60-$75 plus $40 food/drink min. **Credit** AmEx, DC, Disc, MC, V. **Map** p405 E22. Michael Feinstein, cabaret's crown prince, draws A-list talent to this swank room in the Regency hotel. The shows and the drinks are pricey, but you usually get what you pay for. Recent performers have included Chita Rivera, Rita Moreno and Diahann Carroll, as well as Hollywood types (Lynda Carter, Tony Danza) dabbling in music.

★ Oak Room

Algonquin, 59 W 44th Street, between Fifth & Sixth Avenues, Midtown (1-212 840 6800/ reservations 1-212 419 9331/www.algonquin hotel.com). Subway B, D, F, V to 42nd Street-Bryant Park; 7 to Fifth Avenue. **Shows** 9pm Tue-Thur; 9pm, 11.30pm Fri, Sat. **Cover** $50-$65 plus $30 drink minimum; $70 dinner compulsory at 9pm Fri & Sat shows. **Credit** AmEx, DC, Disc, MC, V. **Map** p404 E24.

ARTS & ENTERTAINMENT

This banquette-lined room is the perfect place in which to enjoy cabaret eminences such as Karen Akers and Andrea Marcovicci, plus rising stars such as the luminous Maude Maggart and the formidable jazz singer Paula West.

▶ *For the Algonquin hotel, see p168.*

Standards

Don't Tell Mama
343 W 46th Street, between Eighth & Ninth Avenues, Theater District (1-212 757 0788/ www.donttellmamanyc.com). Subway A, C, E to 42nd Street-Port Authority. **Shows** times vary; 2-3 shows per night. *Piano bar* 9pm-4am daily. **Cover** $5-$20 plus 2-drink min. *Piano bar* free plus 2-drink min. **Average drink** $8. **Credit** AmEx, DC, Disc, MC, V. **Map** p404 C23.
Showbiz pros and piano bar buffs adore this dank but homey Theater District stalwart, where acts range from the strictly amateur to potential stars of tomorrow. The nightly line-up may include pop, jazz and musical theatre singers, as well as female impersonators, comedians and musical revues.

Duplex
61 Christopher Street, at Seventh Avenue South, West Village (1-212 255 5438/www.theduplex. com). Subway 1 to Christopher Street-Sheridan Square. **Shows** 7pm, 9pm daily. *Piano bar* 9pm-4am daily. **Cover** $5-$20 plus 2-drink min. **Average drink** $8. **Credit** AmEx, DC, MC, V. **Map** p403 D28.
This cosy, brick-lined room, located upstairs from a piano bar in the heart of the West Village, is a good-natured testing ground for new talent. The eclectic offerings often come served with a generous dollop of good, old-fashioned camp.

Laurie Beechman Theater
407 W 42nd Street, at Ninth Avenue, Theater District (1-212 695 6909/www.westbankcafe. com). Subway A, C, E to 42nd Street-Port Authority. **Shows** times vary; 1-2 shows per night. *Open mic* 10.30pm-2am Fri. **Cover** $15-$25 plus $15 food or drink min. **Average drink** $10. **Credit** AmEx, DC, MC, V. **Map** p404 C24.
Tucked away beneath the West Bank Café, the Beechman is home to many local favourites. Among the names worth catching are Lisa Asher and the irrepressible Brandon Cutrell; the latter also hosts the After Party, a racy open-mic show-tune showcase that pulls in the crowds on Friday nights.

★ Metropolitan Room
34 W 22nd Street, between Fifth & Sixth Avenues, Flatiron District (1-212 206 0440/ www.metropolitanroom.com). Subway F, R, V, W to 23rd Street. **Shows** times vary. **Cover** $15-$35 plus 2-drink min. **Average drink** $10. **Credit** AmEx, DC, MC, V. **Map** p404 E26.

The Met Room has established itself as the must-go venue for high-level nightclub singing that won't bust your wallet. Regular performers range from rising musical-theatre stars to established cabaret acts (including Baby Jane Dexter and English songstress Barb Jungr), plus legends such as Tammy Grimes, Julie Wilson and Annie Ross.

COMEDY

Each style of humour in New York's diverse comedy scene reflects and attracts a different kind of audience, offering visitors the chance to immerse themselves in varying slices of local life while watching top talent. Mingle with the buttoned-up date crowd in slick showrooms such as **Carolines on Broadway**, learn about the latest trends from hipsters at the **Upright Citizens Brigade Theatre**, or get rowdy with ribald partiers at Village spots such as the **Comedy Cellar**. Want something more specific? Comb websites for the popular niche showcases of African American, Latino, Italian or female comics.

★ Ars Nova
511 W 54th Street, between Tenth & Eleventh Avenues, Hell's Kitchen (1-212 489 9800/www.arsnovanyc.com). Subway C, E to 50th Street. **Shows** times vary. **Cover** $10-$20. **Average drink** $5. **Credit** (tickets only) AmEx, Disc, MC, V. **Map** p405 C22.
Thoughtful, professional productions are married in the impeccably curated programme at Ars Nova. The space isn't bad, either: rather than dusty bar glasses and dripping basement fixtures, crowds are treated to comfortable cabaret seating and a professional light and sound artist. The Tragedy Tomorrow series on Tuesdays is a good bet.

Broadway Comedy Club
318 W 53rd Street, between Eighth & Ninth Avenues, Theater District (1-212 757 2323/ www.broadwaycomedyclub.com). Subway C, E to 50th Street. **Shows** 9pm Mon-Thur, Sun; 10pm, midnight Fri; 9pm, 11pm, midnight Sat. **Cover** $10-$20 plus 2-drink min. **Average drink** $6. **Credit** AmEx, DC, Disc, MC, V. **Map** p404 D23.

INSIDE TRACK
SINGING ALONG

Most non-hotel cabaret rooms have open-mic nights where show-tune lovers can briefly seize the spotlight. However, those who prefer to sing communally should head to the venerable piano bar **Marie's Crisis** (59 Grove Street, between Seventh Avenue South & Bleecker Street).

Ars Nova.

The BCC features TV faces and other regulars from the club circuit. From Wednesday to Saturday, it's also home to Chicago City Limits (1-212 888 5233, www.chicagocitylimits.com), which moved to Manhattan in 1979, although the group's classic Second City format of topical sketches, songs and audience-inspired improv is a little dated.

Carolines on Broadway
1626 Broadway, between 49th & 50th Streets, Theater District (1-212 757 4100/ www.carolines.com). Subway N, R, to 49th Street; 1 to 50th Street. **Shows** times vary. **Cover** $15-$50 plus 2-drink min. **Average drink** $8. **Credit** AmEx, DC, MC, V. **Map** p404 D23.
This New York City institution's long-term relationships with national headliners, sitcom stars and cable-special pros ensure that its stage always features marquee names. You probably won't see anything especially edgy or underground, but you'll never see anything less than professional.

Comedy Cellar
117 MacDougal Street, between Bleecker & W 3rd Streets, Greenwich Village (1-212 254 3480/www.comedycellar.com). Subway A, B, C, D, E, F, V to W 4th Street. **Shows** 9pm, 11pm Mon-Thur, Sun; 8pm, 9.45pm, 11.30pm Fri; 7.30pm, 9.15pm, 11pm, 12.45am Sat. **Cover** $10-$15 plus 2-item min. **Average drink** $6. **Credit** AmEx, DC, MC, V. **Map** p403 E29.
Despite being dubbed one of the best stand-up clubs in the city year after year, the Comedy Cellar has maintained a hip, underground feel. It gets incredibly crowded, but the bookings, which typically include no-nonsense comics Colin Quinn, Jim Norton and Marina Franklin, are enough to distract you from your bachelorette party neighbours.

Comic Strip Live
1568 Second Avenue, between 81st & 82nd Streets, Upper East Side (1-212 861 9386/ www.comicstriplive.com). Subway 4, 5, 6 to 86th Street. **Shows** 8.30pm Mon-Thur; 8.30pm, 10.30pm Fri; 8pm, 10.30pm, 12.30am Sat; 8pm Sun. **Cover** $20-$25 plus 2-drink min. **Average drink** $10. **Credit** AmEx, DC, Disc, MC, V. **Map** p405 F19.
The Upper East Side isn't exactly a breeding ground for edgy entertainment, so you'll be grateful to find this fabled, long-running showcase. Established in 1975, CSL once launched the careers of Eddie Murphy and Chris Rock. The fare is more standard these days, but the club does attract a lot of stand-ups from the late-night talk-show circuit.

★ Comix
353 W 14th Street, between Eighth & Ninth Avenues, Meatpacking District (1-212 524 2500/ www.comixny.com). Subway A, C, E to 14th Street. **Shows** times vary. **Cover** $10-$40 plus 2-item min. **Average drink** $9. **Credit** AmEx, DC, Disc, MC, V. **Map** p403 C27.
This large, sleek club gives audiences space to spread out and order from the contemporary American menu. Big names such as Richard Lewis

have graced the stage, as have lesser-known but equally talented local and alt stand-ups.

▶ *Downstairs sits the cover-free Ochi's Lounge, home to emerging acts and experimental shows.*

Dangerfield's

1118 First Avenue, between 61st & 62nd Streets, Upper East Side (1-212 593 1650/www.danger fields.com). Subway N, R, W to Lexington Avenue-59th Street; 4, 5, 6 to 59th Street. **Shows** 8.45pm Mon-Thur, Sun; 8.30pm, 10.30pm Fri; 8pm, 10.30pm, 12.30am Sat. **Cover** $15-$20. **Average drink** $7. **Credit** AmEx, DC, Disc, MC, V. **Map** p405 F22.

New York's oldest comedy club is a bit of a time warp. The decor and gentility are throwbacks to the era of its namesake Rodney, who founded it as a cabaret in 1969. But the good thing is that, instead of putting eight to ten comics in a showcase, Dangerfield's gives three or four stand-ups the chance to settle into longer acts. And it's still the only club with no drink minimum.

EastVille Comedy Club

85 E 4th Street, between Bowery & Second Avenue, East Village (1-212 260 2445/www.east villecomedy.com). Subway F, V to Lower East Side-Second Avenue. **Shows** 8.30pm Mon-Thur, Sun; 8.30pm, 10.30pm, 12.30am Fri, Sat. **Cover** $10-$18 plus 2-drink min. **Average drink** $6. **Credit** AmEx, DC, MC, V. **Map** p403 F29.

The East Village got its first bona fide chuckle-hut-style stand-up club with the recent opening of EastVille. The venue puts up much of the same club-circuit talent that populate the city's other rooms, plus up-and-coming comics from the downtown alt scene.

Gotham Comedy Club

208 W 23rd Street, between Seventh & Eighth Avenues, Chelsea (1-212 367 9000/www.gotham comedyclub.com). Subway F, N, R, V to 23rd Street. **Shows** 8.30pm Mon-Thur, Sun; 8.30pm, 10.30pm Fri; 8pm, 10pm, 11.45pm Sat. **Cover** $15-$22 plus 2-drink min. **Average drink** $7. **Credit** AmEx, DC, MC, V. **Map** p404 D26.

Chris Mazzilli's vision for his club involves elegant surroundings, professional behaviour and mutual respect. That's why the talents he fosters, such as Jim Gaffigan, Tom Papa and Ted Alexandro, keep coming back here long after they've found national

fame. It's also why crowds return to see who Mazzilli is championing – and who might just 'drop by'.

Magnet Theater

254 W 29th Street, between Seventh & Eighth Avenues, Chelsea (1-212 244 8824/www.magnet theater.com). Subway A, C, E to 34th Street-Penn Station; 1 to 28th Street. **Shows** times vary. **Cover** free-$7. **Average drink** $5. **Credit** AmEx, DC, MC, V. **Map** p404 D25.

In the past year, the community of house teams and solo performers at Armando Diaz's upstart black box has grown strong, cementing the Magnet as one of the best places to watch improv in the city. You won't see faces from VH1 onstage, but you will see thoughtful, patient improv.

People's Improv Theater

2nd Floor, 154 W 29th Street, between Sixth & Seventh Avenues, Chelsea (1-212 563 7488/ www.thepit-nyc.com). Subway 1 to 28th Street. **Shows** times vary. **Cover** $5-$12; free Wed. **Average drink** $3. **Credit** (online purchases only) Disc, MC, V. **Map** p404 D25.

While talented sketch groups perform on the weekends and improv teams pack 'em in on Wednesday night, it's the teaching programme that put the PIT on the creative map. Teachers from *Saturday Night Live* and *The Daily Show,* accomplished stand-ups and writers, offer a rolling roster of classes.

Stand-Up New York

236 W 78th Street, at Broadway, Upper West Side (1-212 595 0850/www.standupny.com). Subway 1 to 79th Street. **Shows** 8.30pm Mon-Thur; 8pm, 10pm, midnight Fri, Sat; 9pm Sun. **Cover** $15-$20 plus 2-drink min. **Average drink** $9. **Credit** AmEx, DC, MC, V. **Map** p405 C19.

The line-ups at this musty Uptown club, under new management, have started garnering attention for the first time in years. Jay Oakerson and Patrice Oneal have both frequented the small space already, and plans to expand the programming beyond stand-up also look promising.

★ Upright Citizens Brigade Theatre

307 W 26th Street, between Eighth & Ninth Avenues, Chelsea (1-212 366 9176/www.ucb theatre.com). Subway C, E to 23rd Street; 1 to 28th Street. **Shows** times vary. **Cover** $5-$20. **Average drink** $3. **No credit cards.** **Map** p404 D26.

The improv troupes and sketch group anchored at UCBT are the best in the city. Competitive booking practices and a student following have kept it at the top of its game for almost a decade now. Stars of *Saturday Night Live,* VH1 and writers for late-night talk shows gather on Sunday nights to wow crowds in the long-running *ASSSSCAT 3000.* Other teams include Mother and Reuben Williams (both Saturdays) and the Stepfathers (Fridays).

INSIDE TRACK
TV TICKETS

There are more laughs on offer at the recordings of major TV shows in New York, such as *The Late Show with David Letterman* and *Saturday Night Live.* For details of how to score tickets, *see p304.*

Children

Big city attractions for small travellers.

If you want to make your child fall in love with New York City in five minutes flat, head for Times Square after dark, when the electronic billboards are shape-shifting and pulsing. They'll be totally dazzled. So far, so simple. But what next?

Happily, the city is bursting with cultural, culinary and just plain touristy destinations suitable for families. The Statue of Liberty and the top of the Empire State Building are unmissable, but they're just the tips of the iceberg: the selection of sights and activities in this chapter should keep most kids content. Impromptu street concerts, jumbo public art and lively street fairs will probably present themselves en route; and if you or your offspring start to feel overwhelmed, there's always one of the city's green spaces. To keep up with the child-friendly events, pick up a copy of the monthly magazine *Time Out New York Kids*.

About the author
Manhattan-born writer **Julia Israel** is Assistant Editor of the monthly Time Out New York Kids *magazine*.

SIGHTSEEING & ENTERTAINMENT
Animals & nature

See also p104 **Central Park**.

★ Bronx Zoo
For listing, see p145.
This massive institution is home to more than 4,500 creatures. Step aboard the Wild Asia Monorail (open May-Oct, admission $4), which tours 38 acres of exhibits housing elephants, Indo-Chinese tigers, antelope, Mongolian wild horses and more. In 2008, the zoo's Lion House was transformed into Madagascar!, a permanent home to exotic animals from the lush island nation off the eastern coast of Africa. Lemurs, giant crocodiles, lovebirds, radiated tortoises and, coolest (and grossest) of all, hissing cockroaches all live here. *Photos p286.*
► *For other zoos, see p106, p129 and p140.*

New York Aquarium
610 Surf Avenue, at West 8th Street, Coney Island, Brooklyn (1-718 265 3474/www.ny aquarium.com). Subway D to Coney Island-Stillwell Avenue; F, Q to W 8th Street-NY Aquarium.

Open *Apr, May, Sept, Oct* 10am-5pm Mon-Fri; 10am-5.30pm Sat, Sun. *June-Aug* 10am-6pm Mon-Fri; 10am-7pm Sat, Sun. *Nov-Mar* 10am-4.30pm daily. **Admission** $13; $9-$10 reductions; free under-2s. **Credit** AmEx, DC, Disc, MC, V.
Like the rest of Coney Island, this aquarium is a little on the shabby side, but kids always enjoy seeing the famous beluga whale family and the scary sharks. If your little one wants to catch a glimpse of animals chowing down on some grub, the aquarium offers daily shark, penguin, walrus and sea otter feedings (call for exact times and locations).

FREE Prospect Park Audubon Center
Prospect Park, enter from Ocean Avenue, at Lincoln Road, Brooklyn (1-718 287 3400/ www.prospectpark.org). Subway B, Q to Prospect Park. **Open** *Apr-Nov* noon-5pm Thur-Sun. *Dec-Mar* noon-4pm Sat, Sun. **Admission** free. **Map** p410 U12.
Overlooking Prospect Lake, the Audubon Center is dedicated to nature education and wildlife preservation. Start at the visitor centre, and stick around for woodland tours, storytelling, bird-watching, pedalboat rides and other activities.

FREE Queens County Farm Museum
73-50 Little Neck Parkway, Floral Park, Queens (1-718 347 3276/www.queensfarm.org). Subway E, F to Kew Gardens-Union Turnpike, then take

Bronx Zoo. *See p285.*

the Q46 bus to Little Neck Parkway. **Open** 10am-5pm Mon-Fri (outdoors only); 10am-5pm Sat, Sun. **Admission** free (except special events). Stroll through apple and pear orchards, take a guided tour of an 18th-century farmhouse (weekends only) and see sheep and goats at NYC's only working historical farm. On your way in, pick up some feed at the gift store so your little one can treat the animals to a nibble.

Museums

Defying the stuffy cliché, many of Manhattan's most venerable institutions are extremely child-friendly. The **Museum of Modern Art** (*see p100*), the **Metropolitan Museum of Art** (*see p110*) and the **Rubin Museum** (*see p87*) offer workshops for kids of all ages; check their websites for schedules. The Met, with its mummies and Temple of Dendur, a real ancient Egyptian temple, is a particular hit with kids, so long as you don't try to tackle too much of the massive collection.

Even very young children will love exploring the **American Museum of Natural History** (*see p116*). The museum's Fossil Halls are home to huge, reconstructed and beloved dinosaurs, plus the world's largest collection of vertebrate fossils (nearly a million specimens).

Elsewhere, kids and adults will be fascinated by the amazing scale-model *Panorama of the City of New York* at the **Queens Museum of Art** (*see p140*) and by the toy collection at the **Museum of the City of New York** (*see p110*), with teddy bears, games and dolls' houses. The hangar deck at the **Intrepid Sea-Air-Space Museum** (*see p98*), back at its home on Pier 86, houses a family zone where youngsters can learn about the physics involved in a fighter jet's landing and climb a massive cargo net. Downtown, the new **Sports Museum of America** (*see p65*) offers fans of all ages something to cheer about.

★ Brooklyn Children's Museum

145 Brooklyn Avenue, at St Marks Avenue, Crown Heights, Brooklyn (1-718 735 4400/ www.brooklynkids.org). Subway A, C to Nostrand Avenue; C to Kingston-Throop Avenue; 3 to Kingston Avenue. **Open** 11am-1pm (Totally Tots only), 1pm-6pm Wed-Fri; 10am-6pm Sat, Sun. **Admission** $7.50; free under-1s. **Credit** AmEx, DC, Disc, MC, V. **Map** p410 V11. *See p289* **Profile**.

Children's Museum of Manhattan

212 W 83rd Street, between Amsterdam Avenue & Broadway, Upper West Side (1-212 721 1234/www.cmom.org). Subway B, C to 81st Street-Museum of Natural History; 1 to 86th Street. **Open** 10am-5pm Tue-Sun. **Admission**

$10; $7 reductions; free under-1s. **Credit** AmEx, DC, MC, V. **Map** p405 C19.
This must-see children's museum, a mainstay in every Upper West Side child's social agenda, promotes literacy, multiculturalism and creativity through its permanent and temporary interactive exhibitions and programmes. On the second floor, preschoolers can explore 'Adventures with Dora and Diego', a bilingual playspace that transports visitors to some of the Nickelodeon TV show's settings, including Dora's house and her cousin Diego's animal rescue centre. There's also a miniature version of the museum's neighbourhood.

Children's Museum of the Arts

182 Lafayette Street, between Broome & Grand Streets, Soho (1-212 274 0986/www.cmany.org). Subway 6 to Spring Street. **Open** noon-5pm Wed, Fri-Sun; noon-6pm Thur. **Admission** $9; free under-1s. Pay what you wish 4-6pm Thur. **Credit** AmEx, DC, Disc, MC, V. **Map** p403 E30.
The focus at this gallery space is on teaching, creating, collecting and exhibiting kids' artwork. The walls usually showcase an engaging temporary exhibit juxtaposed with works from the museum's collection of over 2,000 pieces of children's art.

★ New York City Police Museum

For listing, see p69.
Kids try out sirens on real SWAT cars, stand in a police line-up, have their mugshots taken and hang out behind bars in the on-site jail cell. Although there are plenty of special weekend events offered by the museum, it's the access to old-school and modern NYPD gear that makes it worth visiting.

New York Hall of Science

For listing, see p140.
Known for the 1964 World's Fair pavilion in which it is housed and the rockets from the US space programme that flank it, this museum has always been worth a trek for its discovery-based exhibits. Since its massive expansion in 2005, it's become a must for curious kids. The new building houses permanent hands-on exhibits that deal with 21st-century concepts such as networks, the science of sports and, in a massive preschool-science area, the urban world. From March to December, the 30,000sq ft outdoor Science Playground teaches children the principles of balance, gravity and energy.

ADVENTURES with DORA & DIEGO

Presented by Nickelodeon™

An interactive exhibit only at the

Children's Museum of Manhattan

CMOM

The Tisch Building
212 West 83rd Street
(btwn Broadway & Amsterdam Ave.)
New York, NY 10024
212.721.1223
www.cmom.org
Open 10am – 5pm
Tuesday – Sunday

Five floors of hands-on exhibits for children from 0 – 12 and their families!

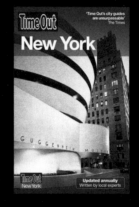

Profile Brooklyn Children's Museum

The world's first kids' museum gets a welcome revamp.

Brooklyn Children's Museum (listings p287) has been around for a long time: 110 years, to be precise. Opened in 1899, it was the first museum in the world designed for kids. But age is no barrier to success. In late 2008, it reopened after a $46 million expansion, and now contains some of the city's freshest child-centric attractions.

Architect Rafael Viñoly's L-shaped design has doubled the original building's size and is ultra-green, with renewable bamboo floors and a groundwater heating and cooling system.

The star exhibit, 'World Brooklyn', is a maze of kid-sized shops, each containing an activity and modelled after a real Brooklyn business managed by a local family; 'We've looked to these people as our storytellers,' says Sharon Klotz, director of exhibitions. The miniature community also has a grocery store equipped with conveyor belt-propelled wares and a theatre showing recorded performances by Brooklyn dance troupes. (Kids can then step on stage to try and replicate the choreography.)

After soaking up the street scenes, young visitors can wander over to 'Neighborhood Nature', a sprawling exhibition spotlighting the borough's diverse ecosystems. Kids can glimpse images of red-winged

blackbirds through a viewing blind, see a pond from the perspective of its resident fish, and watch reptiles, amphibians and other assorted small critters in terrariums and a tide-pool touch tank. At a mixing board, they can create soundscapes by blending natural noises with man-made ones.

Nearby, the 'Totally Tots' area is geared towards the under-5s. The sun-drenched play space includes a water station with levées, pumps and streams; a dune-like sand zone with mounds at varying heights for kids of different ages; and a baby hub, where those 18 months and under can play with soft sculptures, squishy barriers and low-mounted mirrors. A breast-feeding nook for the littlest museum-goers and their mothers, set behind a curtain in the back corner, is just one of many welcome new amenities, including a bright new café.

Still, it's not all change. Catering to local nostalgia, the curators took care to retain some favourite attractions – including the museum's resident 20-foot-long Burmese python, Fantasia. As usual, she'll be simultaneously delighting kids and creeping them out. Ophidiophobics, you have been warned...

NEARBY PARK LIFE
If your little ones haven't seen enough wildlife here, take them for a runaround in nearby **Prospect Park** and the **Audubon Center** (*see p129 and p285*).

Performing arts

The New York City Ballet's **Nutcracker** (*see p359* New York State Theater) is a Christmas family tradition. In spring, **Ringling Bros and Barnum & Bailey**'s three-ring circus comes to Madison Square Garden (*see p260*). In summer, **Madison Square Park** (*see p93*) has children's concerts and there's an award-winning playground and the excellent Shake Shack on-site.

Big Apple Circus
Damrosch Park, Lincoln Center, 62nd Street, between Columbus & Amsterdam Avenues, Upper West Side (1-212 268 2500/www.big applecircus.org). Subway 1 to 66th Street-Lincoln Center. **Shows** *Oct-Jan.* Phone or check website for schedule. **Tickets** $28-$86. **Credit** AmEx, DC, Disc, MC, V. **Map** p405 C21.
New York's travelling circus was founded in 1977 as an intimate answer to the Ringling Bros. The clowns at this not-for-profit organisation are among the most creative in the country. The circus performs a special late show on New Year's Eve, at the end of which the entire audience joins the performers in the ring.

★ Bowery Kids
For listing, see p280 Bowery Poetry Club. **Shows** *Sept-July* noon Sun. **Tickets** $10.
While you may happen upon a magic show or play, the children's line-up at this Lower East Side performance space is dominated by kiddie rock concerts. Children are free to jump up and down, sing along and munch on healthy snacks sold at an on-site café while the reverb gets to them.

Carnegie Hall Family Concerts
For listing, see p330. **Tickets** $9.
Even kids who profess to hate classical music are usually impressed by a visit to Carnegie Hall. The Family Concert series features first-rate classical, world music and jazz performers and runs from November to March (recommended for ages five to 12).

Just Kidding at Symphony Space
For listing, see p334. **Shows** *Oct-early May* Sat (times vary). **Tickets** $18-$27; $12-$17 reductions.
Tell your munchkins to forego their weekly dose of cartoons. In Manhattan, kids spend Saturday mornings grooving to live concerts instead. Symphony Space's Just Kidding series features both local and nationally recognised talent. One Sunday a month, the venue also hosts a children's author (usually a household name) for a Q&A, reading and signing.

Manhattan Children's Theatre
52 White Street, between Broadway & Church Street, Tribeca (1-212 226 4085/www. manhattanchildrenstheatre.org). Subway N, Q, R, W, 4, 5, 6 to Canal Street; 1 to Franklin Street. **Shows** *Sept-May* noon Sat, Sun. **Tickets** $20-$50. **No credit cards. Map** p402 E31.
At the company's 74-seat playhouse, kids climb onto rows of padded benches set up in descending stadium formation, which means everyone (even the tiniest tot in the back) enjoys an unobstructed view. The folks at MCT take their shows quite seriously, as their source material – either classic or contemporary children's literature – illustrates.

★ New Victory Theater
For listing, see p351.
As New York's only full-scale young people's theatre, the New Victory presents international theatre and dance companies at junior prices. Shows often sell out well in advance, so reserve seats early.

Puppetworks
338 Sixth Avenue, at 4th Street, Park Slope, Brooklyn (1-718 965 3391/www.puppet

Central Park. *See p293.*

works.org). Subway F to 7th Avenue. **Shows**
12.30pm, 2.30pm Sat, Sun. **Tickets** $8; $7
under-12s. **No credit cards. Map** p410 T11.
The Brooklyn company puts on musicals adapted
from fairy tales and children's stories that feature a
cast of marionettes operated by two puppeteers
(the voice and music track is pre-recorded). The company also demonstrates how the puppets work at
the beginning of each performance.
► *For the Swedish Cottage Marionette Theater,
see p293.*

Teatro SEA Los Kabayitos Puppet & Children's Theatre

*107 Suffolk Street, between Delancey & Rivington
Streets, Lower East Side (1-212 529 1545/
www.sea-ny.org). Subway F to Delancey Street;
J, M, Z to Essex Street.* **Shows** *times vary.*
Tickets $15; $12.50 reductions. **Credit** AmEx,
DC, MC, V. **Map** p403 G29.
Spanish and English feature prominently in every
show at this cheery theatre, which adapts both
Spanish and American fairytales for its puppet pro-
ductions. Budding linguists get the chance to hone
their skills – especially after curtain calls, when
actors mingle with the audience.

Theatreworks/NYC

*Lucille Lortel Theatre, 121 Christopher Street,
between Bleecker & Hudson Streets, West
Village (1-212 647 1100/www.theatreworks
usa.org). Subway 1 to Christopher Street.*
Shows *Nov, Dec, Mar, Apr, July, Aug*
(show times vary). **Tickets** $25; free mid
July-late Aug. **Credit** AmEx, DC, MC, V.
Map p403 D28.
The respected travelling company Theatreworks/
USA has developed a reputation for producing
dependable mostly musical adaptations of kid-lit
classics; a New York branch was formed in 2005.

PARKS & PLAY SPACES

Most New Yorkers don't have their own garden
– instead, they let off steam in public parks. The
most popular of all is **Central Park** (*see p104*),
which has places and programmes just for kids.

Battery Park City Parks

*Hudson River, between Chambers Street &
Battery Place, Battery Park City (1-212 267
9700/www.bpcparks.org). Subway A, C, 1, 2, 3 to
Chambers Street; 1 to Rector Street.* **Open** 6am-
1am daily. **Admission** free. **Map** p402 D32.
Besides watching the boats along the Hudson, kids
can enjoy one of New York's best playgrounds, an
open field for ball games, Frisbee and lazing, and a
park house that has balls, board games and toys.
Kids' events are held from May to October and don't
miss the picnic garden near the Chambers Street
entrance, where children love to interpret (and climb
on) sculptor Tom Otterness's *Real World* installation.

Chelsea Piers

For listing, see p341.
A roller rink, gym, pool, toddler gym, ice-skating
rink, batting cages and rock-climbing walls are all
found in this vast and hugely energetic complex.

Mamalú Café, Play & Munch Ground

*232 North 12th Street, between Driggs & Union
Avenues, Williamsburg, Brooklyn (1-718 486
6312/www.mamalunyc.com). Subway L to Bedford
Avenue; G to Nassau Avenue.* **Open** 9am-7pm
Mon-Thur; 9am-8pm Fri, Sat; 10am-7pm Sun
(open play not available during classes; phone for
schedule). **Admission** $5 per child. **Map** p411 V7.
This restaurant/indoor playground's 800sq ft play
space, with climbable furniture and library, make it
a favourite with hip Williamsburg families.

Time Out
Travel Guides

Worldwide

All our guides are
written by a team of
local experts with a
unique and stylish
insider perspective.
We offer essential tips,
trusted advice and
honest reviews for
everything you need
to know in the city.

Over 50 destinations
available at all good
bookshops and at
timeout.com/shop

Time Out Guides

Riverbank State Park

Hudson River, at 145th Street, Hamilton Heights (1-212 694 3600). Subway 1 to 145th Street. **Open** 6am-11pm daily. *Ice skating Nov-Jan; hours vary.* **Admission** free. *Rink* $1. *Skate rental* $4. **Map** p408 B10.

A 28-acre park featuring a skating rink and other athletic facilities, along with the popular Totally Kid Carousel (June-Aug), designed by children.

Central Park

For more information and a calendar of events, visit www.centralparknyc.org. Don't miss the beautiful antique **Friedsam Memorial Carousel** (closed Mon-Fri Dec-Apr; $2 per ride). There are 21 playgrounds in the park; the large **Heckscher Playground**, in the south-west corner (between Seventh Avenue and Central Park South, from 61st to 63rd Streets), sprawls over more than three acres and boasts an up-to-date adventure area and handy restrooms.

Central Park Zoo

For listing, see p106.

The stars here are the penguins and the polar bear, which live in glass habitats so you can watch their underwater antics. The Zoo's annual Chillout! Weekend (*see p265*) offers frosty fun in high summer. The on-site Tisch Children's Zoo houses species that enjoy being petted.

Conservatory Water

Central Park, entrance on Fifth Avenue, at 74th Street. Subway 6 to 68th Street-Hunter College. **Map** p405 E20.

Nicknamed Stuart Little Pond after EB White's story-book mouse, this is a mecca for model-yacht racers. When the boatmaster is around, you can rent a remote-controlled vessel (Apr-Oct 11am-7pm Mon-Fri, Sun; 2-7pm Sat, weather permitting, $10/hr). Kids are drawn to two statues near the pond: the bronze rendering of Lewis Carroll's Alice, the Mad Hatter and the White Rabbit is an irresistible climbing spot, while the Hans Christian Andersen statue is a gathering point for free storytelling sessions (11am-noon Sat, early June-late Sept). *Photos pp290-291.*

Henry Luce Nature Observatory

For listing, see p106.

Inside the Gothic Belvedere Castle, telescopes, microscopes and hands-on exhibits teach kids about the plants and animals living in the park. With ID, you can borrow a Discovery Kit: binoculars, a bird-watching guide and other cool tools to explore nature in all its glory.

★ Swedish Cottage Marionette Theater

Central Park West, at 81st Street (1-212 988 9093). Subway B, C to 81st Street-Museum of Natural History. **Shows** *Oct-June* 10.30am, noon Tue-Fri; 1pm Sat. *July, Aug* 10.30am, noon Mon-Fri. **Tickets** $6; $5 reductions. **No credit cards. Map** p405 D19.

Tucked just inside the western boundary of Central Park is a curiously incongruous old wooden structure. Designed as a schoolhouse, the building was Sweden's entry in the 1876 Centennial Exposition in Philadelphia (it was moved to NYC a year later). Inside is one of the best-kept secrets (and deals) in town: a tiny marionette theatre with regular shows.

★ Trump Wollman Rink & Victorian Gardens

For Trump Wollman Rink listing, see p343. **Victorian Gardens** *1-212 982 2229/ www.victoriangardensnyc.com. Subway N, R, W to Fifth Avenue-59th Street.* **Open** *mid May-mid Sept* 11am-7pm Mon-Fri; 10am-9pm Sat; 10am-8pm Sun. **Admission** $6.50 Mon-Fri; $7.50 Sat, Sun. Free children under 36in tall. Games & rides cost extra. **Credit** AmEx, DC, Disc, MC, V. **Map** p405 D21.

Skating in Central Park amid snowy trees, with grand apartment buildings towering in the distance, is a New York tradition, and a classic image of the city that never seems to tarnish with passing years. This popular (read: crowded) rink offers lessons and skate rentals, plus a snack bar where you can warm up with hot chocolate. In summer the site hosts the Victorian Gardens, a nostalgic amusement park geared towards younger children. It's hardly white-knuckle stuff, but the mini-teacup carousel and Rio Grande train are bound to be hits with little kids.

▶ *For more skating rinks, see p343.*

RESTAURANTS & CAFES

★ Alice's Teacup

102 W 73rd Street, at Columbus Avenue, Upper West Side (1-212 799 3006/www.alicesteacup. com). Subway B, C to 72nd Street. **Open** 8am-8pm daily. **Credit** AmEx, DC, Disc, MC, V. **Map** p405 C20.

Beloved by Disney-adoring children, this magical spot offers much more than tea (though the three-tiered version, comprising an assortment of sandwiches, scones and desserts, truly is a treat). The brunch menu is fit for royalty, with Alice's Curious French Toast (it's drenched in fruit coulis, crème

> **INSIDE TRACK**
> **CENTRAL PARK PRETZELS**
>
> For added entertainment when strolling around in Central Park, buy a hot pretzel and let your child feed little pieces of it to the park's resident pigeons.

anglaise and syrup) and scones in scrumptious flavours like blueberry and pumpkin. In the afternoon, the special after-school snack menu features own-made graham crackers and honey, and banana bread topped with jam. At a little shop in the front of the eaterie, you can outfit your fairy-princess-in-training with a pair of glittery wings.

Other locations 156 E 64th Street, at Lexington Avenue, Upper East Side (1-212 486 9200); 220 E 81st Street, between Second & Third Avenues, Upper East Side (1-212 734 4832).

★ Bubby's

120 Hudson Street, at North Moore Street, Tribeca (1-212 219 0666/www.bubbys.com). Subway A, C, E to Canal Street; 1 to Franklin Street. **Open** 8am-11pm Mon-Thur; 8am-midnight Fri; 9am-4pm, 6pm-midnight Sat; 9am-4pm, 6-10pm Sun. **Credit** AmEx, DC, MC, V (no credit cards weekend brunch). **Map** p402 E31.

On weekend mornings, a 'We love kids!' attitude and a no-reservations policy add up to pleasant, barely controlled chaos. Children and adults alike will enjoy savoury treats such as alphabet chicken soup, mac and cheese, salads and slow-cooked barbecue fare. If you're Brooklyn-bound, dine at the enormous Dumbo location, which is directly across the street from a swell playground with Manhattan skyline views.

Other locations 1 Main Street, between Plymouth & Water Streets, Dumbo, Brooklyn (1-718 222 0666).

Dylan's Candy Bar

1011 Third Avenue, at 60th Street, Upper East Side (1-646 735 0078/www.dylanscandybar.com). Subway N, R, W, 4, 5, 6 to Lexington Avenue-59th Street. **Open** 10am-10pm Mon-Thur; 10am-11pm Fri, Sat; 10am-9pm Sun. **Credit** AmEx, DC, MC, V. **Map** p405 F22.

Think of this sweet shop as Candyland's supply room. The colourful, three-floor emporium, with packaged candy in the basement, bulk selections at ground level, and a café/ice-cream parlour on the top floor, will satisfy your entire family's sugar craving. After you've treated the kids to some Bubblegum-flavoured ice-cream upstairs, pick up the shop's speciality, Clodhopper chocolate fudge-covered graham clusters, in a cool plastic 'paint can' to take home.

▶ *Would-be Charlie Buckets should head to Jacques Torres Chocolate; see p248.*

Kitchenette

156 Chambers Street, between West Broadway & Greenwich Street, Tribeca (1-212 267 6740/www.kitchenetterestaurant.com). Subway A, C, 1, 2, 3 to Chambers Street. **Open** 7.30am-11pm Mon-Fri; 9am-11pm Sat, Sun. **Credit** AmEx, DC, MC, V. **Map** p402 E31.

On Sunday mornings, packs of parents and kids head to this home-style-cooking haven, or its uptown sister, to partake of one of the top brunches in the city. There are many imaginative egg dishes, but your carb-loving tot can likely make a meal out of a fluffy, fist-size biscuit with a dollop of strawberry butter. Kitchenette's no disappointment at night, either: try the honey-fried chicken or BBQ salmon.

Other locations 1272 Amsterdam Avenue, between 122nd & 123rd Streets, Upper West Side (1-212 531 7600).

Perch Café

365 Fifth Avenue, between 5th & 6th Streets, Park Slope, Brooklyn (1-718 788 2830/www.the perchcafe.com). Subway D, F, G, M, N, R, W to Fourth Avenue-9th Street. **Open** 7am-10pm Mon-Fri; 8am-9pm Sat, Sun. **Credit** AmEx, DC, Disc, MC, V ($10 minimum). **Map** p410 T11.

You don't get much more child-friendly than Perch Café. Built-in banquettes and sleek sofas are roomy enough for the whole family, and there's plenty of space for a pushchair both inside and in the back garden. Patrons love the chilli-crusted shrimp over grits, the fried chicken and the double-chocolate cupcakes. Your kids will also enjoy weekday on-site sing-along concerts ($5 per family) by adored local musicians.

S'MAC

345 E 12th Street, between First & Second Avenues, East Village (1-212 358 7912/www.smac nyc.com). Subway L to First Avenue. **Open** 11am-11pm Mon-Thur, Sun; 11am-1am Fri, Sat. **Credit** AmEx, DC, Disc, MC, V. **Map** p403 F28.

Ten varieties of mac and cheese range from simple all-American (mild enough for picky types) to a more complex dish – with brie, roasted figs and shiitake mushrooms, or mac and manchego with fennel and shallots. There's a size for everyone: 'nosh' (great for kids), 'major munch' (a hearty adult serving) and 'mongo' (if you want leftovers to take with you). Children are offered a regular bowl in lieu of the sizzling skillet in which meals are typically served.

BABYSITTING

Baby Sitters' Guild

1-212 682 0227/www.babysittersguild.com. **Bookings** 9am-9pm daily. **No credit cards** (except when paying through hotel).

Long- or short-term sitters cost from $25 per hour and up (four-hour minimum), plus transportation ($4.50, or $10 after midnight). Sitters are available around the clock, and speak 16 languages between them.

Pinch Sitters

1-212 260 6005/www.nypinchsitters.com. **Bookings** 8am-5pm Mon-Fri. **No credit cards**. Charges are $20 per hour (four-hour minimum), plus the babysitter's cab fare after 9pm ($10 maximum). A $35 fee is levied for cancellations with less than 24 hours' notice.

Clubs

As one door closes, another one opens.

New York helped to spawn what we now call dance music, and at one time was the clubbing capital of the world. However, despite this storied history, Gotham's relationship with its after-hours scene is complex and slightly messy. On the one hand, the city's clubbers crave a healthy, progressive and fun scene. On the other, though, the local government seems to want it eradicated. Originally enacted in 1926 and still on the books today, an arcane local law forbids three or more people dancing in any venue without a cabaret licence, a state of affairs that effectively means

many bars and clubs are flouting the law whenever dancing breaks out on their dancefloors. Still, despite this little local difficulty, the scene here is still vibrant – after all, not for nothing is New York nicknamed the city that never sleeps.

THE LOCAL SCENE

There was much excitement when the city recently signalled that it was ready to consider revamping the aforementioned cabaret-license law. But don't get *too* buzzed. We've been down this road before: specifically in spring of 2003, when Gretchen Dykstra, then the Department of Consumer Affairs commissioner, announced plans to drop the cabaret laws in favour of something called a 'nightlife licence'. Much celebrating ensued – until fine print revealed that the proposed legislation was even worse, since it effectively allowed the nightlife police to shut down bars and clubs for pretty much any reason they felt like. Luckily, that little bit of three-card Monte didn't pass, and as of press time, the cabaret regulations are still on the books.

The situation illustrates the love-hate relationship that New York has towards nightlife. Granted, things aren't as bad as in the dark ages (the Giuliani era) of nightlife, when deputy mayor Rudy Washington once proudly stated: 'We've been closing down these little buckets of blood for about three years and paralysing them.' But club closings still happen on a regular basis: the ultra-fun Brooklyn boîte Studio B was recently shuttered by the

Department of Buildings, and the police still storm into niteries on occasion, demanding IDs from patrons and all manner of paperwork from club management. If they don't produce those papers fast enough, that's the end of the night.

But we're here to praise NYC nightlife, not to bury it – and the praise comes easily. In the annual Club World Awards 2008 (www.club worldawards.com), the city's offerings scooped some of the top prizes. Trophy-holders include **Cielo** (Best Club), a lovely, intimate jewel-box that features residents on the level of Louie Vega and François K, along with DJ royalty from around the world; **Dance.Here.Now** (Best Party), a weekly shindig at the same club, which ropes in superstars along the lines of Danny Tenaglia and Victor Calderone to play in the tiny room; and **Pacha** (Best Superclub), which, despite its mainstream trappings, features a healthy dose of underground sounds.

There's plenty more beyond those hallowed halls, too, if you know where to look. **P.S.1 Warm Up**, a weekly summertime soirée held in a courtyard at Queens' P.S.1 Contemporary Art Center, attracts thousands of people who like nothing better than to get down to some pretty twisted DJs. The Meatpacking District's casual **APT** regularly scores some of the world's best spinners to play at what's essentially nothing more than a bar with a sound system. Newcomer **Santos Party House** might be the best club to hit Manhattan in years. And if you're really lucky, you might

About the author
As well as editing the Clubs section in Time Out New York *magazine,* **Bruce Tantum** *is a DJ in venues across the city.*

ARTS & ENTERTAINMENT

APT. *See p299.*

even hear about an illegal warehouse party hidden away in the outer boroughs – though, having said that, you'd better hope that the cops don't hear about it too.

CLUBS

Bunker

Public Assembly (back room), 70 N 6th Street, between Kent & Wythe Avenues, Williamsburg, Brooklyn (1-718 782 5188/www.beyond booking.com/thebunker). Subway L to Bedford Avenue. **Open** 7pm-4am Fri. **Cover** $10-$15. **Average drink** $8. **Credit** DC, MC, V. **Map** p411 U7.
Gotham's electronic music fans were in a tizzy when Tonic, the long-time home of the Bunker, closed in 2007, but the shindig is now happily ensconced in Williamsburg's Public Assembly (former home of Galapagos Art Space; *see p320*). And, as befits the party that helped to kick off the current craze for all things minimal and techno in NYC, residents DJ Spinoza and Derek Plaslaiko are still scoring with big guns from labels like Spectral Sound and Kompakt regularly packing the bunker-like room.

★ Cielo

18 Little W 12th Street, between Ninth Avenue & Washington Street, Meatpacking District (1-212 645 5700/www.cieloclub.com). Subway A, C, E to 14th Street; L to Eighth Avenue. **Open** 10pm-4am Mon; 11pm-4am Wed, Sat; hrs vary Tue, Thur, Fri, Sun. **Cover** $12-$40. **Average drink** $10. **Credit** AmEx, DC, MC, V. **Map** p403 C28.
You'd never guess from the Paris Hilton wannabes hanging out in the neighbourhood that the attitude inside this exclusive club is close to zero. Grab a cocktail, then move to the sunken dancefloor where hip-to-hip crowds gyrate to deep beats from top DJs, including NYC old-schoolers François K, Tedd Patterson and Louie Vega, as well as international spinners ranging from Berlin's Ellen Allien to Dimitri from Paris. Cielo, which features a crystal-clear sound system, has won a bevy of 'best club' awards in its half decade of existence – and it deserves them all.

Element

225 E Houston Street, at Essex Street, Lower East Side (1-212 254 2200/www.elementny.com). Subway F, V to Lower East Side-Second Avenue. **Open** 10pm-4am Fri, Sat. Phone or check website for events on other nights. **Cover** $10-$20. **Average drink** $9. **Credit** AmEx, DC, MC, V. **Map** p403 G29.
A former bank, goth hotspot and studio of Jasper Johns, this hulking space offers a massive dancefloor encircled by a perfect-view balcony and a relatively mellow VIP area. The venue opened as a hipster haven but, for better or worse, it has lost a bit of that edge lately, which might be considered a good thing

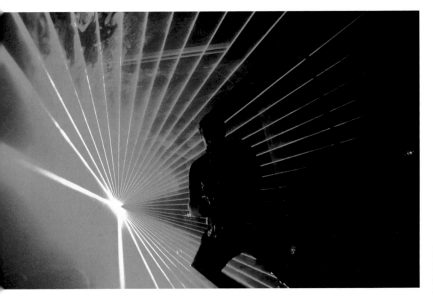

if you're looking for a no-frills night of hip hop or reggae. Be sure to check out the downstairs lounge, Vault (accessible via a separate entrance), which features underground sounds of all sorts.

★ Love

179 MacDougal Street, at 8th Street, Greenwich Village (1-212 477 5683/www.musicislove.net). Subway A, B, C, D, E, F, V to W 4th Street; R, W to 8th Street-NYU. **Open** 10pm-4am Thur-Sat; hrs vary Wed, Sun. **Cover** $10-$20. **Average drink** $8. **Credit** AmEx, V. **Map** p403 E28.
The focus here is squarely on the music (ranging from techno and electro to deep house and hip hop) and building a scene. It's hardly a revolutionary concept, but in today's nightlife world of going for the quick buck, Love stands out from the crowd. The main room is a sparsely furnished box, but the DJ line-up is pretty impressive – the likes of the seminal Chicago house DJ Derrick Carter and Body & Soul's Joe Claussell have all graced the decks here. Lately, the boîte has been branching out beyond house music by hosting nights devoted to drum 'n' bass and dubstep; played over Love's stunning sound system, it all sounds great.

Marquee

289 Tenth Avenue, between 26th & 27th Streets, Chelsea (1-646 473 0202/www.marqueeny.com). Subway C, E to 23rd Street. **Open** 10.30pm-4am Tue-Sat. **Cover** $20. **Average drink** $9. **Credit** AmEx, DC, Disc, MC, V. **Map** p404 C26.
The owners tore the roof off a former garage, and custom-made everything here: the vaulted ceiling,

the glass-beaded chandelier, even the champagne buckets. The centrepiece is a spectacular double-sided staircase that leads to a mezzanine level overlooking the action below. The club accommodates up to 600 people, but despite having been around for a few years, is still so hot that you'll have trouble getting past the velvet rope. Don't expect much musically, though – as with many venues where the scene trumps the tunes, it's largely middle-of-the-road fare (Christina Aguilera and Paris Hilton both had their album release parties here).

Pacha

618 W 46th Street, between Eleventh & Twelfth Avenues, Hell's Kitchen (1-212 209 7500/ www.pachanyc.com). Subway C, E to 50th Street. **Open** 10pm-4am Fri, Sat. **Cover** $20-$25. **Average drink** $9. **Credit** AmEx, DC, MC, V. **Map** p404 B23.
The worldwide glam clubbing chain Pacha, with outposts in nightlife capitals such as Ibiza, London and Buenos Aires, hit the US market in 2005 with this swanky NYC joint helmed by superstar spinner Erick Morillo. The spot attracts heavyweights ranging from local hero Danny Tenaglia to big-time visiting jocks such as Jeff Mills and Josh Wink, but like most big clubs, it pays to check the line-up in advance if you're into underground beats.

Pyramid

101 Avenue A, between 6th & 7th Streets, East Village (1-212 228 4888/www.thepyramid club.com). Subway F, V to Lower East Side-Second Avenue; L to First Avenue; 6 to Astor

ARTS & ENTERTAINMENT

Downtown Rises Again

A new Manhattan club could signal the scene's revival.

Back in the late 1970s and the '80s, Downtown New York was a capital of the world's clubbing scene. The Mudd Club, the Pyramid, the World, Area and many other spots filled the streets of Manhattan south of 14th Street, creating a playground for thrillseekers looking for something a bit more progressive, artistic, egalitarian and fun than the commercial uptown boîtes.

That, though, was a generation or two ago. In recent years, much of the interesting after-dark action has been pushed to the city's outskirts, particularly in the form of unofficial warehouse parties. Which is why the arrival of new Downtown spot **Santos Party House** (*see right*) stirred up so much excitement when it hit the scene in spring 2008.

Launched in Tribeca by a team that includes rocker Andrew WK, Santos is right around the corner from where the beloved Mudd Club once stood. However, the joint isn't the sort of velvet-roped, bottle-servicey lounge you would expect to find in the neighbourhood, but a real-deal underground club. Take it from one who knows. 'I used to go to Mudd Club a lot,' says DJ legend Nicky Siano, who holds a weekly Sunday-night residency, 'and the vibe at Santos, where the management is open to just about anything, is as close to that as I've seen in years. It's like old times, when the

creative people were the ones in charge instead of the bean counters.'

Although the club was three years in the making, you'd never guess it from the decor. Santos doesn't look like much – both floors are basically black, square rooms done out in a bare-bones, generic-club style. But the bi-level club is certainly committed to keeping Downtown's underground scene (or what's left of it) alive and kicking, with top spinners of off-kilter house and cosmic disco regularly taking to the decks. Besides Siano and his soulful-house night, the mighty DFA label is currently holding down Wednesdays with left-of-centre disco and techno; Rong Music's DJ Spun and Rub-n-Tug's Eric Duncan rock Saturdays with a similar mix; and there's also a funk and soul party helmed by A Tribe Called Quest's Q-Tip and talented spinner Rich Medina.

In addition to the residents, visitors can expect a healthy array of visiting bands and DJs, all with an emphasis on beats that rarely reach the mainstream. The street-level room's sound system is one of the biggest and baddest in all of Gotham clubland. And the crowd is one of the best in the city, with tattered art-punks mingling with fashionistas who are tripping over the sort of nightlife habitués who rarely see the daylight. Squint a bit, and you just might believe that the glory days are back.

Place. **Open** 10pm-4am Mon, Thur, Fri, Sat; 8pm-2am Tue, Wed, Sun. **Cover** $6-$10. **Average drink** $7. **No credit cards. Map** p403 G28.
In a clubbing era that's long gone, the Pyramid was a cornerstone of forward-thinking queer club culture. In what could be considered a sign of the times, the venue's sole remaining gay soirée is Friday night's non-progressive '80s dance-fest, 1984. Otherwise, the charmingly decrepit space features the long-running drum 'n' bass bash Konkrete Jungle, as well as an interesting rotating roster of goth and new-wave affairs.
▶ *For more on the gay nightlife scene, see p311.*

★ Santos Party House
100 Lafayette Street, at Walker Street, Tribeca (recorded information 1-212 714 4646/ www.santospartyhouse.com). Subway J, M, Z, N, Q, R, W, 6 to Canal Street. **Open** hrs vary. **Cover** $5-$20. **Average drink** $9. **Credit** AmEx, DC, Disc, MC, V. **Map** p402 E31.
See p298 **Downtown rises again**.

Sapphire
249 Eldridge Street, between Houston & Stanton Streets, Lower East Side (1-212 777 5153/ www.sapphirenyc.com). Subway F, V to Lower East Side-Second Avenue. **Open** 7pm-4am daily. **Cover** $5. **Average drink** $7. **Credit** AmEx, DC, Disc, MC, V. **Map** p403 F29.
Sapphire's bare walls and minimal decorations are as raw as it gets – and not particularly appealing – yet the energetic, unpretentious clientele is oblivious to the (lack of) aesthetic. A dance crowd packs the place all week – various nights feature house, hip hop, reggae and disco.

Sullivan Room
218 Sullivan Street, between Bleecker & W 3rd Streets, Greenwich Village (1-212 252 2151/ www.sullivanroom.com). Subway A, B, C, D, E, F, V to W 4th Street. **Open** 10pm-4am Mon, Tue, Thur-Sat; sometimes Wed, Sun. **Cover** $5-$20. **Average drink** $8. **Credit** AmEx, Disc, DC, MC, V. **Map** p403 E29.
Where's the party? It's right here in this unmarked subterranean space, which hosts some of the best deep-house, tech-house and breaks bashes the city has to offer. It's an utterly unpretentious place with little of the glitz of bigger clubs – but hell, all you really need are some thumpin' beats and a place to move your feet, right? Keep a special lookout for the nights hosted by local stalwarts Sleepy and Boo.

205 Club
205 Chrystie Street, at Stanton Street, Lower East Side (1-212 477 6688/www.myspace.com/ 205club). Subway F, V to Second Avenue-Lower East Side. **Open** 9pm-4am Tue-Sun. **Cover** free-$10. **Credit** AmEx, DC, MC, V. **Map** p403 F29.

Out of the ashes of 6s & 8s arises Club 205, and it's the cabaret-licenced venue's best incarnation yet. That's not so much because of the club's decor – the street level has a definite dive-bar ambience, while the basement, despite an effort to convey a Factory-esque vibe, is basically just a basement. No matter, though, because the subterranean space contains a top-tier Phazon sound system, which lures some of the city's best DJs. Musically, you'll hear a lot of electro, space-disco and other hipster-friendly sounds, but the bookers toss in plenty of curveballs too (hip hop has been big here lately), so best to check the MySpace page to find out what you'll be getting into.

Webster Hall
125 E 11th Street, between Third & Fourth Avenues, East Village (1-212 353 1600/ www.websterhall.com). Subway L to Third Avenue; N, Q, R, W, 4, 5, 6 to 14th Street-Union Square. **Open** 10pm-5am Thur-Sat. **Cover** free-$30. **Average drink** $6. **Credit** AmEx, DC, MC, V. **Map** p403 F28.
Should you crave the sight of big hair, muscle shirts and gold chains, Webster Hall offers all that and, well, not much more. The grand four-level space, originally a 19th-century dance hall, is nice enough, and the DJs aren't bad (spinning disco, hip hop, soul, Latin, trance, progressive house or pop hits), but it's hard to forget who you're sharing the dancefloor with. True, the massive club has put a little effort into glamming up its image lately – spinners along the line of progressive-house heroes Sasha and Digweed have been featured recently – but wet T-shirt and striptease contests also abound.
▶ *See p325 for concerts at Webster Hall.*

LOUNGES & DJ BARS
APT
419 W 13th Street, between Ninth Avenue & Washington Street, Meatpacking District (1-212 414 4245/www.aptwebsite.com). Subway A, C, E to 14th Street; L to Eighth Avenue. **Open** 9pm-4am daily. **Cover** free-$10. **Average drink** $9. **Credit** AmEx, DC, MC, V. **Map** p403 C27.
Kicking back in APT's formerly exclusive street-level space (the neat design is by India Mahdavi) is like being at an impromptu party in some trust-fund babe's Upper East Side townhouse. Below, people looking for the perfect beat gather in a minimalist, faux-wood-panelled rectangular room. The place features an amazing array of DJs; top spinners, such as locals DJ Spun and the Negroclash crew, and superstars like cosmic-disco dons the Idjut Boys and house-music hero Tony Humphries regularly regale the tipplers with a wide range of underground sounds. *Photos pp296-297.*

Le Souk
47 Avenue B, between 3rd & 4th Streets, East Village (1-212 777 5454/www.lesoukny.com).

ARTS & ENTERTAINMENT

Subway F, V to Lower East Side-Second Avenue.
Open 6pm-4am daily. **Cover** free. **Average drink** $9. **Credit** DC, MC, V. **Map** p403 G29.
You might not suspect a Middle Eastern eaterie and hookah bar to be one of the mainstays of New York's clubbing scene, but if you're at all into straight-up house music, make sure you stop by Le Souk on a Sunday any time between mid afternoon and, say, mid Monday morning. That's when you'll find local vets Astro&Glyde and Swamy manning the decks, along with top guests. And when we say top, we mean it: folks on the level of Sasha and Paul Oakenfold have been known to tickle the Technics here. There are DJs on other nights too, but really, it's all about Sundays here.

ROVING & SEASONAL PARTIES

New York has a number of peripatetic and season-specific shindigs. Nights, locations and prices vary, so call or hit websites for updates.

Giant Step
www.giantstep.net.
Giant Step parties have been among the best of the nu-soul scene since the early '90s – back before there was a nu-soul scene. Sadly, the gang doesn't throw as many fêtes as it once did, now preferring to concentrate on live shows and record promotions. But on the rare occasion that Giant Step does decide to pack a dancefloor, you'd be a fool to miss it: the music is always great, and the multicultural crowd always gorgeous beyond belief.

P.S.1 Warm Up
P.S.1 Contemporary Art Center, 22-25 Jackson Avenue, at 46th Avenue, Long Island City,
Queens (1-718 784 2084/www.ps1.org). Subway E, V (V weekdays only) to 23rd Street-Ely Avenue; G to 21st Street-Jackson Avenue; 7 to 45th Road-Court House Square. **Open** *July-Sept* 2-9pm Sat.
Cover (incl museum admission) $10. **Average drink** $6. **No credit cards. Map** p412 V5.
Back in 1997, who could have guessed that the courtyard of the MoMA-affiliated P.S.1 Contemporary Art Center would play host to some of the most anticipated, resolutely underground clubbing events in the city? Since the Warm Up series kicked off that year, summer Saturdays truly haven't been the same. Thousands of dance music fanatics make the pilgrimage to Queens to pack the space, swig beer, dance and generally make a mockery of the soirée's arty setting. The sounds range from spiritually inclined soul to full-bore techno, spun by local and international stars.
▶ *See p136 for further details of the P.S.1 exhibition space.*

★ 718 Sessions
1-212 978 8869/www.dannykrivit.net.
DJ Danny Krivit, best known for his part in the legendary Body & Soul party (which also returns from time to time), plays old-school, soulful house for a diverse crowd at various venues in the city.

★ Turntables on the Hudson
www.turntablesonthehudson.com.
This ultra-funky affair lost its long-time home at the Lightship Frying Pan when the city put the kibosh on the vessel's parties (no surprise there), but they still pop up all over the place – sometimes on the Hudson, sometimes not. DJs Nickodemus, Mariano and their guests do the dub-funky, world-beat thing, and live percussionists add to the flavour. As good as it gets.

P.S.1 Warm Up.

Film & TV

The reel deal.

By now, the whole world is on first-name terms with New York's canonical legends: Marty, Woody, Spike, the no-nonsense poets. Let Hollywood hog all the glamour it wants – this is the place where movies come to get real.

So welcome to your own New York story. Who are you going to be? Do you feel like strutting through Lincoln Center Plaza à la Bill Murray in *Ghostbusters*? Or maybe sulking on the subway like Christopher Walken in *King of New York*? You're here, so, whatever you do, make sure you play a part.

FILM

Few cities offer the film lover as many options as New York. If you insist, you can check out the blockbusters at the mobbed multiplexes on 42nd Street. But Gotham's gems are its smaller art houses and museums, world-famous rep and cutting-edge cinemas. You can see acclaimed Romanian films before many Romanians do, or hear legendary directors introduce their films. For listings, see *Time Out New York* magazine.

Art & revival houses

Angelika Film Center
18 W Houston Street, at Mercer Street, Soho (1-212 995 2000/www.angelikafilmcenter.com). Subway B, D, F, V to Broadway-Lafayette Street; R, W to Prince Street; 6 to Bleecker Street. **Tickets** $12; $8 reductions. **Credit** AmEx, DC, MC, V. **Map** p403 E29.
When it opened in 1989, the Angelika immediately became a player in the then-booming Amerindie scene, and the six-screen cinema still puts the emphasis on edgier fare, both domestic and foreign. The complex is packed at weekends, so come extra early or visit the website to buy advance tickets.

Anthology Film Archives
32 Second Avenue, at 2nd Street, East Village (1-212 505 5181/www.anthologyfilmarchives.org). Subway F, V to Lower East Side-Second Avenue;

6 to Bleecker Street. **Tickets** $8; $5 reductions. **No credit cards.** **Map** p403 F29.
This red-brick building feels a little like a fortress – and, in a sense, it is one, protecting the legacy of NYC's fiercest experimenters. Anthology is committed to screening the world's most adventurous fare, from 16mm found-footage works to digital video dreams. Dedicated to the preservation, study and exhibition of independent and avant-garde film, it houses a gallery and film museum plus two screens.

★ BAM Rose Cinemas
Brooklyn Academy of Music, 30 Lafayette Avenue, between Ashland Place & St Felix Street, Fort Greene, Brooklyn (1-718 636 4100/www.bam.org). Subway B, Q, 2, 3, 4, 5 to Atlantic Avenue; C to Lafayette Street; D, M, N, R to Pacific Street; G to Fulton Street. **Tickets** $11; $7.50 reductions. **Credit** AmEx, DC, MC, V. **Map** p410 T10.
Brooklyn's premier art-film venue does double duty as a rep house for well-programmed classics on 35mm and a first-run multiplex for indie films. It's recently started to host an annual best-of-Sundance programme: far more convenient than going to Utah.

Cinema Village
22 E 12th Street, between Fifth Avenue & University Place, Greenwich Village (1-212 924 3363/www.cinemavillage.com). Subway L, N, Q, R, W, 4, 5, 6 to 14th Street-Union Square. **Tickets** $10; $5.50-$7.50 reductions. **Credit** DC, MC, V. **Map** p403 E28.
A classic marquee that charmed Noah Baumbach long before he made *The Squid and the Whale*, this three-screener specialises in indie flicks, cutting-edge documentaries and foreign films. Check out the subway turnstile that admits ticket holders to the lobby.

About the author
Joshua Rothkopf *is a film critic at* Time Out New York *magazine. His writing has also appeared in* Penthouse, Details *and the* Village Voice.

City Secrets Film Forum's Faux Plaques

The best seats in the house don't always go to the A-listers.

With its premier programming and rich repertory offerings (ranging from Hitchcock to Ousmane Sembene), **Film Forum** is the destination of choice for film students and aficionados. But it would take an obsessive movie trivia addict to crack, let alone notice, one particular industry in-joke.

'One of the benefits of donating to Film Forum at a "higher level" is getting to dedicate a seat plaque to yourself or anyone you desire,' says programmer Mike Maggiore. 'Two of my favourite seat plaques are located next to each other in the second theatre on your right, row 18, seats B and C: "Through the generosity of Karl Mundt" and "In loving memory of Doris Crane". Both were donated by Frances McDormand and Joel Coen. Mundt is the name of John Goodman's insurance salesman/psycho in *Barton Fink,* and Crane is the name of McDormand's boozy, bingo-obsessed murder victim in *The Man Who Wasn't There*.'

★ Film Forum

209 W Houston Street, between Sixth Avenue & Varick Street, West Village (1-212 727 8110/ www.filmforum.com). Subway 1 to Houston Street. **Tickets** $10.50; $5.50 reductions. **Credit** (online purchases only) MC, V. **Map** p403 D29.
The city's leading tastemaking venue, Film Forum is programmed by a fest-scouring staff that takes its duties as seriously as a Kurosawa samurai. A recent renovation included new seats, all the better to take in the hottest films from Cannes, Venice and beyond.

★ IFC Center

323 Sixth Avenue, at 3rd Street, Greenwich Village (1-212 924 7771/www.ifccenter.com). Subway A, B, C, D, E, F, V to W 4th Street. **Tickets** $12; $8 reductions. **Credit** AmEx, DC, MC, V. **Map** p403 D29.
The long-darkened 1930s Waverly was once again illuminated in 2005 when it was reborn as a modern three-screen art house, showing the latest indie hits, choice midnight cult items and occasional foreign classics. You may rub elbows with the actors on the screen, many introduce their work on opening night.
▶ *A high-toned café provides sweets, lattes and substantials.*

★ Landmark Sunshine Cinema

141-143 E Houston Street, between First & Second Avenues, East Village (1-212 330 8182).
Subway F, V to Lower East Side-Second Avenue. **Tickets** $12; $8 reductions. **Credit** AmEx, DC, Disc, MC, V. **Map** p403 F29.
Once a renowned Yiddish theatre, this comfortable, date-friendly venue has snazz and chutzpah to spare. Intimate cinemas and excellent sound are a beautiful complement to the indie fare; here, too, is New York's most consistently excellent midnight series.
▶ *If you're here for a late show, it's worth remembering that nearby Katz's Deli is open until the wee hours at weekends; see p185.*

Leonard Nimoy Thalia

Symphony Space, 2537 Broadway, at 95th Street, entrance on 95th Street, Upper West Side (1-212 864 5400/www.symphonyspace.org). Subway 1, 2, 3 to 96th Street. **Tickets** $11; $7 reductions. **Credit** AmEx, DC, MC, V. **Map** p406 C17.
The famed Thalia art house, featured in *Annie Hall* (when it was screening *The Sorrow and the Pity*), was recently upgraded, but it's still trying to find its identity. Even so, the classics are reliable: a month of Hepburn and Tracy, for instance.

Quad Cinema

34 W 13th Street, between Fifth & Sixth Avenues, Greenwich Village (1-212 255 8800/www.quad cinema.com). Subway F, V to 14th Street; L to Sixth Avenue. **Tickets** $10.50; $7.50 reductions. **Credit** AmEx, DC, Disc, MC, V. **Map** p403 E28.

ARTS & ENTERTAINMENT

The Quad's four small screens show a wide range of foreign and American indies. However, the real draws at this Greenwich Village operation are the latest offerings related to gay sexuality and politics.
▶ *There's gay-movie action of a very different type at the Chelsea Classics film series, held at the Clearview Cinemas in Chelsea; see p313.*

Two Boots Pioneer Theater

155 E 3rd Street, at Avenue A, East Village (1-212 591 0434/www.twoboots.com/pioneer). Subway F, V to Lower East Side-Second Avenue. **Tickets** $10; $6.50 reductions. **Credit** (online purchases only) AmEx, Disc, MC, V. **Map** p403 G29. This East Village alternative film centre recently underwent a curatorial restaffing. The venue's strengths – low-budget indies and horror revivals – remain in full effect, but the first-run fare tends to be hit or miss.

Museums & societies

★ Film Society of Lincoln Center

Walter Reade Theater, 70 Lincoln Center Plaza, between Broadway & Amsterdam Avenue, Upper West Side (1-212 875 5601/www.filmlinc.com). Subway 1 to 66th Street-Lincoln Center. **Tickets** $11; $7 reductions. **Credit** (online purchases only) MC, V. **Map** p405 C21. Founded in 1969 to promote contemporary film, the FSLC now also hosts the prestigious New York Film Festival. Programmes are usually thematic with an international perspective. Until autumn 2009,

when Lincoln Center's state-of-the-art Elinor Bunin-Munroe Film Center opens on the south side of 65th Street with two screens, a gallery and café, all of your film-going needs will be met here.

★ Museum of Modern Art

For listing, see p100. **Tickets** free with museum admission, or $10; $6-$8 reductions; free under-16s. **Credit** AmEx, DC, MC, V. Renowned for its superb programming of art films and experimental work, MoMA draws from a vast vault. Buy tickets in person at the museum, the lobby desk or the film desk (see www.moma.org or call 1-212 708 9480). And take in some paintings or sculptures while you're there.

Museum of the Moving Image

1-718 784 0077/www.movingimage.us. **Tickets** prices vary. **Credit** AmEx, DC, MC, V. The Museum of the Moving Image in Queens (*see p137*) is closed for renovations. It reopens in late 2009 (with stadium seating, larger screens and state-of-the-art sound). Screenings and other events have moved to various off-site Manhattan venues.
▶ *For Queens' cinematic heritage, see p138.*

Foreign-language specialists

There is a wealth of specifically foreign language film operations. There's the **French Institute Alliance Française** (22 East 60th Street, 1-212 355 6100), German movies courtesy of the **Goethe-Institut** (*see p107*); the **Japan**

Anthology Film Archives. *See p301.*

Society (*see p103*) and **Scandinavia House** (*see p92*) live up to expectations; and the **Asia Society & Museum** (*see p108*) offers works from Asian countries plus Asian-American productions. Tickets are in the $10-$12 region.

Film festivals

Each spring, the Museum of Modern Art and the Film Society of Lincoln Center sponsor the highly regarded **New Directors/New Films** series, presenting works by on-the-cusp filmmakers. Together with Lincoln Center's *Film Comment* magazine, the FSLC puts on the popular **Film Comment Selects**, showcasing films yet to be distributed in the US. And from late September to early October, the FSLC hosts the **New York Film Festival** (1-212 875 5050, www.filmlinc.com), a worthy showcase packed with premières, features and short flicks from around the globe.

January brings the annual **New York Jewish Film Festival** (1-212 875 5600, www.thejewishmuseum.org) to Lincoln Center's Walter Reade Theater. In spring, Robert De Niro's **Tribeca Film Festival** (22 Apr-3 May, 1-212 941 2400, www.tribecafilmfestival.org) draws around 400,000 fans to screenings of independent movies. The **New York Lesbian & Gay Film Festival** (1-212 571 2170, www.newfest.org) takes place 4-14 June. And summer sees several outdoor film festivals; *see below* **Inside track**.

TV

Studio tapings

Colbert Report
513 W 54th Street, between Tenth & Eleventh Avenues, Hell's Kitchen (www.comedycentral. com). Subway C, E to 50th Street. **Tapings** 6pm Mon-Thur. **Map** p405 C22.

**INSIDE TRACK
OUTDOOR MOVIES**

With summer arrives the wonderful New York tradition of free outdoor movie festivals. Look out for the **Bryant Park Summer Film Festival** in Midtown Manhattan (1-212 512 5700, www.bryant park.org); **Movies with a View** in Brooklyn Bridge Park (1-718 802 0603, http://brooklynbridgepark.org); the **River to River Festival** across Lower Manhattan (*see p263*); and **Summer on the Hudson** in Riverside Park South (1-212 408 0219).

Mocking correspondent Stephen Colbert's parody of Bill O'Reilly's right-wing political talk show – the 't' is silent in both 'Colbert' and 'Report' – tells viewers why everyone else's opinions are 'just plain wrong'. Reserve tickets online at least six months ahead, or try your luck getting standby tickets on the day at 4pm. You must be at least 18 and have a photo ID.

Daily Show with Jon Stewart
513 W 54th Street, between Tenth & Eleventh Avenues, Hell's Kitchen (www.thedailyshow.com). Subway C, E to 50th Street. **Tapings** 5.45pm Mon-Thur. **Map** p105 C22.
Many viewers believe they get a fairer view of current affairs from Stewart's irreverent take than they do from the network news. Reserve tickets at least three months ahead online; as ticket distribution may be in excess of studio capacity, admission is not guaranteed. You must be over 18 and have photo ID.

Late Night with Conan O'Brien
30 Rockefeller Plaza, Sixth Avenue, between 49th & 50th Streets, Midtown (1-212 664 3056/ www.nbc.com). Subway B, D, F, V to 47th-50th Streets-Rockefeller Center. **Tapings** 5.30pm Mon-Fri. **Map** p404 E23.
You'll need to call at least four weeks in advance for tickets to this late-night staple, although a few same-day tickets are distributed at the studio at 9am (49th Street entrance). You must be over 16 with photo ID. Note that O'Brien is due to leave the show in spring 2009 in order to replace Jay Leno on *The Tonight Show* in LA; Jimmy Fallon looks set to step into O'Brien's *Late Night* shoes.

Late Show with David Letterman
1697 Broadway, between 53rd & 54th Streets, Midtown (1-212 975 1003/www.lateshow audience.com). Subway B, D, E to Seventh Avenue. **Tapings** 4.30pm, 7pm Mon; 4.30pm Tue-Thur. **Map** p405 D22.
Letterman's sardonic humour has been a defining feature of the late-night landscape for decades. Seats are hard to get: fill out a request form online, or try to get a standby ticket by calling 1-212 247 6497 at 11am on the day. You must be 18 with photo ID.

Saturday Night Live
30 Rockefeller Plaza, Sixth Avenue, between 49th & 50th Streets, Midtown (1-212 664 3056/www.nbc. com/snl). Subway B, D, F, V to 47th-50th Streets-Rockefeller Center. **Tapings** Dress rehearsal at 8pm; live show at 11.30pm. **Map** p405 D22.
Tickets to this long-running comedy sketch show are assigned by lottery every autumn. Send an email to snltickets@nbcuni.com in August, or try the standby lottery on the day. Line up by 7am (but get there much earlier) under the NBC Studio marquee (49th Street side of 30 Rockefeller Plaza). You must be over 16 with photo ID.

Gay & Lesbian

Three cheers for the queers.

In the small hours of 28 June 1969, homo tipplers at the Stonewall Inn in Greenwich Village decided that they'd had enough with the series of harassing raids that police regularly made on gay bars in the area. This time, when cops once again crashed their party, the bar's patrons fought back, resisting arrest and protesting in huge numbers at the police's actions.

Since that historic night, widely seen as the birth of the gay rights movement, progress has continued at breakneck speed in New York. The constant formation and dissolution of gay organisations, from ACT UP to the Lesbian Avengers, has run alongside the arrival and departure of storied nightclubs, from the Saint to the Roxy. The city's laws now foster a healthy gay existence, criminalising anti-gay violence, forbidding workplace discrimination and affording same-sex couples full domestic partnership rights. On the 40th anniversary of the Stonewall riots, New York is still one of the gayest cities in the world, welcoming to lesbian, gay, bisexual and transgender folks from near and far.

GAY NEIGHBOURHOODS

Although it's hard to get consensus on anything from New Yorkers, most would agree that the hottest 'gaybourhood' is currently **Hell's Kitchen** (aka Clinton). In this western swath of Midtown by the Theater District, slick new bars, eateries and boutiques catering to gay men have been opening at a fast and furious rate. You'll find most of the drinking, dining and strutting on Ninth Avenue in the 40s and 50s.

Chelsea, which borders Hell's Kitchen to the south (with a little break in between, in the 30s), was Manhattan's gay top dog for more than a decade. Some would argue it's still the hub of gay life in NYC; however, as inevitably happens in gay ghettos, the area's cool factor has dissipated as its population has aged (you'll see male couples pushing baby strollers), and the area has become more mainstream due to the throngs of straight folks who want in on the fun. The slew of boy bars and clubs are joined by eateries, gyms, parties and muscled

About the author
Keith Mulvihill *edited the* Time Out New York Shortlist 2009, *and frequently writes about travel for the* New York Times.

characters cruising along Eighth Avenue. This is, after all, the area that inspired *Chelsea Boys*, the spot-on comic-strip series penned by New Yorkers Glen Hanson and Allan Neuwirth.

Just south of here is the original gay bohemia: the **West Village**, home to the famed Christopher Street and the deep, still-palpable roots of gay liberation. It's also the end point of the annual Gay Pride March (*see p263*), which wends its way past the lovely townhouses of Christopher Street and over to the Hudson River. On any given night, Pier 45 attracts scores of whooping Latino and African-American gay and transgender youths, to flirt, cruise and find kindred spirits. Across town, in the **East Village**, is a steadfast network of nightspots that cater to dykes and gays on the creative, edgy side; it's the type of place where you might rub elbows with latex-clad club kids, none-too-polished drag queens and skinny, electronica-lovin', twentysomething boys.

In Brooklyn, leafy **Park Slope** is a long-time enclave for lesbians and gay men of all types. During the first weekend in June, the Slope hosts the borough's annual **Brooklyn Pride March**, a (very) scaled-down version of the NYC event. Hip **Williamsburg** is also home to a large queer population. And over in

Pride March.

ARTS & ENTERTAINMENT

Queens, the diverse locale of **Jackson Heights** has several LGBT bars and clubs and a large South American queer population. The **Queens Pride March**, held here in mid June, is a less corporate, more soulful version of Manhattan's main Pride event.

FESTIVALS & PARTIES

Sex parties are part of any gay scene, and New York is no exception. Men of all ages, shapes and sizes frequent private sex and fetish soirées (see *HX* magazine for listings), including Brooklyn's **SPAM** (1-718 789 4053, www.submitparty.com). **Gay Male S/M Activists** (www.gmsma.org) holds frequent parties and workshops on kinky play, with its central star attraction being the annual **Folsom Street East festival** held in June in the Meatpacking District. The underground (and frequently shuttered) **Bijou** (82 E 4th Street, behind the red door) is a sleazily popular post-nightclub hook-up spot, where porn on a big screen is just a warm-up for the private-play booths. Libidinous lesbians should head to one of the friendly, dyke-owned **Babeland** boutiques (*see p249*), which hold occasional workshops, or the perpetually wild monthly women's sex party **Submit** (1-718 789 4053, www.submitparty.com), where a den of slings, shower rooms and handcuffs awaits more adventurous punters.

Gay Pride Week, New York's biggest queer event, takes place in June, bringing a swirl of parties and performances. Although some jaded New Yorkers find the celebration a little passé, there are still a half-million or so spectators and participants at the **Pride March** (*see p263*), which takes five hours to wind down Fifth Avenue from Midtown to the West Village. August, meanwhile, brings **Pride in the City** (www.prideinthecity.com), the official black LGBT pride event that delivers picnics, dance soirées, concerts, queer health forums and a huge beach party out in the Rockaways of Queens. But don't despair if you miss the big gatherings – gay pride is never in short supply.

BOOKS & MAGAZINES

Because of the popularity of large bookstore chains that sell everything (but may not know their Sedaris from their Sappho), the number of gay bookstores has unfortunately dropped significantly in recent years. **Oscar Wilde** is the only one left, although **Bluestockings** also has a good stock of LGBT titles.

Time Out New York's Gay & Lesbian section offers its own weekly guide to happenings all around the city. Both of New York's weekly gay

entertainment magazines – *HX* (www.hx.com) and *Next* (www.nextmagazine.com) – include extensive boy-centric information on bars, clubs, restaurants, events, meetings and sex parties. The monthly *Go!* (www.gomag.com), 'a cultural road map for the city girl', gives the lowdown on the lesbian nightlife and travel scene. *Gay City News* (www.gaycity news.com) provides feisty political coverage with an activist slant; its thin rival, the *New York Blade* (published by *HX*), has stories about gay news picked up from the local and international press. All are free and widely available in street boxes, at gay and lesbian bars and in bookstores. *MetroSource* (www.metrosource.com; $4.95) is a bi-monthly glossy with a fashion victim slant and tons of listings.

Bluestockings

172 Allen Street, between Rivington & Stanton Streets, Lower East Side (1-212 777 6028/ www.bluestockings.com). Subway F, V to Lower East Side-Second Avenue. **Open** 11am-11pm daily. **Credit** AmEx, DC, MC, V. **Map** p403 F29.
This radical bookstore, Fairtrade café and activist resource centre stocks LGBT literature and regularly hosts queer events (often with a feminist slant), including dyke knitting circles, trans-politics forums and women's open mic nights.
▶ *For readings here, see p278.*

★ Oscar Wilde Bookshop

15 Christopher Street, between Sixth & Seventh Avenues, West Village (1-212 255 8097/www. oscarwildebooks.com). Subway 1 to Christopher Street-Sheridan Square. **Open** 11am-7pm daily. **Credit** AmEx, DC, MC, V. **Map** p403 D28.
Purportedly the world's first gay bookstore when it opened in 1967, Oscar Wilde has gone through many changes of hands. Kim Brinster, its current owner, is passionate about stocking all manner of queer titles both new and used, including rare first editions and signed volumes. Magazines and DVDs are also sold.

INSIDE TRACK
GAY MARRIAGE

Although New York State's highest court declared gay marriage illegal in 2006, recent events may help to bring about change. In May 2008, NY Governor David Paterson directed all state agencies to comply with an earlier court ruling and recognise legally performed out-of-state same-sex marriages. Keep your eyes peeled for further news.

ARTS & ENTERTAINMENT

ARTS & ENTERTAINMENT

CENTRES & HELPLINES

Gay & Lesbian National Hotline
1-888 843 4564/www.glnh.org. **Open** 4pm-midnight Mon-Fri; noon-5pm Sat.
This phone service offers excellent peer counselling, legal referrals, details of gay and lesbian organisations, and information on bars, restaurants and hotels. Younger callers can contact the toll-free GLBT National Youth Talk Line (1-800 246 7743).

Gay Men of African Descent
103 E 125th Street, at Park Avenue, Harlem (1-212 828 1697/www.gmad.org). Subway 4, 5, 6 to 125th Street. **Open** hours vary; phone for schedule. **Map** p407 E13.
This vibrant centre for same-gender-loving men of colour is a great resource for health information. Based in Harlem, it hosts meetings and events, from HIV support group gatherings to queer youth celebrations and community outreach projects.

Gay Men's Health Crisis
119 W 24th Street, between Sixth & Seventh Avenues, Chelsea (1-212 367 1000/AIDS advice hotline 1-212 807 6655/www.gmhc.org). Subway F, V, 1 to 23rd Street. **Open** *Hotline* 10am-9pm Mon-Fri; recorded information at other times. *Office* 11am-8pm Mon-Fri. **Map** p404 D26.
GMHC was the world's first organisation dedicated to helping people with AIDS. Its threefold mission is to push for better public policies; to educate the public to prevent the spread of HIV; and to provide services and counselling to people living with HIV. Local support groups meet here in the evening.

Lesbian, Gay, Bisexual & Transgender Community Center
208 W 13th Street, between Seventh & Eighth Avenues, West Village (1-212 620 7310/www.gay center.org). Subway A, C, E, 1, 2, 3 to 14th Street; L to Eighth Avenue. **Open** 9am-11pm daily. **Map** p403 D27.
The Center celebrated 25 years in 2008 and provides information and a gay support network. It's a friendly resource that offers guidance to gay tourists; it's also used as a venue for 300-plus groups. The National Museum & Archive of Lesbian & Gay History and the Pat Parker/Vito Russo Library are housed here, as is an art gallery and small internet room (11am-9pm Mon-Fri, noon-6pm Sat, Sun; $3/hr).

★ Lesbian Herstory Archives
484 14th Street, between Eighth Avenue & Prospect Park West, Park Slope, Brooklyn (1-718 768 3953/www.lesbianherstory archives.org). Subway F to 15th Street-Prospect Park. **Open** times vary; phone or check website for details. **Map** p410 T12.
The Herstory Archives contain more than 20,000 books (cultural theory, fiction, poetry, plays), 1,600 periodicals and assorted memorabilia. The cosy brownstone also hosts occasional screenings, readings and social gatherings, plus an annual open house in early June to coincide with Brooklyn Pride.

NYC Gay & Lesbian Anti-Violence Project
Suite 200, 240 W 35th Street, between Seventh & Eighth Avenues, Garment District (24hr bilingual hotline 1-212 714 1141/1184/ www.avp.org). Subway A, C, E, 1, 2, 3 to 34th Street-Penn Station. **Open** 10am-6pm Mon-Fri. **Map** p404 D25.
The Project works with local police to provide support to victims of anti-gay crime, plus volunteers who offer advice on seeking help from police. Long- and short-term counselling services are available. The Project is also the place to call (in addition to the police) to report any sort of gay bias attack.

WHERE TO STAY

Chelsea Mews Guest House
344 W 15th Street, between Eighth & Ninth Avenues, Chelsea (1-212 255 9174). Subway A, C, E to 14th Street; L to Eighth Avenue. **Rates** $150-$200 double. **Rooms** 8. **No credit cards.** **Map** p403 C27.
Built in 1840, this guesthouse caters to gay men. The rooms are comfortable and well furnished and, in most cases, share a bathroom with only one neighbour. Bikes and a laundry service are complimentary. The charming Anne Frank Suite (room 110) has two twin beds and a private bathroom.
Internet (wireless; free). No smoking. Room service.

Chelsea Pines Inn
317 W 14th Street, between Eighth & Ninth Avenues, Chelsea (1-212 929 1023/1-888 546 2700/www.chelseapinesinn.com). Subway A, C, E to 14th Street; L to Eighth Avenue. **Rates** (incl breakfast) $140-$350 double. **Rooms** 25. **Credit** AmEx, DC, Disc, MC, V. **Map** p403 C27.
On the border of Chelsea and the West Village, Chelsea Pines welcomes gay guests of all persuasions. The 25 rooms are clean and comfortable, with classic film themes; most have private bathrooms, and all are equipped with a radio, a TV, a fridge and free Wi-Fi.
Concierge. Internet (wireless; free). No smoking. TV: DVD.

★ Colonial House Inn
318 W 22nd Street, between Eighth & Ninth Avenues, Chelsea (1-212 243 9669/1-800 689 3779/www.colonialhouseinn.com). Subway C, E to 23rd Street. **Rates** (incl breakfast) $150-$207 double. **Rooms** 20. **Credit** DC, MC, V. **Map** p404 C26.
This beautifully renovated 1850s townhouse sits on a quiet street in Chelsea. Run by (and primarily

for) gay men, it's a great place to stay, even if some of the cheaper rooms are a bit snug. Bonuses include a fireplace in three of the deluxe rooms, a rooftop deck for all (nude sunbathing is allowed) and an owner, Mel Cheren, who's famous in the music world as the CEO of West End Records and the financial backer of the legendary Paradise Garage club.
Internet (wireless; $10/hr). No smoking. Parking ($37.50).

East Village B&B

244 E 7th Street, between Avenues C & D, East Village (no phone/evbandb@juno.com). Subway F, V to Lower East Side-Second Avenue; L to First Avenue. **Rates** (incl breakfast) $120-$150 double. **Rooms** 2. **No credit cards.** **Map** p403 G28.

This lesbian-owned accommodation gem is tucked neatly into a turn-of-the-20th-century apartment building on a quiet East Village block. The space has gleaming wood floors, exposed brick walls and slick retro (1970s) furniture, as well as an eclectic art collection. The bedrooms all are done up in bold colours and white walls; one of the bathrooms includes a small tub, while the living room has a TV and a CD player.
Internet (wireless; free). No smoking.

Incentra Village House

32 Eighth Avenue, between Jane & W 12th Streets, West Village (1-212 206 0007/www.incentravillage.com). Subway A, C, E to 14th Street; L to Eighth Avenue. **Rates** $169-$219 double. **Rooms** 13. **Credit** AmEx, DC, MC, V. **Map** p403 D28.

City Secrets Toilet Art

How Keith Haring brightened up a New York restroom.

Artist Keith Haring was deeply involved with well-loved institution **LGBT Community Center** (*see p308*) in the 1980s. During a fund-raiser on 27 May 1989, he and 50 other artists decided to paint every room in the building in honour of the 20th anniversary of the Stonewall Riots. For his part, Haring tackled a 12ft x

8ft x 25ft chunk of ceiling and upper walls in a men's restroom on the second floor, a space that's now used mostly for storage. If you get the chance, feast your eyes on the *Once Upon a Time* mural; you'll spy giant cocks aplenty, and Haring's signature figures knocking boots in every way imaginable.

ARTS & ENTERTAINMENT

Two cute 1841 townhouses in the Meatpacking District make up this nicely restored and gay-run guesthouse. The spacious rooms have private bathrooms and kitchenettes; some also have fireplaces. A 1939 Steinway baby grand graces the parlour and sets a tone of easy sophistication.
Disabled-adapted rooms. Internet (wireless; free). No smoking. TV: DVD.

Ivy Terrace

230 E 58th Street, between Second & Third Avenues, Midtown East (1-516 662 6862/www. ivyterrace.com). Subway N, R, W to Lexington Avenue-59th Street; 4, 5, 6 to 59th Street. **Rates** (incl breakfast) $195-$300 double. **Rooms** 6. **Credit** AmEx, DC, Disc, MC, V. **Map** p405 F22.
This lovely lesbian-run B&B has six cosy rooms with high ceilings and wooden floors. Some have old-fashioned sleigh beds; the Zen room is more modern. The owners serve breakfast each morning, but you're also free to make your own meals: each room has a gas stove and a full-size fridge for those essential midnight feasts.
Internet (wireless; free). No smoking.

RESTAURANTS & CAFES

The sight of same-sex couples holding hands across a candlelit table is pretty commonplace in New York. But if you want to increase the odds of being in the majority when you dine, check out the following gay-friendly places.

★ Counter

105 First Avenue, between 6th & 7th Streets, East Village (1-212 982 5870). Subway F, V to Lower East Side-Second Avenue. **Open** 5pm-midnight Mon-Thur; 5pm-1am Fri; 11am-1am Sat; 11am-midnight Sun. **Average main course** $15. **Credit** AmEx, DC, Disc, MC, V. **Map** p403 F28.
This hip, lesbian-owned vegetarian bistro has a wine bar with more than 200 organic and biodynamic offerings; the organic martinis are also a big draw. Locally grown produce is used whenever possible; the kitchen even caters to purists, with raw dishes on the menu alongside healthy cooked fare such as the East Side Burger made of mushroom pâté, seitan and herbs. There's a popular brunch at weekends.

★ Elmo

156 Seventh Avenue, between 19th & 20th Streets, Chelsea (1-212 337 8000/www.elmo restaurant.com). Subway 1 to 18th Street. **Open** 11am-midnight Mon-Thur; 11am-1am Fri, Sat; 10am-midnight Sun. **Average main course** $15. **Credit** AmEx, DC, MC, V. **Map** p403 D27.
The attraction at this spacious, brightly decorated eaterie is the good, reasonably priced food. Then there's the bar, which provides a view of the dining room that's jammed with guys in clingy tank tops.

And that's before you come to the basement venue, which holds readings, comedy and drag shows plus the occasional chic lesbian soirée.

44 & X Hell's Kitchen

622 Tenth Avenue, at 44th Street, Hell's Kitchen (1-212 977 1170/www.44andx.com). Subway A, C, E to 42nd Street-Port Authority. **Open** 11.30am-2.30pm, 5.30-11.45pm Mon-Wed; 11.30am-2.30pm, 5.30pm-12.15am Thur, Fri; 11.30am-2.45pm, 5.30pm-12.15am Sat; 11.30am-2.45pm, 5.30-10.45pm Sun. **Average main course** $25. **Credit** AmEx, DC, MC, V. **Map** p404 C24.
Fabulous queens pack out the sleek dining space, one of the first bright spots on quickly gentrifying Tenth Avenue. It's situated alongside the Theater District and the Manhattan Plaza high-rises, so it tends to attract actors (and those seeking them). The food's great – classics such as creamy mac 'n' cheese and American specialities including filet mignon.

HK

523 Ninth Avenue, at 39th Street, Hell's Kitchen (1-212 947 4208/www.hkhellskitchen.com). Subway A, C, E to 34th Street-Penn Station. **Open** 9am-1am Mon-Thur, Sat, Sun; 9am-3am Fri. **Average main course** $15. **Credit** AmEx, DC, MC, V (no credit cards 9am-5pm Sat, Sun). **Map** p404 C24.
Located on a gritty corner, this swankily lit hotspot opens its glass sides in warm months and lets tables spill out on to the pavement. Enjoy an extensive list of strong cocktails and cuisine that ranges from creative salads and pasta dishes to burgers, soups, fish dishes and more.
▶ *Next door is the HK Lounge (see p313), a modish and violently hip drinking venue.*

Lucky Cheng's

24 First Avenue, between 1st & 2nd Streets, East Village (1-212 995 5500/www.planetlucky chengs.com). Subway F, V to Lower East Side-Second Avenue. **Open** 6pm-2am Mon-Thur, Sun; 6pm-4am Fri, Sat. **Price** $32 per person dinner/show. **Credit** AmEx, DC, Disc, MC, V. **Map** p403 F29.
This Asian drag queen theme palace is a popular dinner-and-show kind of place that attracts straight and

queer folks alike. The sassy ladies serve up pan-Asian fare, put on a show and then lead the post-meal karaoke. On Friday evenings, the gay night Acid Disko takes over the space with glamorous gusto.

★ Rocking Horse Café
182 Eighth Avenue, between 19th & 20th Streets, Chelsea (1-212 463 9511/www.rocking horsecafe.com). Subway C, E to 23rd Street. **Open** noon-11pm Mon-Thur, Sun; noon-midnight Fri, Sat. **Average main course** $16. **Credit** AmEx, DC, MC, V. **Map** p403 D27.
Eclectic Mexican cuisine is what originally established the Rocking Horse Café as a unique eating place in Chelsea, but the bar now holds a distinguished reputation for the tongue-numbingly stiff frozen margaritas they serve. Decked out in bright colours, it's also still good for ogling beautiful boys doing the Eighth Avenue strut.

Superfine
126 Front Street, between Jay & Pearl Streets, Dumbo, Brooklyn (1-718 243 9005). Subway F to York Street. **Open** 11.30am-3pm, 6-11pm Tue-Fri; 6-11pm Sat; 11.30am-3pm, 6-10pm Sun. **Average main course** $15. **Credit** AmEx, DC, Disc, MC, V. **Map** p411 T9.
Owned by a couple of super-cool lesbians, this eaterie, bar and gallery serves Mediterranean cuisine in its massive, hip space. The mellow vibe and pool table draw a mixed, local crowd. The southwestern themed Sunday brunches are delicious and justifiably popular. For bar hours, *see p224*.

BARS

Whatever your nightlife pleasure – sleek martini lounge or kinky leather cave, dive bar or kitschy neighbourhood hangout – you are sure to find a queer watering hole that suits in New York. Most offer happy hours, drink specials, live shows, go-go dancers and rotating theme nights, such as bingo parties or 'talent' contests.

All bars, gay or straight, enforce the state-wide drinking age of 21; always carry picture ID as you might be asked to show it, even if your 21st birthday is a distant memory.

Lower East Side & the East Village

★ Cock
29 Second Avenue, between 2nd & 3rd Streets (no phone). Subway F, V to Lower East Side-Second Avenue. **Open** 11pm-4am daily. **Cover** $5-$10. **Average drink** $5. **No credit cards.** **Map** p403 F29.
This wonderfully dark and sleazy fag-rock spot has nightly soirées featuring cruising, cocktail guzzling and heavy petting among the rail-thin, messy-haired young boys who frequent it. Drag performers and holiday-pegged theme nights often rock the house.

DTOX
31 Second Avenue, at 2nd Street (no phone). Subway F, V to Lower East Side-Second Avenue. **Open** 8pm-4am daily. **Average drink** $8. **Credit** AmEx, DC, Disc, MC, V. **Map** p403 F29.
This newest spot on the block is much prettier than its neighbours, the Cock and Urge, but don't let that mislead you into thinking that dirty thoughts are checked at the door. The classy lounge vibe is perfect for sparking new friendships.

★ Eastern Bloc
505 E 6th Street, between Avenues A & B (1-212 777 2555/www.easternblocnyc.com). Subway F, V to Lower East Side-Second Avenue. **Open** 7pm-4am daily. **Average drink** $7. **No credit cards.** **Map** p403 G28.
This cool little space has a red-scare Commie feel – in the sexiest of ways – with TV screens that show Bettie Page films, and Soviet-era posters. Bartenders are cuties, and there are nightly themes and happy hours to get the ball rolling.

Nowhere
322 E 14th Street, at First Avenue (1-212 477 4744). Subway L to First Avenue. **Open** 3pm-4am daily. **Average drink** $5. **No credit cards.** **Map** p403 F27.
A friendly, spacious bar, Nowhere attracts attitude-free crowds – and the place is filled with everyone from dykes to bears, thanks to a fun line-up of theme nights. The pool table's also a big draw.
► *The same folks run the nearby Phoenix (447 E 13th Street, between First Avenue & Avenue A, 1-212 477 9979).*

Urge
33 Second Avenue, at 2nd Street (1-212 533 5757/www.theurgenyc.com). Subway F, V to Lower East Side-Second Avenue. **Open** 4pm-4am daily. **Average drink** $7. **Credit** DC, MC, V. **Map** p403 F29.
Forget Chelsea: you can satisfy your bulging bicep fixation at this East Side bi-level haunt for muscle queens and downtown hipsters. The bar offers the perfect vantage point from which to survey the prey – both in the room and on the bar, where go-go boys strut in thongs and black boots. Check out the drag acts on Sundays or go for broke on Bingo Mondays. Hosted by Flotila DeBarge, Ass Wednesday brings out guys showing their stuff to win $100 in cash.

West Village

Chi Chiz
135 Christopher Street, at Hudson Street (1-212 462 0027). Subway 1 to Christopher Street-Sheridan Square. **Open** 2pm-4am daily. **Average drink** $6. **No credit cards.** **Map** p403 D29.

Cattyshack. See p314.

One of a string of eight neighbourhood gay pubs along Christopher Street, this is a cruisey spot for men of colour, just steps from the way-gay Pier 45. Popular nights include Monday karaoke and Thursday pool tournaments.

★ Cubbyhole
281 W 12th Street, at 4th Street (1-212 243 9041/www.cubbyholebar.com). Subway A, C, E to 14th Street; L to Eighth Avenue. **Open** 4pm-4am Mon-Fri; 2pm-4am Sat, Sun. **Average drink** $6. **No credit cards. Map** p403 E28.
This friendly lesbian spot is always chock-full of flirtatious girls (and their dyke-friendly boy pals), with the standard set of Melissa Etheridge or KD Lang blaring in the background. Chinese lanterns, tissue paper fish and old holiday decorations emphasise the festive, home-made charm.

Henrietta Hudson
438 Hudson Street, at Morton Street (1-212 924 3347/www.henriettahudson.com). Subway 1 to Christopher Street-Sheridan Square. **Open** 5pm-2am Mon, Tue; 4pm-4am Wed-Fri; 1pm-4am Sat, Sun. **Average drink** $7. **Credit** AmEx, DC, MC, V. **Map** p409 D29.
A much-loved lesbian bar, this glam lounge attracts young hottie girls from all over the New York area, especially the nearby 'burbs. Every night's a different party, with hip hop, pop, rock and live shows among the musical pulls. Super-cool New Yorker Lisa Cannistraci is in charge. *Photos pp314-315.*

Monster
80 Grove Street, at Sheridan Square (1-212 924 3558/www.manhattan-monster.com). Subway 1 to Christopher Street-Sheridan Square. **Open** 4pm-4am Mon-Fri; 2pm-4am Sat, Sun. **Average drink** $5. **No credit cards. Map** p403 D28.
Upstairs, locals gather to sing showtunes in the piano lounge, adorned with strings of lights and rainbow paraphernalia. And, honey, you haven't lived 'til you've witnessed a bunch of tipsy queers belting out the best of Broadway. The downstairs disco caters to a young, fun outer-borough crowd.

Stonewall Inn
53 Christopher Street, between Seventh Avenue South & Waverly Place (1-212 488 2705/www.thestonewallinnyc.com). Subway 1 to Christopher Street-Sheridan Square. **Open** 2pm-4am daily. **Average drink** $7. **Credit** AmEx, DC, MC, V. **Map** p403 D28.
This gay landmark is next door to the location of the 1969 gay rebellion against police harassment. After a long closure, it's been remodelled in a way that both preserves its historic dignity and strives to attract a new generation. It now has a decidedly collegiate feel; there's a small stage for drag performances and occasional *American Idol*-type contests, with a more intimate dance space upstairs. Special nights range from dance soirées to bingo gatherings.
▶ *While you're here, check out George Segal's sculptures in nearby Christopher Park; see p85.*

Chelsea

★ Barracuda
275 W 22nd Street, between Seventh & Eighth Avenues (1-212 645 8613). Subway C, E to 23rd Street. **Open** 4pm-4am daily. **Average drink** $6. **No credit cards. Map** p404 D26.
This long-time staple has a lot less attitude than most of the competition. Guys from the nabe converse in the low-lit bar up front or relax in the lounge in the back, a hodgepodge of ultra-mod furnishings out of an Austen Powers film. Drag queens perform during the week; there's never a cover charge.

★ Eagle
554 W 28th Street, between Tenth & Eleventh Avenues (1-646 473 1866/www.eaglenyc.com). Subway C, E to 23rd Street. **Open** 10pm-4am Mon-Sat; 5pm-4am Sun. **Average drink** $6. **No credit cards. Map** p404 C26.
Whatever your kink, this fetish bar will satisfy with its array of beer blasts, foot-worship fêtes and leather soirées, plus simple pool playing and cruising nights. In summer, it hosts rooftop barbecues.

G Lounge
225 W 19th Street, between Seventh & Eighth Avenues (1-212 929 1085/www.glounge.com). Subway 1 to 18th

Street. **Open** 4pm-4am daily. **Average drink** $9. **No credit cards. Map** p403 D27.

The 'hood's original slick boy lounge, a rather moodily lit cave with a cool brick and glass arched entrance, wouldn't look out of place in an Ian Schrager boutique hotel. It's a favourite after-work cocktail spot, where an excellent roster of DJs stays on top of the mood.

Gym Sports Bar

167 Eighth Avenue, at 18th Street (1-212 337 2439/www.gymsportsbar.com). Subway A, C, E to 14th Street; L to Eighth Avenue. **Open** 4pm-2am Mon-Thur; 4pm-4am Fri; 1pm-4am Sat; 1pm-2am Sun. **Average drink** $8. **Credit** AmEx, DC, Disc, MC, V. **Map** p403 D27.

This popular spot is all about games – of the actual sporting variety, that is. Catch theme parties that revolve around gay sports leagues, play at the pool tables and video games, or watch the pro events from rodeo competitions to figure skating (everyone's favourite) shown on big-screen TVs.

Rush

579 Sixth Avenue, at 16th Street (1-212 243 6100). Subway F, V to 14th Street. **Open** 10pm-4am daily. **Average drink** $7. **No credit cards. Map** p404 D26.

Young studs enthusiastically pack in to this three-floor place, decked out with mirrored walls and flashing lights, for the cheap drinks and the brash beats. College dudes flock here on weekends to catch go-go boys, rotating drag hostesses and, on Saturdays, DJ Steve Sidewalk. Drink specials and hunks abound during the week.

Midtown

HK Lounge

409 W 39th Street, between Ninth & Tenth Avenues (1-212 947 4208/www.hkhellskitchen. com). Subway A, C, E to 34th Street-Penn Station. **Open** 5pm-4am daily. **Average drink** $9. **Credit** AmEx, DC, MC, V. **Map** p404 C24.

This Hell's Kitchen beauty is attached to the equally atmospheric HK eaterie. It's an intimate, cool cave of couches, gargantuan potted plants, low tables and dim lighting, and the site of occasional performances and special DJ evenings. Perfect for a post-theatre cosmo.

★ Therapy

348 W 52nd Street, between Eighth & Ninth Avenues (1-212 397 1700/www.therapy-nyc.com). Subway C, E to 50th Street. **Open** 5pm-2am Mon-Wed, Sun; 5pm-4am Thur-Sat. **Average drink** $8. **Credit** AmEx, DC, MC, V. **Map** p404 C23.

Therapy is just what the analyst ordered. The minimalist, dramatic two-level space offers up comedy and musical performances, some clever cocktails (including the Freudian Sip) and a crowd of beautiful boys. You'll find good food and a cosy fireplace to boot.

Vlada

331 W 51st Street, between Eighth & Ninth Avenues (1-212 974 8030/www.vladabar.com). Subway C, E to 50th Street. **Open** 4pm-4am daily. **Average drink** $7. **Credit** AmEx, DC, Disc, MC, V. **Map** p404 C23.

This Hell's Kitchen favourite is a narrow, modern and hyper-stylish lounge that attracts scores of handsome men for house-made infused vodka cocktails, nibbly bits such as paninis and cheese plates, and entertainment from drag shows to stand-up.

Uptown

Candle Bar

309 Amsterdam Avenue, at 74th Street (1-212 874 9155). Subway 1, 2, 3 to 72nd Street. **Open** 4pm-4am Mon-Fri; 3pm-4am Sat, Sun. **Average drink** $6. **No credit cards. Map** p406 C15.

An Upper West Side mainstay, the Candle Bar is a dank, cruisy neighbourhood kind of place, with regulars and a well-used pool table. Catch nightly drink specials, from Buds to potent margaritas.

★ No Parking

4168 Broadway, between 176th Street & 177th Streets (1-212 923 8700/www.noparking bar.com). Subway 1, 2, 3 to 168th Street. **Open** 5pm-3am Mon-Thur, Sun; 5pm-4am Fri, Sat. **Average drink** $6. **No credit cards. Map** p409 B6.

If you're feeling frisky, head straight to No Parking in Washington Heights, where a beefy doorman frisks you before entering. Don't be scared, though: the only pistols these cute locals are packing are the fun kind. The bar also boasts a crew of awesome R&B, disco and hip hop video DJs.

> ### INSIDE TRACK
> ### CHELSEA CLASSICS
>
> Chelsea's famous for its boy bars and muscle marys. But for a change of pace, don't miss the campy **Chelsea Classics** film series at Clearview Cinemas (260 W 23rd Street, between Seventh & Eighth Avenues). Held on Thursdays at 7pm and 9.30pm (with occasional Saturday screenings) and hosted by local drag queens such as Hedda Lettuce, it offers campy cinematic treats such as *The Witches of Eastwick* and *Mommie Dearest.*

ARTS & ENTERTAINMENT

ARTS & ENTERTAINMENT

Henrietta Hudson. *See p312.*

Suite

992 Amsterdam Avenue, at 109th Street (1-212 222 4600/www.suitenyc.com). Subway 1, 2, 3 to 110th Street. **Open** 5pm-4am daily. **Average drink** $7. **Credit** (minimum $15) AmEx, DC, Disc, MC, V. **Map** p406 C15.

Suite offers a relaxed and comfortable Uptown atmosphere for local gay residents and Columbia students alike. The nightly drag performances have a fun, let's-put-on-a-show feel.

Brooklyn

★ Cattyshack

249 Fourth Avenue, between Carroll & President Streets, Park Slope (1-718 230 5740/www.catty shackbklyn.com). Subway M, R to Union Street. **Open** 2pm-4am Mon-Fri; noon-4am Sat, Sun. **Average drink** $7. **No credit cards**. **Map** p410 T11.

This hoppin', bi-level space is all industrial-chic, spare-design charm. It's a full-time lesbian joint, courtesy of former Meow Mix cat Brooke Webster, and its theme nights, excellent DJs and breezy roof deck bring in crowds from all over town and beyond.

▶ *See p129 for more on Park Slope's lesbian chic.*

Excelsior

390 Fifth Avenue, between 6th & 7th Streets, Park Slope (1-718 832 1599/www.excelsior brooklyn.com). Subway F, M, R to Fourth

Avenue-9th Street. **Open** 6pm-4am Mon-Fri; 2pm-4am Sat, Sun. **Average drink** $6. **No credit cards**. **Map** p410 T11.

Homey Excelsior has a spacious deck and garden out back, and inside, an eclectic jukebox and an excellent selection of beers on tap. This straight-friendly spot attracts gay men, lesbians and their hetero pals looking to catch up without the fuss found in trendy lounge bars.

Ginger's Bar

363 Fifth Avenue, between 5th & 6th Streets, Park Slope (1-718 788 0924). Subway M, R to Fourth Avenue-9th Street. **Open** 5pm-4am Mon-Fri; 2pm-4am Sat, Sun. **Average drink** $6. **No credit cards**. **Map** p410 T11.

The front room of Ginger's, with its dark-wood bar, looks out on to a bustling street. The back, which has an always-busy pool table, evokes a rec room, while the patio feels like a friend's yard. This local hang is full of all sorts of dykes, many with their dogs – or favourite gay boys – in tow.

★ Metropolitan

559 Lorimer Street, at Metropolitan Avenue, Williamsburg (1-718 599 4444). Subway G to Metropolitan Avenue; L to Lorimer Street. **Open** 3pm-4am daily. **Average drink** $6. **No credit cards**. **Map** p411 V8.

Hip Williamsburg has its fair share of queers, but this is its sole gay standby. Stop in to refresh with an icy brew while you're tooling around the neighbourhood;

you'll find an eminently mellow crowd (featuring lots of beards, of the facial-hair variety), a host of video games, a patio and drinks specials.

CLUBS

Clubs come and go in this town – that's nothing new – but the gay scene is changing. 'Things are trending away from the giant dance club, and almost all of the clubs that were entirely gay have closed,' says Brian Moylan, editor-in-chief of *Next*. 'Instead of the big nightclubs, we have a growing gay lounge scene.' DTOX (*see p311*), which opened in summer 2008, is one such example.

A number of non-gay-specific clubs have weekly or monthly queer nights, and some of the big clubs – such as Pacha (*see p297*), for instance – have gay nights now and then. However, if it's an all-gay, all-the-time night you're after, check out dance bar Splash (*see below*). For more clubs, plus additional information about some of those listed below, *see pp295-300*.

★ Big Apple Ranch
Fifth floor, 39 W 19th Street, between Fifth & Sixth Avenues, Flatiron District (1-212 358 5752/www.bigappleranch.com). Subway R, W to 23rd Street; 1 to 18th Street. **Open** 8pm-1am Sat. **Cover** $10. **Average drink** $6. **No credit cards. Map** p403 E27.

Saddle up! All your urban cowboy (or *Brokeback Mountain*) fantasies can be played out at this country and western bash, a chance to put on your chaps and show some skin. The dance venue also runs lessons at 8pm and hosts a party every Saturday.

GirlNation
Nation, 12 W 45th Street, between Fifth & Sixth Avenues, Midtown (1-212 391 8053). Subway B, D, F, V to 47-50 Street-Rockefeller Center. **Open** 10pm-4am Sat. **Cover** $5-$11. **Average drink** $7. **Credit** AmEx, DC, Disc, MC, V. **Map** p404 E24.

This lesbian bash is the place to be on Saturday nights. The two-level space, on a quiet, business-minded block of Midtown, gets rowdy and super-fun with its diverse and very cute crowd of girls, who flock here from all over the city to dance, drink and flirt themselves senseless.

Saint at Large
1-212 674 8541/www.saintatlarge.com.
The now-mythical Saint was one of the first venues where New York's gay men could enjoy dancefloor freedom. The club closed, but the clientele keeps the memory alive with special events and one huge and *très* important annual circuit party: the fetishy Black Party in March, with mind-blowing themes that revolve around kink and sex shows. The White Party, its angelic answer, has been on hiatus for a while; check the website for updates on its buzzed-about reappearance.

Snapshot
Bar 13, 35 E 13th Street, at University Place, Greenwich Village (1-212 979 6677/www.snap shotnyc.com). Subway L, N, Q, R, W, 4, 5, 6 to 14th Street-Union Square. **Open** 9pm-4am Tue. **Cover** $8. **Average drink** $5. **Credit** AmEx, DC, Disc, MC, V. **Map** p403 E28.

This party for hip young dykes and their pals has been injecting a sense of excitement into Tuesday evenings for a few years. There's plenty of room for lounging and dancing (to fresh-faced DJs); the outdoor roof deck is an atmospheric spot for a smoke. Watch for Proud as Fuck, its cool annual Pride party.

Splash
50 W 17th Street, between Fifth & Sixth Avenues, Flatiron District (1-212 691 0073/ www.splashbar.com). Subway F, V to 14th Street; L to Sixth Avenue. **Open** 4pm-4am daily. **Cover** $5-$25. **Average drink** $9. **No credit cards. Map** p403 E27.

This NYC queer institution offers 10,000sq ft of dance and lounge space, plus the famous onstage showers, where hunky go-go boys get wet and wild. The super-muscular bartenders here seem bigger than ever, and nationally known DJs still rock the house, while local drag celebs give good face, and in-house VJs flash hypnotic snippets of classic musicals spliced with video visuals.

Music

Whatever's on your playlist, the live scene here won't disappoint.

New York's musical heritage is seamlessly long, wildly varied and justly revered. From the bebop revolution of the '40s to the punk scene at CBGB three decades later, from the emergence of the Gershwins to the birth of hip hop, the city holds a stellar place in musical history.

But don't let New York's past overshadow its present. Storied venues remain, from palatial Radio City Music Hall to the cosy Village Vanguard, but the city also fosters a rich supply of upstarts, hopefuls and local weirdos who propel the scene forward. See *Time Out New York* magazine for weekly listings.

Rock, Roots & Jazz

Even as the recording industry crumbles, Manhattan and Brooklyn remain packed with music venues, from hole-in-the-wall dives to resplendent Midtown theatres. Plan accordingly and you can catch more than one world-class show on any given night. For smaller gigs, the best bets lie across Downtown Manhattan and parts of Brooklyn. Rock music dominates the Lower East Side and Williamsburg, while a few jazz clubs thrive in Greenwich Village. And you don't have to look far for hip hop, soul, blues, folk, world music and everything in between.

To help you navigate the scene, we've organised the city's most notable venues by genre. These categories are necessarily loose: some spots will feature scraggly rock one night and jazz the next, for instance. Tickets are usually available from clubs in advance and at the door, though a few small and medium-size venues also sell tickets through local record stores. For larger events, buy online through the venue's website or through **Ticketmaster** or **Ticket Web** (for both, *see p258*). And remember to phone ahead for information and show times, which often change without notice.

About the authors

Steve Smith *is the Music Editor of* Time Out New York *magazine and a contributing writer for the* New York Times, *and maintains the blog* Night After Night (www.nightafternight.com). TONY *Music Writer* **Jay Ruttenberg** *has also contributed to* Spin *and the* New York Times.

ARENAS

Izod Center

For listing, see p336 Meadowlands Sports Complex.
New Jersey's answer to Madison Square Garden has played host to the likes of the Police, Dylan and the Jonas Brothers. Radio-sponsored pop and hip hop extravaganzas also take place here, pulling in predictably enormous crowds. Sometimes, shows that sell out at the Garden are easier to access here, just a bus ride away.

Madison Square Garden

For listing, see p336.
Some of music's biggest acts – the White Stripes, Justin Timberlake, Madonna, for instance – come out to play at the world's most famous basketball arena. Whether you'll actually be able to get a look at them depends on your seat number or the quality of your binoculars. There's also a smaller theatre within the complex.

Nassau Coliseum

For listing, see p336.
Long Island's arena hosts mainstream acts such as Bon Jovi and the Spice Girls, punctuated by teen shows (Vans Warped Tour, *American Idol* Live!) and garish Bollywood showcases.

ROCK, POP & SOUL

★ Apollo Theater

253 W 125th Street, between Adam Clayton Powell Jr Boulevard (Seventh Avenue) & Frederick Douglass Boulevard (Eighth Avenue), Harlem

*(1-212 531 5300/www.apollotheater.org). Subway
A, B, C, D, 1 to 125th Street.* **Box office** 10am-
6pm Mon, Tue, Thur, Fri; 10am-8.30pm Wed;
noon-6pm Sat. **Tickets** $20-$100. **Credit** AmEx,
DC, Disc, MC, V. **Map** p407 D13.

Apollo Theater.

Visitors may think they know this venerable theatre
from TV's *Showtime at the Apollo*. But as the saying goes, the small screen adds about ten pounds:
the city's home of R&B and soul music is actually
quite cosy. Known for launching the careers of Ella
Fitzgerald and D'Angelo, among others, the Apollo
continues to mix veteran talents like Dianne Reeves
with younger artists such as the Roots and Duffy.

BB King Blues Club & Grill
*237 W 42nd Street, between Seventh & Eighth
Avenues, Theater District (1-212 997 4144/
www.bbkingblues.com). Subway A, C, E to 42nd
Street-Port Authority; N, Q, R, S, W, 1, 2, 3, 7
to 42nd Street-Times Square.* **Box office**
10.30am-midnight daily. **Tickets** $12-$150.
Credit AmEx, DC, Disc, MC, V. **Map** p404 D24.
BB's Times Square joint stages one of the most
varied music schedules in town. Cover bands and
tributes fill the gaps between big-name bookings
such as Ralph Stanley and Little Richard, but the
venue has also hosted extreme metal (Napalm Death,
Obituary) and neo-soul (Angie Stone, Raekwon). For
many shows, the best seats are at the dinner tables
at the front, but the menu prices are steep (and watch
out for drink minimums). On Sunday, the Harlem
Gospel Choir's buffet brunch raises the roof.

Beacon Theatre
*2124 Broadway, at 74th Street, Upper West Side
(1-212 465 6500/www.beacontheatrenyc.com).
Subway 1, 2, 3 to 72nd Street.* **Box office** 11am-
7pm Mon-Sat; noon-6pm Sun. **Tickets** $15-$175.
Credit AmEx, DC, MC, V. **Map** p405 C20.
This spacious theatre hosts a variety of popular
acts, from 'Weird Al' Yankovic to ZZ Top; once a
year, the Allman Brothers take over for a lengthy
residency. While the vastness can be daunting to
performers and audience alike, the gaudy, gilded
interior and uptown location make you feel as
though you're having a real night out on the town.

Blender Theater at Gramercy
*127 E 23rd Street, between Park & Lexington
Avenues, Gramercy Park (1-212 777 6800).
Subway R, W, 6 to 23rd Street.* **Box office** at
Fillmore New York at Irving Plaza; *see p319.*
Tickets $10-$30. **Credit** AmEx, DC, MC, V.
Map p404 E26.
The Blender looks exactly like what it is, a run-down
former movie theatre, yet it has a decent sound system and good sightlines. Concert-goers can lounge
in raised seats on the top level or get closer to the
stage. Bookings have included indie stalwarts (the
mighty Mekons, Múm), established stars (Dr John)
and the occasional hip hop show (Fabolous, Q-Tip).

★ Bowery Ballroom

6 Delancey Street, between Bowery & Chrystie Street, Lower East Side (1-212 533 2111/www.boweryballroom.com). Subway B, D to Grand St; J, M, Z to Bowery; 6 to Spring Street. **Box office** at Mercury Lounge; *see p323.* **Tickets** $10-$35. **Credit** (bar only) AmEx, DC, MC, V. **Map** p403 F30.

It's probably the best venue in the city for seeing indie bands, either on the way up or holding their own. Still, the Bowery also manages to bring in a diverse range of artists from home and abroad. Expect a clear view and bright sound from any spot. The spacious downstairs lounge is a great place to relax and socialise between (or during) sets.

Bowery Poetry Club

For listing, see p280 **Bowery Poetry Club**. The name of this colourful joint reveals its roots, but it's also the truest current iteration of the East Village's arts scene: all kinds of jazz, folk, hip hop and improv theatre acts can be found here.

Cake Shop

152 Ludlow Street, between Rivington & Stanton Streets, Lower East Side (1-212 253 0036/www.cake-shop.com). Subway F, V to Lower East Side-Second Avenue. **Open** 5pm-2am daily. **Tickets** $6-$8. **Credit** DC, Disc, MC, V. **Map** p403 G29.

It can be difficult to see the stage in this narrow, stuffy basement space, but the Cake Shop gets big points for its keen indie and underground-rock bookings, among the best and most adventurous in town. The venue lives up to its name, selling vegan pas-

tries and coffee upstairs, while the back room at street level sells record-store ephemera.

Canal Room

285 W Broadway, at Canal Street, Tribeca (1-212 941 8100/www.canalroomlive.com). Subway A, C, E, 1 to Canal Street. **Box office** 10am-6.30pm Mon-Fri. **Tickets** $10-$25. **No credit cards. Map** p403 E30.

Performers at the mid-sized Canal Room include young songwriters, *Billboard* veterans with cult followings (Glenn Tilbrook, Colin Hay) and tribute bands. When the shows are packed, things can get uncomfortable and the door people tend to be a bit uptight. There are also DJ nights on the schedule.

Club Europa

98-104 Meserole Avenue, at Manhattan Avenue, Greenpoint, Brooklyn (1-718 383 5723/www.europaclub.com). Subway G to Nassau Avenue. **Open** 5pm-4am daily. **Tickets** $8-$25. **Credit** DC, MC, V. **Map** p411 V7.

You'll hear anything from cutting-edge metal to bubblegum pop in this Polish nightclub. It's a bit cheesy but has offered some solid bookings (Om and High on Fire appeared recently) and dancetastic light shows. At the bar, Eastern Euro beauties sling cheap drinks.

Fillmore New York at Irving Plaza

17 Irving Place, at 15th Street, Gramercy Park (1-212 777 6800/www.irvingplaza.com). Subway L, N, Q, R, W, 4, 5, 6 to 14th Street-Union Square. **Box office** noon-6.30pm Mon-Fri; 1-4pm Sat. **Tickets** $10-$65. **Credit** AmEx, DC, MC, V. **Map** p403 E27.

Joe's Pub. *See p320.*

With the rise of clubs such as Webster Hall, the pleasantly worn Irving Plaza lost its monopoly on concerts by mid-size touring bands. What to do? Rebrand! The renovations that came with the name were largely cosmetic, and nobody actually calls the club 'Fillmore New York'. Still, it's a great place to see big stars keeping a low profile (Gnarls Barkley, Wu-Tang Clan) and medium heavies on their way up.

Galapagos Art Space
16 Main Street, at Water Street, Dumbo, Brooklyn (1-718 222 8500/www.galapagos artspace.com) Subway A, C to High Street; F to York Street. **Shows** times vary. **Cover** $5-$12. **Credit** AmEx, DC, MC, V. **Map** p411 S9.
Galapagos established itself in Williamsburg years before the neighbourhood's renaissance – and, like all colonisers, eventually got squeezed out of the scene it helped create. The new, much larger and LEED-certified space in Dumbo promises a grander mix of the cultural offerings for which Galapagos is known and loved: music, performance art, burlesque, drag queens and other weird stuff.

Hammerstein Ballroom
Manhattan Center, 311 W 34th Street, between Eighth & Ninth Avenues, Garment District (1-212 279 7740/www.mcstudios.com). Subway A, C, E to 34th Street-Penn Station. **Box office** noon-intermission, show days only. **Tickets** $10-$150. **Credit** AmEx, DC, MC, V. **Map** p404 C25.
Lines can wind across the block, drinks prices are high, and those seated in the balcony should bring binoculars. Still, this cavernous space regularly draws big performers in the limbo between club and arena shows. The once-poor sound quality has been rectified, but unless you land tickets on the floor, it takes an amazing act to make a night special.

Highline Ballroom
431 W 16th Street, between Ninth & Tenth Avenues, Chelsea (1-212 414 5994/www.highline ballroom.com). Subway A, C, E to 14th Street; L to Eighth Avenue. **Box office** 11am-10pm daily. **Cover** $15-$50; $10 food/drink min. **Credit** AmEx, DC, Disc, MC, V. **Map** p403 C27.
This recently hatched club is perfect on paper: the sound is top-of-the-heap and sightlines are pretty good. The bookings are also impressive, ranging from world music (Tinariwen) to hip hop (Dizzee Rascal) via old-guard stars (Lou Reed) and indie favourites (Art Brut). The overall vibe, however, can feel more LA than New York – as such, the club works best with cool R&B (Raphael Saadiq, say).

Hiro Ballroom at Maritime Hotel
371 Ninth Avenue, at 16th Street, Chelsea (1-212 242 4300/http://hiroballroom.com). Subway A, C, E to 14th Street; L to Eighth Avenue. **Open** 10pm-4am Thur-Sun. **Cover** $10-$40. **Credit** AmEx, DC, MC, V. **Map** p403 C27.
Hiro Ballroom reeks of Manhattan chic, with a flamboyant, futuristic sushi bar atmosphere – James Bond might feel comfortable checking out a band here. The room feels much fancier than the price of admission suggests, but beware the velvet rope: most shows are part of larger dance nights, which can bring tacky crowds and snooty door guys.

★ Joe's Pub
Public Theater, 425 Lafayette Street, between Astor Place & E 4th Street, East Village (1-212 539 8770/www.joespub.com). Subway N, R, W to 8th Street-NYU; 6 to Astor Place. **Box office** 1-6pm Mon, Sun; 1-7pm Tue-Sat. **Tickets** $12-$30. **Credit** AmEx, DC, MC, V. **Map** p403 E28.
Probably the city's premier small spot for sit-down audiences, Joe's Pub brings in impeccable talent of all genres and origins. While some well-established names play here (Gilberto Gil, Ute Lemper), Joe's also lends its stage for up-and-comers (Christina Courtin, a new-to-America Amy Winehouse). A small but solid menu and deep bar selections seal the deal – just keep an eye on the drink prices. *Photo p319.*
▶ *Joe's is named for Joseph Papp, the founder of its parent, the Public Theater; see p353.*

Knitting Factory
74 Leonard Street, between Broadway & Church Street, Tribeca (1-212 219 3132/www.knitting factory.com). Subway A, C, E to Canal Street; 1 to Franklin Street. **Box office** 5-11pm Mon-Fri; 2-11pm Sat, Sun. **Tickets** $5-$20. **Credit** (bar only) AmEx, DC, MC, V. **Map** p402 E31.
This three-floor circus was once known as NYC's home of avant-garde jazz. Ownership changes have shifted the emphasis; still, great artists pop in from time to time, and the space retains a soft spot for the great, the weird and the underappreciated. The smaller Tap Bar and claustrophobic Old Office, both under the main room (and with separate admissions), often have good DJs in among the busy flow of bands taking part. The venue is currently planning an expansion into Brooklyn and mid-America.

Lakeside Lounge
162 Avenue B, between 10th & 11th Streets, East Village (1-212 529 8463/www.lakeside lounge.com). Subway L to First Avenue; N, Q, R, W, 4, 5, 6 to 14th Street-Union Square. **Shows** 9.30pm Mon-Thur, Sun; 10pm Fri, Sat. **Cover** free. **Credit** AmEx, DC, MC, V. **Map** p403 G28.
Because this comfortable joint is co-owned by guitarist and producer Eric Ambel, the roadhouse and roots acts that play tend to be fun. Local country-tinged talents often appear, and bigger names such as Amy Rigby stop by occasionally. The bar, the jukebox and the photo booth are all attractions in their own right – and there's never a cover charge.

ARTS & ENTERTAINMENT

Beyond the Gate

On the site of a legendary Village stage, a genre-busting venue mixes things up.

Between 1958 and 1993, the Village Gate hosted an avalanche of 20th-century icons: Miles Davis, Nina Simone, Allen Ginsberg, Aretha Franklin, Jimi Hendrix and many others. After the Gate closed, the building welcomed not gig-goers but folks looking for aspirin and athlete's foot powder – a CVS pharmacy took over the site. The store is still there, but the corner is regaining its reputation as a musical intersection thanks to the 2008 arrival below the old Village Gate of **(Le) Poisson Rouge** (*see p322*).

The sleek new space, replete with table service and a dinner menu, is a far cry from the basement where Bob Dylan wrote 'A Hard Rain's A-Gonna Fall'. But what really sets it apart is the adventurous booking policy of David Handler and Justin Kantor, its young founders. The pair met while studying at Manhattan School of Music and pursue classical music and arty pop with equal zeal – sometimes on the same bill.

The idea began with the duo's desire to 'present classical music in an edgy environment where patrons could also drink and let loose,' Kantor explains. 'After sitting down and hashing out the details,

we realised that we had come up with something that could really fill a gap in NYC nightlife.' Borrowing a page from the popular Wordless Music Series (www.wordlessmusic.org), which has since booked shows at the venue, Handler and Kantor have paired young classical artists such as pianist Simone Dinnerstein with compatible indie musicians such as singer-songwriter Essie Jain. The cabaret setting demystifies the often stuffy classical world – and helps young patrons avoid a trip uptown.

Still, the place promises to be more than a classical-indie meeting ground. In its short existence, performances have been devoted to jazz (Charlie Haden), experimental electronic sounds (Matmos) and children's music (Ralph's World). And, of course, the building still reverberates with the eclectic ghosts of its previous incarnation. It remains to be seen whether (Le) Poisson Rouge lives up to the site's heavyweight heritage, but Kantor is hopeful. 'I'd like to see a real mix of people enjoying our offerings,' he says. 'Maybe we'll find the future Diaghilev, Stravinsky and Picasso sharing ideas over an absinthe at our bar.'

ARTS & ENTERTAINMENT

Pete's Candy Store.

★ (Le) Poisson Rouge

158 Bleecker Street, at Thompson Street, Greenwich Village (1-212 796 0741/www.le poissonrouge.com). Subway A, B, C, D, E, F, V to W 4th Street. **Open** *noon-2am Mon-Wed, Sun; noon-4am Thur-Sat.* **Box office** *noon-5pm Mon-Sat.* **Tickets** $10-$20. **Credit** AmEx, DC, Disc, MC, V. **Map** p403 E29
See p321 **Beyond the Gate.**

Living Room

154 Ludlow Street, between Rivington & Stanton Streets, Lower East Side (1-212 533 7235/www.livingroomny.com). Subway F to Lower East Side-Second Avenue; J, M, Z to Delancey-Essex Streets. **Open** *6.30pm-2am Mon-Thur, Sun; 6.30pm-4am Fri, Sat.* **Cover** *free; 1-drink min.* **No credit cards.** **Map** p403 G29.

Many local clubs claim to be the place where Norah Jones got her start, but the Living Room is the real McCoy – she even donated a piano as a way of saying thanks. That was in the venue's old (and drab) location; since moving to the Lower East Side's version of Main Street, the stream of singer-songwriters has taken on a bit more gleam, and the warmly lit environs always seem to be bustling. Upstairs is Googie's Lounge, an even more intimate space.

★ Maxwell's

1039 Washington Street, at 11th Street, Hoboken, NJ (1-201 798 0406/www.maxwells nj.com). PATH train to Hoboken, then taxi, Red Apple bus or NJ Transit 126 bus to 11th Street. **Open** *5pm-midnight Mon-Thur; 5pm-1am Fri, Sat; 11.30am-4pm, 5pm-midnight Sun.* **Tickets** $7-$25. **Credit** AmEx, DC, Disc, MC, V. **Map** p403 C28.

The trip to Maxwell's can be a hassle, but the 15-minute walk from the PATH train can make you feel like you're in small-town America. The restaurant in front is big and friendly; for dessert you can feast on indie-rock fare from popular indie acts (the Fiery Furnaces, Times New Viking) and garage favourites (Black Lips). Hometown heroes Yo La Tengo stage their more or less annual Hanukkah shows here.

★ Mercury Lounge
217 E Houston Street, between Essex & Ludlow Streets, Lower East Side (1-212 260 4700/ www.mercuryloungenyc.com). Subway F, V to Lower East Side-Second Avenue. **Tickets** $8-$15. **Credit** (bar only) AmEx, DC, Disc, MC, V. **Map** p403 G29.
The unassuming, boxy Mercury Lounge is both an old standby and pretty much the number-one indie rock club in town, with solid sound and sightlines (and a cramped bar in the front room). There are four-band bills most nights, though they can seem stylistically haphazard and set times are often later than advertised. Some of the bigger shows sell out in advance, mainly through online purchases.

Music Hall of Williamsburg
66 N 6th Street, between Kent & Wythe Avenues, Williamsburg, Brooklyn (1-718 486 5400/ www.williamsburgmusichall.com). Subway L to Bedford Avenue. **Box office** 11am-6pm Sat. **Tickets** $12-$35. **Credit cards** (online tickets only) AmEx, DC, Disc, MC, V. **Map** p411 U7.
When, in 2007, the local promoter Bowery Presents found itself in need of a Williamsburg outpost, it gave the former Northsix a facelift and took over the bookings. It's basically a Bowery Ballroom in Brooklyn – and bands such as Spiritualized and Celebration headline, often on the day after they've played the Bowery.

New Jersey Performing Arts Center
1 Center Street, at the waterfront, Newark, NJ (1-888 466 5722/www.njpac.org). NJ Transit or PATH to Newark Penn Station, then 10min walk or Newark Light Rail to NJPAC. **Box office** 10am-6pm Mon-Sat; noon-5pm Sun. **Tickets** $12-$100. **Credit** AmEx, DC, Disc, MC, V.
Visible from Manhattan (and quite easy to access – detailed instructions are on the website), the NJPAC offers disco legends (Donna Summer), Broadway stars such as Brian Stokes Mitchell in cabaret performances, crowd-pleasing swing and soul music, and even some classical events. Summer is chock-full of family-oriented outdoor entertainment.

Nokia Theatre Times Square
1515 Broadway, at 44th Street, Theater District (1-212 930 1950/www.nokiatheatrenyc.com). Subway N, Q, R, S, W, 1, 2, 3, 7 to 42nd Street-Times Square. **Box office** noon-6pm Mon-Sat. **Tickets** $20-$80. **Credit** AmEx, DC, MC, V. **Map** p404 D24.
This large, corporate club begs for character but finds redemption in its creature comforts. The sound and sightlines are both good, and there's even edible food. Those who wish to look into a musician's eyes can stand in the ample front section; foot-weary fans can sit in the cinema-like section at the back. It's a comfortable place to see a well-known band that hasn't (yet) reached stadium-filling fame.

Pete's Candy Store
709 Lorimer Street, between Frost & Richardson Streets, Williamsburg, Brooklyn (1-718 302 3770/www.petescandystore.com). Subway L to Lorimer Street. **Open** 5pm-2am Mon-Wed, Sun; 5pm-4am Thur-Sat. **Cover** free. **Credit** AmEx, DC, MC, V. **Map** p411 V7.
An overlooked gem, tucked away in an old candy shop, Pete's is gorgeous, tiny and always free. The performers are generally unknown and crowds can be thin, but it can be a comfortable place to catch a singer-songwriter. Worthy underdogs – Jeffrey Lewis, Simone White – may stop by for casual sets.

Pianos
158 Ludlow Street, between Rivington & Stanton Streets, Lower East Side (1-212 505 3733/ www.pianosnyc.com). Subway F to Delancey Street; J, M, Z to Delancey-Essex Streets. **Open** 3pm-4am daily. **Cover** free-$12. **Credit** AmEx, DC, MC, V. **Map** p403 G29.
In recent years, a lot of the cooler bookings have moved from Pianos to Brooklyn or down the block to venues such as Cake Shop (*see p319*). Still, while sound is often lousy and the room can get uncomfortably mobbed, there are always good reasons to go back – very often the under-the-radar emerging rock bands that make local music scenes tick.

★ Radio City Music Hall
1260 Sixth Avenue, at 50th Street, Midtown (1-212 247 4777/www.radiocity.com). Subway B, D, F, V to 47th-50th Streets-Rockefeller Center. **Box office** 11.30am-6pm Mon-Sat. **Tickets** $25-$125. **Credit** AmEx, DC, MC, V. **Map** p404 D23.
Few rooms scream 'New York City!' more than this gilded hall, which has recently drawn Goldfrapp, Mary J Blige and Alanis Morissette as headliners. The greatest challenge for any performer is not to be upstaged by the awe-inspiring art deco surroundings. On the other hand, those same surroundings lend historic heft to even the flimsiest showing.

Roseland
239 W 52nd Street, between Broadway & Eighth Avenue, Theater District (1-212 247 0200/www. roselandballroom.com). Subway B, D, E to Seventh Avenue; C to 50th Street. **Box office** at Fillmore New York at Irving Plaza; *see p319*.

ARTS & ENTERTAINMENT

Tickets $17-$75. **Credit** (advance purchases only) AmEx, DC, MC, V. **Map** p404 D23.
This slightly depressing Times Square club is bigger than Irving Plaza and smaller than the Hammerstein Ballroom. Any artist who can fill the room performs here, with past acts including My Morning Jacket, Massive Attack and the Fratellis.

Sidewalk Café
94 Avenue A, at 6th Street, East Village (1-212 473 7373). Subway F, V to Lower East Side-Second Avenue; 6 to Astor Place. **Open** 8am-2.30am Mon-Thur, Sun; 24hrs Fri, Sat. **Cover** free; 2-drink min. **Credit** AmEx, DC, Disc, MC, V. **Map** p403 G28.
Despite its cramped, awkward layout, the Sidewalk Café is the focal point of the city's anti-folk scene – though that category means just about anything from piano pop to wry folk. Nellie McKay, Regina Spektor and the Moldy Peaches all started here.

SOB's
204 Varick Street, at Houston Street, Tribeca (1-212 243 4940/www.sobs.com). Subway 1 to Houston Street. **Box office** 11am-6pm Mon-Fri; noon-5pm Sat. **Tickets** $10-$30. **Credit** (food & bar only) DC, Disc, MC, V. **Map** p403 D29.
The titular Sounds of Brazil (SOB, geddit?) are just some of many global genres that keep this spot hopping. Hip hop, soul, reggae and Latin beats figure in the mix, with Seu Jorge, Zap Mama and Wyclef Jean each appearing of late. The drinks are expensive, but the sharp-looking clientele doesn't seem to mind.

Southpaw
125 Fifth Avenue, between Sterling & St Johns Places, Park Slope, Brooklyn (1-718 230 0236/ www.spsounds.com). Subway B, Q, 2, 3, 4, 5 to Atlantic Avenue; D, M, N, R to Pacific Street. **Open** 8pm-2am Tue-Sun. **Tickets** $7-$20. **No credit cards. Map** p410 T11.
This cool space welcomes prime outfits that would otherwise play in slightly larger Manhattan rooms (the Raveonettes, the Dirtbombs), and also hosts the Rub, a monthly Saturday night funk and hip hop party. Like its Park Slope neighbourhood, Southpaw tends to draw cool, mellow audiences; with all the elbow room, getting to the (huge) bar is no problem.

Terminal 5
610 W 56th Street, between 11th & 12th Avenues, Hell's Kitchen (1-212 260 4700/ www.terminal5nyc.com). Subway A, B, C, D, 1 to 59th Street-Columbus Circle. **Box office** at Mercury Lounge; see p323. **Tickets** $15-$90. **Credit** (online purchases & bar only) AmEx, Disc, MC, V. **Map** p405 C22.
Opened by Bowery Presents at the end of 2007, this three-floor, 3,000-capacity venue is the largest midtown venue to set up shop in more than a decade. Bookings include bands that not long ago were

Radio City Music Hall. *See p323.*

playing smaller Bowery confines (Wolf Parade, Hot Chip), plus bigger stars (MIA) and scruffy veterans with loyal fan bases (Ween, Iggy & the Stooges).

★ Town Hall
123 W 43rd Street, between Sixth Avenue & Broadway, Theater District (1-212 840 2824/ www.the-townhall-nyc.org). Subway B, D, F, V to 42nd Street-Bryant Park; N, Q, R, S, W, 1, 2, 3, 7 to 42nd Street-Times Square. **Box office** noon-6pm Mon-Sat. **Tickets** $15-$85. **Credit** AmEx, DC, MC, V. **Map** p404 D24.
Acoustics at the 'people's auditorium' are superb, and there's no doubting the gravitas of Town Hall's surroundings. Adam Green, Ornette Coleman and Ani DiFranco have performed here in recent times, and smart indie songwriters such as the Magnetic Fields have set up shop for a number of nights.

Union Hall
702 Union Street, at Fifth Avenue, Park Slope, Brooklyn (1-718 638 4400/www.unionhall ny.com). Subway M, R to Union Street. **Open** 4pm-4am Mon-Fri; noon-4am Sat, Sun. **Tickets** $5-$20. **Credit** AmEx, DC, MC, V. **Map** p410 T11.
The spacious main floor of this Brooklyn bar has a garden, food service and a bocce ball court. Tucked

in the basement is a comfortable space dominated by the more delicate side of indie rock, with infrequent sets by indie comics such as Eugene Mirman.

Union Pool
484 Union Avenue, at Meeker Avenue, Williamsburg, Brooklyn (1-718 609 0484/ www.myspace.com/unionpool). Subway L to Lorimer Street; G to Metropolitan Avenue. **Open** 5pm-4am daily. **Tickets** $5-$12. **Credit** (bar only) AmEx, DC, MC, V. **Map** p411 V8

Wind through the kitschy backyard space of this modest Williamsburg bar and you'll find yourself back indoors, facing a modest stage in a small room. Local stars check in from time to time (Karen O debuted her Native Korean Rock & the Fishnets side-project here), but it's dominated by well-plucked smaller indie acts such as the Boggs. *Photo p326.*

Webster Hall
125 E 11th Street, between Third & Fourth Avenues, East Village (1-212 353 1600/ www.websterhall.com). Subway L to Third Avenue; N, Q, R, W, 4, 5, 6 to 14th Street-Union Square. **Box office** 11am-5pm Mon-Fri. **Tickets** free-$30. **Credit** AmEx, DC, MC, V. **Map** p403 F28.

A great-sounding alternative for bands (and fans) who've had their fill of the comparably sized Irving Plaza, Webster Hall is booked by Bowery Presents, the folks who run Bowery Ballroom and Mercury Lounge. Expect to find high-calibre indie acts (Animal Collective, Battles, the Gossip), but be sure to show up early if you want a decent view.

JAZZ & EXPERIMENTAL

In the last two weeks in June, look out for the **JVC Jazz Festival** (1-212 501 1390, www.festivalproductions.net). This New York City institution fills Carnegie and Avery Fisher Halls with big-draw talent, and also sponsors gigs in Harlem and downtown clubs.

Barbès
376 9th Street, at Sixth Avenue, Park Slope, Brooklyn (1-347 422 0248/www.barbes brooklyn.com). Subway F to Seventh Avenue. **Open** 5pm-2am Mon-Thur; 5pm-4am Fri; 2pm-4am Sat; 2pm-2am Sun. **Tickets** free-$10. **Credit** (bar only) DC, Disc, MC, V. **Map** p410 T11.

Show up early if you want to get into Park Slope's global-bohemian club – it's tiny. Run by musically inclined French expats, the boîte brings in traditional swing and jazz of more daring stripes, plus world music-derived hybrids (Las Rubias del Norte) and acts that often defy categorisation (One Ring Zero). Chicha Libre, a Brooklyn band reviving psychedelic Peruvian music, holds down Mondays.

Birdland
315 W 44th Street, between Eighth & Ninth Avenues, Theater District (1-212 581 3080/ www.birdlandjazz.com). Subway A, C, E to 42nd Street-Port Authority. **Open** 5pm-1am daily. **Tickets** $20-$50; $10 food/drink min. **Credit** AmEx, DC, Disc, MC, V. **Map** p404 C24.

Its name is synonymous with jazz (Kurt Elling, Jim Hall), but Birdland is also a prime cabaret destination (Christine Andreas, Christine Ebersole) and the bookings in both fields are excellent. The Chico O'Farrill Afro-Cuban Jazz Orchestra owns Sundays, and David Ostwald's Louis Armstrong Centennial Band hits on Wednesdays; Mondays see cabaret's waggish Jim Caruso and his Cast Party.

Blue Note
131 W 3rd Street, between MacDougal Street & Sixth Avenue, Greenwich Village (1-212 475 8592/www.bluenote.net). Subway A, B, C, D, E, F, V to W 4th Street. **Shows** 8pm, 10.30pm Mon-Thur; 8pm, 10.30pm, 12.30am Fri, Sat; 12.30pm, 2.30pm, 8pm, 10.30pm Sun. **Tickets** $10-$75; $5 food/drink min. **Credit** AmEx, DC, MC, V. **Map** p403 E29.

The Blue Note prides itself on being 'the jazz capital of the world'. Bona fide musical titans (Cecil Taylor, Charlie Haden) rub against hot young talents (the Bad Plus), while the close-set tables in the club get patrons rubbing up against each other. The Late Night Groove series and the Sunday brunches are the best bargain bets.

Carnegie Hall
For listing, see p330.
Carnegie Hall means the big time. In recent years, though, the 599-seat, state-of-the-art Zankel Hall has greatly augmented the venue's pop, jazz and

---

INSIDE TRACK
BACKSTAGE PASSES

Curious music lovers can go behind the scenes at several major concert venues. **Backstage at the Met** (1-212 769 7020, www.metoperafamily.org/education) shows you around the famous house during the opera season, which runs from September to May; **Lincoln Center Tours** (1-212 875 5350) escorts you inside Avery Fisher and Alice Tully Halls, as well as the New York State Theater; **Carnegie Hall** (1-212 247 7800) guides you through what is perhaps the world's most famous concert hall; and for a $16 fee, you may sit in on rehearsals of the **New York Philharmonic** (1-212 875 5656), usually held on the Thursday before a concert.

Union Pool. See p325.

world music offerings. Between both halls, the complex has welcomed Dave Brubeck, Bobby McFerrin and Fred Hersch, among other high-wattage names.

Cornelia Street Café

29 Cornelia Street, between Bleecker & W 4th Streets, Greenwich Village (1-212 989 9319/ www.corneliastreetcafe.com). Subway A, B, C, D, E, F, V to W 4th Street. **Open** 10am-midnight daily. **Tickets** $8-$12; $7 drink min. **Credit** AmEx, DC, Disc, MC, V. **Map** p403 D29.
Upstairs at the Cornelia Street Café is a cosy little eaterie. Downstairs is an even cosier music space hosting adventurous jazz, poetry, world music and folk. Regular mini-festivals spotlight blues, songwriters and new concert-theatre works.

55 Bar

55 Christopher Street, between Seventh Avenue South & Waverly Place, West Village (1-212 929 9883/www.55bar.com). Subway 1 to Christopher Street-Sheridan Square. **Open** 3pm-4am daily. **Tickets** free-$15. **No credit cards. Map** p403 D28.
This tiny Prohibition-era dive is one of New York's most artist-friendly rooms, thanks to its knowledgeable, appreciative audience. You can catch emerging talent almost every night at the free-of-charge early shows; late sets regularly feature established artists such as Chris Potter and Mike Stern.

★ Iridium Jazz Club

1650 Broadway, at 51st Street, Theater District (1-212 582 2121/www.iridiumjazzclub.com). Subway 1 to 50th Street; N, R, W to 49th Street. **Shows** 8pm, 10pm Mon; 8.30pm, 10.30pm Tue-Sun. **Tickets** $25-$50; $10-$25 food/drink min. **Credit** AmEx, DC, Disc, MC, V. **Map** p404 D23.
One of the nicer places to dine while being hit with top-shelf jazz, Iridium is located bang in the middle

of Broadway's bright lights. Recent guests have included the Art Ensemble of Chicago and Mose Allison, but don't miss the residencies: Mondays belong to wise-cracking guitarist Les Paul, while Tuesdays offer the Mingus Big Band. Book ahead.

★ Jazz at Lincoln Center

Broadway, at 60th Street, Upper West Side (1-212 258 9800/www.jalc.org). Subway A, B, C, D, 1 to 59th Street-Columbus Circle. **Shows** 7.30pm, 9.30pm Mon-Thur, Sun; 7.30pm, 9.30pm, 11.30pm Fri, Sat. **Box office** 10am-6pm Mon-Sat; noon-6pm Sun. **Tickets** $10-$120. *Dizzy's Club Coca-Cola* $5-$40; $5-$10 food/drink min. **Credit** AmEx, DC, MC, V. **Map** p405 D22.
The jazz arm of Lincoln Center is actually several blocks away from the main campus, high atop the Time Warner Center. It includes three rooms: the Rose Theater is a traditional mid-sized space, but the crown jewels are the Allen Room and the smaller Dizzy's Club Coca-Cola, with stages framed by enormous windows looking on to Columbus Circle and Central Park. The venues feel like a Hollywood cinematographer's vision of a Manhattan jazz club. Some of the best players in the business regularly grace the spot; among them is Wynton Marsalis, Jazz at Lincoln Center's famed artistic director.
▶ *See p263 for details of Midsummer Night Swing.*

Jazz Gallery

290 Hudson Street, between Dominick & Spring Streets, Soho (1-212 242 1063/www.jazz gallery.org). Subway A, C, E to Spring Street. **Shows** times vary. **Tickets** $10-$15. **Credit** (online purchases only) AmEx, Disc, MC, V. **Map** p403 D30.
The fact that there's no bar here should be a tip-off: the Jazz Gallery is a place to witness true works of art, from the sometimes obscure but always interesting jazzers who play the club (Henry Threadgill

and Steve Coleman, to name a couple) to the photos and artefacts displayed on the walls. The diminutive room's acoustics are sublime. *Photo p328*.

Jazz Standard

116 E 27th Street, between Park Avenue South & Lexington Avenue, Flatiron District (1-212 576 2232/www.jazzstandard.com). Subway 6 to 28th Street. **Shows** 7.30pm, 9.30pm Mon-Thur; 7.30pm, 9.30pm, 11.30pm Fri, Sat. **Tickets** $15-$30. **Credit** AmEx, DC, Disc, MC, V. **Map** p404 E26.
Jazz Standard's airy, multi-tiered floor plan makes for splendid sightlines to match the sterling sound. In keeping with the rib-sticking chow upstairs at Danny Meyer's Blue Smoke barbecue joint, the jazz is often of the groovy, hard-swinging variety, with musicians such as trumpeter Dave Douglas and pianist Gonzalo Rubalcaba.

★ Lenox Lounge

288 Malcolm X Boulevard (Lenox Avenue), between 124th & 125th Streets, Harlem (1-212 427 0253/www.lenoxlounge.com). Subway 2, 3 to 125th Street. **Open** Mon, Wed, Thur, Sun 4.30pm-midnight; 4.30pm-2.30am Fri, Sat. **Cover** free-$20; $16 drink min. **Credit** DC, Disc, MC, V. **Map** p407 D13.
This classy art deco lounge once hosted Billie Holiday and has drawn stars since the late 1930s. Saxist Patience Higgins's Sugar Hill Jazz Quartet jams into the wee hours on Monday nights.
► *For the bar, see p223.*

Merkin Concert Hall

For listing, see p330.
Just north of Lincoln Center, the recently refurbished Merkin provides a polished platform for classical and jazz composers. Chamber music, jazz, folk, cabaret and experimental performers take the stage at the intimate venue. Popular annual series include the New York Festival of Song, WNYC's New Sounds Live and Broadway Close Up.

92nd Street Y

1395 Lexington Avenue, at 92nd Street, Upper East Side (1-212 415 5500/www.92y.org). Subway 6 to 92nd Street. **Box office** 9am-7pm Mon-Thur; 9am-5pm Fri. **Tickets** from $20. **Credit** AmEx, DC, MC, V. **Map** p406 F17.
Best known for the series Jazz in July and spring's Lyrics & Lyricists, this multi-disciplinary cultural centre also offers gospel, mainstream jazz and singer-songwriters. The small, handsome theatre provides a fine setting for the sophisticated fare.

★ Smalls

183 W 10th Street, between Seventh Avenue South & W 4th Street, West Village (1-212 252 5091/www.smallsjazzclub.com). Subway 1 to Christopher Street-Sheridan Square. **Open** 7.30pm-4am daily. **Cover** $20. **No credit cards**. **Map** p403 D28.
The resurrected version of this storied, youth-friendly jazz spot offers a big concession for the grown-ups: a liquor licence and a fully stocked bar.

Everything Under the Sun

When summer arrives, New York's music scene goes outside to soak it up.

The main fixture on the summer calendar is **Central Park Summerstage** (*see p261*), a New York institution that has an ear for every sound under the sun. Many of the shows are free, with a handful of benefits (Crosby, Stills & Nash, the National) covering for them.

Not far from here is **Lincoln Center** (*see p330*), where the multi-tiered floor plan allows for several outdoor stages. The most popular venues are the North Plaza, which houses the Midsummer Night Swing concerts (*see p263*), and the Damrosch Park Bandshell, which rolls out the red carpet for the likes of Sonny Rollins.

There's also plenty of action downtown. The **South Street Seaport** has been booking the ridiculously hip likes of No Age as part of the **River to River Festival** (1-212 732 7678, www.seaport musicfestival.com; *see p261*), while the historic fort of **Castle Clinton** in Battery

Park (1-212 344 7220) welcomes stars when the weather is warm. (Tickets must be picked up in person on the day of a show, and they always go fast.)

Brooklyn's equivalent to the Central Park SummerStage is the **Celebrate Brooklyn! Performing Arts Festival** at the **Prospect Park Bandshell** (*see p263*). Adventurous booking runs the global gamut, from exotic visitors to familiar blues titans. Also in Brooklyn, the **Seaside Summer & Martin Luther King Jr Concert Series** (1-718 469 1912, www.brooklynconcerts.com) offers free funk, soul, R&B, Caribbean, Latin and gospel sounds in Coney Island and Brooklyn respectively. And further out in Long Island (and definitely not free), **Nikon at Jones Beach Theater** (1-516 221 1000, www.livenation.com) offers big-name acts in an unbeatable beachside amphitheatre location.

ARTS & ENTERTAINMENT

Jazz Gallery. See p326.

One thing hasn't changed, though: it's still a place to catch the best and brightest up-and-comers as well as moonlighting stars such as the Bad Plus's Ethan Iverson and veteran baritone saxist Charles Davis.

Smoke

2751 Broadway, between 105th & 106th Streets, Upper West Side (1-212 864 6662/www.smoke jazz.com). Subway 1 to 103rd Street. **Shows** 8pm, 10pm, 11.30pm Mon-Sat; 6.30pm, 8pm, 10pm, 11.30pm Sun. **Cover** *Mon-Wed, Sun* free; $20 food/drink min per person per set; *Thur-Sat* $20-$30; $10 min per person per set. **Credit** AmEx, DC, Disc, MC, V. **Map** p406 C16.

Not unlike a swanky living room, Smoke is a classy little joint that acts as a haven for local jazz legends and touring artists looking to play an intimate space. Early in the week, evenings are themed: on Sunday, it's Latin jazz; Tuesday, organ jazz. On weekends, renowned jazzers hit the stage, relishing the opportunity to play informal gigs uptown.

★ Stone

Avenue C, at 2nd Street, East Village (no phone/ www.thestonenyc.com). Subway F, V to Lower East Side-Second Avenue. **Shows** 8pm, 10pm Tue-Sun. **Cover** $10. **No credit cards**. **Map** p403 G29.

Don't call sax star John Zorn's not-for-profit venture a 'club'. You'll find no food or drinks here, and no nonsense, either: the Stone is an art space dedicated to 'the experimental and the avant-garde'. If you're down for some rigorously adventurous sounds (Anthony Coleman, Okkyung Lee, Tony Conrad), Zorn has made it easy: no advance sales, and all ages admitted (under-19s get discounts). The bookings are left to a different artist-cum-curator each month.

Sweet Rhythm

88 Seventh Avenue South, between Bleecker & Grove Streets, West Village (1-212 255 3626/www.sweetrhythmny.com). Subway 1 to Christopher Street-Sheridan Square. **Shows** 8pm, 10pm Mon-Thur, Sun; 8pm, 10pm, midnight Fri, Sat. **Cover** $10-$25; $10 food/drink min per person per set. **Credit** AmEx, DC, MC, V. **Map** p403 D28.

Sweet Rhythm is more of a show destination than a general hangout. A variety of jazz sounds dominates (swing, standards, bop) and big names such as Sonny Fortune and Rashied Ali drop in occasionally, but blues and world music are also on offer and Tuesdays are devoted to vocalists.

Swing 46

349 W 46th Street, between Eighth & Ninth Avenues, Theater District (1-212 262 9554/ www.swing46.com). Subway A, C, E to 42nd Street-Port Authority. **Open** 5pm-midnight Mon-Thur, Sun; 5pm-3am Fri, Sat. **Cover** $5-$15. **Credit** AmEx, DC, MC, V. **Map** p404 C23.

Swing isn't just a trend at this supper club: whether peppy or sappy, these cats mean it. Bands with names like the Flying Neutrinos and the Flipped Fedoras await, so be sure to wear your dancin' shoes. Dance lessons are available for the inexperienced.

Uptown Jazz Lounge at Minton's Playhouse

20 W 118th Street, between St Nicholas Avenue & Adam Clayton Powell Jr Boulevard (Seventh Avenue), Harlem (1-212 864 8346/ www.uptownatmintons.com). Subway B, C to 116th Street. **Shows** 9pm, 10.30pm, midnight Mon-Thur, Sun; 10pm, 11.30pm, 1am Fri, Sat.

Cover *Mon-Thur, Sun* free; 2-drink min. *Fri, Sat* $10; 2-drink min. **Credit** AmEx, DC, MC, V. **Map** p407 D14.

Few clubs in the city can boast as rich a history as Minton's, which Miles Davis once dubbed 'the black jazz capital of the world'. After being boarded up for more than 30 years, the club reopened in 2006 and now presents five house bands from Sunday to Thursday. On weekends, when it's more crowded, you can see guest acts, which have included the likes of percussionist Joe Chambers.

► *See p120 for more on West Harlem's bar and music scene.*

★ Village Vanguard

178 Seventh Avenue South, at Perry Street, West Village (1-212 255 4037/www.village vanguard.com). Subway A, C, E, 1, 2, 3 to 14th Street; L to Eighth Avenue. **Shows** 9pm, 11pm daily. **Tickets** $25 Mon-Thur; $35 Fri-Sun. **Credit** (online purchases only) AmEx, MC, V. **Map** p403 D28.

More than 75 years old but still going strong, the Village Vanguard is one of New York's real jazz meccas. History surrounds you: John Coltrane, Miles Davis and Bill Evans have all grooved in this hallowed hall. Big names both old and new continue to fill the schedules; the 16-piece Vanguard Jazz Orchestra has been the Monday-night regular for more than 40 years. Reservations are recommended; the venue takes only cash or travellers' cheques at the door.

Zebulon

258 Wythe Avenue, between Metropolitan Avenue & North Third Street, Williamsburg, Brooklyn (1-718 218 6934/www.zebulonca feconcert.com). Subway L to Bedford Avenue. **Open** 5.30pm-4am Mon-Fri; 4pm-4am Sat, Sun. **Cover** free. **Credit** AmEx. **Map** p411 U7.

While emphasising young firebrands (Gold Sparkle Band, Tyshawn Sorey) over the establishment, this killer jazz spot also welcomes the daring wing of the local rock scene (such as great singer-songwriter Hannah Marcus). While the café opens in the afternoon, don't expect live music until closer to 10pm.

WORLD, COUNTRY & ROOTS

See also 324 **SOB's** *and p317* **BB King Blues Club & Grill**.

BAMcafé at Brooklyn Academy of Music

For listing, see p330 Brooklyn Academy of Music. Among the cornucopia of live entertainment programmes at BAM is the BAMcafé above the lobby, which comes to life on weekend nights with country, spoken word, hip hop, world music and more. The Brooklyn Next series focuses on up-and-coming performers from the musically rich borough.

Nublu

62 Avenue C, between 4th & 5th Streets, East Village (1-646 546 5206/www.nublu.net). Subway F, V to Lower East Side-Second Avenue. **Open** 8pm-4am daily. **Cover** $5-$10. **No credit cards. Map** p40 G29.

Nublu's prominence on the local globalist club scene has been inversely proportional to its size. A pressure-cooker of creativity, the venue gave rise to the Brazilian Girls, who started jamming at one late-night session and haven't stopped yet, as well as starting NYC's romance with the northern Brazilian style *forró*. Even on weeknights, events usually start no earlier than 10pm – but if you show up early (and find the unmarked door), the bar is well stocked.

Rodeo Bar & Grill

375 Third Avenue, at 27th Street, Gramercy Park (1-212 683 6500/www.rodeobar.com). Subway 6 to 28th Street. **Shows** 9pm Mon, Tue, Sun; 10pm Wed, Thur; 11pm Fri, Sat. **Cover** free. **Credit** AmEx, DC, MC, V. **Map** p404 F26.

The unpretentious crowd, roadhouse atmosphere and absence of a cover charge help make the Rodeo the city's best roots club, with a steady stream of rockabilly, country and related sounds. Watch out for the peanut shells spread across the floor, and the frat boys from nearby Murray Hill.

Classical

The **Metropolitan Opera** continues to command headlines in 2009, not least because it's the only big gun currently firing on all cylinders. The **New York Philharmonic** will spend the spring of 2009 bidding farewell to Lorin Maazel, its current music director, and preparing for the autumn arrival of Alan Gilbert, his young successor. And in late 2008, the **New York City Opera**'s plans were thrown into disarray when Gerard Mortier, the controversy-courting head of Paris Opera who was due to take up the reins for the 2009/10 season, resigned due to budget cuts.

Arguably the most important development in New York's classical scene of late has occurred off the beaten path in Greenwich Village. In short order, **(Le) Poisson Rouge** (*see p322*)

> ### INSIDE TRACK
> ### MET'S CHEAP SEATS
>
> Most tickets at the **Met** (*see p332*) will be expensive for those not used to forking out for the arts. However, 200 prime seats for all Monday-through-Thursday performances are held until the last hour, then sold for a mere $20 apiece.

has become a go-to venue for edgy rock, jazz, electronica… and bold chamber-music groups such as Signal and NOW Ensemble. It's also home to Ronen Givony's innovative **Wordless Music Series** (www.wordlessmusic.org), which draws young, curious crowds to hear uncompromising new music of all types.

The standard New York concert season lasts from September to June, but there are plenty of summer events and performances (*see p260*). Box office hours may change in summer, so phone ahead or check websites for times.

You can buy tickets directly from most venues, whether by phone, online or at the box office. However, a surcharge is generally added to tickets not bought in person. For more on tickets, *see p258*.

MAJOR CONCERT HALLS

Brooklyn Academy of Music
30 Lafayette Avenue, between Ashland Place & St Felix Street, Fort Greene, Brooklyn (1-718 636 4100/www.bam.org). Subway B, Q, 2, 3, 4, 5 to Atlantic Avenue; C to Lafayette Street; D, M, N, R to Pacific Street; G to Fulton Street. **Box office** noon-6pm Mon-Sat; noon-4pm Sun (show days). *Phone bookings* 10am-6pm Mon-Fri; noon-6pm Sat; noon 4pm Sun. **Admission** prices vary. **Credit** AmEx, DC, MC, V. **Map** p410 T10.

America's oldest performing arts academy continues to present some of the freshest programming in the city. Every autumn and winter, the Next Wave Festival offers avant-garde music, dance and theatre, while spring brings lauded European opera. The nearby BAM Harvey Theater offers a smaller, more atmospheric setting for new creations by composers such as Tan Dun and Meredith Monk, as well as innovative stagings of baroque opera. Meanwhile, the resident Brooklyn Philharmonic Orchestra continues to provide interesting programming under the direction of Michael Christie.

▶ *See p133 for more on BAM's history.*

★ Carnegie Hall
154 W 57th Street, at Seventh Avenue, Midtown (1-212 247 7800/www.carnegie hall.org). Subway N, Q, R, W to 57th Street. **Box office** *In person* 11am-6pm Mon-Sat; noon-6pm Sun. *Phone bookings* 9am-9pm daily. **Admission** prices vary. **Credit** AmEx, DC, Disc, MC, V. **Map** p405 D22.

Artistic director Clive Gillinson continues to put his stamp on Carnegie Hall. The stars, both soloists and orchestras, continue to shine most brightly in the Isaac Stern Auditorium, inside this renowned concert hall. But it's the spunky upstart Zankel Hall that has generated the most buzz, offering an eclectic mix of classical, contemporary, jazz, pop and world music. Next door, the Weill Recital Hall hosts intimate concerts and chamber music

programmes. In 2009, look out for 'Honor', a spring celebration of African-American artistry.

Merkin Concert Hall
Kaufman Center, 129 W 67th Street, between Broadway & Amsterdam Avenue, Upper West Side (1-212 501 3330/www.kaufman-center.org). Subway 1 to 66th Street-Lincoln Center. **Box office** noon-7pm Mon-Thur, Sun; noon-4pm Fri. **Admission** $10-$50. **Credit** (advance purchases only) AmEx, MC, V. **Map** p405 C21.

Tucked on a side street in the shadow of Lincoln Center, this newly refurbished gem offers a robust mix of early music and avant-garde programming, plus an increasing amount of jazz, folk and some more eclectic fare.

92nd Street Y
For listing, see p327.

The Y has always stood for solidly traditional orchestral, solo and chamber masterpieces. But the organisation also fosters the careers of young musicians and explores European and Jewish-American music traditions, with innovative results.

Lincoln Center

Columbus Avenue, at 65th Street, Upper West Side (1-212 546 2656/www.lincolncenter.org). Subway 1 to 66th Street-Lincoln Center. **Map** p405 C21.

Built in the 1960s, this massive complex is the nexus of Manhattan's performing arts scene. Lincoln Center hosts lectures and symposia in the **Rose Building**, in addition to events in the main halls: **Alice Tully Hall**, **Avery Fisher Hall**, **Metropolitan Opera House**, **New York State Theater**, **Vivian Beaumont Theater** and **Mitzi E Newhouse Theater**. Also situated here are the **Juilliard School** (*see p335*) and the **Fiorello H La Guardia High School of Music & Art and Performing Arts** (108 Amsterdam Avenue, between 64th & 65th Streets, www.laguardiahs.org), which frequently hosts professional performances.

Big stars such as Valery Gergiev, William Christie and the Takács Quartet are Lincoln Center's meat and potatoes. Lately, though, the divide between the flagship Great Performers season and the more audacious, multidisciplinary **Lincoln Center Out of Doors Festival** (*see p264*) has begun to narrow. Freshest of all is the **Mostly Mozart Festival** (late July-Aug), a formerly moribund four-week summer staple that has been thoroughly reinvented with progressive bookings and innovative juxtapositions.

The main entry point for Lincoln Center is at Columbus Avenue, at 65th Street, but the

Profile Renée Fleming

New Yorkers can expect to see a lot more of the popular diva in 2009.

A prominent lyric soprano for more than two decades, Renée Fleming has been a creative force at the Metropolitan Opera since the mid-1990s. Without question the reigning American opera singer worldwide, the diva has performed on *The Late Show with David Letterman*, and top chef Daniel Boulud has even named a dessert after her. But these trappings of celebrity have made it easy to overlook Fleming's artistic contributions. During Peter Gelb's first two seasons as general manager of the Met, Fleming's presence seemed to diminish among the subway-station posters and Times Square simulcasts – not to mention the furore over recent arrivals like Anna Netrebko and Natalie Dessay.

However, it's impossible to overlook her now. In September 2008, Fleming's face was plastered all over the city as the Met's figurehead, crowned with the leonine mane she'd wear in Massenet's *Thaïs* in December. Starring in the Met's opening-night gala, she performed in one act apiece from Verdi's *La Traviata* and Massenet's *Manon*, and Richard Strauss's *Capriccio*.

That Gelb soldiered on with a glamorous event put in place by the previous regime, was proof of his fervent wish to keep Fleming busy here. 'She is under such demand to do more lucrative recitals and different types of projects,' Gelb explains. 'One of my first acts as manager was to have lunch with her and persuade her to increase her performances.' In March 2009, Fleming appears at the Met in one of her signature roles in Dvorak's *Rusalka*, and is strongly tipped to feature in the 2009/10 season. She will also sing in the New York Philharmonic's opening gala in autumn 2009.

The 2008 Met gala saw Fleming in costumes designed by Karl Lagerfeld, John Galliano and Christian Lacroix. It also saw the launch of a $200 perfume, La Voce by Renée Fleming; part of the proceeds benefit the Met. Fleming accepts the glitz pragmatically because, as she says, media attention for the arts is drying up. 'A hundred years ago, singers were advertising fragrances and even cigarettes, because they were huge stars.'

LUCK OF THE DEBUT One of Fleming's key roles is **Countess Almaviva** (*Le nozze di Figaro*), a part she played in her debut performance at the Met when she stepped in for an ailing Dame Felicity Lott.

venues that follow are spread out across the square of blocks from 62nd to 66th Streets, between Amsterdam and Columbus Avenues.

Centercharge (1-212 721 6500) sells tickets for events at Alice Tully Hall, Avery Fisher Hall and the Juilliard School, as well as for the Lincoln Center Out of Doors Festival.

★ Alice Tully Hall
1-212 875 5050. **Box office** 11am-6pm Mon-Sat; noon-6pm Sun. **Admission** free-$75. **Credit** AmEx, DC, Disc, MC, V.

Home to the Chamber Music Society of Lincoln Center (1-212 875 5788, www.chambermusicsociety.org), Alice Tully Hall somehow feels cosy despite a capacity of 1,096 seats. Following extensive remodelling, the hall is set to reopen in February 2009 with a festive series of events.

★ Avery Fisher Hall
1-212 875 5030. **Box office** 10am-6pm Mon-Sat; noon-6pm Sun. **Admission** $20-$114. **Credit** AmEx, DC, Disc, MC, V.

This handsome, comfortable 2,700-seat hall is the headquarters of the New York Philharmonic (1-212 875 5656, www.nyphilharmonic.org), the country's oldest symphony orchestra (founded in 1842) and one of its finest. The sound, which ranges from good to atrocious depending on who you ask, stands to be improved, although the timing of the improvements hasn't been confirmed. Inexpensive early-evening 'rush hour' concerts and open rehearsals are presented on a regular basis. The Great Performers series features top international soloists and ensembles.

★ Metropolitan Opera House
1-212 362 6000/www.metopera.org. **Box office** 10am-8pm Mon-Sat; noon-6pm Sun. **Admission** $25-$320. **Credit** AmEx, DC, Disc, MC, V.

The grandest of the Lincoln Center buildings, the Met is a spectacular place to see and hear opera. It hosts the Metropolitan Opera from September to May, with major visiting companies appearing in summer. Opera's biggest stars appear here regularly, and artistic director James Levine has turned the orchestra into a true symphonic force. Audiences are knowledgeable and fiercely devoted, with subscriptions remaining in families for generations.

The Met had already started becoming more inclusive before current impresario Peter Gelb took the reins in 2006. Now, the company is placing a priority on creating novel theatrical experiences while assembling a new company of physically graceful, telegenic stars (Anna Netrebko, Rolando Villazón, Juan Diego Flórez) for a programme of high-definition movie-theatre broadcasts. In 2009, look out for new productions of *La Rondine* and *La Sonnambula*, as well as the final run of Otto Schenk's *Ring* Cycle.

★ New York State Theater
1-212 870 5570. **Box office** 10am-7.30pm Mon; 10am-8.30pm Tue-Sat; 11.30am-7.30pm Sun. **Admission** $16-$120. **Credit** AmEx, DC, Disc, MC, V.

As well as the New York City Ballet (www.nycballet.com), the State Theater is also home to the New York City Opera (www.nycopera.com). The company has long tried to overcome its second-best reputation by being both ambitious and defiantly populist: rising young American singers often take their first bows here, and casts and productions have until recently tended to be younger and sexier than those of its more patrician counterpart. The theatre is closed for renovation during much of 2009, with a grand reopening no doubt in store for the autumn.
► *See p359 for further details of the New York State Theater and the New York City Ballet.*

★ Walter Reade Theater
1-212 875 5600/tickets 1-212 496 3809/www.filmlinc.com. **Box office** 12.30-6pm Mon-Fri; 30mins before shows Sat, Sun. **Admission** $11; $7-$8 reductions. **No credit cards.**

The Walter Reade Theater's acoustics are less than fabulous (it's mainly a cinema). Still, the Great Performers series offers Sunday morning events fuelled by pastries and hot beverages sold in the lobby, and composer-lecturer Robert Kapilow's 'What Makes It Great?' series provides an entertaining introduction to major classical works.

OPERA

The Metropolitan Opera and the New York City Opera may be the leaders of the pack, but they're hardly the only game in town. Call the organisations or check online for information on prices, schedules and venues. Music schools (*see p335*) also have regular opera programmes.

Amato Opera Theater
319 Bowery, at 2nd Street, East Village (1-212 228 8200/www.amato.org). Subway B, D, F, V to Broadway-Lafayette Street; 6 to Bleecker Street. **Admission** $35; $30 reductions. **Credit** AmEx, DC, Disc, MC, V. **Map** p403 F29.

New York's beloved mom-and-pop opera shop offers charming, fully staged productions in a theatre just 20ft wide – it's almost like watching opera in your living room. Though well-established singers once performed here, casting can be indifferent.

American Opera Projects
South Oxford Space, 138 South Oxford Street, between Atlantic Avenue & Hanson Place, Fort Greene, Brooklyn (1-718 398 4024/www.operaprojects.org). Subway B, Q, 2, 3, 4, 5 to Atlantic Avenue; C to Lafayette Avenue;

INSIDE TRACK
MUSIC IN THE PARKS

The **Metropolitan Opera** (*see p332*) stages free opera performances in Central Park and other NYC parks in June every year. Grab a blanket, pack a picnic (no alcohol or glass bottles) and show up in the afternoon to nab a good spot. And in July and August, the **New York Philharmonic**'s Concerts in the Parks (*see p332* **Avery Fisher Hall**) offers a varied programme around the five boroughs' larger parks. Again, arrive early. Admission to both series is free.

D, M, N, R to Pacific Street; G to Fulton Street. **Admission** prices vary. **No credit cards.** **Map** p410 T10.

AOP is not so much an opera company as a living, breathing workshop that allows you the opportunity to follow a new work from gestation to completion. Shows can be anything from a table reading of new librettos to a complete orchestral production.

Dicapo Opera Theatre

184 E 76th Street, between Lexington & Third Avenues, Upper East Side (1-212 288 9438/ www.dicapo.com). Subway 6 to 77th Street. **Admission** $60 (plus $12.50 handling charge). **Credit** AmEx, MC, V. **Map** p405 F20.

This top-notch chamber-opera troupe benefits from City Opera-quality singers performing in a delightfully intimate setting in the basement of St Jean Baptiste Church. Dicapo has recently augmented its diet of standard classics with a sprinkling of offbeat works and even premières, thanks in part to composer Tobias Picker's arrival as artistic adviser.

Gotham Chamber Opera

Harry de Jur Playhouse, 466 Grand Street, at Pitt Street, Lower East Side (1-212 598 0400/ www.gothamchamberopera.org). Subway B, D to Grand Street; F to East Broadway; F, J, M, Z to Delancey-Essex Streets. **Admission** $30-$65. **Credit** AmEx, DC, MC, V. **Map** p403 G30.

This fine young company specialises in chamber opera: that doesn't mean scaled-down versions of big-stage classics, but rather those rarely staged shows specifically designed for smaller forces in intimate settings.

OTHER VENUES

★ Bargemusic

Fulton Ferry Landing, between Old Fulton & Water Streets, Dumbo, Brooklyn (1-718 624 2083/www.bargemusic.org). Subway A, C to
High Street; F to York Street; 2, 3 to Clark Street. **Admission** $25-$40. **Credit** DC, MC, V. **Map** p411 S9.

This former coffee bean barge usually presents four chamber concerts a week (plus one jazz programme), set against a panoramic view of lower Manhattan. It's a magical experience (and the programming has recently grown more ambitious), but wrap up in winter. When the weather warms, enjoy a drink on the upper deck during the intermission.

★ Frick Collection

For listing, see p109. **Admission** $25.

Concerts in the Frick Collection's elegantly appointed concert hall are a rare treat, generally featuring both promising debutants and lesser-known but world-class performers. Concerts are broadcast live in the Garden Court, where tickets aren't required.

Gilder Lehrman Hall

Morgan Library & Museum, 225 Madison Avenue, at 36th Street, Murray Hill (1-212 685 0008/www.themorgan.org). Subway 6 to 33rd Street. **Admission** prices vary. **Credit** DC, MC, V. **Map** p404 E25.

This elegant, 280-seat gem of a concert hall is perfect for song recitals and chamber groups. The St Luke's Chamber Ensemble and Glimmerglass Opera were quick to establish a presence here.

Kitchen

For listing, see p360.

A meeting place for the avant-garde in music, dance and theatre for more than 30 years, the Kitchen has played a less prominent role in the local scene during recent seasons. Still, edgy contemporary sounds can be found here; tickets range from free to $25.

★ Metropolitan Museum of Art

For listing, see p110.

When it comes to established virtuosos and revered chamber ensembles, the Met's programming is rich and full (and ticket prices can be correspondingly high). The museum has established a youthful resident ensemble, Metropolitan Museum Artists in Concert.

▶ *Seasonally inspired early music concerts are held uptown in the stunning Fuentidueña Chapel at the Cloisters; see p122.*

★ Miller Theatre at
Columbia University

Broadway, at 116th Street, Morningside Heights (1-212 854 7799/www.millertheatre.com). Subway 1 to 116th Street-Columbia University. **Box office** noon-6pm Mon-Fri (plus 2hrs before performance on show days). **Admission** $20; $12 reductions. **Credit** AmEx, DC, MC, V. **Map** p407 C14.

The Miller Theatre single-handedly made contemporary classical music sexy in New York City. The

ARTS & ENTERTAINMENT

credit belongs to former executive director George Steel, who proved that presenting challenging fare in a casual, unaffected setting could attract young audiences – and hang on to them. Steel departed for the Dallas Opera in late 2008; it'll be interesting to see what happens here next.

Symphony Space

2537 Broadway, at 95th Street, Upper West Side (1-212 864 5400/www.symphonyspace.org). Subway 1, 2, 3 to 96th Street. **Box office** 11am-7pm Tue-Sun. **Admission** prices vary ($2 surcharge per order). **Credit** AmEx, DC, MC, V. **Map** p406 C17.

Despite its name, programming at Symphony Space is anything but orchestra-centric: recent seasons have featured sax quartets, Indian classical music and a cappella ensembles. The annual Wall to Wall marathons serve up a full day of music free of charge, all focused on a particular composer.

Tenri Cultural Institute

43A W 13th Street, between Fifth & Sixth Avenues, Greenwich Village (1-212 645 2800/ www.tenri.org). Subway F, V to 14th Street; L to Sixth Avenue; L, N, Q, R, W, 4, 5, 6 to 14th Street-Union Square. **Admission** prices vary. **No credit cards. Map** p403 E27.

A not-for-profit organisation devoted to promoting the Japanese language and appreciation of international art, Tenri also regularly hosts concerts by New York's leading contemporary music ensembles, such as the American Modern Ensemble, in its clean, effortlessly cosy gallery space.

CHURCHES

From sacred to secular, a thrilling variety of music is performed in New York's churches. Superb acoustics, out-of-this-world choirs and serene surroundings make these houses of worship particularly attractive venues. A bonus is that some concerts are free or very cheap.

Cathedral Church of St John the Divine

For listing, see p117 **Cathedral Church of St John the Divine.**

This stunning neo-Gothic, 3,000-seat sanctuary provides a heavenly atmosphere for the church's own choir and visiting ensembles. Acoustics, however, are murky.

Christ & St Stephen's Church

120 W 69th Street, between Columbus Avenue & Broadway, Upper West Side (1-212 787 2755/ www.csschurch.org). Subway 1, 2, 3 to 72nd Street. **Admission** prices vary. **No credit cards. Map** p405 C21.

This small, pleasant West Side church offers one of the most diverse concert rosters in the city.

Church of the Ascension

12 W 11th Street, between Fifth & Sixth Avenues, Greenwich Village (1-212 358 1469/ www.voicesofascension.org). Subway N, R, W to 8th Street-NYU. **Admission** $10-$50. **Credit** MC, V (advance purchases only). **Map** p403 E28.

There's a first-rate professional choir, the Voices of Ascension, at this little Village church. You can catch the choir at Lincoln Center on occasion, but home turf is the best place to hear it.

Church of St Ignatius Loyola

980 Park Avenue, at 84th Street, Upper East Side (1-212 288 2520/www.saintignatius loyola.org). Subway 4, 5, 6 to 86th Street. **Admission** $10-$40. **Credit** AmEx, DC, Disc, MC, V. **Map** p406 E18.

The Sacred Music in a Sacred Space series is a high point of Upper East Side music culture. Lincoln Center also holds concerts here, capitalising on the church's fine acoustics and prime location.

Corpus Christi Church

529 W 121st Street, between Amsterdam Avenue & Broadway, Morningside Heights (1-212 666 9266/www.mb1800.org). Subway 1 to 116th Street-Columbia University. **Admission** prices vary. **Credit** DC, MC, V. **Map** p407 C14.

Fans of early music can get their fix from Music Before 1800, a series that regularly imports the world's leading antiquarian artists and ensembles.

Good Shepherd-Faith Presbyterian Church

152 W 66th Street, between Amsterdam Avenue & Broadway, Upper West Side (1-212 799 1259/www.jupitersymphony.com). Subway 1 to 66th Street-Lincoln Center. **Admission** prices vary. **No credit cards. Map** p405 C21.

This handsome Lincoln Center-area facility plays host to the Jupiter Symphony Chamber Players, an offshoot of a well-respected local orchestra led for years by the late Jens Nygaard. In his honour, the Jupiters now present an affordable mix of chamber music chestnuts and less familiar Romantic gems.

St Bartholomew's Church

109 E 50th Street, between Park & Lexington Avenues, Midtown East (1-212 378 0248/ www.stbarts.org). Subway E, V to Lexington Avenue-53rd Street; 6 to 51st Street. **Admission** prices vary. **Credit** AmEx, DC, MC, V. **Map** p403 E23.

This magnificent church hosts the Summer Festival of Sacred Music, one of the city's most ambitious choral music series. It fills the rest of the year with performances by resident ensembles and guests.

St Thomas Church Fifth Avenue

1 W 53rd Street, at Fifth Avenue, Midtown East (1-212 757 7013/www.saintthomaschurch.org).

Subway E, V to Fifth Avenue–53rd Street.
Admission $15-$70. **Credit** AmEx, DC, MC, V.
Map p405 E22.
The country's only fully accredited choir school for boys keeps the great Anglican choral tradition alive and well in New York. St Thomas's annual performance of Handel's *Messiah* is a must-hear that's well worth the rather steep ticket price.

Trinity Church/ St Paul's Chapel

Trinity Church, Broadway, at Wall Street; St Paul's Chapel, Broadway, at Fulton Street, Financial District (1-212 602 0747/www.trinity wallstreet.org). Subway R, W to Rector Street; 4, 5 to Wall Street. **Admission** *Concerts at One* $2 donation. **No credit cards.**
Map p402 E33.
Historic Trinity, situated in the heart of the Financial District, plays host to the inexpensive Concerts at One series. Performances are held (at 1pm) on Mondays at St Paul's Chapel, and on Thursdays at Trinity Church.
▶ *See p69 for more on the history of St Paul's.*

SCHOOLS

The Juilliard School and the Manhattan School of Music are renowned for their talented students, faculty and artists in residence, all of whom regularly perform for free or at low cost. Lately, Mannes College of Music has made great strides. Noteworthy music and innovative programming can also be found at several other colleges and schools in the city.

Juilliard School

60 Lincoln Center Plaza, Broadway, at 65th Street, Upper West Side (1-212 769 7406/ www.juilliard.edu). Subway 1 to 66th Street-Lincoln Center. **Admission** usually free. **Map** p405 C21.
NYC's premier conservatory stages weekly concerts by student soloists, orchestras and chamber ensembles, as well as elaborate opera productions that can often rival many professional presentations.

Manhattan School of Music

120 Claremont Avenue, at 122nd Street, Morningside Heights (1-212 749 2802 ext 4428/www.msmnyc.edu). Subway 1 to 125th Street. **Admission** usually free. **Map** p407 B14.
The Manhattan School offers master classes, recitals and off-site concerts by its students and faculty as well as visiting professionals. The American String Quartet has been in residence here since 1984 and gives concerts regularly, while the Augustine Guitar Series includes recitals by top soloists.

Mannes College of Music

150 W 85th Street, between Columbus & Amsterdam Avenues, Upper West Side (1-212 580 0210/www.mannes.edu). Subway B, C, 1 to 86th Street. **Admission** usually free. **Map** p406 C18.
In addition to student concerts and faculty recitals, Mannes also mounts its own ambitious, historically themed concert series; the summer is given over to festivals and workshops for instrumentalists. Productions by the Mannes Opera, whose fresh-faced members are drilled by seasoned opera professionals, are a perennial treat.

New York Philharmonic. *See p332.*

ARTS & ENTERTAINMENT

Sports & Fitness

It's all action in Gotham.

Here in New York, we have pro teams to spare in all the major sports. From hockey and basketball (three apiece) to football and baseball (each with only a paltry pair), the city's athletic variety has spawned a surprisingly diverse fan base – and one that isn't shy about loudly championing one franchise over another. There's no need to worry about getting fat on overpriced stadium beer and hot dogs, though: the city also presents myriad opportunities to get active, and maybe see some of the neighbourhood while you're at it. Whether it's falling on your butt in one of three magical ice rinks in winter, cycling through Central Park, or competing in one of the New York Road Runner events, you'll certainly have that satisfying achy feeling in the morning.

About the author
Drew Toal *is the Assistant Editor of* Time Out New York *magazine.*

SPECTATOR SPORTS

Major venues

All advance tickets for events at these venues are sold through **Ticketmaster** (*see p258*).

Madison Square Garden

Seventh Avenue, between 31st & 33rd Streets, Garment District (1-212 465 6741/www.the garden.com). Subway A, C, E, 1, 2, 3 to 34th Street-Penn Station. **Open** *Box office* 9am-6pm Mon-Fri; 10am-6pm Sat; noon-1hr before event begins Sun. **Tickets** prices vary. **Credit** AmEx, DC, Disc, MC, V. **Map** p404 D25.
The New York Rangers (hockey) and New York Knicks and New York Liberty (basketball) call this home. *See p339 and p341.*
► *For more on the stadium's history, see p94.*

Meadowlands Sports Complex

East Rutherford, NJ (1-201 935 3900/ www.meadowlands.com). NJ Transit Meadowlands Sports Complex bus from Port Authority Bus Terminal. **Open** *Box office* 11am-6pm Mon-Sat; 2hrs prior to event Sun. **Tickets** prices vary. **Credit** *Giants & Jets games & Meadowlands Racetrack.* **No credit cards.** *All other events* AmEx, DC, Disc, MC, V.

The IZOD Center, the Meadowlands Racetrack (*see p340*) and Giants Stadium are all part of this massive multi-venue complex across the river. All are serviced by the same bus.

Nassau Veterans Memorial Coliseum

1255 Hempstead Turnpike, Uniondale, Long Island (1-516 794 9303/www.nassau coliseum.com). LIRR (www.lirr.org) train from Penn Station to Hempstead, then N70, N71 or N72 bus. **Tickets** prices vary. **Credit** AmEx, DC, Disc, MC, V.
Where the New York Islanders hockey team keep sports in Long Island alive, and where you can also catch the occasional monster truck rally alongside the usual cavalcade of sellout music gigs.

Prudential Center

165 Mulberry Street, between Edison Place & Lafayette Street, Newark, NJ (1-973 757 6000/ www.prucenter.com). PATH to Newark. **Tickets** prices vary. **Credit** AmEx, DC, Disc, MC, V.
The new home of the New Jersey Devils hockey team.

Baseball

It wasn't the end of the world when, in 1958, the Dodgers left Brooklyn for Los Angeles and the Giants departed the Polo Grounds for San Francisco. After all, locals still had the mighty **New York Yankees** to cheer (or, of course, boo). And then, in 1962, the **New York Mets**

Fields of Dreams

With some trepidation, the Mets and Yankees say hello to their new homes.

In spring 2008, there was a record-breaking scrum for Mets tickets as fans scrambled to relive 45 years of 7-train magic at Shea Stadium. Meanwhile, eulogies to Yankee Stadium filled the airwaves (and column inches) as 'the House that Ruth Built', in constant use since 1923, was finally put to rest. But while New York's baseball fans have said goodbye to two iconic venues, they'll be saying hello to two new ones in 2009.

Plans for the Yankees' and Mets' new stadiums date back to the Giuliani administration. In December 2001, the outgoing mayor disagreed with detractors who thought the money was better spent elsewhere. 'Baseball is a tremendously big business. It's like keeping the Stock Exchange here. This is by far, without any doubts, one of the best deals in sports.'

The new Yankee Stadium will have the same field dimensions as the old one, including the short right-field fence that proved such a boon to the Babe, but the amenities have been bumped up considerably. Fans will no longer be able to grumble about the dearth of leg room in the cramped seats: space between rows has been increased by five to ten inches. Refreshments go far beyond the old beer-in-a-plastic-cup formula – there's now a martini bar and a fancy steak house. Already the most expensive stadium ever built in the US, it had surpassed its estimated $1 billion budget by 30 per cent in early 2008.

Running at a mere $800 million, the Mets' new Citi Field is being designed to recall (architecturally, at least) stadiums of yore: the vanished Ebbets Field, which the Brooklyn Dodgers once called home, and the old Polo Grounds, where the Mets played their first two seasons. The difference is that it's designed to provide full, panoramic views and boasts flashy features like an interactive Mets museum.

But in the current climate of fiscal belt-tightening and soaring construction costs, who's going to foot the bill for all these improvements? The fans. Both baseball teams are actually cutting the number of seats, sacrificing affordable seating for super-expensive luxury boxes and pricing out many families. Although the teams will still offer some cheaper bleacher seats, the reduced number available is likely to drive the scalpers' price right back up – and the irony of having the most expensive sports venue (Yankee Stadium) in the country located in one of the nation's poorest areas (the Bronx) isn't lost on anyone.

Budget setbacks aside, at least one potential 'curse' has been removed from Yankee Stadium. In April 2008, after a tip-off, construction workers used jackhammers to remove a David Ortiz jersey that had been buried under concrete on the site by a colleague who roots for the rival Boston Red Sox. The jersey was later auctioned for charity on eBay for $175,110.

ARTS & ENTERTAINMENT

Model of the new Yankee Stadium.

Gleason's Gym.

arrived in town, transforming themselves from the league's laughing stock to World Series winners in a mere seven years.

The Yankees have had a long tradition of success, although the team has endured its share of problems as the next generation of Steinbrenners takes over the country's most storied franchise – in 2008, the team missed the playoffs for the first time in 13 years. The Mets have shelled also out plenty of money on high-priced free agents, but the policy hasn't helped them to post-season success: in 2008, as in 2007, the team was eliminated on the last day of the regular season and missed the playoffs. Both teams move into new stadiums for 2009 (*see p337* **Fields of Dreams**); if the prices are too high, head to Brooklyn or Staten Island for a minor-league game. The season runs April to September, with playoffs in October.

Brooklyn Cyclones
KeySpan Park, 1904 Surf Avenue, between West 17th & 19th Streets, Coney Island, Brooklyn (1-718 449 8497/www.brooklyn cyclones.com). Subway D, F, Q to Coney Island-Stillwell Avenue. **Open** *Box office* 10am-5pm Mon-Fri; 10am-4pm Sat. **Tickets** $7-$16. **Credit** AmEx, DC, Disc, MC, V.

★ New York Mets
Citi Field, Flushing, Queens (1-718 507 8499/ www.mets.com). Subway 7 to Willets Point-Shea Stadium. **Open** *Box office* 9am-5.30pm Mon-Fri; 9am-2pm Sat, Sun. **Tickets** phone or check website for details. **Credit** AmEx, DC, Disc, MC, V.

★ New York Yankees
Yankee Stadium, River Avenue, at 161st Street, Bronx (1-718 293 6000/www.yankees.com). Subway B, D, 4 to 161st Street-Yankee Stadium. **Open** *Box office* 9am-5pm Mon-Sat; 10am-4pm Sun; also during games. **Tickets** $12-$325. **Credit** AmEx, DC, Disc, MC, V. **Map** p408 B8.

Staten Island Yankees
Richmond County Bank Ballpark, 75 Richmond Terrace, at Bay Street, Staten Island (1-718 720 9265/www.siyanks.com). Staten Island Ferry to St George Terminal. **Open** *Box office* 9am-5pm Mon-Fri; also during games. **Tickets** $5-$13. **Credit** AmEx, DC, Disc, MC, V.

Basketball

The damage had already been done, but beleaguered **New York Knicks** coach Isiah Thomas was finally given the boot in the 2007-2008 season and the team can maybe now take some meaningful steps forward behind Phoenix run-and-gun enthusiast Mike D'Antoni. Something had better happen: although Knicks fans are among the league's most loyal, the patience of Garden stalwarts such as Spike Lee has been severely tested of late. For their part, the **New Jersey Nets**

need to rebuild, and are hoping that the proposed move to their new digs in Brooklyn (now slated for 2010) still happens.

The NBA season runs from late October/ early November to mid April; at this point, the best teams enter two months of playoffs. Also during the summer, the ladies of the WNBA's **New York Liberty** hold court at Madison Square Garden, playing there from May to September.

New York Knicks

Madison Square Garden (for listing, see p336). www.nyknicks.com. **Tickets** $45-$150.

New York Liberty

Madison Square Garden (for listing, see p336). www.nyliberty.com. **Tickets** $10-$260.

New Jersey Nets

IZOD Center (for listing, see p336 Meadowlands Sports Complex). *1-800 765 6387/www.nj nets.com.* **Tickets** $10-$210.

Boxing

★ Church Street Boxing Gym

25 Park Place, between Broadway & Church Street, Financial District (1-212 571 1333/ www.nyboxinggym.com). Subway 2, 3 to Park Place; 4, 5, 6 to Brooklyn Bridge-City Hall. **Open** phone or check website for details. **Tickets** $30. **Credit** (online purchases only) MC, V. **Map** p402 E32.

This workout gym and an amateur boxing venue has seen famous fighters such as Evander Holyfield and Mike Tyson train here before Garden bouts. About ten times a year, the gym hosts Friday Night Fights – some of the best fight tickets in town.

Gleason's Gym

77 Front Street, between Main & Washington Streets, Dumbo, Brooklyn (1-718 797 2872/ www.gleasonsgym.net). Subway F to York Street. **Open** phone or check website for details. **Tickets** $20. **Credit** DC, Disc, MC, V. **Map** p411 T11. Although it occupies an second-floor warehouse in a now-groovy neighbourhood, Gleason's is *the* professional boxer's address in New York. The 'sweet scientists' who have trained in the city's most storied gym include Muhammad Ali and Jake 'Raging Bull' LaMotta. Gleason's used to host regular white-collar boxing matches, but the legality of these bouts was still being debated at press time.

Madison Square Garden

For listing, see p336. **Tickets** $30-$305. The Garden still hosts some great pro fights (such as 2007's Cotto-Judah rumble), plus the city's annual Golden Gloves amateur championships.

Football

Uniquely, New York lays claim to two NFL teams, and win-loss records seem to have no bearing on the attendance at either. Every game from here to eternity is effectively sold out for both the **New York Giants**, 2007 Super Bowl champions, and the **New York Jets**, still in search of 21st-century success. But there are usually extra tickets floating around before the game: unclaimed seats for the visiting team, or season-ticket holders who can't make it that day.

The NFL season runs from September to December, with the playoffs in January. Outside these months, fans of the fast, high-scoring Arena Football League should head to Nassau Coliseum to witness the inimitable **New York Dragons**, who play from February through to May.

New York Dragons
Nassau Veterans Memorial Coliseum (for listing, see p336). 1-866 235 8499/www.newyork dragons.com. **Tickets** $30-$60.

New York Giants
Giants Stadium (for listing, see p336) Meadowlands Sports Complex). 1-201 935 8222/www.giants.com. **Tickets** $30-$105.

New York Jets
Giants Stadium (for listing, see p336 Meadowlands Sports Complex). 1-516 560 8100/www.newyorkjets.com. **Tickets** $75-$115.

Hockey

The NHL is still in the process of making the game a little more fan-friendly, a necessary step since the strike a few seasons back. The **New York Rangers** have put a star-studded team on the ice and the **New Jersey Devils**, now in their new home at the Prudential Center in Newark, have been one of professional sports' most consistent franchises this past decade (mostly thanks to super-goalie Martin Brodeur). That leaves the **New York Islanders**, a decent team that are nevertheless consigned to fighting for scraps in the competitive Atlantic Division. Tickets for all three teams are on sale throughout the season, which runs from October to April before two months of playoffs.

New Jersey Devils
Prudential Center (for listing, see p336 Meadowlands Sports Complex). www.newjerseydevils.com. **Tickets** $20-$90.

New York Islanders
Nassau Veterans Memorial Coliseum (for listing, see p336). www.newyorkislanders.com. **Tickets** $19-$120.

New York Rangers
Madison Square Garden (for listing, see p336). www.newyorkrangers.com. **Tickets** $8-$349.

Horse racing

Thoroughbreds run at all three major racetracks near Manhattan.

Aqueduct Racetrack
110-00 Rockaway Boulevard, at 110th Street, Jamaica, Queens (1-718 641 4700/www.ny ra.com). Subway A to Aqueduct Racetrack. **Races** *Thoroughbred* late Oct-late Apr Wed-Sun. **Admission** *Clubhouse* $1. *Skyline Club* $2. Free early Jan-early Mar. **No credit cards.**
The Wood Memorial, New York's most important Kentucky Derby prep race, is usually in early April.

★ Belmont Park
2150 Hempstead Turnpike, Elmont, Long Island (1-516 488 6000/www.nyra.com). From Penn Station, take LIRR (www.lirr.org) to Belmont Park. **Races** *Thoroughbred* May-July, Sept, Oct Wed-Sun. **Admission** *Clubhouse* $5. *Grandstand* $2. **No credit cards.**
This big beauty of an oval is home to the third and longest leg of US horse racing's Triple Crown, the infamous mile-and-a-half Belmont Stakes in June. *Photo p342.*

Meadowlands Racetrack
For listing, see p336 Meadowlands Sports Complex. *1-201 843 2446/www.thebigm.com.* **Races** *Thoroughbred* Sept-Nov. *Harness* Oct-Aug. Phone or check website for details. **Admission** *Clubhouse* $3. *Grandstand* $1. **No credit cards.** Meadowlands Racetrack offers an established programme of both harness (trotting) and thoroughbred racing. Top harness racers compete for more than $1 million in the prestigious Hambletonian race.

Soccer

David Beckham's arrival in LA may not have stirred American interest in soccer in the way it was hoped, but New York is still home to a multitude of 'football' fans. You'll find pick-up games in many of the city's parks, and the pro **RedBulls** play at Giants Stadium, which also occasionally hosts top European teams for exhibition matches. Check www.meadow lands.com for the schedule. The **New Jersey Ironmen** play a more confined brand of soccer indoors at the Prudential Center.

Ironmen
Prudential Center (for listing, see p336). 1-800 476 6636/www.njironmen.com. **Tickets** prices vary; phone for details.

RedBulls
Giants Stadium (for listing, see p336 Meadowlands Sports Complex). 1-201 583 7000/www.metrostars.com. **Tickets** $22-$40.

Tennis

★ US Open

USTA National Tennis Center, Flushing Meadows-Corona Park, Queens (1-866 673 6849/www.usopen.org). Subway 7 to Willets Point-Shea Stadium. **Tickets** $22-$120. **Credit** AmEx, DC, MC, V.

Tickets go on sale late in the spring for this late-summer grand-slam thriller, which the USTA says is the highest-attended annual sporting event in the world. Check the website for match schedules and more ticket information.

PARTICIPATION SPORTS & FITNESS

With constantly multiplying fitness facilities, plus parkland, rivers and blocks of streets to roam, New York offers plenty of opportunities to get moving.

All-in-one sports centre

★ Chelsea Piers

Piers 59-62, W 17th to 23rd Streets, at Eleventh Avenue, Chelsea (1-212 336 6666/www.chelseapiers.com). Subway C, E to 23rd Street. **Open** times vary; phone or check website for details. **Map** p403 C27.

This six-block stretch of riverfront real estate provides an Olympics-level variety of physical diversions in a bright, clean and well-maintained facility. Visitors can practise their swings at the Golf Club (Pier 59, 1-212 336 6400); bowlers can show the locals how to roll at the 300 lanes (between Piers 59 and 60, 1-212 835 2695); and ice skaters (and pint-sized hockey players) can carve up the indoor Sky Rink (Pier 61, 1-212 336 6100). The Field House (Pier 62, 1-212 336 6500) has a rock-climbing wall, a gymnastics training centre, batting cages, basketball courts, indoor playing fields, a toddler adventure centre and more. At the Sports Center Health Club (Pier 60, 1-212 336 6000), open to non-members, you'll find an expansive gym complete with comprehensive weight deck and 100 cardiovascular machines plus classes in everything from triathlon training in the 25-yard pool to boxing.

Bowling

Bowlmor Lanes

110 University Place, between 12th & 13th Streets, Greenwich Village (1-212 255 8188/www.bowlmor.com). Subway L, N, Q, R, W, 4, 5, 6 to 14th Street-Union Square. **Open** 11am-2am Mon, Thur; 11am-1am Tue, Wed; 11am-3.30am Fri, Sat; 11am-midnight Sun. **Cost** $9.45-$12.95 per person per game; $6 shoe rental. Under-21s not admitted after 5pm Tue-Sun. **Credit** AmEx, DC, MC, V. **Map** p403 E28.

Renovation turned a seedy but historic Greenwich Village alley (Richard Nixon bowled here) into a hip downtown nightclub. Monday evening's Night Strike features glow-in-the-dark pins and a techno-spinning DJ in addition to unlimited bowling from 10pm to 2am ($24 per scenester; includes shoes).

Leisure Time Lanes

550 Ninth Avenue, between 40th & 41st Streets, Midtown (1-212 268 6909/www.leisuretimebowl.com). Subway A, C, E, 1, 2, 3, 7, N, W, R, Q to 42nd Street-Port Authority. **Open** 10am-midnight Mon-Wed; 10am-2am Thur; 10am-3am Fri; 11am-3am Sat; 11am-11pm Sun. **Cost** from $6.50 per game. **Credit** AmEx, DC, MC, V. **Map** p404 C24.

Leisure Time, smack in the middle of the Port Authority, has seriously upgraded its facilities in recent years and is now the site of the New York media bowling league (of which *Time Out New York* is an enthusiastic member). We particularly enjoy the giant beer cylinders.

Cycling

Everyone knows that the only people driving cars in this city are cabbies and people from Jersey; biking is the preferred mode of travel for many residents. On the west side, you can now cycle along the river all the way from Battery Park up to the George Washington Bridge (at 178th Street). A word of caution: cycling in the city is a serious business. Riders must stay alert and abide by traffic laws, especially as drivers and pedestrians often don't.

Bike hire

Gotham Bike Shop *112 West Broadway, between Duane & Reade Streets, Tribeca (1-212 732 2453/www.gothambikes.com). Subway A, C, 1, 2, 3 to Chambers Street.* **Open** 10am-6.30pm Mon-Wed, Fri, Sat; 10am-7.30pm Thur; 10.30am-5pm Sun. **Fees** $10/hr; $30/24hrs (incl helmet). **Credit** AmEx, DC, MC, V (credit card & ID required for rental). **Map** p402 E31.

Loeb Boathouse *Central Park, entrance on Fifth Avenue, at 72nd Street (1-212 517 2233/www.centralparknyc.org). Subway 6 to 68th Street-Hunter College.* **Open** 10am-6pm daily, weather permitting. **Fees** $10-$15/hr (includes helmet). **Credit** AmEx, DC, Disc, MC, V (credit card & ID required for rental). **Map** p405 E20.

Metro Bicycles *1311 Lexington Avenue, at 88th Street, Upper East Side (1-212 427 4450/www.metrobicycles.com). Subway 4, 5, 6 to 86th Street.* **Open** 9.30am-6.30pm Mon-Sat; 9.30am-6pm Sun. **Fees** $7/hr; $35/day. **Credit** AmEx, DC, Disc, MC, V. **Map** p406 E18. **Other locations** check website.

Bike-path maps
Department of City Planning Bookstore
22 Reade Street, between Broadway & Elk Street (1-212 720 3667). Subway J, M, Z to Chambers Street; R, W to City Hall; 4, 5, 6 to Brooklyn Bridge-City Hall. **Open** 10am-4pm Mon-Fri. **Map** p402 E31.

This free NYC Cycling Map, covering cycle lanes in all five boroughs, is available here, or you can download it as a PDF at www.nyc.gov/planning.

Transportation Alternatives *Suite 1002, 10th Floor, 127 W 26th Street, between Sixth & Seventh Avenues, Chelsea (1-212 629 8080/www.transalt.org). Subway N, R, W, 1 to 28th Street; C, E, F, V, N, R, W, 1 to 23rd Street.* **Open** 9.30am-5.30pm Mon-Fri. **Map** p404 D26.

TA is a not-for-profit citizens' group that lobbies for more bike-friendly streets. You can visit the office get free maps, or download them from the website.

Organised bike rides
Bike the Big Apple *1-877 865 0078/www.bikethebigapple.com.*
Trips include a Lower East Side and Brooklyn ride that makes stops at chocolate and beer factories.

Fast & Fabulous *1-212 567 7160/www.fastnfab.org.*
This 'queer and queer-friendly' group leads tours that usually meet in Central Park and head out of the city.

Five Borough Bicycle Club *1-212 932 2300 ext 115/www.5bbc.org.*
This local club always offers a full slate of leisurely rides around the city, as well as jaunts that head further afield. Best of all, most trips are free.

Time's Up! *1-212 802 8222/www.times-up.org.*
An alternative-transportation advocacy group, Time's Up! sponsors rides year-round, including Critical Mass, in which hundreds of cyclists and skaters meet at Union Square Park (7pm on the last Friday of every month) and go tearing through the city, often ending up in Greenwich Village and lending the streets a vibrant party atmosphere.

▶ *For bike tours, see p56. For Bike New York: The Great Five Boro Bike Tour, see p261.*

Gyms

Many gyms offer single-day membership. If you can schedule a workout during off-peak hours, there will probably be less competition for the machines. Call for class details. *See also p341* **Chelsea Piers**.

Crunch
25 Broadway, at Morris Street, Financial District (1-212 269 1067/www.crunch.com). Subway 4, 5 to Bowling Green. **Open** 5am-9pm Mon-Fri; 8am-2pm Sat, Sun. **Fees** $16 day pass. **Credit** AmEx, DC, Disc, MC, V. **Map** p402 E33.

Belmont Park. *See p340.*

The reasonable day membership at this funky chain includes its diverse roster of classes, including creative variations on yoga, bootcamps, boxing and dance. Note that the fees vary according to location. **Other locations** throughout the city.

New York Sports Club

151 E 86th Street, between Lexington & Third Avenues, Upper East Side (1-800 301 1231/ www.nysc.com). Subway 4, 5, 6 to 86th Street. **Open** 5.30am-11pm Mon-Thur; 5.30am-10pm Fri; 8am-9pm Sat, Sun. **Fees** $25 day pass. **Credit** AmEx, DC, Disc, MC, V. **Map** p406 F18.

A day membership at New York Sports Club includes aerobics classes and access to the weights room, cardio machines, steam room and sauna. The 62nd and 86th Street branches feature squash courts. **Other locations** throughout the city.

Horse riding

Kensington Stables

51 Caton Place, at East 8th Street, Kensington, Brooklyn (1-718 972 4588/www.kensington stables.com). Subway F to Fort Hamilton Parkway. **Open** 10am-dusk daily. **Fees** *Guided trail ride* $37/hr. *Private lessons* $57/hr. Reservations required. **Credit** AmEx, DC, Disc, MC, V. **Map** p410 U13.

Take a guided ride through the miles of lovely trails that wind through Prospect Park (*see p129*), including the rugged Ravine District, which was designed in the 19th century to be traversed by horseback.

Ice skating

FREE Pond at Bryant Park

Bryant Park, Sixth Avenue, between 40th & 42nd Streets, Midtown (1-212 768 4242/www.bryant park.org). Subway B, D, F, V to 42nd Street-Bryant Park; 7 to Fifth Avenue. **Open** late Oct-mid Jan; phone or check website for details. Closed mid Jan-late Oct. **Fees** free. **Skate rental** $10. **No credit cards. Map** p404 E24.

You can't beat the price at Bryant Park's seasonal 17,000 sq ft rink – it's free if you have your own skates. Between Thanksgiving and Christmas it's surrounded by a holiday crafts fair.

Rockefeller Center Ice Rink

1 Rockefeller Plaza, from 49th to 50th Streets, between Fifth & Sixth Avenues, Midtown (1-212 332 7654/www.therinkatrockcenter.com). Subway B, D, F, V to 47-50th Streets-Rockefeller Center. **Open** Oct-Apr; phone or check website for details. Closed May-Sept. **Fees** $14-$17; $7-$12 reductions. **Skate rental** $8-$10. **Credit** AmEx, DC, Disc, MC, V. **Map** p404 E23.

Rock Center may be the most recognisable place to skate, but you might as well paint a sign on your back that reads 'Ain't from around here'. The rink

opens with an energetic ice show in mid October, but attracts the most visitors when the Christmas tree is lit and looming over the skating crowds.

Trump Wollman Rink

Central Park, midpark at 62nd Street (1-212 439 6900/www.wollmanskatingrink.com). Subway N, R, W to Fifth Avenue-59th Street. **Open** late Oct-Mar 10am-2.30pm Mon, Tue; 10am-10pm Wed, Thur, Sun; 10am-11pm Fri, Sat. Closed Apr-late Oct. **Fees** *Mon-Thur* $9.50; $4.75 reductions. *Fri-Sun* $12; $5 reductions. **Skate rental** $5. **No credit cards. Map** p405 E21.

Less crowded – especially after the holidays – than Rock Center, the rink offers a lovely setting beneath the trees of Central Park.

In-line skating

There is plenty of animosity between bikers, motorists and pedestrians in the city but in-line skaters manage to transcend that ongoing battle. Join a group skate, or go it alone. The gear shop **Blades, Board & Skate** (156 W 72nd Street, between Broadway & Columbus Avenue, 1-212 787 3911) rents by the day ($20).

Empire Skate Club of New York

1-212 774 1774/www.empireskate.org.
This club organises in-line and roller skating events around town, including island-hopping tours and night rides (weather permitting): meet outside Blades, Board & Skate (*see above*) at 8pm.

Kayaking

Kayaking is a great way to explore New York Harbor and the Hudson River. Given the tricky currents, the tidal shifts and the hairy river traffic, it's best to go on an organised excursion.

FREE Downtown Boathouse

Pier 96, Clinton Cove Park, 56th Street & West Side Highway, Hell's Kitchen (no phone/ www.downtownboathouse.org). Subway A, C, E, 1 to Columbus Circle. **Open** *mid May-mid Oct* 10am-6pm Sat, Sun. **Classes** 6-8pm Wed. **Fee** free. **Map** p405 B22.

Weather permitting, this volunteer-run organisation offers free kayaking (no appointment necessary) in front of the boathouses, at three locations (9am-6pm at Pier 40; 10am-5pm at 72nd Street). All trips are offered on a first-come, first-served basis, and you must be able to swim.

Other locations Pier 40, West Side Highway, at W Houston Street; Riverside Park promenade, at 72nd Street.

Manhattan Kayak Company

Pier 66, Twelfth Avenue, at 26th Street, Chelsea (1-212 924 1788/www.manhattankayak.com).

ARTS & ENTERTAINMENT

Subway C, E to 23rd Street. **Open** phone or check website for schedule & prices. **Credit** AmEx, DC, Disc, MC, V. **Map** p404 B26.

Run by veteran kayaker Eric Stiller, Manhattan Kayak offers a range of classes from beginners' to advanced as well as tours. Adventures include an easy 90min Paddle & Pub Tour ($60) that ends at a bar, and a 3.5hr circumnavigation of the Statue of Liberty ($125).

Running

The path ringing the Central Park reservoir is probably the most popular jogging trail in the entire city, but there are dozens of parks and paths waiting to be explored. For information on runners' sightseeing tours, *see p57* **Running commentary**.

New York Road Runners

9 E 89th Street, between Fifth & Madison Avenues, Upper East Side (1-212 860 4455/ www.nyrrc.org). Subway 4, 5, 6 to 86th Street. **Open** 10am-8pm Mon-Fri; 10am-5pm Sat; 10am-3pm Sun. **Fees** prices vary. **Credit** AmEx, DC, MC, V. **Map** p406 E18.

Hardly a weekend passes without some sort of run or race sponsored by the NYRR, which is responsible for the New York City Marathon. Most races take place in Central Park and are open to the public. The club also offers classes and clinics.

NYC Hash House Harriers

1-212 427 4692/www.hashnyc.com. **Fees** $15 (covers food & beer after the run).

This energetic, slightly wacky group has been running in the Big Apple for more than 20 years and always welcomes newcomers. A 'hash' is part training run, part scavenger hunt, part keg party. Participants follow a three- to five-mile trail that a member (called 'the hare') marks with chalk or other visual clues. After the exercise, you retire to a local watering hole where you may also be asked to sing.

Stunts

New York City Professional Stunt Training Center

1920 Amethyst Street, off Rhinelander Avenue, Bronx (1-212 752 5105/www.hollywood stunts.com). Subway 2, 5 to Bronx Park East. **Open** phone for details. **Fees** $65/2hr session; $2,800/3wk course ($25 registration fee). **Credit** AmEx, DC, Disc, MC, V.

It doesn't so much matter whether or not you actually *are* a badass, as long as you look like one. Founded by professional stuntman Bob Cotter, this Bronx school offers an intensive course covering unarmed combat, window penetration, car hits and firearms use, among other skills.

Swimming

The Harlem, Vanderbilt and West Side **YMCAs** (www.ymcanyc.org) have pools, as do some private gyms and many hotels. The city of New York also maintains several facilities. Its outdoor pools are free and open from late June to Labor Day (the first Monday in September): **Hamilton Fish** (Pitt Street, between Houston & Stanton Streets, 1-212 387 7687); **Asser Levy Pool** (23rd Street, between First Avenue & FDR Drive, 1-212 447 2020); **Tony Dapolito Recreation Center** (Clarkson Street, at Seventh Avenue South, 1-212 242 5228). **Recreation Center 54** (348 54th Street, between First & Second Avenues, 1-212 754 5411) has an indoor pool. Finally, the **Floating Pool Lady** (Barretto Point Park, 1-718 430 4601) – a seven-lane pool facility set on a barge – has moved from Brooklyn to Hunts Point, Bronx. For a complete list visit www.nycgovparks.org.

Table tennis

New York Table Tennis Foundation

384 Broadway, between Walker & White Streets, Chinatown (1-646 772 2922/www.nyttf.com). Subway J, M, Z, N, Q, R, W, 6 to Canal Street. **Fees** $9 per person per hr. **No credit cards.** **Map** p403 E27.

If you harboured any doubts as to just how seriously some people regard table tennis, then you should stop by at this spacious basement club in Chinatown – picture the secret army training scene in *Enter the Dragon*, but with paddles instead of swords. While it caters to more serious players, beginners are also welcome. Head instructor Robert Chen gives lessons at a workshop on Saturdays and Sundays (11am-2pm, $20).

Tennis

From April through to November, the city authorities maintain excellent municipal courts throughout the five boroughs. Single-play (one-hour) tickets cost $7. For a list of city courts, visit www.nycgovparks.org.

INSIDE TRACK RESERVOIR JOGS

Follow in the fitness footsteps of Jackie Kennedy Onassis, who used to jog around the reservoir that carries her name. The path commands spectacular views of the skyscrapers surrounding Central Park, especially when you reach the northern bank and look southwards.

Theatre & Dance

Broadway… and beyond.

Broadway has recently acquired new lustre. In the 1990s, the Great White Way was largely a tourist trap, the best shows having migrated to the smaller stages known as Off Broadway and Off-Off Broadway. But in the 21st century, wildly successful musicals such as *The Producers* and *Wicked* have helped spur a commercial renaissance, while injections of new blood in the likes of *Spring Awakening* and *Avenue Q* have added youthful vitality. And as *Doubt*, and *August: Osage County* recently proved, there's still room for serious drama.

As far as dance is concerned, New York has long been the centre of the universe, and it's still on top in terms of sheer volume. Yet there are now more visiting international troupes that have been helped by funding from their home countries, funding that simply isn't available to American artists.

ARTS & ENTERTAINMENT

Theatre

Although Broadway has regenerated itself in recent years, the creative picture isn't entirely rosy. Because shows are so expensive to stage, producers tend to favour the familiar. For a while, there was a trend towards recycling pop songs of yesteryear into so-called 'jukebox musicals'. And recently, there has been a spate of adaptations of hit movies, especially films aimed at a family audience. The last three years have yielded *Legally Blonde*, *The Little Mermaid*, *Mary Poppins*, *Xanadu* and *Young Frankenstein*; the most anticipated shows of the 2008/09 season are *Shrek*, *Billy Elliot* and *9 to 5*.

So is Broadway the place to see the best theatre in New York? The answer is yes – and no. Many of a given season's best offerings do open on Broadway, or transfer there after Off Broadway runs. But savvy and intrepid theatre-goers know that for challenging, innovative, experimental and controversial theatre, they must often look further downtown. Broadway's lights may dazzle, but the theatre beyond Times

Square – from venerable Off Broadway not-for-profits to funky Off-Off dives – can provide a deeper and more lasting illumination.

BUYING TICKETS

If you have a major credit card, then buying tickets should simply be a matter of picking up the phone. Nearly all Broadway and Off Broadway shows are served by one of the city's 24-hour ticketing agencies, listed in the shows' print advertisements or in the capsule reviews that run every week in *Time Out New York magazine*. Venue information lines can also refer you to ticket agents, sometimes by merely transferring your call.

About the authors

Adam Feldman reviews theatre and cabaret for Time Out New York *magazine, and is president of the New York Drama Critics' Circle.* **Elizabeth Zimmer**, *the former Dance Editor of the* Village Voice, *now writes for publications including New York's* Metro *and* The Australian.

INSIDE TRACK 'RUSH' TICKETS

Some of the cheapest tickets on Broadway are 'rush' tickets, those purchased the day of a show not from TKTS but the theatre's box office. These tickets cost an average of $25, but not all theatres offer them. Some venues reserve them for students, while others use a lottery system that's held two hours before the performance. Still, if a show is sold out, it's worth waiting for standby tickets just before curtain-up.

Spring Awakening. *See p348.*

Theatre box offices usually charge a small fee for phone orders.

For cheap seats, your best bet is the **Theatre Development Fund/TKTS** booth (in Father Duffy Square, at Broadway and 47th Street), where you can get tickets on the day of the performance for as much as 50 per cent off face value. The booth sells tickets for evening shows every day from 3pm to 8pm, except Tuesdays (2-8pm) and Sundays (3-7pm); it also sells same-day matinée tickets on Wednesdays, Saturdays (both 10am-2pm) and Sundays (11am-3pm). Ssee the TDF website, listed below, for detailed hours and information.

Be sure to get to the TKTS booth early, as lines can be long. And beware of scam artists trying to sell tickets to those waiting in line: they're often fake. There are further TKTS branches at the corner of Front and John Streets in South Street Seaport, and One MetroTech Center, at the corner of Jay Street and Myrtle Avenue in Downtown Brooklyn, both of which also sell matinée tickets the day before a show. Consider purchasing a set of vouchers from the Theatre Development Fund if you're interested in seeing more than one Off-Off Broadway show or dance event.

Theatre Development Fund

520 Eighth Avenue, Suite 801, between 36th & 37th Streets, Garment District (1-212 912 9770/ www.tdf.org). Subway N, Q, R, S, W, 1, 2, 3, 7 to 42nd Street-Times Square. **Open** 10am-5.30pm Mon-Fri. **No credit cards. Map** p404 D24.
For $36, TDF offers four vouchers, each valid for one admission to an Off-Off Broadway theatre, dance or music event at venues such as 59E59, Performance Space 122 and the Joyce. Bring a pass-port or driver's licence when you buy the booklet, and note that a voucher doesn't guarantee a seat on a given night; you'll need to wait at the theatre and hope for the best.

BROADWAY

Subway C, E, 1 to 50th Street; N, Q, R, S, W, 2, 3, 7 to 42nd Street-Times Square.

Technically speaking, 'Broadway' is the theatre district that surrounds Times Square on either side of Broadway (the actual avenue), mainly between 41st and 53rd Streets. This is where you'll find the grandest theatres in town: wood-panelled, frescoed jewel boxes, mostly built between 1900 and 1930. Officially, 38 of them – those with more than 500 seats – are designated as being part of Broadway (plus the Vivian Beaumont Theater, uptown at Lincoln Center). Full-price tickets can set you back more than $100; the very best seats may go up to $350.

The big shows are still there, and hard to miss. However, in recent years, meaty and provocative new dramas such as *August: Osage County* and *The Coast of Utopia* have had remarkable success, as have serious revivals of classic dramas. Each season also usually includes several small, artistically adventurous musicals to balance out the rafter-rattlers.

Long-running shows

Straight plays can provide some of Broadway's most stirring experiences, but they're less likely than musicals to enjoy long runs. Check *Time Out New York* magazine for current listings and reviews. (The playing schedules listed below are subject to change.)

Avenue Q

Golden Theater, 252 W 45th Street, between Broadway & Eighth Avenue, Theater District (1-212 239 6200/www.avenueq.com). Subway A, C, E to 42nd Street-Port Authority. **Box office** 10am-8pm Mon-Sat; noon-7pm Sun. **Shows** 8pm Mon, Tue, Thur, Fri; 2pm, 8pm Sat; 2pm, 7pm

Sun. **Length** 2hrs 15mins; 1 intermission.
Tickets $66.50-$251.50. **Credit** AmEx, DC,
Disc, MC, V. **Map** p404 D24.
Mixing puppets and live actors with irreverent jokes
and snappy songs, this clever, good-hearted musical comedy – *Sesame Street* for grown-ups – began
Off Broadway and became a surprise hit. It garnered
several 2004 Tonys and has travelled across the
country as well as to London's West End.

Hairspray

*Neil Simon Theatre, 250 W 52nd Street, between
Broadway & Eighth Avenue, Theater District (1-
212 307 4100/www.hairsprayonbroadway.com).
Subway C, E, 1 to 50th Street.* **Box office** 10am-
8pm Mon-Sat; noon-6pm Sun. **Shows** 7pm Tue;
2pm, 8pm Wed, Sat; 8pm Thur, Fri; 3pm Sun.
Length 2hrs 35mins; 1 intermission. **Tickets**
$75-$240. **Credit** AmEx, DC, Disc, MC, V.
Map p404 D23.
John Waters' kitschy film about a plump girl with
hopes as high as her hairdo has become an eye-
popping song-and-dance stage extravaganza that's
bigger, brighter and funnier than the original. If you
loved the recent movie remake, here's a chance to
see the show that inspired it. If the last number does-
n't set your toes a-tapping, you need to get new toes.

In the Heights

*Richard Rodgers Theatre, 226 W 46th Street,
between Broadway & Eighth Avenue, Theater
District (1-212 307 4100/www.intheheightsthe
musical.com). Subway N, Q, R, S, W, 1, 2, 3, 7 to
42nd Street-Times Square.* **Box office** 10am-
8pm Mon-Sat; noon-6pm Sun. **Shows** 7pm Tue,
Wed; 8pm Thur, Fri; 2pm, 8pm Sat; 2pm, 7pm
Sun. **Length** 2hrs 25mins; 1 intermission.
Tickets $41.50-$251.50. **Credit** AmEx, DC,
Disc, MC, V. **Map** p404 D24.
This bouncy musical has plenty of good old-
fashioned Broadway heart, and that heart has a
thrilling new beat: the invigorating pulse of modern
Latin rhythms, mixed with the percussive dynamism
of hip hop. Lin-Manuel Miranda's joyous score gives
classic musical theatre themes (love, self-definition,
overcoming adversity) a contemporary urban twist,
and helps pull Broadway into the present tense.

Jersey Boys

*August Wilson Theatre, 245 W 52nd Street,
between Broadway & Eighth Avenue, Theater
District (1-212 239 6200/www.jerseyboys
info.com/broadway). Subway C, E, 1 to 50th
Street.* **Box office** 10am-8pm Mon-Sat; noon-
6pm Sun. **Shows** 7pm Tue; 2pm, 8pm Wed, Sat;
8pm Thur, Fri; 3pm Sun. **Length** 2hrs 15mins;
1 intermission. **Tickets** $96.50-$351.50. **Credit**
AmEx, DC, Disc, MC, V. **Map** p404 D23.
The Broadway musical finally does right by the
jukebox with this nostalgic behind-the-music tale,
presenting the Four Seasons' infectiously energetic

1960s tunes (including 'Walk Like a Man' and 'Big
Girls Don't Cry') as they were intended to be per-
formed. A dynamic cast under the sleek direction of
Des McAnuff ensures that Marshall Brickman and
Rick Elice's script feels canny instead of canned.

★ South Pacific

*Vivian Beaumont Theater (at Lincoln Center), 150
W 65th Street, at Broadway, Upper West Side
(1-212 239 6200/www.lct.org). Subway 1 to 66th
Street-Lincoln Center.* **Box office** 10am-8pm
Mon-Sat; noon-6pm Sun. **Shows** 7pm Tue; 2pm,
8pm Wed, Sat; 8pm Thur, Fri; 3pm Sun. **Length**
2hrs 50mins; 1 intermission. **Tickets** $75-$125.
Credit AmEx, DC, Disc, MC, V. **Map** p405 C21.
This revival of Rodgers and Hammerstein's 1949
World War II musical is faultlessly decorous. The
staging is elegant; the cast acts with restraint and
sings beautifully; the 30-piece orchestra swells with
pride. The score sounds terrific, and the audience
swoons. Indeed, everything about the production
lovingly whispers 'masterpiece musical theatre'.

★ Spring Awakening

*Eugene O'Neill Theatre, 230 W 49th Street,
between Broadway & Eighth Avenue, Theater
District (1-212 239 6200/www.springawakening.
com). Subway N, Q, R, S, W, 1, 2, 3, 7 to 42nd
Street-Times Square.* **Box office** 10am-8pm Mon-
Sat; noon-6pm Sun. **Shows** 8pm Mon; 7pm Tue;
2pm, 8pm Wed, Sat; 8pm Thur, Fri. **Length** 2hrs
20mins; 1 intermission. **Tickets** $31.50-$251.50.
Credit AmEx, DC, Disc, MC, V. **Map** p404 D23.
Singer-songwriter Duncan Sheik and playwright
Steven Sater have taken Frank Wedekind's 1891
play about confused German teens stumbling
towards a tragic adolescence, and created the
most exciting rock musical in a generation. High in
concept – actors in 19th-century costumes whip
microphones from their jackets and launch into
foot-stomping rock numbers – this show is a leap
forward for the Broadway musical.

Wicked

*Gershwin Theatre, 222 W 51st Street, between
Broadway & Eighth Avenue, Theater District
(1-212 307 4100). Subway C, E, 1 to 50th
Street.* **Box office** 10am-8pm Mon-Sat; noon-
6pm Sun. **Shows** 7pm Tue; 2pm, 8pm Wed, Sat;
8pm Thur, Fri; 3pm Sun. **Length** 2hrs 45mins;
1 intermission. **Tickets** $51.25-$301.25. **Credit**
AmEx, DC, Disc, MC, V. **Map** p404 D23.
Based on novelist Gregory Maguire's 1995 riff on
The Wizard of Oz mythology, *Wicked* is a witty
prequel to the classic children's book and legendary
movie. The show's combination of pop dynamism
and sumptuous spectacle has made it the most
popular show on Broadway. Teenage girls, especially, have responded in force to the story of how a
green girl named Elphaba comes to be known as the
Wicked Witch of the West.

OFF BROADWAY

As the cost of mounting a show on Broadway continues to soar, many serious playwrights are opening their shows in the less financially demanding Off Broadway houses. The theatres have between 100 and 499 seats; tickets usually run from $40 to $70. Here, we've listed some reliable long-running shows, plus a few of the best theatres and repertory companies.

Long-running shows

Altar Boyz

New World Stages, 340 W 50th Street, between Eighth & Ninth Avenues, Theater District (1-212 239 6200/www.altarboyz.com). Subway C, E, 1 to 50th Street. **Box office** 1-6pm Mon, Sun; 1-7.30pm Tue-Sat. **Shows** 8pm Mon, Tue, Thur, Fri; 2pm, 8pm Sat; 3pm, 7pm Sun. **Length** 1hr 30mins; no intermission. **Tickets** $25-$75. **Credit** AmEx, DC, MC, V. **Map** p404 D23.

The Altar Boyz sing about Jesus in the unlikely idiom of boy-band pop, complete with five-part harmony, synchronised steps and some prefab streetwise posturing. Mad props where mad props are due: the show's young stars really work their crosses off.

Blue Man Group

Astor Place Theater, 434 Lafayette Street, between Astor Place & E 4th Street, East Village (1-212 254 4370/www.blueman.com). Subway N, R, W to 8th Street-NYU; 6 to Astor Place. **Box office** noon-7.45pm daily. **Shows** 8pm Mon-Thur; 7pm, 10pm Fri; 2pm, 5pm, 8pm Sat, Sun. **Length** 2hrs; no intermission. **Tickets** $69-$79. **Credit** AmEx, DC, Disc, MC, V. **Map** p403 F28.

Three deadpan men with extraterrestrial imaginations (and head-to-toe blue body paint) carry this long-time multimedia favourite. A weird, exuberant trip through the trappings of modern culture, the show is as smart as it is ridiculous.

Stomp

Orpheum Theater, 126 Second Avenue, between St Marks Place & E 7th Street, East Village (1-212 477 2477). Subway N, R, W to 8th Street-NYU; 6 to Astor Place. **Box office** 1-7pm Tue-Fri. **Shows** 8pm Tue-Fri; 3pm, 8pm Sat; 3pm, 7pm Sun. **Length** 1hr 30mins; no intermission. **Tickets** $40-$69. **Credit** AmEx, DC, MC, V. **Map** p403 F28.

This show is billed as a 'percussion sensation' because there's no other way to describe it. Using garbage-can lids, buckets, brooms, sticks and just about anything they can get their hands on, these aerobicised dancer-musicians make a lovely racket.

Repertory companies & venues

Atlantic Theater Company

336 W 20th Street, between Eighth & Ninth Avenues, Chelsea (Telecharge 1-212 239 6200/ www.atlantictheater.org). Subway C, E to 23rd Street. **Box office** 6-8pm Tue-Fri; noon-2pm, 6-8pm Sat; 1-3pm Sun. **Tickets** $35-$65. **Credit** AmEx, DC, Disc, MC, V. **Map** p403 D27.

Created in 1985 as an offshoot of acting workshops taught by playwright David Mamet and film star William H Macy, the dynamic Atlantic Theater Company has presented nearly 100 plays, including Martin McDonagh's *The Lieutenant of Inishmore* and Duncan Sheik and Steven Sater's *Spring Awakening* (see p348). Both productions transferred to Broadway.

International WOW Company. *See p355.*

ARTS & ENTERTAINMENT

★ Brooklyn Academy of Music

Harvey Theater, 651 Fulton Street, between Ashland & Rockwell Places, Fort Greene, Brooklyn (1-718 636 4100/www.bam.org). Subway B, Q, 2, 3, 4, 5 to Atlantic Avenue; D, M, N, R to Pacific Street; G to Fulton Street. **Box office** noon-6pm Mon-Fri; noon-4pm Sat, Sun. **Tickets** $30-$90. **Credit** AmEx, DC, Disc, MC, V. **Map** p410 T10.

BAM's beautifully distressed Harvey Theater – along with its grand old opera house (two blocks away on Lafayette Avenue) – is the site of the annual multidisciplinary Next Wave Festival (*see p266*), as well as other international offerings. Recent headliners include Sir Ian McKellen in Shakespeare's *King Lear* and Fiona Shaw in Beckett's *Happy Days*.

Classic Stage Company

136 E 13th Street, between Third & Fourth Avenues, East Village (Ticket Central 1-212 677 4210/www.classicstage.org). Subway L, N, Q, R, W, 4, 5, 6 to 14th Street-Union Square. **Box office** noon-5pm Mon-Fri. **Tickets** $55-$75. **Credit** AmEx, DC, MC, V. **Map** p403 F27.

With a purview that includes Greek tragedies, medieval mystery plays and Elizabethan standards, Classic Stage Company (under artistic director Brian Kulick) makes the old new again with performances including open rehearsals, staged readings and full-blown productions.

59E59

59 E 59th Street, between Madison & Park Avenues, Upper East Side (1-212 279 4200/ www.59e59.org). Subway N, R, W to Lexington Avenue-59th Street; 4, 5, 6 to 59th Street. **Box office** noon-7pm daily. **Tickets** $15-$60. **Credit** AmEx, DC, MC, V. **Map** p405 E22.

This chic, state-of-the-art venue, which comprises an Off Broadway space and two smaller theatres, is home to the Primary Stages company. It's also where you'll find the annual Brits Off Broadway festival, which imports some of the UK's best work for brief summer runs.

Flea Theater

41 White Street, between Broadway & Church Street, Tribeca (1-212 226 2407/www.theflea. org). Subway A, C, E, J, M, N, Q, R, W, Z, 1, 6 to Canal Street. **Box office** noon-6pm Mon-Sat. **Tickets** $15-$60. **Credit** AmEx, DC, MC, V. **Map** p402 E31.

Founded in 1997, Jim Simpson's cosy, well-appointed venue has presented avant-garde experimentation (such as the work of Mac Wellman) and politically provocative satires (mostly by AR Gurney).

Irish Repertory Theatre

132 W 22nd Street, between Sixth & Seventh Avenues, Chelsea (1-212 727 2737/www.irish repertorytheatre.com). Subway F, V, 1 to 23rd Street. **Box office** 10am-6pm Mon-Fri; 11am-6pm Sat, Sun. **Tickets** $55-$60. **Credit** AmEx, DC, MC, V. **Map** p404 D26.

This company puts on compelling shows by Irish and Irish-American playwrights. Fine revivals of classics by the likes of Oscar Wilde and George Bernard Shaw alternate with productions by lesser-known modern authors.

Lincoln Center Theater

Lincoln Center, 150 W 65th Street, at Broadway, Upper West Side (1-212 239 6200/www.lct.org). Subway 1 to 66th Street-Lincoln Center. **Box office** 10am-8pm Mon-Sat; noon-6pm Sun. **Tickets** $35-$125. **Credit** AmEx, DC, Disc, MC, V. **Map** p405 C21.

The majestic and prestigious Lincoln Center Theater complex has a pair of amphitheatre-style drama venues. The Broadway house, the 1,138-seat Vivian Beaumont Theater is home to star-studded and elegant major productions. (When the Beaumont is tied up in long runs, such as the current *South Pacific* (*see p348*), LCT presents its larger works at available Times Square theatres.) Downstairs from the Beaumont is the 338-seat Mitzi E Newhouse Theater, an Off Broadway space devoted to new work by the upper layer of American playwrights. In an effort to shake off its reputation for stodginess, Lincoln Center is launching LCT3, which will present the work of emerging playwrights and directors at other theatres; ultimately, there are plans for a devoted space. *See p352* **The next stage**.

▶ *For music and festivals at Lincoln Center, see p264 and p330.*

Mint Theater Company

3rd Floor, 311 W 43rd Street, between Eighth & Ninth Avenues, Theater District (1-212 315 0231/www.minttheater.org). Subway A, C, E to 42nd Street-Port Authority. **Box office** noon-6pm Mon-Sat; 11am-3pm Sun. **Tickets** $45-$55. **Credit** AmEx, DC, MC, V. **Map** p404 D24.

The Mint specialises in theatrical archaeology, unearthing obscure but worthy plays for a full airing. Recent productions have included rarities by AA Milne, DH Lawrence and JB Priestley.

New Victory Theater

209 W 42nd Street, between Seventh & Eighth Avenues, Theater District (1-646 223 3020/ Telecharge 1-212 239 6200/www.newvictory. org). Subway N, Q, R, S, W, 1, 2, 3, 7 to 42nd Street-Times Square. **Box office** 11am-5pm Mon, Sun; noon-7pm Tue-Sat. **Tickets** $12.50-$35. **Credit** AmEx, DC, MC, V. **Map** p404 D24.

The New Victory is a perfect symbol of the transformation of Times Square. Built in 1900 by Oscar Hammerstein, grandfather of the famous lyricist, Manhattan's oldest theatre became a strip club and adult cinema in the 1970s and '80s. Renovated by the city in 1995, the building now

ARTS & ENTERTAINMENT

The Next Stage

Lincoln Center launches a platform for emerging talent.

Paige Evans and André Bishop.

André Bishop, Artistic Director of Lincoln Center Theater, conveys a professorial air. But get him on to the subject of **LCT3**, the theater's new Off-Off Broadway-style wing where all tickets cost $20, and the cusses fly. *Time Out New York* spoke with Bishop and co-conspirator Paige Evans.

TONY: This is your baby, right?
André Bishop: Lincoln Center Theater has needed to do this for years. This is the opposite of the sort of analogy I should be making, but since we're doing *South Pacific* right now, fuck it. You know how in *The King and I*, Mrs Anna desperately wants a house outside the walls of the palace? That's been my situation about this theatre.

TONY: Why does Lincoln Center Theater need yet another space? You already have two.
AB: There's nothing worse than putting the wrong play in front of the wrong audience. It's just a trip to hell. Also, the institution needs to cultivate a new generation of artists who will work in our larger theatres. And I wanted someone other than stodgy old me, someone younger and peppier to run it.

TONY: The shows aren't typical Lincoln Center fare.
AB: It's tough here – the members won't go away, which is great! But we have to work to broaden our audience. Just because it's 20 bucks doesn't mean they will show up.

TONY: What's your grand vision for LCT3?
Paige Evans: A lot of productions. Just having two puts too much focus on each one. Also, I hope our commissioning programme will generate work we can produce.
AB: And we need a permanent space! In London, they let you bring beer to your seat. That's what the audience needs: beers in the seats.

functions as a kind of kiddie Brooklyn Academy of Music, offering a full season of smart, adventurous, reasonably priced and family-friendly plays.

New World Stages
340 W 50th Street, between Eighth & Ninth Avenues, Theater District (1-646 871 1730/ www.newworldstages.com). Subway C, E, 1 to 50th Street. **Box office** 1-6pm Mon, Sun; 1-7.30pm Tue-Sat. **Tickets** $25-$75. **Credit** AmEx, DC, MC, V. **Map** p404 C23.
Formerly a movie multiplex, this centre – one of the last bastions of commercial Off Broadway in New York – boasts a shiny, space-age interior and five stages, presenting everything from campy revues such as *Naked Boys Singing* to new musicals such as *Altar Boyz* (*see p349*).

★ New York Theatre Workshop
79 E 4th Street, between Bowery & Second Avenue, East Village (1-212 460 5475/www.ny tw.org). Subway F, V to Lower East Side-Second Avenue; 6 to Astor Place. **Box office** 1-6pm Tue-Sun. **Tickets** $45-$65. **Credit** AmEx, DC, MC, V. **Map** p403 F29.
Founded in 1979, the New York Theatre Workshop works with emerging directors eager to take on challenging pieces. Besides plays by world-class artists like Caryl Churchill (*Far Away, A Number*) and Tony Kushner (*Homebody/Kabul*), this company also premièred *Rent*, Jonathan Larson's Pulitzer Prize-winning musical.

★ Playwrights Horizons
416 W 42nd Street, between Ninth & Tenth Avenues, Theater District (Ticket Central 1-212 279 4200/www.playwrightshorizons.org). Subway A, C, E to 42nd Street-Port Authority. **Box office** noon-8pm daily. **Tickets** $50-$70. **Credit** AmEx, DC, MC, V. **Map** p404 C24.
More than 300 important contemporary plays have premièred here, among them dramas such as *Driving Miss Daisy* and *The Heidi Chronicles* and musicals such as Stephen Sondheim's *Assassins* and *Sunday*

in the Park with George. Recent seasons have included works by Craig Lucas (*Small Tragedy*) and an acclaimed musical version of *Grey Gardens.*

★ Public Theater

425 Lafayette Street, between Astor Place & E 4th Street, East Village (1-212 539 8500/Telecharge 1-212 239 6200/www.publictheater.org). Subway N, R, W to 8th Street-NYU; 6 to Astor Place. **Box office** 1-6pm Mon, Sun; 1-7.30pm Tue-Sat. **Tickets** $50-$70. **Credit** AmEx, DC, MC, V. **Map** p403 F28.

The civic-minded Oskar Eustis is artistic director of this local institution dedicated to the work of new American playwrights but also known for its Shakespeare productions (Shakespeare in the Park). The building, an Astor Place landmark, has five stages, and is home to one of the city's most dynamic troupes: LAByrinth Theater Company, co-founded by actor Philip Seymour Hoffman.
▶ *The building is also home to Joe's Pub; see p320.*

Roundabout Theatre Company

American Airlines Theatre, 227 W 42nd Street between Seventh & Eighth Avenues, Theater District (1-212 719-1300/www.roundabout theatre.org). Subway N, Q, R, S, W, 1, 2, 3, 7 to 42nd Street-Times Square. **Box office** noon-6pm Tue-Sun. **Tickets** $63.75-$111.50. **Credit** AmEx, DC, MC, V. **Map** p404 D24.

Devoted entirely to revivals, the Roundabout pairs beloved chestnuts with celebrity casts; it was the force behind recent stagings of *Sunday in the Park with George* by Stephen Sondheim and James Lapine, and Shaw's *Pygmalion*. In addition to its Broadway flagship, the company also mounts shows at Studio 54 (254 W 54th Street, between Broadway & Eighth Avenue) and Off Broadway's Laura Pels Theatre (111 W 46th Street, between Sixth & Seventh Avenues).

St Ann's Warehouse

38 Water Street, between Dock & Main Streets, Dumbo, Brooklyn (1-718 254 8779/www.stanns warehouse.org). Subway A, C to High Street; F to York Street. **Box office** 1-7pm Tue-Sat. **Tickets** $25-$75. **Credit** AmEx, DC, Disc, MC, V. **Map** p411 S9.

The adventurous theatergoer's alternative to BAM, St Ann's Warehouse offers an eclectic lineup of theatre and music. Recent shows have included high-level work by the Wooster Group and National Theatre of Scotland.

Second Stage Theatre

307 W 43rd Street, at Eighth Avenue, Theater District (1-212 246 4422/www.2st.com). Subway A, C, E to 42nd Street-Port Authority. **Box office** 10am-7pm Mon; 10am-8pm Tue-Sat; 10am-3pm Sun. **Tickets** $56-$70. **Credit** AmEx, DC, Disc, MC, V. **Map** p404 D24.

Occupying a beautiful Rem Koolhaas-designed space near Times Square, Second Stage specialises in American playwrights, including the New York prèmieres of Mary Zimmerman's *Metamorphoses* and Edward Albee's *Peter and Jerry*. Following in the footsteps of the Roundabout and the Manhattan Theatre Club, the company has announced plans to expand into Broadway's Helen Hayes Theatre.

FREE Shakespeare in the Park at the Delacorte Theater

Park entrance on Central Park West, at 81st Street, then follow the signs (1-212 539 8750/ www.publictheater.org). Subway B, C to 81st Street-Museum of Natural History. **Tickets** free. **Map** p405 D19.

The Delacorte Theater in Central Park is the fair-weather sister of the Public Theater (*see above*). When not producing Shakespeare in the East Village, the Public offers the best of the Bard outdoors during the New York Shakespeare Festival (June-Sept). Free tickets (two per person) are distributed at both theatres at 1pm on the day of the performance. Around 9am is normally a good time to begin waiting, although the line can start forming as early as 6am when big-name stars are on the bill. You can also enter an online lottery for tickets.
▶ *See p104 for other Central Park attractions.*

Signature Theatre Company

555 W 42nd Street, between Tenth & Eleventh Avenues, Midtown (box office 1-212 244 7529/ www.signaturetheatre.org). Subway A, C, E to 42nd Street-Port Authority. **Box office** 1-7pm Tue-Sat; noon-6pm Sun. **Tickets** $20-$65. **Credit** AmEx, DC, MC, V. **Map** p404 C24.

This award-winning company focuses on the works of a single playwright each season. Signature has delved into the oeuvres of Edward Albee, August Wilson, John Guare and Paula Vogel. In 2009/10, the company is scheduled to present work by Suzan-Lori Parks (*Topdog/Underdog*). A smart corporate sponsorship deal helps keep ticket prices remarkably low.

★ Soho Rep

46 Walker Street, between Broadway & Church Street, Tribeca (1-212 868 4444/box office 1-212 941 8632/www.sohorep.org). Subway A, C, E, N, R, 6 to Canal Street; 1 to Franklin Street. **Box office** 9am-8pm Mon-Fri; 10am-8pm Sat; 10am-6pm Sun. **Tickets** 99¢-$30. **Credit** AmEx, DC, MC, V. **Map** p402 E31.

A couple of years ago, this Off-Off mainstay moved to an Off-Broadway contract, but tickets for most shows are still cheap for Off Broadway. Artistic director Sarah Benson's programming is diverse and adventurous: the 2007/8 lineup included a four-hour performance installation by the Nature Theater of Oklahoma, and the New York prèmiere of Sarah Kane's brutal, controversial 1995 play *Blasted*.

ARTS & ENTERTAINMENT

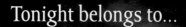

Theatre Row

410 W 42nd Street, between Ninth & Tenth Avenues, Theater District (1-212 868 4444/box office 1-212 279 4200/www.theatrerow.org). Subway A, C, E to 42nd Street-Port Authority. **Box office** 9am-8pm Mon-Fri; 10am-8pm Sat; 10am-6pm Sun. **Tickets** $18-$60. **Credit** AmEx, DC, MC, V. **Map** p404 C24.

A complex of five venues, Theatre Row hosts new plays and revivals by the trendy and celebrity-friendly New Group (*Aunt Dan and Lemon, Hurlyburly*), as well as scores of other productions by assorted companies.

Vineyard Theatre

108 E 15th Street, at Union Square East, Union Square (1-212 353 0303/box office 1-212 353 0303/www.vineyardtheatre.org). Subway L, N, Q, R, W, 4, 5, 6 to 14th Street-Union Square. **Box office** 10am-6pm Mon-Fri. **Tickets** $45-$60. **Credit** AmEx, DC, MC, V. **Map** p403 E27.

This theatre produces excellent new plays and musicals, including the downtown cult hit *[title of show]* (yes, that's its actual name) and the Tony Award-winning *Avenue Q* (*see 347*), both of which transferred to Broadway.

OFF-OFF BROADWAY

Technically, 'Off-Off Broadway' denotes a show that is presented at a theatre with fewer than 100 seats, usually for less than $25. It's where some of the most daring writers and performers

– who aren't necessarily card-carrying union professionals – create their edgiest work: **Radiohole** (www.radiohole.com), the **International WOW Company** (www.internationalwow.org) and the cheekily named **National Theater of the United States of America** (www.ntusa.org) are among many troupes that offer inspired, envelope-pushing theatre. The **New York International Fringe Festival** (1-212 279 4488, www.fringenyc.org), held every August, offers a great opportunity to experience the wacky side of the stage.

If you like your entertainment on the seedy-sexy side, check out New York's burgeoning burlesque scene, a winking throwback to the days when the tease was as important as the strip. Two reliable purveyors of retro smut are **Le Scandal** at the Cutting Room (19 W 24th Street, 1-212 388 2988) and **Monday Night Burlesque** at Public Assembly (70 North 6th Street, Williamsburg, Brooklyn, 1-718 782 5188); also, keep an eye out for **Pinchbottom** (www.pinchbottom.com) and **Starshine Burlesque** (www.starshineburlesque.com). Weekly listings for burlesque shows can be found in *Time Out New York* magazine.

Repertory companies & venues

For **Dixon Place**, which offers a dizzying variety of theatre, music and dance pieces by emerging artists, *see p360*.

Starshine Burlesque.

ARTS & ENTERTAINMENT

ARTS & ENTERTAINMENT

Brick

575 Metropolitan Avenue, between Lorimer Street & Union Avenue, Williamsburg, Brooklyn (1-718 907 3457/www.bricktheater.com). Subway G to Metropolitan Avenue; L to Lorimer Street. **Box office** opens 15mins before curtain. **Tickets** $15-$20. **No credit cards. Map** p411 V8.
This chic, brick-lined venue presents a variety of experimental work. Its Summer Theme Festival Series has covered such tongue-in-cheek categories as 'Hell', 'pretension' and 'moral values'.

HERE

145 Sixth Avenue, between Broome & Spring Streets, Soho (1-212 647 0202/Smarttix 1-212 868 4444/www.here.org). Subway C, E to Spring Street. **Box office** 4-10pm daily. **Tickets** $20-$35. **Credit** AmEx, DC, MC, V. **Map** p403 E30.
This recently renovated Soho arts complex, dedicated to not-for-profit arts enterprises, has been the launching pad for such well-known shows as Eve Ensler's *The Vagina Monologues*. More recently, it's showcased the talents of puppeteer Basil Twist, singer Joey Arias and the brilliantly imaginative playwright-performer Taylor Mac.

★ Performance Space 122

150 First Avenue, at 9th Street, East Village (1-212 477 5288/www.ps122.org). Subway L to First Avenue; 6 to Astor Place. **Box office** 11am-6pm daily. **Tickets** $18-$25. **Credit** AmEx, DC, MC, V. **Map** p403 F28.
One of New York's most interesting venues, this not-for-profit arts centre presents experimental theatre, performance art, music, film and video. Whoopi Goldberg, Eric Bogosian and John Leguizamo have all developed projects here. Australian trendsetter Vallejo Gantner serves as artistic director, and has been working to give the venue a more international scope. The dance programming is also noteworthy; *see p360*.

Dance

For the classically minded, the **New York City Ballet** (NYCB) offers the unparalleled repertory of the prestigious George Balanchine, who established the School of American Ballet in 1934 and whose choreography transformed ballet in the 20th century. In 2007, NYCB's then-resident choreographer, Christopher Wheeldon, launched his own company, Morphoses, to extend ballet's appeal by experimenting with movement, music and visual art.
When it comes to modern dance, the scene is as eclectic and extensive as you'd expect. The companies of modern dance icons Martha Graham, Alvin Ailey, Merce Cunningham and Trisha Brown are based here, while exceptional artists such as Sarah Michelson, Neil Greenberg,

John Jasperse and Ann Liv Young keep finding new ways to expand the definition of dance. And in the city where the Judson Dance Theater spawned the 'postmodern' dance movement in the 1960s, there remains a host of smaller venues that serve as incubators for emerging companies: **Dance Theater Workshop**, **Performance Space 122** and **Danspace Project** are essential.
Elsewhere, you'll find a variety of ethnic dance at venues such as **Symphony Space** and **City Center**, while the **Japan Society** (*see p103*) is a fine place for discovering both avant-garde experimenters and pure traditional dance. The **French Institute: Alliance Française** (22 East 60th Street, 1-212 355 6100), meanwhile, is collaborating with numerous local organisers and venues to bring French dance and other art forms to our stages.
There are two major dance seasons – March to June, and October to December. That's not to say that dance is dead from July to September; there are outdoor performances at the open-air **Central Park SummerStage** (*see p261*), the Lincoln Center **Out of Doors Festival** (*see p264*) and the **River to River Festival** (*see p263*) in lower Manhattan. In the early autumn, two dance festivals – DancenOw/NYC, at Dance Theater Workshop, and **Fall for Dance**, at City Center – get audiences back into the groove after the summer repose.

TRADITIONAL VENUES

Ailey Citigroup Theater

405 W 55th Street, at Ninth Avenue, Hell's Kitchen (1-212 405 9000/www.alvinailey.org). Subway A, B, C, D, 1 to 59th Street-Columbus Circle; N, R, Q, W to 57th Street. **Tickets** $10-$50. **Credit** AmEx, DC, Disc, MC, V. **Map** p405 C22.
The elegant new home of the Alvin Ailey American Theater, the Joan Weill Center for Dance, contains this flexible downstairs venue; when not in use as rehearsal space by the company or for the home seasons of Ailey II, its terrific junior ensemble, it is rented to a great range of groups (including the annual 92nd Street Y's Harkness Dance Festival in

---

INSIDE TRACK
DANCE CLASSES

If you too yearn to get your move on, there are dozens of dance schools that offer classes in everything from ballet to hip hop. You'll find information about classes and workshops in *Time Out New York* magazine. Walk-ins are welcome at most spaces.

New York City Ballet.

the spring). Passers-by sit on the building's patio and watch classes through tall windows.

Baryshnikov Arts Center

450 W 37th Street, at Tenth Avenue, Midtown (1-646 731 3200/www.bacnyc.org). Subway A, C, E to 34th Street-Penn Station. **Tickets** free-$25. **Credit** AmEx, DC, MC, V. **Map** p404 C25.
Russian émigré star Mikhail Baryshnikov – still dancing though he's over 60 – has rebranded himself as a company director (of Hell's Kitchen Dance) and impresario. His home base, on a stark overpass near the Lincoln Tunnel, includes several inviting studios, a 200-seat performance space and great facilities for rehearsal and workshops.

Brooklyn Academy of Music

For listing, see p330.
Showcasing superb local and visiting companies, BAM is one of New York's most prominent cultural institutions. The 2,100-seat Howard Gilman Opera House, with its Federal-style columns and carved marble, is a stunning dance venue. The Mark Morris Dance Group generally performs here in the spring. The 1904 Harvey Theater (651 Fulton Street, between Ashland & Rockwell Places, Fort Greene, Brooklyn), formerly the Majestic, has hosted modern dance choreographers such as John Jasperse and Sarah Michelson. Yearly events include the Dance-Africa Festival, held every Memorial Day weekend (late May).
▶ *BAM's Next Wave Festival highlights established and lesser-known experimental dance groups, many from abroad; see p266.*

Chez Bushwick

304 Boerum Street, between White & Bogart Streets, Bushwick, Brooklyn (1-718 418 4405/ www.chezbushwick.net). Subway L to Morgan Avenue. **Tickets** $5. **No credit cards**. **Map** p411 W8.
Jonah Bokaer, young alum of the Merce Cunningham company turned choreographer, media artist and budding impresario, offers cheap rehearsal space and performances by a stream of interesting international dancers in this bright Brooklyn loft space.

Joyce Theater

175 Eighth Avenue, at 19th Street, Chelsea (1-212 242 0800/www.joyce.org). Subway A, C, E to 14th Street; 1 to 18th Street; L to Eighth Avenue. **Tickets** $19-$59. **Credit** AmEx, DC, Disc, MC, V. **Map** p403 D27.
This intimate space is one of the finest theatres in town. Companies and choreographers that present work here, among them Ballet Hispanico, Pilobolus Dance Theater and Doug Varone, tend to be more traditional than experimental. During the summer the Joyce continues its programming with the New York City Tap Festival and offerings from Pilobolus and the Tulsa Ballet in 2009. At the Joyce Soho, emerging companies present work most weekends. **Other locations** 155 Mercer Street, between Houston & Prince Streets, Soho (1-212 334 7479).

Metropolitan Opera House

For listing, see p332.
A range of international companies, from the Paris Opera Ballet to the Kirov, performs at the Met. In

spring, the majestic space is home to American Ballet Theatre, which presents full-length traditional story ballets, contemporary classics by Frederick Ashton and Antony Tudor, and the occasional world première by the likes of Twyla Tharp. The acoustics are wonderful, but the theatre is immense: get as close to the stage as you can afford.

★ New York City Center
131 W 55th Street, between Sixth & Seventh Avenues, Midtown (1-212 581 7907/ www.nycitycenter.org). Subway B, D, E to Seventh Avenue; F, N, Q, R, W to 57th Street. **Tickets** $15-$150. **Credit** AmEx, DC, MC, V. **Map** p405 D22.
Before Lincoln Center changed the cultural geography of New York, this was the home of the American Ballet Theatre, the Joffrey Ballet and the New York City Ballet. City Center's lavish decor is golden – as are the companies that pass through here. The ABT graces the stage every autumn, while the Alvin Ailey American Dance Theater, the Paul Taylor Dance Company and Morphoses/The Wheeldon Company, as well as the Fall for Dance Festival and visitors from abroad, offer superb performances throughout the year; London's DV8 Physical Theatre is due, with a world première, in September 2009.

New York State Theater
Lincoln Center, 64th Street, at Columbus Avenue, Upper West Side (1-212 870 5570/www.nyc ballet.com). Subway 1 to 66th Street-Lincoln Center. **Tickets** $30-$110. **Credit** AmEx, DC, Disc, MC, V. **Map** p405 C21.
The neo-classical New York City Ballet headlines at this opulent, just-renovated theatre, which Philip Johnson designed to resemble a jewellery box. The winter season begins just before Thanksgiving and features more than a month of performances of *The Nutcracker*, then continues until the end of February with repertory performances. The nine-week spring season usually begins in April. The works are by Balanchine; Jerome Robbins; Peter Martins, the company's ballet master in chief; former resident Christopher Wheeldon; emerging Russian dance maker Alexei Ratmansky; and a handful of others. Weekly cast lists are available online.

ALTERNATIVE VENUES

Abrons Arts Center
466 Grand Street, at Pitt Street, Lower East Side (1-212 598 0400/www.henrystreet.org/arts). Subway F to Delancey-Essex; B, D to Grand Street. **Tickets** $10-$125. **Credit** DC, MC, V. **Map** p403 G30.
As many dance lovers (and performers) move to Brooklyn in search of cheap rent and more space, this out-of-the-way proscenium theatre just across the river in the Lower East Side has become a viable venue. Once the headquarters of

the Alwin Nikolais Dance Theater, it now serves a diverse community with, among other things, Urban Ballet Theater's multicultural seasonal offering, *Nutcracker in the Lower.*

Brooklyn Arts Exchange
421 Fifth Avenue, at 8th Street, Park Slope, Brooklyn (1-718 832 0018/www.bax.org). Subway F, M, R to Fourth Avenue-9th Street. **Tickets** $8-$15. **Credit** DC, Disc, MC, V. **Map** p428.
This multi-arts, not-for-profit organisation presents dance concerts by emerging choreographers. There are also performances just for children.

CPR – Center for Performance Research
Greenbelt, Unit 1, 361 Manhattan Avenue, at Jackson Street, Williamsburg, Brooklyn (1-718 577 2700/www.cprnyc.org). Subway L to Graham Avenue. **Tickets** free-$25. **No credit cards.** **Map** 411 V8.
Based in a brand-new LEED-certified green building with a 45ft x 45ft performing space, CPR, founded and curated by choreographers Jonah Bokaer and John Jasperse, represents a new trend of artists taking control of the means of production.

Dance New Amsterdam (DNA)
280 Broadway, at Chambers Street, Financial District (1-212 625 8369/www.dnadance.org). Subway J, M, R, W, Z, 4, 5, 6 to City Hall. **Tickets** $8-$25. **Credit** AmEx, DC, Disc, MC, V. **Map** p402 E31.
Housed in the historic Sun Building, DNA has a 135-seat theatre that hosts about 50 performances a year by groups like the Sean Curran Company and Liz Lerman Dance Exchange, as well as mixed bills by emerging choreographers.

★ Dance Theater Workshop
Bessie Schönberg Theater, 219 W 19th Street, between Seventh & Eighth Avenues, Chelsea (1-212 924 0077/www.dancetheaterworkshop.org).

INSIDE TRACK
CITY CENTER'S SPITTOONS

It's widely known that the 1923 building that houses **New York City Center** was home to the Shriners for years. Less well known is the fact that the men used the mezzanine lobby, complete with leather armchairs and brass cuspidors (receptacles for spit) by each seat, as a smoking lounge. Masons are no longer hurling phlegm around, but their spittoons have been reincarnated as flower vases, now proudly on display in the main lobby.

Subway 1 to 18th Street. **Tickets** $15-$26.
Credit AmEx, DC, MC, V. **Map** p403 D27.
Dance Theater Workshop hosts work by contemporary choreographers, both local and foreign. This space features a 194-seat theatre, two dance studios and an artists' media lab.

★ Danspace Project
*St Mark's Church in-the-Bowery, 131 E
10th Street, at Second Avenue, East Village
(information 1-212 674 8112/reservations 1-866
811 4111/www.danspaceproject.org). Subway L
to Third Avenue; 6 to Astor Place.* **Tickets** $12-
$22. **No credit cards. Map** p403 F28.
This gorgeous, high-ceilinged sanctuary for downtown dance is at its most sublime when the music is live. The choreographers who take on the four-sided performance space tend towards pure movement rather than technological experimentation. The venue also hosts a free series of works-in-progress.

Dixon Place
*161 Chrystie Street, at Delancey Street, Lower
East Side (1-212 219 0736/www.dixonplace.org).
Subway F, V to Lower East Side-Second Avenue;
J, M, Z to Bowery-Delancey Streets.* **Tickets** free-
$15. **No credit cards. Map** p403 F30.
More than 22 years after it started hosting experimental performances in a living room-like loft on the Bowery, this plucky organisation was finally poised to open its gorgeous new space a few blocks away on the Lower East Side as this guide went to press. A lounge, mainstage theatre and studio all support the work of emerging artists. Summer events include the annual HOT! festival of lesbian and gay arts.

Flea
*41 White Street, between Church Street &
Broadway, Tribeca (1-212 352 3101/www.the
flea.org). Subway A, C, E, N, R, Q, W, 6 to Canal
Street; 1 to Franklin Street.* **Tickets** free-$40.
Credit AmEx, DC, Disc, MC, V. **Map** p402 E31.
Two stages host a variety of offerings including well-attended free monthly series, Dance Conversations at the Flea, curated by Nina Winthrop.

Harlem Stage/Aaron Davis Hall
*City College, Convent Avenue, at W 135th Street,
Harlem (1-212 650 7100/www.harlemstage.org).
Subway 1 to 137th Street-City College.* **Tickets**
free-$45. **Credit** AmEx, DC, Disc, MC, V.
Map p407 C12.
Performances at this centre celebrate African-American life and culture. Troupes that have graced the modern, spacious theatres include the Bill T Jones/Arnie Zane Dance Company and the Alvin Ailey junior company, Ailey II.

Kitchen
*512 W 19th Street, between Tenth & Eleventh
Avenues, Chelsea (1-212 255 5793/www.the*

kitchen.org). *Subway A, C, E to 14th Street; L to
Eighth Avenue.* **Tickets** free-$15. **Credit** AmEx,
DC, MC, V. **Map** p403 C27.
The Kitchen offers experimental dance and installations by inventive, often provocative artists. Cutting-edge choreographers such as Dean Moss and Sarah Michelson have presented work here; now they mentor younger upstairs.

La MaMa E.T.C.
*74A E 4th Street, between Bowery & Second
Avenue, East Village (1-212 475 7710/www.la
mama.org). Subway F, V to Lower East Side-
Second Avenue; 6 to Astor Place.* **Tickets** $15-
$25. **Credit** AmEx, DC, MC, V. **Map** p403 F29.
This experimental theatre hosts the La MaMa Moves dance festival every spring, featuring up-and-coming artists; it also presents international troupes.

Merce Cunningham Studio
*11th Floor, 55 Bethune Street, between
Washington & West Streets, West Village
(1-212 255 8240/www.merce.org). Subway
A, C, E to 14th Street; L to Eighth Avenue.*
Tickets $10-$50. **Credit** AmEx, DC, Disc, MC,
V. **Map** p403 C28.
Located in the Westbeth complex on the far edge of the West Village, the Cunningham Studio is rented to independent choreographers, so quality varies. The stage and seating area are in a large dance studio, so be prepared to take off your shoes.

FREE Movement Research at the Judson Church
*Judson Church, 55 Washington Square South, at
Thompson Street, Greenwich Village (1-212 539
2611/www.movementresearch.org). Subway A, B,
C, D, E, F, V to W 4th Street.* **Tickets** free.
Map p403 E28.
This free performance series, staged in a historic religious building, is a great place to check out up-and-coming artists and experimental works. Performances are held every Monday, from September to May.

Performance Space 122
For listing, see p356.
Emerging choreographers present new works in the auditorium of this former public school. Ron Brown and Doug Varone started out here.

Symphony Space
For listing, see p334.
The World Music Institute hosts traditional dancers from around the globe at this multi-disciplinary performing arts centre, but Symphony Space also stages works by contemporary choreographers, especially with its boundary-breaking spring Thalia dance season.
► *See p302 for more on the Thalia.*

Escapes & Excursions

City Island.
See p365.

Escapes & Excursions

A change of scene is closer than you think.

Had enough of the city? You're in luck. New York is well placed for both coast and countryside, and there are plenty of worthwhile destinations within relatively easy reach of the five boroughs. Bucolic areas such as New York State's Hudson Valley, north of Manhattan, can be reached in little more than an hour; and although New Jersey is the butt of some unkind jokes from New Yorkers, even hardened urbanites concede it has some lovely beaches that can be accessed in little more time than it takes to get the bus crosstown. What's more, many getaway spots are accessible by public transport, allowing you to avoid the often expensive car-rental rates and the heavy summer traffic in and out of town.

Hit the Trails

The city's parks are great for a little casual relaxation. But if you're hankering for a real fresh-air escape, set off on one of these day hikes, between one and three hours away. Bring water and snacks: refuelling options are scarce.

BREAKNECK RIDGE

The trek at Breakneck Ridge is a favourite of local hikers for its accessibility, its variety of trails and its awe-inspiring views of the Hudson Valley. The trail head is a two-mile walk along the highway from the Cold Spring stop on Metro-North's Hudson line (on weekends, the train stops closer to the trail at the Breakneck Ridge stop). You can spend anywhere from two hours to a full day hiking Breakneck, so make sure you plan your route in advance.

You'll find the start of the trail on the river's eastern bank, atop a tunnel that was drilled out for Route 9D: it's marked with small white paint splotches (called 'blazes' in hiking parlance) on nearby trees. Be warned, though, that Breakneck got its name for a reason. The initial trail ascends 500 feet in just a mile and a half, and gains another 500 feet by a series of dips and rises over the next few miles. If you're not in good shape, you might want to think about an alternative hike. But if you do choose this path, there are plenty of dramatic overlooks where you can stretch out on a rock.

After the difficult initial climb, Breakneck Ridge offers options for all levels of hikers, and several crossings in the first few miles provide alternative routes back down the slope. Trail information and maps of all the paths, which are clearly marked with differently coloured blazes along the way, are available from the New York-New Jersey Trail Conference; it's strongly recommended that you carry them.

Tourist information

New York-New Jersey Trail Conference
1-201 512 9348/www.nynjtc.org.

Getting there

By train Take the Metro-North Hudson train from Grand Central to the Cold Spring stop. You can get closer to the start of the trail by catching the line's early train to the Breakneck Ridge stop (Sat & Sun only). The journey takes 1hr 10mins, and a round-trip ticket costs $19.48-$27.50 ($9.98-$13.50 reductions). Contact the MTA (www.mta.info) for schedules.

HARRIMAN STATE PARK

Just across the Hudson and south-west of the sprawling campus of West Point is Harriman State Park. You can access its more than 200 miles of trails and 31 lakes from stops on the Metro-North Port Jervis line.

Of the various trail options, our favourite is the **Triangle Trail**, an eight-mile jaunt that begins just past the parking lot at Tuxedo station (about an hour from Penn Station). Triangle leads up steadily more than 1,000 feet towards the summit of Parker Cabin Mountain before turning south to offer views of two lakes, Skenonto and Sebago. From there, it heads down steadily, steeply at times, before ending after roughly five miles at a path marked with red dashes on white. It's a long distance to cover, but the terrain is varied and there are shortcuts. On a hot day, however, the best detour is to take a dip in one of the lakes followed by a nap in the sun.

Tourist information

Harriman State Park *1-845 786 2701/ www.nysparks.state.ny.us.*
New York-New Jersey Trail Conference *1-201 512 9348/www.nynjtc.org.*

Getting there

By train Take the Metro-North/NJ Transit Port Jervis train, Penn Station to Tuxedo line (with a train switch in Secaucus, NJ). The journey takes 1hr 15mins, and a round-trip ticket costs $13.50 ($6.75 reductions). Contact the MTA (www.mta.info) for schedules.

OTIS PIKE WILDERNESS

If you're looking for ocean views and a less aggressive hike, consider Fire Island's Otis Pike Wilderness Area. The journey takes 90 minutes on the LIRR from Penn Station to Patchogue, on Long Island, followed by a 45-minute ferry ride south to the Watch Hill Visitor Center, but the pristine beaches and wildlife are worth the effort. The stretch of preserved wilderness from Watch Hill to Smith Point is home to deer, rabbits, foxes and numerous types of seabirds, including the piping plover, which nests during the summer. Just be sure you stay out of the plovers' nesting grounds, which are marked with signs, and don't feed any wildlife you see along the way.

Breakneck Ridge

City Island.

Apart from a few sand dunes, Fire Island is completely flat, although walking on the beaches and sandy paths can be slow going. After traversing the boardwalk leading from the Watch Hill Center, hike along Burma Road, a path that runs across the entire island, and in seven miles you'll arrive at the Wilderness Visitor Center at Smith Point.

Tourist information

Fire Island National Seashore *1-631 289 4810/www.nps.gov/fiis.*

Getting there

By train/ferry Take the LIRR Montauk Line, Penn Station to Patchogue. Call 1-718 217 5477 for fares and schedules. For the Davis Park Ferry from Patchogue to Watch Hill, call 1-631 475 1665. The journey should take around 2hrs 30mins in total.

Head for the Ocean

SANDY HOOK

The first thing you should know about Sandy Hook, New Jersey, is that there's a nude beach at its north end (Gunnison Beach, at parking lot G). The sights it affords compels boaters with

binoculars to anchor close to shore, and there's also a cruisy gay scene – but there's much more to this 1,665-acre natural wonderland than sunbathers in the buff. With all that the expansive Hook has to offer, it's a little like an island getaway on the city's doorstep.

Along with seven miles of dune-backed ocean beach, the **Gateway National Recreation Area** is home to the nation's oldest lighthouse (the only one remaining from colonial times), as well as extensive fortifications from the days when Sandy Hook formed the outer line of defence for New York Harbor. Other historic sites beyond the lighthouse include the **Fort Hancock Museum**, located in one of the elegant century-old officer's houses that form an arc facing Sandy Hook Bay, and the abandoned forts are worth a look.

Elsewhere, natural areas such as the **Maritime Holly Forest** attract an astounding variety of birds. In fact, large stretches of beach are closed in summer to allow the endangered piping plover a quiet place to mate. The park really does offer a bit of everything, including surfers catching waves within sight of the Manhattan skyline.

There's even a cool way to get there. Rather than take to the roads and their awful traffic only to find at the end of the drive that the parking lots are full, hop on the ferry from Manhattan, and turn an excursion to the beach into a scenic mini-cruise. Once you dock at Fort

Hancock after the hour-long crossing, it's a short walk to most of the beaches; and if you've still got energy for more, shuttle buses will transport you to any one of the other six strands along the peninsula.

Eating & drinking

Hot dogs and other typical waterside snacks are available from concession stands at the beach areas. But for more ambitious grub – Caesar salad with grilled tuna, for instance – head to the **Sea Gull's Nest** (1-732 872 0025), the park's one restaurant; it's located at Area D, about three miles south of the ferry dock.

Alternatively, blanket picnics in the sand are permitted, so you can bring along goodies for dining alfresco. There are tables and grills for barbecues at Guardian Park at the south end of Fort Hancock.

Tourist information

Sandy Hook Gateway National Recreation Area *1-732 872 5970/ www.nps.gov/gate.*

Getting there

By boat Board the ferry weekdays and weekends (June-Sept) from E 35th Street at the East River or at Pier 11 in the Financial District (at the eastern end of Wall Street). Contact Sea Streak (1-800 262 8743, www.seastreak.com) for reservations, fares and departure times. The ride takes 45 minutes.

CITY ISLAND

A small-town vibe pervades City Island (population: fewer than 5,000), the slightly gritty backdrop for films such as *Margot at the Wedding* and *A Bronx Tale*. Yet in its heyday, around World War II, it was home to no fewer than 17 shipyards. Seven America's Cup-winning yachts were built on the island; and, residents add, the Cup was lost in 1983, the very same year they stopped building the boats here. You'll find a room devoted to the island's past as a centre of maritime history at the **City Island Nautical Museum** (190 Fordham Street, between Minnieford & King Avenues, 1-718 885 0008, open 1-5pm Sun only). Housed in a quaint former schoolhouse, it's stocked with model ships, Revolutionary War artefacts and tributes to such local heroes as Ruby Price Dill, the island's first kindergarten teacher.

Accessible by subway and bus from Manhattan, City Island, in the Bronx, just east of Pelham Bay Park, in the Long Island Sound, is also worth a summer evening trip. With crab shanties on every corner and boats bobbing in the background, the maritime community exudes a striking New England charm. There

Dia:Beacon.

are still a handful of yacht clubs in operation on these shores and a few sailmakers in the phone book, but City Islanders are far more likely to head into Manhattan for work nowadays. Few commercial fishermen are left, though you'd hardly guess it walking into the **Boat Livery** (663 City Island Avenue, at Sutherland Street, 1-718 885 1843): this bait-and-tackle shop and bar has changed little over the past decades.

If you're here late at night, don't miss the eerie midnight views of nearby Hart Island. The former site of an insane asylum, a missile base and a narcotics rehab center, Hart is also home to NYC's public cemetery, where you can sometimes spot Rikers Island inmates burying the unnamed dead. How's that for a fishy tale?

Eating & drinking

Over on Belden Point are **Johnny's Reef** (2 City Island Avenue, 1-718 885 2086) and **Tony's Pier Restaurant** (1 City Island Avenue, 1-718 885 1424); both have outdoor seating. Grab a couple of beers and a basket of fried clams, sit at one of the picnic benches and watch the boats sail by. If you're hankering for French fare, tuck into excellent escargots at **Le Refuge Inn** (586 City Island Avenue, 1-718 885 2478), located in a former oysterman's home.

Getting there

By train/bus Take the 6 train to Pelham Bay Park and transfer to the Bx29 bus to City Island.

Museum Escapes

DIA:BEACON

Take a model example of early 20th-century industrial architecture. Combine it with some of the most ambitious and uncompromising art of the past 50 years. What do you get? One of the finest, most luxuriant aesthetic experiences on earth. Indeed, for the 24 artists whose work is on view, and for the visiting public, Dia Art Foundation's outpost in the Hudson Valley is a blessing indeed.

The Dia Art Foundation's founders, Heiner Friedrich and his wife Philippa de Menil (an heir to the Schlumberger oil fortune), acquired many of their holdings in the 1960s and '70s. The pair had a taste for the minimal, the conceptual and the monumental, and supported artists with radical ideas about what art was, what it could do and where it should happen. Together with others of their generation, the Dia circle (Robert Smithson, Michael Heizer, Walter De Maria, Donald Judd and Dan Flavin) made it difficult to consider a work of art apart from its context – be it visual, philosophical or historical – ever again. Since 2003, that context has been the Riggio Galleries, a massive museum on a 31-acre tract of land overlooking the Hudson River. Despite the cavernous galleries it had in Chelsea, the organisation never had adequate space in which to put its hugely scaled collection on permanent display until its move out here.

An 80-minute train ride from Grand Central, the 300,000-square-foot complex of three brick buildings was erected in 1929 as a box-printing factory for snack-manufacturing giant Nabisco (the National Biscuit Company). No less than 34,000 square feet of north-facing skylights provide almost all of the illumination within. Nowhere does that light serve the art here better than in the immense gallery in which 72 of the 102 canvases that make up Andy Warhol's rarely exhibited *Shadows* (1978-79) hang end to end like a strangely mesmerising series of solar flares.

But what really sets the Dia:Beacon experience apart from other museums is its confounding intimacy. The design of the galleries and gardens by California light-and-space artist Robert Irwin, in collaboration with the Manhattan architectural collective OpenOffice, seems close to genius. Not only does it make this enormous museum feel more like a private house, it also allows the gallery's curators to draw correspondences between artworks into an elegant and intriguing narrative of connoisseurship.

Further information

Dia:Beacon Riggio Galleries
3 Beekman Street, Beacon, NY (1-845 440 0100/ www.diabeacon.org). **Open** *Mid Apr-mid Oct* 11am-6pm Mon, Thur-Sun. *Mid Oct-mid Apr* 11am-4pm Mon, Fri-Sun. **Admission** $10; $7 reductions; free under-12s. **Credit** AmEx, MC, V.

Getting there

By train Take the Metro-North train from Grand Central Terminal to Beacon station. The journey takes 1hr 20 minutes, and the round-trip fare is $24-$31.50. Discount rail and admission packages are available; for details, see www.mta.info.

COOPERSTOWN

A mecca for baseball devotees, Cooperstown, north of Manhattan, isn't known for much besides its famous hall of rawhide ephemera, old pine tar-stained lumber and October memories. For the large number of folks who don't care a lick about America's national pastime but are forced along for the ride, a weekend focused on baseball minutiae sounds about as thrilling a prospect as a DIY colonoscopy. Happily, though, there's more than Major League history to be found at this single-stop-light village (population 2,000) on the shores of Lake Otsego. The area's wooded hills are a welcome respite for those who would like nothing better than to take a Louisville Slugger to the head of their baseball-obsessed companions.

The **National Baseball Hall of Fame & Museum** draws around 300,000 visitors a year. The actual hall is exactly what it claims to be: a corridor full of plaques. And as such, it's the museum that's the real diamond here. A time line begins with Abner Doubleday's first (and much-disputed) layout of the game in 1839 and works through to Barry Bonds' historic (and also much-disputed) eclipse of Hank Aaron's home run record in 2007, providing some context for the goods. You'll see everything from Babe Ruth's locker to hate mail sent to Jackie Robinson in 1951 and the glove worn by Willie Mays when he made his fabled over-the-shoulder basket catch in the 1954 World Series.

Local shopping is devoted primarily to baseball, so if you're looking for vintage memorabilia or limited-edition collectibles, the **Cooperstown Bat Company** (118 Main Street, at Chestnut Street, 1-607 547 2415) is

INSIDE TRACK
ESSENTIAL INFORMATION

For information on these and other out-of-town trips, check the **New York State Tourist Board**'s website at www.iloveny.com. For details on leaving the city on public transport, a better option than driving, *see pp372-374*.

worth checking out. For a dose of history that has nothing to do with sports, take a walk through the **Christ Episcopal Churchyard Cemetery** (46 River Street, at Church Street, 1-607 547 9555), where the Cooper family is buried.

As well as baseball, this is brewing country. The nearby **Brewery Ommegang** (656 County Highway 33, 1-800 544 1809, www.ommegang. com), set in a Belgian-style farmhouse, brews five award-winning Belgian ales, from the light and citrusy Witte Ale to the unusually strong and chocolatey Three Philosophers. You can see how the whole process works at the 136-acre farmstead. The **Cooperstown Brewing Co** (110 River Street, at E Main Street, Milford, NY; 1-607 286 9330, www.cooperstownbrewing.com) offers tours and informal tastings of its ales, porters and stouts.

On your way out of town, stop at **Howe Caverns** (255 Discovery Drive, Howes Cave, 1-518 296 8900, www.howecaverns.com; admission $18, $10-$15 reductions), located between Cooperstown and Albany. Don't get lost in this vast complex of underground caves made from limestone deposited hundreds of millions of years ago. The highlight is Lake Venus, hidden 156 feet below the ground and open for boat rides – a trip that appeals to sports fans and spelunkers alike.

Eating & drinking

In town, the **Doubleday Café** (93 Main Street, at Pioneer Street, 1-607 547 5468) offers good American grub. At **Alex & Ika** (149 Main Street, at Chestnut Street, 1-607 547 4070, closed Mon, Tue), hostess Ika Fognell and chef Alex Webster serve creative dishes like spicy habanero shrimp cake and sake-seared salmon (the Japanese also love baseball). The local dive, **Cooley's Stone House Tavern** (49 Pioneer Street, at Main Street, 1-607 544 1311), is a beautifully restored tavern that dates from before the Civil War, and is a good spot for a nightcap. For the two brewpubs in the area, *see above*.

Hotels

Check in at the **Inn at Cooperstown** (16 Chestnut Street, at Main Street, 1-607 547 5756, www.innatcooperstown.com, $105-$525) and request a room on the recently renovated third floor. Four-poster beds, afternoon tea and a smouldering fireplace provide a cosy backdrop for the seemingly endless array of board games.

If you're looking for something a little more swanky, stay at the grand lakeside **Otesaga Hotel** (60 Lake Street, at Pine Boulevard, 1-800 348 6222, www.otesaga.com, $410-$650) and play a round on the par-72 golf course.

Further information

Cooperstown/Otsego County Tourism *1-607 643 0059/www.thisiscooperstown.com.* **National Baseball Hall of Fame & Museum** *25 Main Street, at Fair Street (1-888 425 5633/www.baseballhalloffame.org).* **Open** *Memorial Day-Labor Day* 9am-9pm daily. *Labor Day-Memorial Day* 9am-5pm daily. **Admission** $16.50; $6-$11 reductions.

Getting there

By car Take I-87N to I90 to exit 25A. Take I-88W to exit 24. Follow Route 7 to Route 20W to Route 80S to Cooperstown. The journey should take around 4hrs.

Over the Hills…

NEW PALTZ

A mere 90 minutes' bus ride from Manhattan lies an unexpectedly rugged, wooded landscape that provides plenty of diversion for hikers, rock climbers and anyone who appreciates beautiful scenery. Situated at the top of the Shawangunk Ridge, an area that the local rock climbing community has nicknamed the Gunks (www.gunks.com), **Mohonk Mountain House** overlooks the half-mile-long Lake Mohonk, in the Hudson Valley.

Mohonk is a National Historic Landmark that has been owned by the same family for almost 140 years. Spending the night at this 265-room Victorian castle doesn't exactly qualify as roughing it, but rustic charm nonetheless abounds. Photographs of long-gone relatives dot the wall, fires roar in winter, and the rooms display a refreshing absence of TVs.

The hotel's room rates include three meals, plus afternoon tea and cookies, and there's also a full-service spa. However, the best excuse to visit Mohonk is to get outside and explore its 85 miles of hiking trails, which are set in 2,200 acres of forests. All of the hiking trails are well marked and maps are provided, offering hikers everything from a beginner path to some serious rock scrambles located along a network of paths situated on lakeside cliffs.

One of the most popular hikes is a relatively easy trek up to Sky Top Tower, a stone structure that was built about 85 years ago in honour of one of the resort's founders. From the top, there are fantastic views of the surrounding area. But if you want to take your adventure up a notch, contact Alpine Endeavors (1-845 658 3094, www.alpineendeavors.com). This local climbing outfitter will provide all the necessary equipment and certified guides.

After your chosen activity, you can ease your muscles in the resort's spa. The Mohonk Red massage (80 minutes for $170), named after the red witch hazel that's grown on the property, includes a mix of Swedish massage, Hawaiian lomi lomi massage and traditional Thai stretches. Each session ends with a 'Guided Power Nap', but you probably won't need help in that department. Weary hikers can lounge in the solarium while sipping an elixir of berries and herbs and soak in the heated outdoor mineral pool, which is filled with Dead Sea salts and surrounded by 100-foot trees. Serenity found.

Further information

Mohonk Mountain House *1000 Mountain Rest Road (1-800 772 6646, www.mohonk.com).* **Rates** $480-$2000.

Getting there

By bus Take the Greyhound service from Port Authority Bus Terminal to Beacon Station. The journey takes 1hr 20 minutes, and the round-trip fare is $36.50. Contact Greyhound (1-800 231 2222, www.greyhound.com) for bus schedules.

The Boardwalk Goes Boutique

The formerly faded seaside belle of Atlantic City is back in fashion.

To many sentimental Americans, the New Jersey coastal town of Atlantic City is synonymous with a kind of '40s-vintage dinner-jacket-and-cigarettes glamour. In reality, it's a struggling gambling resort that long ago fell from its heyday perch. So why would anyone who doesn't have a craps addiction choose to visit? Because after a desperate, decade-long revitalisation, two ambitious, non-gaming hotels have opened, hoping to attract a clientele that would rather spend money than simply lose it.

The **Chelsea** (111 S Chelsea Avenue, at Pacific Avenue, 1-800 548 3030, www.the chelsea-ac.com; $95-$450 doubles) claims to be the first casino-free boutique hotel to arrive on the Boardwalk since the 1960s. The developer, Curtis Bashaw, has converted two chain lodgings (a Howard Johnson and a Holiday Inn) into one aspirational destination: the 331 rooms, decorated in a campy retro style that recalls Mrs Robinson's lair, are joined by two restaurants by Philly restaurateur Stephen Starr, the Chelsea Prime steakhouse and upscale diner Teplitzky's.

Perhaps the real coup of Bashaw's vision was his wooing of Beatrice Inn impresarios Paul Sevigny and Matt Abramcyk to design the hotel's nightlife programme, coolly dubbed the Fifth Floor. This den of sin is home to intimate bars-cum-performance-venues (the Terrace Lounge, the Living Room, the Bar and the Game Room), plus a rooftop pool that might make Soho House members envious. There's also a saltwater swimming pool in the courtyard and free bike rentals.

An even more luxurious option is the **Water Club** (1 Renaissance Way, 1-800 800 8817, www.thewaterclubatborgata. com, $300-$800), a 43-floor tower operated by hotel/casino the **Borgata** (1 Borgata Way, 1-609 317 1000, www. theborgata.com). The opulence here is of the exotic-orchids, earth-toned-decor, designer spa variety. Sipping a cocktail and munching on executive chef Geoffrey Zakarian's farm-fresh crudités in one of the outdoor poolside cabanas, you might even forget where you are. Miami? Mexico? It's a far cry from the image most of us have of the New Jersey resort.

But for players, the poker tables aren't too far off. The Borgata, connected to the Water Club, is the most Vegas-style of Atlantic City's casinos. As well as gambling, on any given night there are concerts and comedy shows (Cyndi Lauper, James Taylor and Robin Williams have recently appeared) and an embarrassment of restaurants: Wolfgang Puck American Grille and Bobby Flay Steak, to name a couple.

But if all the decadence makes you want to get out for some local flavour, ask the concierge to get you a table at **Chef Vola's** (111 S Albion Place, between Pacific Avenue and the Boardwalk, 1-609 345 2022). At this family-run Italian restaurant, hidden in a residential basement close to the hotels, customers must be personally recommended.

To reach Atlantic City, take the Greyhound bus (1-800 231 2222, www. greyhound.com) from Port Authority. The journey takes 2hrs 40mins, and a round-trip ticket is $35.

New York's most beautiful Garden

No trip to New York is complete without a visit to The New York Botanical Garden. With 250 spectacular acres of year-round natural beauty, it has something for everyone.

THE NEW YORK BOTANICAL GARDEN
TICKETS: WWW.NYBG.ORG • INFO: 718.817.8700
20 MINUTES ON METRO-NORTH FROM GRAND CENTRAL

Directory

Getting Around

ARRIVING & LEAVING

By air

Three major airports serve the New York City area (along with smaller MacArthur Airport on Long Island). For a list of transport services between New York City and its major airports, call 1-800 247 7433.

Public transport is the cheapest method of travelling between city and airport, but it can be frustrating and time-consuming – none of the local airports is particularly close or convenient.

Private bus or van services are usually the best bargains, but you'll need to allow extra time: vans will be picking up other passengers. As well as the choices for each airport below, Blue SuperShuttle (1-212 209 7000, 1-800 258 3826, www.supershuttle.com) vans offer door-to-door service between NYC and the three major airports.

Yellow cabs can be flagged on the street or picked up from designated locations in airports. They are more expensive but take you to your destination for a fixed, zoned price, with any tolls on top. (Not so in reverse.) You may also reserve a car service in advance to pick you up or drop you off (see p374). Avoid the car-service drivers and unlicensed 'gypsy cabs' at the baggage-claim areas – it's illegal.

Airports

John F Kennedy International Airport

1-718 244 4444/www.panynj.gov.
At $2, the **bus and subway link** from JFK is dirt-cheap, but it can take up to two hours to get to Manhattan. At the airport, look for the yellow shuttle bus to the Howard Beach station (free), then take the A train to Manhattan. JFK's AirTrain now offers faster service between all eight terminals and the A, E, J and Z subway lines, as well as the Long Island Rail Road, for $5. For more, see www.airtrainjfk.com.

Private bus and van services are a good compromise between value and convenience. New York Airport Service (1-212 875 8200, www.nyairportservice.com) runs frequently between Manhattan and

JFK (one way $15, round trip $27) from early morning to late night, with stops near Grand Central Terminal (Park Avenue, between 41st & 42nd Streets), near Penn Station (33rd Street, at Seventh Avenue), inside the Port Authority Bus Terminal (see 373) and outside a number of Midtown hotels (for an extra charge). Buses also run from JFK to La Guardia (one way $13).

A **yellow cab** from JFK to Manhattan will charge a flat $45 fare, plus toll (usually $4) and tip (if service is fine, give at least $5). (The fare to JFK from Manhattan will be about the same. Check www.nyc.gov/taxi for the latest cab rates.

La Guardia Airport

1-718 533 3400/www.panynj.gov.
Seasoned New Yorkers take the **M60 bus** ($2), which runs between the airport and 106th Street at Broadway. The ride takes 40-60mins (depending on traffic) from 4.30am to 1.30am daily. The route crosses Manhattan at 125th Street in Harlem. Get off at Lexington Avenue for the 4, 5 and 6 trains; at Malcolm X Boulevard (Lenox Avenue) for the 2 and 3; or at St Nicholas Avenue for the A, B, C and D trains. You can also disembark on Broadway at 116th or 110th Street for the 1 and 9 trains.

Less time-consuming options: New York Airport Service **private buses** (1-212 875 8200, www.nyairportservice.com) run frequently between Manhattan and La Guardia (one way $12, round trip $21). **Taxis and car services** charge about $30, plus toll and tip.

MacArthur Airport

1-631 467 3210/www.macarthurairport.com.
Getting to Manhattan from this airport in Islip, Long Island, 50 miles away, will be more expensive, unless you take the **Long Island Rail Road**. Fares are generally $13; a shuttle from the airport to the station is $5. For **cars**, Colonial Transportation (1-631 589 3500) will take up to four to Manhattan for $170, including tolls and tip.

Newark Liberty International Airport

1-973 961 6000/www.newarkairport.com.

Newark has good mass transit access to NYC. The best bet is a 40min, $15 trip by **New Jersey Transit** to or from Penn Station. The airport's monorail, AirTrain Newark (www.airtrainnewark.com), is linked to the NJ Transit and Amtrak train systems.

Bus services operated by Coach USA (1-877 894 9155, www.coachusa.com) run between Newark and Manhattan, stopping outside Grand Central Station (41st Street, between Park & Lexington Avenues), and inside Port Authority (one way $15, round trip $25); buses leave every 15-30mins. A **car or taxi** will run at about $60, plus toll and tip.

Major airlines

Air Canada *1-888 247 5373/www.aircanada.com.*
American Airlines *1-800 433 7300/www.aa.com.*
British Airways *1-800 247 9297/www.britishairways.com.*
Continental Airlines *1-800 523 3273/www.continental.com.*
Delta Air Lines *1-800 221 1212/www.delta.com.*
JetBlue Airways *1-800 538 2583/www.jetblue.com.*
Northwest/KLM *1-800 225 2525/www.nwa.com.*
United Airlines *1-800 241 6522/www.united.com.*
US Airways *1-800 428 4322/www.usairways.com.*
Virgin Atlantic *1-800 862 8621/www.virgin-atlantic.com.*

By bus

Buses aren't quick and can be uncomfortable, but you probably won't need to book. **Greyhound** (1-800 231 2222, www.greyhound.com) offers long-distance bus travel to destinations across North America. **New Jersey Transit** (1-800 772 2222, www.njtransit.com) runs a bus service to nearly everywhere in the Garden State and parts of New York State. Finally, **Peter Pan** (1-800 343 9999, www.peterpanbus.com) runs extensive services to cities across the North-east; its tickets are also valid on Greyhound buses. Most out-of-town buses come and go from Port Authority.

George Washington Bridge Bus Station *4211 Broadway, between 178th & 179th Streets, Washington Heights (1-212 564 8484/www.panynj.gov). Subway A, 1 to 181st Street.* **Map** p409 B6.
A few bus lines serving New Jersey and Rockland County are based here.
Port Authority Bus Terminal *625 Eighth Avenue, between 40th & 42nd Streets, Garment District (1-212 564 8484/www.panynj.gov). Subway A, C, E to 42nd St-Port Authority.* **Map** p410 S13.
This unlovely terminus is the hub for many commuter and long-distance services. Watch out for petty criminals, especially at night, and note that the food concessions don't open until around 7am.

By car

If you drive into the city, you may face delays, from 15 minutes to two hours, at bridge and tunnel crossings (check www.nyc.gov and www.panynj.gov). Tune your radio to **WINS** (1010 AM) for traffic reports. The average toll is $4. Try to time your arrival and departure against the commuter flow.

If you drive to NYC, consider heading for a garage, parking your car and leaving it there. Street parking is problematic and car theft not unheard of. Garages are dear but plentiful. If you want to park for less than $15 a day, try a garage outside Manhattan and take public transport into the city.

By train

America's national rail service is run by Amtrak. Nationwide routes are slow and infrequent, but there are some good fast services linking the eastern seaboard cities. For commuter rail services, *see below*.

Grand Central Terminal
From 42nd to 44th Streets, between Vanderbilt & Lexington Avenues, Midtown East. Subway S, 4, 5, 6, 7 to 42nd Street-Grand Central. **Map** p404 E24.
Grand Central is home to Metro-North, which runs trains to more than 100 stations in New York State and Connecticut. Schedules are available at the terminal.
Penn Station *31st to 33rd Streets, between Seventh & Eighth Avenues, Garment District. Subway A, C, E, 1, 2, 3 to 34th Street-Penn Station.* **Map** p404 D25.
Amtrak, Long Island Rail Road and New Jersey Transit trains depart from this terminal.

PUBLIC TRANSPORT

Changes to schedules can occur at short notice – pay attention to the posters on subway station walls and announcements you may hear in trains and on subway platforms.

Metropolitan Transportation Authority (MTA) *Travel info 1-718 330 1234/updates 1-718 243 7777/www.mta.info.*
The MTA runs the subway and bus lines, as well as services to points outside Manhattan. News of service interruptions and MTA maps are on its website. Be warned: backpacks and handbags may be subject to random searches.

Fares & tickets

The standard fare across the subway and bus network is $2. Although you can pay cash on the buses, you'll need a **MetroCard** to enter the subway system. You can buy them from booths or vending machines in the stations; from the NY Convention & Visitors Bureau; from the New York Transit Museum in Brooklyn; and from many hotels. Free transfers between the subway and buses are available only with a MetroCard.

Up to four people can use a **pay-per-use MetroCard**, sold in denominations from $4 (two trips) to $80. A $20 card offers 12 trips for the price of ten.

However, if you're planning to use the subway or buses often, an **unlimited-ride MetroCard** is great value. These cards are offered in four denominations, available at station vending machines but not at booths: a single-day Fun Pass ($7.50), a seven-day pass ($25), a 14-day pass ($47), and a 30-day pass ($81). All are good for unlimited rides, but you can't share a card with your travel companions.

City buses

White and blue MTA buses are fine if you're not in a hurry. They have a digital destination sign on the front, along with a route number preceded by a letter (M for Manhattan). Maps are posted on most buses and at all subway stations; they're also available from **NYC & Company** (*see p383*). The Manhattan bus map is reprinted in this guide; *see p413*. All local buses are equipped with wheelchair lifts.

The $2 fare is payable with a MetroCard (*see above*) or exact change (coins only; no pennies).

MetroCards allow for an automatic transfer from bus to bus, and between bus and subway. If you pay cash, and you're travelling uptown or downtown and want to go crosstown (or vice versa), ask the driver for a transfer when you get on – you'll be given a ticket for use on the second leg of your journey, valid for two hours. MTA's express buses usually head to the outer boroughs for a $5 fare.

Subway

Far cleaner and safer than it was 20 years ago, the city's subway system is one of the world's largest and cheapest, with a flat fare of $2. Trains run around the clock; however, with sparse service and fewer riders at night, it's advisable to take a cab after 10pm. The most current subway map is at the back of the book (*see pp414-416*); you can also ask MTA workers in service booths for a free copy.

If you are travelling either late at night or early in the morning, board the train from the designated off-peak waiting area, usually near the middle of the platform; this area is more secure than the ends of the platforms or the outermost cars, which are often less populated at night. Hold your bag with the opening facing you, keep your wallet in a front pocket and don't wear flashy jewellery. Petty crime levels increase during the holidays.

Trains are identified by letters or numbers, colour-coded according to the line on which they run. Stations are most often named after the street on which they're located. Entrances are marked with a green globe (open 24 hours) or a red globe (limited hours). Many stations have separate entrances for the uptown and downtown platforms – look before you pay.

Local trains stop at every station on the line; express trains stop at major stations only.

Train

The following commuter trains service NY's hinterland.

Long Island Rail Road *1-718 217 5477/www.lirr.org.*
Provides rail services from Penn Station, Brooklyn and Queens.
Metro-North *1-212 532 4900/ 1-800 638 7646/www.mnr.org.*
Commuter trains service towns north of Manhattan and leave from Grand Central Terminal.

DIRECTORY

New Jersey Transit *1-973 275 5555/www.njtransit.com.* Service from Penn Station reaches most of New Jersey, some points in New York State and Philadelphia.
PATH Trains *1-800 234 7284/ www.pathrail.com.*
PATH (Port Authority Trans-Hudson) trains run from six stations in Manhattan to various places across the Hudson in New Jersey, including Hoboken, Jersey City and Newark. The 24-hour service is automated; entry costs $1.75 (change or bills). Manhattan PATH stations are marked on the subway map (*see p416*).

Taxis

Yellow cabs are rarely in short supply, except at rush hour and in nasty weather. If the centre light atop of the taxi is lit, the cab is available and should stop if you flag it down. Jump in and then tell the driver where you're going. (New Yorkers generally give cross-streets rather than addresses.) By law, taxis cannot refuse to take you anywhere inside the five boroughs or to New York airports. Use only yellow medallion (licensed) cabs; avoid unregulated gypsy cabs.

Taxis will carry up to four passengers for the same price: $2.50 plus 40¢ per fifth of a mile, with an extra 50¢ charge from 8pm to 6am and a $1 surcharge during rush hour (4-8pm Mon-Fri). The average fare for a three-mile ride is $9-$11, depending on the time and traffic (the meter adds 20¢/minute while the car is idling). Cabbies rarely allow more than four passengers in a cab (it's illegal, unless the fifth person is a child under seven).

Not all drivers know their way around the city, so it helps if you know where you're going. If you have a problem, take down the medallion and driver's numbers, posted on the partition. Always ask for a receipt – there's a meter number on it. To complain or to trace lost property, call the **Taxi & Limousine Commission** (1-212 227 0700, 8am-4pm Mon-Fri) or visit www.nyc.gov/taxi. Tip 15-20 per cent, as in a restaurant.

Late at night, cabs tend to stick to fast-flowing routes. Try the avenues and key streets (Canal, Houston, 14th, 23rd, 34th, 42nd, 57th, 72nd and 86th). Bridge and tunnel exits are good for a steady flow of taxis returning from airports, and cabbies will usually head for nightclubs and big hotels. Otherwise, try the following:

Chinatown Chatham Square, where Mott Street meets the Bowery, is an unofficial taxi stand. You can also try hailing a cab exiting the Manhattan Bridge at Bowery and Canal Street.
Lincoln Center The crowd heads to Columbus Circle; those in the know go to Amsterdam Avenue.
Lower East Side Katz's Deli (Houston Street, at Ludlow Street) is a cabbies' hangout; also try Delancey Street, where cabs come in over the Williamsburg Bridge.
Midtown Try Penn Station, Grand Central Terminal and the Port Authority Bus Terminal.
Soho On the west side, try Sixth Avenue; east side, the intersection of Houston Street and Broadway.
Times Square There are 30 taxi stands: look for yellow globes on poles.
Tribeca Cabs head up Hudson Street. The Tribeca Grand (2 Sixth Avenue, between Walker & White Streets) is another good bet.

Car services

Car services are regulated by the **Taxi & Limousine Commission**. Unlike cabs, drivers can make only pre-arranged pickups. Don't try to hail one, and be wary of those that offer you a ride.

The following companies will pick you up anywhere in the city, at any time, for a set fare.

Carmel *1-212 666 6666.*
Dial 7 *1-212 777 7777.*
Limores *1-212 777 7171.*

DRIVING

Taking to the streets is not for the faint of heart. It's best to restrict your driving to evening hours, when traffic is lighter and there's more street parking.

Car rental

Car rental is cheaper in the city's outskirts, and in New Jersey and Connecticut, than in Manhattan; book ahead for weekends, or rent from an independent agency such as Aamcar (*see below*).

Companies outside New York State exclude loss/damage waiver insurance from their rates. Rental companies in New York State are required by law to insure their own cars (the renter pays the first $100 in damage to the vehicle). UK residents may find cheaper rental insurance on www.insurance 4carhire.com.

You will need a credit card to rent a car in the US, and you usually have to be at least 25 years old. All the car-rental companies listed below will add sales tax (8.375 per cent).

Aamcar *1-800 722 6923/1-212 222 8500/www.aamcar.com.*
Alamo *US: 1-800 462 5266/www.alamo.com. UK: 0870 400 4562/www.alamo.co.uk.*
Avis *US: 1-800 230 4898/www.avis.com. UK: 0870 606 0100/www.avis.co.uk.*
Budget *US: 1-800 527 0700/www.budget.com. UK: 0844 581 9998/www.budget.co.uk.*
Dollar *US: 1-800 800 3665/www.dollar.com. UK: 0800 252 897/www.dollar.co.uk.*
Enterprise *US: 1-800 261 7331/www.enterprise.com. UK: 0870 350 3000/ www.enterprise.com/uk.*
Hertz *US: 1-800 654 3131/www.hertz.com. UK: 0870 844 8844/www.hertz.co.uk.*
National *US: 1-800 227 7368. UK: 0116 217 3884. Both: www.nationalcar.com.*
Thrifty *US: 1-800 847 4389/www.thrifty.com. UK: 01494 751500/www.thrifty.co.uk.*

Parking

Make sure you read parking signs and never park within 15 feet of a fire hydrant (to avoid a $115 ticket and/or having your car towed). Parking is off-limits on most streets for at least a few hours daily. The **Department of Transportation** (dial 311) provides information on daily changes to regulations. If precautions fail, call 1-718 935 0096 for towing and impoundment information.

CYCLING

Aside from the pleasurable cycling in Central Park, and along the wide bike paths around the perimeter of Manhattan (now virtually encircled by paths), biking in the city streets is not recommended for urban beginners. Still, zipping through bumper-to-bumper traffic holds allure for those with the requisite skills and gear. For bike rentals and citywide bike paths, *see p341*.

WALKING

One of the best ways to take in NYC is on foot. Most of the streets are laid out in a grid pattern and relatively easy to navigate.

Resources A-Z

ADDRESSES

Addresses follow the standard US format. The room, apartment or suite number usually appears after the street address, followed on the next line by city name and zip code.

AGE RESTRICTIONS

Buying/drinking alcohol 21
Driving 16
Sex 17
Smoking 18

ATTITUDE & ETIQUETTE

New Yorkers have a reputation for being rude, but 'outspoken' is more apt: they are unlikely to hold their tongues in the face of injustice or inconvenience but they can also be very welcoming and will often go out of their way to offer advice or help.

Some old-school restaurants and swanky clubs operate dress codes (jacket and tie, for example, or no baseball caps or ripped jeans; phone to check). However, on the whole anything goes sartorially.

BUSINESS

Courier services

DHL *1-800 225 5345/ www.dhl.com.*
FedEx *1-800 247 4747/ www.fedex.com.*
UPS *1-800 742 5877/ www.ups.com).*

Messenger services

A to Z Couriers *1-212 253 6500/www.atozcouriers.com.*

Breakaway *1-212 947 4455/ www.breakawaycourier.com.*

Office services

All-Language Translation Services *77 W 55th Street, between Fifth & Sixth Avenues, Midtown (1-212 986 1688/www.all-language.com). Subway F to 57th Street.* **Open** 24hrs daily. **Credit** AmEx, DC, MC, V. **Map** p405 E22.
Copy Specialist *44 E 21st Street, at Park Avenue South, Gramercy Park (1-212 533 7560). Subway N, R, W to 23rd Street.* **Open** 8.30am-7pm Mon-Fri; 10am-4pm Sat. **Credit** AmEx, DC, MC, V. **Map** p404 E26.
FedEx Kinko's *1-800 463 3339/ www.fedex.com.*
There are outposts of this efficient computer and copy centre all over the city; many open 24 hours a day.

CONSUMER

Better Business Bureau *1-212 533 6200/www.new york.bbb.org.*
New York City Department of Consumer Affairs *42 Broadway, between Beaver Street & Exchange Place, Financial District (311 local, 1-212 639 9675 out of state/www. nyc.gov/consumer). Subway 4, 5 to Bowling Green.* **Open** 9am-5pm Mon-Fri. **Map** p402 E33.
File complaints on consumer-related matters here.
New York City 311 Call Center *311.*
This non-emergency three-digit number is a means for residents to get answers and register complaints about city issues, from parking regulations up to real-estate auctions and consumer tips.

CUSTOMS

US Customs allows foreigners to bring in $100 worth of gifts (the limit is $800 for returning Americans) without paying duty. One carton of 200 cigarettes (or 50 cigars) and one litre of liquor (spirits) are allowed. Plants, meat and fresh produce of any kind cannot be brought into the country. You will have to fill out a form if you carry more than $10,000 in currency. You will be handed a white form on your inbound flight to fill in, confirming that you haven't exceeded any of these allowances.

If you need to bring prescription drugs into the US, make sure the container is clearly marked, and bring your doctor's statement or a prescription. Marijuana, cocaine and most opiate derivatives, along with a number of other drugs and chemicals, are not permitted: the possession of them is punishable by a stiff fine and/or imprisonment. Check in with the **US Customs Service** (www.customs.gov) before you arrive if you're unsure.

UK Customs allows returning visitors to bring only £145 worth of 'gifts, souvenirs and other goods' into the country duty-free, along with the usual duty-free goods.

DISABLED

Under New York City law, all facilities constructed after 1987 must provide complete access for the disabled – restrooms, entrances and exits included. In 1990, the Americans with Disabilities Act made the same requirement federal law. In the wake of this legislation, many older buildings have added

DIRECTORY

disabled-access features. There has been widespread (though imperfect) compliance with the law, but call ahead to check facilities.

New York City can still be very challenging for disabled visitors. One useful resource is *Access for All*, a guide to New York's cultural institutions published by **Hospital Audiences Inc** (1-212 575 7660, www.hospaud.org). The online guide tells how accessible each location really is and includes information on the height of telephones and water fountains; hearing and visual aids; and passenger-loading zones and alternative entrances. HAI's service for the visually impaired provides recordings of commentaries of theatre performances.

All Broadway theatres are equipped with devices for the hearing-impaired; call **Sound Associates** (1-212 582 7678, 1-888 772 7686) for more information. There are a number of other stage-related resources for the disabled. **Telecharge** (1-212 239 6200) reserves tickets for wheelchair seating in Broadway and Off Broadway venues while Theatre Development Fund's **Theater Access Project** (1-212 221 1103, www.tdf.org) arranges sign-language interpretation and captioning in American Sign Language for both Broadway and Off Broadway shows. **Hands On** (1-212 740 3087, www.handson.org) does the same.

Lighthouse International
111 E 59th Street, between Park & Lexington Avenues, Upper East Side (1-212 821 9200/ www.lighthouse.org). Subway N, R, W to Lexington Avenue-59th Street; 4, 5, 6 to 59th Street. **Open** 10am-6pm Mon-Fri; 10am-5pm Sat. **Map** p405 E29.
In addition to running a store that sells handy items for the vision-impaired, Lighthouse also provides helpful information for blind residents of and visitors to NYC.
Mayor's Office for People with Disabilities *100 Gold Street, between Frankfort & Spruce Streets, Financial District (1-212 788 2830). Subway J, M, Z to Chambers Street; 4, 5, 6 to Brooklyn Bridge-City Hall.* **Open** 9am-5pm Mon-Fri. **Map** p402 F32.
This city office provides a broad range of services for the disabled.
New York Society for the Deaf *315 Hudson Street, between Vandam & Spring Streets, Soho (1-212 366 0066/www.fegs.org).*

Subway C, E to Spring Street; 1 to Houston Street. **Open** 9am-5pm Mon-Thur; 9am-4.30pm Fri. **Map** p403 D30.
Information and a range of services for the deaf and hearing-impaired.
Society for Accessible Travel & Hospitality
1-212 447 7284/www.sath.org.
This not-for-profit group educates the public about travel facilities for people with disabilities and to promote travel for the disabled worldwide. Membership ($45 a year, $30 for seniors and students) includes access to an information service and a quarterly magazine.

DRUGS

Possession of marijuana can result in anything from a $100 fine and a warning (for a first offence, 25g or less) to felony charges and prison time (for greater amounts and/or repeat offenders). Penalties, ranging from class B misdemeanors to class C felonies, are greater for the sale and cultivation of marijuana.

Possession of 'controlled substances' (cocaine, ecstasy, heroin, etc) is not taken lightly, and charges come with stiff penalties – especially if you are convicted of possession with intent to sell. Convictions carry anything from a mandatory one- to three-year prison sentence to a maximum of 25 years.

ELECTRICITY

The US uses 110-120V, 60-cycle alternating current rather than the 220-240V, 50-cycle AC. The transformers that power or recharge newer electronic devices such as laptops are designed to handle either current and may need nothing more than an adaptor for the wall outlet. Other appliances may also require a power converter. Adaptors and converters can be purchased at airport shops, pharmacies, department stores, and at branches of Radio Shack (see www.radioshack.com for locations).

EMBASSIES & CONSULATES

Check the phone book for a complete list of consulates and embassies. *See also p375* **Travel advice**.

Australia *1-212 351 6500.*
Canada *1-212 596 1628.*
Great Britain *1-212 745 0200.*
Ireland *1-212 319 2555.*
New Zealand *1-212 832 4038.*

EMERGENCIES

In an emergency only, dial 911 for an **ambulance**, **police** or **fire**, or call the operator (dial 0). For hospitals, *see below*; for helplines, *see p377*; for the police, *see p381*.

GAY & LESBIAN

For gay/lesbian resources, *see pp305-315*.

HEALTH

Public healthcare is virtually non-existent in the US, and private healthcare is very expensive. Make sure you have comprehensive medical insurance before you leave.

For HIV testing, *see p377* **Chelsea Clinic**; for HIV/AIDS counselling, *see p377* **Helplines**. For a list of hospitals, *see below*. For other hospitals, consult the *Yellow Pages* directory.

Accident & emergency

You will be billed for any emergency treatment. Call your travel insurance company before seeking treatment to find out which hospitals accept your insurance. The following hospitals have emergency rooms:

Cabrini Medical Center *227 E 19th Street, between Second & Third Avenues, Gramercy Park (1-212 995 6000). Subway L to Third Avenue; N, Q, R, W, 4, 5, 6 to 14th Street-Union Square.* **Map** p403 F27.
Mount Sinai Hospital *Madison Avenue, at 100th Street, Upper East Side (1-212 241 7171). Subway 6 to 103rd Street.* **Map** p406 E16.
New York – Presbyterian Hospital/Weill Cornell Medical Center *525 E 68th Street, at York Avenue, Upper East Side (1-212 746 5454). Subway 6 to 68th Street.* **Map** p405 G21.
St Luke's – Roosevelt Hospital *1000 Tenth Avenue, at 59th Street, Upper West Side (1-212 523 6800). Subway A, B, C, D, 1 to 59th Street-Columbus Circle.* **Map** p405 C22.
St Vincent's Hospital *153 W 11th Street, at Seventh Avenue, West Village (1-212 604 7998). Subway F, V, 1, 2, 3 to 14th Street; L to Sixth Avenue.* **Map** p403 D28.

Clinics

Walk-in clinics offer treatment for minor ailments. Most clinics will require immediate payment for treatments and consultations, though some will send their bill directly to your insurance company if you're a US resident. You will have to file a claim to recover the cost of any prescription medication.

D•O•C•S *55 E 34th Street, between Madison & Park Avenues, Murray Hill (1-212 252 6000). Subway 6 to 33rd Street.* **Open** *Walk-in* 8am-8pm Mon-Thur; 9am-7pm Fri; 9am-3pm Sat; 9am-2pm Sun; also by appointment. **Base fee** from $175. **Credit** AmEx, DC, Disc, MC, V. **Map** p404 E25.
Primary-care facilities, affiliated with Beth Israel Medical Center, offering by-appointment and walk-in services. If you need X-rays or lab tests, go as early as possible (no later than 6pm) Monday to Friday. **Other locations** 202 W 23rd Street, at Seventh Avenue (1-212 352 2600).

NY Urgent Medical Services *Suite 1D, 952 Fifth Avenue, between 76th & 77th Streets, Upper East Side (1-212 737 1212/ www.travelmd.com). Subway 6 to 77th Street.* **Open** 24hrs daily; appointments required. **Fees** *Weekday hotel visit* $300. *Weekday office visit* $175 (higher for nights & weekends). **Credit** AmEx, DC, MC, V. **Map** p405 E19.
Specialist medical attention in your Manhattan hotel room or private residence, from a simple prescription to urgent medical care.

Dentists

New York County Dental Society *1-212 573 8500/www.nysdental.org.* **Open** 9am-5pm Mon-Fri.
Can provide local referrals and operates an emergency line at the number above outside of office hours; alternatively use the search facility on the Association's website.

NYU College of Dentistry *345 E 24th Street, between First & Second Avenues, Gramercy Park (1-212 998 9872/after-hours emergency care 1-212 998 9800). Subway 6 to 23rd Street.* **Open** 8.30am-7pm Mon-Thur; 8.30am-3pm Fri. **Base fee** $90. **Credit** DC, Disc, MC, V. **Map** p404 F26.
If you need your teeth fixed on a budget, the final-year students here are slow but proficient, and an experienced dentist is always on hand to supervise.

Opticians

See p251.

Pharmacies

For a list of pharmacies (including 24-hour locations, *see p251*). Note that pharmacies in New York will not refill foreign prescriptions and may not sell the same products as you'll be used to at home.

STDs, HIV & AIDS

Chelsea Clinic *303 Ninth Avenue, at 28th Street, Chelsea (1-212 720 7128). Subway C, E to 23rd Street.* **Open** 8.30am-4.30pm Mon-Fri; 9am-2pm Sat. **Map** p404 B26.
Hours of local walk-in clinics may change at short notice, so be sure to call ahead before visiting. Arrive early, because day-to-day testing is offered on a first-come, first-served basis. (Check the phone book or see www.nyc.gov for other free clinics.)

Women's health

Liberty Women's Health Care of Queens *37-01 Main Street, at 37th Avenue, Flushing, Queens (1-718 888 0018/www. libertywomenshealth.com). Subway 7 to Flushing-Main Street.* **Open** by appointment only. **Credit** DC, MC, V. **Map** p412 W4.
This facility provides surgical and non-surgical abortions until the 24th week of pregnancy. Liberty uses abdominal ultrasound before, during and after the abortion to ensure safety.

Parkmed Eastern Women's Center *7th Floor, 800 Second Avenue, between 42nd & 43rd Streets, Midtown East (1-212 686 6066/www.easternwomenscenter. com). Subway S, 4, 5, 6, 7 to 42nd Street-Grand Central.* **Open** by appointment only. **Credit** AmEx, DC, Disc, MC, V. **Map** p404 F24.
Urine pregnancy tests are free. Counselling, contraception services and non-surgical abortions are also available at the centre.

Planned Parenthood of New York City *Margaret Sanger Center, 26 Bleecker Street, at Mott Street, Greenwich Village (1-212 965 7000/1-800 230 7526/ www.ppnyc.org). Subway B, D, F, V to Broadway-Lafayette Street; N, R, W to Prince Street; 6 to Bleecker Street.* **Open** 8am-4.30pm Mon, Tue; 8am-6.30pm Wed-Fri; 7.30am-4pm Sat. **Credit** AmEx, DC, MC, V. **Map** p403 F29.
The best-known network of family-planning clinics in the US. Counselling and treatment are available for a full range of needs,

including abortion, contraception, HIV testing and treatment of STDs. **Other locations** 44 Court Street, between Joralemon & Remsen Streets, Brooklyn Heights, Brooklyn (1-212 965 7000).

HELPLINES

All numbers are open 24 hours unless otherwise stated.

Alcoholics Anonymous *1-212 647 1680.* **Open** 9am-10pm daily.
Childhelp USA's National Child Abuse Hotline *1-800 422 4453.*
Cocaine Anonymous *Recorded information 1-212 262 2463.*
Drug Abuse Information Line *1-800 522 5353.* **Open** 8am-10pm daily.
National STD & AIDS Hotline *1-800 232 4636.*
Pills Anonymous *Recorded information 1-212 874 0700.*
Safe Horizon Crisis Hotline *1-212 227 3000/ www.safehorizon.org.*
Counselling for victims of domestic violence, rape or other crimes.
Samaritans *1-212 673 3000.*
Special Victims Liaison Unit of the NYPD *Rape hotline 1-212 267 7273.*
St Luke's – Roosevelt Hospital Crime Victims Treatment Center *1-212 523 4728.* **Open** 9am-5pm Mon-Fri.

ID

Always carry picture ID: even people well over 18 or 21 may be carded when buying tobacco or alcohol, ordering drinks in bars, or entering clubs.

INSURANCE

Non-nationals and US citizens should have travel and medical insurance before travelling. For a list of New York urgent-care facilities, *see p376.*

INTERNET

Cyber Café *250 W 49th Street, between Broadway & Eighth Avenue, Theater District (1-212 333 4109). Subway C, E, 1, 9 to 50th Street; N, R, W to 49th Street.* **Open** 8am-11pm Mon-Fri; 11am-11pm Sat, Sun. **Cost** $6.40/30mins; 50¢/printed page. **Credit** AmEx, DC, MC, V. **Map** p404 D23.
This is a standard internet access café that also happens to serve great coffee and snacks.

DIRECTORY

DIRECTORY

FedEx Kinko's *1-800 463 3339/ www.fedex.com.*
Outposts of this ubiquitous and very efficient computer and copy centre are peppered throughout the city; many are open 24 hours a day.
New York Public Library *www.nypl.org.*
The branch libraries throughout the five boroughs are great places to email and surf the web for free. However, the scarcity of computer stations may make for a long wait, and user time is limited. The **Science, Industry and Business Library**, 188 Madison Avenue, at 34th Street, has more than 40 workstations that you can use for up to an hour per day.
NYCWireless *www.nycwireless.net.*
This group has established dozens of hotspots in the city for free wireless access. (For example, most parks below 59th Street are covered.) Visit the website for information and a map.
Starbucks *www.starbucks.com.*
Many branches offer wireless access through AT&T (up to two hours of free access per day with activation of a Starbucks card).
For a list of websites providing further information, *see p385.*

LEFT LUGGAGE

There are left-luggage facilites at Arrivals halls in **JFK Airport** (in Terminal 1, call 1-718 751 2947; in Terminal 4, call 1-718 751 4020). And at **Penn Station**, Amtrak offers checked baggage services ($4.50 per bag per day) for some of its ticketed passengers. Due to heightened security, luggage storage is not available at the Port Authority Bus Terminal, Grand Central, or LaGuardia and Newark Airports.
One Midtown alternative is to leave bags with **Schwartz Travel**, (355 W 36th Street, between Eighth & Ninth Avenues), between Penn Station and the Port Authority. Fees are $6-$10 per bag per day. Some hotels may allow you to leave suitcases with the front desk before check-in or after check-out; if so, be sure to tip the concierge.

LEGAL HELP

If you're arrested for a minor violation (disorderly conduct, loitering, etc) and you're very polite to the officer during the arrest (and carry proper ID), then you'll probably be fingerprinted,

photographed at the station and given a ticket with a date to show up at criminal court. After that, you'll most likely get to go home.
Arguing with a police officer or engaging in more serious criminal activity (such as possession of a weapon, drunken driving, illegal gambling or prostitution, for example) might get you 'processed', which means a 24- to 30-hour journey through the system. If the courts are backed up (and they usually are), you'll be held temporarily at a precinct pen. You can make a phone call after you've been fingerprinted. When you get through central booking, you'll arrive at 100 Centre Street for arraignment. A judge will decide whether you should be released on bail and will set a court date. If you can't post bail, then you'll be held at Rikers Island.

Legal Aid Society *1-212 577 3300/www.legal-aid.org.* **Open** 9am-5pm Mon-Fri.
Sandback, Birnbaum & Michelen Criminal Law *1-800 640 2000.* **Open** 24hrs daily.
If no one at this firm can help you, then you'll be directed to lawyers who can.

LIBRARIES

See p100 **New York Public Library.**

LOST PROPERTY

For property lost in the street, contact the police. For lost credit cards or travellers' cheques, *see p380.*

Grand Central Terminal *1-212 340 2555.* **Open** 7am-6pm Mon-Fri; 8.45am-5pm Sat. Call if you've left something on a Metro-North train.
JFK Airport *1-718 244 4225, or contact your airline.*
La Guardia Airport *1-718 533 3988, or contact your airline.*
Newark Liberty International Airport *1-973 961 6243, or contact your airline.*
Penn Station: Amtrak *1-212 630 7389.* **Open** 7.30am-4pm Mon-Fri.
Penn Station: Long Island Rail Road *1-212 643 5103.* **Open** 7am-11pm daily.
Penn Station: New Jersey Transit *1-973 275 5555.* **Open** 6am-10pm Mon-Fri; 8am-8pm Sat; 9am-8pm Sun.

Subway & buses *New York City Metropolitan Transit Authority, 34th Street-Penn Station, near the A-train platform, Garment District (1-212 712 4500).* **Open** 8am-4pm Mon, Tue, Fri; 11am-7pm Wed, Thur. **Map** p404 D25. Call if you've left something on a subway train or a bus.
Taxis *1-212 826 3211/www. nyc.gov/taxi.* Call for items left in a cab.

MEDIA

Daily newspapers

The **Daily News** has drifted politically from the Neanderthal right to a more moderate but always tough-minded stance under the ownership of noted real-estate mogul Mort Zuckerman.
Founded in 1801 by Alexander Hamilton, the **New York Post** is the nation's oldest continuously published daily newspaper. It has swerved sharply to the right under current owner Rupert Murdoch, includes more gossip than any other local paper, and its headlines are often sassy and sensational.
As Olympian as ever after more than 150 years, the **New York Times** remains the city's, and the nation's, paper of record. It has broadest and deepest coverage of world and national events and, as the masthead proclaims, it delivers 'All the News That's Fit to Print'. The mammoth **Sunday Times** can weigh a full 5lb and includes a very well-regarded magazine, as well as book review, travel, real-estate and various other sections.
The **Amsterdam News**, one of the nation's oldest black newspapers, offers a trenchant African-American viewpoint. New York also supports three Spanish-language dailies: **El Diario**, **Hoy** and **Noticias del Mundo**. **Newsday** is a Long Island-based daily with a tabloid format but a sober tone. Free tabloids **AM New York** and **New York Metro** offer locally slanted news, arts and entertainment listings. **USA Today** keeps weary travellers abreast of national news.

Weekly newspapers

Downtown journalism is a battlefield, with the **New York Press** pitted against the **Village Voice**. The *Press* is full of youthful energy and irreverence, as well as cynicism and self-absorption. The *Voice* is sometimes passionate and ironic but just as often strident and predictable. Both are free. The **New York Observer** focuses on the doings of the upper echelons of business, finance, media and politics. **Our Town, Chelsea Clinton News**, the **West Sider** and **Manhattan Spirit** are free sister publications featuring neighbourhood news and local political gossip. In a class all of its own is the hilarious, satirical national weekly **The Onion**.

Magazines

New York magazine is part news weekly, part lifestyle reporting and part listings. Since the 1920s the **New Yorker** has been known for its fine wit, elegant prose and sophisticated cartoons. Today, it's a forum for serious long-form journalism.

Based on the tried and trusted format of its London parent magazine, **Time Out New York** is an intelligent, irreverant, indispensable weekly guide to what's going on in the city: arts, restaurants, bars, shops and more.

Since its launch in 1996, the bimonthly **Black Book Magazine** has covered New York's high fashion and culture with intelligent bravado. **Gotham**, a monthly from the publisher of glossy gab-rags **Hamptons** and **Aspen Peak**, unveiled its larger-than-life celeb-filled pages in 2001. And for two decades now, **Paper** has offered buzz on bars, clubs, downtown boutiques and more.

Radio

Nearly 100 stations serve the New York area. On the AM dial, you can find talk radio and phone-in shows that attract everyone from priests to sports nuts. Flip to FM for free jazz, the latest Franz Ferdinand single or any other auditory craving. Radio highlights are printed weekly in *Time Out New York*, and daily in the *Daily News*.

College radio is innovative and commercial-free but reception is often compromised by Manhattan's high-rise topography. **WNYU-FM 89.1** and **WKCR-FM 89.9** are, respectively, the stations of New York University and Columbia. **WFUV-FM 90.7**, Fordham University's station, airs a variety of shows, including *Beale Street Caravan*, the world's most widely distributed blues programme.

American **commercial radio** is rigidly formatted, which makes most pop stations extremely tedious and repetitive during the day. Tune in on evenings and weekends for more interesting programming. Always popular, **WQHT-FM 97.1**, 'Hot 97,' is a commercial hip hop station with all-day rap and R&B. **WKTU-FM 103.5** is the premier dance music station. **WWPR-FM 105.1**, 'Power 105,' plays top hip hop, and a few old-school hits. **WBLS-FM 107.5** showcases classic and new funk, soul and R&B. **WBGO-FM 88.3** is strictly jazz. **WAXQ-FM 104.3** offers classic rock. **WXRK-FM 92.3**'s alternative music attracts and appals listeners with its 6-10am weekday sleaze-fest.

WQEW-AM 1560, 'Radio Disney', has kids' programming. **WNYC-FM 93.9** and **WQXR-FM 96.3** serve up a range of classical music. **WCAA-FM 105.9** and **WQBU-FM 92.7** spin Spanish and Latin.

WABC-AM 770, WCBS-AM 880, WINS-AM 1010 and **WBBR-AM 1130** offer news throughout the day, plus traffic and weather reports. **WNYC-AM 820/FM 93.9**, a commercial-free, public radio station, provides news and current-affairs commentary and broadcasts the BBC World Service. **WBAI-FM 99.5** is a left-leaning community radio station. **WLIB-AM 1190** is the flagship station of Air America, a far more liberal answer to right-wing talk radio.

WFAN-AM 660 airs Giants, Nets, Mets and Devils games. **WCBS-AM 880** covers the Yankees. **WEPN-AM 1050** is devoted to news and sports talk and is the home of the Jets, Knicks and Rangers. **WBBR-AM 1130** broadcasts Islanders games.

Television

Six major **networks** broadcast nationwide. All offer ratings-driven variations on a theme. **CBS** (Channel 2 in NYC) has the top investigative show, *60 Minutes*, on Sundays at 7pm; overall, programming is geared to a middle-aged demographic, but CBS also screens shows like *CSI* and the reality series *Survivor*. **NBC** (4) is the home of *Law & Order*, the long-running sketch-comedy series *Saturday Night Live* (11.30pm Sat), and popular primetime shows including *Heroes*, *Scrubs* and *My Name is Earl*. **Fox-WNYW** (5) is popular with younger audiences for shows such as *The Simpsons*,

Family Guy, *24*, *Prison Break* and *American Idol*. **ABC** (7) is the king of daytime soaps, family-friendly sitcoms and hits like *Desperate Housewives*, *Lost* and *Ugly Betty*.

Public TV is on channels 13, 21 and 25. Documentaries, arts shows and science series alternate with Masterpiece Theatre and reruns of British shows like *Inspector Morse*. Channel 21 broadcasts *BBC World News* at 6am, 7pm and 11pm daily.

For channel numbers for **cable TV** channels, such as Time Warner Cable, Cablevision and RCN, check a local newspaper.

FSN (Fox Sports Network), **MSG** (Madison Square Garden), **ESPN** and **ESPN2** are all-sports stations. **Comedy Central** is all comedy, airing *South Park*, *The Daily Show with Jon Stewart* and its hugely popular spin-off *The Colbert Report*. **Cinemax**, the **Disney Channel**, **HBO**, the **Movie Channel** and **Showtime** are often available in hotels. They show uninterrupted feature films, exclusive specials and series like *Entourage* and *Curb Your Enthusiasm*.

Time Out New York offers a rundown of TV highlights.

MONEY

Over the past few years, much of American currency has undergone a subtle facelift, partly to deter increasingly adept counterfeiters. However, 'old' money still remains in circulation. All denominations except for the $1 bill have recently been updated by the US Treasury. Coins include copper pennies (1¢) and silver-coloured nickels (5¢), dimes (10¢) and quarters (25¢). Half-dollar coins (50¢) and the gold-coloured dollar coins are less common. All paper money is the same size, so make sure you fork over the right bill. It comes in denominations of $1, $2, $5, $10, $20, $50 and $100 (and higher, but you'll never see those bills). The $2 bills are quite rare. Try to keep low denominations on you because getting change may be a problem with anything bigger than a $20 bill.

ATMs

The city is full of ATMs, located in bank branches, delis and many small shops. Most accept American Express, MasterCard, Visa and major bank cards. Some UK banks charge up to £4 per transaction plus a variable payment to cover themselves against any exchange rate fluctuations.

DIRECTORY

Most ATM cards now double as charge cards, if they bear Maestro or Cirrus logos. You can get cashback on this at supermarkets, British customers included (theoretically, and for a percentage charge). In practice you'll find that this only works at certain outlets.

Banks & currency exchange

Banks are generally open from 9am to 5pm Monday to Friday, though some stay open longer and/or on Saturdays. You need photo ID, such as a passport, to cash travellers' cheques. Many banks will not exchange foreign currency; bureaux de change, limited to tourist-trap areas, close at around 6pm or 7pm. It's best to arrive in the city with a few dollars in cash, then pay mostly with credit cards or travellers' cheques (accepted in most larger stores and restaurants, but do ask first and carry ID). In emergencies, most large hotels will offer 24-hour exchange facilities, but the rates won't be great.

Chase Bank *1-212 935 9935/ www.chase.com.*
Chase's website gives information on foreign currency exchange, branch locations and credit cards. For foreign currency delivered in a hurry, call the number listed above.
Commerce Bank *1-888 751 9000/www.commerceonline.com.*
All 17 Manhattan branches of the Commerce Bank are open seven days a week.
People's Foreign Exchange *3rd Floor, 575 Fifth Avenue, at 47th Street, Midtown East (1-212 883 0550). Subway E, V to Fifth Avenue-53rd Street; 7 to Fifth Avenue.* **Open** 9am-6pm Mon-Fri; 10am-3pm Sat, Sun. **Map** p404 E23.
People's offers foreign currency exchange on bank notes and travellers' cheques of any denomination for a $2 fee.
Travelex *29 Broadway, at Morris Street, Financial District (1-212 363 6206). Subway 4, 5 to Bowling Green.* **Open** 9am-5pm Mon-Fri.
Map p402 E33.
A complete range of foreign-exchange services is offered.
Other locations 1590 Broadway, at 48th Street (1-212 753 0117).

Credit cards

Credit cards are essential for renting cars and booking hotels, and handy for buying tickets over the phone and the internet.

The five major cards accepted in the US are American Express, Diners Club, Discover, MasterCard and Visa. MasterCard (abbreviated as MC throughout this book) and Visa (V) are the most popular, with American Express (AmEx) also widely accepted. Thanks to a 2004 deal between MC and Diners Club (DC), all businesses that accept MC can now accept DC. If cards are lost or stolen, call the following numbers:

American Express
1-800 528 2122.
Diners Club *1-800 234 6377.*
Discover *1-800 347 2683.*
MasterCard/Maestro
1-800 826 2181.
Visa/Cirrus *1-800 336 8472.*

Tax

Sales tax is 8.375 per cent in New York City, and is applicable to restaurant bills, services and the purchase of just about anything, except most store-bought foods, clothing and shoes (the latter two are exempt from the 4 per cent city tax, but items over $110 are still subject to a 4.375 per cent state tax). In the US, sales tax is almost never included in the price of the item, but added on to the final bill at the till. There is no tax refund option for foreign visitors.

Travellers' cheques

Like credit cards, travellers' cheques are also routinely accepted at banks, stores and restaurants throughout the city. Bring your driver's licence or passport for

identification. If cheques are lost or stolen, call the following numbers:

American Express
1-800 221 7282.
Thomas Cook *1-800 223 7373.*
Visa *1-800 336 8472.*

Wire services

If you run out of cash, you can have funds wired to you from home through the following companies:

MoneyGram *1-800 666 3947/ www.moneygram.com.*
Western Union *1-800 325 6000/www.westernunion.com.*

OPENING HOURS

Banks and government offices, including post offices, close on federal holidays. Retail in the city shuts down on Christmas Day and New Year's Day, although movie theatres and some restaurants remain open. Most museums are closed on Mondays, but may open when a public holiday falls on a Monday. New York's subway runs 24 hours a day, 365 days a year, but always check station signs for track or schedule changes, especially during weekends and holidays.

Banks 9am-5pm Mon-Fri; sometimes also Sat mornings.
Businesses 9am-5pm Mon-Fri.
Post offices 9am-5pm Mon-Fri (a few open as early as 7.30am and close as late as 8.30pm); sometimes also Sat mornings. The James Farley branch at 31st Street and Eighth Avenue is open 24 hours a day, 365 days a year.

SIZE CHART

Women's clothing				Women's shoes		
UK	Europe	US		UK	Europe	US
4	32	2		3	36	5
6	34	4		4	37	6
8	36	6		5	38	7
10	38	8		6	39	8
12	40	10		7	40	9
14	42	12		8	41	10
16	44	14		9	42	11

Men's suits				Men's shoes		
UK	Europe	US		UK	Europe	US
34	44	34		7	40	7.5
36	46	36		7.5	41	8
38	48	38		8	42	8.5
40	50	40		8.5	43	9
42	52	42		9.5	44	10
44	54	44		10.5	45	11
46	56	46		11.5	46	12

Pubs & bars 4pm-2am Sun-Thur, noon-4am Fri and Sat (hours vary widely); last call is at 4am.
Shops 9am or 10am-7pm Mon-Sat (some to 9pm). Many are also open on Sun, usually 10am-6pm.

POLICE

In an emergency only, dial 911. The NYPD stations below are in central, tourist-heavy areas of Manhattan. For the location of your nearest police precinct or information about police services, call 1-646 610 5000.

Midtown North Precinct *306 W 54th Street, between Eighth & Ninth Avenues, Hell's Kitchen (1-212 760 8300).*
17th Precinct *167 E 51st Street, between Third & Lexington Avenues, Midtown East (1-212 826 3211).*
Midtown South Precinct *357 W 35th Street, between Eighth & Ninth Avenues, Garment District (1-212 239 9811).*
Central Park Precinct *86th Street & Transverse Road, Central Park (1-212 570 4820).*

POSTAL SERVICES

Stamps are available at all US post offices, from drugstore vending machines and at most newsstands. It costs 42¢ to send a 1oz letter within the US. Each additional ounce costs 17¢. Postcards mailed within the US cost 27¢. Airmailed letters or postcards to Canada and Mexico cost 72¢ for the first ounce; to all other countries it's 94¢ for the first ounce. The cost of additional ounces varies by country.

For faster Express Mail, you must fill out a form, either at a post office or by arranging a pickup; 24-hour delivery to major US cities is guaranteed. International delivery takes two to three days, with no guarantee. Call 1-800 275 8777 for more information.

General Post Office *421 Eighth Avenue, between 31st & 33rd Streets, Garment District (24hr information 1-800 275 8777/www.usps.com). Subway A, C, E to 34th Street-Penn Station.* **Open** 24hrs daily. **Credit** DC, MC, V. **Map** p404 D25.
Queues are long, but stamps are available from vending machines. Branches are usually open 9am-5pm Mon-Fri; hours vary Sat.
General Delivery *390 Ninth Avenue, between 31st & 33rd Streets, Garment District (1-212*

330 3099). Subway A, C, E to 34th Street-Penn Station. **Open** 10am-1pm Mon-Sat. **Map** p404 C25.
US residents without local addresses can receive their mail here; it should be addressed to the recipient, General Delivery, 390 Ninth Avenue, New York, NY 10001. You will need to show a passport or ID card when picking up letters.
Poste Restante *Window 29, 421 Eighth Avenue, between 31st & 33rd Streets, Garment District (1-212 330 2912). Subway A, C, E to 34th Street-Penn Station.* **Open** 8am-6pm Mon-Sat. **Map** p404 D25.
Foreign visitors can receive mail here; mail should be addressed to the recipient, General Post Office, Poste Restante, 421 Eighth Avenue, attn: Window 29, New York, NY 10001. Be sure to bring ID to collect anything.

RELIGION

Here are just a few of New York's many places of worship. Check the phone book for more listings.

Abyssinian Baptist Church *For listing, see p120.*
Cathedral Church of St John the Divine *For listing, see p117.*
Church of St Paul & St Andrew, United Methodist *263 W 86th Street, between Broadway & West End Avenue, Upper West Side (1-212 362 3179/www.spsanyc.org). Subway 1 to 86th Street.* **Map** p406 C18.
Islamic Cultural Center of New York *1711 Third Avenue, between 96th & 97th Streets, Upper East Side (1-212 722 5234). Subway 6 to 96th Street.* **Map** p406 F17.
Madison Avenue Presbyterian Church *921 Madison Avenue, at 73rd Street, Upper East Side (1-212 288 8920/www.mapc.com). Subway 6 to 72nd Street.* **Map** p405 E20.
New York Buddhist Church *331-332 Riverside Drive, between 105th & 106th Streets, Upper West Side (1-212 678 0305/ www.newyorkbuddhistchurch.org). Subway 1 to 103rd Street.* **Map** p406 B16.
St Patrick's Cathedral *For listing, see p102.*
UJA–Federation of New York Resource Line *1-212 753 2288/www.ujafedny.org.* **Open** 9am-5pm Mon-Thur; 9am-4pm Fri. This hotline provides referrals to other Jewish organisations, groups, temples, philanthropic activities and synagogues.

SAFETY & SECURITY

New York's crime rate, particularly for violent crime, has waned during the past decade. Most crime occurs late at night in low-income neighbourhoods. Don't arrive thinking your safety is at risk wherever you go; it is unlikely that you will ever be bothered.

Still, a bit of common sense won't hurt. Don't flaunt your money and valuables, and try not to look obviously lost. Avoid deserted and poorly lit streets; walk facing oncoming traffic so no one can drive up alongside you undetected, and close to or on the street; muggers prefer to hang back in doorways and shadows. If you are threatened, hand over your valuables at once, then dial 911.

Be extra alert to pickpockets and street hustlers – especially in crowded areas like Times Square.

SMOKING

The 1995 NYC Smoke-Free Air Act makes it illegal to smoke in virtually all indoor public places, including the subway and cinemas; for a list of exceptions, *see p224* **Inside Track**.

STUDY

Student life in NYC is unlike it is anywhere else in the world; the city provides an endless extracurricular education, as well as a nonstop playground. Foreign students should get hold of an International Student Identity Card (ISIC) in order to secure discounts. These can be bought from your local student-travel agent (ask at your student union or an STA Travel office). For student-oriented features, listings and guidance, check the *Time Out New York Student Guide*, available in August for free on campuses. Manhattan's main universities include: the **City University of New York**'s 23 colleges (1-212 794 5555, www.cuny.edu); **Columbia University** (2960 Broadway, at 116th Street, Morningside Heights, 1-212 854 1754, www.columbia.edu); the **Cooper Union** (Cooper Square, at Fourth Avenue, East Village, 1-212 353 4100, www.cooper.edu); **Fordham University** (113 W 60th Street, at Columbus Avenue, Upper West Side, 1-212 636 6000, www.fordham.edu); the **New School** (55 W 13th Street, between Fifth & Sixth Avenues, Greenwich

Village, 1-212 229 5620, www.newschool.edu); **New York University** (70 Washington Square South, Greenwich Village, 1-212 998 1212, www.nyu.edu); and performing arts school **Julliard** (60 Lincoln Center Plaza, at Broadway, Upper West Side, 1-212 799 5000, www.julliard.edu).

TELEPHONES

As a rule, you must dial 1 + the area code before a number, even if the place you are calling is in the same area code. The area codes for Manhattan are 212 and 646; Brooklyn, Queens, Staten Island and the Bronx are 718 and 347; 917 is now reserved mostly for mobile phones and pagers. Long Island area codes are 516 and 631; codes for New Jersey are 201, 551, 848, 862, 609, 732, 856, 908 and 973. Numbers preceded by 800, 877 and 888 are free of charge when dialled from within the US.

Collect calls are also known as reverse-charge calls. To make one, dial 0 followed by the number, or dial AT&T's 1-800 225 5288, MCI's 1-800 265 5328 or Sprint's 1-800 663 3463. For **directory assistance**, dial 411 or 1 + area code + 555 1212. Doing so may cost nothing, depending on the payphone you are using; carrier fees may apply. Long-distance directory assistance may also incur long-distance charges. For a directory of toll-free numbers, dial 1-800 555 1212. In an **emergency** dial 911. All calls are free (including those from pay- and mobile phones). For **international calls** dial 011 + country code (Australia 61; New Zealand 64; UK 44), then the number. For the **operator** dial 0.

Pagers & mobiles

Most US mobile phones will work in NYC but since the US doesn't have a standard national network, visitors should check with their provider that their phone will work here, and whether they need to unlock a roaming option. Visitors from other countries will need a tri-band handset and a roaming agreement, and may find charges so high that rental (*see p232*), or, depending on the length of their stay, purchase of a US phone (or SIM card) will make better economic sense.

If you carry a mobile phone, make sure you turn it off at restaurants, plays, movies, concerts and museums. New Yorkers are quick

to show their annoyance at an ill-timed ring. Some establishments now even post signs designating 'cellular-free zones'.

Public payphones & phonecards

Public payphones are easy to find. Some of them even work (non-Verizon phones tend to be poorly maintained). Phones take any combination of silver coins: local calls usually cost 50¢ for three minutes. If you're not used to US phones, then note that the ringing tone is long; the engaged tone, or 'busy signal', is much shorter and higher pitched.

To call long-distance or to make an international call from a payphone, you need to go through a **long-distance company**. Most of the payphones in New York automatically use AT&T, but phones in and around transportation hubs usually contract other long-distance carriers, and charges can be outrageous. MCI and Sprint are respected brand names (*see left* **Collect calls**). Make the call by either dialling 0 for an operator or dialling direct, which is cheaper. To find out how much it will cost, dial the number, and a computerised voice will tell you how much money to deposit. You can pay for calls with your credit card.

The best way to make long-distance calls is with a phonecard, available from any post-office branch or from chain stores like Duane Reade or Rite Aid (*see p251* **Pharmacies**). Many delis and newspaper kiosks sell phonecards.

TIME & DATES

New York is on **Eastern Standard Time**, which extends from the Atlantic coast to the eastern shore of Lake Michigan and south to the Gulf of Mexico. This is five hours behind Greenwich Mean Time. Clocks are set forward one hour in early March for Daylight Saving Time (**Eastern Daylight Time**) and back one hour at the beginning of November. Going from east to west, Eastern Time is one hour ahead of Central Time, two hours ahead of Mountain Time and three hours ahead of Pacific Time. In the United States, the date is written as month, day and year; so 2/8/08 is 8 February 2008. Forms that foreigners may need to fill in, however, are often the other way round.

TIPPING

In restaurants, it is customary to tip at least 15 per cent, and since NYC tax is 8.375 per cent, a quick way to calculate the tip is to double the tax. In many restaurants, when you are with a group of six or more, the tip will be included in the bill. For tipping on taxi fares, *see p374*.

TOILETS

The media had a field day when the first pay toilet to open in the city since 1975 received its 'first flush' by officials in a special ceremony in 2008. 'Public Toilet No.1', as the New York Post christened it, is in Madison Square Park (Madison Avenue, between 23rd & 24th Streets, Subway N, R, W, 6 to 23rd Street) and should be followed by around 20 across the city within the next couple of years. It costs 25¢ to enter the large stainless steel and tempered glass box (dawdlers and OCD sufferers beware: the door opens after 15 minutes). Below is a list of other convenient rest stops.

Downtown

Battery Park *Castle Clinton Subway 1 to South Ferry; 4, 5 to Bowling Green.*
Tompkins Square Park *Avenue A, at 9th Street. Subway L to First Avenue; 6 to Astor Place.*
Washington Square Park *Thompson Street, at Washington Square South. Subway A, B, C, D, E, F, V to W 4th Street.*

Midtown

Bryant Park *42nd Street, between Fifth and Sixth Avenues. Subway B, D, F, V to 42nd St-Bryant Park; 7 to Fifth Avenue.*
Grand Central Terminal *42nd Street, at Park Avenue, Lower Concourse. Subway S, 4, 5, 6, 7 to 42nd Street-Grand Central.*
Penn Station *Seventh Avenue, between 31st and 33rd Streets, Subway A, C, E, 1, 2, 3 to 34th Street-Penn Station.*

Uptown

Avery Fisher Hall *Broadway, at 65th Street. Subway 1 to 66th Street-Lincoln Center.*
Charles A Dana Discovery Center *Central Park, north side of Harlem Meer, 110th Street, at Malcolm X Blvd (Lenox Avenue). Subway 2, 3 to 110th Street-Central Park North.*

Delacorte Theater *Central Park, midpark, at 81st Street. Subway B, C to 81st Street-Museum of Natural History.*

TOURIST INFORMATION

NYC & Company *810 Seventh Avenue, between 52nd & 53rd Streets, Midtown (1-800 NYC VISIT/www.nycvisit.com). Subway B, D, E to Seventh Avenue.* **Open** 8.30am-6pm Mon-Fri; 9am-5pm Sat, Sun. **Map** p404 D23.
The city's official (private, non-profit) visitors' and information centre doles out maps, leaflets, coupons and advice, and provides information on tour operators and travel agents.
Other locations 33-34 Carnaby Street, London W1V 1CA, England (020 7437 8300).
Times Square Visitors Center *1560 Broadway, between 46th & 47th Streets, Theater District (1-212 869 1890). Subway N, Q, R, S, W, 1, 2, 3, 7 to 42nd Street-Times Square.* **Open** 8am-8pm daily. **Map** p404 D24.
This centre offers discount coupons for Broadway tickets, MetroCards, free maps and other useful goods and services, predominantly for the Theater District. Staff are multilingual. There are also ATMs, photo booths and free internet stations on site.

VISAS & IMMIGRATION

Visas

Some 27 countries currently participate in the Visa Waiver Program (VWP). Citizens of Andorra, Australia, Austria, Belgium, Brunei, Denmark, Finland, France, Germany, Iceland, Ireland, Italy, Japan, Liechtenstein, Luxembourg, Monaco, the Netherlands, New Zealand, Norway, Portugal, San Marino, Singapore, Slovenia, Spain, Sweden, Switzerland and the UK do not need a visa for stays in the US shorter than 90 days (business or pleasure) as long as they have a machine-readable passport valid for the full 90-day period and a return ticket.
If you do not qualify for entry under the VWP, that is if you are not from one of the eligible countries or are visiting for any purpose other than pleasure or business, you will need a visa. Media workers and students: this includes you. If you in the slightest doubt, check ahead. You can obtain the application

forms from your nearest US embassy or consulate or from its website. Find out several months ahead how long the application process is currently taking.
Canadians travelling to the US will need visas only in special circumstances.
Whether or not you have a visa, you should not travel on a passport with six months or less to run.
If you lose your passport inside the US, contact your consulate (*see p376*).

Immigration

Your airline will give all visitors an immigration form to be presented to an official when you land. Fill it in clearly and be prepared to give an address at which you are staying (a hotel is fine).
Upon arrival, you may have to wait an hour or, if you're unlucky, considerably longer, in Immigration, where owing to tightened security you can expect slow-moving queues. You may be expected to explain your visit; be polite and prepared. Note that all visitors to the US are now photographed and fingerprinted on arrival on every trip. You will usually be granted an entry permit.

US Embassy Visa Information *US: 1-202 663 1225/UK: 09055 444546, 60p per minute/http://travel.state.gov/visa.*

WEIGHTS & MEASURES

Despite attempts to bring in metric measurements, you'll find Imperial used in almost all contexts in New York and throughout America. People think in ounces, inches, gallons and miles.

WHEN TO GO

There is no bad time to visit New York, and visitor numbers are fairly steady year-round. However, the weather can be unpleasantly hot and humid in summer (especially August) and, although winter snow (usually heaviest in January and February) is picturesque before it gets dirty and slushy, these months are often brutally cold. Late spring and early autumn bring pleasantly moderate temperatures that are perfect for walking and exploring.

Public holidays

New Year's Day (1 Jan); Martin Luther King, Jr Day (3rd Mon in Jan); Presidents Day (3rd Mon in Feb); Memorial Day (last Mon in May); Independence Day (4 July); Labor Day 1st Mon in Sept); Columbus Day (2nd Mon in Oct); Veterans Day (11 Nov); Thanksgiving Day (4th Thur in Nov; Christmas Day (25 Dec).

WORKING IN NEW YORK

Non-nationals cannot work in the United States without the appropriate visa; these are hard to get and generally require you to prove that your job could not be done by a US citizen. Contact your local embassy for further details. Some student visas allow part-time work after the first academic year.
UK students who want to spend a summer vacation working in the States should contact the **British Universities North America Club** (BUNAC) for help in securing a temporary job and also the requisite visa (16 Bowling Green Lane, London, EC1R 0QH, England; 020 7251 3472, www.bunac.org/uk).

THE LOCAL CLIMATE

Average temperatures and monthly rainfall in New York.

	High (°C/°F)	Low (°C/°F)	Rainfall (mm/in)
Jan	2 / 36	-5 / 23	94 / 3.7
Feb	4 / 40	-4 / 24	75 / 3.0
Mar	9 / 48	0 / 32	104 / 4.1
Apr	14 / 58	6 / 42	103 / 4.1
May	20 / 68	12 / 53	114 / 4.5
June	25 / 77	17 / 63	88 / 3.5
July	28 / 83	20 / 68	106 / 4.2
Aug	27 / 81	19 / 66	103 / 4.1
Sept	23 / 74	14 / 58	103 / 4.1
Oct	17 / 63	8 / 47	89 / 3.5
Nov	11 / 52	3 / 38	102 / 4.0
Dec	6 / 42	-2 / 28	98 / 3.9

DIRECTORY

Further Reference

BOOKS

Edward F Bergman *The Spiritual Traveler: New York City*
Sacred and peaceful spaces in New York City.
William Corbett
New York Literary Lights
The city's literary past.
Suzanne Gerber
Vegetarian New York City
Going meat-free in the city.
Colleen Kane (ed)
Sexy New York City
Discover erotica in the Naked City.
Chuck Katz *Manhattan on Film 2*
Walking tours of New York City.
Earl Steinbicker (ed)
Daytrips: New York
50 breaks within reach of town.
Linda Tarrant-Reid
Discovering Black New York
Museums, landmarks and more.
Time Out
New York Eating & Drinking 2009
The annual critics' guide to thousands of places to eat and drink in the five boroughs.
Time Out
1000 Things To Do in New York
Original and inspirational ideas to appeal to jaded residents and newly arrived visitors alike.

Architecture

Richard Berenholtz
New York, New York
Miniature panoramic images of the city through the seasons.
Stanley Greenberg
Invisible New York
A photographic account of hidden architectural triumphs.
New York City Landmarks Preservation Commission
Guide to New York City Landmarks
Lives up to its title.
Karl Sabbagh *Skyscraper*
How the tall ones are built.
Robert AM Stern et al
New York 1930
A massive coffee-table slab with stunning pictures.
Norval White & Elliot Willensky
The AIA Guide to New York City
A comprehensive directory of important buildings.
Gerard R Wolfe *New York: A Guide to the Metropolis*
Historical and architectural walking tours.

Culture & recollections

Irving Lewis Allen
The City in Slang
NY bred words and phrases.
Candace Bushnell
Sex & the City; Trading Up
Smart women, superficial NY.
George Chauncey *Gay New York*
The evolution of gay culture from 1890 to 1940.
Martha Cooper & Henry Chalfant *Subway Art*
A definitive survey of city graffiti.
Josh Alan Friedman
Tales of Times Square
Sleaze and decay in the old days.
Nelson George *Hip Hop America*
The real history of hip hop, from Grandmaster Flash to Puff Daddy.
Robert Hendrickson
New Yawk Tawk
A dictionary of NYC slang.
Jane Jacobs *The Death and Life of Great American Cities*
A hugely influential critique of modern urban planning.
Gillian McCain & Legs McNeil
Please Kill Me
An oral history of the punk scene.
Frank O'Hara *The Collected Poems of Frank O'Hara*
The great NYC poet found inspiration in his hometown.
Thurston Moore & Byron Coley *No Wave*
Musicians reminisce about the downtown post-punk underground scene in this nostalgia trip co-edited by the Sonic Youth frontman.
Andrés Torres
Between Melting Pot and Mosaic
African-American and Puerto Rican life in the city.
Heather Holland Wheaton
Eight Million Stories in a New York Minute
The shortest of short stories: none more than 300 words.
EB White *Here Is New York*
A clear-eyed love letter to Gotham.

Fiction

Kurt Andersen
Turn of the Century
Millennial Manhattan as seen through the eyes of media players.
Paul Auster
The New York Trilogy: City of Glass, Ghosts and *The Locked Room*
A search for the madness behind the method of Manhattan's grid.

Kevin Baker *Dreamland*
A poetic novel about Coney Island's glory days.
James A Baldwin
Another Country
Racism under the bohemian veneer of the 1960s.
Michael Chabon *The Amazing Adventures of Kavalier and Clay*
Jewish comic-book artists battling with crises of identity in the 1940s.
Bret Easton Ellis *Glamorama*
A satirical view of dazzling New York City nightlife.
Jack Finney *Time and Again*
An illustrator travels back to 19th-century NY.
Larry Kramer *Faggots*
A devastating satire of gay NY.
Phillip Lopate (ed)
Writing New York
An excellent anthology of short stories, essays and poems.
Patrick McGrath *Trauma*
A first-person account of psychic decay that floats a critique of post-9/11 social and political amnesia.
Tim McLoughlin (ed)
Brooklyn Noir
Crime tales set in Brooklyn.
Toni Morrison *Jazz*
Life in 1920s Harlem.
Richard Price *Lush Life*
A contemporary murder story set on the Lower East Side.
David Schickler
Kissing in Manhattan
The lives of quirky tenants in a teeming Manhattan block.
Hubert Selby Jr
Last Exit to Brooklyn
Dockland degradation, circa 1950s.
Edith Wharton *Old New York*
Four novellas of 19th-century New York City.
Colson Whitehead *The Colossus of New York: A City in 13 Parts*
A lyrical tribute to city life.
Tom Wolfe
The Bonfire of the Vanities
Rich/poor, black/white – an unmatched slice of 1980s NYC.

History

Herbert Asbury
The Gangs of New York: An Informal History of the Underworld
A racy journalistic portrait of the city at the turn of the 19th century.
Robert A Caro *The Power Broker*
A biography of Robert Moses, New York's mid-20th-century master builder, and his chequered legacy.

DIRECTORY

Federal Writers' Project
The WPA Guide to New York City
A wonderful evocation of the 1930s
by writers who were employed
under FDR's New Deal.
Sanna Feirstein
Naming New York
How Manhattan places got
their names.
Mitchell Fink & Lois Mathias
*Never Forget: An Oral History of
September 11, 2001*
First-person accounts.
Clifton Hood *722 Miles: The
Building of the Subways and How
They Transformed New York*
The birth of the world's longest
rapid transit system.
Kenneth T Jackson (ed)
The Encyclopedia of New York City
An ambitious and useful
reference guide.
David Levering Lewis
When Harlem Was in Vogue
A study of the Harlem Renaissance.
Jonathan Mahler *Ladies and
Gentlemen, the Bronx is Burning*
A gritty snapshot of New York City
in 1977.
Shaun O'Connell *Remarkable,
Unspeakable New York*
A history of New York as literary
inspiration.
Mitchell Pacelle *Empire*
The story of the fight to build the
Empire State Building.
Clayton Patterson (ed)
Resistance
This collection of essays reflects on
the Lower East Side's history as a
radical hotbed.
Jacob A Riis
How the Other Half Lives
A pioneering photojournalistic
record of squalid tenement life.
Luc Sante *Low Life*
Opium dens and brothels in New
York from the 1840s to the 1920s.
Russell Shorto *The Island at the
Center of the World*
How the Dutch colony shaped
Manhattan – and America.
**Mike Wallace & Edwin G
Burrows** *Gotham: A History of
New York City to 1898*
The first volume in a planned
mammoth history of NYC.

FILMS

Annie Hall (1977)
Woody Allen co-stars with Diane
Keaton in this appealingly neurotic
valentine to Manhattan.
Breakfast at Tiffany's (1961)
Audrey Hepburn as the cash-poor,
time-rich socialite Holly Golightly.
Dog Day Afternoon (1975)
Al Pacino as a Brooklyn bank
robber in Sidney Lumet's classic.

Do the Right Thing (1989)
The hottest day of the summer
leads to racial strife in Bedford-
Stuyvesant in Spike Lee's drama.
The French Connection (1971)
As detective Jimmy 'Popeye' Doyle,
Gene Hackman ignores all traffic
lights to chase down drug
traffickers in William Friedkin's
much-imitated thriller.
Gangs of New York (2002)
Martin Scorsese's compelling,
epic retelling of Herbert Asbury's
history of criminal New York in
the mid-19th century.
The Godfather (1972) &
The Godfather: Part II (1974)
Francis Ford Coppola's brilliant
commentary on capitalism in
America is told through the
violent saga of Italian gangsters.
Mean Streets (1973)
Robert De Niro and Harvey Keitel
shine as small-time Little Italy
hoods in Scorsese's breakthrough
film, which still shocks today.
Midnight Cowboy (1969)
Street creatures 'Ratso' Rizzo
and Joe Buck face an unforgiving
Times Square in John Schlesinger's
darkly amusing classic.
Spider-Man (2002)
The comic book web-slinger from
Forest Hills comes to life in Sam
Raimi's pitch-perfect crowd pleaser.
Taxi Driver (1976)
Robert De Niro is a crazed cabbie
who sees all of New York as a den
of iniquity in Scorsese's drama.

MUSIC

Beastie Boys
'No Sleep Till Brooklyn'
These now middle-aged hip
hoppers began showing their love
for their fave borough decades ago.
Leonard Cohen
'Chelsea Hotel #2'
Of all the songs inspired by
the Chelsea, this bleak vision of
doomed love is on a level of its own.
Billy Joel
'New York State of Mind'
This heartfelt ballad exemplifies
the city's effect on the souls of its
visitors and residents.
Charles Mingus *Mingus Ah Um*
Mingus brought the gospel to jazz
and created a NY masterpiece.
Public Enemy *It Takes a Nation
of Millions to Hold Us Back*
A ferociously political tour de force
from the Long Island hip hop group
whose own Chuck D once called rap
'the CNN for black America'.
The Ramones *Ramones*
Four Queens roughnecks, a few
buzzsaw chords, and clipped
musings on turning tricks and

sniffing glue – it transformed
rock 'n' roll.
Frank Sinatra 'Theme from
"New York, New York"'
Trite and true, Frank's bombastic
love letter melts those little-town
blues.
Bruce Springsteen
'My City of Ruins'
The Boss praises the city's
resilience post-September 11
with this track from *The Rising*.
The Strokes *Is This It*
The effortlessly hip debut of this
hometown band garnered praise
and worldwide attention.
The Velvet Underground
The Velvet Underground & Nico
Lou Reed and company's first
album is still the gold standard
of downtown cool.
Wu Tang Clan Few artists
embodied '90s hip hop like the Wu,
its members – RZA, GZA and the
late ODB among them – coining a
cinematic rap aesthetic that
influences artists to this day.

WEBSITES

www.timeoutnewyork.com
The *Time Out New York* website
covers all the city has to offer.
When planning your trip, check the
individual Arts & Entertainment,
Museums & Culture and Shopping
sections for up-to-the-minute
listings. Search Eating & Drinking
for thousands of restaurant and bar
reviews written by our critics.
www.clubplanet.com
Follow the city's nocturnal scene
and buy tickets to big events.
www.forgotten-ny.com
Remember old New York here.
www.hipguide.com
A very short 'n' sweet site for those
looking for what's considered hip.
www.hopstop.com
Calculates door-to-door directions
on public transportation.
www.livebroadway.com
'The Official Website of Broadway'
is the source for theatres, tickets
and tours.
**www.manhattanusersguide.
com** An insiders' guide to what's
going on around town.
www.mta.info
Subway and bus service changes
are always posted here.
www.nyc.gov
City Hall's official New York City
website has lots of useful links.
www.nycvisit.com
NYC & Company, the local
convention and visitors' bureau.
www.nytimes.com
'All the News That's Fit to Print'
from the *New York Times*.

Index

Note: page numbers in **bold** indicate section(s) giving key information on a topic; *italics* indicate photos.

INDEX

INDEX

INDEX

INDEX

INDEX

Advertisers' Index

Please refer to the relevant pages for contact details

INDEX

Put New York City in your pocket.

If you haven't been on a New York City Transit subway or bus, then you haven't seen NYC. And MetroCard® gives you access to it all. Not to mention it's the least expensive and most convenient way to get around. And with MetroCard Deals, you can see a lot more of NYC for a lot less.

Ride the subways and local buses as many times as you want with a 1-Day Fun Pass, a 7-Day MetroCard, or a Pay-Per-Ride MetroCard, usable by up to four people.

Buy MetroCard at subway station vending machines with debit/credit cards or cash. You can also buy it at many hotels and at the New York Transit Museum's locations in Brooklyn Heights and Grand Central Terminal.

Visit our multilingual website at **www.mta.info** and click on the MetroCard icon for more information, MetroCard Deals, and tips for travel and sightseeing.

No matter where you decide to go, let us help you get there with Trip Planner, our online service for bus and subway travel information. Trip Planner gives you point-to-point directions and provides schedules, service advisories, and more.

800-METROCARD (800-638-7622)
212-METROCARD (in NYC)

New York City Transit *Going your way*

www.mta.info

Maps

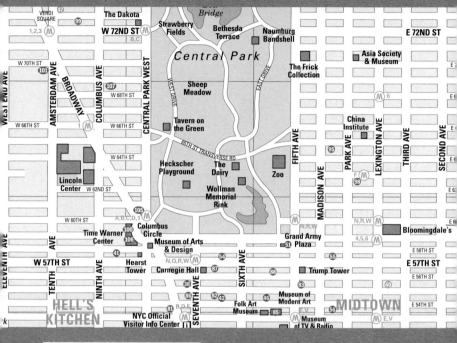

Major sight or landmark . . . .
Hospital or college . . . .
Railway station . . . .
Parks . . . .
River . . . .
Freeway 476
Main road . . . .
Main road tunnel . . . .
Pedestrian road . . . .
Airport . . . . ✈
Church . . . . ✚
Subway station . . . . Ⓜ
Area name . . . . SOHO

Street Index

STREET INDEX

Street Index

STREET INDEX

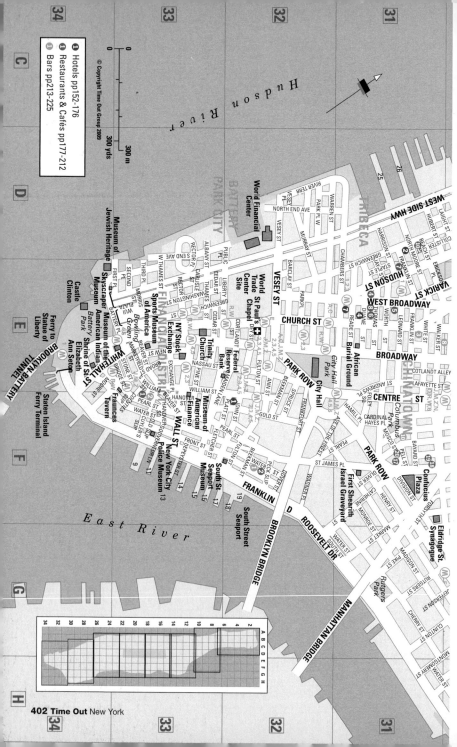

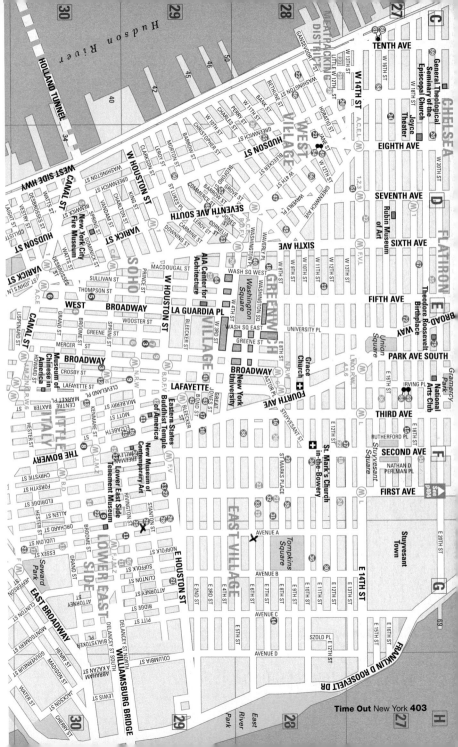

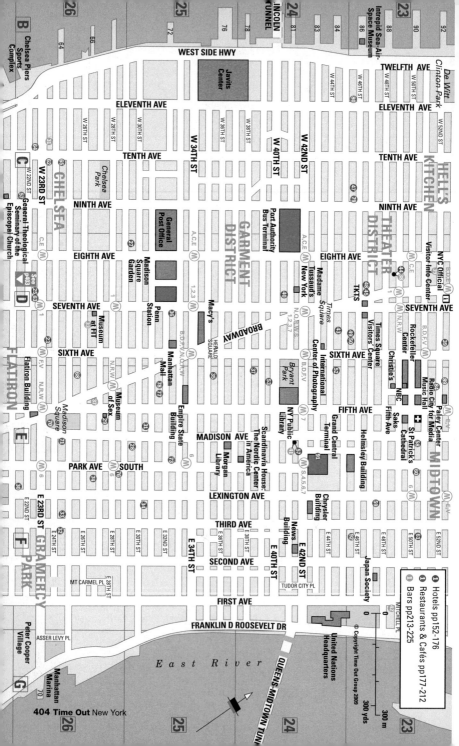

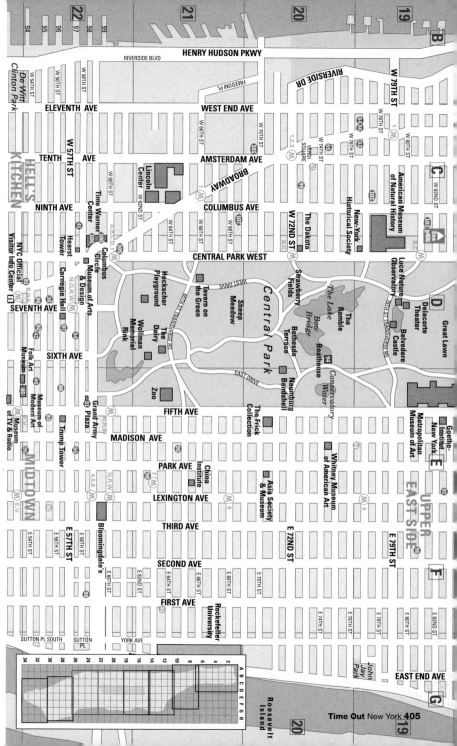

18   **17**   **16**   **15**

B

Soldiers' & Sailors' Monument

HENRY HUDSON PKWY

RIVERSIDE DRIVE

Riverside Park

Cathedral of St. John the Divine

- ❶ Hotels pp152-176
- ❶ Restaurants & Cafés pp177-212
- ❶ Bars pp213-225

Symphony Space

WEST END AVE

BROADWAY

AMSTERDAM AVE

COLUMBUS AVE

MANHATTAN AVE

Cathedral Close

MORNINGSIDE DR

C

UPPER WEST SIDE

W 88TH ST

W 86TH ST

W 84TH ST

BROWNE BLVD

W 92ND ST

W 94TH ST

W 90TH ST

W 96TH ST

W 98TH ST

W 100TH ST

W 102ND ST

W 103RD ST

W 105TH ST

W 106TH ST

W 107TH ST

W 109TH ST

W 111TH ST

W 113TH ST

DUKE ELLINGTON BLVD

CATHEDRAL PARKWAY

See p405

CENTRAL PARK WEST

D

Great Lawn

Central Park

The Reservoir

86TH ST TRANSVERSE RD

WEST DRIVE

96TH ST TRANSVERSE RD

The Pool

WEST DRIVE

CENTRAL PARK NORTH

ADAM CLAYTON POWELL JR BLVD

ST NICHOLAS AVE

MALCOLM X BLVD

Harlem Meer

Conservatory Garden

Charles A Dana Discovery Center

SPANISH HARLEM

EAST DRIVE

EAST DRIVE

Metropolitan Museum of Art

Goethe-Institut New York

Neue Galerie

Guggenheim Museum

Cooper-Hewitt National Design Museum

Jewish Museum

FIFTH AVE

MADISON AVE

PARK AVE

E 96TH ST

E 98TH ST

LEXINGTON AVE

Museum of the City of NY

El Museo del Barrio

E 105TH ST

E 107TH ST

E 109TH ST

E 111TH ST

E 113TH ST

E

EAST SIDE

UPPER

THIRD AVE

SECOND AVE

FIRST AVE

E 100TH ST

E 102ND ST

E 103RD ST

F

YORKVILLE

E 86TH ST

E 84TH ST

E 88TH ST

E 90TH ST

E 92ND ST

E 94TH ST

FRANKLIN D ROOSEVELT DR

Jefferson Park

G

EAST END AVE

Gracie Mansion

Carl Schurz Park

FRANKLIN D ROOSEVELT DR

406 Time Out New York

18   **17**   **16**   **15**

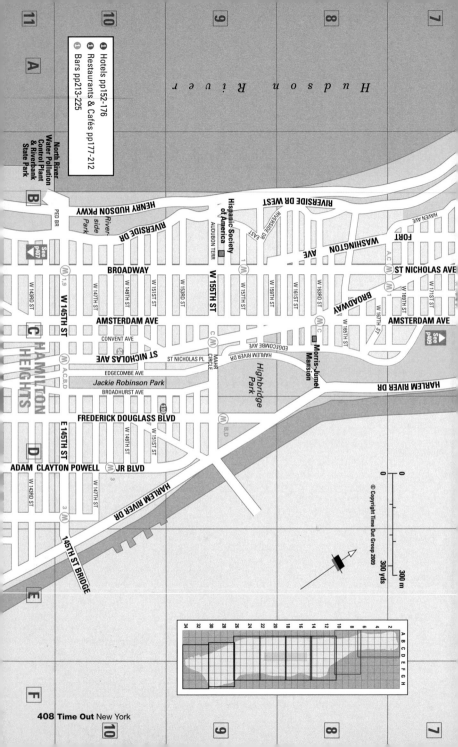

Hudson River

Hotels pp152-176
Restaurants & Cafés pp177-212
Bars pp213-225

North River
Water Pollution
Control Plant
& Riverbank
State Park

PED BR

HENRY HUDSON PKWY

Riverside Park

RIVERSIDE DR

See p407

BROADWAY

W 143RD ST
W 145TH ST
W 147TH ST
W 149TH ST
W 151ST ST
W 153RD ST
W 155TH ST

Hispanic Society of America

AUDUBON TERR

RIVERSIDE DR WEST

RIVERSIDE DR EAST

W 157TH ST
W 159TH ST
W 161ST ST
W 163RD ST

WASHINGTON AVE

HAVEN AVE

FORT

ST NICHOLAS AVE

BROADWAY

W 165TH ST
W 167TH ST
W 169TH ST
W 171ST ST

AMSTERDAM AVE

AMSTERDAM AVE

See p409

W 145TH ST

CONVENT AVE

ST NICHOLAS AVE

ST NICHOLAS PL

CONVENT AVE

MARR CIRCLE

HARLEM RIVER DR

EDGECOMBE AVE

Morris-Jumel Mansion

W 185TH ST

Highbridge Park

HARLEM RIVER DR

HAMILTON HEIGHTS

EDGECOMBE AVE

Jackie Robinson Park

BROADHURST AVE

FREDERICK DOUGLASS BLVD

E 145TH ST

W 149TH ST
W 151ST ST

ADAM CLAYTON POWELL JR BLVD

W 143RD ST
W 147TH ST

145TH ST BRIDGE

HARLEM RIVER DR

0
0

300 m
300 yds

© Copyright Time Out Group 2009

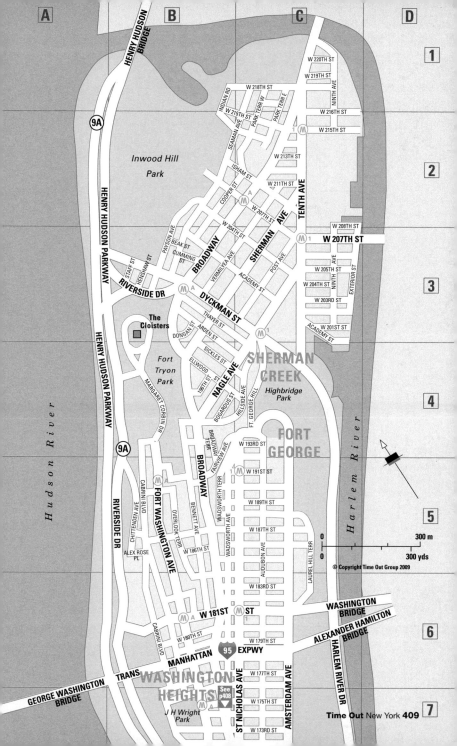

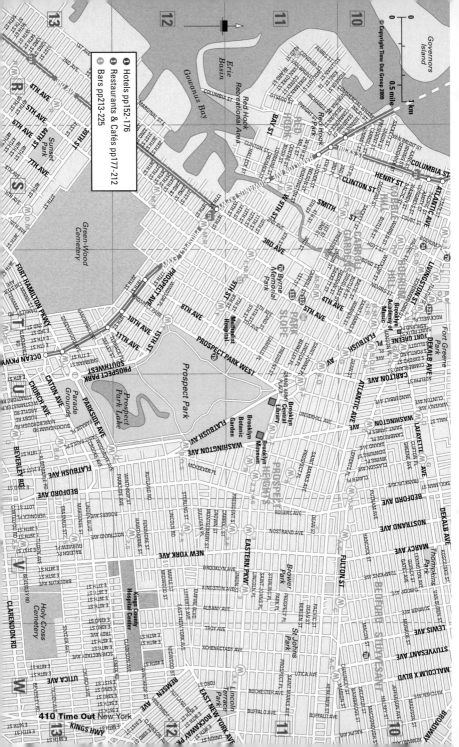

Hotels pp152-176
Restaurants & Cafés pp177-212
Bars pp213-225

© Copyright Time Out Group 2009

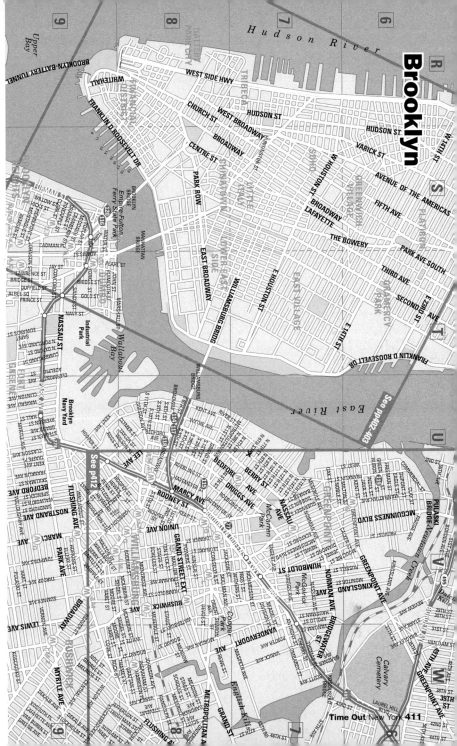

Queens

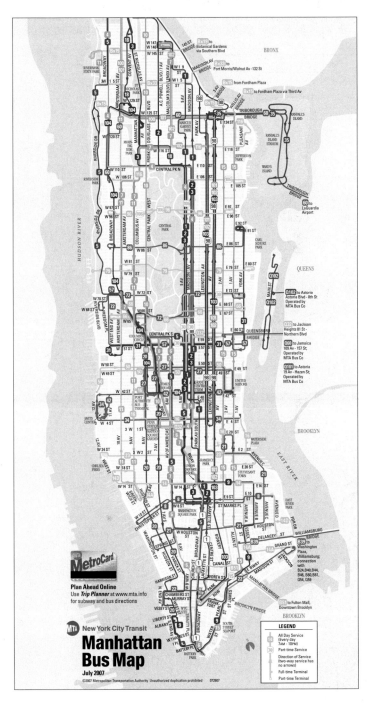

MTA New York City Transit

Manhattan Bus Map

July 2007

©2007 Metropolitan Transportation Authority. Unauthorized duplication prohibited. 072607

Plan Ahead Online
Use *Trip Planner* at www.mta.info
for subway and bus directions

LEGEND

All Day Service
(Every day
7AM - 10PM)

Part-time Service

Direction of Service
(two-way service has
no arrows)

Full-time Terminal

Part-time Terminal

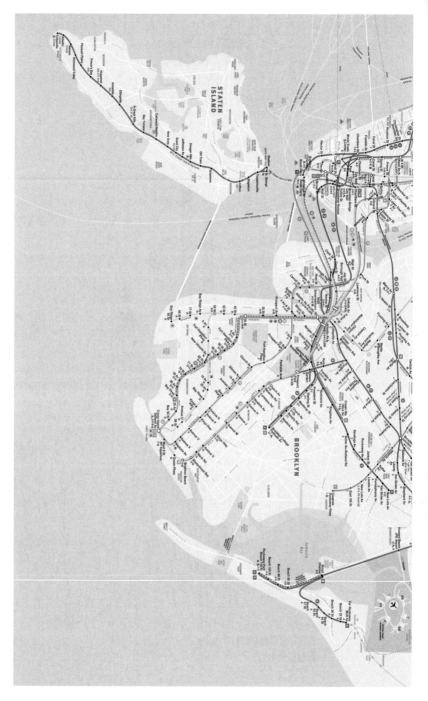

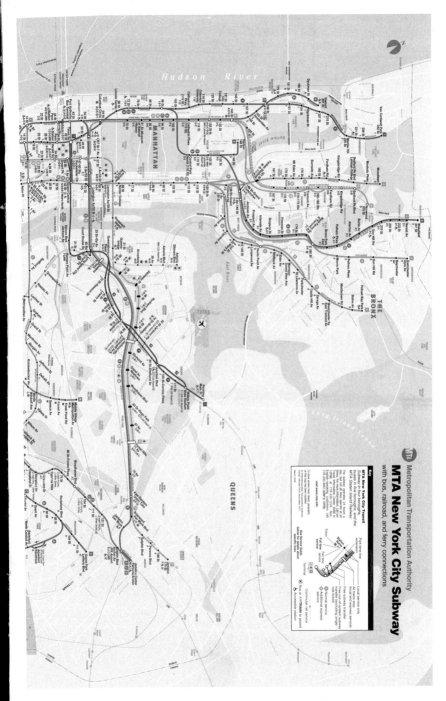

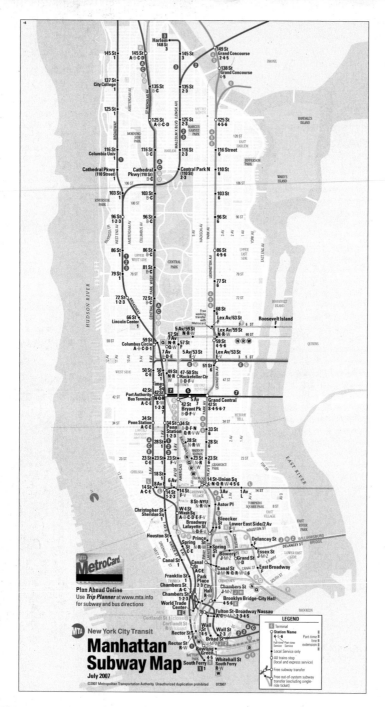

MTA MetroCard

Plan Ahead Online
Use *Trip Planner* at www.mta.info
for subway and bus directions

MTA New York City Transit

Manhattan Subway Map

July 2007

©2007 Metropolitan Transportation Authority Unauthorized duplication prohibited   072607